long nights
and log fires

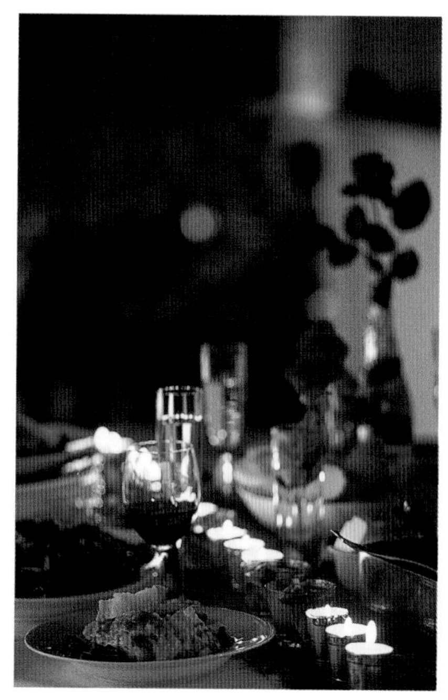

long nights
and log fires

Warming comfort food for family and friends

RYLAND
PETERS
& SMALL

LONDON NEW YORK

Senior Designer Toni Kay
Commissioning Editor Julia Charles
Picture Research Emily Westlake
Production Toby Marshall
Art Director Leslie Harrington
Publishing Director Alison Starling

Indexer Hilary Bird

First published in the United Kingdom
in 2009 by Ryland Peters & Small
20–21 Jockey's Fields
London WC1R 4BW
www.rylandpeters.com

10 9 8 7 6 5 4 3 2 1

ISBN: 978 1 84597 918 8

A catalogue record for this book is available from the British Library.

Printed and bound in China.

Notes

- All spoon measurements are level, unless otherwise stated.
- All herbs used in the recipes in this book are fresh unless specified as dried.
- Eggs are medium unless otherwise specified. Uncooked or partially cooked eggs should not be served to the very old, frail, young children, pregnant women or those with compromised immune systems.
- When a recipe calls for the grated zest of lemons or limes or uses slices of fruit, buy unwaxed fruit and wash well before using. If you can only find treated fruit, scrub well in warm soapy water before using.
- Ovens should be preheated to the specifed temperature. Recipes in this book were tested in a regular oven. If using a fan-assisted oven, follow the manufacturer's instructions for adjusting temperatures.

contents

6 introduction
8 soups and snacks
36 supper dishes
66 one-pot wonders
86 roasts
100 sides and salads
122 bakes and desserts
156 drinks
174 index
176 credits

come in from the cold...

Chilly days and long dark evenings were made for staying indoors and taking the time to prepare hearty, warming and sustaining food for family and friends. When the cold wind blows and the snow piles up outside, where better to be than at the heart of a warm kitchen, enjoying the aromas of good home cooking wafting from the oven? This book is intended to be as warming as a log fire on a cold winter's night and offers a wealth of delicious recipes for comfort food and warming drinks.

What could be more welcome on a freezing cold day that a steaming hot bowl of soup? It's time to give your tired old soup-making repertoire a new lease of life – here you'll find old favourites such as Leek and Potato Soup but also some tasty and original ideas like Pumpkin Soup with Sage and Honey or Parsnip, Chorizo and Chestnut Soup. Warm and sustaining savoury snacks are a must to keep energy reserves up in the colder months. With quick and easy recipes to try from Parmesan and Bacon Pancakes with Chive Butter to Smoked Trout Rarebit, you'll never be stuck for inspiration again.

Casual supper dishes are perfect for two people or for weekday family meals. Recipes include Herby Sausages on Polenta with Red Onion and Redcurrant Jelly, or Chicken, Leek and Tarragon Pot Pie. One-pot wonders were made for cooking on winter days – from slow-cooked French classics such as Boeuf Bourguignon to exotic Moroccan tagines, once assembled these casserole-style dishes can be put in the oven and left to cook themselves.

A roast has to be everyone's idea of a delicious, homely family meal and one that many of us remember fondly from our childhoods. You can recreate that same warm ambience with the recipes included here – from Italian-style Roast Pork with White Wine, Garlic and Fennel to the 'king of roasts', Roast Fillet of Beef with Herbed Yorkshire Puddings. Roasting can bring out the best in poultry, game and fish too. Try Roast Chicken with Bay Leaves, Thyme and Lemon, Roasted Pheasant Breasts with Bacon, Shallots and Mushrooms or delicious Roasted Salmon Wrapped in Prosciutto.

Interesting side dishes can turn a simple roast or rustic casserole into something very special. Forget dull and soggy boiled vegetables – enticing recipes here include Garlic Sautéed Green Beans and Vichy Carrots with Fresh Ginger, plus indulgent Creamy Potato Gratin and Baked Spinach Mornay. And who says a salad is just for summer? Use quality seasonal produce to create light meals or accompaniments such as Butternut Squash and Pancetta Salad with Mixed Spice Dressing and Winter-spiced Salad with Pears, Honeyed Pecans and Ricotta.

Baking is such a satisfying and comforting pastime as well as being very cost-effective. Make a batch of Stem Ginger Biscuits and fill the barrel so that family can help themselves during the week. Keep a Sticky Marzipan and Cherry Loaf in the cake tin and offer visitors who come in from the cold a slice of something home-baked with a warming cup of tea.

Finally, you'll find a tempting array of warming drinks guaranteed to stave off the winter blues. Included are flavoured coffees, spiced teas, indulgent hot chocolates and milky bedtime drinks and, as it's the party season, plenty of recipes for punches and cocktails. Try traditional tipples such as Egg Nog and Orange-mulled Wine or choose from a selection of elegant cocktails – Brandy Alexander, White Russian or a sparkling Champagne cocktail – all guaranteed to bring some festive cheer to the coldest of winter evenings.

soups and snacks

chestnut and Puy lentil soup with whipped celeriac cream

This is a spectacularly rich, satisfying soup with a light-as-air, foamy topping. You can prepare the soup ahead and it's a particularly good way to use up a tasty turkey or ham stock. You don't have to peel your own chestnuts, but they do taste wonderful and it's a nice, cosy thing to do if you've got company in the kitchen. If you prefer to serve the soup on its own without the celeriac cream, save some of the chopped chestnut for garnishing, frying the pieces in a little butter and sprinkling over the soup before serving.

350 g peeled chestnuts (fresh or vacuum-packed)

4 tablespoons light olive oil

1 leek, trimmed and thinly sliced

1 large carrot, finely diced

1 celery stick, thinly sliced

1 garlic clove, crushed

1 teaspoon Spanish sweet paprika (pimentón dulce) or paprika

1.5–1.75 litres fresh turkey, duck, ham, chicken or game stock or stock made with 2 beef or chicken stock cubes

175 g green Puy lentils, rinsed

2 tablespoons dry Marsala, Madeira or amontillado sherry

½–1 teaspoon Worcestershire or dark soy sauce

sea salt and freshly ground black pepper

celeriac cream

500 g celeriac

568 ml semi-skimmed milk

25 g butter

freshly grated nutmeg, to taste

freshly snipped chives, to garnish

Serves 6–8

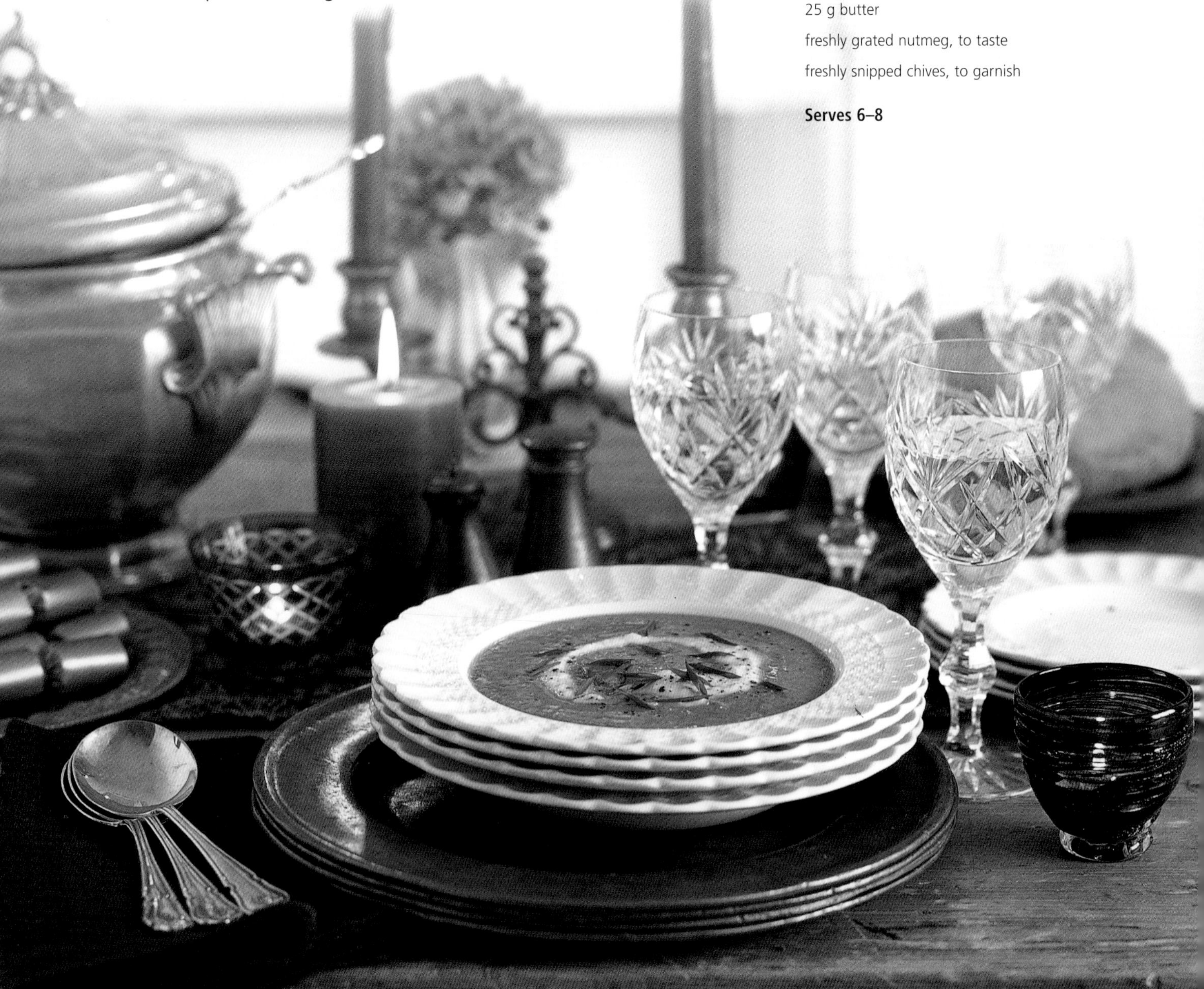

Wash the chestnuts and make a cut with a sharp knife in the curved side of each one. Put in a saucepan of boiling water, bring back to the boil and boil for 3 minutes. Turn the heat off and remove the chestnuts 2 at a time, letting them cool for a few seconds, then peeling off both the hard outer shell and inner brown papery skin. If they become harder to peel, bring the water back to the boil again. Chop the chestnuts roughly.

Heat the oil in a large saucepan, add the leek, carrot and celery, stir well and cook over medium heat until the vegetables start to soften (about 5–6 minutes). Stir in the garlic and pimentón and cook for a minute, then add the chestnuts and 1 litre of the stock and bring to the boil. Add the lentils to the vegetables, then cook for about 35–40 minutes until the vegetables are soft. Cool for 10 minutes, then pass the soup in batches through a food processor. Return the soup and remaining stock to the pan, add the Marsala and reheat gently. Add more stock if necessary and season to taste with salt, pepper and Worcestershire sauce.

Meanwhile, to make the celeriac cream, remove the tough outer skin from the celeriac and cut it into cubes. Put in a saucepan, add enough of the milk to cover and bring to the boil. Partially cover the pan and simmer for about 20–25 minutes, until the celeriac is soft. Remove the celeriac with a slotted spoon, leaving the liquid behind, and whizz it in a food processor. Season with salt, pepper and a little freshly grated nutmeg. Remove half the purée and add half the remaining milk to the purée in the food processor. Whizz until smooth, light and foamy, adding the extra milk if needed.

Serve the soup in bowls with a generous swirl of celeriac purée on the top and garnish with snipped chives. Serve with some crusty sourdough or multigrain bread.

pumpkin soup
with honey and sage

This is based on a delicious soup that is served at a restaurant called Tom's Kitchen, run by top London chef Tom Aikens. His version contains chicken stock but this recipe is vegetarian, but you could base it on chicken stock too.

75 g unsalted butter

1 small–medium onion, roughly chopped

1 carrot, finely chopped

1 garlic clove, crushed

1 kg pumpkin or butternut squash, deseeded, peeled and cut into cubes

2 heaped tablespoons clear honey

3 sprigs of sage, plus extra crisp-fried leaves (optional), to serve

750 ml vegetable stock

75 ml double cream

freshly squeezed lemon juice, to taste

sea salt and freshly ground black pepper

Serves 4–6

Gently melt the butter in a large lidded saucepan or flameproof casserole. Add the onion, carrot and garlic, stir, cover and cook over low heat for about 4–5 minutes. Add the cubed pumpkin, honey and sage, stir, replace the lid and continue to cook very gently for about 10 minutes. Pour in the stock, bring to the boil and cook for a further 10 minutes until the vegetables are soft. Turn off the heat and allow the soup to cool slightly, then remove the sage and strain the soup, retaining the liquid. Put half the cooked vegetables in a food processor with just enough of the reserved cooking liquid to blend into a smooth purée.

Transfer to a clean saucepan and repeat with the remaining vegetables, adding the purée to the first batch. Whizz the remaining liquid in the food processor to pick up the last bits of purée and add that too. Bring the soup slowly to the boil, then stir in the cream without boiling further. Season to taste with lemon juice, salt and pepper.

Serve with an extra swirl of cream or scatter some crisp-fried sage leaves on top and serve with wholemeal or multigrain bread.

roasted tomato soup with rarebit toasts

This hearty home-made tomato soup packs a real flavour punch. It's very easy to make and much, much tastier than any shop-bought versions. It's also highly nutritious, packed with antioxidants and therefore one of the best remedies to help fight off winter colds and coughs. Roasting the tomatoes does add to the cooking time but it's well worth the effort as something magical happens during the roasting process and the flavour is concentrated, retaining the natural sweetness of fresh tomatoes. The rarebit toasts are a deliciously indulgent addition but the soup can be more simply served with a swirl of cream or crème fraîche if preferred.

1 kg Italian tomatoes, such as Roma, halved

2 small red onions, quartered

6 sprigs of fresh lemon thyme

1 teaspoon sugar

1 teaspoon sea salt

2 garlic cloves, sliced

2 tablespoons olive oil

500 ml vegetable stock

sea salt and freshly ground black pepper

rarebit toasts

100 g mature Cheddar cheese

3 tablespoons wheat beer

1 tablespoon Worcestershire sauce

4 slices of baguette

Serves 4

Preheat the oven to 170°C (325°F) Gas 3. Put the tomatoes, onion, lemon thyme, sugar, salt, garlic and oil in a large bowl. Use your hands to toss the ingredients to combine and evenly coat them in the oil. Tip the mixture out onto a baking tray and roast in the preheated oven for 1½ hours. Discard the lemon thyme sprigs then put the tomatoes, onions and any tasty juices in a food processor or blender and process until smooth, adding a little stock if the mixture is too thick to process. Transfer to a large saucepan, add the stock and cook over gentle heat for 10 minutes. Season to taste and keep warm.

Preheat the grill to high. Put the Cheddar, beer and Worcestershire sauce in a small saucepan and set over low heat. Stir until the cheese has melted and the mixture is smooth. Toast the bread under the hot grill on one side only. Spread about 2 tablespoons of the cheese mixture on each untoasted side of bread and grill until it is bubbling and golden. Ladle the soup into warmed serving bowls and sit a rarebit toast on top of each to serve.

slow-cooked onion and cider soup
with Gruyère toasts

Alongside tomatoes, onions are almost certainly the most important ingredient in the kitchen. They are so versatile and give depth of flavour to so many dishes. The sweet onion mixture here could also be added to an egg custard and baked in a pastry case with some soft goats' cheese to make a savoury tart, or spread on a pizza base and topped with black olives and fresh thyme.

50 g butter

1 kg white onions, thinly sliced

4 garlic cloves

1 litre vegetable stock

375 ml sweet cider

2 egg yolks

4 thin slices of baguette

100 g Gruyère cheese, thinly sliced

Serves 4

Put the butter in a saucepan and set over medium heat. Add the onions and garlic, partially cover with a lid and cook for 20 minutes, stirring often so that the onions become silky soft without burning. Add the stock and cider and bring to the boil. Reduce the heat to low and cook for about 40 minutes, until thick and golden. Remove from the heat and slowly whisk in the egg yolks. Cover and keep warm.

Preheat the grill to high. Toast the bread under the hot grill until lightly golden on one side only. Put the cheese slices on the untoasted side and grill until the cheese is golden brown and bubbling. Ladle the soup into warmed serving bowls and sit a Gruyère toast on top of each to serve.

spicy red vegetable soup

The colour of this fiery red vegetable soup is matched by a pleasing chilli kick, which can be adjusted according to your palate – just add extra chillies as required. It's a really rewarding recipe so don't be put off by the cooking time.

60 ml light olive oil

1 tablespoon soft brown sugar

1 red pepper, deseeded and chopped

1 kg Roma or plum tomatoes, quartered

1 red onion, chopped

1 large red chilli, deseeded and chopped

2 garlic cloves, chopped

250 ml vegetable or chicken stock

4 slices of rye bread

50 g soft goats' cheese

Serves 4

Preheat the oven to 180°C (350°F) Gas 4.

Put the olive oil, sugar, pepper, tomatoes, onion, chilli and garlic in a roasting tin and use your hands to toss until coated in oil. Cook in the preheated oven for 2 hours, stirring often, until the vegetables are really soft and starting to turn brown.

Remove the vegetables from the oven. Put the stock in a saucepan and add the vegetables. Spoon the mixture, in batches, into a food processor or blender and process until smooth. Return the soup to a clean saucepan and warm over low heat for a few minutes until heated through.

Toast the rye bread and, while it's still warm, spread over the cheese. Ladle the soup into warmed serving bowls and sit a soft cheese toast on top of each to serve.

creamy cauliflower and Gruyère soup

Try and find a small, whole head of cauliflower that is creamy-white and soft for this indulgent soup. This recipe does not involve straining the puréed mixture (a messy and laborious job) so you want to avoid cooking with a gnarly, old head for a good result.

2 tablespoons butter

1 white onion, roughly chopped

1 celery stalk, chopped

1 small cauliflower, about 1 kg, cut into small pieces

1.5 litres vegetable or chicken stock

250 ml double cream

200 g Gruyère cheese, grated, plus extra to serve

sea salt and freshly ground black pepper

freshly chopped parsley and toasted wholemeal bread, to serve

Serves 4

Heat the butter in a saucepan set over high heat. Add the onion and celery and cook for 5 minutes, until the onion has softened but not browned.

Add the cauliflower pieces and stock and bring to the boil. Let boil for 25–30 minutes, until the cauliflower is really soft and breaking up in the stock.

Transfer the mixture to a food processor or blender and process in batches until smooth. Return the purée to a clean saucepan. Add the cream and cheese and cook over low heat, stirring constantly, until the cheese has all smoothly melted into the soup.

Season to taste with a little salt and pepper. Ladle into warmed serving bowls. Serve sprinkled with chopped parsley and extra grated cheese with wholemeal toast on the side.

carrot and lentil soup

You'll need to use a variety of lentil here that will soften to a mush when cooked for a short time. French green lentils, or Puy, will not work. Orange or red varieties are what's needed and they also create the rich autumnal colour. The taste of this soup belies the simplicity of its ingredients. Carrots can be very sweet and lentils are nutty and wholesome so they make a perfect pair. Try adding a couple of tablespoons of mild curry powder to the onions at the early stage of cooking.

3 tablespoons butter

1 red onion, chopped

1 garlic clove, chopped

2 tablespoons sun-dried tomato paste

500 g carrots, peeled and grated

250 g red lentils, rinsed

1.5 litres chicken or vegetable stock

125 ml natural yoghurt

a handful of coriander leaves, chopped

Serves 4

Heat the butter in a large saucepan set over high heat. Add the onion and garlic and cook for 4–5 minutes, stirring often. Add the sun-dried tomato paste and stir-fry for 1 minute. Add the carrots, lentils and stock to the pan and bring to the boil. Cook at a rapid simmer for 40 minutes, until the lentils are soft.

Spoon the mixture, in batches, into a food processor or blender and process until smooth. Return the soup to the saucepan and warm over low heat.

Ladle the soup into warmed serving bowls and serve with a dollop of yoghurt and a sprinkling of chopped coriander.

classic lamb, chickpea and lentil soup with cumin

Variations of this soup can be found throughout the Islamic world. In Morocco alone there are at least a dozen versions of this soup, differentiated by their regional recipes and by the pulses and vegetables used in the soup. It is one of the classic dishes prepared at religious feasts and it is traditionally served to break the fast during Ramadan, the month of fasting. Thick and hearty, with a consistency that comes somewhere between a soup and a stew, it can be served as a meal on its own with thick, crusty bread or flat breads.

2–3 tablespoons olive oil
2 white onions, chopped
2 celery stalks, diced
2 small carrots, peeled and diced
2–3 garlic cloves, left whole but smashed
1 tablespoon cumin seeds
450 g lean lamb, cut into bite-sized cubes
2–3 teaspoons ground turmeric
2 teaspoons paprika
2 teaspoons ground cinnamon
2 teaspoons sugar
2 fresh or dry bay leaves
2 tablespoons tomato purée
1 litre lamb or chicken stock
400-g tin chickpeas, drained and rinsed
400-g tin chopped tomatoes, drained of juice
100 g brown or green lentils, rinsed
a small bunch of flat leaf parsley, chopped
a small bunch of coriander, chopped
sea salt and freshly ground black pepper
1 lemon, cut into quarters, to garnish

Serves 4–6

Heat the oil in a deep, heavy-based saucepan. Add the onions, celery and carrots and cook until the onions begin to colour. Add the garlic and cumin seeds and toss in the lamb. Cook until lightly browned. Add the spices, sugar and bay leaves and stir in the tomato purée. Pour in the stock and bring the liquid to the boil. Reduce the heat, cover with a lid, and simmer for 1 hour, until the meat is tender.

Add the chopped tomatoes, chickpeas and lentils to the pan and cook gently for a further 30 minutes, until the lentils are soft and the soup is almost as thick as a stew. Top up with a little water, if necessary, as the lentils will absorb most of it. Season the soup with salt and pepper and add most of the parsley and coriander.

Serve the soup piping hot, sprinkled with the remaining parsley and coriander and with wedges of lemon to squeeze over it and plenty of bread for dipping.

potato, bacon and Savoy cabbage soup

This hearty recipe was inspired by a Polish soup called zurek which uses a fermented flour batter. This simplified recipes uses fine oatmeal instead but it still thickens the soup up very nicely.

2 tablespoons extra virgin olive oil

8 rashers of smoked, streaky bacon, sliced

1 white onion, chopped

2 garlic cloves, crushed

⅛ teaspoon ground allspice

300 g potatoes, peeled and cubed

¼ Savoy cabbage, shredded

400 ml chicken or vegetable stock

400 ml milk

2 tablespoons fine oatmeal

freshly ground black pepper

Serves 4

Heat the olive oil in a heavy-based saucepan or casserole dish. Add the bacon and fry for 2–3 minutes, until cooked. Turn the heat down and add the onion and garlic. Cover and cook for about 3 minutes, or until the onion is starting to soften.

Add the allspice and potatoes, cover and cook for a further 2–3 minutes to start softening the potatoes. Add the cabbage and stir until it has wilted into the rest of the ingredients. Pour in the stock and milk and bring to the boil.

Mix the oatmeal with 3–4 tablespoons cold water until smooth and gradually whisk into the soup to thicken.

Ladle the soup into warmed serving bowls and grind over some black pepper to serve.

parsnip, chorizo and chestnut soup

This is a thick and unctuous soup; the kind you want to wolf down after a long walk or building a snowman in the depths of winter. It's very heavy so a little goes a long way; it can be served as a meal in itself – offering it as a starter is likely to leave everyone too full-up for another course!

125 g raw chorizo, cubed

1 white onion, chopped

3 garlic cloves, sliced

1 celery stick, chopped

1 carrot, peeled and chopped

3 parsnips, peeled and chopped

¼ teaspoon dried chilli flakes

1 teaspoon ground cumin

200 g peeled, cooked chestnuts (fresh or vacuum-packed)

1 litre chicken, ham or vegetable stock

sea salt and freshly ground black pepper

Serves 4–6

Put the chorizo in a large saucepan and heat gently for 2–3 minutes until the oil seeps out and the chorizo becomes slightly crispy. Lift out the chorizo with a slotted spoon, trying to leave as much oil behind as you can and set to one side.

Add the onion, garlic, celery, carrot and parsnips to the pan, stir well, cover and cook gently for 10 minutes, or until softening. Add the chilli flakes and cumin, season well with salt and pepper and stir to release the aroma. Add the chestnuts and hot stock, then cover and simmer over low heat for 25–30 minutes until everything is very tender.

Transfer the contents of the pan to a blender (or use a handheld blender) and liquidize until smooth. Reheat the chorizo in a small frying pan.

Ladle the soup into warmed serving bowls and scatter with the crispy chorizo to serve.

monkfish, fennel and saffron bourride

A bourride is a little like a bouillabaisse but thickened with a gorgeous, garlicky aïoli. The aïoli in this recipe is spiced up with harissa, a Moroccan chilli and spice paste (see note on page 61), and is heavenly spread on anything. It's an impressive soup for dinner parties and can be served as a main course if liked.

3 tablespoons olive oil
1 white onion, chopped
1 fennel bulb, finely chopped
1 leek, white part sliced
300 g new potatoes (unpeeled), thinly sliced
¼ teaspoon saffron threads
2 fresh thyme sprigs
2 large tomatoes, thinly sliced
600 g monkfish fillets, skinned and sliced
1 litre fish stock
toasted bread, to serve
75 g Gruyère cheese, finely grated, to serve
sea salt and freshly ground black pepper

harissa aïoli

2 egg yolks
1 teaspoon Dijon mustard
200 ml extra virgin olive oil
2 garlic cloves, crushed
2 teaspoons harissa paste
1 tablespoon freshly squeezed lemon juice

Serves 4–6

Heat the olive oil in a large saucepan set over low heat. Add the onion, fennel and leek and cook for 5 minutes. Add the potatoes, saffron and thyme, stirring just once or twice, and cook until the potatoes start to soften.

Add the tomatoes and monkfish in a layer on top and, without stirring, pour in the stock. It should come at least halfway up the fish; if not, top up with water. Bring to the boil over gentle heat with the lid on and cook for 10–12 minutes until the fish is cooked and the potatoes are tender.

Meanwhile, to make the aïoli, put the egg yolks and mustard in a mixing bowl and whisk with electric beaters. Trickle in the olive oil, whisking until it emulsifies and thickens. Season with salt and pepper, then stir in the garlic, harissa and lemon juice. Transfer half the aïoli to a serving small dish.

Siphon off 2–3 ladlefuls of the liquid in the saucepan, add it to the remaining aïoli and stir well until combined. Stir back into the saucepan. Warm over low heat and season to taste, but don't allow the soup to boil.

Ladle the soup into warmed serving bowls and serve with toast, extra aïoli and finely grated Gruyère on the side.

smoked haddock and bean soup

Smoked haddock provides that warm smoky flavour that cold wintry nights call for. Beans are a perfect ingredient for soups – they are so quick and easy to throw in and thicken soups up nicely. Here a combination of cannellini and butter beans is used.

4 tablespoons olive oil

1 red onion, thinly sliced

600 ml fish stock

3 fresh or dried bay leaves

finely grated zest of 1 lemon

300 g smoked haddock, skinned and cubed

400-g tin cannellini beans, drained and rinsed

400-g tin butter beans, drained and rinsed

4 tablespoons crème fraîche

water or milk, to thin (optional)

sea salt and freshly ground black pepper

Serves 4

Heat the olive oil in a large saucepan and add the onion. Fry for 1 minute then cover and cook over low heat for 10 minutes, stirring every now and then until soft.

Pour in the stock, add the bay leaves and lemon zest and bring to a gentle simmer. Add the smoked haddock and cook for 3–4 minutes until opaque. It will continue to cook in the residual heat.

Liquidize half the cannellini beans and half the butter beans with 200 ml water in a blender and stir into the soup. Stir in the remaining whole beans and add the crème fraîche. Season with salt. If the soup is too thick, add a little milk or water to thin it down.

Ladle the soup into warmed serving bowls and grind over some black pepper to serve.

leek and potato soup

Sometimes the classics are the best and with leek and potato this is certainly true. If you are using nice clean leeks, you can slice them lengthways and simply rinse them under the tap, but if you are lucky enough to have some from the garden place them in a sink full of warm water and swirl them around to dissolve the mud and encourage it to come out.

50 g butter

4 leeks (about 500 g), chopped

3 floury potatoes (about 250 g), peeled and chopped

1 white onion, finely chopped

500 ml vegetable stock

300 ml milk

2 dried bay leaves

2 tablespoons freshly snipped chives, to serve

sea salt and freshly ground black pepper

Serves 4–6

Melt the butter in a large, heavy-based saucepan and add the leeks, potatoes, onion and a large pinch of salt. Cover and cook over low heat for 15 minutes until soft and translucent. Stir occasionally so that the vegetables don't catch on the bottom of the pan.

Add the stock, milk and bay leaves and bring to the boil. Turn the heat down and simmer, covered, for 20 minutes until the potato is so soft it is falling apart.

Transfer the soup to a blender, removing the bay leaves as you unearth them, and liquidize until smooth. Strain the blended soup through a sieve back into the pan to get it extra smooth and velvety. Bring back to the boil.

Ladle the soup into warmed serving bowls, scatter with chives and add a few grinds of black pepper to serve.

mushroom soup with Madeira and hazelnuts

The earthiness of mushrooms blends well with the sweetness of Madeira wine. The hazelnuts add a thickness to the soup and another complimentary flavour, but omit them if you prefer.

50 g butter

1 large white onion, chopped

3 garlic cloves, crushed

25 g blanched hazelnuts

3 tablespoons freshly chopped parsley

350 g chestnut or field mushrooms, sliced

25 g dried porcini mushrooms

100 ml Madeira

1 litre vegetable or chicken stock, warmed

Serves 4–6

Melt the butter in a large saucepan and add the onion and garlic. Cover and cook over low heat for 10 minutes, or until soft. Stir occasionally so that they don't colour. Meanwhile, toast the hazelnuts in a dry frying pan and roughly chop, then set aside.

Add half the parsley and all the mushrooms to the saucepan and turn the heat up to medium. Cover and cook, stirring, for about 15 minutes until they are softened.

Put the dried mushrooms in a heatproof bowl with 100 ml of the hot stock and set aside to soak for about 15 minutes to rehydrate.

Add the Madeira to the pan and cook until it evaporates. Add the remaining stock and the dried mushrooms with their soaking liquid, cover and cook for 10 minutes.

Transfer half the soup to a blender, along with half the hazelnuts and liquidize until smooth, then stir back into the pan and heat through.

Ladle the soup into warmed serving bowls and scatter the remaining parsley and toasted hazelnuts over the top to serve.

Parmesan and rosemary wafers

These are a must for any good drinks party, as the crispness of the cheese is wonderful and the infusion of the rosemary divine. Everyone will be constantly nibbling, so make lots. They can be prepared in advance but must be kept chilled in an airtight container until you are ready to serve.

2 sprigs of rosemary, needles stripped and finely chopped

200 g Parmesan cheese, coarsely grated

2 baking trays, lined with non-stick baking paper

Makes 24

Preheat the oven to 200°C (400°F) Gas 6. Put the rosemary into a bowl and stir in the Parmesan. Put teaspoons of the mixture in little heaps on the baking trays and flatten out into circles, making sure that they are not too close, as they will spread. Bake in the preheated oven for 8–10 minutes until golden, remove and let cool. Gently peel off the paper and serve.

oven-roasted spiced nuts

This recipe gives you control of the salt, the type of nut and the spice mix. When cool, mix in anything else you fancy, such as dried fruits or seeds.

40 g unsalted butter

1 tablespoon garam masala, Chinese five-spice, Cajun, or another spice mix, hot or mild

1 egg white

500 g mixed skinned nuts, such as almonds, Brazils, hazelnuts and pecans

1 teaspoon fine sea salt

Makes about 500 g

Preheat the oven to 150°C (300°F) Gas 2. Melt the butter in a small saucepan and stir in the spices. Let cool slightly, then whisk in the egg white until foamy. Add the nuts and toss well to coat. Spread the nuts out evenly in a thin layer in a roasting tin and roast slowly in the preheated oven for 30 minutes to 1 hour, stirring from time to time, until they are golden and toasted. Remove from the oven and toss the nuts with the salt.

Let cool completely, then store for at least 1 day before eating. They will keep in an airtight container for up to 2 weeks.

dukkah

No Egyptian home is complete without a jar of this wonderful seed and nut mixture in the larder. It is normally eaten as a snack – bread is dipped first into olive oil, then into the dukkah. Serve it with breadsticks and the most delicious olive oil you can find. It is also great used as a coating for chicken or fish instead of breadcrumbs.

150 g whole shelled hazelnuts

100 g whole shelled almonds

100 g sesame seeds

75 g coriander seeds

50 g ground cumin

1 teaspoon sea salt

½ teaspoon freshly ground black pepper

to serve

extra virgin olive oil

breadsticks or strips of toasted flatbread

Makes about 500 g

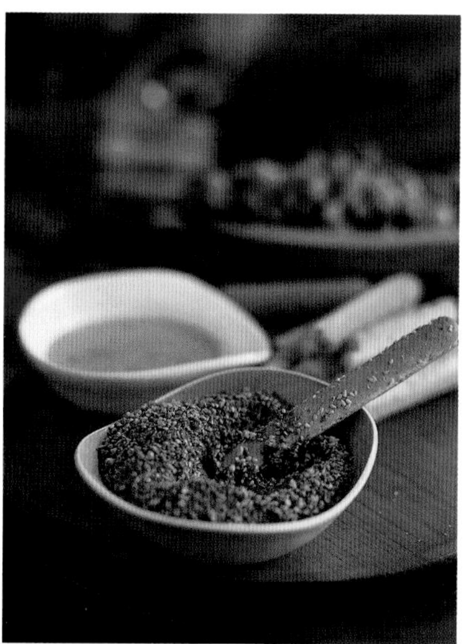

Preheat the oven to 200°C (400°F) Gas 6. Put the hazelnuts, almonds and sesame seeds in an ovenproof dish in the preheated oven and toast for 5–10 minutes. Remove from the oven, then tip onto a plate to cool completely. If they aren't cool enough, they will turn oily when ground.

Toast the coriander seeds in a dry frying pan for 1–2 minutes until you can smell the aroma, tip onto the cooling nuts, then add the ground cumin to the pan. Toast for 30 seconds then transfer to the plate.

When cold, put the nuts, spices, salt and pepper in a food processor and blend to a coarse, powdery meal – still dry-looking, but not totally pulverized. Spoon into a bowl and serve with a bowl of olive oil and breadsticks or flatbreads cut into strips.

beef and ale pâté

This spicy pâté is real party fare. It was inspired by 'tinga', Mexican shredded beef, and relies on slow cooking and a few key flavours. Even though it calls for a cheap cut of beef, it pays to use the best quality you can find. Serve it as you would a dip.

150 g dried pinto beans

2 tablespoons olive oil

5 large, mild red chillies

3 whole garlic cloves, peeled

1 large, dried mulatto or ancho chilli (optional)

600 g chuck steak, trimmed of fat and cut into 2-cm chunks

2 x 330-ml bottles of ale

sea salt and freshly ground black pepper

8 tablespoons chopped coriander, to garnish

plain tortilla chips, to serve

Serves 4–6

Soak the beans in cold water overnight. Drain, put in a saucepan and cover with plenty of water. Bring to the boil and continue to boil for 10 minutes. Drain the beans and set aside.

Heat the olive oil in a large, heavy-based saucepan set over medium/low heat. Cut the green stalk ends from 3 of the red chillies. Put these chillies and the garlic in the saucepan and gently cook for 3 minutes. If using, cut the dried chilli in half and remove the seeds and stalk. Add the flesh to the saucepan and continue cooking for 2 minutes. Increase the heat to medium/high, add the steak and cook, stirring occasionally, for 5 minutes until the meat is browned.

Add the ale and beans to the saucepan and bring to the boil. Reduce the heat to a slow simmer, cover and cook for 1½ hours, stirring occasionally. Uncover the pan and cook for 1 hour until the meat is falling apart. Put the meat with its accompanying ingredients and a little of the cooking liquid in a food processor and process briefly until you have a coarse pâté. Season to taste.

Spoon into serving dishes. Cut the remaining red chillies into thin strips and scatter over the pâté with the coriander. Serve warm or at room temperature with plain tortilla chips.

trio of honey-baked camembert with calvados and herbs

3 x 250-g boxes of Camembert cheese

3 tablespoons calvados or brandy

3 tablespoons dark chestnut honey

1 garlic clove, sliced

3 sage leaves

3 sprigs of rosemary

3 fresh bay leaves

to serve

celery sticks

walnut bread

chilled French breakfast radishes

Serves about 15

Another great recipe for entertaining, this molten cheese dish is spiked with perfumed honey, pungent calvados and garlic. Serve with crunchy celery sticks, warm crusty walnut bread and chilled French breakfast radishes.

Preheat the oven to 200°C (400°F) Gas 6.

Unwrap the cheeses and return them to their boxes. Using a skewer, make 6 or 7 holes in each cheese. Mix the calvados and honey together and spoon the mixture into and over the holes. Stud with the garlic slices and lightly press the sage, rosemary and bay onto each cheese. Bake in the preheated oven for about 7 minutes.

Remove the boxes from the oven. Using sharp scissors, quickly make 3 cuts on the surface of each cheese, from the centre out, and gently open the 'petals' a little. Take the cheeses out of their boxes, put them on a cheeseboard or plate and serve straight away, with the celery sticks, walnut bread and radishes on the side for dipping.

trio of vegetable dips with spelt toasts

Have you ever been lucky enough to share a plate of mixed dips at a Turkish restaurant? It's the vibrant colours that first grab your attention, quickly followed by the delicious flavours. These dips are all made with root vegetables, all too often lurking at the bottom of your veggie box. They have a creamy texture, so the crisp toasts are a nice nutty contrast.

spelt toasts

100 g spelt, rinsed under cold water

1 tablespoon dried active yeast

250 g spelt flour

½ teaspoon sea salt

plain flour, for dusting

Makes about 40 toasts

Put the spelt in a saucepan with 1 litre water and bring to the boil. Reduce the heat to low, cover with a lid and cook for 45 minutes. Remove the lid and boil rapidly until almost all the liquid has evaporated.

Meanwhile, put the yeast in a bowl with 4 tablespoons warm water, stir, cover and let rest in a warm place until the mixture is frothy. While it is still warm, put the spelt in a bowl with the spelt flour, salt, 125 ml hand-hot water and the yeast and stir to bring the mixture together to form a sticky dough. Put the dough on a lightly floured work surface and gently knead for about 1 minute. Carefully transfer the dough to a lightly oiled bowl, cover with a tea towel and let rise in a warm place for about 1–1¼ hours, until it has risen and doubled in size.

Preheat the oven to 200°C (400°F) Gas 6. Tip the dough out onto a lightly oiled baking tray and, using floured hands, form the dough into a loaf. Bake the bread in the preheated oven for 40 minutes. Carefully slide the loaf off the tray and directly onto the oven shelf, then bake for a further 5 minutes. Remove from the oven and let cool. To serve, slice into ½-cm wide pieces and toast under a hot grill until golden and crispy on both sides.

roasted parsnip and garlic dip

25 g chilled butter, cubed • 90 ml double cream • ½ teaspoon sea salt • ¼ teaspoon white pepper • 500 g parsnips, peeled and sliced • 1 garlic bulb, cut in half

Serves 6–8

Preheat the oven to 180°C (350°F) Gas 4. Lightly butter a small baking dish. Put the cream in a bowl and add the salt and pepper. Put the parsnips in the dish with the garlic. Pour the cream over the top, cover with foil and cook in the preheated oven for 45 minutes. Remove the garlic and let cool. When cool enough to handle, squeeze the garlic directly into the bowl of a blender and discard the skin. Add the remaining ingredients and process until smooth. Transfer to a dish and cover until ready to serve.

beetroot and caraway dip

3 medium beetroots, uncooked • 1 tablespoon horseradish sauce • 90 g sour cream • 1 teaspoon caraway seeds • sea salt and white pepper

Serves 6–8

Put the beetroots in a large saucepan and cover with cold water. Bring to the boil and let boil for 45–50 minutes, until tender and easily pierced with a skewer. Drain and let cool. When cool enough to handle, peel and discard the skins. Roughly chop and put in a blender with the other ingredients and process until smooth. Season to taste, transfer to a dish and cover until ready to serve.

spiced carrot dip

250 ml vegetable stock • 4 medium carrots, chopped • 2 tablespoons light olive oil • 1 small red onion, chopped • 2 garlic cloves, chopped • 1 large red chilli, chopped • 1 teaspoon fenugreek seeds • 1 teaspoon ground cumin • sea salt and white pepper

Serves 6–8

Put the stock in a saucepan, add the carrots, oil, onion and garlic. and bring to the boil. Reduce the heat to low and simmer for 15–20 minutes, until almost all the liquid has evaporated and the carrots are soft. Add the chilli, fenugreek and cumin and cook for 2 minutes. Put in a blender and process until blended but with a rough texture. Season to taste, transfer to a dish and cover until ready to serve.

warm cheese scones with Cheddar and pickled pears

These little scones are particularly good served warm and filled at the last minute. If you have any leftover pickled pears you could serve them with cold meats or a cheese platter. Gruyère could be substituted for the Cheddar if liked.

pickled pears

700 g firm pears

300 g soft brown sugar

500 ml cider vinegar

½ onion studded with 4 cloves

2 bay leaves, bruised

1 cinnamon stick

cheese scones

500 g self-raising flour, plus extra for dusting

150 g butter

100 g Cheddar cheese, grated

2 teaspoons salt

2 teaspoons bicarbonate of soda

1 teaspoon Dijon mustard

1 teaspoon cayenne pepper

200 ml milk

200 g mature Cheddar cheese, shaved into thin slices

a 4-cm biscuit cutter (optional)

2 –3 baking trays

Makes 30 small scones

To make the pickled pears, peel, quarter and core the pears. Put all the other ingredients in a large saucepan and gently bring to the boil. When the sugar has dissolved, add the pears and simmer for about 5–8 minutes until just tender. Remove the pears from the liquid with a slotted spoon and transfer them to a shallow dish. Set aside to cool. Continue boiling the liquid until it reduces by half and becomes a syrup. Discard the onion, bay leaves and cinnamon and gently pour the syrup over the pears to coat.

To make the scones, preheat the oven to 200°C (400°F) Gas 6. Rub the flour and butter together in a bowl until it resembles fine breadcrumbs then add 50 g of the grated cheese. Add the salt, bicarbonate of soda, mustard and cayenne pepper and mix to combine. Next add enough milk to bring the dry ingredients together and form a pliable dough. Flour a work surface, turn the dough out and knead it lightly. Pat it out to a thickness of 1–1½ cm. Use a biscuit cutter or an unturned glass to stamp out small rounds. Sprinkle the remaining grated cheese over the scones, transfer to baking trays and bake for 10 minutes until lightly browned. Let cool a little on a wire rack. Slice the pickled pears into small pieces. Cut the scones ¾ of the way through, put a slice of cheese and a piece of pickled pear inside each one and serve immediately.

potato and parsnip croquettes

Use a floury potato for these croquettes, such as Desirée, as it fluffs up nicely when boiled and mashed. The parsnip adds an interesting flavour dimension, as it is a little bitter and sweet at the same time. Serve warm with mild mustard on the side for dipping.

500 g floury potatoes, peeled and quartered

1 parsnip, peeled and quartered

25 g butter, plus 1 tablespoon for frying

2 tablespoons finely chopped parsley

2 eggs

100 g dry breadcrumbs from a day-old loaf of bread

2 tablespoons plain flour, for dusting

vegetable oil, for shallow-frying

sea salt and freshly ground black pepper

sweet German mustard, to serve

Makes 18 croquettes

Put the potatoes and parsnip in a large saucepan and cover with boiling water. Set over high heat and boil for 12–15 minutes until tender. Drain and return to the warm pan. Add the 25 g butter and mash well until the mixture is lump-free. Stir in the parsley and season well with salt and pepper. Cover and refrigerate until the mixture is completely chilled.

Break the eggs into a bowl and beat well to combine. Put the breadcrumbs in a separate bowl. Lightly flour your hands and work surface. Take 1 heaped tablespoon of mixture and form it into a small sausage, tapping the ends on the floured work surface so that they are flattened rather than tapered. Dip the croquette in the beaten egg, then roll it in the crumbs until coated. Put it on a baking tray lined with baking paper. Repeat until all of the potato mixture has been used and then refrigerate until ready to cook.

Put the 1 tablespoon butter in a frying pan and pour in sufficient oil to come halfway up the sides of the pan. Heat the pan over medium heat until the butter begins to sizzle. To test if the oil is hot enough, sprinkle a few breadcrumbs into it – they should sizzle on contact. Cook the croquettes in batches for 2–3 minutes, turning often, until golden and crisp all over. Remove from the oil using a slotted spoon and drain on kitchen paper to remove excess oil. Serve warm with the mustard on the side for dipping.

crispy onion rings
with Parmesan aïoli

These are a good thing to cook at the same time as the croquettes (see recipe left), especially if you don't cook fried food often. You don't have to be too fussy and cook one ring at a time – they taste just as delicious cooked in clumps. Enjoy them warm with the aïoli on the side for dipping.

2 red onions, sliced into ½-cm thick rings

2 white onions, sliced into ½-cm thick rings

250 ml buttermilk (or 250 ml full-fat milk combined with 1 tablespoon freshly squeezed lemon juice)

55 g chickpea flour

60 g cornflour

1 teaspoon sea salt

2 eggs

500 ml vegetable oil

Parmesan aïoli

2 egg yolks

2 garlic cloves, crushed

2 teaspoons freshly squeezed lemon juice

200 ml light olive oil

25 g Parmesan cheese, very finely grated

sea salt and white pepper

Serves 4

To make the aïoli, put the egg yolks, garlic and lemon juice in a small bowl and whisk until just combined. Whisk constantly as you add the oil, very slowly at first but building up to a steady stream. Stir in the Parmesan and season with salt and pepper. Set aside.

Put the onion slices in a large bowl and gently toss to separate the rings. Add the buttermilk and stir. Set aside for 1 hour. Put the chickpea flour, cornflour and salt in a bowl. Make a small well in the centre. Use a slotted spoon to remove the onions from the buttermilk (reserving the buttermilk) and transfer them to a colander to drain off any excess liquid. Put 125 ml of the reserved buttermilk in a bowl and beat in the eggs until just combined. Pour this mixture into the flour mixture and beat well with a wooden spoon to form a smooth, thick batter.

Put the oil in a frying pan and set over medium/high heat. Toss a handful of onion rings into the batter and lift them out with a slotted spoon (letting any excess batter drip back into the bowl). Put them in the frying pan. Cook for about 1–2 minutes, until golden. Remove from the oil with a slotted spoon and drain on kitchen paper. Repeat with the remaining onion rings. Serve warm with the Parmesan aïoli for dipping.

baked mushrooms
with Manchego béchamel

Modern Spanish tapas bars are very popular just now. Hopefully it's not just a passing trend and that they are here to stay, as tapas dishes are shared comfort food at its very best. Mushrooms really are nature's cups just waiting to be filled. Look for ones that will be two to three small mouthfuls when cooked – wild field mushrooms or the large portobello mushrooms are both ideal. These are very rich, so a crisp fennel salad is the perfect accompaniment.

2 teaspoons butter

2 teaspoons plain flour

125 ml full-fat milk

50 g Manchego cheese, finely grated

12 wide, flat field mushrooms

¼ teaspoon Spanish smoked paprika (pimentón)

fennel salad

1 small fennel bulb

1 handful of flat leaf parsley leaves

2 teaspoons extra virgin olive oil

2 teaspoons freshly squeezed lemon juice

sea salt and freshly ground black pepper

Serves 4–6

Put the butter in a small saucepan and set over high heat. Cook until it is melted and sizzling. Before the butter burns, add the flour and stir quickly to form a thick paste. Remove from the heat and add a little of the milk, stirring constantly until thick and smooth. Return the pan to medium heat and add the remaining milk, whisking constantly until all the milk is incorporated and the mixture is smooth and thick. Remove from the heat and let cool.

Preheat the oven to 220°C (425°F) Gas 7. Remove the stalks from the mushrooms and sit the mushrooms in a small baking dish, gill-side up. Spoon the cheese sauce into the caps and sprinkle the paprika over the top. Cook in the preheated oven for 20 minutes, until the mushrooms are soft and the sauce is golden and bubbling.

While the mushrooms are cooking, slice the fennel bulb as thinly as possible, chop the fronds finely and put them in a bowl with the parsley, oil and lemon juice. Toss to combine, season to taste and serve with the warm mushrooms.

crispy oven wedges
with home-made pesto sauce

When was the last time you stirred some freshly made pesto into a big bowl of hot spaghetti? It's an aromatic and heady experience. Food manufacturers like us to believe that pesto keeps in a jar or plastic tub in the fridge, but in fact it soon oxidizes, turning bitter, brown and oily, and quickly becomes a lesser version of its glorious former self. This vibrant pesto made with handfuls of garden-fresh basil and parsley will knock your socks off and surpass anything you can buy in supermarkets.

2 large floury potatoes, cut into thick wedges

2 tablespoons light olive oil

pesto sauce

2 handfuls of basil leaves

1 handful of flat leaf parsley leaves

1 garlic clove, chopped

1 tablespoon freshly squeezed lemon juice

50 g pine nuts, lightly toasted

65 ml extra virgin olive oil

50 g Parmesan cheese, finely grated

Serves 4

To make the pesto, put the herbs, garlic, lemon juice and pine nuts in a food processor and process until finely chopped. With the motor running, add the oil in a steady stream until it is all incorporated. Transfer the mixture to a bowl, stir in the Parmesan and cover until ready to serve.

Bring a large saucepan of water to the boil and add the potatoes. Boil them for 5 minutes, then drain and let cool completely.

Preheat the oven to 220°C (425°F) Gas 7. Pour the oil into a roasting tin and put it in the oven for 5 minutes to heat up. Arrange the potato wedges in the tin in a single layer. Cook in the preheated oven for about 15 minutes, turning in the middle of the cooking time, until crisp and golden all over. Transfer to a plate and serve with the pesto on the side for dipping.

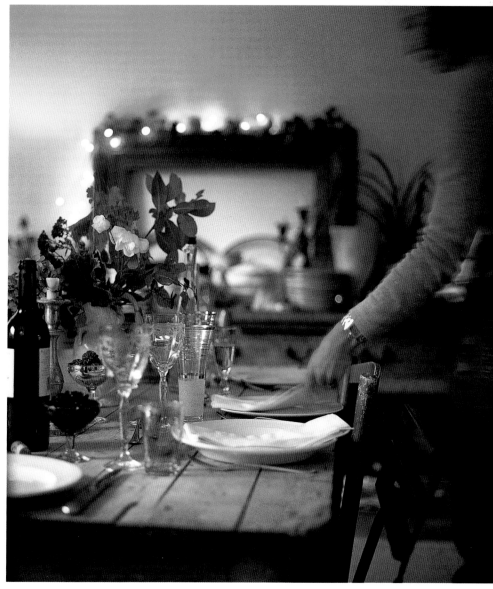

Parmesan and bacon pancakes with chive butter

Served warm from the pan, this combination of smoky bacon pancakes and chive butter makes a lovely fireside treat on a chilly day.

1 tablespoon vegetable oil, plus extra for brushing

3 rashers of bacon, snipped into small pieces, or 75 g pancetta, cubed

115 g self-raising flour

25 g Parmesan cheese, grated

a pinch of sea salt

1 egg, beaten

150 ml full-fat milk

freshly ground black pepper

chive butter

85 g butter, at room temperature

2–2½ tablespoons freshly snipped chives

freshly ground black pepper

Makes about 20 small pancakes

To make the chive butter, put the butter in a bowl and beat in the chives. Season to taste with pepper. Spoon the mixture into a ramekin or small serving bowl, cover and chill until ready to serve.

Put the flour, cheese and salt in a large bowl and season well with pepper. Make a well in the middle. Add the egg and half the milk and gradually work in the flour to make a smooth batter. Beat in the remaining milk to make a smooth batter.

Heat the oil in a large, non-stick frying pan and fry the bacon for about 3 minutes, until crispy. Remove the bacon from the pan and drain off any grease. Wipe the pan with kitchen paper and leave set over low heat.

Drop tablespoonfuls of batter into the pan, sprinkle a little bacon on top and cook for 1–2 minutes, until bubbles appear on the surface. Flip over the pancakes and cook for a further 30 seconds–1 minute, until they are golden. Keep warm while you cook the remaining mixture. Serve warm with the chive butter for spreading.

mini croque-monsieurs

Crisp croque-monsieur sandwiches, oozing with melting Gruyère cheese and ham, are a favourite in French cafés. These miniature versions are the perfect hot savoury to serve at teatime. They're very simple to make and you can prepare them ahead of time and toast when you are ready to serve.

1 baguette
2 teaspoons Dijon mustard
115 g Gruyère cheese, grated
85 g prosciutto or other ham
butter, at room temperature
chopped flat leaf parsley, to garnish
freshly ground black pepper

Makes 12 sandwiches

Cut 24 thin slices of baguette, each about about 7 mm thick. Spread half of the slices with mustard, then top with half the cheese and put a piece of prosciutto on top. Top with the remaining slices of bread.

Preheat the grill to high. Lightly butter the sandwiches on both sides, then arrange them on a grill pan. Grill until golden, then turn over and grill until just golden on the second side. Sprinkle with the remaining cheese and grill for 1 minute, or until the cheese is melted and bubbling. Sprinkle with parsley, grind over some pepper and serve immediately.

smoked trout rarebit

These hearty rarebits provide just the right combination of indulgence and sustenance. Wonderfully comforting, with an oozing, melted topping, they make a warming snack or light lunch.

2 smoked trout fillets, skinned and flaked

4 thick slices of wholegrain bread

175 g Cheddar or Gruyère cheese, grated

3½ tablespoons dry white wine

1 shallot, finely chopped

freshly ground black pepper

chopped fresh parsley, to serve

Serves 4

Preheat the grill to high. Toast the bread on one side only, until golden.

Meanwhile, put the cheese and wine in a saucepan and set over low heat. Gently heat, stirring constantly, until the cheese has melted.

When the bread is golden on one side, turn the slices over and arrange a quarter of the smoked trout on each. Spoon some melted cheese mixture over the top and scatter with some chopped shallot. Season with a little pepper and return the toasts to the hot grill. Cook until golden and bubbling. Sprinkle with a little parsley and serve immediately.

fluffy potato pancakes with smoked salmon

These blini-style pancakes are made with mashed potato rather than flour: the result is light and particularly delicious with salty salmon and cool crème fraîche.

500 g floury potatoes, peeled and halved

150 ml crème fraîche or sour cream

3 eggs, separated

4 tablespoons freshly snipped chives

4 tablespoons unsalted butter

salt and freshly ground black pepper

to serve

500 g sliced smoked salmon

300 ml crème fraîche or sour cream

2 tablespoons freshly snipped chives

4 blini pans or 1 large non-stick frying pan and 4 ring moulds

Serves 4

Put the potatoes in a large saucepan of water, bring to the boil and cook until tender. Drain, return to the pan and mash until soft. Beat in the cream and egg yolks. Season well and mix in the chives. Whisk the egg whites until stiff and fold them into the potato mixture.

Heat four blini pans and add ½ tablespoon butter to each*. When the butter is foaming, spoon about 4 tablespoons of the mixture into each pan. Cook until browning and set, then flip over and cook for 1 minute more. Repeat with the remaining butter and potato mixture. Serve the pancakes topped with salmon, crème fraîche and some chives.

*If using a non-stick frying pan and 4 ring moulds, drop 4 tablespoons of the mixture into each mould. Cook as above and repeat until all the mixture has been used.

smoked salmon and chive soufflé omelette

150 ml full-fat milk
1 small white onion, sliced
1 small carrot, sliced
1 clove
1 fresh or dried bay leaf
250 g smoked salmon
75 g butter
1 tablespoon plain flour
3 large eggs, separated
6 tablespoons sour cream
4 tablespoons freshly snipped chives
2 tablespoons freshly chopped parsley
2 tablespoons freshly grated Parmesan cheese
salt and freshly ground black pepper

Serves 2–4

This light-as-air omelette is a perfect brunch, lunch or supper dish and makes an interesting change from the usual scrambled eggs with smoked salmon.

Put the milk in a saucepan with the onion, carrot, clove and bay leaf. Heat until almost boiling, then turn off the heat and let stand for 10 minutes. Add half the smoked salmon and simmer for 5 minutes until it is opaque. Remove the fish to a plate and flake it with a fork. Strain and reserve the milk.

Melt half the butter in a small saucepan and stir in the flour. Gradually whisk in the reserved milk and bring the mixture to the boil, stirring all the time until a thickened sauce. Remove from the heat.

Put the egg yolks and half the sour cream in a bowl, beat well, then stir into the sauce. Carefully stir in the cooked smoked salmon, chives and parsley and season to taste. Whisk the egg whites in a bowl until stiff and fold into the sauce.

Preheat the oven to 200°C (400°F) Gas 6. Melt the remaining butter in frying pan with a heatproof handle and pour in the salmon mixture. Cook over a medium heat until just beginning to set, then scatter over the remaining salmon and spoon over the remaining sour cream. Carefully flip one half of the omelette over to cover the salmon. Scatter with Parmesan and finish off in the preheated oven for 5 minutes. Serve immediately, straight from the pan.

smoked salmon and chive soufflé omelette

150 ml full-fat milk

1 small white onion, sliced

1 small carrot, sliced

1 clove

1 fresh or dried bay leaf

250 g smoked salmon

75 g butter

1 tablespoon plain flour

3 large eggs, separated

6 tablespoons sour cream

4 tablespoons freshly snipped chives

2 tablespoons freshly chopped parsley

2 tablespoons freshly grated Parmesan cheese

salt and freshly ground black pepper

Serves 2–4

This light-as-air omelette is a perfect brunch, lunch or supper dish and makes an interesting change from the usual scrambled eggs with smoked salmon.

Put the milk in a saucepan with the onion, carrot, clove and bay leaf. Heat until almost boiling, then turn off the heat and let stand for 10 minutes. Add half the smoked salmon and simmer for 5 minutes until it is opaque. Remove the fish to a plate and flake it with a fork. Strain and reserve the milk.

Melt half the butter in a small saucepan and stir in the flour. Gradually whisk in the reserved milk and bring the mixture to the boil, stirring all the time until a thickened sauce. Remove from the heat.

Put the egg yolks and half the sour cream in a bowl, beat well, then stir into the sauce. Carefully stir in the cooked smoked salmon, chives and parsley and season to taste. Whisk the egg whites in a bowl until stiff and fold into the sauce.

Preheat the oven to 200°C (400°F) Gas 6. Melt the remaining butter in frying pan with a heatproof handle and pour in the salmon mixture. Cook over a medium heat until just beginning to set, then scatter over the remaining salmon and spoon over the remaining sour cream. Carefully flip one half of the omelette over to cover the salmon. Scatter with Parmesan and finish off in the preheated oven for 5 minutes. Serve immediately, straight from the pan.

supper dishes

sticky pork fillet with a pecorino crust, mustard mash and balsamic onions

Tender pork with a golden, rosemary-flecked cheese crust, fluffy mustard-speckled mashed potatoes and sticky, savoury-sweet onions add up to cloud nine dining.

2 x 400-g pieces of whole pork fillet

3 tablespoons extra virgin olive oil

150 g pecorino cheese, finely grated

a small bunch of rosemary, chopped

sea salt and freshly ground black pepper

mustard mash

900 g floury potatoes, peeled and cubed

2 tablespoons wholegrain mustard (or to taste)

2 garlic cloves, crushed

3–4 tablespoons full-fat milk

4–5 tablespoons extra virgin olive oil

balsamic onions

2 tablespoons extra virgin olive oil

6 red onions, peeled and thinly sliced

80 ml balsamic vinegar

Serves 4

Preheat the oven to 200°C (400°F) Gas 6.

Brush the pork fillets with 1 tablespoon of the olive oil. Mix the pecorino and rosemary together and spread over a sheet of baking paper. Roll the pork fillets in the mixture, pressing down well so they are evenly coated. Put them in a roasting tin and drizzle with the remaining oil. Roast in the preheated oven for 30 minutes, or until the pork is cooked through and the crusts are golden. Leave to rest in a warm place.

To make the mash, boil the potatoes in a large saucepan of salted water until soft. Drain, return to the warm pan and mash. Beat in the mustard, garlic, milk and olive oil. Cover and keep warm.

To make the onions, heat the olive oil in a frying pan and add the onions. Cook for 3–4 minutes, until light golden and starting to soften. Add the balsamic vinegar and 40–50 ml water. Cook slowly for about 10 minutes, or until the onions are soft and sticky, then season to taste. Slice the pork and serve with mash and balsamic onions.

poulet sauté au vinaigre

Typically, this traditional French dish is thickened and enriched with butter but this recipe uses extra virgin olive oil instead. The one thing that definitely isn't up for negotiation is the use of excellent-quality red wine vinegar. Cheap vinegar is far too astringent for this dish and will produce a harsh and unpleasant sauce – a far cry from the mouth-watering result you should get.

90 ml extra virgin olive oil

a 2-kg chicken, cut into 8 pieces

500 g very ripe cherry tomatoes
(or a 400-g tin cherry tomatoes in juice, drained before using)

2 garlic cloves, crushed

200 ml very good-quality red wine vinegar

300 ml chicken stock

a small bunch of flat leaf parsley, chopped

sea salt and freshly ground black pepper

mixed salad leaves, to serve

Serves 4–6

Heat 3 tablespoons of the olive oil in a large frying pan. Season the chicken all over and cook for 3–4 minutes on each side, or until golden. Add the tomatoes and garlic to the pan. Cook for 10–15 minutes, squashing the tomatoes down with the back of a spoon, until they are thick and sticky and have lost all their moisture.

Pour in the vinegar and leave it to bubble for 10–15 minutes, until the liquid has almost evaporated. Pour in the stock, and cook for a further 15 minutes or so, until reduced by half. Stir in the remaining olive oil and the parsley. Spoon onto serving plates and add a generous handful of mixed salad leaves to serve.

herby sausages on polenta with red onion and redcurrant gravy

This is an Italian take on sausage and mash with a bit of British redcurrant jelly thrown in because it makes onion gravy lovely and sticky. If you've tried polenta before and weren't blown away, try it again now: the secret is plenty of butter, cheese and seasoning.

12 good-quality sausages with herbs
sea salt and freshly ground black pepper

red onion and redcurrant gravy

2 tablespoons extra virgin olive oil
2 red onions, thinly sliced
2 rosemary sprigs, broken up
2 teaspoons plain flour
2 tablespoons redcurrant jelly
300 ml red wine
300 ml beef stock
25 g butter

polenta

150 g traditional or quick-cook polenta
50 g butter
75 g freshly grated Parmesan cheese

Serves 4

Put 750 ml water in a large saucepan. Set over high heat, cover with a lid and heat until simmering. Pour the polenta into the pan of simmering water and beat out any lumps. Reduce the heat to low and let it bubble for 30–40 minutes. (If you are using quick-cook polenta, cook according to the packet instructions.)

To make the gravy, heat the olive oil in a frying pan and cook the onions and rosemary over medium heat, stirring constantly. When the onions are just starting to soften, reduce the heat, cover and leave to soften slowly in their own juices. After 10–15 minutes, stir in the flour and cook for about 1 minute until it is no longer pale. Add the redcurrant jelly, wine and stock and bring to the boil. Leave to bubble away gently for 15 minutes while you cook the sausages.

Preheat the grill to high. Put the sausages on a grill pan lined with foil and cook for about 15 minutes, turning halfway through, until well browned and cooked through.

Beat the butter and Parmesan into the polenta and season well. Beat the butter into the gravy and season to taste. Spoon the polenta into dishes, top with 3 sausages and pour over the hot gravy to serve.

sausages with celeriac rösti

Swiss rösti are crisply fried cakes of grated potato, not unlike hash-browns, that are traditionally served with snitzels or roast meats. There is no doubting that celeriac is unattractive and can be tough to peel but get over that and you will be richly rewarded. Not unlike celery in taste, it gives a base note that enhances the ingredients it is cooked with, in this case potato.

8 good-quality pork sausages

2 tablespoons olive oil

Dijon mustard, to serve

celeriac rösti

3 medium potatoes, unpeeled and halved

1 small head of celeriac (about 800 g), peeled and quartered

3 tablespoons butter

3 tablespoons olive oil

sea salt and freshly ground black pepper

Serves 4

Put the potatoes and celeriac in a saucepan and cover with cold water. Bring to the boil, then immediately remove from the heat and cover with a tight-fitting lid. Set aside for 10 minutes. Drain well and let cool completely.

Grate the potatoes and celeriac into a bowl with 1 teaspoon of salt and some pepper. Toss to combine.

Heat half of the butter and 1 tablespoon of the oil in a large non-stick frying pan set over high heat, swirling the butter around to coat the bottom of the pan. Add the potato mixture and gently press down to form a large cake. Cook for 5 minutes over high heat. Pour 1 tablespoon of olive oil around the very edge of the pan and gently shake the pan often to prevent the rösti from sticking to the bottom. Reduce the heat to medium and cook for 10 minutes, shaking the pan often.

Take a plate slightly larger than the pan. Place it on top of the pan then carefully invert the rösti onto the plate. Add the remaining oil and butter to the pan, then carefully slide the rösti back into the pan, cooked side up, and cook for 10 minutes.

Meanwhile, to cook the sausages, heat the oil in a frying pan set over medium heat. Prick the sausages with a fork, add them to the pan and cook for about 20 minutes, turning often, until well browned, and cooked through.

Spoon the rösti directly from the pan onto serving plates and serve with the sausages and a little mustard on the side.

sage pork chops
with kale colcannon

This is comfort food at its very best – easy to prepare yet tasty sage-crumbed pork chops are served with a mound of creamy Irish-style colcannon mash on the side. This colcannon recipe uses curly kale, a close relative of the cabbage. It is a true cold weather vegetable that actually relies on frost to enhance its flavour. So as the weather gets colder, the kale gets better, making it the perfect choice for late autumn.

60 g plain flour

3 eggs

2 tablespoons Worcestershire sauce

4–6 sage leaves, finely chopped

100 g fresh breadcrumbs

100 g Parmesan cheese, finely grated

4 pork chops

60 ml vegetable oil

kale colcannon

500 g curly kale

2 tablespoons butter

2 rashers of bacon, thinly sliced

6–8 spring onions, thinly sliced

4 large floury potatoes, quartered

125 g butter, cut into cubes

Serves 4

Put the flour on a flat plate. Mix the eggs and Worcestershire sauce in a bowl and, in a separate bowl, combine the sage, breadcrumbs and Parmesan. Press a pork chop into the flour, coating the meat evenly, then dip it in the egg mixture, then press firmly to coat in the crumb mix. Repeat this process with the remaining 3 pork chops. Transfer the chops to a plate, cover and refrigerate until needed.

To make the colcannon, cook the kale in a large saucepan of boiling water for 5 minutes. Drain well, chop finely and set aside.

Put the 2 tablespoons of butter in a frying pan and set over medium heat. Add the bacon and cook for 5 minutes, stirring occasionally, until the bacon turns golden. Add the spring onions and cook for a further 2 minutes. Stir in the kale and remove the pan from the heat.

Put the potatoes in a large saucepan of lightly salted cold water. Bring to the boil and cook for 20 minutes, until soft when pierced with a skewer but not breaking apart. Drain the potatoes well and return them to the warm pan. Add the butter and mash well. Beat with a wooden spoon until smooth. Stir the kale mixture into the potatoes, cover and keep warm.

Heat the vegetable oil in a large frying pan set over medium heat. Add the pork chops and cook for 6–7 minutes, so they gently sizzle in the oil and a golden crust forms. Turn the pork chops over and cook for 5 minutes on the other side. Serve with a generous portion of the kale colcannon.

polenta baked with Italian sausage and cheese

A real winter warmer to eat by a roaring fire. This is sublime comfort food, loaded with sausage and strings of melting cheese. If you can't find Italian sausages, choose those with the highest meat content and bags of flavour. Spicy Spanish chorizo would also be great in this dish.

300 g traditional or quick-cook polenta

500 g fresh Italian sausages (or good, strongly flavoured butcher's sausages)

1 tablespoon olive oil

1 red onion, finely chopped

150 ml vegetable or meat stock

3 tablespoons chopped fresh rosemary and sage, mixed

350 g Taleggio cheese, chopped or grated

150 g Parmesan cheese, grated

a few pieces of butter

sea salt and freshly ground black pepper

a shallow ovenproof dish, buttered

Serves 6

To make the polenta, bring 1 litre salted water to the boil, then slowly sprinkle in the polenta through your fingers, whisking all the time to prevent lumps. Cook, stirring with a wooden spoon, for 45 minutes over low heat. Transfer from the pan to a wooden board and shape into a mound. Let cool and set. (If you are using quick-cook polenta, cook according to the packet instructions.)

Slice the sausages very thickly. Heat the olive oil in a frying pan, add the sausages and fry until browned on all sides. Add the onion and cook for 5 minutes until softening. Add the stock and half the chopped herbs, salt and pepper.

Preheat the oven to 180°C (350°F) Gas 4.

Cut the polenta into 1.5 cm slices. Arrange a layer of polenta in the prepared dish. Add half the sausage mixture, half the Taleggio and half the Parmesan, in layers. Cover with another layer of polenta, add layers of the remaining sausage mixture, Taleggio and Parmesan and dot with a few pieces of butter. Sprinkle with the remaining herbs. Bake in the preheated oven for 40 minutes until brown and bubbling. Serve warm.

meatballs in red pepper sauce

The combination of tomato, orange and chilli gives this dish a Spanish flavour. Any part of this dish – sauce and/or meatballs – can be made a day ahead; in fact, it's better that way. Serve with roasted or sautéed potatoes.

meatballs

50 g fresh breadcrumbs

3 tablespoons milk

1 small white onion

a handful of flat leaf parsley leaves

2 garlic cloves

800 g mince, preferably a mix of beef and pork

1½ teaspoons fine sea salt

1 teaspoon dried oregano

1 teaspoon ground cumin

½ teaspoon Spanish smoked paprika (pimentón)

1 egg, beaten

3 tablespoons extra virgin olive oil

red pepper sauce

2 red peppers

2 tablespoons extra virgin olive oil, plus extra for rubbing

several sprigs of thyme

1 fresh or dried bay leaf

1 white onion, grated

6 garlic cloves, crushed

¼ teaspoon cayenne pepper (optional)

5 tablespoons red wine

½ an orange

1 litre passata (sieved tomatoes)

sea salt and freshly ground black pepper

kitchen string

a large ovenproof dish

Makes about 25 meatballs

Preheat the oven to 220°C (425°F) Gas 7.

To make the sauce, rub the peppers with olive oil, then put them on a sheet of foil on a baking tray (make the foil large enough to fold over and enclose the peppers after roasting). Roast in the preheated oven for about 30–40 minutes, until tender and charred. Remove from the oven, enclose in the foil and set aside. When cool enough to handle, remove the skins and seeds, chop the flesh coarsely and set aside. Lower the oven temperature to 200°C (400°F) Gas 6.

Meanwhile, tie up the thyme and bay leaf with kitchen string. Heat 2 tablespoons of the oil in a heavy-based frying pan. Add the onion and a pinch of salt and cook until soft, 2–3 minutes. Add the garlic and cayenne, if using, and cook, stirring, for 1 minute. Stir in the wine and squeeze in the orange juice (reserve the rest of the orange) and cook for 30 seconds. Add the passata, a good pinch of salt, the bunch of herbs and the reserved orange. Simmer gently for about 20–30 minutes, until thick. Season to taste. Stir in the red peppers, remove the herbs and orange and transfer to a baking dish large enough to hold the meatballs in a single layer. This can be made a day ahead.

To make the meatballs, put the breadcrumbs, milk, onion, parsley, garlic, mince, salt, oregano, cumin, paprika and beaten egg in a large bowl. Mix well (your hands are best). Shape spoonfuls of the meat mixture into golf ball-sized balls and set on a baking tray.

To cook, heat the 3 tablespoons of the oil in a large, heavy-based frying pan. Working in batches, cook the meatballs for about 5 minutes per batch, until browned evenly. Using a slotted spoon, transfer the browned meatballs to the sauce in the baking dish. When all the meatballs are browned, gently spoon some sauce over each one, then cover the baking dish with foil and bake in the preheated oven for 20 minutes. Serve hot with sautéed potatoes.

quick Thai chicken curry

You can add any vegetables to this basic curry recipe, such as mushrooms, French beans, fresh spinach, bamboo shoots, courgette or carrot – it's perfect for using up odds and ends.

400-ml tin coconut milk

50 g green Thai curry paste

1 tablespoon vegetable oil

1 chicken breast (about 400 g), cut into bite-sized pieces

½ teaspoon kaffir lime leaf purée

1 teaspoon Thai fish sauce

100 g mixed fresh vegetables of your choice (see introduction)

a handful of basil leaves

jasmine rice

200 g Thai jasmine rice

25 g unsalted butter

a pinch of sea salt

a wok (optional)

Serves 2

To make the jasmine rice, put the rice in a large saucepan with a tight-fitting lid. Add 375 ml cold water, the butter and salt. Bring to the boil then reduce the heat to a simmer. Cover and cook for about 20 minutes or until the rice has absorbed all the liquid (add a little more water if the rice is not yet tender).

Meanwhile, pour the coconut milk into a separate saucepan and gently bring it to near boiling point. Remove the pan from the heat and stir in the Thai curry paste. Set aside.

Pour the oil into a wok or large frying pan and stir-fry the chicken pieces over high heat for about 2 minutes, until golden. Pour the coconut milk mixture over the fried chicken pieces and add the kaffir lime leaf purée and fish sauce. Add the vegetables, stir and simmer gently for about 12 minutes, or until everything is cooked through.

Remove the rice from the heat and let it sit for 5 minutes. Fluff it up with a fork just before serving. Scatter the basil over the curry and serve with a small bowl of jasmine rice on the side.

chicken jalfrezi

This versatile curry recipe can also be made with beef, lamb, prawns or fish instead of chicken. If using fish, choose a firm white variety such as swordfish, marlin, monkfish or kingfish.

2 tablespoons vegetable oil

1½ large white onions, sliced

2 garlic cloves, chopped

3-cm piece of fresh ginger, peeled and chopped or grated

2 red or green chillies, chopped

1 teaspoon ground turmeric

2 cardamom pods, lightly crushed

2 teaspoons mild curry powder

1 teaspoon ground coriander

1 teaspoon ground cumin

1 kg chicken, cut into chunks

1½ x 400-g tins chopped tomatoes

freshly squeezed juice of 2 limes and 1 lemon

a bunch of coriander, chopped, to serve

sea salt and freshly ground black pepper

Serves 6

Heat the oil in a large saucepan. Add the onion, garlic and chillies and cook until soft, making sure they do not brown. Add the turmeric, cardamom, curry powder, ground coriander and cumin and cook for 2 minutes. Add the chicken, sprinkle with salt and pepper and stir until coated with the spices. Cook for 5 minutes until the chicken is opaque on the outside. Add the tomatoes, mix well, cover with a lid and simmer for 30 minutes, stirring from time to time. Add the lime and lemon juices, simmer for 3 minutes and sprinkle with chopped coriander to serve.

beef en croûte
with mustard sauce

This is a French classic that's perfect for smart dinners. The sauce is delicious but also very rich – a little goes a long way.

4 tablespoons olive oil

3 shallots, finely chopped

2 garlic cloves, chopped

150 g portobello mushrooms, sliced

1.25 kg fillet of beef, trimmed

500 g ready-made puff or shortcrust pastry, thawed if frozen

2 eggs, beaten

sea salt and freshly ground black pepper

mustard sauce

2 tablespoons smooth Dijon mustard

2 tablespoons wholegrain mustard

100 ml white wine

400 ml double cream

reserved juices from roasting the beef fillet

Serves 8

Put 2 tablespoons of the oil into a frying pan and set over low heat. Add the shallots, garlic and mushrooms and gently sauté for about 15 minutes, stirring frequently, until soft but not browned and all the liquid has evaporated. Season with salt and pepper, let cool, then cover and chill.

Preheat the oven to 220°C (425°F) Gas 7.

Put 1 tablespoon of the remaining oil into a roasting tin and put it in the preheated oven to heat for 5 minutes.

Rub the beef fillet all over with the remaining oil and salt and pepper, and transfer to the hot roasting tin. Cook in the hot tin for 15 minutes, then remove. Transfer the fillet to a plate, reserving the meat juices for the mustard sauce, and let cool until completely cold. At this stage, you can make the mustard sauce in the roasting tin and reheat it when you need it or make later in a saucepan.

To make the mustard sauce, add the mustards, white wine and double cream to the roasting tin with the meat juices. Bring to the boil, then simmer for 5 minutes. Remove from the heat, cover and set aside until ready to serve.

Roll out the pastry to a rectangle large enough to wrap around the beef fillet. Brush lightly with a little of the beaten egg. Spoon the mushroom mixture evenly over the pastry, leaving a 5 cm border around the outside. Put the cold beef fillet in the middle of the pastry, on top of the mushrooms, and either roll the pastry around the fillet or wrap, as if covering a parcel. Try not to have too much pastry at the ends, and trim to avoid areas of double pastry. Turn the parcel so that the seam is underneath and transfer to a lightly oiled baking tray. Brush all over with the remaining beaten egg and chill for 2 hours.

Preheat the oven to 200°C (400°F) Gas 6. Cook on the middle shelf of the preheated oven for 20 minutes. Reduce the oven temperature to 180°C (350°F) Gas 4 and continue cooking for 15 minutes for rare, 35 minutes for medium and 50 minutes for well done. If you are cooking to well done, you may need to reduce the oven temperature further to prevent the pastry from burning while the beef cooks through.

When ready to serve, reheat the mustard sauce if necessary, plate slices of the beef and pour a little of the sauce around the outside. Serve immediately with sautéed green beans on the side, if liked.

pan-fried tuna steaks with warm vincotto-dressed lentils

The combination of earthy lentils and sweet, rich vincotto (grape must) is stunning. This recipe works well with good quality balsamic vinegar too, but vincotto definitely has the edge.

300 g Puy or beluga lentils

3 tablespoons olive oil

1 white onion

100 g pancetta lardons

2 tablespoons vincotto or good quality balsamic vinegar

4 fresh tuna steaks

sea salt and freshly ground black pepper

freshly squeezed juice of ½ a lemon

Serves 4

Cook the lentils according to the packet instructions. Meanwhile, heat 2 tablespoons of the olive oil in a frying pan and gently fry the onion for a few minutes, until softened but not coloured. Add the pancetta and cook until crisp. Drain the lentils and add them to the pan. Stir in the vincotto and keep warm.

Brush the tuna with the remaining olive oil and season well. Heat a ridged grill pan or non-stick frying pan. Cook the tuna steaks for 1–2 minutes on each side, depending on how thick they are. (Take care not to overcook the fish as it will be unpleasantly tough and chewy.) Squeeze a little lemon juice over the fish and serve with the warm lentils.

pan-fried tuna steaks with warm vincotto-dressed lentils

The combination of earthy lentils and sweet, rich vincotto (grape must) is stunning. This recipe works well with good quality balsamic vinegar too, but vincotto definitely has the edge.

300 g Puy or beluga lentils

3 tablespoons olive oil

1 white onion

100 g pancetta lardons

2 tablespoons vincotto or good quality balsamic vinegar

4 fresh tuna steaks

sea salt and freshly ground black pepper

freshly squeezed juice of ½ a lemon

Serves 4

Cook the lentils according to the packet instructions. Meanwhile, heat 2 tablespoons of the olive oil in a frying pan and gently fry the onion for a few minutes, until softened but not coloured. Add the pancetta and cook until crisp. Drain the lentils and add them to the pan. Stir in the vincotto and keep warm.

Brush the tuna with the remaining olive oil and season well. Heat a ridged grill pan or non-stick frying pan. Cook the tuna steaks for 1–2 minutes on each side, depending on how thick they are. (Take care not to overcook the fish as it will be unpleasantly tough and chewy.) Squeeze a little lemon juice over the fish and serve with the warm lentils.

chunky fish stew with cheese toasts

1 small white onion, finely chopped

2 garlic cloves, 1 crushed; 1 peeled and halved

a pinch of dried thyme

125 g fennel, hard core removed and finely chopped

1 tablespoon olive oil

50 ml Noilly Prat, dry Martini or dry white wine

400 g passata (sieved tomatoes)

1 pinch of saffron threads

freshly squeezed juice and finely grated zest of 1 orange

200 g skinless cod fillet, cut into large chunks

sea salt and freshly ground black pepper

4 thin slices of baguette

50 g Emmental or Gruyère cheese, finely grated

Serves 2

If you have ever tasted the classic French fish soup bouillabaisse and enjoyed the flavour, then this is a good cheat's version. The combination of saffron, orange and fennel gives the stew its distinctive flavour.

Put the olive oil in a large saucepan and set over low heat. Add the chopped onion, crushed garlic, thyme and fennel and gently sauté, stirring occassionally, for about 6–8 minutes or until soft but not browned. Add the Noilly Prat and let bubble, uncovered, until the liquid has reduced to almost nothing.

Add the passata, saffron, orange juice and zest and 200 ml cold water. Increase the heat to medium and cook for 10 minutes. Add the cod fillet and cook gently for a further 2 minutes, then taste and season as necessary.

Meanwhile, preheat the grill to high. Toast the baguette slices under the hot grill until lightly golden on both sides. Rub the halved garlic over each slice and sprinkle with the grated cheese.

Ladle the stew into warmed serving bowls. Sit two cheese-topped toasts on top and serve immediately.

herb and nut crusted salmon fillets

Serve this deliciously easy yet impressive fish dish with a pile of buttery leeks and creamy mashed potatoes flavoured with a little wholegrain mustard.

1 tablespoon mixed red, green and white dry peppercorns, crushed

4 salmon fillets (about 175 g each), skin on

250 g fresh wholemeal breadcrumbs

75 g shelled walnuts, chopped

8 tablespoons mixed chopped green herbs

finely grated zest of 1 orange

freshly grated nutmeg, to taste

125 g butter, melted

1 egg yolk, beaten

salt and freshly ground black pepper

tartare sauce

150 ml good quality mayonnaise

1 tablespoon chopped capers

1 tablespoon chopped gherkins

1 tablespoon chopped parsley

1 shallot, finely chopped

1 teaspoon freshly squeezed lemon juice

sea salt and freshly ground black pepper

Serves 4

Rub the crushed peppercorns all over the flesh side of the salmon fillets. Put them in a baking dish, skin-side up, cover and set aside.

Mix the breadcrumbs with the walnuts, herbs and orange zest and add ground nutmeg to taste. Set a frying pan over high heat, add the butter and, when foaming, stir in the breadcrumb mixture. Cook until the butter is absorbed and the breadcrumbs are beginning to brown. Season well and set aside.

Preheat the oven to 200°C (400°F) Gas 6.

Brush the salmon skin with egg yolk and press on the breadcrumbs. Bake in the preheated oven for 15–20 minutes, until the fish is opaque and the breadcrumbs crisp.

To make the tartare sauce, mix all the ingredients together in a small bowl and serve as a spooning sauce with the fish.

roast onion and celeriac ravioli
with warm walnut pesto

Walnuts and celeriac make a magical combination, especially when the celeriac is roasted with onion and tucked inside ravioli, as it is here. However, if time is short, try this lovely pesto tossed through pasta tubes such as rigatoni or penne.

pasta

400 g Italian '00' flour

4 eggs, beaten

filling

1 celeriac, peeled and cubed

1 large white onion, finely chopped

1 garlic clove, peeled and crushed

1 teaspoon thyme leaves

2 tablespoons clear honey

3 tablespoons extra virgin olive oil

sea salt and freshly ground black pepper

semolina, to dust

walnut pesto

100 g walnuts

2 garlic cloves, peeled and crushed

3 tablespoons finely chopped rosemary needles

50 g pecorino or Parmesan cheese, finely grated

4 tablespoons walnut oil

Serves 4

To make the pasta, sift the flour into a bowl or food processor. Add the eggs and bring the mixture together to make a soft but not sticky dough. Turn out on to a lightly floured surface and knead for 4–5 minutes, until smooth. Wrap in clingfilm and refrigerate for at least 30 minutes.

Preheat the oven to 200°C (400°F) Gas 6.

To make the filling, put the celeriac, onion, garlic and thyme in a roasting tin. Drizzle with the honey and olive oil, season well and toss to coat in the mixture. Roast in the preheated oven for about 25 minutes, or until the celeriac is soft and golden. Leave to cool slightly, then mash coarsely.

To make the pesto, chop the walnuts, garlic and rosemary very finely in a food processor or by hand. Stir in the pecorino and walnut oil. Season to taste.

Roll out the chilled pasta dough to a thickness of 1 mm using a pasta machine or a rolling pin. Cut the pasta into two long pieces of equal size. Place teaspoonfuls of the filling at even intervals across one half of the pasta. Brush around the filling with a little water and cover with the second sheet. Press lightly around the filling to seal, then cut into squares using a sharp knife or pastry wheel. Lay out the ravioli on a sheet of baking paper lightly dusted with semolina.

Bring a large saucepan of salted water to the boil and drop in the ravioli. Cook for 2–3 minutes, until the pasta rises to the surface and is soft but still retains a little bite. Drain and toss immediately with the walnut pesto. Serve at once.

pasta with broccoli, ricotta and walnuts

The light texture and creamy flavour of ricotta cheese makes the perfect backdrop to walnuts and broccoli in this deliciously simple and quick pasta dish.

100 g shelled walnut halves

1 head of broccoli, about 400–500 g

3 tablespoons light olive oil

3 garlic cloves, thinly sliced

1 handful of flat leaf parsley, chopped

finely grated zest and freshly squeezed juice of 1 lemon

200 g fresh ricotta cheese

400 g spaghetti

sea salt and freshly ground black pepper

Serves 4

Preheat the oven to 180°C (350°F) Gas 4.

Spread the walnuts out on a baking tray and roast in the preheated oven for about 8 minutes, shaking the tray occasionally, until they start to brown.

To prepare the broccoli, trim off the gnarly part, about 2 cm from the stem end, and discard. Thinly slice the stem until you reach the point where it starts to branch into florets. Slice off the individual florets. Heat the oil in a frying pan, add the stems and cook for about 2–3 minutes, turning often, then add the florets and cook for about 5 minutes, until the broccoli has softened. Add the garlic, parsley, lemon zest and walnuts and cook for 5 minutes, stirring often. Reduce the heat to medium and stir in the ricotta and lemon juice. Season well leave in the pan to keep warm.

Cook the spaghetti according to the packet instructions. Drain and return it to the warm pan with the sauce. Stir gently to combine and serve immediately.

mushroom and thyme ragù with hand-torn pasta

This recipe calls for a mixture of mushrooms – button, field and shiitake have been used here but do look out for other exotic varieties, many of which can now be bought year-round. Chestnut, cremini and oyster mushrooms would also work well with the rich, comforting flavours of fresh thyme, red wine and cinnamon.

2 tablespoons light olive oil

2 tablespoons butter

1 white onion, chopped

2 garlic cloves, chopped

3 large field mushrooms, stalks removed and caps chopped

200 g button mushrooms

100 g fresh shiitake mushrooms, quartered

3 thyme sprigs

250 ml red wine

1 cinnamon stick

250 ml vegetable or beef stock

400 g fresh lasagne sheets, cut or torn into thick strips

sea salt and freshly ground black pepper

freshly grated Parmesan cheese, to serve

Serves 4

Heat the oil and butter in a heavy-based saucepan set over medium heat. Add the onion and garlic and cook for 4–5 minutes, until the onions have softened. Increase the heat to high, add the mushrooms and thyme and cook for a further 8–10 minutes, stirring often, until the mushrooms darken and soften.

Add the red wine and cinnamon to the pan and boil rapidly for 5 minutes. Pour in the stock and season well. Reduce the heat to low and let the mixture gently simmer, uncovered, for 35–40 minutes.

Cook the pasta in a saucepan of salted boiling water for 2–3 minutes, until it rises to the surface. Drain well and place in serving bowls. Spoon the mushroom ragù over the top, sprinkle with Parmesan and serve immediately.

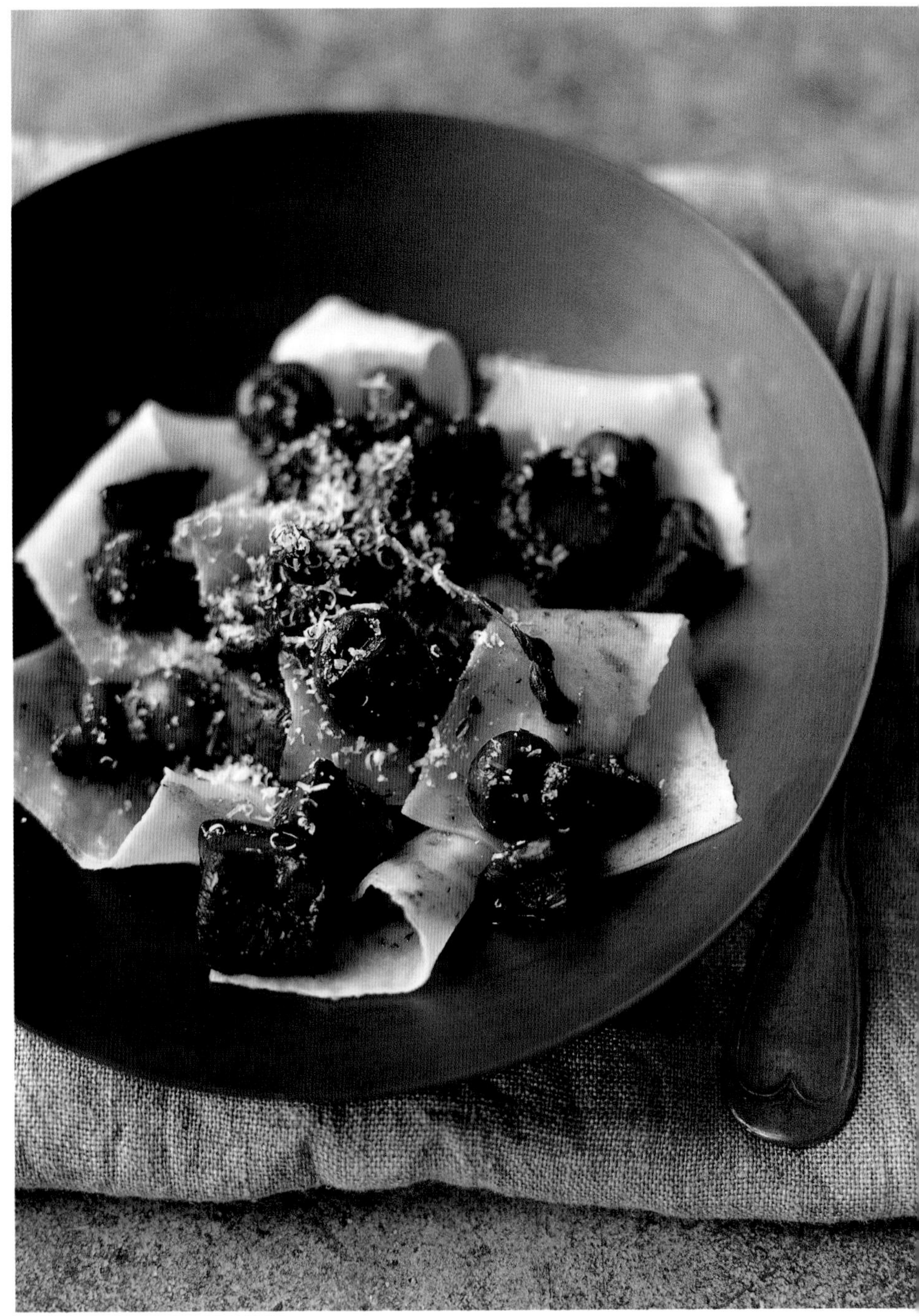

spaghetti with butternut squash, sage and pecorino

65 ml light olive oil

400 g butternut squash, peeled, deseeded and sliced into thin wedges

2 garlic cloves, chopped

10–12 small sage leaves

400 g spaghetti

1 handful of flat leaf parsley, chopped

50 g pecorino or Parmesan cheese, grated

sea salt and freshly ground black pepper

Serves 4

This tasty pasta is inspired by the classic Italian dish of pumpkin-filled ravioli with sage butter, except this is an inside-out version and therefore much easier to make! Butternut squash is used here, but you could also use pumpkin.

Put the oil in a frying pan and set over high heat. Add the squash and cook for 5–6 minutes, turning often, until golden but not breaking up. Add the garlic and sage to the pan and cook for 2–3 minutes. Remove from the heat and set aside to allow the flavours to develop.

Cook the pasta according to the packet instructions. Drain well and return it to the warm pan with the squash mixture. Add the parsley and half of the pecorino. Season well and toss gently to combine. Sprinkle the remaining pecorino over the top and serve immediately.

Swiss chard, feta cheese and egg pie

The pastry here is based on the Turkish version of pizza dough (pide), which is often filled or topped with the freshest of vegetables such as tomatoes, spinach or chard, or tangy feta cheese and sometimes with an egg or two cracked on top before being baked. It's very easy to see where the inspiration for this delicious open pie came from!

3 tablespoons olive oil

2 garlic cloves, sliced

1 red onion, thinly sliced

500 g Swiss chard, chopped

4 eggs

200 g feta cheese, crumbled

sea salt and freshly ground black pepper

pastry

250 g plain flour

150 g unsalted butter, cut into cubes

2 egg yolks

2–3 tablespoons iced water

Serves 6

To make the pastry, put the flour and butter in the bowl of a food processor and put the bowl in the freezer for 10 minutes. Pulse the ingredients a few times until just combined. With the motor of the food processor running, add the egg yolks and just enough iced water so that the mixture is on the verge of coming together. Do not overbeat, as this will make the pastry tough. Remove the dough from the bowl and use lightly floured hands to quickly form it into a ball. Wrap in clingfilm and let rest in the fridge for 30 minutes.

Put 2 tablespoons of the oil in a frying pan and set over high heat. Add the onion and garlic and cook for 2 minutes, until it softens and just flavours the oil. Add the Swiss chard to the pan and cook for about 5 minutes, stirring often, until it wilts and softens. Season well, leave in the pan and set aside to cool.

Preheat the oven to 220°C (425°F) Gas 7.

Roll the pastry dough out on a sheet of lightly floured baking paper to form a circle about 35 cm in diameter, trimming away any uneven bits. Roll the edge over to form a 1-cm border, then roll over again. Transfer the pastry to a baking tray. Spoon the Swiss chard mixture over the top. Put the eggs in a bowl and prick the yolks with a fork. Pour them over the Swiss chard then scatter the feta over the top. Drizzle the remaining oil over the pie and cook in the preheated oven for about 20 minutes, until the pastry is golden and the top of the pie is just starting to turn brown. Let cool for 10 minutes before cutting into slices to serve.

egg, bacon and spinach pie

Autumn is a great time for pies. The weather is often fickle and you have the option of serving a slice of pie with creamy mash or with a tomato salad if the days are still mild. Any leftovers will keep in the fridge for a few days so you can enjoy them as late supper.

500 g fresh spinach

1 tablespoon butter

3 rashers of rindless streaky bacon, cut into thin strips

1 white onion, finely chopped

6 eggs, lightly beaten

50 g Parmesan cheese, finely grated

1 egg, lightly beaten with 1 tablespoon cold water

shortcrust pastry

250 g plain flour

150 g butter, cut into small cubes

1 egg yolk

a loose-based tart tin, 20 cm diameter, lightly greased

Serves 6

Put the flour and butter into the bowl of a food processor and put the bowl into the freezer for 15 minutes. Lightly beat the egg yolk with 2 tablespoons water and refrigerate for 15 minutes. Process the butter and flour until the mixture looks like ground almonds, then add the egg yolk mixture and process for just a few seconds to combine. Tip the mixture into a bowl and use your hands to bring the dough together to form one large ball. It should be a bit crumbly. Wrap in clingfilm and refrigerate for 30 minutes.

Preheat the oven to 180°C (350°F) Gas 4.

Wash the spinach well, leaving some of the water on the leaves. Put it in a large non-stick frying pan and set over high heat. Cook for 2 minutes, until wilted. Transfer to a colander and drain well. When cool enough to handle, use your hands to squeeze out as much water as possible from the spinach and place it in a large bowl.

Heat the butter in the frying pan set over high heat. When sizzling, add the bacon and onion and cook for 5 minutes until golden. Spoon the mixture into the bowl with the spinach. Add the eggs and Parmesan and season well. Stir to combine.

Put the prepared tart tin on a baking tray. Cut two-thirds from the dough and roll it out between two layers of baking paper. Line the bottom of the tart tin with the pastry. Spoon the spinach mixture on top of the pastry base. Roll the remaining pastry out into a circle slightly larger than the tart tin. Place this on top of the pie, allowing any excess pastry to hang over the edge and gently press down around the edges to seal. Brush with the egg and water mixture and bake in the preheated oven for 1 hour, until golden brown.

Let the pie cool for about 10–15 minutes before cutting into wedges. Serve with boiled and buttered new potatoes, if liked.

chicken, leek and tarragon pot pie

When autumn really sets in it is good to know you can rely on one shining beacon of fresh-grown produce: the leek. While most other vegetables are waiting for spring to make it to the dinner table again, summer-planted leeks will be ready to enjoy long after the summer has gone. Do look out for anise-flavoured fresh tarragon as it's particularly good with chicken and cream and works a treat here. The pastry recipe isn't as intimidating as it looks so do try it at least once before resorting to frozen ready-made pastry.

3 tablespoons butter

750 g chicken thigh fillets, cut into bite-sized pieces

4 leeks (white parts only), thickly sliced

3 tablespoons plain flour

250 ml chicken stock

125 ml single cream

2 tablespoons finely chopped tarragon

2 tablespoons roughly chopped flat leaf parsley

sea salt and freshly ground black pepper

pie pastry

185 g plain flour

2 tablespoons butter

2 tablespoons sour cream

1 egg, lightly beaten

a large, deep pie dish (about 1.5 litre capacity)

Serves 4

Put half of the butter in a large frying pan and set over high heat. When the butter is sizzling, add the chicken and cook for 2–3 minutes, turning often until browned all over. Transfer to a bowl.

Add the remaining butter to the pan and cook the leeks over medium heat for 2 minutes. Cover with a lid, reduce the heat, and gently cook for 2–3 minutes, until very soft.

Return the chicken to the pan and increase the heat to high. Sprinkle the flour into the pan and cook for 2 minutes, stirring constantly so that the flour thickly coats the chicken and leeks. Gradually add the chicken stock, stirring all the time. Bring to the boil, then stir in the cream, tarragon and parsley. Season well. Reduce the heat and gently simmer until thickened. Remove from the heat and let cool. Spoon the mixture into the pie dish.

To make the pastry, put the flour, butter and a pinch of salt in a food processor and process for a few seconds. With the motor running, add the sour cream, half of the beaten egg and 1–2 tablespoons cold water. Mix until the dough comes together. Roll into a ball, wrap in clingfilm and refrigerate for 30 minutes.

Preheat the oven to 180°C (350°F) Gas 4. Put the dough between two pieces of baking paper and roll out to a thickness of 5 mm, making sure the dough is more than big enough to cover the dish. Fold the dough over the top of the pie, leaving the edges to overhang. Cut several slits in the top of the pie and gently press down around the edges with the tines of a fork to seal. Brush the remaining beaten egg over the top. Put the pie dish on a baking tray and cook in the preheated oven for about 30 minutes, until the pastry is golden.

steak and wild mushroom pies

This glorious recipe can be baked as six individual pies or one large pie, as preferred, and can be completely made ahead of time. Make the beef stew in advance, top with the pastry and refrigerate until ready to put in the oven. Mixed dried wild mushrooms are available in most supermarkets.

50 g dried wild mushrooms

6 tablespoons olive oil or beef dripping

1 white onion, finely chopped

3 garlic cloves, chopped

1 large carrot, finely chopped

2 celery stalks, finely chopped

125 g cubed pancetta or streaky bacon

8 juniper berries, crushed

3 fresh or dried bay leaves

2 tablespoons chopped thyme

2 tablespoons plain flour

1 kg stewing beef, trimmed and cut into large cubes

300 ml red wine

2 tablespoons redcurrant jelly

600 g ready-rolled puff pastry, thawed if frozen

1 egg, beaten

sea salt and freshly ground black pepper

a large casserole (optional)

6 individual pie dishes or 1 large pie dish

Serves 6

Put the dried mushrooms in a bowl, just cover with hot water and let soak for 30 minutes. Meanwhile, heat half the oil in a large casserole or saucepan, add the onion, garlic, carrot and celery and cook for 5–10 minutes until softening. Stir in the pancetta and fry with the vegetables until just beginning to brown. Add the juniper berries, bay leaves and thyme, sprinkle in the flour, mix well and set aside.

Heat the remaining olive oil in a large frying pan and fry the beef quickly (in batches) on all sides until crusty and brown. Transfer to the casserole as you go. When done, deglaze the frying pan with the wine, let bubble, then scrape up the sediment from the bottom of the pan. Pour over the meat and vegetables. Drain the mushrooms and add to the casserole with 150 ml of the soaking water and the redcurrant jelly. Season well and bring to the boil on the hob, then let gently simmer for 1½ hours until the meat is tender. Let cool overnight.

Next day, preheat the the oven to 220°C (425°F) Gas 7.

Spoon the beef mixture into 6 small pie dishes. Cut out 6 circles of pastry, 3 cm wider than the dishes. Alternatively, use a large pie dish and roll the pastry 3 cm wider than the dish. Brush the edges of the dishes with egg, sit the pastry on top and press over the rim to seal. Brush with more egg, but don't pierce the tops (the steam must be trapped inside). Put the pies on 2 baking trays and chill for 30 minutes. Bake in the preheated oven for 20–25 minutes (or 45 minutes–1 hour for the large pie) until the pastry is risen, crisp and golden.

goats' cheese, leek and walnut tart

250 g ready-made puff pastry, thawed if frozen

50 g butter

4 small leeks, trimmed and sliced

200 g goats' cheese log with rind, sliced

sea salt and freshly ground black pepper

freshly chopped parsley, to serve

walnut paste

125 g shelled walnut pieces

3 garlic cloves, crushed

6 tablespoons walnut oil

3 tablespoons chopped parsley

a 28-cm diameter dinner plate or similar (to use as a template)

Serves 4–6

This light, creamy open tart is easy to make because there is no need to line a tin or bake blind – simply roll out the pastry and top it as you would a pizza. Goats' cheese and walnuts are a great combination, especially combined here with soft earthy leeks.

Preheat the oven to 200°C (400°F) Gas 6.

Roll the pastry out thinly on a lightly floured work surface. Cut out a 28 cm circle using the dinner plate as a template. Set on a baking tray and chill or freeze for at least 15 minutes.

Melt the butter in a large saucepan and add the leeks, stirring to coat. Add a few tablespoons of water and a teaspoon of salt, and cover with a lid. Steam very gently for at least 20 minutes, until just softening. Remove the lid and cook for a few minutes to evaporate any excess liquid. Let cool.

To make the walnut paste, blend the walnuts and garlic in a food processor with 2 tablespoons water. Mix in the walnut oil and stir in the parsley. Spread this over the pastry, avoiding the rim.

Spoon the leeks into the pastry base and top with the goats' cheese. Drizzle with any remaining walnut paste. Season well and sprinkle with olive oil. Bake in the preheated oven for 20 minutes, until the pastry is golden and the cheese bubbling and brown. Sprinkle with parsley and serve immediately.

potato and Parmesan tart

Real comfort food for a miserable wet weekend! This is a deliciously creamy tart, which makes a casual supper dish when served with smoked salmon or a few rashers of crisply fried bacon.

400 g ready-made shortcrust pastry, thawed if frozen

900 g waxy potatoes, such as Desirée, thinly sliced (do not rinse the potatoes as their starch will help to thicken the cream)

50 g butter, cut into pieces

125 g freshly grated Parmesan cheese

4 tablespoons snipped chives

freshly grated nutmeg, to taste

1 egg, beaten

300 ml double cream

sea salt and freshly ground black pepper

a deep tart tin or dish (about 1 litre capacity)

foil or baking paper and baking weights

Serves 4–6

Preheat the oven to 200°C (400°F) Gas 6.

Roll out the pastry thinly on a lightly floured work surface. Use the pastry to line the tin or dish, then prick the base all over with a fork. Chill or freeze for 15 minutes.

Line the pastry case with foil, then fill with baking weights. Set on a baking tray and bake blind in the preheated oven for about 10–12 minutes. Remove the foil and the baking weights and return the pastry case to the oven for a further 5–8 minutes to dry out completely. Reduce the oven temperature to 160°C (325°F) Gas 3.

Reserve 50 g of the Parmesan. Layer the sliced potatoes and butter in the baked case, seasoning each layer with some of the remaining Parmesan, chives, nutmeg, salt and pepper.

Put the egg and cream into a bowl, beat well, then pour the mixture over the potatoes. Sprinkle the reserved Parmesan over the top. Bake in the still-hot oven for about 1 hour (it may take up to 15 minutes longer, depending on the type of potato used) or until the potatoes are tender and the top is dark golden brown.

Let cool for 10 minutes before serving with smoked salmon or fried bacon, if liked

Note You could speed up the cooking time by precooking the filling in the microwave. Mix the sliced potatoes, pieces of butter, 75 g of the Parmesan, nutmeg, half the cream, salt and pepper in a non-metallic bowl. Cover, leaving a small hole for steam to escape, and microwave for 10 minutes on HIGH. Mix in the remaining cream and egg. Carefully spoon the mixture into the pastry case, sprinkling with chives as you go. Finish with the remaining Parmesan cheese and bake for about 30 minutes, until tender.

red curry of roasted autumn vegetables

The vegetables here are very earthy and distinctive, sweet and nutty and the parsnip has that delicious slightly bitter edge. Thai basil is more intensely anise flavoured than other varieties. It may be hard to find so try a few leaves of fresh tarragon if you have difficulty sourcing it. Do shop around and experiment to find a Thai curry paste that you really like.

4 small new potatoes, halved

1 large carrot, cut into bite-sized pieces

1 tablespoon light olive oil

400 g pumpkin, peeled and cut into 2–3 cm pieces

1 parsnip, peeled and cut into batons

1 red onion, cut into 8 wedges

400 ml coconut milk

2 tablespoons Thai red curry paste

2 tablespoons brown sugar

2 tablespoons Thai fish sauce

250 ml chicken or vegetable stock

a handful of basil leaves (preferably Thai basil)

jasmine rice, to serve (see page 45)

Serves 4

Preheat the oven to 220°C (425°F) Gas 7. Put a baking tray in the oven for 10 minutes to heat.

Put the potatoes and carrot on the hot tray in a single layer, drizzle with the oil and roast in the preheated oven for 10 minutes. Add the pumpkin, parsnip and onion to the tray and roast for a further 20 minutes.

Meanwhile, put 250 ml of the coconut milk in a heavy-based saucepan and set over high heat. Bring to the boil then add the curry paste and stir well. Let boil for 4–5 minutes, until the oil starts to separate from the milk. Add the sugar and fish sauce and cook for 2 minutes, until the mixture is very dark.

Add the remaining coconut milk and chicken stock to the pan. Return to the boil then stir in the roasted vegetables and basil. Cook over low heat for 5 minutes to heat the vegetables through, then serve with bowls of fluffy jasmine rice.

potato and Parmesan tart

Real comfort food for a miserable wet weekend! This is a deliciously creamy tart, which makes a casual supper dish when served with smoked salmon or a few rashers of crisply fried bacon.

400 g ready-made shortcrust pastry, thawed if frozen

900 g waxy potatoes, such as Desirée, thinly sliced (do not rinse the potatoes as their starch will help to thicken the cream)

50 g butter, cut into pieces

125 g freshly grated Parmesan cheese

4 tablespoons snipped chives

freshly grated nutmeg, to taste

1 egg, beaten

300 ml double cream

sea salt and freshly ground black pepper

a deep tart tin or dish (about 1 litre capacity)

foil or baking paper and baking weights

Serves 4–6

Preheat the oven to 200°C (400°F) Gas 6.

Roll out the pastry thinly on a lightly floured work surface. Use the pastry to line the tin or dish, then prick the base all over with a fork. Chill or freeze for 15 minutes.

Line the pastry case with foil, then fill with baking weights. Set on a baking tray and bake blind in the preheated oven for about 10–12 minutes. Remove the foil and the baking weights and return the pastry case to the oven for a further 5–8 minutes to dry out completely. Reduce the oven temperature to 160°C (325°F) Gas 3.

Reserve 50 g of the Parmesan. Layer the sliced potatoes and butter in the baked case, seasoning each layer with some of the remaining Parmesan, chives, nutmeg, salt and pepper.

Put the egg and cream into a bowl, beat well, then pour the mixture over the potatoes. Sprinkle the reserved Parmesan over the top. Bake in the still-hot oven for about 1 hour (it may take up to 15 minutes longer, depending on the type of potato used) or until the potatoes are tender and the top is dark golden brown.

Let cool for 10 minutes before serving with smoked salmon or fried bacon, if liked

Note You could speed up the cooking time by precooking the filling in the microwave. Mix the sliced potatoes, pieces of butter, 75 g of the Parmesan, nutmeg, half the cream, salt and pepper in a non-metallic bowl. Cover, leaving a small hole for steam to escape, and microwave for 10 minutes on HIGH. Mix in the remaining cream and egg. Carefully spoon the mixture into the pastry case, sprinkling with chives as you go. Finish with the remaining Parmesan cheese and bake for about 30 minutes, until tender.

red curry of roasted autumn vegetables

The vegetables here are very earthy and distinctive, sweet and nutty and the parsnip has that delicious slightly bitter edge. Thai basil is more intensely anise flavoured than other varieties. It may be hard to find so try a few leaves of fresh tarragon if you have difficulty sourcing it. Do shop around and experiment to find a Thai curry paste that you really like.

4 small new potatoes, halved

1 large carrot, cut into bite-sized pieces

1 tablespoon light olive oil

400 g pumpkin, peeled and cut into 2–3 cm pieces

1 parsnip, peeled and cut into batons

1 red onion, cut into 8 wedges

400 ml coconut milk

2 tablespoons Thai red curry paste

2 tablespoons brown sugar

2 tablespoons Thai fish sauce

250 ml chicken or vegetable stock

a handful of basil leaves (preferably Thai basil)

jasmine rice, to serve (see page 45)

Serves 4

Preheat the oven to 220°C (425°F) Gas 7. Put a baking tray in the oven for 10 minutes to heat.

Put the potatoes and carrot on the hot tray in a single layer, drizzle with the oil and roast in the preheated oven for 10 minutes. Add the pumpkin, parsnip and onion to the tray and roast for a further 20 minutes.

Meanwhile, put 250 ml of the coconut milk in a heavy-based saucepan and set over high heat. Bring to the boil then add the curry paste and stir well. Let boil for 4–5 minutes, until the oil starts to separate from the milk. Add the sugar and fish sauce and cook for 2 minutes, until the mixture is very dark.

Add the remaining coconut milk and chicken stock to the pan. Return to the boil then stir in the roasted vegetables and basil. Cook over low heat for 5 minutes to heat the vegetables through, then serve with bowls of fluffy jasmine rice.

harissa-spiced chickpeas with halloumi and spinach

Halloumi is a firm Greek cheese that is delicious eaten when hot and melting. It has a long shelf-life before it is opened, which means you can keep a pack tucked away in the fridge and rustle up this delicious supper dish at short notice. Harissa is a fiery chilli paste used in North African cooking.

1 tablespoon olive oil

1 white onion, finely chopped

1 garlic clove, crushed

1 tablespoon harissa paste* (see note right)

400-g tin chickpeas, drained

400-g tin chopped tomatoes

125 g halloumi cheese, cut into cubes

100 g baby spinach leaves

sea salt and freshly ground black pepper

freshly squeezed juice of ½ a lemon

freshly grated Parmesan cheese, to serve

warmed naan bread, to serve

Serves 2

Pour the oil into a large saucepan and set over low heat. Add the onion and garlic and gently sauté until softened. Add the harissa paste, chickpeas and chopped tomatoes and stir to combine. Bring to the boil then reduce the heat and let simmer for about 5 minutes.

Add the halloumi cheese and spinach, cover and cook over a low heat for a further 5 minutes. Season to taste and stir in the lemon juice. Spoon onto serving plates and sprinkle with the Parmesan cheese. Serve immediately with warmed naan bread for mopping up the sauce.

***Note:** If you don't have harissa paste, you can make your own by mixing together ½ teaspoon cayenne pepper, 1 tablespoon ground cumin, 1 tablespoon tomato purée and the freshly squeezed juice of 1 lime.

winter vegetable gratin

200 g celeriac, peeled and cut into 3-cm pieces
1 carrot, peeled and cut into rounds
1 parsnip, peeled and cut into semi-circles
1 small swede, peeled and cut into chunks
2 potatoes, cut into 3–cm pieces
250 ml single cream
1 garlic clove, crushed
1 teaspoon mustard powder
50 g fresh rye or brown breadcrumbs
2 tablespoons finely grated Parmesan cheese
2 teaspoons marjoram leaves
25 g butter, melted
sea salt and freshly ground black pepper

a shallow ovenproof dish, buttered

Serves 6

This is a great way to use up any combination of root vegetables, especially those that are often overlooked like swede and parsnip.

Preheat the oven to 180°C (350°F) Gas 4.

Bring a large saucepan of lightly salted water to the boil. Add the celeriac, carrot, parsnip, swede and potatoes. Cook for 10 minutes, drain well and transfer to a large bowl.

Put the cream, garlic and mustard powder in a small saucepan and set over medium heat. Cook, stirring constantly, for about 10 minutes until the mixture is thick and coats the back of a spoon. Season to taste and pour over the vegetables. Spoon the vegetables into the prepared baking dish.

Put the breadcrumbs, Parmesan and marjoram in a bowl and mix to combine. Sprinkle the breadcrumb mixture over the vegetables and drizzle the melted butter over the top.

Cook in the preheated oven for about 40 minutes, until the breadcrumbs are golden and the mixture around the edge of the baking dish has formed a golden crust. Serve warm, not hot, as a vegetarian main or as a side dish with any roast meat.

tomato and aubergine gratin with tomato and chilli pesto

2 aubergines
500 g ripe tomatoes
about 150 ml olive oil
4 tablespoons freshly chopped basil
125 g freshly grated Parmesan cheese
sea salt and freshly ground black pepper

tomato and chilli pesto

1 large red pepper
55 g basil leaves
1 garlic clove, crushed
2 tablespoons pine nuts, toasted
2 very ripe tomatoes
6 sun-dried tomatoes in oil, drained
3 tablespoons tomato purée
1 teaspoon mild chilli powder
55 g Parmesan or pecorino cheese, grated
150 ml extra virgin olive oil

a shallow ovenproof dish, buttered

Serves 4

A deliciously spicy and satisfying vegetarian dish. Any leftover tomato and chilli pesto can be spooned into a jar, covered with a thin layer of olive oil and kept in the refrigerator for up to 2 weeks. It's great with pasta or grilled meat and fish.

Using a sharp knife, cut the aubergine into 5 mm slices. Sprinkle with salt and put in a colander to drain for 30 minutes. Rinse well and pat dry with kitchen paper.

Preheat the oven to 220°C (425°F) Gas 7.

To make the tomato and chilli pesto, put the red pepper on a baking tray and cook in the preheated oven for about 15 minutes, turning often until the skin is starting to blacken and puff up. Transfer it to a clean plastic bag and let cool. When the pepper is cool enough to handle peel off most of the blackened skin, pull out the stalk and scrape out the seeds. Put the flesh in a food processor with the basil, garlic, pine nuts, tomatoes, sun-dried tomatoes, tomato purée, chilli powder and Parmesan and blend until smooth. With the machine running, slowly pour in the olive oil until well blended. Set aside until needed.

Preheat the oven to 200°C (400°F) Gas 6.

Heat the grill. Brush the aubergines with olive oil and grill on both sides until brown. Drain on kitchen paper. Cut the tomatoes in half through the middle. Arrange a layer of aubergines in the baking dish, followed, by a few spoonfuls of pesto, then a layer of tomatoes and the basil. Sprinkle with Parmesan. Season well, then repeat, finishing with a layer of aubergines. Sprinkle over the remaining Parmesan.

Bake in the preheated oven for 25–30 minutes until browned and bubbling on top. Cool slightly, then serve warm with plenty of bread and a green salad, if liked.

taleggio and potato tortilla
with red pepper tapenade

The creamy Taleggio cheese packs a super-rich taste punch and makes this tortilla more than enough for four to enjoy as a light supper. The red pepper tapenade is a very versatile recipe to have in your repertoire. It can be tossed through cooked pasta, spooned over grilled vegetables and stirred into soup.

1 tablespoon olive oil

10–12 small, waxy new potatoes, thickly sliced

1 small red onion, roughly chopped

250 ml vegetable stock

1 handful of flat leaf parsley, chopped

100 g Taleggio cheese, chopped

2 eggs, lightly beaten

red pepper tapenade

1 large red pepper

1 garlic clove, chopped

50 g pine nuts, lightly toasted

2 tablespoons olive oil

50 g Parmesan cheese, finely grated

Serves 4

To make the tapenade, preheat the oven to 220°C (425°F) Gas 7. Put a baking tray in the oven for a few minutes to heat.

Put the red pepper on the baking tray and cook in the preheated oven for about 15 minutes, turning often until the skin is starting to blacken and puff up. Transfer to a clean plastic bag and let cool. When cool enough to handle, peel off the skin, chop the flesh and put it in a food processor. Add the garlic, pine nuts and oil and process until smooth. Spoon into a bowl, add the Parmesan and stir to combine.

Put the oil, potatoes and onion in a frying pan with a heatproof handle. Set over high heat and cook for 1 minute. Add the stock and cook for about 10 minutes, until the stock has evaporated. Stir in the parsley and sprinkle the pieces evenly over the potatoes. Pour the eggs into the pan and cook for about 2–3 minutes, until the tortilla starts to puff up around the edges.

Preheat the grill to high. Put the frying pan under the hot grill and cook the tortilla for 1–2 minutes, until the top is golden but still wobbly in the centre. Spread some of the tapenade over a serving plate and carefully slide the tortilla onto the plate. Cut into slices and serve warm with extra tapenade on the side for spooning.

mountain eggs

This simple yet satisfying dish is popular in the Swiss Alps, where they cook and serve it in small, individual frying pans. Ham is traditional, but it is also very good with slices of chorizo sausage.

4 teaspoons olive oil

4 large cooked potatoes, thickly sliced

200 g smoked ham, chopped

4 eggs

4 slices Emmental cheese or 100 g grated Emmental

sea salt and freshly ground black pepper

chopped flat leaf parsley, to serve (optional)

Serves 4

Heat 1 teaspoon of oil in each of 4 small frying pans. Add the potatoes and cook for 2 minutes on each side. Stir in the ham.

Crack an egg into each pan. Top with the sliced or grated cheese, sprinkle with salt and pepper and cook for 2–3 minutes until the egg is just set and the cheese is melting.

Serve immediately, sprinkled with chopped parsley, if using.

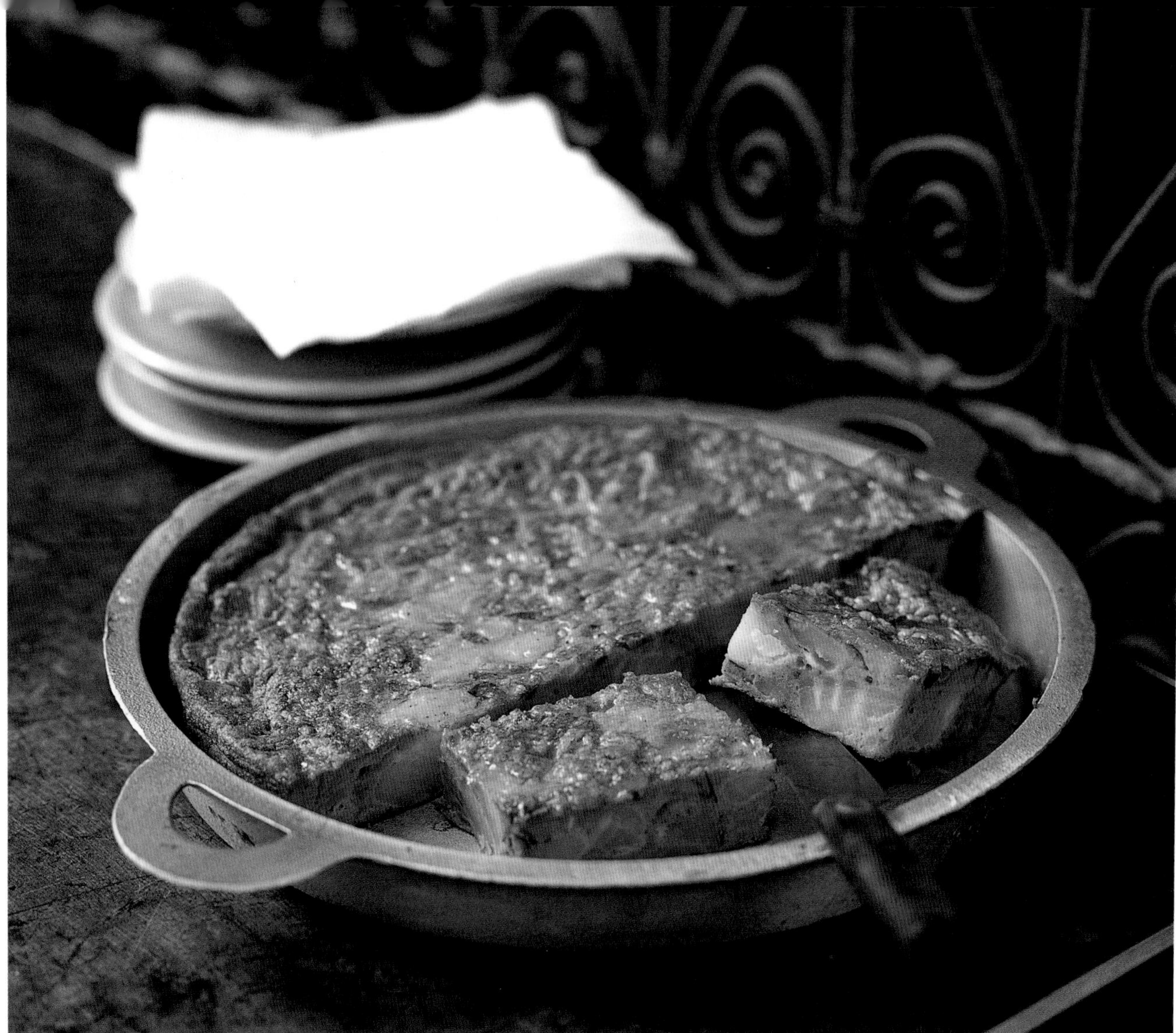

spicy potato omelette

- 4–6 medium potatoes, unpeeled and halved
- 6–8 eggs
- 1 teaspoon ground turmeric
- 1 teaspoon ground cumin
- 1 teaspoon paprika
- ½ teaspoon ground coriander
- 1 handful of flat leaf parsley, finely chopped
- 1 tablespoon olive oil
- sea salt and freshly ground black pepper

Serve 4–6

This Spanish-style potato omelette can be cut into thin strips and served as a light supper or as a side dish with grilled food. The entire omelette can be cooked on the hob and browned under the grill, or it can be baked in the oven.

Put the potatoes in a large saucepan with plenty of salted water and bring to the boil. Cook until tender. Drain and refresh under cold running water. When cool enough to handle, peel off the skins and transfer to a bowl and mash well. Beat the eggs into the potatoes and add the spices and parsley. Season to taste.

Heat the oil in a frying pan with a heatproof handle. Tip in the potato mixture making sure it spreads evenly in the pan. Cover and cook over low heat for 10–15 minutes, until the omelette has puffed up and is firm to the touch.

Preheat the grill to high. Place the pan under the grill for 3–4 minutes to brown the top of the omelette. Cut into slices and serve warm.

one-pot wonders

Portuguese lamb stew with piri piri

A huge, colourful stew is very inviting, and this one makes a nice change from the standard repertoire. The marinade is authentic, as is the spicing; the fiery chilli heat comes from Portuguese piri piri sauce. Be sure to buy imported Portuguese sauce, not the inferior chain-restaurant brand more widely available; it makes a huge difference to the taste. This dose has been approved by both a panel of chilli-lovers and the chilli-wary, so it's fine. But piri piri is very hot and heat varies from one brand to another, so beware if you've never tried it. You can always add more after cooking if it's not hot enough. Serve with Plain, Buttery Couscous (see page 77) or boiled rice.

1 kg boneless lamb, cubed

2 tablespoons olive oil

1½ tablespoons plain flour

500 g waxy potatoes, peeled and cut into large chunks

500 g carrots, cut into large pieces

1–2 teaspoons piri piri sauce, to taste

750 g courgettes, cut into thick rounds

1 red pepper, deseeded and cut into pieces

400-g tin chickpeas, drained

sea salt and freshly ground black pepper

marinade

1 white onion, chopped

6 tablespoons sherry vinegar

1½ teaspoons Spanish smoked paprika (pimentón)

4 garlic cloves, sliced

1 large handful of chopped coriander

1 large handful of chopped flat leaf parsley

1 tablespoon coarse sea salt

a large, flameproof casserole

Serves 6

To make the marinade, combine all of the ingredients in a large non-reactive dish. Mix well. Add the lamb and turn to coat thoroughly. Cover with clingfilm and refrigerate for at least 3 hours or overnight.

Preheat the oven to 190°C (375°F) Gas 5.

Heat the oil in a large flameproof casserole. When very hot, add the lamb and all of the marinade. Sprinkle with the flour and stir to coat well. Cook the lamb for 3–5 minutes to sear, then stir in 250 ml water. Add the potatoes, carrots, some salt and piri piri and mix well. Cover with a lid and cook in the preheated oven for 50 minutes.

Add the courgettes and red pepper and cook for a further 40 minutes. Remove from the oven and stir in the chickpeas. Season to taste, adding more piri piri if necessary. Serve hot with couscous or rice.

Languedoc beef stew with red wine, herbs and olives

This is an adaptation of the classic French beef daube. Adding a little extra wine right at the end lifts the winey flavour after the long, slow cooking.

1 kg thickly sliced braising or stewing steak

25 g plain flour

5–6 tablespoons olive oil

1 large white onion, thinly sliced

2 large garlic cloves, crushed

1 tablespoon tomato purée

300 ml full-bodied fruity red wine

125 ml fresh beef stock

1 teaspoon herbes de Provence

1 thin strip of orange zest

2 fresh or dry bay leaves

100 g black olives, stoned

3 heaped tablespoons roughly chopped flat leaf parsley

sea salt and freshly ground black pepper

slow-roasted carrots

500 g carrots

a pinch of cayenne pepper

2 tablespoons olive oil

a large flameproof casserole

a large, shallow ovenproof dish

Serves 4–6

Trim any excess fat from the beef, then cut the meat into large cubes. Put the flour in a shallow dish and season with salt and pepper. Dip the cubes of beef in the flour to coat.

Heat 2 tablespoons oil in a frying pan, add the beef and fry on all sides until it is browned – do this in batches, adding extra oil as you go. Transfer the beef to a large flameproof casserole. Heat the remaining oil in the frying pan, add the onion and cook for 3–4 minutes until softened but not browned. Add the garlic and tomato purée and cook for 1 minute, stirring. Add 250 ml of the wine, the stock, herbes de Provence, orange zest and bay leaves. Bring to the boil, then pour the sauce into the casserole with the beef. Heat the casserole over medium heat and bring the sauce back to the boil. Reduce the heat, cover and simmer very gently for 2½–3 hours until the meat is completely tender. Check the contents of the casserole occasionally to ensure there is enough liquid (add a little extra stock or water if it's dry).

About two-thirds of the way through the cooking time, prepare the slow-roasted carrots. Preheat the oven to 180°C (350°F) Gas 4. Cut the carrots into long, thick diagonal slices. Put the carrots, salt and cayenne pepper in a large, shallow ovenproof dish, pour the oil over and toss well. Bake in the preheated oven for 45–60 minutes until the carrots are soft and their edges caramelized.

About 30 minutes before the stew is ready, stir in the olives. Just before serving, season to taste then stir in the parsley and the remaining wine and cook for a further 5 minutes. Serve with the slow-roasted carrots on the side.

smoky hotpot of great northern beans

This is a hearty hotpot packed with autumnal vegetables and rich with smoky paprika. Great northern beans are large and white, resembling butter beans in shape but with a distinctive, delicate flavour. If you can't find them, large butter beans will do just as well.

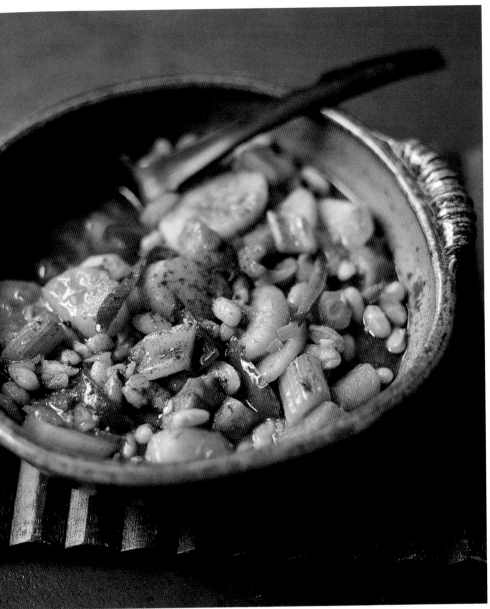

100 g dried great northern beans or large butter beans

2 tablespoons olive oil

1 large white onion, chopped

2 garlic cloves, chopped

2 teaspoons Spanish smoked paprika (pimentón)

1 celery stick, chopped

1 carrot, chopped

2 medium waxy potatoes, cut into dice

1 red pepper, deseeded and chopped

500 ml vegetable stock

sea salt and freshly ground black pepper

crusty bread, to serve

Serves 4

Soak the dried beans in cold water for at least 6 hours or overnight. Drain and put in a large saucepan with sufficient just-boiled water to cover. Cook for 30 minutes until softened. Drain and set aside until needed.

Put the oil in a large saucepan and set over medium heat. Add the onion and cook for 4–5 minutes until softened. Add the garlic and paprika to the pan and stir-fry for 2 minutes. Add the celery, carrot, potatoes and red pepper and cook for 2 minutes, stirring constantly to coat the vegetables in the flavoured oil. Add the stock and beans and bring to the boil. Reduce the heat and partially cover the pan with a lid. Let simmer for 40 minutes, stirring often, until all the vegetables are cooked. Season to taste and serve with plenty of crusty bread.

vegetable ragù
with spiced couscous

This is a substantial dish packed with nutritious root vegetables. The method for making the spiced couscous is not the traditional Moroccan way, but it does produce a full-flavoured version that makes the perfect accompaniment to this ragù.

3 tablespoons olive oil

25 g butter

1 red onion, chopped

1 celery stick, roughly chopped

6 garlic cloves, lightly smashed

500 ml passata (sieved tomatoes)

500 ml vegetable stock

2 tablespoons oregano leaves

1 parsnip, peeled and chopped

2 carrots, peeled and chopped

6 small, waxy, new potatoes

spiced couscous

375 ml vegetable stock

25 g butter

280 g couscous

1 teaspoon each of ground cumin, ground coriander and Spanish smoked paprika (pimentón)

¼ teaspoon cayenne pepper

Serves 4

Put the oil and butter in a large saucepan and set over high heat. When the butter sizzles, add the onion, celery and garlic. Reduce the heat, partially cover the pan and cook for 10 minutes, stirring often, until the vegetables are soft and lightly browned. Add the passata, stock and oregano and bring to the boil. Reduce the heat to a simmer and cook, uncovered, for about 20 minutes. Add the parsnip, carrots and potatoes to the pan and cook for a further 15–20 minutes until the vegetables are tender.

To make the spiced couscous, put the stock and butter in a medium saucepan and set over high heat. Bring to the boil, then reduce the heat to low and keep the stock warm. Put the couscous and spices in a large heavy-based saucepan and cook over medium/high heat until the spices are aromatic and just start to turn a dusky brown. Turn off the heat. Pour the warm stock into the pan. Stir, cover with a tight-fitting lid and let sit for 10 minutes. Fluff up the couscous with a fork, cover again and let sit for a further 5 minutes. Tip the couscous out into a bowl and fluff up to separate as many grains as possible. To serve, spoon the couscous onto serving plates and top with the vegetable ragù.

boeuf bourguignon

Although Boeuf Bourguignon sounds as if it should be made from red Burgundy, you'll get a better result if you use a fuller-bodied red wine from the Rhône or Languedoc. Ideally, it should be made a day ahead to allow the flavours to fully develop, but it's not essential to do so.

900 g braising beef or steak

3 tablespoons olive oil

130 g cubed pancetta

3 white onions, finely chopped

2 large garlic cloves, finely chopped

1½ tablespoons plain flour

450 ml full-bodied red wine, plus an extra splash if needed

a bouquet garni made from a few sprigs of thyme, parsley stalks and a fresh or dried bay leaf

25 g butter

250 g chestnut mushrooms, cleaned and halved

2 tablespoons finely chopped flat leaf parsley

salt and freshly ground black pepper

a large, flameproof casserole

Serves 6

Pat the beef dry, trim off any excess fat or sinew and cut into large cubes. Put 1 tablespoon of the oil in a large frying pan and set over medium heat. Add the pancetta and fry until lightly browned. Remove from the pan with a slotted spoon and transfer to a large, flameproof casserole. Add the beef to the frying pan in 2 batches and brown it in the fat that remains in the pan. Transfer to the casserole with the pancetta. Add the remaining oil to the pan and fry the onion gently, covered, until soft and caramelized (about 25 minutes), adding the garlic halfway through the cooking time. Stir the flour into the onions, cook for 1 minute, then add the wine and bring to the boil. Pour over the meat in the casserole, add the bouquet garni and return to the boil. Turn down the heat and simmer over very low heat for 2–2½ hours, until the meat is just tender. Turn off the heat and leave the casserole overnight.

The next day bring the casserole back to boiling point, then turn down low again. Heat the butter in a frying pan and fry the mushrooms until lightly browned (about 5 minutes). Tip the mushrooms into the stew, stir and cook for another 10–15 minutes. Season the casserole to taste, adding an extra splash of wine if you don't think the flavour is quite pronounced enough. Sprinkle over chopped parsley before serving with Pomme Purée (see page 104) or boiled new potatoes.

pork in cider

with potatoes and apples

If it has apples and cream in it, then it must be a dish from Normandy in France. The cider is a good clue as well, and it provides a luxuriously rich sauce for the long-simmered pork. This is a great dish for all the family, as children (and adults) enjoy sweet things to accompany their meat. Any leftover cider can be enjoyed with the meal.

90 g unsalted butter

2 white onions, sliced

1 tablespoon sunflower oil

1 pork middle leg roast, about 1.75 kg

1.5 litres dry cider

2 thyme sprigs

800 g new potatoes, peeled and halved lengthways

125 ml double cream

coarse sea salt and freshly ground black pepper

5 tart apples, such as Braeburn or Cox's, peeled, cored and sliced

a large, flameproof casserole

Serves 4

Put 30 g of the butter in a large flameproof casserole and set over low heat. Add the onions and cook gently until softened but not browned, about 5 minutes. Remove with a slotted spoon and set aside. Add the oil to the casserole and increase the heat. Add the pork and cook until browned all over. Remove and season well.

Preheat the oven to 150°C (300°F) Gas 2.

Add some of the cider to the casserole, heat and scrape the bottom of the pan. Return the pork and onions to the casserole and add the remaining cider and the thyme. Season lightly and bring to the boil. Boil for 1 minute, skim off any foam that rises to the surface, then lower the heat and cover with a lid. Transfer to the preheated oven and cook for 4 hours. Turn the pork regularly, tasting and adjusting the seasoning half-way through cooking. About 1 hour before the end of the cooking time, add the potatoes and return to the oven.

Remove the casserole from the oven, transfer the pork and potatoes to serving plates and cover with foil to keep warm. Set the casserole over high heat and cook to reduce the liquid slightly, about 10–15 minutes. Season to taste.

To cook the apples, put the remaining butter in a large frying pan and set over high heat. Add the apples and cook until browned and tender, 5–10 minutes. Do not crowd the pan; use 2 pans if necessary. To serve, slice the pork and arrange on plates with the potatoes and apples. Stir the cream into the sauce and serve immediately.

Mexican pork and beans

This is a version of chili that's not too spicy and made with pork instead of beef. Serve it with a big bowl of green rice and some warmed tortillas for a fun family feast.

1 white onion, coarsely chopped

4 garlic cloves, coarsely chopped

1 red pepper, deseeded and coarsely chopped

1 fresh fat red chilli, deseeded and chopped

2 teaspoons mild chilli powder

1 teaspoon Spanish smoked paprika (pimentón)

1 teaspoon ground cumin

1 teaspoon ground coriander

½ teaspoon ground cinnamon

1 teaspoon dried oregano

300 ml lager beer

500 g pork or beef steak

4 tablespoons sunflower oil

400-g tin chopped tomatoes

350 ml passata (sieved tomatoes)

400-g tin pinto beans or black-eyed peas, drained and rinsed

25 g very dark chocolate, chopped

sea salt and freshly ground black pepper

green rice

300 g basmati rice

4 tablespoons any coarsely chopped green herbs

100 g frozen chopped spinach, thawed

1 tablespoon sunflower oil

to serve

2 avocados, chopped and tossed with lime juice

4–6 soft flour tortillas, warmed

tomato salsa

sour cream or crème fraîche

Serves 4–6

Put the onion, garlic, red pepper, fresh chilli, chilli powder, paprika, cumin, coriander, cinnamon and oregano in a food processor. Add half the lager and blend to a purée.

Trim the pork steaks, then cut into large cubes. Heat the oil in a large saucepan, and working in batches, add the pork and fry until browned. Transfer to a plate.

Add the purée to the pan and cook, stirring continuously, over moderate heat for 5 minutes – making sure it doesn't catch and burn. Add the remaining lager, tomatoes, passata, pork and any juices. Season well and bring to the boil. Reduce the heat and simmer gently, half-covered, for 30–35 minutes until the pork is tender and the sauce thickened. Gently stir in the beans and chocolate and heat through.

To make the green rice, bring a very large saucepan of cold salted water to the boil. Rinse the rice under cold running water until the water runs clear. Drain. Add the rice to the boiling water, return to a rolling boil and stir once. Boil for exactly 8 minutes then drain well, return to the pan, stir in the herbs, spinach and oil, then quickly put on a tight-fitting lid. Let steam in its own heat for another 10 minutes, then lightly fluff up with a fork.

Serve the Mexican pork with the green rice and your choice of trimmings.

chili with all the trimmings

Forget the stuff that's slopped on jacket potatoes – this is the real thing, made with chopped steak instead of mince and spiced with several types of chilli. This is great party food because it should be served in bowls and eaten with a spoon – easy to do even if you are perched on the edge of a sofa!

1 chipotle chilli (dried smoked jalapeño)

4 tablespoons olive oil

4 peppers (1 red, 1 yellow, 1 orange and 1 green), deseeded and chopped

1 large red onion

2 celery sticks, chopped

½–1 fresh green chilli, finely chopped

800 g chuck steak, cut in small cubes

3 garlic cloves

250 ml red wine, fresh beef stock or water

¼ teaspoon dried chilli flakes

2 teaspoons ground cumin

2 teaspoons dried oregano

2 x 400-g tins chopped tomatoes

3 x 400-g tins kidney beans, drained and rinsed

1 fresh or dried bay leaf

coarse sea salt and freshly ground black pepper

to serve

2 avocados, chopped and tossed with lime juice

a bunch of spring onions, chopped

a bunch of coriander, chopped

8–12 soft flour tortillas, warmed

sour cream or crème fraîche

freshly grated cheese, such as mild Cheddar or Double Gloucester

lime wedges

Tabasco sauce

Serves 6–8

Put the chipotle in a small bowl and just cover with hot water. Soak for at least 15 minutes, or as long as it takes to prepare the other ingredients.

Heat 2 tablespoons of the oil in a large saucepan. Add the peppers, onion, celery, green chilli and a good pinch of salt and cook until soft, 5–7 minutes, stirring often. Remove from the pan and set aside. Increase the heat, add the remaining oil and the meat. Cook, stirring often until browned, 1–2 minutes. Add the garlic and another pinch of salt and cook, stirring constantly for 1 minute. Add the wine and bring to the boil for 1 minute.

Return the peppers to the pan and stir in the chilli flakes, cumin and oregano. Add the tomatoes, beans, bay leaf and a good pinch of salt and stir well. Remove the chipotle from the soaking liquid, chop finely and stir into the pan, along with the soaking liquid. Cover and simmer gently until the meat is tender, 15–20 minutes. Season to taste.

At this point, the chili is ready, but you should set it aside for at least 2–3 hours before serving to let the flavours develop or, ideally, make a day in advance and chill until needed. Serve hot, with all the trimmings in separate bowls.

classic lamb tagine with almonds, prunes and apricots

A tagine is a stew which gets its name from the conical, lidded, earthenware cooking dish traditionally used in Morocco. There's no need to worry if you don't have a tagine, a lidded casserole is fine.

1–2 tablespoons olive oil

2 tablespoons blanched almonds

2 red onions, finely chopped

2–3 garlic cloves, finely chopped

a thumb-sized piece of fresh ginger, peeled and finely chopped

a pinch of saffron fronds

2 cinnamon sticks

1–2 teaspoons coriander seeds, crushed

500 g boned lamb, from the shoulder, leg or shanks, trimmed and cubed

12 stoned prunes and 6 dried apricots, soaked in cold water for 1 hour and drained

3–4 strips orange rind

1–2 tablespoons dark, runny honey

1 handful of coriander leaves, chopped

sea salt and freshly ground black pepper

Plain, Buttery Couscous (see opposite), to serve

a flameproof casserole or tagine

Serves 4–6

Heat the oil in the base of a flameproof casserole. Add the almonds and cook, stirring, until they turn golden. Add the onions and garlic and fry until they begin to colour. Stir in the ginger, saffron, cinnamon sticks and coriander seeds. Add the lamb to the casserole and cook for about 1–2 minutes, stirring to make sure it is coated in the onion and spices.

Pour in enough water to just cover the meat then bring it to the boil. Reduce the heat, put the lid on the casserole and simmer for 1 hour, until the meat is tender. Add the prunes, apricots and orange rind, replace the lid and simmer for a further 15–20 minutes. Stir in the honey, season to taste, cover, and simmer for a further 10 minutes. Make sure there is enough liquid in the pot as you want the sauce to be syrupy and slightly caramelized, but not dry.

Stir in half of the fresh coriander and serve immediately, sprinkled with the remaining coriander and accompanied by a mound of couscous.

lamb tagine with chestnuts, saffron and pomegranate seeds

This is a lovely winter dish, decorated with ruby-red pomegranate seeds. Whole, meaty chestnuts are often used in Arab-influenced culinary cultures as a substitute for potatoes. You can use freshly roasted nuts or ready-peeled, vacuum-packed or frozen chestnuts.

2 tablespoons ghee (clarified butter)

2 white onions, finely chopped

4 garlic cloves, finely chopped

a thumb-sized piece of fresh ginger, peeled and finely chopped

a pinch of saffron threads

1–2 cinnamon sticks

1 kg lean lamb, from the shoulder or leg, cut into bite-sized pieces

250 g peeled chestnuts

1–2 tablespoons dark, runny honey

sea salt and freshly ground black pepper

seeds of 1 pomegranate, pith removed

1 handful of mint leaves, chopped

1 handful of coriander leaves, chopped

Plain, Buttery Couscous (see below), to serve

a flameproof casserole or tagine

Serves 4

Heat the ghee in a flameproof casserole or tagine. Add the onions, garlic and ginger and sauté until they begin to colour. Add the saffron and cinnamon sticks, and toss in the lamb. Pour in enough water to almost cover the meat and bring it to the boil. Reduce the heat, cover with a lid and simmer gently for about 1 hour.

Add the chestnuts and stir in the honey. Cover with the lid again and cook gently for a further 30 minutes, until the meat is very tender. Season to taste and then stir in some of the pomegranate seeds, mint and coriander. Sprinkle the remaining pomegranate seeds and herbs over the lamb, and serve with a mound of couscous.

plain, buttery couscous

Traditionally, plain, buttery couscous, piled high in a mound, is served as a dish on its own after a tagine or roasted meat. It is held in such high esteem that religious feasts and celebratory meals would be unthinkable with it. The par-boiled couscous available outside Morocco is extremely easy to prepare, making it a practical accompaniment for many dishes.

350 g couscous, rinsed and drained

½ teaspoon sea salt

400 ml warm water

2 tablespoons sunflower or olive oil

40 g butter, broken into little pieces

2–3 tablespoons blanched, flaked almonds

Serves 4–6

Preheat the oven to 180°C (350°F) Gas 4.

Tip the couscous into an ovenproof dish. Stir the salt into the water and pour it over the couscous. Leave the couscous to absorb the water for about 10 minutes.

Using your fingers, rub the oil into the couscous grains to break up the lumps and aerate them. Scatter 25 g of the butter over the surface and cover with a piece of foil or wet greaseproof paper. Put the dish in the preheated oven for about 15 minutes, until the couscous is heated through. Meanwhile, prepare the almonds. Melt the remaining butter in a heavy-based frying pan over medium heat, add the almonds and cook, stirring, until they turn golden. Remove from the pan and drain on kitchen paper.

Take the couscous out of the oven and fluff up the grains with a fork. Tip it onto a plate and pile it high in a mound, with the almonds scattered over the top.

spicy carrot and chickpea tagine
with turmeric and coriander

Pulses of all kinds and, in particular, chickpeas, make nourishing and simple to prepare winter meals. To avoid lengthy preparation and cooking, use tinned chickpeas.

3–4 tablespoons olive oil
1 white onion, finely chopped
3–4 garlic cloves, finely chopped
2 teaspoons ground turmeric
1–2 teaspoons cumin seeds
1 teaspoon ground cinnamon
½ teaspoon cayenne pepper
½ teaspoon freshly ground black pepper
1 tablespoon dark, runny honey
3–4 medium carrots, sliced on the diagonal
2 x 400-g tins chickpeas, rinsed and drained
sea salt and freshly ground black pepper
1–2 tablespoons rosewater (optional)
1 handful of coriander leaves, finely chopped
natural yoghurt, to serve
lemon wedges, to serve

a flameproof casserole or tagine

Serves 4

Heat the oil in a flameproof casserole or tagine. Add the onion and garlic and gently sauté until soft. Add the turmeric, cumin, cinnamon, cayenne, black pepper, honey and carrots. Pour in enough water to cover the base of the casserole and cover with a lid. Cook gently for 10–15 minutes.

Add the chickpeas, check that there is still enough liquid at the base of the tagine, adding a little water if necessary. Cover with the lid, and cook gently for a further 5–10 minutes. Season to taste, sprinkle the coriander over the top and add a dollop of yoghurt. Serve with lemon wedges.

winter vegetable tagine with apple and mint

3 tablespoons olive oil

1 white onion, chopped

2 garlic cloves, chopped

½ teaspoon turmeric

½ teaspoon paprika

1 teaspoon ground cumin

1 cinnamon stick

400-g tin chopped tomatoes

1 large carrot, peeled and cut into thick batons

1 parsnip, peeled and cut into 2–3 cm pieces

1 turnip, peeled and cut into 1-cm thick rounds

125 g sweet potato, peeled and cut into cubes

1 green apple, peeled, cored and cut into 8 wedges

1 small handful of mint leaves, roughly chopped

sea salt and freshly ground black pepper

Plain, Buttery Couscous (see page 77), to serve

a flameproof casserole or tagine

Serves 4

Put the oil in a flameproof casserole and set over medium heat. Cook the onion and garlic, stirring, for 2–3 minutes. Add the turmeric, paprika, cumin and cinnamon and cook for about 2 minutes, until aromatic but not burning.

Add 750 ml water and the tomatoes and season well. Bring to the boil, add the carrot and parsnip and cook over medium heat, uncovered, for 30 minutes. Add the turnip, sweet potato and apple and cook for 20–30 minutes, until all the vegetables are tender, then stir in the mint. Serve hot with a mound of couscous.

Aromatic, sweet, succulent and juicy with the addition of the fruit, this is a perfect introduction to the aromatic spices and flavours typical of Moroccan food. The rich spices work very well with the full-flavoured winter root vegetables used here. They all grow underground so have been given a breath of air by the addition of some crisp green apple and fresh mint.

a big pot of cassoulet

This hearty dish from south-west France will become a firm favourite. It is big and filling, and traditionally made with a type of haricot bean (lingots). However, dried butter beans with their creamy texture work just as well, but remember you'll need to soak them before you start cooking. All the components of the dish can be made a day in advance, then assembled on the day. It reheats very well (top up with a little more liquid if it looks dry) and is a boon for entertaining a crowd without any fuss. Make this for large gatherings on cold winter days.

675 g dried butter beans

500 g smoked Italian pancetta, fat bacon or belly pork, in a piece

4 tablespoons olive oil

4 boneless duck breasts, halved crossways, or chicken legs or thighs

750 g fresh Toulouse sausages or Italian coarse pork sausages, cut into 3 pieces each

2 white onions, chopped

1 large carrot, chopped

4–6 large garlic cloves, crushed

3 fresh or dried bay leaves

2 teaspoons dried thyme

2 whole cloves

3 tablespoons tomato purée

12 sun-dried tomatoes in oil, drained and coarsely chopped

75 g fresh white breadcrumbs (ciabatta is good too)

50 g butter

sea salt and freshly ground black pepper

green salad, to serve

a large, deep casserole

Serves 6–8

Put the butter beans in a very large bowl, cover with plenty of cold water (to cover them by their depth again) and let them soak for at least 6 hours or ideally overnight.

Drain the beans well and tip into a large saucepan. Cover with fresh water, bring to the boil, then simmer for about 1 hour or until just cooked. Drain well (reserving the cooking liquid).

Trim and discard the rind from the pancetta, and cut the flesh into large pieces. Heat 2 tablespoons of the oil in a frying pan. Add the pancetta and, working in batches, brown and transfer to a plate. Heat the remaining oil in the pan, add the duck breasts and fry them skin-side down until the skin is golden. Transfer to the same plate as the pancetta. Brown the sausages in the same way and add to the plate.

Add the onions to the pan, then the carrot, garlic, bay leaves, thyme, cloves, tomato purée and sun-dried tomatoes. Cook for 5 minutes until softening.

Preheat the oven to 180°C (350°F) Gas 4.

To assemble the dish, put half the beans in a large, deep casserole. Add an even layer of all the browned meats, then the onion and tomato mixture. Season well. Cover with the remaining beans, then add enough reserved hot cooking liquid until the beans are almost covered. Sprinkle evenly with breadcrumbs and dot with butter.

Bake the cassoulet in the preheated oven for about 1 hour, until a golden crust has formed. Serve warm straight out of the dish with a green salad on the side, if liked.

smoky sausage and bean casserole

The Italians use a mixture of onions, carrots and celery sautéed in olive oil as the base for many classic soups and casseroles. This holy trinity of veggies is known as a *soffritto* and it's right at home here in a hearty stew with sausages and beans. This is perfect one-pot comfort food.

1 tablespoon olive oil
12 chippolata sausages
1 garlic clove, chopped
1 leek, thinly sliced
1 carrot, diced
1 celery stick, diced
400-g tin chopped tomatoes
1 teaspoon Spanish smoked paprika (pimentòn)
2 tablespoons maple syrup
2 fresh thyme sprigs
400-g tin cannellini beans, drained and rinsed
sea salt and freshly ground black pepper
4 slices of toasted sourdough bread, to serve

a flameproof casserole or heavy-based saucepan

Serves 4

Heat the oil in a flameproof casserole or heavy-based saucepan set over high heat. Add the sausages in two batches and cook them for 4–5 minutes, turning often until cooked and evenly browned all over. Remove from the casserole and set aside.

Add the garlic, leek, carrot and celery and cook for 5 minutes, stirring often. Add the tomatoes, paprika, maple syrup, thyme, beans and 500 ml water and return the sausages to the pan.

Bring to the boil, then reduce the heat to medium and simmer for 40–45 minutes, until the sauce has thickened. Season well.

Put a slice of toasted sourdough bread on each serving plate, spoon the casserole over the top and serve.

Variation: Try replacing the sausages with 500 g pork neck fillet cut into 2–3-cm pieces. Cook the pork in batches for 4–5 minutes each batch, turning often so each piece is evenly browned. Return all the pork to the pan, as you would the sausages, and simmer for 45–50 minutes until the pork is tender.

coq au vin

This classic French recipe is a terrific dish for a dinner party because it tastes even better the day after it's made so you can prepare it ahead. The French would always use a local wine to make it but any good, dry, fruity red would work.

300 g shallots
3 tablespoons plain flour
6 large skinless, boneless chicken breasts
3 tablespoons olive oil
125 g chopped streaky bacon or pancetta cubes
2 garlic cloves, thinly sliced
50 ml brandy
3 fresh thyme sprigs
1 fresh or dried bay leaf
1 x 750-ml bottle dry, fruity red wine
250 g small button mushrooms
1 tablespoon butter, softened (optional)
3 tablespoons chopped flat leaf parsley
sea salt and freshly ground black pepper
Pomme Purée (see page 104), to serve

a large, lidded frying pan

Serves 6

Cut the shallots into even-sized pieces, leaving the small ones whole and halving or quartering the others.

Put 2 tablespoons flour in a shallow dish and season it with salt and pepper. Dip the chicken breasts in the flour and coat both sides. Heat 2 tablespoons of the olive oil in a large lidded frying pan. Add the chicken and fry for 2–3 minutes on each side until lightly browned (you may need to do this in several batches).

Remove the chicken from the pan, discard the oil and wipe the pan with kitchen paper. Return the pan to the heat and pour in the remaining oil. Add the chopped bacon or pancetta cubes and the shallots and fry until lightly browned. Stir in the garlic, then return the chicken to the pan. Put the brandy in a small saucepan and heat it until almost boiling. Set it alight with a long kitchen match and carefully pour it over the chicken. Let the flames die down, then add the thyme and bay leaf and pour in enough wine to just cover the chicken. Bring back to simmering point, then reduce the heat, half cover the pan and simmer very gently for 45 minutes. (If you're making this dish ahead of time, take the pan off the heat after 30 minutes, let cool and refrigerate overnight.) Add the mushrooms to the pan and cook for another 10–15 minutes.

Remove the chicken from the pan, set aside and keep it warm. Using a slotted spoon, scoop the shallots, bacon pieces or pancetta cubes and mushrooms out of the pan and keep them warm. Increase the heat under the pan and let the sauce simmer until it has reduced by half. If the sauce needs thickening, mash 1 tablespoon soft butter with 1 tablespoon flour to give a smooth paste, then add it bit by bit to the sauce, whisking well after each addition, until the sauce is smooth and glossy.

Return the shallots, pancetta and mushrooms to the pan. Season to taste. To serve, cut each chicken breast into 4 slices and arrange them on warmed serving plates. Spoon a generous amount of sauce over the chicken and sprinkle with chopped parsley. Serve immediately with creamy Pomme Purée on the side.

pumpkin and Gorgonzola risotto

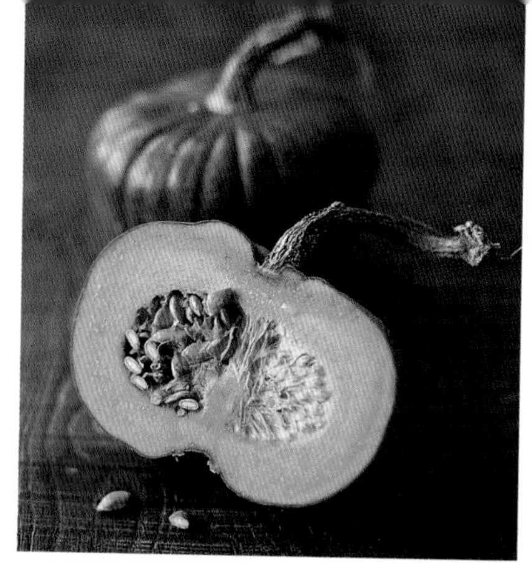

The secret of making a good Italian risotto is to use quality ingredients – fresh butter, best quality risotto rice and a good flavourful stock are all essential. Roasted pumpkin retains its deep flavour and unique texture here as it's cooked separately, then added to a basic risotto. Tart yet creamy Gorgonzola cheese makes the perfect pairing with the sweet pumpkin. You could substitute any firm, dense winter squash – such as butternut or hubbard.

600 g pumpkin, peeled, deseeded and diced

1 tablespoon olive oil

1 litre vegetable stock

2 tablespoons unsalted butter

1 leek, halved lengthways and thinly sliced

1 garlic clove, chopped

330 g Arborio (risotto) rice

50 g Gorgonzola, crumbled

sea salt and freshly ground black pepper

a small roasting tin

Serves 4

Preheat the oven to 180°C (350°F) Gas 4.

Put the pumpkin in a small roasting tin, drizzle with the olive oil, season and toss to coat in the oil. Roast in the preheated oven for about 30 minutes, until soft and golden.

Put the stock in a saucepan and heat until gently simmering. Melt the butter in a saucepan set over high heat and add the leek and garlic. Cook for 4–5 minutes, stirring often, until the leeks have softened.

Add the rice to the pan and stir for 1 minute, until the rice is well coated with oil. Add 125 ml of the hot stock to the rice and cook, stirring constantly, until the rice has absorbed most of the liquid. Repeat this process until all the stock has been used. This will take about 20–25 minutes. The rice should be soft but still have a slight bite to the centre. Add the roasted pumpkin to the pan. Remove from the heat, stir in the Gorgonzola and serve immediately.

roasted butternut squash risotto

Risotto is a relatively simple dish to make but a good deal of stirring is required. Remember to keep the stock hot and the heat constant. Roasting the squash first brings out its sweetness and the pumpkin seeds add a spicy crunch.

500 g butternut squash, peeled, deseeded and diced

3 tablespoons olive oil

1½ teaspoons dried chilli flakes

25 g pumpkin seeds

850 ml vegetable stock

1 small onion, finely chopped

150 g Arborio (risotto) rice

100 ml white wine

50 g Parmesan cheese, finely grated

crème fraîche, to serve (optional)

sea salt and freshly ground black pepper

a small roasting tin

Serves 2

Preheat the oven to 230°C (450°F) Gas 8.

Put the squash in a small roasting tin with 1 tablespoon of the olive oil and ½ teaspoon of the chilli flakes. Season well and toss to coat in the oil. Roast in the preheated oven for about 20 minutes, until soft and golden.

Heat 1 tablespoon of the remaining olive oil in a small frying pan and toast the pumpkin seeds with the remaining chilli flakes for about 1–2 minutes until lightly browned. Set aside until needed.

Whilst the squash is cooking in the oven, make the risotto. Pour the vegetable stock into a large pan and heat to a simmer. Pour the remaining oil into a saucepan and set over medium heat. Gently sauté the onions for about 1 minute, or until softened but not coloured. Add the rice, stir for 2–3 minutes, then add the wine and let simmer until reduced by half. Add another ladleful of hot stock. Let the risotto continue to simmer gently, adding another ladleful or two of stock each time the liquid has been absorbed into the rice. Stir, continuously, until the rice has absorbed all the stock.

Once the rice is cooked and tender, stir in the roasted squash and the Parmesan and season to taste. Serve immediately, topped with a dollop of crème fraîche, if using, and sprinkled with the spicy toasted pumpkin seeds.

mushrooms, cognac and cream risotto

Here is a rich, creamy risotto that is very substantial and comforting. The cognac adds a touch of indulgent luxury, making it perfect for a special supper or entertaining.

100 g unsalted butter

275 g large, open-cap mushrooms, thinly sliced

1 tablespoon Cognac or other brandy

3 tablespoons single cream

900 ml vegetable stock

1 tablespoon olive oil

8 shallots, finely chopped

2 garlic cloves, crushed

275 g Arborio (risotto) rice

100 g Parmesan cheese, freshly grated

a handful of fresh flat leaf parsley, coarsely chopped

sea salt and freshly ground black pepper

shavings of Parmesan cheese, to serve

Serves 4

Heat half the butter in a frying pan until foaming, then add the mushrooms and cook for 5 minutes. Season. Add the Cognac, boil until reduced by half, then stir in the cream. Let simmer for about 5 minutes, until the sauce has thickened slightly. Set aside.

Put the stock in a saucepan. Heat until almost boiling, then reduce the heat until barely simmering to keep it hot.

Heat the remaining butter and oil in a frying pan or heavy-based saucepan set over medium heat. Add the shallots and cook for 1–2 minutes, until softened but not browned. Add the garlic.

Add the rice and stir for about 1 minute, until the grains are well coated and glistening.

Add 1 ladleful of hot stock and simmer, stirring continuously, until it has been absorbed. Continue to add the stock at intervals and cook as before, until the liquid has been absorbed and the rice is tender but firm to the bite. This should take about 18–20 minutes.

Add the mushroom mixture, grated Parmesan and parsley. Season to taste. Remove from the heat, cover and let rest for 2 minutes before serving. Spoon into bowls, top with Parmesan shavings and serve.

country chicken

1 chicken, about 2 kg, cut into 8 pieces

8 shallots

5 fresh or dried bay leaves

250 g bacon, chopped

2 tablespoons olive oil

1½ tablespoons wholegrain mustard

1 bunch of tarragon, coarsely chopped

100 ml white wine

sea salt and freshly ground black pepper

cooked tagliatelle, to serve

Serves 4

A simple-to-make yet delicious roast chicken dish that is served with pasta.

Preheat the oven to 180°C (350°F) Gas 4.

Put the chicken in a bowl and add the shallots, bay leaves, bacon and oil. Season well, mix and transfer to a roasting tin. Cook in the preheated oven for 30 minutes.

Put the mustard, tarragon and wine in a small bowl and mix well. Remove the chicken from the oven and pour off any excess fat. Pour the mustard mixture over the chicken and return it to the oven for a further 10 minutes. Serve with the tagliatelle.

roasts

italian-style roast pork
with white wine, garlic and fennel

A great recipe for weekend entertaining or a family get-together. You can leave the meat gently bubbling away for hours in the oven and you will have a fantastic roast at the end of the day. An Italian wine like Pinot Grigio is best, but you could use any dry white wine.

3 kg boned, rolled shoulder of pork
2 tablespoons fennel seeds
1 tablespoon coarse sea salt
1 teaspoon black peppercorns
1 teaspoon crushed dried chillies
6 garlic cloves, roughly chopped
freshly squeezed juice of 2 lemons
2 tablespoons olive oil
175 ml dry white wine

to serve
sautéed or mashed potatoes
green beans or a mixed leaf salad

a large roasting tin with a rack
an ovenproof dish

Serves 8

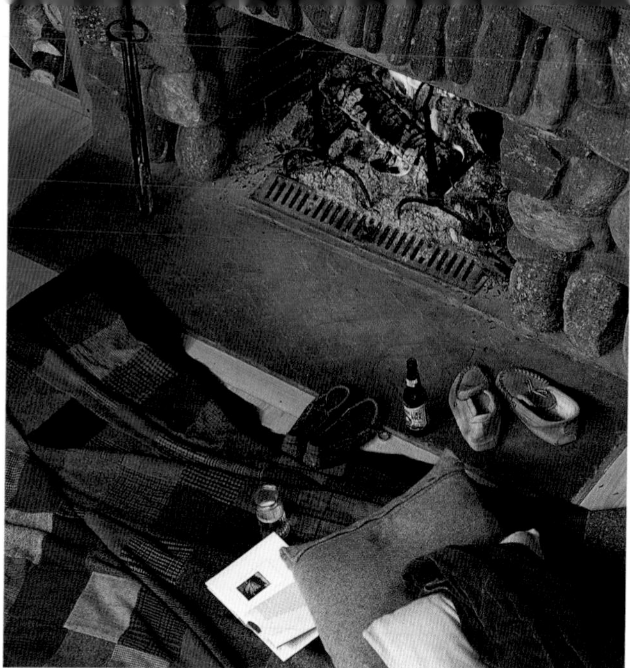

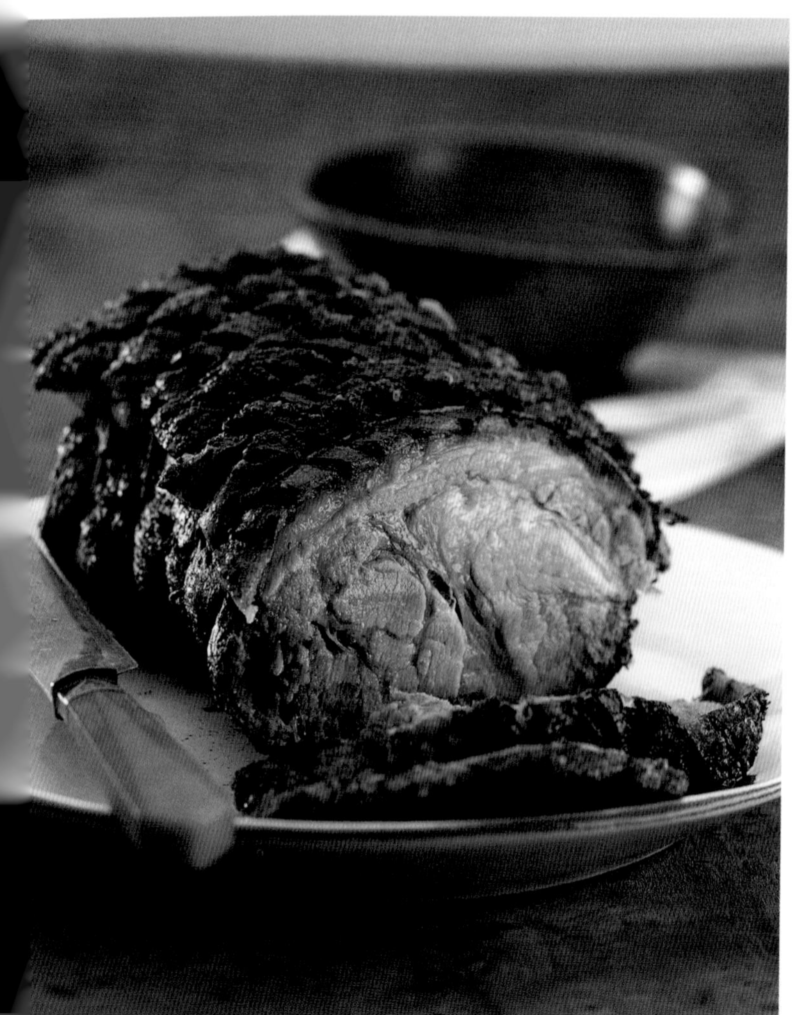

Preheat the oven to 230°C (450°F) Gas 8.

Cut deep slits in the pork skin with a sharp knife. Grind the fennel seeds, salt, peppercorns and chillies in a mortar using a pestle. Add the chopped garlic and pound to a rough paste. Using your hands, smother the paste all over the pork working it into the slits. Put the pork on a wire rack and place it over a roasting tin. Cook, skin-side up in the preheated oven for 30 minutes. Remove the pork from the oven and reduce the heat to 120°C (250°F) Gas ½.

Turn the pork over and pour half the lemon juice and all of the olive oil over it. Return the pork to the oven and cook for at least 7 hours, checking it every couple of hours. You should be aware that the meat is cooking – it should be sizzling quietly. Ovens vary, so you may want to increase the temperature slightly. About halfway through the cooking time, spoon off the excess fat and squeeze the remaining lemon juice over the meat. About 30 minutes before the pork is due to be cooked, remove it from the oven and increase the heat to 220°C (425°F) Gas 7. Transfer the pork, skin side up, to a clean ovenproof dish and when the oven is hot, return the pork to the oven for about 15–20 minutes to crisp up the crackling. Remove from the oven and let rest.

Pour off any excess fat from the original roasting tin and add the wine and 175 ml water. Heat gently on the hob, working off any sticky burnt-on bits from the edges of the tin and simmer for 10 minutes. Strain the juices through a sieve and keep them warm.

Carve the pork into thick slices. Put a few slices on warmed plates and pour some of the pan juices over the top. Serve with sautéed potatoes and a mixed leaf salad or mashed potatoes and green beans, as preferred.

pork loin roasted with rosemary and garlic

This classic Tuscan dish is redolent of the early morning markets where 'porchetta' is sold crammed into huge buns, this dish re-creates all those tastes and smells in your oven at home. Use plenty of rosemary so that the sweet pork flesh will be suffused with its pungent aroma.

1.75 kg loin of pork on the bone (ask the butcher to remove the rind and score it for crackling, but to give you the bones.)

6 garlic cloves

4 tablespoons rosemary needles

300 ml dry white wine

a few sprigs of rosemary

olive oil, for brushing

sea salt and freshly ground black pepper

2 roasting tins

kitchen string

Serves 6

Preheat the oven to 230°C (450°F) Gas 8.

Weigh the meat and calculate the total cooking time, allowing 25 minutes for every 500 g.

Turn the loin fat-side down. Make deep slits all over. Put the garlic, rosemary and at least a teaspoon of salt and pepper into a food processor and blend to a paste. Push this paste into all the slits in the meat and spread the remainder over the surface of the meat. Roll up and tie securely with kitchen string.

Put the pork in a hot frying pan and brown all over. Set in a roasting tin. Pour the wine over the pork and tuck in the rosemary sprigs.

Put the bones in the other roasting tin, convex side up. Rub the skin with a little oil and salt, then drape it over the bones. Put the tin on the top shelf of the oven, and the pork loin on the bottom or middle shelf. Roast for 20 minutes. Reduce the heat to 200°C (400°F) Gas 6, and roast for the remaining calculated time, basting the pork loin every 20 minutes. Rest the pork for 15 minutes before carving. Serve slices of pork with shards of crackling and spoon the pan juices over the top. Serve with roast potatoes, if liked.

roasted pork
with apple and fennel puddings

They may sound a little unusual but these savoury puddings packed with vegetables and sweet raisins make a wonderful accompaniment to pork.

1.5 kg piece of pork loin, skin on
2 tablespoons white wine vinegar
1 tablespoon sea salt

apple and fennel puddings
3 tablespoons butter
1 white onion, chopped
1 celery stick, thinly sliced
1 tart green apple, grated
1 fennel bulb, grated
100 g fresh breadcrumbs
60 g raisins
1 egg, lightly beaten
250 ml chicken or vegetable stock
45 g flaked almonds

a large roasting tin with a rack
an ovenproof dish, lightly buttered

Serves 6

Make small incisions on the skin of the pork with a sharp knife, but don't cut through to the meat. Rub the vinegar and sea salt into the skin and set aside for 1 hour at room temperature. (This will help the skin dry out making for better crackling.)

Preheat the oven to 220°C (425°F) Gas 7. Put the pork on a cooking rack over a roasting tin. Pour 250 ml water into the tin and cook in the preheated oven for 30 minutes. Reduce the oven temperature to 180°C (350°F) Gas 4 and cook for a further 1½ hours, until the pork skin is golden and crisp. Keep adding water to the roasting tin during the cooking time as necessary. Remove the pork from the oven, cover with foil and let rest for 10 minutes.

To make the puddings. Heat the butter in a frying pan set over medium heat. When the butter is sizzling, add the onion and celery and cook for 4–5 minutes, stirring often. Add the apple and fennel and cook for 1 minute, stirring well. Remove the pan from the heat and add all the remaining ingredients, except for the almonds. Stir well. Spoon the mixture into the baking dish, sprinkle the almonds on top and cook in a preheated oven at 180°C (350°F) Gas 4 for 1 hour. Serve slices of the pork with slices of the pudding and Slow-cooked Sprouts with Pancetta and Chestnuts (see page 108).

roast turkey with lemon and herb stuffing

Family tradition will dictate the best way to present a festive turkey. This recipe has a light herb and lemon bread stuffing made with plenty of butter. It absorbs lots of juices and is fabulous served cold the next day. Allow 40 minutes at the end of cooking for the turkey to rest before carving.

6 kg turkey, with giblets (trussed weight)

1 white onion, coarsely chopped

a sprig of thyme

1 bay leaf

125 g salted butter

sea salt and freshly ground black pepper

lemon and herb stuffing

2 eggs

125 g butter, melted

a handful of parsley leaves

1 teaspoon lemon thyme leaves

grated zest and juice of 1 lemon

225 g fresh white breadcrumbs

sea salt and freshly ground black pepper

squares of muslin, baking paper or foil (enough to cover the breast and drumsticks)

a large roasting tin

Serves 10–12

To make a stock, the day before, put the giblets, minus the liver, but with the neck chopped in half, in a saucepan. Add the onion, thyme and bay leaf. Cover with water and bring slowly to the boil, removing any foam as it rises. Simmer for 2 hours and strain. Taste and, if necessary, reduce to strengthen the flavour. Set aside.

To make the stuffing, put the eggs, butter, parsley, thyme, lemon zest and juice in a liquidizer and blend to a smooth purée. Pour it over the crumbs and mix well. Season to taste and set aside. Wipe out the neck area and body cavity of the turkey with a damp cloth and season the inside. Spoon in the stuffing, allowing plenty of room for it to expand. This is especially true when stuffing the neck.

Put half the butter in a saucepan and melt gently. Using your hands, spread the remaining butter all over the skin. Soak the muslin or paper in the melted butter and drape over the bird, with a double layer covering the drumsticks.

Preheat the oven to 220°C (425°F) Gas 7. Put the turkey in a large roasting tin in the middle of the oven and roast for 35 minutes. Reduce the oven temperature to 170°C (335°F) Gas 3 and roast for about 3½ hours. Return the oven temperature to 220°C (425°F) Gas 7. Remove the coverings from the bird and cook for 30 minutes to crisp and brown the skin. Remove the turkey from the oven, cover with a tent of foil and leave to rest in a warm place for 40 minutes.

Remove the foil and using oven gloves, tip out any free juices from the cavity, then lift the turkey onto the serving platter. Return it to the oven, leaving the door open until the temperature has dropped and will no longer cook the bird. Pour off the gravy juices, preferably into a gravy separator or jug to lift off the fat. Reheat with the seasoned stock. Use to fill a gravy boat, reserving the rest in a Thermos for second helpings.

Serve with the traditional trimmings of your choice, such as bacon rolls, chipolatas, sausage meat patties, bread sauce, Brussels sprouts and roast potatoes.

pot roast brisket with red wine

200 ml full-bodied red wine, such as Zinfandel

200 ml fresh beef stock or made with ½ a beef stock cube, cooled

2 tablespoons red wine vinegar

1 large garlic clove, crushed

1 fresh or dried bay leaf

1 white onion, chopped

a few of sprigs of thyme or ½ teaspoon dried thyme

1.5 kg boned, rolled brisket of beef

2–3 tablespoons sunflower or light olive oil

2 tablespoons dry Marsala or Madeira

sea salt and freshly ground pepper

a large flameproof casserole

Serves 6

Brisket has a rich flavour that lends itself well to braising. You can use any full-bodied red wine, but Zinfandel has just the right gutsy rustic character.

Put the wine, stock, wine vinegar, garlic, bay leaf, onion and thyme in a large jug and mix. Put the meat in a plastic bag, pour in the marinade. Knot the top of the bag or seal with a wire tie. Leave the meat to marinate in the fridge for at least 4 hours or preferably overnight.

Preheat the oven to 200°C (400°F) Gas 6.

Remove the meat from the marinade and dry thoroughly with kitchen paper. Strain the marinade and reserve the liquid. Heat the oil in a flameproof casserole. Brown the meat all over in the hot oil then add 3–4 tablespoons of the strained marinade. Put a lid on the casserole and roast for 2 hours. Check from time to time that the pan juices are not burning. Add more marinade if necessary, but the flavour of this dish comes from the well-browned sticky juices, so do not add too much extra liquid. If on the other hand more liquid has formed, spoon some out. Simmer the remaining marinade over low heat until it loses its raw, winey taste.

Once the meat is cooked, set it aside in a warm place. Spoon any fat off the surface of the pan juices and add the Marsala and the cooked marinade. Bring to the boil, scraping off all the brown tasty bits from the side of the casserole and adding a little extra water if necessary. Season to taste. Serve slices of the meat with the sauce spooned over the top or in a gravy boat for pouring.

roast beef with winter vegetables and garlic crème

Unlike roast pork, where the fat and skin form tasty crackling, excess fat on beef can be off-putting. Choose a lean fillet and cook it quickly for a lovely rare roast.

800 g beef rib-eye fillet

1 tablespoon freshly ground black pepper

1 bunch of baby carrots, unpeeled and tops trimmed

2 small red onions, cut into thin wedges

1 turnip, cut into quarters

½ small celeriac, cut into thick batons

1 large parsnip, cut into semi circles

1 tablespoon light olive oil

garlic crème

1 bulb of garlic

3 egg yolks

1 teaspoon Dijon mustard

1 teaspoon red wine vinegar

250 ml light olive oil

Serves 4

Preheat the oven to 180°C (350°F) Gas 4.

To make the garlic crème, wrap the garlic firmly in foil and cook in the preheated oven for 40 minutes. Remove and let cool. Cut in half and squeeze the soft flesh directly into the bowl of a food processor. Add the egg yolks, mustard and vinegar and process until smooth. With the motor running, add the olive oil in a steady stream until all the oil is incorporated. Transfer to a small bowl, cover and chill until needed.

Rub the pepper all over the beef. Cover and refrigerate, for at least 3 hours or overnight.

When ready to cook the beef, preheat the oven to 220°C (425°F) Gas 7. Put a baking tray in the oven to heat. Put the vegetables on the baking tray, drizzle with olive oil and roast in the preheated oven for 30 minutes, turning once. Cover with foil to keep warm.

Set a frying pan over high heat. When smoking hot, add the fillet and sear for 4 minutes, turning every minute. Put it in a roasting tin and roast in the still-hot oven for 10 minutes. Turn the beef and cook for a further 5 minutes. Cover with foil and let rest for 10 minutes before carving. Serve with the roast vegetables and garlic crème.

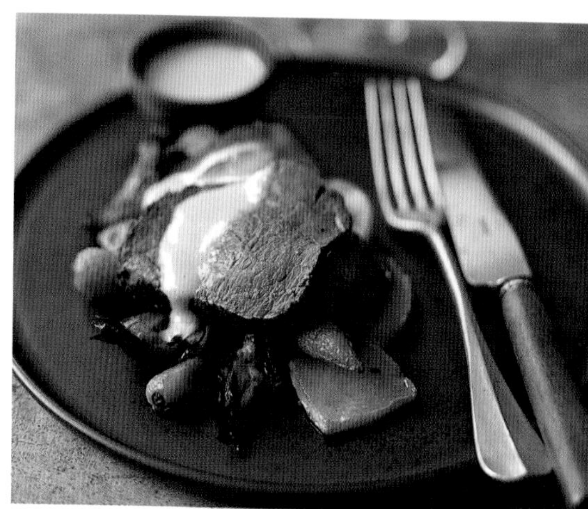

roast fillet of beef
with soy and butter sauce

The soy and butter sauce may sound unconventional, but it makes a very light, savoury, meaty sauce that is much more wine friendly than some of the very intense winey reductions you get in restaurants.

1 teaspoon coarse sea salt

2 teaspoons black peppercorns

½ teaspoon ground allspice

1 tablespoon plain flour

1 kg fillet of beef

1 tablespoon sunflower oil or light olive oil

40 g soft butter

2 tablespoons Madeira or dry Marsala

375 ml fresh beef stock or stock made with ¾ beef stock cube

1½ tablespoons Japanese soy sauce, such as Kikkoman

a large cast-iron casserole or deep roasting tin

Serves 6

Preheat the oven to 225°C (425°F) Gas 7.

Put the salt and peppercorns in a mortar and grind with a pestle until finely ground. Mix in the allspice and flour. Remove any fat or sinew from the beef fillet and dry thoroughly with kitchen paper. Put the seasoning and flour on a plate and roll the beef in the mixture, patting it evenly into the surface and shaking off any excess. Set the casserole over medium/high heat, add the oil and half the butter and brown the beef quickly on all sides. Transfer to the preheated oven and roast for 20–40 minutes, depending how thick your beef fillet is and how rare you like it. Remove from the oven and set aside for 10–15 minutes, lightly covered with foil. Pour off any excess fat in the pan, leaving about 1 tablespoon. Pour in the Madeira and let it bubble up for a few seconds, then add the stock and soy sauce. Bring to the boil, turn the heat down a little and reduce by half. Pour any juices that have accumulated under the meat into the pan, whisk in the remaining butter and season with black pepper (you shouldn't need any salt).

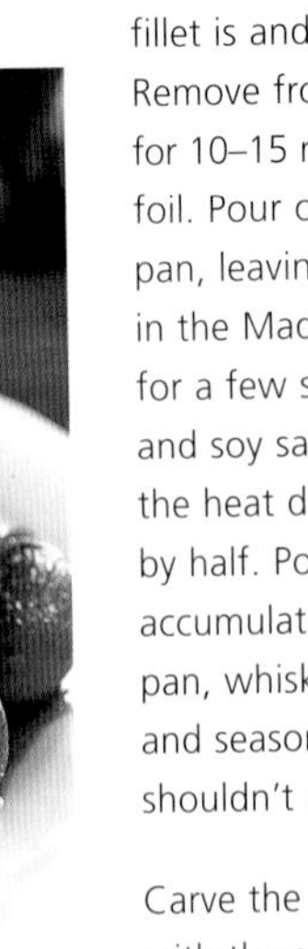

Carve the meat into slices and serve with the sauce and some roast new potatoes and green beans, if liked.

perfect roast fillet of beef
with herbed Yorkshire puddings

The fillet is the most tender cut of beef and is best cooked until rosy pink inside. Resting the meat before carving will ensure a juicy result. The Yorkshire puddings are essential!

1 kg fillet of beef

olive oil

200 g thinly sliced pancetta or thinly sliced dry-cure streaky bacon

sea salt and freshly ground black pepper

herbed Yorkshire puddings

225 g plain white flour

½ teaspoon salt

2 large rosemary sprigs, chopped

1 tablespoon chopped fresh thyme

4 eggs

600 ml milk

8 tablespoons beef dripping, duck fat or vegetable oil

kitchen string

a 12-hole muffin tin or Yorkshire pudding tin

Serves 6

To make the Yorkshire puddings, sift the flour and salt into a food processor or blender. Add the rosemary and thyme, eggs and milk. Blend until smooth and pour into a jug. Cover and refrigerate for at least 1 hour.

Trim the fillet of all fat and membrane and neatly tie at regular intervals to give a good shape. Rub all over with olive oil, salt and pepper. Wrap with the pancetta. Cover and set aside for 20 minutes at room temperature.

Preheat the oven to 230°C (450°F) Gas 8.

Put the meat in a roasting tin and cook in the preheated oven for 25 minutes for medium rare; 20 for very rare; 35 for medium. Remove from the oven, cover loosely with foil and let rest in a warm place for 10–15 minutes (this will make it easier to carve and give the meat an even pink colour).

Lower the oven temperature to 200°C (400°F) Gas 6 and cook the puddings while the meat is resting. Put the dripping into the holes of the muffin tin and heat in the oven for a couple of minutes. Stir the batter and pour into the hot pans – it should sizzle as soon as it hits the fat. Return to the oven and bake for 15–20 minutes until well-risen and deep golden brown – do not open the oven during cooking if you want a perfect result!

Carve the meat into thick slices and serve with the Yorkshire puddings and the juices from the meat.

pot roast leg of lamb

with rosemary and onion gravy

This is the perfect cook-and-forget roast. The lamb is cooked until tender on a bed of rosemary and onions. The meat juices are then puréed with the soft onions to make a rich gravy.

1.5 kg leg of lamb

2 tablespoons olive oil

3 garlic cloves, crushed

2 tablespoons chopped rosemary needles

3 large rosemary sprigs

2 fresh bay leaves

4 large white onions, thinly sliced

300 ml dry white wine

2 teaspoons Dijon mustard

sea salt and freshly ground black pepper

Creamy Potato Gratin (see page 104), to serve (optional)

a large flameproof casserole

Serves 6

Trim the lamb of any excess fat. Heat the oil in a casserole in which the lamb will fit snugly. Add the lamb and brown it all over. Remove to a plate and let cool.

Crush the garlic and chopped rosemary needles together in a mortar with a pestle. Using a sharp knife, make small incisions all over the lamb. Push the paste deep into these incisions. Season well.

Preheat the oven to 160°C (325°F) Gas 3.

Put the rosemary sprigs, bay leaves and onions in the casserole and put the lamb on top. Mix the wine with the mustard, then pour into the casserole. Bring to the boil, cover tightly, then cook in the preheated oven for 1½ hours, turning the lamb twice.

Increase the oven temperature to 200°C (400°F) Gas 6 and remove the lid from the casserole. Cook for another 30 minutes. The lamb should be tender and cooked through. Transfer the lamb to a serving dish and keep warm.

Skim the fat from the cooking juices and remove the bay leaves and rosemary sprigs. Add a little water if too thick, then bring to the boil, scraping the bottom of the pan to mix in the sediment. Pour the liquid into a blender and whizz until smooth. Season to taste. Serve the lamb with the gravy, and Creamy Potato Gratin, if liked.

roasted rack of lamb with a spicy crust

3 tablespoons cumin seeds

2 tablespoons coriander seeds

2 teaspoons black peppercorns

4 cloves

4 small dried red chillies

2 tablespoons sea salt

grated zest and juice of 2 lemons

4 tablespoons olive oil

3 racks of lamb, 6 cutlets each

200 ml red wine

Petits Pois à la Française (see page 106) and Perfect Mashed Potatoes (see page 103), to serve (optional)

a large roasting tin

Serves 8

Racks of lamb are so convenient as they cook much more quickly than a large leg of lamb. Do trim as much fat off as possible as it doesn't get a chance to crisp up under the spicy crust. Allow two to three cutlets per person, depending on the size.

Heat a frying pan and add the cumin and coriander seeds, peppercorns, cloves and chillies. Cook for 1 minute, stirring. Tip into a mortar and crush coarsely with a pestle. Transfer to a small bowl and stir in the salt, lemon zest and juice and oil.

Put the racks of lamb into a large roasting tin. Rub the spice mixture well into the lamb. Cover and chill overnight.

Preheat the oven to 200°C (400°F) Gas 6.

Cook the lamb in the preheated oven for 20 minutes then reduce the oven temperature to 180°C (350°F) Gas 4. Cook for a further 20 minutes for rare lamb; 25 minutes for medium; 35 minutes for well done. Remove the lamb from the oven, transfer to a carving board and let rest for 5 minutes in a warm place.

Meanwhile, add the wine and 200 ml water to the roasting tin and set over high heat. Stir to scrape up all the roasted bits on the bottom, and boil until reduced by half.

To serve, cut the lamb into cutlets, spoon the sauce over the top and serve with Petis Pois and Perfect Mashed potatoes, if liked.

baked and glazed ham

Ham is an easy dish to prepare for a large gathering and children love it. Buy a ready-boned gammon to make carving simple. This size ham will allow you some leftovers to serve cold during the following week.

1 kg gammon, soaked overnight

2 tablespoons English or Dijon mustard

2 tablespoons demerara sugar

1 teaspoon crushed cloves

freshly ground black pepper

a large roasting tin, lightly oiled

Serves 4

Preheat the oven to 160°C (325°F) Gas 3.

Put the gammon in a large roasting tin and cover with a sheet of foil. Cook in the preheated oven for 1 hour.

Remove from the oven and discard the foil. Drain off the cooking juices and peel off the skin, leaving a layer of fat. Using a knife, score the fat with a criss-cross pattern.

Spread the mustard evenly over the ham. Mix the sugar, cloves and pepper in a small bowl, then sprinkle the mixture all over the ham, pressing it down into the fat with your hands.

Return the ham to the oven and bake for a further 20 minutes. Serve hot, warm or cold.

roast chicken with bay leaves, thyme and lemon

This poor man's version of a dish in which truffle slices are stuffed under the chicken skin makes a nice change from ordinary roast chicken. The bay leaves and thyme delicately flavour the flesh, while the tart lemon keeps it lively.

1 chicken, about 1.5 kg

2 lemons, 1 quartered, 1 sliced

6 large fresh bay leaves

2 thyme sprigs

1–2 tablespoons extra virgin olive oil or 30 g unsalted butter

1 teaspoon dried thyme

1 white onion, sliced into rounds

250 ml dry white wine

1 tablespoon unsalted butter

coarse sea salt and freshly ground black pepper

Vichy Carrots (see page 106) and Crunchy Roast Potatoes (see page 102), to serve (optional)

a large roasting tin with a rack

Serves 4

Season the inside of the chicken and stuff with the lemon quarters, 2 of the bay leaves and the thyme. Using your fingers, separate the skin from the breast meat to create a little pocket and put 1 bay leaf on each side of the breast, underneath the skin. Put the remaining 2 bay leaves under the skin of the thighs. Rub the outside of the chicken all over with oil or butter, season generously and sprinkle all over with the dried thyme.

Preheat the oven to 220°C (425°F) Gas 7.

Put the chicken on its side on a rack set over a roasting tin. Add water to the tin to a depth of 1 cm and add the sliced lemon and onion. Cook in the preheated oven for 40 minutes, then turn the chicken on its other side. Continue roasting the chicken until cooked through and the juices run clear when a thigh is pierced with a skewer, about 40 minutes more. Add extra water to the tin if necessary during cooking. Remove from the oven, remove the chicken from the rack to a plate and let rest, covered in foil, for 10 minutes. Add 250 ml water, or the wine if using, to the pan juices and cook over high heat, scraping the bottom of the tin, for 3–5 minutes. Stir in the butter. Carve the chicken, spoon over the pan juices and serve with Vichy Carrots and Crunchy Roast Potatoes, if liked.

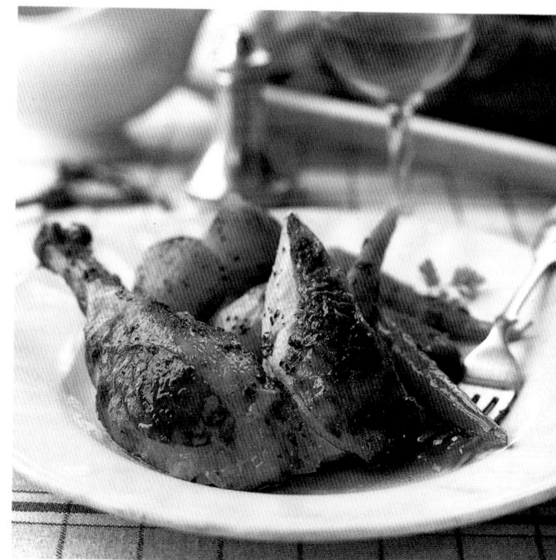

roasted pheasant breasts
with bacon, shallots and mushrooms

Pheasant is by far the most plentiful and popular of game birds. While cooking a whole pheasant is more economical, it does involve all that last-minute carving and it never looks as good when plated as a breast does. If you are offered a choice between hen and cock pheasant, buy the hen – the meat will be more tender. As pheasant season is October through to January, this makes an extra special seasonal treat.

6 boneless and skinless pheasant breasts
12 slices smoked, rindless bacon
6 thyme sprigs
3 fresh bay leaves, halved
25 g unsalted butter
1 tablespoon olive oil
12 shallots
100 ml dry sherry
6 portobello mushrooms, quartered
6 thick slices French bread
200 g watercress
sea salt and cracked black pepper

a large roasting tin

Serves 6

Preheat the oven to 190°C (375°F) Gas 5.

Wrap 2 slices of bacon around each breast, inserting a thyme sprig and half a bay leaf between the pheasant and the bacon.

Put the butter and oil in a large roasting tin and set over high heat. Add the breasts, shallots, sherry, mushrooms and season. Turn the breasts in the mixture until they are well coated. Transfer the tin to the preheated oven and roast for 25 minutes. Remove from the oven and let rest for 5 minutes. Put the bread onto serving plates, then add a little watercress, the mushrooms, shallots and pheasant. Spoon over any cooking juices and serve immediately.

roast monkfish with pancetta, rosemary and red wine gravy

Monkfish makes an excellent alternative to a meaty roast, especially when it is served with a robust red wine gravy. It also makes an impressive main course for a dinner party.

8 rosemary sprigs

7 garlic cloves

50 g butter at room temperature, plus an extra 25 g, chilled and cut into cubes

2 small monkfish tails (about 450 g each), skinned, boned and each divided into 2 fillets

110 g very thinly sliced pancetta or dry-cure streaky bacon, rind removed

2 tablespoons olive oil

8 shallots, quartered

175 ml full-bodied fruity red wine, such as Merlot

125 ml chicken or vegetable stock

sea salt and freshly ground black pepper

Smashed Roast New Potatoes (see page 102) and a green salad, to serve

a roasting tin

Serves 4–6

Strip the needles from 4 of the rosemary sprigs, chop them finely and transfer to a bowl. Crush 1 garlic clove and add it to the rosemary along with the softened butter. Season and beat well.

Preheat the oven to 200°C (400°F) Gas 6.

Lay out the monkfish fillets in pairs with the thin end of 1 fillet next to the thick end of the other. Spread the rosemary and garlic butter over one side of each fillet, then press each pair together with the buttered sides in the middle. Wrap the slices of pancetta around each pair of fillets, enclosing them completely. Put 1 tablespoon olive oil in a roasting tin, then add the monkfish. Put the remaining garlic cloves, rosemary and shallots around the monkfish, then drizzle over the remaining oil. Roast in the preheated oven for 25 minutes, turning the shallots and garlic halfway through, until the pancetta or bacon is nicely browned.

Remove the monkfish from the tin, lightly cover with foil and set aside. Leaving the shallots and garlic in the tin, pour off all but 1 tablespoon of the oil and butter, then set the tin over medium heat. Heat for a few minutes, stirring, then pour in the wine. Let it bubble up and reduce by half, then add the stock. Continue to let it bubble until the liquid is reduced by half again. Strain the gravy through a sieve and return it to the pan. Reheat gently, then whisk in the chilled butter. Season to taste

Cut the monkfish into thick slices, arrange on serving plates and spoon over the red wine gravy. Serve with Smashed Roast New Potatoes and a green salad, if liked.

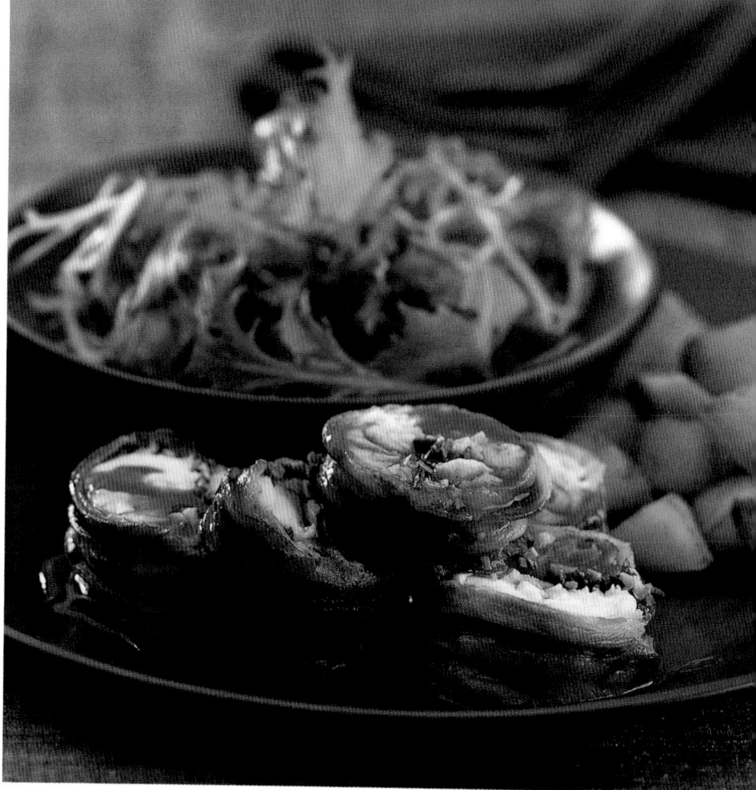

roasted salmon wrapped in prosciutto

What makes this dish such a joy is that you will have no last-minute dramas with the fish falling to pieces, because the prosciutto not only adds flavour and crispness, it also parcels up the salmon and makes it easier to handle.

4 thin slices Fontina cheese, rind removed

4 skinless salmon fillets (about 175 g each)

4 fresh or dried bay leaves

8 thin slices prosciutto

sea salt and freshly ground black pepper

Garlic Sautéed Green Beans (see page 115), to serve (optional)

Serves 4

Preheat the oven to 200°C (400°F) Gas 6. Trim the Fontina slices to fit on top of the salmon fillets. Put a bay leaf on top of each fillet, then a slice of the Fontina. Wrap 2 slices of prosciutto around each piece of salmon, so that it is covered. Transfer to a baking tray.

Cook in the preheated oven for about 10–15 minutes, until the fish is cooked through and the prosciutto crispy. Serve with Garlic Sautéed Green Beans, if liked.

sides and salads

smashed roast new potatoes

This is great way to roast baby new potatoes. You will need tiny little ones to make these perfect roasties. The initial blast of a really hot oven is what makes the potatoes so soft and fluffy on the inside and about to burst out of their crispy skins.

16 small new potatoes, unpeeled

2 tablespoons light olive oil

a few rosemary sprigs

sea salt flakes, to sprinkle

a non-stick roasting tin

Serves 4

Preheat the oven to 230°C (450°F) Gas 8. Put the roasting tin in the oven to heat up for 10 minutes.

Put the potatoes in a large bowl with about 1 tablespoon of the oil and toss to coat. Put the potatoes in the hot roasting tin and roast in the preheated oven for 20 minutes.

Remove the tin from the oven and turn the potatoes over. Gently press down on each potato with the back of large metal spoon until you hear the potato skin pop.

Drizzle the remaining oil over the potatoes, add the rosemary sprigs and sprinkle with the salt. Return to the oven for a further 10 minutes, until the potatoes are crispy and golden brown.

Variation: Remove the potatoes from the oven and spoon over a soft French cheese (such as a sweet and nutty brie), while the potatoes are still warm. The cheese will melt and transform these into an indulgence treat. Delicious served with a Baked and Glazed Ham (see page 97).

crunchy roast potatoes

Use an old, floury potato, such as Maris Piper or King Edward. The idea is to get a crisp, crunchy outside and a light and fluffy inside.

1.5 kg floury potatoes, peeled and halved or quartered

5–6 tablespoons rapeseed or vegetable oil

sea salt flakes, to sprinkle

a non-stick roasting tin

Serves 6

Preheat the oven to 200°C (400°F) Gas 6.

Place the potatoes in a large saucepan. Cover with cold water and bring to the boil. Add a little salt, boil for 5 minutes, then drain. Pour the oil into a roasting tin and tip in the potatoes, turning them in the oil.

Roast the potatoes in the preheated oven for 45 minutes, turning them halfway through the cooking time. Turn the heat up to 220°C (425°F) Gas 7 and continue to cook until the potatoes are crisp (about another 15–20 minutes).

sides and salads

smashed roast new potatoes

This is great way to roast baby new potatoes. You will need tiny little ones to make these perfect roasties. The initial blast of a really hot oven is what makes the potatoes so soft and fluffy on the inside and about to burst out of their crispy skins.

16 small new potatoes, unpeeled

2 tablespoons light olive oil

a few rosemary sprigs

sea salt flakes, to sprinkle

a non-stick roasting tin

Serves 4

Preheat the oven to 230°C (450°F) Gas 8. Put the roasting tin in the oven to heat up for 10 minutes.

Put the potatoes in a large bowl with about 1 tablespoon of the oil and toss to coat. Put the potatoes in the hot roasting tin and roast in the preheated oven for 20 minutes.

Remove the tin from the oven and turn the potatoes over. Gently press down on each potato with the back of large metal spoon until you hear the potato skin pop.

Drizzle the remaining oil over the potatoes, add the rosemary sprigs and sprinkle with the salt. Return to the oven for a further 10 minutes, until the potatoes are crispy and golden brown.

Variation: Remove the potatoes from the oven and spoon over a soft French cheese (such as a sweet and nutty brie), while the potatoes are still warm. The cheese will melt and transform these into an indulgence treat. Delicious served with a Baked and Glazed Ham (see page 97).

crunchy roast potatoes

Use an old, floury potato, such as Maris Piper or King Edward. The idea is to get a crisp, crunchy outside and a light and fluffy inside.

1.5 kg floury potatoes, peeled and halved or quartered

5–6 tablespoons rapeseed or vegetable oil

sea salt flakes, to sprinkle

a non-stick roasting tin

Serves 6

Preheat the oven to 200°C (400°F) Gas 6.

Place the potatoes in a large saucepan. Cover with cold water and bring to the boil. Add a little salt, boil for 5 minutes, then drain. Pour the oil into a roasting tin and tip in the potatoes, turning them in the oil.

Roast the potatoes in the preheated oven for 45 minutes, turning them halfway through the cooking time. Turn the heat up to 220°C (425°F) Gas 7 and continue to cook until the potatoes are crisp (about another 15–20 minutes).

perfect mashed potatoes

The secret of perfect mash is the right potato – a floury variety that fluffs up properly. Older potatoes work better than new and make sure that they are thoroughly cooked or the mash will be lumpy. Mash will keep warm in a very cool oven – 120°C (250°F) Gas ½ – for up to 2 hours if covered with buttered foil. Otherwise, cool and reheat gently, beating in melted butter and hot milk. If adding herbs, add just before serving.

750 g floury potatoes, peeled and quartered

55 g unsalted butter

75–100 ml milk

3 tablespoons chopped spring onions, sautéed in butter (optional)

2 tablespoons creamed horseradish (optional)

sea salt and freshly ground black pepper

Serves 4

Preheat the oven to 150°C (300°F) Gas 2.

Put the potatoes in a saucepan of salted cold water and bring to the boil. As soon as the water comes to the boil, reduce to a simmer (it's important not to cook the potatoes too quickly) and cook for about 20 minutes. When perfectly done, the point of a sharp knife should glide into the centre.

Drain in a colander, then set over the hot pan to steam and dry out. Tip the potatoes back into the hot pan and crush with a potato masher or pass them through a mouli or ricer into the pan. Melt the butter in the milk. Using a wooden spoon, beat the butter and milk into the mash – an electric hand-mixer sometimes helps here. Add the spring onions and horseradish, if using. Season well, pile into a warm dish and serve immediately.

buttermilk mash

This simple variation on classic mashed potatoes has creamy buttermilk and Parmesan added to give extra flavour.

750 g floury potatoes, peeled and quartered

125 ml buttermilk

3 tablespoons unsalted butter

50 g Parmesan cheese, finely grated

Serves 4

Put the potatoes in a large saucepan of salted cold water and bring to the boil. Cook for about 20 minutes, until tender. Drain and return to the warm pan with the buttermilk and butter. Mash well then beat with a wooden spoon until really smooth. Stir in the Parmesan and season well with sea salt and black pepper.

pomme purée

This decadent French way of cooking potatoes makes a chic alternative to classic mashed potatoes.

1 kg red-skinned potatoes, such as Desirée, peeled and cut into quarters or eighths

50 ml double cream

75–100 ml full-fat milk

75 g unsalted butter, cut into cubes and at room temperature

sea salt and freshly ground black pepper

a potato ricer or mouli

Serves 6

Put the potatoes in a saucepan, pour over boiling water, add 1 teaspoon salt and bring back to the boil. Turn down the heat and simmer gently for about 12–15 minutes until you can easily pierce them with a skewer. Drain them in a colander, then return them to the pan over very low heat and leave them for 1–2 minutes to dry off.

Mix the cream and milk together and heat until just below boiling point in a separate saucepan. Tip the potatoes back into the colander, then pass them through a potato ricer back into the pan. Pour in half the cream mixture and beat with a wooden spoon, then gradually beat in the remaining cream mixture and the butter. Season well with salt and pepper.

creamy potato gratin

Cream and potatoes are almost all you'll find in this classic French dish. If the recipe included cheese, it wouldn't be a true dauphinois. Serve as a partner for simple roast meat or poultry.

2 kg waxy salad-style potatoes, cut into half if large

2 litres full-fat milk

1 fresh bay leaf

30 g unsalted butter

550 ml whipping cream

a pinch of freshly grated nutmeg

coarse sea salt, to sprinkle

an ovenproof baking dish

Serves 4–6

Preheat the oven to 180°C (350°F) Gas 4.

Put the potatoes in a large saucepan with the milk and bay leaf. Bring to the boil, then lower the heat, add a pinch of salt and simmer gently for about 5–10 minutes.

Drain the potatoes. When cool enough to handle (but still hot), slice into rounds about 3 mm thick.

Spread the butter in the bottom of the baking dish. Arrange half the potato slices in the dish and sprinkle with salt. Put the remaining potato on top and sprinkle with more salt. Pour in the cream and sprinkle with the grated nutmeg.

Bake in the preheated oven until golden and the cream is almost absorbed, but not completely, 45 minutes. Serve hot.

harissa potatoes

These spicy potatoes made with harissa, a Moroccan chilli paste, make an interesting alternative to more classic potato side dishes. Serve them with any roast meat or poultry or grilled fish.

3 tablespoons olive oil

1 onion, sliced

750 g waxy potatoes, thickly sliced

5 garlic cloves, sliced

1 heaped teaspoon harissa, or more to taste

1 teaspoon ground cumin

1 teaspoon coarse sea salt

1 tablespoon freshly squeezed lemon juice

a large handful of coriander leaves, chopped

sea salt and freshly ground black pepper

Serves 4

Heat the oil in a large frying pan with a lid. Add the onion and cook for 1 minute, then add the potatoes and cook for 2–3 minutes more, stirring often. Add the garlic, harissa, cumin and salt and mix well. Add enough water to cover by half, then cover with a lid and simmer gently for 20 minutes. Uncover and continue simmering until cooked through and the liquid has been almost completely absorbed, 5–8 minutes more.

Stir in the lemon juice and coriander, season to taste and serve.

French fries

Choose evenly sized potatoes so that the fries you end up with are roughly the same width and length. Use an electric deep-fryer or a deep saucepan for frying, and add the uncooked fries to the oil in small batches. If using a saucepan, use a sugar thermometer to check the temperature of the oil.

1 kg floury potatoes, such as Desirée or King Edwards

sea salt

sunflower or peanut oil, for deep-frying

an electric deep-fryer (optional)

Serves 4

Cut the potatoes into 1 cm slices, then cut these slices into 1 cm thick sticks. Put them in a bowl of cold water and let soak for 15 minutes. Drain well and dry thoroughly using a clean, dry tea towel.

Pour 5 cm depth of oil into a deep, heavy saucepan. Heat gently until the oil reaches 150°C (300°F) on a sugar thermometer.

Alternatively, use an electric deep-fryer and follow the manufacturer's instructions. Cook the fries, in batches, for 5–6 minutes until lightly golden and cooked through. Drain on kitchen paper and set aside until required.

Increase the heat of the oil to 180°C (350°F) and cook the fries again, in batches, for 1–2 minutes until crisp and golden. Drain on kitchen paper, transfer to a large bowl and season lightly with salt. Serve hot.

Variation Shoestring Potatoes
Cut the potatoes into 2 mm slices, then again into 2 mm thick strips. Rinse well under cold running water and dry thoroughly using a clean, dry tea towel. Heat 5 cm depth of oil in a deep, heavy frying pan until it reaches 180°C (350°F) on a sugar thermometer. Add the potato strips and fry, in batches, for 2–3 minutes until crisp and golden. Drain on kitchen paper. Serve hot, sprinkled with salt.

vichy carrots with fresh ginger

These buttery carrots almost caramelize as they cook, so the ginger adds a spicy punch to cut through the rich sweetness.

1 kg carrots

2 tablespoons finely chopped fresh ginger

55 g unsalted butter

½ teaspoon sea salt

2 teaspoons caster sugar

freshly ground black pepper

3 tablespoons chopped coriander or parsley

Serves 8

Cut the carrots into batons or thick rounds and put in a saucepan with the ginger, butter, salt and sugar. Half-cover with water, bring to the boil and boil steadily, stirring once or twice, until the water has almost disappeared and the carrots are tender.

Reduce the heat and let the carrots brown a little and caramelize. Season with black pepper and stir in the coriander or parsley. Serve immediately.

petits pois à la Française

Equally good when made with fresh or frozen peas, this recipe is great for large numbers. The lettuce adds sweetness to the peas. Perfect with fish or lamb.

250 g green peas, fresh or frozen

1 large onion, thinly sliced

1 small lettuce, such as Little Gem, shredded

55 g unsalted butter

1 teaspoon caster sugar

2 tablespoons chopped mint

2 tablespoons chopped parsley

sea salt and freshly ground black pepper

Serves 4

Mix the peas, onion and lettuce together in a casserole or heavy-based saucepan. Add 150 ml water, the butter, sugar, salt and pepper. Cover tightly with a lid and simmer for 30 minutes, until the peas are tender. Stir in the mint and parsley, season to taste, then serve.

carrots with cream and herbs

Thyme is omnipresent in French cuisine. Here, it transforms what would otherwise be ordinary boiled carrots into something subtly sumptuous. The crème fraîche helps too. You can substitute steamed baby leeks for the carrots, but stir in a tablespoon or so of butter when adding the crème fraîche.

800 g carrots, ideally baby ones

50 g unsalted butter

a sprig of thyme

2 tablespoons crème fraîche

several sprigs of chervil

a small bunch of chives

fine sea salt

Serves 4

If using larger carrots, cut them diagonally into 5 cm slices. Put in a large saucepan (the carrots should fit in almost a single layer for even cooking). Add the butter and set over low heat. Cook to melt and coat, about 3 minutes. Half fill the saucepan with water, then add a pinch of salt and the thyme. Cover and cook until the water is almost completely evaporated, about 10–20 minutes.

Stir in the cream and add salt to taste. Using kitchen scissors, snip the chervil and chives over the top, mix well and serve.

Variation In early spring, when turnips are sweet, they make a nice addition to this dish. Peel and quarter large turnips, or just peel baby ones – the main thing is to ensure that all the vegetable pieces (carrot and turnip) are about the same size so that they cook evenly. Halve the carrot quantity and complete with turnips. Sprinkle with a large handful of just-cooked shelled peas before serving for extra crunch and a pretty colour.

mushrooms marinated with raisins and apple cider vinegar

Mushroom fans will love this tasty mix of juicy mushrooms in a sweet and sour chilli-spiked marinade. Add a crumbling of salty cheese, such as feta, and you have a pretty special vegetarian main course.

60 ml olive oil
2 shallots, peeled and finely chopped
2 garlic cloves, peeled and crushed
500 g mushrooms, halved
20 ml apple cider vinegar
2 tablespoons raisins
2 tablespoons runny honey
a pinch of dried chilli flakes
oregano leaves, to garnish (optional)

Serves 4–6

Heat 3 tablespoons of the olive oil in a frying pan. Add the shallots and garlic and gently fry over low heat for 2–3 minutes, until softened. Add the mushrooms and cook for 4–5 minutes, until golden. Add the vinegar and raisins, and let bubble for 1–2 minutes. Stir in the honey, remaining olive oil and chilli flakes. Cook for a further minute. Remove from the heat and let cool. Leave to marinate for half an hour before serving. Garnish with oregano, if using.

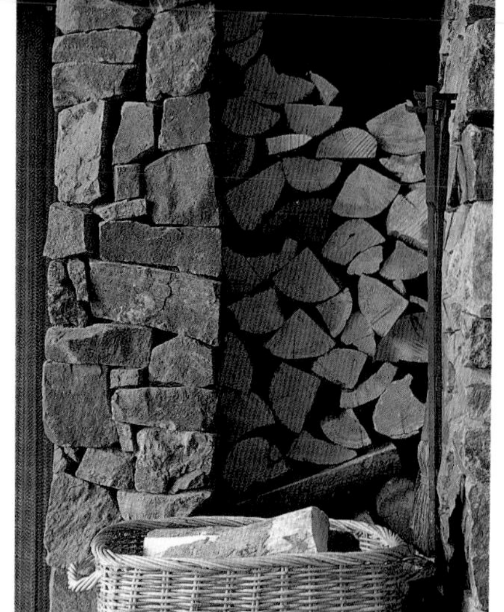

slow-cooked Brussels sprouts
with pancetta and chestnuts

You won't be surprised to learn that Brussels sprouts are a member of the cabbage family as they look just like little baby cabbages. But unlike cabbage they have a sweet and nutty flavour, especially when they are young. Use baby sprouts in this rather festive dish, which is lovely as a side with roast turkey, pork or beef. If you can't find pancetta, use chopped lean bacon rashers instead.

200 g fresh chestnuts
60 ml light olive oil
50 g pancetta, chopped into 1-cm pieces
1 small onion, finely chopped
2 garlic cloves, thinly sliced
60 ml chicken or vegetable stock
60 ml dry white wine
1 tablespoon freshly squeezed lemon juice
400 g young Brussels sprouts, trimmed

Serves 2

Preheat the oven to 200°C (400°F) Gas 6.

Cut a small slit, without cutting into the flesh, along one side of the chestnuts. Put them on a baking tray and roast in the preheated oven for 15–20 minutes, until the skins start to split. Remove from the oven and let cool a little. Peel and rub off the skin and set aside.

Heat the oil in a heavy-based saucepan over medium heat. Add the pancetta, onion and garlic and cook for 3–4 minutes. Pour in the stock, wine and lemon juice and bring to the boil. Add the sprouts to the pan, cover, reduce the heat and simmer gently for 20 minutes. Turn the sprouts over and add the chestnuts to the pan. Cover and cook for a further 20 minutes, until almost all the liquid has evaporated and the sprouts are tender. Serve immediately.

savoy cabbage with bacon and cream

Based loosely on a traditional French dish that includes pheasant, this recipe is a very elegant way to dress up a rustic vegetable. It seems to go best with poultry and potatoes, both roasted. In fact, it's an idea to make extra cabbage and potatoes because they can be mashed together the next day, formed into patties and fried in a mix of butter and olive oil for a leftover feast.

1 bay leaf

1 Savoy cabbage, about 1.25 kg

2 tablespoons unsalted butter

1 tablespoon extra virgin olive oil

100 g thinly sliced pancetta, chopped

a sprig of sage, leaves stripped and thinly sliced

4 tablespoons crème fraîche or double cream

sea salt and freshly ground black pepper

Serves 4

Bring a large saucepan of water to the boil with the bay leaf and a large pinch of salt. Quarter the cabbage and blanch it in the boiling water for 2–3 minutes. Drain well. Core the cabbage quarters, then slice crossways. Set aside until needed.

Heat the butter and oil in a large frying pan. Add the pancetta and sage and cook over high heat, stirring often, for 1 minute. Add the blanched cabbage and a pinch of salt and cook, stirring often, for 2–3 minutes.

Stir in the cream and cook until warmed through, about 1 minute. Mix to thoroughly combine, season to taste and serve hot.

cauliflower with garlic and anchovies

If you thought cauliflower was boring think again. The Italians have a way with vegetables and know how to cook them beautifully. This deliciously savoury recipe breathes new life into what is so often a tired old vegetable side dish. Perfect with roast meats and poultry. The Tabasco is optional but does add a nice spicy kick.

2 cauliflowers, about 600 g

1 bay leaf

3 celery stalks, plus a handful of leaves

3–5 tablespoons extra virgin olive oil

6 anchovy fillets in oil, drained and coarsely chopped

3–4 garlic cloves, finely chopped

freshly squeezed juice of ½ a lemon

sea salt and freshly ground black pepper

Tabasco sauce (optional)

Serves 4

Separate the cauliflowers into florets. Bring a large saucepan of water to the boil with the bay leaf. Add a generous amount of salt, then the cauliflower. Cook for 2–3 minutes just to blanch. Drain and set aside.

Chop the celery stalks finely and set aside. Chop the leaves separately and set aside. Heat 3 tablespoons of the oil in a large frying pan. Add the celery stalks and cook for 1 minute. Add the cauliflower and a good pinch of salt. Cook for 2–3 minutes over medium-high heat, without stirring. The cauliflower should brown.

Add the remaining oil if it seems to need it (this dish can be slightly oily), then the anchovies, and cook for 2–3 minutes more. Add the garlic, stir well and cook for just 30 seconds – do not let the garlic burn. Remove from the heat and stir in the celery leaves. Add the lemon juice and season to taste. Add a few drops of Tabasco, if using. Serve hot or at room temperature.

spiced cauliflower with red pepper and peas

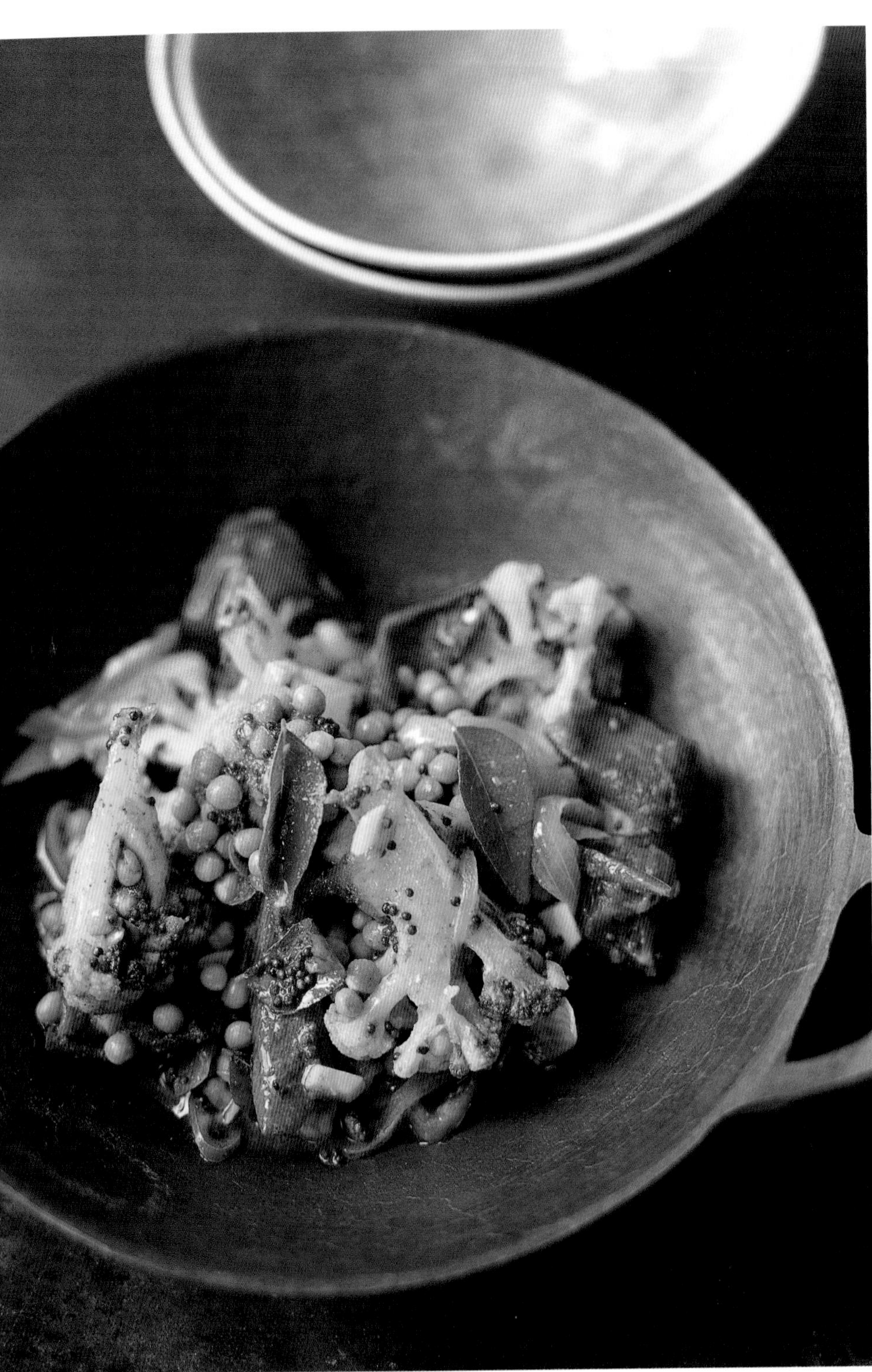

This is a spicy treat that's perfect if you like things hot. The vegetable dishes you find in Indian cuisine are among the most delicious in the world. Many of the recipes embrace the philosophy of cooking fresh produce and letting the flavours speak for themselves.

½ a head of cauliflower, cut into large florets
2 teaspoons ground cumin
1 teaspoon turmeric
3 tablespoons light olive oil
2 teaspoons black mustard seeds
6–8 curry leaves
1 onion, sliced
1 small red pepper, cored, deseeded and sliced
1 tablespoon finely grated fresh ginger
2 garlic cloves, chopped
1 large green chilli, sliced
125 ml vegetable stock
2 ripe tomatoes, chopped
125 g freshly shelled peas
cooked basmati rice, to serve (optional)

Serves 4

Put the cauliflower florets in a large bowl with the cumin and turmeric and toss until evenly coated in the spices.

Put the oil in a large frying pan set over medium/high heat. Add the cauliflower, mustard seeds and curry leaves and cook for 8–10 minutes, turning the pieces often so that they soften and colour with the spices.

Add the onion and red pepper and cook for 5 minutes. Add the ginger, garlic and chilli and stir-fry for 1 minute, then add the stock, tomatoes and peas. Reduce the heat and let simmer gently for 10 minutes until the vegetables are tender and cooked through.

Spoon over basmati rice to serve, if liked.

sweet potatoes with thyme and chilli

Sweet potatoes make such a nice change from the usual vegetable repertoire and their partnership here with chillies and thyme is inspired. Serve them to accompany roast meat or poultry – they are especially good with pan-fried duck breasts.

3 large sweet potatoes, about 850 g

30 g unsalted butter

2 tablespoons extra virgin olive oil

a small bunch of thyme

1 fresh red chilli, deseeded (optional) and finely chopped

coarse sea salt

a large roasting tin

Serves 4

Preheat the oven to 220°C (425°F) Gas 7.

Cut the potatoes into large chunks. Put them in a large roasting tray and toss with the butter and oil. Strip the thyme leaves from the stems and sprinkle the leaves and chilli over the potatoes. Season well with salt and add 125 ml water. Bake in the preheated oven until just browned and tender, about 35–40 minutes. Serve hot.

Note This is not very spicy. To make it hotter, keep the chilli seeds in or add an extra chilli.

cauliflower gratin

The secret of delicious cauliflower is to blanch it first; if you parboil it with a bay leaf, the unpleasant cabbage aroma disappears. This classic recipe goes especially well with pork or can be enjoyed on it's own as a light supper.

1 large cauliflower, separated into large florets

1 fresh bay leaf

500 ml double cream

1 egg, beaten

2 teaspoons Dijon mustard

160 g finely grated Comté* cheese

coarse sea salt

a baking dish, greased with butter

Serves 4–6

Preheat the oven to 200°C (400°F) Gas 6.

Bring a large saucepan of water to the boil, add the bay leaf, salt generously, then add the cauliflower. Cook until still slightly firm, about 10 minutes. Drain and set aside.

Put the cream in a saucepan and bring to the boil. Boil for 10 minutes. Add a spoonful of hot milk to the beaten egg to warm it, then stir in the egg, mustard and 1 teaspoon salt.

Divide the cauliflower into smaller florets, then stir into the cream sauce. Transfer to the prepared dish and sprinkle the cheese over the top in an even layer. Bake in the preheated oven for about 40–45 minutes, until golden. Serve hot.

***Note** Like Gruyère, Comté is a French mountain cheese but the similarity stops there. Use Emmental or Cantal if Comté is unavailable.

roast beetroot

Banish all thoughts of vinegary pickled beetroot from your mind – when slow-roasted in the oven beetroot is mellow and delicious and makes the perfect accompaniment to many dishes.

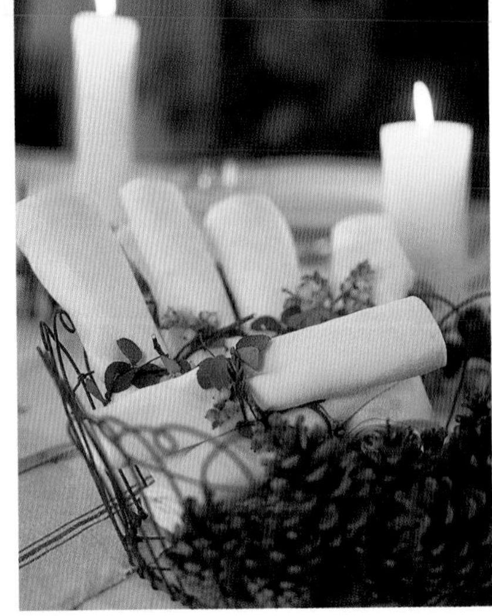

6 beetroot, about 750 g

3 tablespoons balsamic vinegar

2 tablespoons extra virgin olive oil

a small handful of flat leaf parsley, chopped

a small handful of oregano or dill, chopped

a sprig of mint, leaves chopped

coarse sea salt

a large roasting tin

Serves 2–4

Preheat the oven to 200°C (400°F) Gas 6.

Peel the beetroot and trim the stems to about 3 cm. Cut into 4–6 wedges, depending on size. Put the wedges in a roasting tin that will hold them in a single layer. Add the vinegar, oil, parsley, oregano, mint and a good pinch of salt. Toss well.

Cover the dish with foil and roast in the preheated oven for 30 minutes. Remove the foil and continue roasting until just tender when pierced with a knife, about 20 minutes more. There should still be some liquid in the dish; if this evaporates too quickly, add a spoonful or so of water during cooking. Serve hot or at room temperature if preferred.

wilted greens

Here are two foolproof ways with greens. Larger greens are good with sausages and roast beef, smaller leaves make an excellent side with roast fish.

750 g greens, mixed or single, such as baby chard, spinach, mustard greens or rocket

extra virgin olive oil

1 lemon

1 garlic clove (Method two)

fine sea salt and freshly ground black pepper

Serves 2–4

Method one: Best for larger, robust greens, such as chard. Bring a large saucepan of water to the boil. Salt well, add the greens and blanch for 2–3 minutes. Drain and refresh under cold running water. Let dry in a colander, tossing occasionally to let all the water escape (squeeze excess with your hands if necessary). To serve, sprinkle with 2–3 tablespoons oil, the juice of ½ lemon and a good sprinkling of salt and pepper.

Method two: Best for smaller leaves, such as baby spinach and rocket. Crush the garlic clove, but leave whole and spear on the end of a fork. Heat about 2 tablespoons oil in a large frying pan. Add a very large handful of leaves and cook, stirring with the garlic fork, until wilted. Using tongs, transfer the leaves to a large plate and continue adding handfuls until all the greens are wilted. Season with extra oil, a squeeze of lemon juice and plenty of salt and pepper.

butternut squash with pistou

Butternut squash and pistou aren't obvious partners, but the sweetness of squash goes very well with the garlicky basil sauce. This is best served with roast lamb or chicken because the pistou makes a lovely sauce for it all (though you might want to double the quantity to be sure). Experiment with different types of winter squash, such as kabochka (the small Japanese pumpkins with striped green skin and brilliant orange flesh), or other kinds of pumpkin, in place of the butternut.

6 tablespoons extra virgin olive oil

4 garlic cloves

a large handful of fresh basil leaves

2 butternut squash, about 800 g each

fine sea salt

a large roasting tin

Serves 4

Preheat the oven to 200°C (400°F) Gas 6.

To make the pistou, put the oil, garlic, basil leaves and a pinch of salt in a small food processor. Blend well. Transfer to a small bowl.

Trim the stems from the butternut squashes and cut in half lengthways. Scoop out the seeds. Arrange the squash halves in a roasting tin and sprinkle with salt. Brush generously with the pistou, letting it well up a bit in the cavity if you like. Roast in the preheated oven until just browned at the edges and tender when pierced with a knife, 40–45 minutes. Serve hot, with the remaining pistou.

baked spinach mornay

This is really rich and ideally served with simply cooked meat or fish. It is also a great brunch dish, perfect with poached eggs and hot buttered toast.

40 g butter

2 tablespoons plain flour

750 ml full-fat milk

200 g Fontina cheese, cubed

1 onion, chopped

1 garlic clove, chopped

1 kg fresh spinach leaves, chopped

¼ teaspoon freshly grated nutmeg

toasted and buttered sourdough bread, to serve (optional)

Serves 6

Preheat oven to 180°C (350°F) Gas 4.

Put 25 g of the butter in a saucepan and set over medium heat. When sizzling, add the flour and cook for 1 minute, stirring constantly, until a thick paste forms.

Reduce the heat to low and slowly pour the milk into the pan, whisking constantly until all the milk is incorporated and the mixture is smooth and lump-free. Add the cheese and stir until it has melted into the sauce.

Heat the remaining butter in a large frying pan set over high heat. Add the onion and garlic and cook for 2–3 minutes, until the onion has softened. Add the spinach, cover with a lid, and cook for 4–5 minutes, stirring often, until the spinach has wilted. Transfer the spinach to a large bowl. Pour in the cheese sauce and stir to combine. Spoon the mixture into a large baking dish.

Sprinkle the nutmeg over the top and bake in the preheated oven for 30 minutes until the top is golden and bubbling. Serve hot.

roasted early autumn vegetables
with chickpeas

Sometimes we forget how good the simple things can be. These autumn vegetables roasted with whole garlic cloves and thyme sprigs make a substantial side dish or serve them with Plain, Buttery Couscous (see page 77) for a vegetarian main course.

12 small mushrooms

2 ripe tomatoes, halved

1 red pepper, deseeded and cut into strips

1 yellow pepper, deseeded and cut into strips

1 red onion, peeled and cut into wedges

1 small fennel bulb, sliced into thin wedges

1 garlic bulb, broken into individual cloves but left unpeeled

2 teaspoons sea salt

2 tablespoons olive oil

400-g tin chickpeas, drained and rinsed

2 fresh thyme or rosemary sprigs

Plain, Buttery Couscous (see page 77), to serve (optional)

Serves 4

Preheat the oven to 180°C (350°F) Gas 4. Put the mushrooms, tomatoes, red and yellow peppers, onion, fennel and garlic in a large roasting tray. Sprinkle the salt evenly over the vegetables and drizzle with the oil. Roast in the preheated oven for 1 hour.

Remove the tray from the oven and turn the vegetables. Add the chickpeas and thyme sprigs. Return the tray to the oven and roast for a further 30 minutes, until the edges of the vegetables are just starting to blacken and char.

To serve, spoon the Plain, Buttery Couscous, if liked, onto serving plates and top with the warm roasted vegetables with chickpeas.

garlic sautéed green beans

It may seem odd not to cook the beans in a pan of water, but with this method the beans take on a wonderful buttery, garlic flavour, while keeping their crunchy texture.

2 garlic cloves, crushed and finely chopped

25 g unsalted butter

2 tablespoons olive oil

200 g runner beans, trimmed and cut into 3 pieces each

200 g fine green beans, trimmed

200 g sugar snap peas, trimmed

freshly ground black pepper

Serves 8

Put the garlic, butter and oil into a large saucepan and heat gently. When hot, add all the beans and sugar snap peas and cook, stirring frequently, for 5 minutes until tender but still slightly crisp. Sprinkle with plenty of black pepper and serve warm.

beetroot, goats' cheese and pine nut salad with melba toast

Wintry, festive sumptuousness, thanks to the deep red of the beetroot and the bright white of the cheese.

12 slices white bread

750 g small, unpeeled beetroot, trimmed

500 g mixed salad leaves

200 g firm goats' cheese, crumbled

100 g pine nuts, toasted in a dry frying pan

a large handful of basil leaves

2 garlic cloves, crushed and chopped

5 tablespoons olive oil

freshly squeezed juice of 2 lemons

salt and freshly ground black pepper

Serves 12

To make the Melba toast, toast the slices of bread, then remove the crusts. Using a large, sharp knife, split each piece of toast through the middle, to give 2 whole slices of toast with 1 soft bread side each. Cut in half diagonally, then cook under a preheated grill, soft side up, until golden and curled. Watch the toasts carefully, as they can burn quickly.

Preheat the oven to 180°C (350°F) Gas 4.

Put the beetroot into a roasting tin and roast in the preheated oven for 45 minutes. Remove, let cool, then peel and quarter. Put the salad leaves onto a serving dish, add the beetroot and goats' cheese, then sprinkle with pine nuts and torn basil leaves.

Put the garlic, oil and lemon juice in a small bowl. Season, mix well, and pour over the salad. Serve with the Melba toast.

smoked duck, mandarin and pecan salad with Pinot Noir dressing

3 mandarin oranges or other small sweet oranges

100 g lamb's lettuce or watercress

225 g sliced smoked duck breast

100 g candied pecans* or walnuts

Pinot Noir dressing

225 ml Chilean or other inexpensive Pinot Noir, or another fruity red wine

1½ tablespoons light muscovado sugar

100 ml light olive oil

1 medium pomegranate

½–1 teaspoon pomegranate molasses or balsamic vinegar

sea salt and freshly ground black pepper

Serves 6

Wine can be used instead of vinegar to make a deliciously fruity salad dressing. Making a reduction like this is a thrifty way to use up leftover wine and it will keep in the refrigerator for several days. If you can't find a pomegranate, use sun-dried cherries instead.

Peel and slice the oranges horizontally, reserving any juice. Cut the larger slices in half to make half-moon shapes.

To make the dressing, put the wine in a small saucepan, bring to the boil, then lower the heat. Simmer for 10–15 minutes or until the wine has reduced by two-thirds. Remove the pan from the heat, stir in the muscovado sugar and let cool.

Once cool, whisk in the olive oil and season to taste. Cut the pomegranate in half and scoop the seeds into a bowl, catching any juice. Discard the pith and tip the seeds and juice, along with any juice from the oranges, into the dressing. Add the pomegranate molasses or balsamic vinegar to taste. Stir well.

Divide the lamb's lettuce or watercress among 6 plates and arrange the duck breast and orange slices on top. Scatter over the candied pecans or walnuts. Give the dressing a quick whisk, then spoon it over the salad. Serve immediately.

***Note** If you can't find candied pecans, put 100 g pecans in a dry, non-stick frying pan and sprinkle over 1 teaspoon caster sugar. Toast gently over medium heat for a couple of minutes, shaking the pan frequently, until the nuts are crisp and the sugar has caramelized.

chicken, raisin and chilli salad with hazelnut dressing

Everyone will love this moist marinated chicken salad. For the best flavour, be sure to toast the hazelnuts until dark golden. If time is short, you could cheat a little and buy a freshly cooked rotisserie chicken and throw away the evidence!

a 2-kg chicken

1.5 litres chicken or vegetable stock

a handful of raisins

100 g blanched hazelnuts, toasted until dark golden

1 teaspoon dried chilli flakes, or to taste

a small bunch of flat leaf parsley, chopped

sea salt and freshly ground black pepper

hazelnut dressing

6 tablespoons hazelnut oil

2 tablespoons red wine vinegar

1 tablespoon caster sugar

Serves 4–6

Put the chicken in a large saucepan and cover with the stock. Bring to the boil. Turn down the heat and poach the chicken for about 1 hour, or until the juices run clear when the chicken is tested with a skewer at the thickest part of the leg. Leave to cool in the stock, then transfer to a chopping board. Shred the meat into a large bowl. Add the raisins, hazelnuts and chilli flakes.

To make the hazelnut dressing, whisk the hazelnut oil, vinegar and sugar together in a small bowl and season to taste. Add to the chicken along with the parsley, toss well and leave to marinate in a cool place (not the refrigerator) for at least 1 hour. Serve at room temperature.

winter-spiced salad with pears, honeyed pecans and ricotta

You need to be careful when buying ricotta because it can sometimes be very soggy, especially when sold in tubs. Look for the organic varieties or buffalo ricotta which is crumbly rather than creamy. Buffalo mozzarella also works well, as does a soft, fresh goats' cheese. Leave some seeds in the chilli to give a little kick, awaken all the other flavours and contrast with the sweet nuts.

1 star anise

1 cinnamon stick

2 pears, unpeeled, quartered and cored

150 g salad leaves, such as rocket, shredded radicchio or baby Swiss chard

125 g buffalo ricotta

honeyed pecans

50 g pecans

¼ teaspoon dried chilli flakes

¼ teaspoon fennel seeds

3 tablespoons clear honey

dressing

4 tablespoons sunflower oil

1 tablespoon walnut oil

freshly squeezed juice of 1 lemon

1 large red chilli, partly deseeded and chopped

Serves 4

Fill a saucepan with water and add the star anise and cinnamon stick. Bring to the boil and add the pears. Poach for 12 minutes, or until tender.

Put the pecans, a large pinch of salt, the chilli flakes and the fennel seeds in a frying pan and toast until golden and aromatic. Pour in the honey, turn the heat right up and leave to bubble away for a few minutes. Tip onto greaseproof paper and leave to cool.

Meanwhile, to make the dressing, whisk together the sunflower and walnut oils, the lemon juice and chilli.

Transfer the salad leaves to bowls, scatter over the pears and crumble over the ricotta. Drizzle with the dressing. Roughly break up the nuts with your fingers and scatter them over the top. Serve immediately.

salad of winter fruit
with blue cheese and spinach

The number of organically grown apple and pear varieties at your local farmers' market might be a little overwhelming! If you are unsure, ask the stallholder what varieties are good for cooking, for munching on or, as here, slicing directly into a salad bowl with a few other great ingredients.

2 apples, cored and cut into thin wedges

2 firm pears, cored and cut into thin wedges

1 small head of radicchio, leaves separated

100 g fresh spinach leaves

200 g firm blue cheese, crumbled

tarragon vinaigrette

3 tablespoons light olive oil

1 tablespoon tarragon vinegar

¼ teaspoon freshly cracked white or black pepper

sea salt

Serves 4

Combine the apples, pears, radicchio, spinach and blue cheese in a large salad bowl and toss gently to combine.

Whisk the olive oil, tarragon vinegar and pepper in a small bowl and season with a little salt. Pour the dressing over the salad, toss well and serve immediately.

cauliflower and Swiss chard salad

If you've never tried a cauliflower salad, do try this recipe. Cauliflower has a firm, crunchy texture and creamy flavour which makes it perfect for this light and spicy dish with Middle Eastern-style flavourings. It makes a great winter buffet dish and is the perfect accompaniment to a Baked and Glazed Ham (see page 97) and slices of cold leftover turkey.

65 ml light olive oil

1 small head of cauliflower, separated into large florets

1 teaspoon ground cumin

6 large Swiss chard leaves, chopped into 2-cm wide strips

1 red onion, cut into wedges

2 garlic cloves, chopped

400-g tin chickpeas, rinsed and drained

65 ml tahini (sesame seed paste)

2 tablespoons freshly squeezed lemon juice

¼ teaspoon freshly cracked white pepper

sea salt

Serves 4

Put the oil in a frying pan and set over high heat, add the cauliflower florets and cook for 8–10 minutes, turning often, until they are a dark, golden brown. Add the cumin and cook, stirring, for 1 minute. Add the Swiss chard, onion and garlic to the pan and cook for a further 2–3 minutes. Add the chickpeas and stir. Season to taste with salt.

Combine the tahini, lemon juice and white pepper in a small bowl and add a little salt to taste. Whisk to combine. Transfer the vegetables to a bowl and drizzle the dressing over the top to serve.

chickpea salad with onions and paprika

225 g dried chickpeas, soaked in plenty of cold water overnight

1 red onion, cut in half lengthways, then in half crossways, and sliced with the grain

4 garlic cloves, finely chopped

1 teaspoon ground cumin

1–2 teaspoons paprika

3 tablespoons olive oil

freshly squeezed juice of 1 lemon

a small bunch of flat leaf parsley, coarsely chopped

a small bunch of coriander, coarsely chopped

125 g firm goats' cheese or feta, crumbled (optional)

sea salt and freshly ground black pepper

crusty bread, to serve

Serves 4

This hearty Moroccan salad is packed with filling pulses and is particularly good served warm, topped with crumbled goats' cheese. If you don't have time to soak the chickpeas, you can use cooked tinned ones instead, but their texture won't be quite as good.

Drain the chickpeas and put them in a large saucepan. Cover with water and bring to the boil. Reduce the heat and simmer for about 45 minutes, until the chickpeas are tender but not mushy. Drain the chickpeas well and remove any loose skins – you can rub them in a clean tea towel or between your fingertips.

Tip them into a large bowl. Add the onion, garlic, cumin, paprika, olive oil and lemon juice while the chickpeas are still warm. Toss well, making sure the chickpeas are well coated. Season to taste and toss in most of the herbs. Crumble over the goats' cheese, if using, and sprinkle with the rest of the herbs. Serve while still warm with plenty of crusty bread.

spiced tomato and lentil salad

This salad is from Lebanon and Syria, but similar lentil dishes can be found all round the eastern Mediterranean, from Egypt to Turkey. Sumac is a very popular Middle Eastern spice, enjoyed for its sour, almost lemony flavour. Umbrian lentils, although not Middle Eastern, hold their texture well and are particularly flavourful.

200 g brown lentils

5 tablespoons extra virgin olive oil

1 onion, halved and finely sliced

400 g cherry tomatoes, quartered

2 teaspoons sumac*, plus extra to serve

sea salt and freshly ground black pepper

Serves 4–6

Put the lentils into a large bowl, cover with plenty of cold water and soak for 2 hours or according to the packet instructions. Drain, transfer to a saucepan, add a pinch of salt and cover with boiling water. Return to the boil, reduce the heat and simmer for about 15 minutes, until tender but still firm. Drain well and set aside.

Clean the saucepan, add 2 tablespoons of the oil, heat well, then add the onion. Fry gently for about 8 minutes until softened and translucent. Remove from the heat and add the lentils, tomatoes, sumac, salt, pepper and the remaining oil. Stir gently with a wooden spoon and serve as a side dish, with extra sumac served separately.

***Note** If you can't find sumac but would like to try this salad, opt for a completely different, but still Middle Eastern flavour. In the Levant, caraway is used in many ways, and will give this salad a light anise flavour rather than the sour edge provided by the sumac. Add 1 teaspoon caraway seeds when you heat the oil, then proceed with the recipe – a refreshing alternative.

roasted butternut squash and pancetta salad
with pumpkin oil and mixed spice dressing

This combination of roasted squash with a spicy dressing is a knockout. The recipe calls for the type of ground mixed spice usually saved for fruit cakes, which is a well-balanced mixture of cassia, ginger, nutmeg, caraway, cloves and coriander – not to be confused with Jamaican allspice, which is something very different.

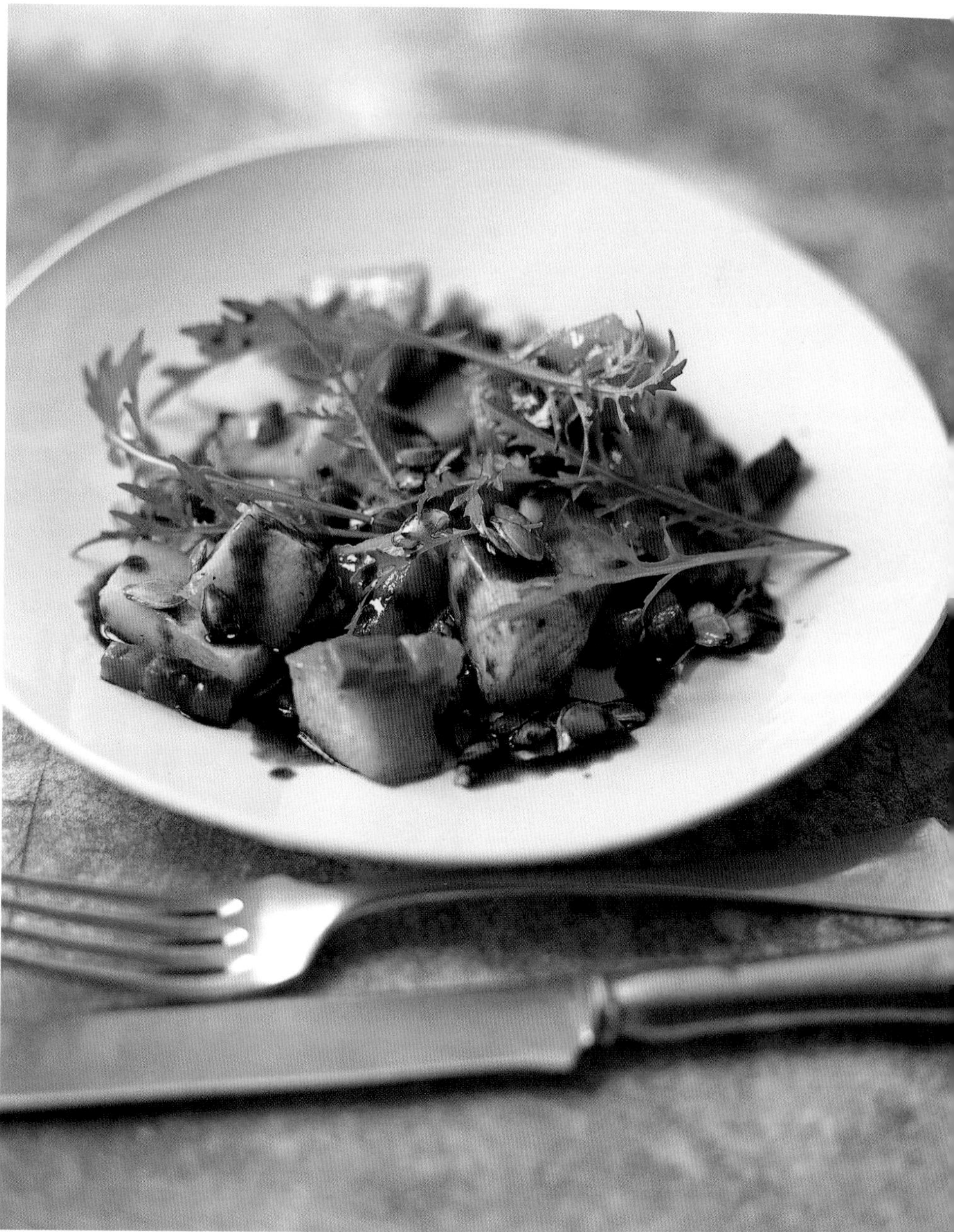

1 large butternut squash, peeled

2 garlic cloves, peeled and crushed

1 teaspoon caster sugar

2 tablespoons pumpkin oil

150 g pancetta lardons

a handful of rocket leaves, to serve

sea salt and freshly ground black pepper

dressing

6 tablespoons pumpkin oil

2 tablespoons red wine vinegar

1–2 tablespoons runny honey

½ teaspoon ground mixed spice

Serves 4

Preheat the oven to 200°C (400°F) Gas 6.

Deseed the butternut squash and pop the seeds into a sieve. Wash them under cold running water until clean, then pat dry with kitchen paper.

Cut the squash flesh into bite-sized chunks. Put in a roasting tin with the seeds and garlic, sprinkle with the sugar and drizzle with the pumpkin oil. Season and toss well. Roast in the preheated oven for 10 minutes. Remove from the oven, scatter the pancetta lardons on top and return to the oven for a further 15 minutes, or until the squash and garlic are soft and golden and the pancetta is crisp.

To make the dressing, put the pumpkin oil, red wine vinegar, honey and mixed spice in a saucepan, whisk to combine and heat gently over low heat. Season to taste.

Put the roasted squash mixture on serving plates, drizzle with the warm dressing and top each serving with a small handful of rocket leaves. Serve immediately.

ginger and cinnamon biscuits

It's easy enough to buy spiced biscuits, but it's worth baking them yourself if only for the gorgeous smell that permeates the kitchen. As well as being a welcome tea time treat, these pretty biscuits make a lovely and inexpensive gift. Simply package in a pretty box and tie with ribbon.

90 g dark muscovado sugar

110 g unsalted butter, cut into cubes

6 tablespoons golden syrup

100 ml double cream

375 g plain flour

1 tablespoon ground ginger

1 tablespoon ground cinnamon

⅛ teaspoon ground cloves (optional)

1 teaspoon baking powder

½ teaspoon salt

2 baking trays lined with baking paper

star-shaped biscuit cutters in various sizes (or any other shapes you like, such as Christmas trees, bells, angels etc).

Makes about 40 biscuits

Sift the sugar through a coarse sieve to remove any lumps and put in a large bowl with the cubed butter. Beat together until smooth, then beat in the golden syrup and cream. Measure out the flour and add the ginger, cinnamon, cloves, baking powder and salt and sift into another bowl. Add the flour and spice mixture to the creamed mixture a third at a time until you have a stiff dough. Form the dough into a flat disc, wrap in foil and refrigerate for 3 hours.

When you're ready to bake the biscuits preheat the oven to 190°C (375°F) Gas 5.

Cut off a quarter of the dough, flour the work surface and rolling pin generously and roll out the dough thinly. Stamp out shapes with your cutters. Carefully prise them off the work surface with a palate knife, lay them on one of the baking trays and bake in the preheated oven for about 8 minutes. Leave them to firm up for 2–3 minutes, then transfer to a wire rack until crisp. Repeat with the remaining pieces of dough, re-rolling the offcuts to give you as many biscuits as possible. The biscuits will keep in an airtight container for up to one week.

bakes and desserts

snowy pine nut cookies

200 g unsalted butter, softened
100 g caster sugar
200 g plain flour
½ teaspoon fine sea salt
200 g pine nuts, roughly chopped
1 teaspoon almond extract
icing sugar, for dusting

2 baking trays, lined with baking parchment

Makes about 20

Rich, buttery and addictive, these delicious little biscuits are dusted with icing sugar while warm and again when cold. Serve with dessert wines, sticky liqueurs or spicy mulled wine.

Preheat the oven to 180°C (350°F) Gas 4.

Put the butter and caster sugar in a large bowl and beat together until soft. Add the flour, salt, pine nuts and almond extract and mix well to combine. Using your hands, form the mixture into about 20 small balls (about 4 cm in diameter) and place them slightly apart on the prepared baking trays as they will spread during baking. Bake in the preheated oven for 12–15 minutes.

Let cool a little before transferring to a wire rack and dust with icing sugar. Dust again when the cookies are cold. The biscuits will keep in an airtight container for up to one week

stem ginger biscuits

The spicy and chewy pieces of stem ginger give a flavour kick to these buttery, melt-in-the-mouth biscuits. Served with a pot of warming lapsang souchong, they are the perfect addition to a cosy fireside tea.

85 g unsalted butter, at room temperature
75 g golden caster sugar
1 egg yolk
½ teaspoon ground ginger
60 g stem ginger in syrup, chopped
25 g ground almonds
115 g self-raising flour

2 baking trays, lined with baking parchment

Makes about 10

Preheat the oven to 160°C (325°F) Gas 3.

Beat the butter and sugar together until pale and creamy, then beat in the egg yolk. Stir in the ground ginger and stem ginger, then the ground almonds. Add the flour and mix well.

Roll the mixture into 10 walnut-sized balls and arrange them on the prepared baking trays, spacing well apart. Flatten slightly with your fingers and bake in the preheated oven for about 20 minutes, until a pale golden brown.

Let the biscuits cool on the baking trays for a few minutes. When firm, use a spatula to transfer them to a wire rack to cool. The biscuits will keep in an airtight container for up to one week.

iced star biscuits

These biscuits are simple to make and are ideal decorations. Pick your favourite biscuit cutters, then once they are baked, have fun icing and finishing.

150 g unsalted butter, at room temperature

100 g caster sugar

finely grated zest and freshly squeezed juice of 1 lemon

75 g cream cheese

300 g plain flour

1 teaspoon ground mixed spice

a good pinch of salt

to decorate

glacé icing or writing icing pens, edible silver balls, string or ribbons

a star-shaped biscuit cutter

several baking trays

Makes about 24

Cream the butter with the sugar and lemon zest. Beat in 2 teaspoons of the lemon juice and the cream cheese. Sift in the flour, mixed spice and salt and mix. When thoroughly combined, remove the dough from the bowl, shape into a ball and wrap in clingfilm. Chill until firm, about 30 minutes. The dough can be kept in the fridge, tightly wrapped, for up to 1 week.

When you're ready to bake the biscuits preheat the oven to 180°C (350°F) Gas 4.

Remove the dough from the fridge and roll out on a lightly floured work surface until 5 mm thick. Dip the biscuit cutter in flour and cut out shapes. Gather up the trimmings and re-roll, then cut out more shapes. Arrange slightly apart on the baking trays. If using as decorations, use a cocktail stick to make a small hole at the top of each shape large enough to thread a ribbon through. Bake in the preheated oven for 12–15 minutes until just turning golden brown at the edges. Remove from the oven, let cool for 3 minutes, then transfer to a wire rack until completely cold. Decorate with glacé icing (see below), or use a writing icing pen. When firm, thread with ribbons. The biscuits will keep in an airtight container for up to 5 days.

Glacé icing – Made with icing sugar and water, plus a little colouring if you like, this icing will dry firm but not as hard as royal icing. Sift 100 g icing sugar into a bowl. Stir in water or lemon juice, a teaspoon at a time, to make a thick icing that can be piped.

cranberry and cherry florentines

These have to be the easiest biscuits in the world to make, but they look impressive and taste delicious.

100 g unsalted butter

100 g unrefined caster sugar

2 teaspoons clear honey

75 g blanched almonds

110 g mixed sun-dried cranberries, cherries and blueberries

100 g plain flour

125 g good-quality dark chocolate (minimum 70% cocoa solids), broken into pieces

2–3 non-stick baking trays or baking trays lined with non-stick baking paper

Makes 20–24

Preheat the oven to 180°C (350°F) Gas 4.

Put the butter, sugar and honey in a saucepan and set over low heat. When the sugar has dissolved, bring almost to boiling point, then take the pan off the heat. Stir in the almonds and fruit, then tip in the flour and mix thoroughly. Spoon heaped teaspoonfuls of the mixture onto the baking trays, leaving plenty of space between each one. Flatten them slightly with the back of your spoon. Bake in the preheated oven for 10–12 minutes until the florentines have spread and are turning brown at the edges. Let cool for about 3 minutes, then prise them off the baking trays and transfer to a wire rack. When they are completely cold, put the chocolate in a heatproof bowl and melt over a pan of barely simmering water, taking care that the bowl doesn't touch the water. Lay the florentines flat-side upwards on a sheet of greaseproof paper and spread the chocolate over them with a flat-bladed knife. Let them sit until the chocolate sets, then store in an airtight tin for up to 5 days.

coffee, macadamia and white chocolate chunk cookies

These big, fat, chunky, chewy cookies are subtly flavoured with coffee and studded with chunks of white chocolate and macadamia nuts.

115 g unsalted butter, at room temperature

200 g caster sugar

1 egg

1 tablespoon instant coffee granules dissolved in 1½ tablespoons just-boiled water

100 g macadamia nuts

100 g white chocolate, roughly chopped

100 g self-raising flour

100 g plain flour

2 baking trays, greased

Makes about 15

Preheat the oven to 190°C (375°F) Gas 5.

Cream together the butter and sugar until soft, then beat in the egg, followed by the coffee. Stir in the macadamia nuts and chocolate and mix together. Combine the flours and sift over the cookie mixture, then stir until thoroughly combined.

Drop heaped tablespoonfuls of the mixture on to the baking trays, spacing them well apart. Bake for about 10 minutes until pale golden and slightly puffed up.

Let the cookies firm up for a few minutes, then transfer to a wire rack to cool. The cookies will keep in an airtight container for up to 3 days.

toasted teacakes

There's something comforting and homely about a plateful of freshly toasted teacakes dripping with butter, and the wonderful smell of spices that they emit. If you've got an old-fashioned toasting fork with a long handle, why not toast the teacakes the traditional way over the open fire?

225 g strong white bread flour

½ teaspoon sea salt

1 teaspoon fast-action dried yeast

15 g soft brown sugar

¼ teaspoon freshly grated nutmeg

60 g mixed dried vine fruits

40 g butter, melted

120 ml full-fat milk, plus extra for brushing

butter, to serve

Makes 8

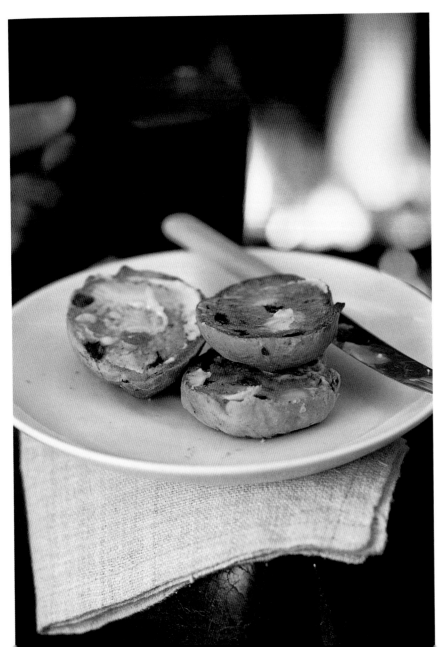

Sift the flour, salt, yeast, sugar and nutmeg into a large bowl. Stir in the dried fruits and make a well in the centre.

Put the milk and butter in a small saucepan and heat until just warm. Pour into the flour mixture and work together to make a soft dough. Turn out on to a lightly floured work surface and knead for about 5 minutes, until smooth and elastic. Place in a bowl, slip the bowl into a large plastic bag, seal and leave to rise for 1 hour, until doubled in size. When risen, tip the dough out on to a lightly floured work surface, punch down, and divide into eight pieces of equal size. Shape each one into a ball, flatten slightly and arrange on a non-stick baking tray, spacing slightly apart. Slip the tray into a large plastic bag and leave the dough to rise again for 45 minutes, until doubled in size.

Preheat the oven to 200°C (400°F) Gas 6.

Brush the top of each teacake with milk, bake in the preheated oven for about 15 minutes, until risen and golden. Transfer to a wire rack to cool. When ready to serve, split, toast on the cut sides and spread generously with butter.

triple chocolate brownies

There are no nuts but plenty of rich chocolate in these moist brownies.

200 g dark chocolate, coarsely chopped

100 g unsalted butter, at room temperature, cut into cubes

225 g caster sugar

½ teaspoon vanilla extract

4 large eggs, at room temperature

60 g plain flour

60 g unsweetened cocoa powder

100 g white chocolate, coarsely chopped

a baking tin, about 25.5 x 20.5 cm, greased and base-lined with baking paper

Makes 24

Preheat the oven to 180°C (350°F) Gas 4.

Melt the chocolate in a heatproof bowl set over a pan of simmering, but not boiling, water. Do not let the base of the bowl touch the water. Stir occasionally until melted, then remove the bowl from the heat and leave to cool until needed.

Beat the butter, sugar and vanilla extract until light and fluffy, then gradually beat in the eggs, beating well after each addition.

Stir in the melted chocolate, then sift the flour and cocoa into the bowl and mix in. Transfer the mixture to the prepared tin and spread evenly. Scatter the chopped white chocolate over the top, then bake in the preheated oven for 20 minutes, or until a skewer inserted halfway between the sides and the centre comes out slightly moist but not sticky with uncooked batter.

Remove the tin from the oven and set on a wire rack. Leave to cool completely, then cut into 24 pieces. Store in an airtight container and eat within 4 days.

crumpets

Home-made crumpets are even more wonderful than the shop-bought kind. Fresh yeast gives the best result – it's often available to buy in small bakers or in-store supermarket bakeries – but if you can't find it, just use fast-action dried yeast instead.

285 ml milk mixed with 285 ml water

15 g fresh yeast or a 7-g sachet of fast-action dried yeast

450 g plain flour

½ teaspoon bicarbonate of soda

1 teaspoon salt

to serve

unsalted butter

raspberry or strawberry jam or honey

2–3 crumpet rings or scone cutters

a flat griddle pan or frying pan, preheated and greased

Makes 12

Warm the milk and water mixture in a small saucepan. If using fresh yeast, put it into a small bowl with a little of the warm liquid, stir well, then add the remaining milk and water. Sift the flour into a mixing bowl, then stir in the warm yeast mixture. If you are using fast-action dried yeast, follow the manufacturer's instructions.

Cover the bowl with a clean tea towel and leave in a warm place for 1 hour. Put the bicarbonate of soda and salt into a bowl, add 2 tablespoons water, mix well, then beat it into the mixture. Set aside for a further 45 minutes.

Put the greased crumpet rings on the prepared griddle pan and set over medium heat. When the rings are hot, spoon 2 tablespoons of the batter into each ring – just enough to cover the base. Let cook for about 4–5 minutes, until the underside is golden, then remove the rings and turn the crumpet over to brown the top.

To serve, toast the crumpets on both sides, spread them with butter and stack on a hot plate. Serve with a dish of jam or honey.

gingerbread mini-muffins

Spicy, sticky and utterly moreish, these cute little muffins are particularly popular with children.

100 g unsalted butter

2 tablespoons black treacle

2 tablespoons honey

100 g dark muscovado sugar

100 ml milk

175 g plain flour

1 teaspoon bicarbonate of soda

1 tablespoon ground ginger

1 teaspoon ground cinnamon

a good pinch of salt

1 large egg, beaten

50 g stem ginger, drained and finely chopped

glacé icing (see page 126), or writing icing pens

3 mini-muffin trays lined with mini-muffin cases, or use double cases set on a baking tray

Makes about 36

Preheat the oven to 180°C (350°F) Gas 4.

Put the butter, treacle, honey, sugar and milk in a saucepan over low heat and melt gently. Remove from the heat and leave to cool for a couple of minutes.

Sift the flour, bicarbonate of soda, ground ginger, cinnamon and salt into a mixing bowl. Pour in the cooled, melted mixture, then the egg. Mix thoroughly with a wooden spoon. Mix in the stem ginger.

Spoon the mixture into the cases. Bake in the preheated oven for about 15 minutes, until firm to the touch.

Leave to cool on a wire rack, then decorate with icing. Store in an airtight container and eat within 3 days.

Christmas mini-muffins

150 g plain flour

1 teaspoon baking powder

a pinch of salt

50 g caster sugar

finely grated zest of ½ an orange

50 g pecan pieces, coarsely chopped, plus 2 tablespoons extra, to decorate

1½ tablespoons raisins or sultanas

50 g fresh or frozen cranberries (no need to thaw)

1 large egg, beaten

50 g unsalted butter, melted

75 ml milk

icing sugar, to dust

3 mini-muffin trays lined with mini-muffin cases, or use double cases set on a baking tray

Makes about 36

Not as sweet as some muffins, these are good for brunch and breakfast along with a cup of good coffee.

Preheat the oven to 180°C (350°F) Gas 4.

Sift the flour, baking powder and salt into a mixing bowl. Stir in the sugar, orange zest, chopped pecans and raisins.

Put the cranberries into the bowl of a food processor and chop roughly. Stir them into the flour mixture. Combine the beaten egg with the melted butter and milk and stir into the flour mixture with a wooden spoon.

Spoon the mixture into the foil cases using 2 teaspoons, then decorate with the extra pecans. Bake in the preheated oven for 12–15 minutes until barely golden and firm to the touch.

Turn out onto a wire rack. Serve warm, dusted with icing sugar. When cold, store in an airtight container and eat within 2 days.

sticky marzipan and cherry loaf

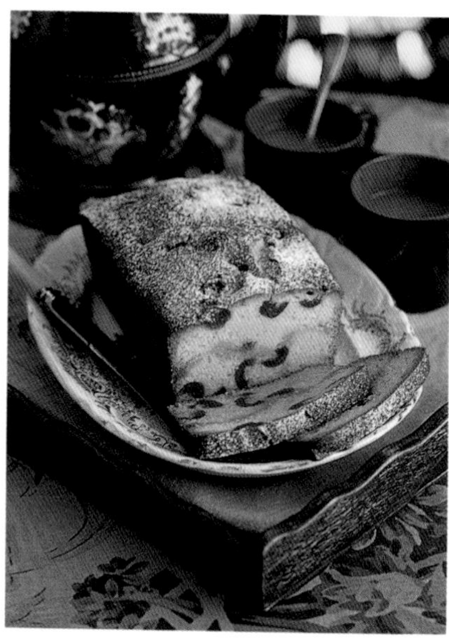

Studded with sweet glacé cherries and with a surprise layer of sticky marzipan running through the centre, this simple loaf cake will become a firm favourite.

175 g butter, at room temperature

175 g caster sugar

3 eggs

175 g self-raising flour

85 g ground almonds

175 g glacé cherries, halved

75 g chilled marzipan, finely grated

icing sugar, for dusting

a loaf tin, about 2 lb capacity, greased and lined

Serves 8–12

Preheat the oven to 180°C (350°F) Gas 4.

Put the butter and sugar in a large bowl and beat until pale and creamy. Beat in the eggs one at a time. Sift in the flour and fold in, then stir in the cherries.

Spoon half the mixture into the prepared loaf tin and level the surface. Sprinkle with the grated marzipan. Top with the remaining mixture and smooth the surface.

Bake in the preheated oven for about 45 minutes, then remove the cake from the oven and cover the top with foil. Return it to the oven and bake for a further 25 minutes, until risen and golden and a skewer inserted in the centre comes out clean. Leave to cool in the tin for about 10 minutes, then transfer to a wire rack to cool. Serve the cake at room temperature.

chocolate brandy cake

A rich chocolate treat to serve in thin slices with coffee or whipped cream for dessert. There's no baking involved as it's made from melting very good bitter chocolate with butter, then mixing with whisked eggs and sugar and flavouring with brandy (or walnut liqueur if you can find it), toasted walnuts and the best dried cranberries you can find.

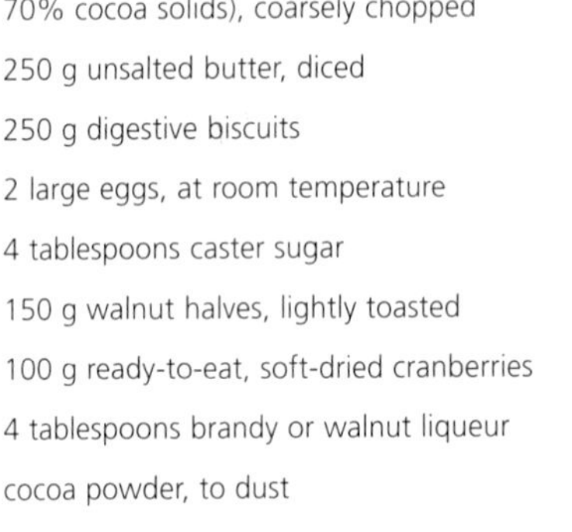

250 g good quality dark chocolate (minimum 70% cocoa solids), coarsely chopped

250 g unsalted butter, diced

250 g digestive biscuits

2 large eggs, at room temperature

4 tablespoons caster sugar

150 g walnut halves, lightly toasted

100 g ready-to-eat, soft-dried cranberries

4 tablespoons brandy or walnut liqueur

cocoa powder, to dust

a springform cake tin, lined with clingfilm

Serves 16

Melt the chocolate and butter in a heatproof bowl set over a pan of steaming but not boiling water. Do not let the base of the bowl touch the water. Stir frequently until melted, then remove the bowl from the heat and leave to cool until needed. Coarsely crush the biscuits with a rolling pin or in a food processor.

Using an electric or rotary whisk, beat the eggs with the sugar until very thick and mousse-like and the whisk leaves a ribbon-like trail when lifted out of the bowl. Whisk in the melted chocolate mixture.

Coarsely chop 100 g of the walnuts and carefully fold in with the cranberries, brandy and the crushed biscuits.

Spoon into the prepared tin and spread evenly. Decorate with the rest of the walnut halves. Cover the top of the tin with clingfilm and chill for at least 4 hours or overnight.

When ready to serve, unclip the tin and remove the clingfilm. Dust with cocoa and serve cut into thin slices. Store in an airtight container in the fridge for up to 1 week.

Swedish saffron cake

This deliciously rich, golden-hued cake uses saffron for the flavour and colour. Serve with whipped cream and a dollop of any red fruit conserve on the side.

125 ml full-fat milk

225 g slightly salted butter

1 teaspoon saffron threads

2 large eggs, at room temperature

200 g golden caster sugar

225 g plain flour

2 teaspoons baking powder

icing sugar, to dust

a 22–23-cm springform tin, greased, base-lined with greaseproof paper and sprinkled with dried breadcrumbs or ground almonds

Serves 8–12

Pour the milk into a saucepan. Add the butter and heat until melted and steaming hot but not boiling. Remove the pan from the heat and sprinkle in the saffron. Cover and leave to infuse for 1 hour.

When ready to bake, preheat the oven to 180°C (350°F) Gas 4.

Put the eggs in a mixing bowl and whisk until just frothy. Whisk in the sugar and continue whisking until the mixture is very thick and mousse-like and the whisk leaves a trail when lifted out of the bowl.

Gently fold in the just-warm saffron mixture. Sift the flour and baking powder into the bowl and fold in gently with a large metal spoon – the mixture will look hopeless at first but it will combine after a minute.

Pour into the prepared tin and bake in the preheated oven for 35–40 minutes until the cake is a good golden brown, slightly shrunk from the sides of the tin and firm to touch.

Put on a wire rack and unclip the tin. Leave to cool completely then serve dusted with icing sugar. Store in an airtight container and eat within 4 days.

coffee and walnut cake

This classic teatime cake is enduringly popular, perhaps because something magical happens when coffee and walnuts come together.

180 g unsalted butter, at room temperature

180 g caster sugar

3 eggs

180 g self-raising flour

2 teaspoons instant coffee granules, dissolved in 1 tablespoon hot water

60 g walnut pieces

coffee frosting

250 g mascarpone cheese

85 g icing sugar, sifted

1½ teaspoons instant coffee granules, dissolved in 2 teaspoons hot water

walnut halves, to decorate

2 x 20-cm diameter sandwich tins, greased and base-lined with greaseproof paper

Serves 8–12

Preheat the oven to 180°C (350°F) Gas 4.

Put the butter and sugar in a mixing bowl and cream together until pale and fluffy. Beat in the eggs one at a time. Sift the flour into the butter mixture and stir to combine. Fold in the walnuts and coffee. Divide the cake mixture between the prepared tins and level out the surface of each.

Bake for 20–25 minutes until golden and the sponge springs back when gently pressed or a skewer inserted in the centre of the cake comes out clean. Transfer to a wire rack, carefully peel off the greaseproof paper and let cool completely before frosting.

To make the frosting, beat together the mascarpone, icing sugar and coffee until smooth and creamy. Spread slightly less than half of the frosting over one of the cooled cakes, then place the second cake on top. Spread the remaining frosting over the top and decorate with walnut halves to finish. Store in an airtight container and eat within 2 days.

pear and ginger crumble cake

This is a deliciously spicy cake with a very moreish texture. Note that ground ginger loses its intensity if left sitting in the storecupboard for too long, so do make sure that what you use here is not past it's use-by date. You can also follow this recipe substituting apples for the pears. If you decide to try it, use ground cinnamon instead of the ginger.

125 g unsalted butter, softened

125 g caster sugar

2 eggs, at room temperature

125 g plain flour

2 teaspoons baking powder

2 firm pears, peeled, cored and sliced

1 tablespoon freshly squeezed lemon juice

double cream, to serve (optional)

ginger crumble

60 g plain flour

1 teaspoon ground ginger

3 tablespoons soft light brown sugar

50 g chilled unsalted butter, cut into cubes

a 20-cm diameter springform cake tin, base-lined with greaseproof paper and greased

Serves 6–8

To make the crumble mixture, put the flour and ginger in a mixing bowl. Add the chilled butter and quickly rub it into the flour using your fingertips. Add the sugar and rub again until the mixture resembles coarse sand. Refrigerate until needed.

Preheat the oven to 180°C (350°F) Gas 4.

Beat the softened butter and sugar until pale and creamy. Add the eggs, 1 at a time, and beat well between each addition. Tip in the.flour and baking powder and beat for 1 minute, until the mixture is smooth and well combined. Pour it into the prepared tin. Toss the pears in a bowl with the lemon juice and put them on top of the cake. Sprinkle the crumble topping over the top and bake in the preheated oven for 40–45 minutes, until the cake is golden on top.

Let cool slightly before removing from the tin and serving warm with double cream, if liked. Store in an airtight container and eat within 2–3 days.

pear and almond tart

This is elegant, both in appearance and flavour. It is ideal for entertaining since the tart shell and almond cream can be made a few hours in advance. Serve with sweetened crème fraîche, or good quality vanilla ice cream.

3–4 ripe pears

100 g unsalted butter

100 g sugar

2 eggs

100 ground almonds

2 tablespoons flour

pastry

200 g plain flour, plus extra for rolling

2 teaspoons caster sugar

100 g chilled unsalted butter, cut into cubes

a pinch of salt

baking paper and baking weights or beans

a 27-cm diameter loose-based tart tin, greased and floured

Serves 6

To make the pastry, put the flour, sugar, butter and salt in a food processor and, using the pulse button, process until the butter is broken down (about 5–10 pulses). Add 3 tablespoons cold water and pulse until the mixture forms coarse crumbs; add 1 more tablespoon if necessary but do not do more than 10 pulses.

Transfer the pastry to a sheet of baking paper, form into a ball and flatten to a disc. Wrap in paper and let stand for 30–60 minutes.

Roll out the pastry on a floured work surface to a disc slightly larger than the tart tin. Carefully transfer the pastry to the tin, patching any holes as you go and pressing gently into the sides. To trim the edges, roll a rolling pin over the top, using the edge of the tin as a cutting surface, and letting the excess fall away. Tidy up the edges and refrigerate until firm, about 30–60 minutes.

Preheat the oven to 200°C (400°F) Gas 6. Prick the pastry all over, line with the baking parchment and fill with baking weights. Bake on a low shelf in the preheated oven for 15 minutes, then remove the paper and weights and bake until just golden, 10–15 minutes more. Let the tart case cool slightly before filling.

To make the almond cream, put the butter and sugar in a bowl and beat with an electric mixer until fluffy. Beat in the eggs, 1 at a time. Using a spatula, fold in the almonds and flour until well mixed.

Lower the oven temperature to 190°C (375°F) Gas 5. Spread the almond cream evenly in the tart shell.

Peel and slice the pears, into 8 or 12 slices, depending on the size of the pears. Arrange the slices on top of the almond cream. Bake in the preheated oven until puffed and golden, about 20–25 minutes. Serve warm.

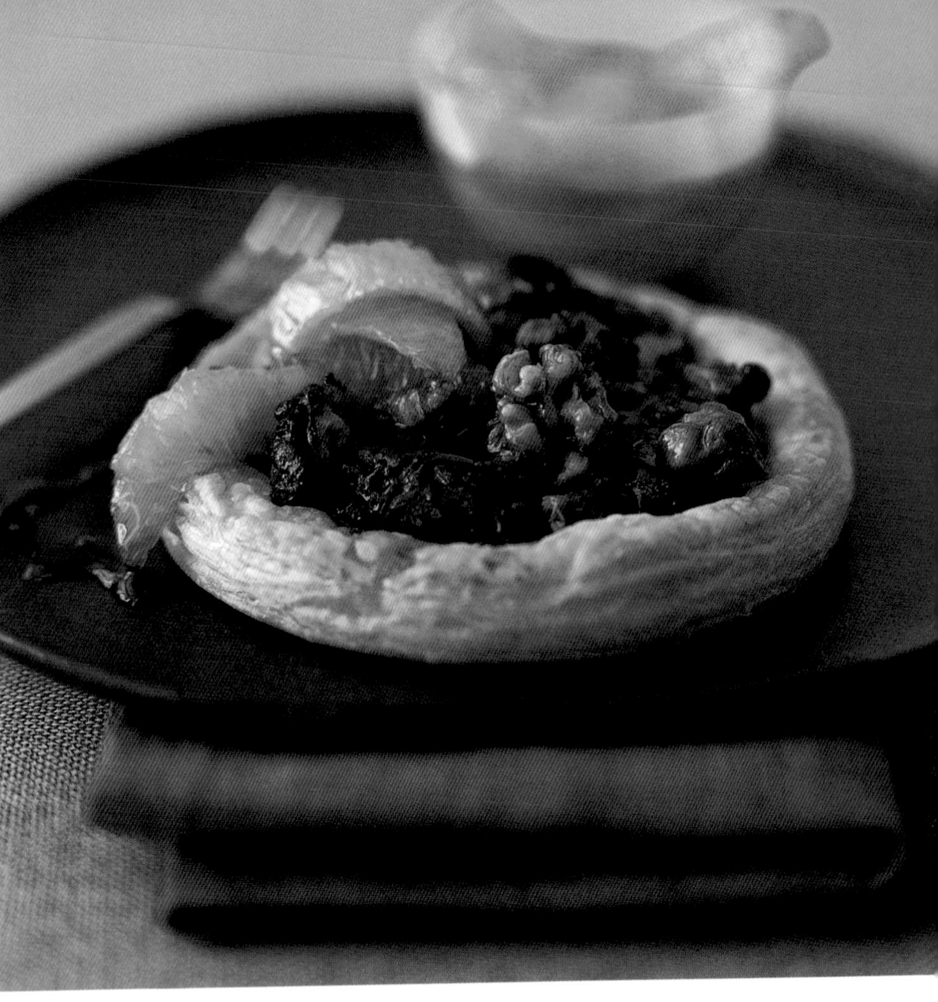

sticky date flaky tarts with caramel oranges

Fresh dates are so sweet and sticky, they make a fantastic quick-and-easy topping for a crisp puff pastry base. The maple syrup and sugar caramelize with the butter and give the tarts a wonderful sheen. Don't serve them too hot, or you will burn your mouth.

1 sheet of ready-rolled puff pastry, defrosted if frozen

caramel oranges

4 small, juicy, thin-skinned oranges

125 g sugar

date topping

55 g unsalted butter

30 g soft light brown sugar

2 tablespoons maple syrup

12–16 fresh Medjool dates

75 g walnut pieces

a 13-cm diameter saucer or similar (to use as a template)

Serves 4

Preheat the oven to 200°C (400°F) Gas 6.

Unroll the pastry on a lightly floured work surface. Cut out 4 circles, using the saucer as a template. Put these on a non-stick baking tray, prick all over, then chill or freeze for 15 minutes.

Meanwhile, make the caramel oranges. Slice the top and bottom off of each orange, then cut off the skin in a spiral, as if you were peeling an apple. Try to remove all the bitter white pith. Slice down between the membranes and flick out each segment. Catch the juice in a bowl.

Put the sugar and 3 tablespoons water into a heavy-based saucepan. Set over low heat until the sugar has completely dissolved and the liquid is clear. Increase the heat and boil until the liquid turns a dark caramel colour. Quickly remove the pan from the heat, stand back and add another 3 tablespoons water – it will hiss and splutter.

Return the pan to a low heat, and stir until all the hardened pieces of caramel have dissolved. Pour in the reserved orange juice and boil hard until very thick and syrupy. Remove from the heat and let cool completely before adding the orange segments. Chill until needed.

To make the date topping, cut the dates in half and remove the pits. Put the butter, sugar and maple syrup in a saucepan and melt over gentle heat, then add the dates and walnuts.

Spoon the mixture over the pastry circles, leaving a small clear rim on the outside of each. Bake in the preheated oven for 15–18 minutes until the pastry is risen and golden. Serve with the caramel oranges.

real treacle tart with caramelized bananas

Treacle tart is often made with golden syrup, white breadcrumbs and lemon juice but this fabulous recipe uses proper black treacle, German rye bread (pumpernickel) and lime juice. The pumpernickel gives it an unusual, wonderful texture.

Preheat the oven to 190°C (375°F) Gas 5.

On a lightly floured work surface, roll out the pastry to a thickness of 5 mm. Use to line the pie plate and prick the base. Using a small sharp knife, make small cuts the width of the pastry edge about a thumb's breadth apart. Fold over every 'flap' diagonally onto itself towards the centre of the tin, pressing the tips, (not the folds) downwards to seal. Chill or freeze the pastry for 10–15 minutes.

Put the treacle and golden syrup in a large saucepan, add the lime juice and zest and ginger, if using, and heat until just warm and runny. Stir in the pumpernickel crumbs. Spread the mixture into the pastry case and bake in the preheated oven for about 30 minutes, or until the filling is just set and the pastry is browning at the edges.

Meanwhile, peel the bananas and cut them into chunks. Melt the butter in a frying pan and add the sugar. Cook for a couple of minutes until the sugar melts, then turn up the heat and cook until it caramelizes. Add the bananas, toss well to coat with the juices and fry over medium heat until starting to colour. Squeeze in some lemon juice, and remove from the heat.

Cool the tart slightly before serving warm with the caramelized bananas and custard, clotted cream or crème fraîche on the side.

375-g packet of ready-made shortcrust pastry

5 tablespoons black treacle

5 tablespoons golden syrup

finely grated zest and juice of 1 large lime

½ teaspoon freshly grated ginger (optional but recommended)

100 g pumpernickel crumbs (use a food processor to make the crumbs)

caramelized bananas

2 large bananas

55 g unsalted butter

3 tablespoons demerara sugar

a squeeze of fresh lemon juice

custard, clotted cream or crème fraîche, to serve

a 20-cm diameter shallow pie plate

Serves 4–6

individual caramelized pear and cranberry tarts

1 sheet of ready-rolled puff pastry, defrosted if frozen

2 large ripe pears, peeled, halved and cored

25 g dried cranberries

25 g unsalted butter, chilled and cut into cubes

milk, to glaze

3 tablespoons granulated sugar or 75 g sugar cubes, crushed (see recipe intro)

1 teaspoon cinnamon

pouring cream or crème fraîche, to serve

a non-stick baking tray

Serves 4

Having a packet of ready-rolled puff pastry in the freezer is a great standby for an instant fruit tart. You can use practically any fruit; peaches, nectarines, apricots, plums, apples or blueberries. To crush sugar cubes, put them in a plastic bag and beat with the end of a rolling pin. They give a deliciously crunchy effect.

Preheat the oven to 220°C (425°F) Gas 7.

Lightly flour a work surface and unroll the pastry. Use a sharp knife or a pizza wheel to cut it into 4 squares of equal size. Place the pastry squares on a non-stick baking tray.

Divide the dried cranberries between the pastry squares and place a pear half in the centre of each one. Scatter with the cubed butter. Brush the edges with a little milk. Mix the sugar or crushed sugar cubes with the cinnamon and sprinkle over the top.

Carefully slide the tarts onto the hot baking tray and return to the preheated oven to cook for about 35–40 minutes, until the pastry is golden brown and crisp and the pears are tender. Serve whilst still warm with pouring cream or crème fraîche.

lemony apple crumble tart

375-g packet of ready-made shortcrust pastry

custard, to serve

crumble topping

75 g plain flour

75 g demerara sugar

75 g unsalted butter, softened

finely grated zest of 1 lemon

spiced apple filling

6 large apples, such as Cox's Orange Pippins or Granny Smiths, peeled and cored

55 g sultanas

finely grated zest and juice of 1 lemon

55 g soft brown sugar

½ teaspoon cinnamon

¼ teaspoon nutmeg

1 tablespoon each plain flour and caster sugar, mixed together

a 23-cm diameter tart tin

baking paper and baking weights or beans

Serves 6

This family favourite is easy to make and children love the crumble topping.

Preheat the oven to 200°C (400°F) Gas 6.

On a lightly floured work surface, roll out the pastry to a thickness of 5 mm. Use to line the tart tin. Prick the base, then chill or freeze for 15 minutes. Line with baking paper and fill with baking weights. Put on a baking tray and bake in the centre of the oven for 10–12 minutes. Remove the baking paper and the weights and return the pastry case to the oven for a further 5–7 minutes. Let cool.

To make the crumble topping, put the flour, sugar, butter and lemon zest into a bowl and rub lightly between your fingers until the mixture resembles fine breadcrumbs. To make the apple filling, chop the apples into small chunks, put into a bowl and toss with the sultanas, lemon zest and juice, sugar and spices. Sprinkle the base of the pastry case with the flour and caster sugar, then arrange the apples on top. Sprinkle the crumble mixture over the apples. Bake in the preheated oven for 15 minutes, then reduce the temperature to 180°C (350°F) Gas 4 and bake for another 30 minutes. Serve warm with custard.

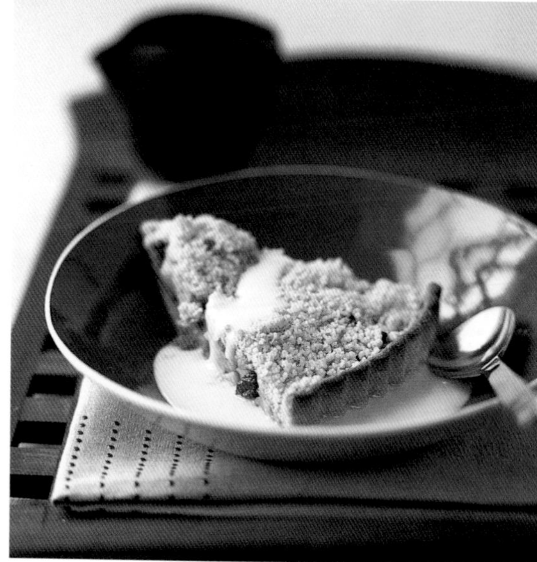

apple and blueberry tarts

These are a cheat's delight – so simple and quick to make and deliciously fresh-tasting. Use Red Delicious apples in autumn at a time when blueberries are in their last few weeks. Both fruits are perfect to cook with and just lovely with the vanilla. Any leftover tarts can be served cold and enjoyed with coffee the next day. Just dust them with some icing sugar and eat them as you would a fruit-filled Danish pastry.

1 sheet of ready-rolled puff pastry, defrosted if frozen

2 tablespoons caster sugar

1 vanilla pod, split in half lengthways

3 sweet dessert apples (such as Red Delicious or Braeburn), each cored and cut into 10–12 thin wedges

1 punnet blueberries (about 150 g)

double cream, to serve

Serves 4

Preheat the oven to 220°C (425°F) Gas 7.

Lightly flour a work surface and unroll the pastry. Use a sharp knife or a pizza wheel to cut it into 4 squares of equal size. Place the pastry squares on a non-stick baking tray.

Put the sugar and 2 tablespoons of water in a saucepan and bring to the boil, stirring until the sugar dissolves. Scrape the seeds from the vanilla pod directly into the sugar syrup, stirring to combine.

Add the apple slices to the pan, reduce the heat to medium and cook for 4–5 minutes, turning the apples so they cook evenly. Add the blueberries and gently stir to coat in the sweet syrup. Arrange the apples and blueberries on top of each pastry square. Bake in the preheated oven for 18–20 minutes, until the pastry is puffed and golden.

Serve warm with the cream spooned over the top.

Variation: For a simple French-style apple frangipane tart, mix 2 tablespoons each of room temperature butter, ground almonds and icing sugar with 1 tablespoon plain flour in a bowl until you have a paste. Stir in 1 egg yolk until smooth. Spread the mixture over each of the pastry squares, leaving a space around the edge, and top with the apple slices. Bake in a preheated oven at 220°C (425°F) Gas 7 for 18–20 minutes, until puffed and golden.

baked plums in puff pastry

with crème fraîche

Make this quick and easy yet elegant dessert with whatever fruit is in season, such as apples, pears, apricots or plums, as used here. Be sure to use just-soft plums, not too ripe. You can prepare the fruit and pastries in advance and assemble just before serving. If necessary, reheat the plums slightly as they are best served warm. How you shape the pastries is up to you – rectangles, squares, triangles or circles all work fine!

1 sheet of ready-rolled puff pastry, defrosted if frozen

1 egg, beaten

caster sugar, for the pastry

6–8 large red plums (not ripe), halved, stoned and quartered

50 g sugar

200 g crème fraîche, sweetened with 1–2 tablespoons caster sugar

a non-stick baking tray

Serves 6

Preheat the oven to 220°C (425°F) Gas 7.

Lightly flour a work surface and unroll the pastry. Use a sharp knife or a pizza wheel to cut it into 6 rectangles of equal size. Place the pastry on a non-stick baking tray.

Brush with the egg and sprinkle each rectangle very generously with sugar. Bake in the preheated oven until puffed and browned. Let cool.

Reduce the oven temperature to 190°C (375°F) Gas 5. Put the plums in a baking dish, sprinkle with the sugar and bake for 20–30 minutes, until tender and slightly browned. Let cool. To assemble, split the pastries in half. Fill with the plums and add a dollop of sweetened crème fraîche. Serve.

roast pumpkin and pecan pie

This recipe may look slightly daunting, but it is worth the effort. Do oven roast the pumpkin if you're cooking it from scratch – it has a much better texture than when you boil it.

pastry

250 g plain flour

1 teaspoon ground ginger

2 tablespoons icing sugar

110 g butter, chilled and cut into cubes

25 g white vegetable fat or shortening

1 egg yolk (reserve the white)

a pinch of salt

pumpkin purée

500 g pumpkin flesh (see method)

1 tablespoon bourbon or dark rum

1 tablespoon light muscovado sugar

¼ teaspoon mixed spice

15 g butter, chilled

pie filling

100 g light muscovado sugar

1 tablespoon maple syrup or clear honey

1½ teaspoons mixed spice

½ teaspoon ground cinnamon

a pinch of salt

1 tablespoon bourbon or dark rum

3 eggs

2 tablespoons plain flour, sifted

150 ml double cream

topping

50 g pecan nuts

1 tablespoon light muscovado sugar

lightly whipped cream, to serve

a 23-cm diameter, 3.5-cm deep tart tin

baking weights or dried beans

Serves 6

To make the pastry, sift the flour, ginger and icing sugar into a mixing bowl. Cut the butter and fat cubes into the flour, then rub lightly with your fingertips until the mixture resembles coarse breadcrumbs. Mix the egg yolk with 2 tablespoons ice-cold water, add to the bowl, mix lightly and pull together into a ball, adding extra water if needed. Shape into a flat disc, put in a plastic bag and refrigerate for at least half an hour.

Preheat the oven to 200°C (400°F) Gas 6.

To make the pumpkin purée, scrape away all the pumpkin seeds and fibrous flesh surrounding them and cut the flesh into even-sized chunks. Put these on a piece of lightly oiled foil. Sprinkle over the bourbon, sugar and mixed spice and dot with the chilled butter. Bring the foil up round the sides and fold over carefully to form a loose but airtight package. Place in a baking dish and cook in the preheated oven for 40 minutes until the pumpkin is soft. Carefully open up the foil, let cool for a few minutes, then tip the pumpkin and the juices into a food processor and whizz until smooth.

Roll out the pastry and lower it into the tart tin. Trim the edges and press the base well into the tin. Prick lightly with a fork and chill for another 30 minutes. Line the pastry case with foil and fill with baking weights. Bake at 200°C (400°F) Gas 6 for about 12 minutes, then remove the foil and weights, brush the base of the case with the reserved egg white to seal it and return to the oven for about 3–4 minutes. Remove it from the oven and lower the temperature to 190°C (375°F) Gas 5.

Add the sugar and maple syrup to the pumpkin purée, then the spices, salt and bourbon. Add the eggs, one by one, beating them in well, then sift in the flour and mix lightly. Add the cream and pour the filling into the flan case. Put the tin on a baking tray and bake in the still-hot oven for about 50 minutes until the filling is just set and firm, reducing the temperature to 180°C (350°F) Gas 4 after 25 minutes.

About 10 minutes before the end of the cooking time, chop the pecan nuts finely. Put them in a saucepan with the sugar and warm gently until the sugar starts to melt. About 5 minutes before the tart is cooked sprinkle the nuts evenly over the surface of the tart and return it to the oven for 5 minutes. Remove from the oven and let cool for 20 minutes before cutting. Serve lukewarm with lightly whipped cream.

dusky apple pie

This rustic apple pie with its spiced crumbly pastry and lemon-infused apple filling is perfect winter comfort food and guaranteed to become a family favourite.

8 tart green apples (such as Granny Smith), peeled, cored and thinly sliced

2 teaspoons freshly squeezed lemon juice

2 thin slices of lemon peel

55 g caster sugar

250 g self-raising flour

185 g brown sugar

1 tablespoon ground cinnamon

1 tablespoon ground ginger

125 g chilled butter, cut into cubes

1 egg, lightly beaten

vanilla ice cream, to serve (optional)

a 20-cm diameter, 4-cm deep loose-based fluted tart tin, lightly greased

Serves 8–10

Put the apple slices in a saucepan with the lemon juice, lemon zest and sugar. Cover and cook over low heat for 15–20 minutes, turning the apples often so they soften and cook evenly. Set aside and let cool.

To make the pastry, put the flour, brown sugar and spices in a food processor and process for a few seconds to combine. With the motor running, add the butter several cubes at a time. Add the egg and 1–2 tablespoons of ice-cold water and process until combined. The dough will look dry and crumbly. Transfer to a bowl and knead to form a ball. Wrap the ball in clingfilm and refrigerate for 30 minutes.

Preheat the oven to 180°C (350°F) Gas 4 and put a baking tray in the oven to heat up. Cut the dough into two portions, with one slightly larger than the other. Roll the larger piece of dough between two sheets of greaseproof paper and use it to line the bottom and sides of the prepared tart tin. (Take care when handling the pastry as it will be quite crumbly.) Trim the edge of the pastry to fit the tin.

Spoon the apples on top of the pastry base. Roll the remaining pastry to a circle large enough to cover the base and place on top of the pie, trimming the edges to fit. Use a small sharp knife to make several slits in the pastry. Put the pie on the hot baking tray and bake in the preheated oven for 50–55 minutes, until the pastry is golden brown.

Remove the pie from the oven and let it rest for 15–20 minutes before cutting into wedges and serving with vanilla ice cream on the side, if liked.

gooseberry and ginger wine crumble

700 g fresh or frozen gooseberries or 2 x 350-g jars of gooseberries in juice, drained

3 tablespoons ginger wine

125 g caster sugar

ginger topping

200 g plain flour

1 teaspoon ground ginger

a pinch of salt

100 g chilled unsalted butter, cut into cubes

100 g caster sugar

thick cream or vanilla ice cream, to serve

a shallow ovenproof dish

Serves 4

Although gooseberries are a summer fruit they pair so perfectly with spicy ginger wine that it's worth freezing a batch in summer ready to bake this delicious crumble once the days start to get shorter. If fresh gooseberries aren't available, good-quality jarred fruit will work fine, but make sure you drain it well as too much liquid will make the crumble rather too soggy.

Preheat the oven to 190°C (375°F) Gas 5 and put a baking tray in the oven to heat.

Place the gooseberries in a non-reactive saucepan, add the ginger wine and sugar and cook gently until the fruit starts to burst. Remove from the heat and tip the gooseberries into a sieve set over a clean saucepan to catch the juices. Next tip the gooseberries into an ovenproof baking dish, covering the base with a single layer.

To make the crumble topping, put the flour, ginger, salt and butter in a food processor and process until the mixture resembles coarse breadcrumbs. (Alternatively you can rub in by hand.) Tip into a mixing bowl and stir in the sugar. (At this stage you can pop it into a plastic bag and chill in the fridge until ready to cook.)

Lightly sprinkle the topping mixture evenly over the prepared gooseberry mixture, mounding it up a little towards the centre. Put the dish on the hot baking tray and bake in the preheated oven for about 25 minutes, until crisp and golden. Let cool for 5 minutes before serving with and thick cream or vanilla ice cream.

apple, prune and armagnac filo crumble

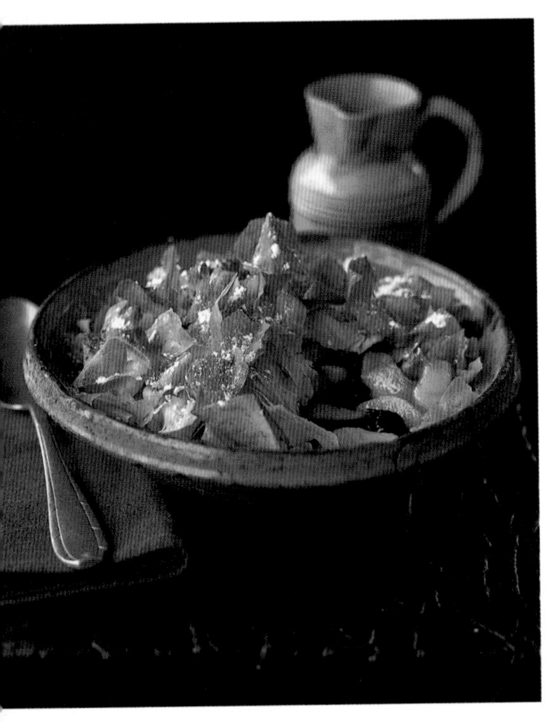

There is a dessert in south-west France called Pastis Gascon, which is a buttery, apple or prune tart with a feather-light topping of sugar-dusted filo pastry, suffused with local fiery Armagnac. This recipe re-interprets it as a crumble.

4 sheets of ready-made filo pastry, thawed if frozen

100 g unsalted butter, melted

4 eating apples

16 ready-to-eat stoned prunes

2–3 tablespoons Armagnac or Cognac

3 tablespoons caster sugar

finely grated zest of 1 lemon

icing sugar, to dust

single cream, to serve

a shallow ovenproof dish

Serves 4

Preheat the oven to 190°C (375°F) Gas 5.

Lay the filo pastry out on a work surface and brush with the melted butter. Leave to set and dry out for 15–20 minutes.

Meanwhile, peel, core and slice the apples and quarter the prunes. Toss them together in a bowl with the Armagnac, sugar and the lemon zest. Pile the fruit into a baking dish, cover with foil and bake in the preheated oven for 20 minutes.

Scrunch the pastry up so that it rips and tears and breaks into small rags. Remove the apple and prune mixture from the oven and lightly scatter the filo pieces on top, making sure it looks quite ragged and spiky. Dust lightly with icing sugar and bake for a further 20 minutes, until golden brown.

Let cool for 5 minutes before serving with single cream for pouring.

mulled winter fruit crumble

Christmas is definitely coming when the smell of this delicious crumble starts to drift around the house. A mixture of either traditional or exotic dried fruits provides a rich base for the light crumble topping. The spicy mulled wine seeps into the fruits as they cook and plumps them up nicely. Serve this as a superior substitute for mince pies!

350 g mixed dried fruits such as sultanas, cranberries, apricots and figs or mango, pineapple and paw-paw

300 ml medium-bodied fruity red wine

1 small muslin bag of mulled wine spices (cinnamon, cloves and allspice)

a thin strip of orange zest

50 g caster sugar

thick cream or vanilla ice cream, to serve

spiced topping

200 g wholemeal flour

¼ teaspoon mixed spice

a pinch of salt

100 g chilled unsalted butter, cut into cubes

100 g demerera sugar

a shallow ovenproof dish

Serves 4

Preheat the oven to 190°C (375°F) Gas 5 and put a baking tray in the oven to heat.

Chop the dried fruits into bite-sized pieces and place them in a non-reactive saucepan. Add the wine, mulling spices, orange zest and caster sugar. Heat gently, then let simmer for 10 minutes. Let cool then spoon into an ovenproof dish and remove the mulling spices and orange zest.

To make the topping, put the flour, mixed spice, salt and butter in a food processor and process until the mixture resembles coarse breadcrumbs. (Alternatively you can rub in by hand.) Tip the mixture into a bowl and stir in the sugar. (At this stage you can pop it into a plastic bag and chill in the fridge ready to cook.)

Lightly sprinkle the crumble topping mixture evenly over the surface of the dried fruits, mounding it up a little towards the centre. Put the dish on the hot baking tray and bake in the preheated oven for about 25 minutes, until crisp and golden on top.

Let cool for 5 minutes before serving with thick cream or vanilla ice cream.

classic blackberry and apple crumble

Who can resist a classic fruit crumble still warm from the oven. It is important to bake this traditional recipe in a moderate oven for a long time as this is what gives the topping its wonderful trademark crunch.

4–5 cooking apples, such as Bramley

250 g fresh or frozen blackberries

4 tablespoons caster sugar

¼ teaspoon mixed spice

finely grated zest and juice of ½ a lemon

crumble topping

200 g chilled unsalted butter

200 g plain flour

a pinch of salt

75 g demerara sugar

single cream or custard, to serve

a shallow, ovenproof dish

Serves 6

Preheat the oven to 180°C (350°F) Gas 4 and put a baking tray in the oven to heat.

Peel, core and slice the apples and put them in a large bowl. Add the blackberries, sugar, mixed spice, lemon zest and juice and toss well to mix. Transfer to an ovenproof dish.

To make the crumble topping, rub the butter into the flour with the salt until the mixture resembles coarse breadcrumbs. Alternatively do this in a food processor. Stir in the sugar. (At this stage the mixture can be popped into a plastic bag and chilled in the fridge until ready to cook.)

Lightly scatter the topping mixture over the fruit. Put the dish on the hot baking tray and bake in the preheated oven for 50–60 minutes, until the golden and bubbling.

Remove from the oven and serve warm with cream for pouring or custard.

plum and hazelnut pandowdy

A pandowdy is made with a sweet dough baked on top of fruit, the crust being 'dowdied' by pushing the sweet dough into the fruit juices to soften it before serving. It can also be served upside down like a Tarte Tatin.

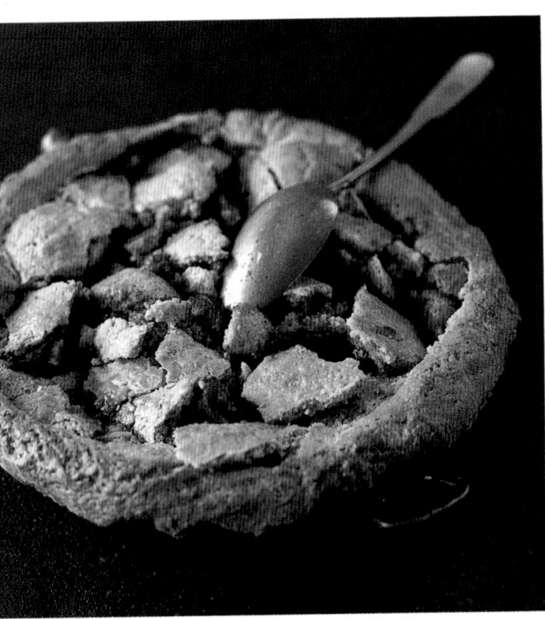

900 g mixed plums, halved, stoned and sliced

125 g light soft brown sugar

½ teaspoon ground cinnamon

finely grated zest and juice of 1 small orange

40 g chilled unsalted butter, cut into cubes

pandowdy crust

250 g plain flour

3 tablespoons caster sugar

1 tablespoon baking powder

100 g chilled unsalted butter, cut into cubes

75 g finely ground hazelnuts

about 200 ml single cream, plus extra to serve

caster sugar, to dust

a 26–28-cm diameter cast-iron skillet

Serves 6

Preheat the oven to 220°C (425°F) Gas 7.

Put the plums in a large bowl with the sugar, cinnamon, orange zest and juice. Tip the fruit into a skillet and dot with butter.

To make the pandowdy crust, sift the flour, sugar and baking powder into a large bowl. Rub the chilled butter into the flour until the mixture resembles coarse breadcrumbs. Add the ground hazelnuts and mix. Stir in all but a couple of tablespoons of the cream with a blunt knife, until the dough comes together. It will be sticky. Knead very lightly until smooth. Working quickly, roll out to a circle ½ cm thick and 1 cm wider than the pan. With the help of the rolling pin, lift the dough over the fruit and over the edge of the pan. Do not press the crust onto the sides of the pan. Make a couple of slits in the dough to allow steam to escape. Brush with the remaining cream and dust with sugar.

Put the pan on a baking tray to catch any leaking juices and bake in the preheated oven for 10 minutes, then reduce the oven temperature to 180°C (350°F) Gas 4 and loosely cover with foil. Bake for a further 35–40 minutes, until the crust is golden. Remove from the oven and 'dowdy' the crust by sharply pushing it under the surface of bubbling fruit with a large spoon.

Serve warm with single cream for pouring.

baked Granny Smith and blueberry pudding

Granny Smith apples are a great all-round cooking apple. Their flesh collapses when cooked, making them perfect for apple sauce but they are also great in sweet puddings, such as this self-saucing one, but they are not ideal for tarts and cakes. This recipe uses fresh blueberries which are now widely available throughout the year, but you could also use blackberries or cranberries.

2 tart green apples, such as Granny Smith

150 g fresh blueberries

125 g plain flour

3 teaspoons baking powder

115 g caster sugar

250 ml buttermilk

1 egg

1 vanilla pod

100 g soft light brown sugar

single cream, to serve (optional)

a medium baking dish, well buttered

Serves 6

Preheat the oven to 180°C (350°F) Gas 4.

Peel and core the apples then thinly slice them directly into the prepared baking dish, arranging them in the bottom of the dish with the blueberries.

Sift the flour, baking powder and caster sugar into a large bowl. Put the buttermilk and egg in a separate bowl. Split the vanilla pod in half lengthways and scrape the seeds from the pod directly into this bowl, then stir to combine. Pour the buttermilk mixture into the flour mixture and beat well.

Pour the mixture over the fruit in the baking dish. Working quickly, put the brown sugar in a jug and add 250 ml boiling water. Stir until the sugar has dissolved. Carefully pour this mixture into the baking dish, pouring into a corner. Bake the pudding in the preheated oven for 45 minutes, until the surface feels dry and springs back when lightly touched. Serve warm with cream for pouring, if liked.

baked brioche pudding
with blackberries

This is an impressive pudding for relatively little work. The sweet and buttery brioche works well with the tangy blackberries. Try and buy very sweet blackberries for this, as they will be softer and juicier. The dark purple juices should bleed into the pudding to create a pretty, marbled effect.

4 brioche rolls or ½ a 400-g brioche loaf

50 g butter, softened

300 g fresh blackberries

3 eggs

125 ml single cream

375 ml full-fat milk

75 g caster sugar

2 tablespoons raw sugar

vanilla ice cream, to serve (optional)

a medium baking dish

Serves 6

Slice the brioche to give you 6–8 thin slices. Lightly butter the slices on one side and arrange them in the bottom of the baking dish, overlapping them slightly. Put half the blackberries on top. Repeat with the remaining brioche slices and blackberries. Put the cream, eggs, milk and caster sugar in a bowl and beat to combine. Pour the mixture over the brioche in the baking dish. Cover with foil and let sit for 30 minutes to allow the brioche to absorb the liquid.

Preheat the oven to 180°C (350°F) Gas 4. Sprinkle the raw sugar over the top of the pudding and bake it in the preheated oven for 40–45 minutes, until the top of the pudding is golden brown. Serve warm with vanilla ice cream, if liked.

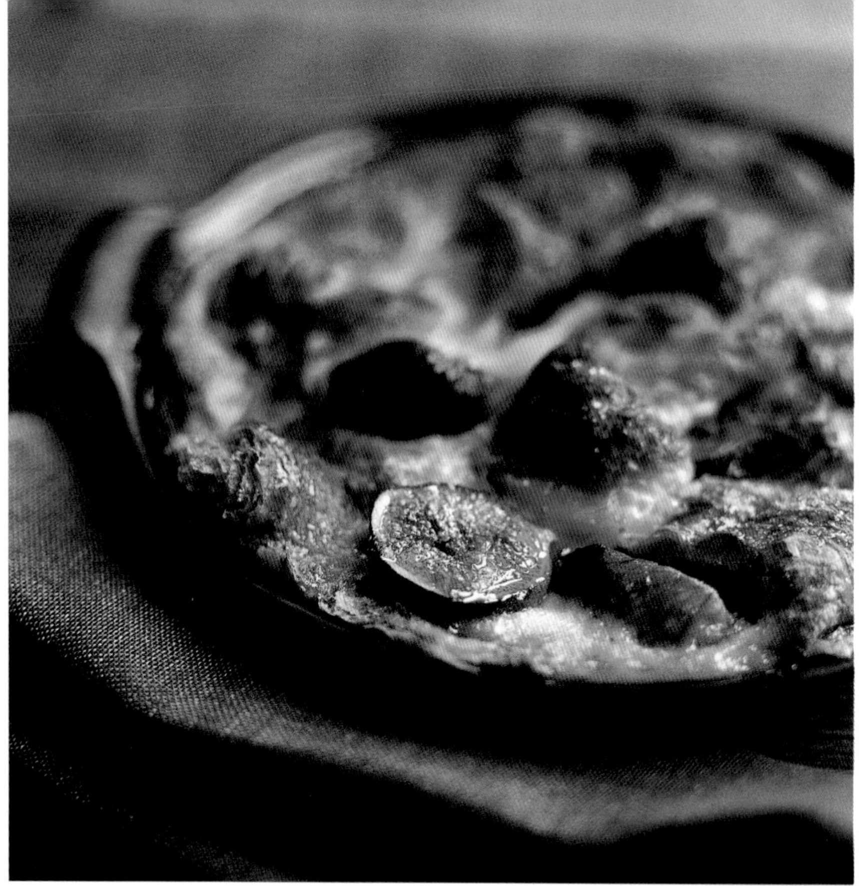

fig and honey croissant pudding

Fresh figs have a sweet, honey-nectar flavour. Once picked, they ripen very quickly and late-season figs are perfect cooked in puddings or enjoyed with cheese.

2 croissants, preferably stale, each torn into 6 pieces

6 fresh figs, halved

60 ml runny honey

3 eggs

250 ml full-fat milk

250 ml single cream

55 g caster sugar

double cream, to serve

a medium ovenproof dish, lightly buttered

Serves 4

Preheat the oven to 180°C (350°F) Gas 4.

Put the croissant pieces in the bottom of the prepared baking dish. Arrange the fig halves in between the croissant pieces and drizzle the honey over the top.

Combine the eggs, milk, cream and sugar in a bowl and pour into the dish. Let stand for about 20 minutes so that the croissants can absorb some of the custard. Bake in the preheated oven for 50 minutes, until the top of the pudding is a dark golden brown.

Let cool a little before cutting into slices and serving with double cream on the side.

Variation: When figs aren't in season, you can lightly spread each piece of croissant with some good-quality fig jam before putting into the dish. Leave out the honey and add 60 g slivered almonds to the egg mixture instead.

poached pear tiramisù

Tiramisù is probably one of the best-loved desserts in the world. It has all the essential elements of a perfect pudding – alcohol, creamy custard and cocoa. Pears work particularly well with anything creamy and cheesey so mascarpone makes an ideal partner. Choose your pears carefully. Soft, sweet varieties such as Packham, do not poach well and will end up as an overly sweet mush. Bosc are good but any fresh firm brown variety will work in this recipe.

6–8 sponge fingers (Italian savoiardi biscuits)

250 ml Marsala or brandy

115 g caster sugar

2 firm brown pears (such as Bosc), peeled, cored and cut into eighths

2 egg whites

4 egg yolks

250 ml mascarpone

cocoa powder, for dusting

4 individual serving dishes

Serves 4

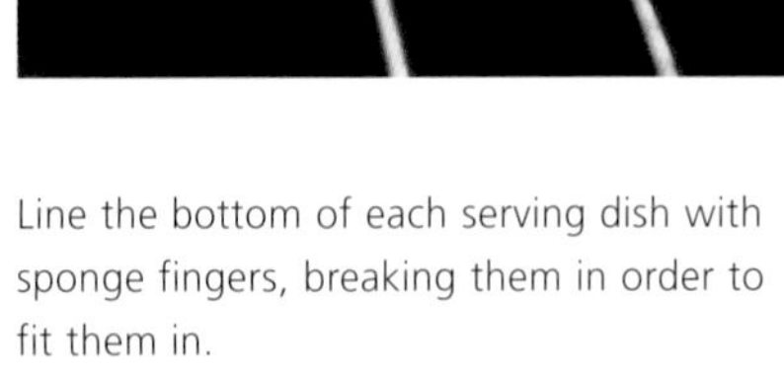

Line the bottom of each serving dish with sponge fingers, breaking them in order to fit them in.

Put the Marsala or brandy, half of the sugar and 125 ml water in a non-stick frying pan and cook over high heat until the mixture boils, stirring until the sugar has dissolved. Add the pears and cook on a gentle simmer for 20 minutes, turning them often until they are soft and glossy and there is about half of the liquid remaining.

Lay the pears on top of the sponge fingers and pour over the poaching liquid. Using electric beaters, beat the egg whites until firm peaks form. Beat the egg yolks with the remaining sugar for 4–5 minutes, until they are pale in colour and doubled in size, then beat the mascarpone into the yolks.

Using a large metal spoon, fold the egg whites into the yolk and sugar mixture and spoon over the pears. Cover each dish with clingfilm and refrigerate until ready to serve. Dust each one with a little cocoa powder just before serving.

Note This pudding contains raw eggs, see note on page 4.

baked apples
with dates and sticky toffee sauce

This has the same sticky toffee sauce that is traditionally used in the famous sponge pudding, but in this recipe the tartness and spiciness of the apples cuts through the sweet, buttery toffee sauce. Sticky toffee sauce is very versatile and can be served with ice cream or spooned over other baked fruit, such as bananas, pears, peaches or apricots. The apples can be prepared in the morning and popped into the oven as soon as you get home.

sticky toffee sauce

75 g unsalted butter

75 g soft dark brown sugar

5 tablespoons double cream

stuffed apples

50 g dried dates, roughly chopped

15 g stem ginger in syrup, drained and finely chopped

30 g walnuts or pecans, roughly chopped

4 large cooking apples, such as Bramley or Russett, cored

single cream or vanilla ice cream, to serve

a medium baking dish or roasting tin

Serves 4

Preheat the oven to 150°C (300°F) Gas 2.

To make the sticky toffee sauce, put the butter, sugar and cream in a saucepan and set over low heat until melted. Bring to the boil and cook for 1 minute. Remove from the heat and set aside.

Mix together the dates, ginger and nuts. Stuff half this mixture into the cored apples and stir the remainder into the toffee sauce.

Arrange the stuffed apples in an ovenproof dish or roasting tin so that they fit tightly. Pour the toffee sauce over the apples and cover the entire dish or tin with foil.

Bake in the preheated oven for 25–30 minutes, basting the apples with the sauce occasionally. Remove the dish from the oven and let the apples cool for a few minutes. Serve whilst still warm, with cream for pouring or vanilla ice cream, as preferred.

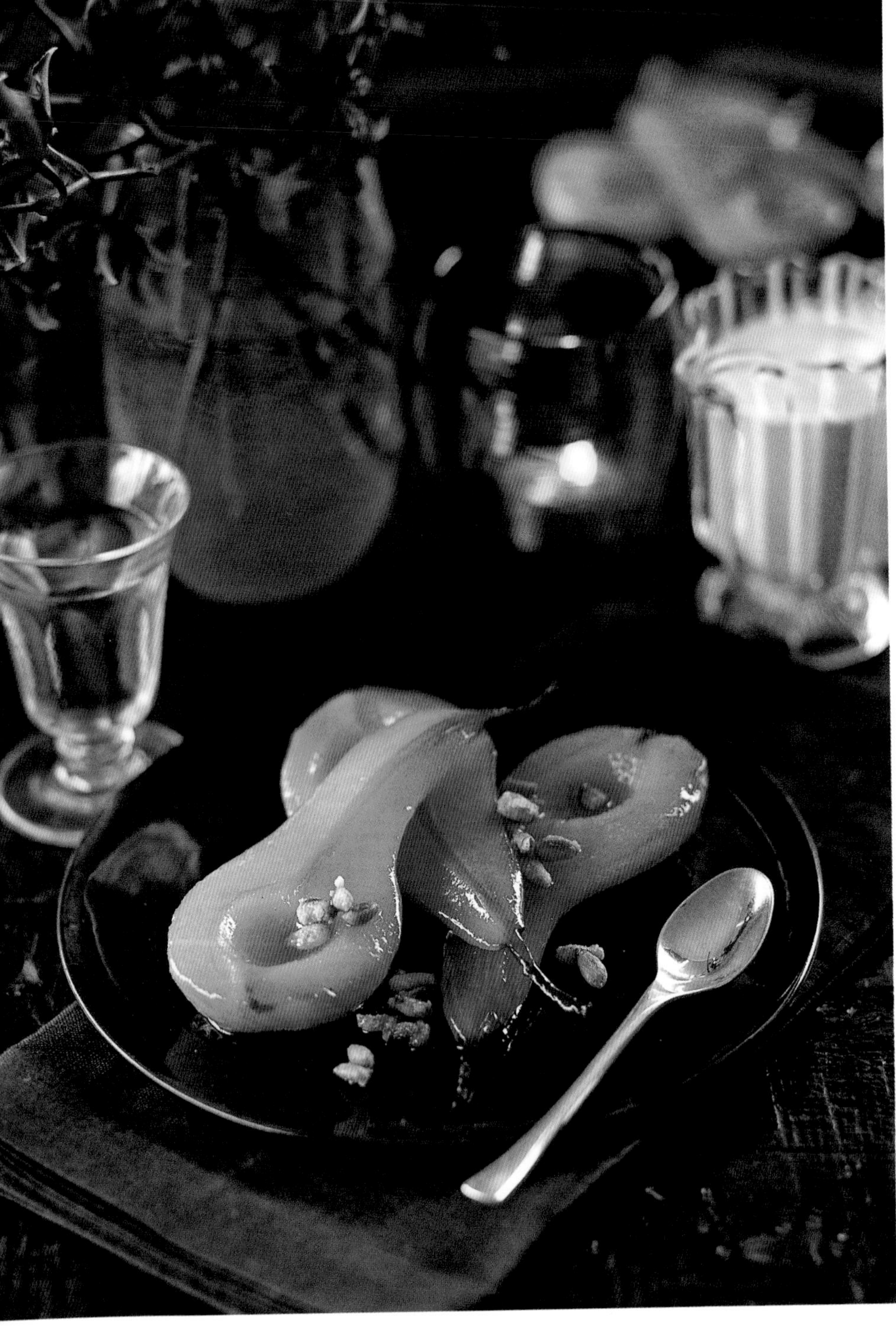

roast pears
with sweet wine, honey and pine nuts

Roasting pears in wine transforms them from everyday fruit into a light but luxurious dessert. The trick is to use an inexpensive wine for cooking and a better wine of the same type to serve with it.

freshly squeezed juice of 1 lemon (about 3 tablespoons)

9 just-ripe, small Conference pears

50 g butter, softened

3 tablespoons fragrant honey

175 ml Premières Côtes de Bordeaux or late-harvested Sauvignon or Semillon

50 g pine nuts

1 dessertspoon unrefined caster sugar

200 ml double cream

2 teaspoons vanilla sugar or ½ teaspoon vanilla extract and 2 teaspoons caster sugar

a large roasting tin or ovenproof dish (big enough to take the pears in a single layer), well buttered

Serves 6

Preheat the oven to 190°C (375°F) Gas 5.

Strain the lemon juice into a small bowl. Cut each pear in half, peel it and cut away the core. Dip it in the lemon juice to stop it discolouring. Place it cut-side upwards in the roasting tin. Arrange the pears so that they fit snugly in one layer. Put a knob of butter in the centre of each half. Drizzle the pears with the honey and pour over the leftover lemon juice and the wine.

Bake in the preheated oven for about 50–60 minutes, turning the pears halfway through. If the pears produce a lot of juice turn the heat up to 200°C (400°F) Gas 6 to concentrate the juices and form a syrup. Remove from the oven and let cool for about 20 minutes.

Meanwhile, toast the pine nuts lightly in a dry frying pan, shaking them occasionally until they start to brown. Sprinkle over the caster sugar and continue to cook until the sugar melts and caramelizes. Sweeten the cream with the vanilla sugar and heat until lukewarm. Arrange 3 pear halves on each plate, trickle over about a tablespoon of warm cream and scatter over the pine nuts. Serve immediately.

rhubarb clafoutis

In summer, many French bistro menus feature clafoutis, a custard-like batter baked with whole cherries. It is one of the finest French puddings, and a cinch to make. The only drawback is that the cherry season is a short one, and it is a shame to limit clafoutis making to just one part of the year. In autumn and winter plums, pears and apples work well, but rhubarb is fantastic. Almost better than the original.

500 g fresh rhubarb, cut into 3 cm slices

200 ml full-fat milk

200 ml double cream

3 eggs

150 g sugar

¼ teaspoon ground cinnamon

a pinch of salt

1 vanilla pod

50 g plain flour

single cream, to serve (optional)

a large baking dish, buttered and sprinkled with sugar

Serves 6

Preheat the oven to 200°C (400°F) Gas 6.

Bring a saucepan of water to the boil, add the rhubarb and cook for 2 minutes, just to blanch. Drain and set aside.

Put the milk, cream, eggs, sugar, cinnamon and salt in a bowl and mix well. Split the vanilla pod lengthways and scrape the seeds into the mixture. Add the flour and whisk well. Arrange the rhubarb pieces in the prepared baking dish. Pour the batter over the top and bake in the preheated oven for 40–45 minutes, until puffed and golden. Serve warm with cream, if liked.

coffee and chestnut roulade

Here coffee custard, enriched with luscious chestnut purée and rolled up inside a light, golden sponge, then drizzled with a bitter-sweet mocha sauce, makes a wickedly indulgent special occasion dessert.

4 eggs

115 g caster sugar, plus extra to sprinkle

115 g self-raising flour

85 g sweetened chestnut purée

coffee custard

3 egg yolks

2 tablespoons caster sugar

3 tablespoons plain flour

120 ml single cream

160 ml milk

2½ teaspoons instant coffee granules dissolved in 1 tablespoon boiling water

mocha sauce

85 g good quality dark chocolate (minimum 70% cocoa solids)

90 ml freshly brewed espresso coffee

180 ml double cream

a 33 x 23-cm Swiss roll tin, greased and lined with greaseproof paper

Serves 6

To make the coffee custard, whisk together the egg yolks, sugar and flour until pale and creamy. Heat the cream and milk in a pan until hot but not boiling, then gradually whisk into the egg mixture. Return to the pan and heat very gently for 5–10 minutes, stirring until thick. Stir in the instant coffee, then pour into a bowl, press clingfilm on to the surface and leave to cool. Chill.

To make the mocha sauce, break the chocolate into pieces and put it in a pan with the espresso and cream. Heat gently, stirring, until smooth and creamy. Pour into a jug and set aside to cool until needed.

Preheat the oven to 220°C (425°F) Gas 7.

Put the eggs and sugar in a bowl and whisk for about 10 minutes until thick and pale and the whisk leaves a trail when lifted. Sift over about one-third of the flour and fold in, then repeat with the remaining thirds of flour. Pour into the prepared Swiss roll tin, tapping the edges so that it spreads out evenly, and bake for about 10 minutes, or until golden.

Lay a clean tea towel on the work surface, sprinkle with caster sugar and turn the cake out onto it. Carefully peel off the paper, then roll the sponge up like a Swiss roll. Leave to cool completely.

To assemble, carefully unroll the cake and spread the coffee custard over the surface, leaving a little space around the edges. Spoon over the chestnut purée, then carefully re-roll using the tea towel to support the cake. Serve in slices, drizzled with the mocha sauce.

caramel custard

These are neither too sweet, nor too heavy; the perfect ending to any meal. Either serve them in their ramekins or inverted onto a plate in a pool of sauce.

750 ml full-fat milk

1 vanilla pod

180 g sugar

5 eggs

a pinch of salt

8 ramekin dishes

a roasting tin large enough to hold the ramekins

Serves 8

Put the milk in a large saucepan and set over medium heat. Split the vanilla pod lengthways and scrape the seeds directly into the milk. Add the vanilla pod to the pan and bring to the boil. Remove from the heat, cover and let stand.

To make the caramel, put 100 g of the sugar, the salt and 4 tablespoons water in a small heavy-based saucepan. Heat until the sugar turns a deep caramel colour, then remove from the heat. When it stops sizzling, pour into the ramekins. Set the ramekins in the roasting tin and add enough boiling water to come half-way up the sides. Set aside.

Preheat the oven to 180°C (350°F) Gas 4.

Add the remaining 80 g sugar and the salt to the saucepan of warm milk and stir until dissolved. Remove the vanilla pod. Crack the eggs into another bowl and whisk until smooth. Pour the warm milk into the eggs and stir well. Ladle into the ramekins.

Carefully transfer the roasting tin with the ramekins to the preheated oven and bake until the custard is set and a knife inserted into the middle comes out clean, about 20–25 minutes. Serve at room temperature.

chocolate and cabernet pots

Combining chocolate with a strong red wine might sound like an unlikely idea, but when you consider the wine's red berry flavours it makes more sense. The ideal wine to use is one that is ripe and fruity but not too oaky, such as a Cabernet.

175 ml medium-bodied fruity red wine, such as Cabernet Sauvignon

40 g caster sugar

200 g good quality dark chocolate (minimum 70% cocoa solids)

280 ml single cream

1 egg

a pinch of ground cinnamon

cocoa powder, for dusting

icing sugar (optional)

6 or 8 small pots, ramekins or espresso coffee cups, each about 100 ml capacity

Serves 6–8

Put the wine and caster sugar in a saucepan and heat gently until the sugar has dissolved. Increase the heat very slightly and simmer gently for about 20–25 minutes, until the wine has reduced by two-thirds to about 4 tablespoons.

Meanwhile, break the chocolate into squares, and put them in a blender. Whizz briefly to break them into smaller pieces.

Put the cream in a saucepan and heat until almost boiling. Pour the hot cream over the chocolate in the blender, then add the hot, sweetened wine. Leave for a few seconds so the chocolate melts. Whizz briefly until the mixture is smooth. Add the egg and cinnamon and whizz again briefly to mix.

Pour the mixture into the ramekins or cups, then chill in the refrigerator for 3–4 hours. Remove the chocolate pots from the refrigerator 20 minutes before serving. To serve, dust each one with a thin layer of cocoa powder then sprinkle with a little sifted icing sugar, if using.

Note This pudding contains raw egg, see note on page 4.

chocolate chilli truffles

Pass round these surprisingly warm and mysterious truffles instead of a dessert.

275 g good quality dark chocolate (minimum 70% cocoa solids)

50 g unsalted butter, cut into cubes

300 ml double cream

¼ teaspoon hot chilli powder

2 tablespoons chilli vodka

cocoa powder, for coating

Candied Bird's Eye Chillies, to garnish (optional)

a shallow roasting tin or straight-sided tray

Makes about 20

Put the chocolate, butter, cream and chilli in a bowl set over a saucepan of simmering water. Heat until melted – the mixture should be just tepid. Stir occasionally (overmixing will make the mixture grainy). Stir in the vodka.

Pour into a shallow tray and refrigerate until firm. Scoop out teaspoonfuls of mixture, roll into rough balls and chill. Sift the cocoa powder onto a plate. Carefully roll each ball in the cocoa. Chill until set. Store in an airtight container in the refrigerator for up to 2 weeks. Serve in little espresso cups with a Candied Bird's Eye Chilli, if liked.

Note Candied Bird's Eye Chillies
These are easy to make and are always quite a talking point served with the truffles. Remember, they are very hot! Dissolve 250 g sugar in 300 ml water in a medium saucepan. Bring to the boil for 1 minute. Add 50 g whole bird's eye chillies and bring to the boil. Simmer for 15 minutes, then turn off the heat and leave to soak in the syrup for 24 hours. Lift out of the syrup with a fork, drain well and arrange on non-stick baking parchment. Use immediately or roll them in sugar to coat and let dry at room temperature for 24 hours. Store in layers in an airtight box for up to 1 month.

drinks

egg nog

Once you've tasted this deliciously light, foamy punch you'll want to make it every year. This recipe is adapted from a recipe in top American bartender Dale Degroff's 'The Craft of the Cocktail'.

3 very fresh large eggs

75 g unrefined caster sugar

100 ml bourbon

100 ml spiced rum

570 ml full-fat milk

275 ml whipping cream

freshly grated nutmeg, to taste

Makes 6–8 cups

Separate the egg yolks carefully from the whites and put them in separate large bowls. Beat the egg yolks with an electric hand-held whisk, gradually adding 50 g of the sugar, until they turn light in colour and moussey in texture. Beat in the bourbon and spiced rum, then stir in the milk and cream.

Clean and dry your whisk thoroughly then whisk the egg whites until beginning to stiffen. Add the remaining sugar to the whites and whisk until they form a soft peak. Fold the whites into the egg nog and grate over a little nutmeg. Ladle out the egg nog into small glasses or cups.

Note This drink contains raw eggs, see note on page 4.

orange-mulled wine

If you've never made mulled wine yourself, you should try. It couldn't be simpler and tastes infinitely better than the ready-mixed versions. The only thing you have to be careful about is that the wine doesn't boil.

2 x 750-ml bottles medium-bodied fruity red wine

1 orange studded with cloves, plus a few orange slices to serve

thinly pared zest of ½ a lemon

2 cinnamon sticks

6 cardamom pods, lightly crushed

a little freshly grated nutmeg or a small pinch of ground nutmeg

100 g soft brown sugar

100 ml orange-flavoured liqueur, such as Cointreau or Grand Marnier, or brandy

Makes 14–16 small cups

Pour the wine into a large saucepan with 500 ml cold water. Add the orange, lemon zest, spices and sugar and heat gently until almost boiling. Turn down to the lowest possible heat so that the liquid barely trembles and simmer for half an hour. Add the orange-flavoured liqueur then reheat gently. Strain into a large, warmed bowl and float a few thin slices of orange on top. Ladle into small cups or heatproof glasses to serve.

mulled cider

This makes a deliciously fruity and lighter alternative to mulled wine.

500 ml traditional dry cider

125 ml Calvados (French apple brandy) or brandy

750 ml cloudy apple juice

75 g soft brown sugar

a thinly pared strip of lemon zest

2 cinnamon sticks

8 cloves

6 even-sized slices of dried apple, halved, to garnish

Makes 10–12 cups

Put the cider, Calvados and apple juice in a large saucepan. Add the sugar, lemon zest, cinnamon sticks and cloves and heat very gently until the sugar has dissolved. Heat until almost boiling, then turn off the heat, add the dried apple slices and leave the pan to sit for 30 minutes to allow the flavours to infuse. Gently reheat the punch, taking care not to let it boil. Ladle into cups or heatproof glasses to serve, adding a slice of dried apple to each serving.

glögg

This comforting, heart-warming drink is served in cafés in Denmark and Sweden to cheer up bleak winter days. It has a miraculous effect.

2 x 750-ml bottles medium-bodied fruity red wine

125 g sugar

150–200 g raisins and slivered almonds

1 cinnamon stick

4 cloves

8 cardamom pods, lightly crushed

2.5 cm piece of fresh ginger, lightly smashed

200 ml schnapps or vodka

100 ml brandy or cognac

a small piece of muslin and some kitchen string

Serves 8

Pour 1 bottle of red wine into a non-reactive bowl or saucepan. Add the sugar, raisins and almonds and stir to dissolve the sugar. Put the spices in the muslin, tie with string and add to the wine. Leave to infuse for a couple of hours if possible.

Heat the wine until almost boiling, then cover and leave to infuse for at least 30 minutes. When ready to serve, remove the spice bag and pour in the remaining bottle of wine, the schnapps and brandy. Reheat until almost boiling and serve hot in cups or heatproof glasses with small spoons to eat the marinated raisins and almonds.

spiced tea

This fragrant tea is particularly reviving after a winter's walk. You can make it as strong or as weak as you prefer. If liked, add a teaspoon of sweetened condensed milk to each cup.

1 cinnamon stick

3 cloves

1 star anise

3–4 cardamom pods, lightly crushed

1 heaped tablespoon Indian leaf tea, such as Darjeeling or Assam

condensed milk, to taste (optional)

Serves 6

Put the cinnamon, cloves, star anise and cardamom pods in a large saucepan, add 1 litre water and bring to the boil. Reduce the heat, cover and simmer gently for 5 minutes, then stir in the loose tea. Stir well, cover and leave to infuse for 5 minutes. Strain into a warmed teapot, and serve as it is, or with a teaspoonful of condensed milk added to each cup, if liked.

mocha maple coffee

Coffee and chocolate make perfect partners as this delicious drink proves. The addition of sweet, maple-flavoured cream makes this an indulgent treat and the perfect after-dinner drink.

500 ml freshly-brewed hot coffee

2 shots crème de cacao or chocolate syrup

125 ml whipping cream

1 teaspoon maple syrup

grated dark chocolate, to sprinkle

Serves 2

Pour the hot coffee into 2 tall heatproof glasses and add a shot of crème de cacao or chocolate syrup to each one.

Lightly whisk the cream and maple syrup together until the mixture is foaming and thickened slightly. Slowly layer the cream over the surface of the coffee using the back of a teaspoon. Sprinkle with grated chocolate and serve immediately.

really good coffee

Good coffee is simple to make and you don't need special pots or machines – just a heatproof jug and a tea strainer. Hot milk makes all the difference for those who take milk in their coffee; it produces a drink that is velvety and keeps hot. Using freshly ground coffee is important – freeze the bag after opening, then use straight from frozen.

4 tablespoons freshly ground coffee

boiling water

hot milk

Serves 2

Pour some hot water into a heatproof jug to warm it up. Empty out and add the appropriate amount of coffee per person. Pour on enough recently boiled water just to cover the coffee grounds. Stir and leave for 1 minute to infuse.

Top up with 300 ml just-boiled water per person and stir well. Cover and let brew for 5 minutes. Either strain through the tea strainer into cups or into another warmed jug. Add hot (not boiled) milk, if using. The coffee will have a crema or creamy foam on top if you have followed all the steps correctly, and will have a full, rich flavour.

pumpkin latte

Perfect for Halloween, this thick, richly spiced latte is flavoured with pumpkin. If you can find some tinned sweetened pumpkin purée, then use this and omit the sugar in the recipe.

375 ml milk

100 g cooked sweet pumpkin, mashed or 100 g tinned sweetened pumpkin purée

3 tablespoons brown sugar (omit if using tinned purée)

¼ teaspoon ground cinnamon

250 ml freshly brewed hot coffee

whipped cream and cinnamon sugar, to serve

Serves 3

Put the milk, pumpkin, sugar (if using) and cinnamon in a saucepan and heat gently, whisking constantly until the mixture just reaches boiling point. Transfer to 3 cups or heatproof glasses and stir in the coffee. Serve topped with lightly whipped cream and a dusting of cinnamon sugar.

egg-nog latte

This warming, festive drink with a hint of coffee makes a lovely alternative to the more traditional egg nog. For a non-alcoholic version, omit the rum.

500 ml milk

1 vanilla pod, split lengthways

2 very fresh eggs

2–3 tablespoons caster sugar, to taste

½ teaspoon ground cinnamon

a pinch of freshly grated nutmeg

2 tablespoons dark rum (optional)

250 ml freshly brewed hot coffee

Serves 4

Put the milk and vanilla pod in a saucepan and heat gently until the milk just reaches boiling point. Put the eggs, sugar and spices in a bowl and whisk until light and frothy. Stir in the milk, then return the mixture to the pan. Heat gently for 2–3 minutes, stirring constantly, until the mixture thickens slightly. Remove from the heat and stir in the rum, if using, and coffee. Pour into 4 heatproof glasses and serve immediately.

spiced white chocolate

The hint of Asian spice is lovely here with the white chocolate and makes a satisfying and warming drink that's just perfect for bedtime.

500 ml milk

4 star anise

a pinch of freshly grated nutmeg, plus extra to dust

100 g white chocolate, finely grated

Serves 2

Put the milk, star anise and nutmeg in a saucepan and bring slowly to the boil. Simmer gently for 5 minutes then remove from the heat and stir in the chocolate until melted. Let cool for 5 minutes then pour into 2 cups or heatproof glasses, dust with a little grated nutmeg and serve.

Variation You could use either dark or milk chocolate in this drink.

mulled bloody mary

This is totally delicious and tastes exactly as you'd imagine a warmed version of the classic brunch drink. It is perfect for a cold winter's morning, especially if you've over-indulged the night before!

1 litre tomato juice

1 lemon

1–2 tablespoons Worcestershire sauce, to taste

80–125 ml vodka

a pinch of celery salt

sea salt and freshly ground black pepper

Serves 4–6

Put the tomato juice in a saucepan. Cut half the lemon into slices and squeeze the juice from the remaining half into the pan. Add the lemon slices, Worcestershire sauce and some salt and pepper to taste. Bring slowly to the boil and simmer gently, uncovered, for 10 minutes.

Remove the saucepan from the heat and let cool for about 20 minutes. Stir in the vodka and some celery salt to taste. Pour into tall heatproof glasses to serve.

malted milk

There are several popular brands of malted milk available, but it is easy enough to make your own healthy version of this soothing hot drink.

500 ml milk

3 tablespoons barley malt extract

freshly grated nutmeg, to serve

Serves 2

Put the milk and malt extract in a saucepan and heat gently until it just reaches boiling point. Whisk the milk with a balloon whisk until frothy then pour it into 2 cups. Grate over a little nutmeg and serve.

honey baba

This is a delicately spiced milk drink infused with a hint of honey. You can always add a little shot of rum to this for a grown-up version.

500 ml milk

2 cinnamon sticks, lightly crushed

2 teaspoons runny honey

cinnamon sugar, to dust

Serves 2

Put the milk and cinnamon sticks in a saucepan and heat gently until the milk just reaches boiling point. Remove from the heat and strain. Add 1 teaspoon honey to each of 2 cups or heat-proof glasses and pour in the cinnamon-infused milk. Dust with a little cinnamon sugar and serve immediately.

hot rum and cider punch

This is a lovely autumnal drink with slices of apple infused with the flavours of the cider, rum and spices. It makes a great punch for a Halloween party. For a family–friendly, non-alcoholic version, replace the cider with apple juice and omit the rum.

1 x 500-ml bottle traditional dry cider

2 slices lemon

1 apple, cored and thinly sliced

1 cinnamon stick, crushed

3 cloves

2 tablespoons soft light brown sugar

80 ml dark rum

Serves 4–6

Put all of the ingredients in a large saucepan and heat gently until the liquid just reaches boiling point. Reduce the heat and simmer very gently for 10 minutes. Remove from the heat and let infuse for 10 minutes. Ladle into cups or heat-proof glasses to serve.

hot buttered rum

This is a simple mulled rum drink with the addition of butter to give it some extra richness. It's perfect for a chilly winter evening.

2 shots dark rum

4 cloves

2 unwaxed lemon slices

2 teaspoons unrefined caster sugar

250 ml just-boiled water

25 g unsalted butter

2 cinnamon sticks

Serves 2

Put the rum into 2 heatproof glasses and add the cloves, lemon slices and sugar. Top up with boiling water and add the butter. Put a cinnamon stick in each glass and use to stir the butter as it melts. Serve immediately.

Christmas milk

This drink has all the flavours of a traditional mince pie in a cup. The star decoration on top is fun, but optional, the drink tastes great either way!

1 litre milk

4 tablespoons raisins

2 tablespoons chopped crystallized ginger

4 teaspoons clear honey

½ an orange, sliced

60 ml whipping cream, whipped

cinnamon sugar, to dust

a piece of thin white card and a star-shaped biscuit cutter, about 5-cm diameter (optional)

Serves 4–6

Using the biscuit cutter as a template, carefully draw a star on the card. Use scissors to cut out the star shape.

Put the milk, raisins, ginger, honey and orange slices in a saucepan. Heat gently until the liquid just reaches boiling point. Divide between 4–6 cups. Spoon the whipped cream over the drinks. Hold the stencil over each drink, making sure that the the star shape is in the centre. Lightly dust with cinnamon sugar and remove the stencil to leave a star decoration on top. Repeat with all the drinks and serve immediately.

saffron milk

This drink is aromatic and exotic. The saffron, with its earthy flavour and striking colour, is pretty as well as delicious. The condensed milk does make this drink very sweet so, if you prefer, reduce the amount used.

430 ml milk

60 ml sweetened condensed milk

¼ teaspoon saffron threads, plus extra to serve

3 green cardamom pods, lightly crushed

Serves 2

Put the milk, condensed milk, saffron and cardamom pods in a saucepan and heat gently, stirring constantly, until the mixture just reaches boiling point. Remove from the heat and let infuse for 5 minutes. Strain the milk into 2 heatproof glasses, sprinkle with a few saffron threads and serve immediately.

Mexican chocolate
with vanilla cream

Mexico is where the world's love affair with chocolate began. It was the Aztecs who first used the cacao bean to make a drink, adding vanilla and spicy chillies but it was the Spanish conquistadors who added sugar and cinnamon and created the hot chocolate we enjoy today. A perfect winter warmer.

125 g dark chocolate (at least 70% cocoa solids), broken into small pieces

1.5 litres milk

4 tablespoons caster sugar

2 teaspoons ground cinnamon

cinnamon sticks, to serve (optional)

vanilla whipped cream

250 ml whipping cream

1 vanilla pod*

Serves 6

To make the vanilla whipped cream, put the cream into a bowl and whisk with an electric beater until light and fluffy, with soft peaks. Split the vanilla pod lengthways and carefully scrape out all the seeds. Gently fold them into the cream.

To make the Mexican chocolate, put the chocolate pieces in a heatproof bowl and set it over a saucepan of gently simmering water to melt – don't let the bottom of the bowl touch the water or the chocolate will be spoiled.

Pour the milk into a large saucepan and stir in the sugar and cinnamon. Heat until gently simmering but do not let it come to the boil. Whisk a ladleful of the milk into the melted chocolate then pour the mixture back into the saucepan, whisking until smooth. Ladle into 6 mugs. Top each with a generous spoonful of vanilla whipped cream and serve hot with a cinnamon stick stirrer, if using.

***Note** Don't throw away the split vanilla pod after use. Put it into a storage jar and cover with sugar to make vanilla sugar that can be used in drinks or for baking.

bellini

This truly indulgent cocktail makes a delicious treat for Christmas Day brunch. Although there are many variations on this recipe, there is one golden rule for the perfect Bellini – always use fresh, ripe peaches to make the juice.

½ a fresh peach, skinned and stoned

12.5 ml crème de pêche

a dash of peach bitters (optional)

champagne, to top up

a peach ball, to garnish

Serves 1

Purée the peach flesh in a blender and spoon it into a champagne flute. Pour in the crème de pêche and the bitters, if using, then top up with champagne, stirring carefully and continuously. Garnish with a peach ball (made using a melon baller) and serve immediately.

Campari fizz

This decadent aperitif combines the herby, bitter taste of Campari and the sweetness of sparkling wine with mouthwatering results.

25 ml Campari

½ teaspoon sugar

chilled sparkling wine, to top up

Serves 1

Pour the Campari into a champagne flute and sweeten with the sugar. Top with chilled sparkling wine and serve immediately.

mimosa

A simple yet effective pairing of champagne and freshly squeezed orange juice, perfect served at any celebratory brunch.

½ glass champagne

freshly squeezed orange juice, to top up

Serves 1

Half-fill a champagne flute with champagne. Top with orange juice, stir gently and serve.

Turkish chocolate

This elegant martini-style cocktail makes a delightful tipple. To decorate the glass, wipe the rim with lemon juice, or dip into egg white, then dip into the cocoa powder.

50 ml vodka

10 ml white crème de cacao

2 dashes of rose water

cocoa powder, for the glass

Serves 1

Add all the ingredients to a shaker filled with ice. Shake the mixture and strain into a chilled martini glass rimmed with cocoa powder, then serve.

champagne cocktail

This classic cocktail has truly stood the test of time, being as popular now as when it was sipped by stars of the silver screen in the 1940s. With a shot of brandy for an extra kick, it is the perfect drink for a festive celebration.

1 white sugar cube

2 dashes of Angostura bitters

25 ml brandy

dry champagne, to top up

Serves 1

Place the sugar cube in a champagne flute and moisten with the Angostura bitters. Add the brandy and stir, then gently top with the champagne and serve.

brandy alexander

The Brandy Alexander is the perfect after-dinner cocktail – luscious, seductive and great for chocolate lovers. It is important to get the proportions just right so that the brandy stands out as the main flavour.

50 ml brandy

12.5 ml crème de cacao

12.5 ml double cream

freshly grated nutmeg, to dust

Serves 1

Add all the ingredients to a cocktail shaker filled with ice. Shake and strain into a chilled martini glass. Dust with grated nutmeg and serve.

black velvet

This one of the most tempting and drinkable cocktails. Pour gently into the glass to allow for the unpredictable nature of both the Guinness and the champagne.

½ a glass Guinness

champagne, to top up

Serves 1

Half-fill a champagne flute with Guinness, gently top with champagne and serve.

vodka espresso

This elegant little cocktail makes the perfect after dinner pick-me-up as it combines freshly made espresso coffee with a dash of vodka.

50 ml vodka

1 measure freshly made strong espresso coffee

a dash of sugar syrup

3 coffee beans, to garnish (optional)

Serves 1

Pour the espresso coffee into a cocktail shaker. Add a generous measure of vodka and sugar syrup to taste. Shake the mixture up sharply and strain into an old fashioned glass filled with ice. The vigorous shaking should have created a foamy 'crema' which will sit on top on the drink. Garnish with three coffee beans, if liked, and serve immediately.

black russian

The Black Russian is a classic that has been around for many years. The sweet coffee flavour of the Kahlúa is sharpened by the vodka to create this stylish after-dinner cocktail.

50 ml vodka

25 ml Kahlúa

a maraschino cherry, to garnish

Serves 1

Add the vodka and Kahlúa to a cocktail shaker filled with ice. Shake and strain into a rocks glass filled with ice, garnish with a cherry and serve.

white russian

This twist on the Black Russian has the addition of cream. It's an indulgent treat that makes the perfect nightcap.

50 ml vodka

25 ml Kahlúa

25 ml single cream

a maraschino cherry, to garnish

Serves 1

Add the vodka and Kahlúa to a cocktail shaker filled with ice. Shake and strain into a rocks glass filled with ice, then gently layer on the cream over the back of a teaspoon. Garnish with a cherry and serve.

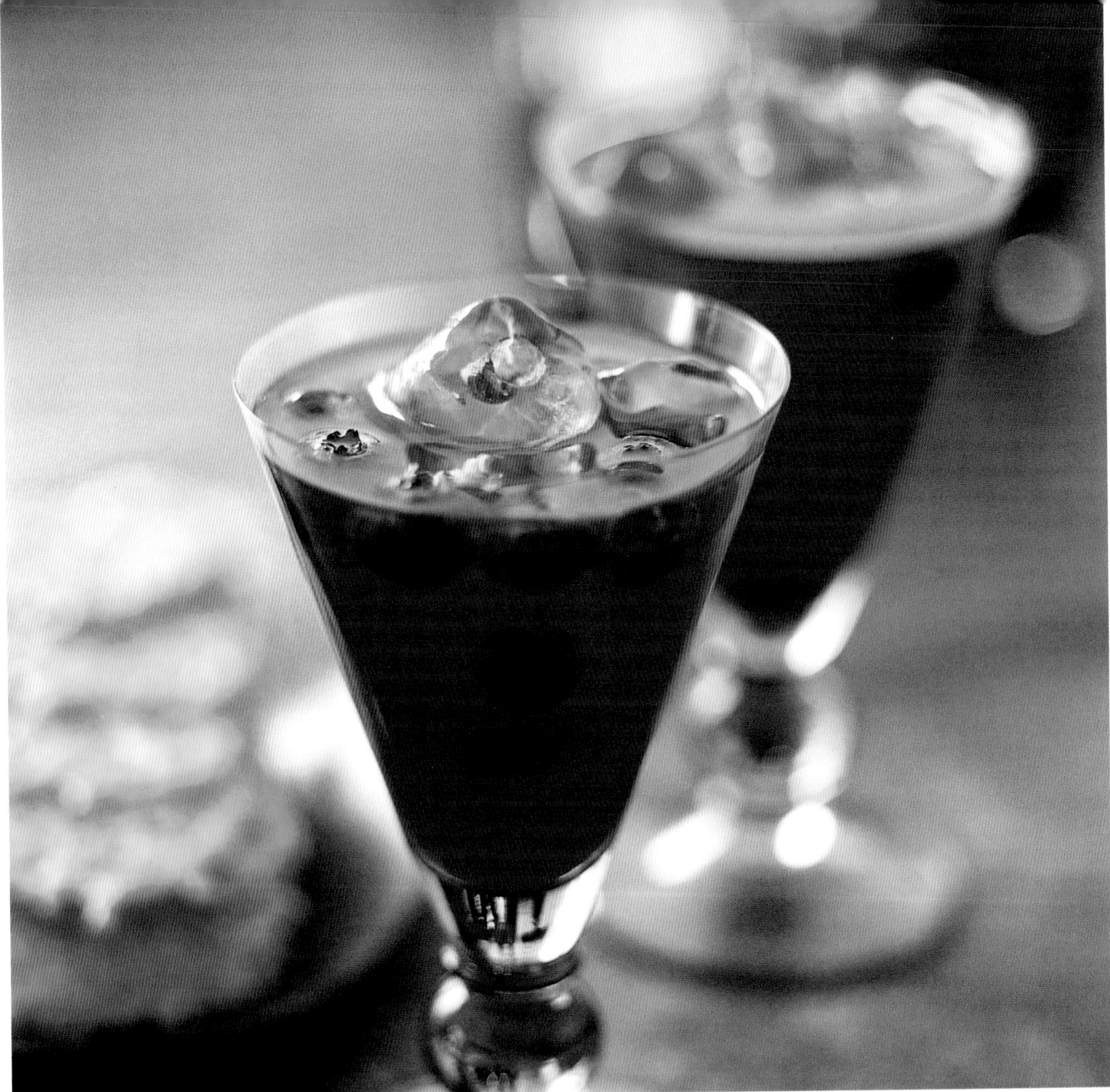

vodka cranberry floaters

This pretty party drink tastes and looks heavenly. The blueberries add a colourful touch to this vodka classic.

25 ml chilled vodka

125 ml cranberry juice

ice cubes, to serve

blueberries, to decorate

Serves 1

Put the vodka in a tall glass and add the cranberry juice. Mix well. Add a few blueberries, then some ice cubes. Serve immediately.

brown cow

This cocktail is perfect for serving to a party crowd as it only requires two ingredients and minimal preparation.

½ bottle Kahlúa, 350 ml

1 litre milk

ice cubes

Serves 8

Put all the ingredients in a large jug and mix. Alternatively, put the Kahlúa in individual glasses, and top up with milk and ice.

New Orleans sazarac

These is a great drink for those who enjoy a warming whisky. It can be topped with water or soda to make a thirst quencher but to fully enjoy the flavours it should be drunk undiluted. If you enjoy the aniseed flavour of Pernod, try adding it to the drink rather than rinsing the glass with it.

50 ml bourbon

25 ml Pernod

1 sugar cube

Angostura bitters

Serves 1

Rinse an old-fashioned glass with Pernod and discard the Pernod. Put the sugar in the glass, saturate with Angostura bitters, then add ice cubes and the bourbon and serve.

hot toddy

This warming blend of spices and sweet honey, is the perfect comforter and will soothe any aches, snuffles that your winter cold may have inflicted upon you. It's also a great life-saver for cold afternoons spent outside watching sport. Next time you have need to pack a Thermos of coffee, think again – mix up a batch of Hot Toddies, and see how popular you are!

5 whole cloves

2 lemon slices

50 ml whisky

25 ml freshly squeezed lemon juice

2 teaspoons honey

75 ml hot water

1 cinnamon stick (optional)

Serves 1

Skewer the cloves into the lemon slices and put them in a heat-proof glass. Pour in the whisky and lemon juice. Add the honey and top up with the water. Stir well and garnish with the cinnamon stick, if using, to serve.

index

A
aïoli, Parmesan, 28–9
almonds: pear and almond tart, 135
apples: apple and blueberry tarts, 140
apple and fennel puddings, 90
apple, prune and Armagnac filo crumble, 144
baked apples with dates, 151
baked Granny Smith and blueberry pudding, 148
classic blackberry and apple crumble, 146
dusky apple pie, 143
lemony apple crumble tart, 139
pork in cider with potatoes and, 72
salad of winter fruit, 119
aubergine and tomato gratin, 63

B
bacon and Parmesan pancakes, 32
bananas, caramelized, 137
beans: beef and ale pâté, 24
a big pot of cassoulet, 80
chili with all the trimmings, 75
Mexican pork and beans, 74
smoked haddock and bean soup, 20
smoky hotpot of great northern beans, 70
smoky sausage and bean casserole, 81
beef: beef and ale pâté, 24
beef en croûte, 46
boeuf bourguignon, 72
chili with all the trimmings, 75
Languedoc beef stew, 69
meatballs in red pepper sauce, 44
perfect roast fillet of beef, 94
pot roast brisket with red wine, 93
roast beef with winter vegetables, 93
roast fillet of beef, 94
steak and wild mushroom pies, 57
beetroot: beetroot and caraway dip, 27
beetroot, goats' cheese and pine nut salad, 116
roast beetroot, 112
Bellini, 168
biscuits, 124–7
black Russian, 171
black velvet, 170
blackberries: brioche pudding with, 149
classic blackberry and apple crumble, 146
bloody Mary, mulled, 163
blueberries: apple and blueberry tarts, 140
baked Granny Smith and blueberry pudding, 148
boeuf bourguignon, 72
bourbon: egg nog, 158
New Orleans sazarac, 173
brandy cocktails, 169, 170
brioche pudding with blackberries, 149
broccoli, pasta with ricotta, walnuts and, 51
brown cow, 172
brownies, triple chocolate, 129
Brussels sprouts with pancetta and chestnuts, 108
buttermilk mash, 103
butternut squash: butternut squash with pistou, 113
roasted butternut squash and pancetta salad, 121
roasted butternut squash risotto, 84
spaghetti with sage, pecorino and, 53

C
cabbage: potato, bacon and Savoy cabbage soup, 17
Savoy cabbage with bacon and cream, 109
cakes, 131–4
Campari fizz, 168
caramel custard, 154
carrots: carrot and lentil soup, 15
carrots with cream and herbs, 106
spiced carrot dip, 27
spicy carrot and chickpea tagine, 78
Vichy carrots with fresh ginger, 106
cassoulet, 80
cauliflower: cauliflower and Swiss chard salad, 119
cauliflower gratin, 111
creamy cauliflower and Gruyère soup, 14
with garlic and anchovies, 109
with red pepper and peas, 110
celeriac: celeriac rösti, 41
roast onion and celeriac ravioli, 50
champagne cocktails, 168–70
cheese: baked spinach mornay, 115
cauliflower gratin, 111
creamy cauliflower and Gruyère soup, 14
harissa-spiced chickpeas with halloumi, 61
mini croque-monsieurs, 33
mountain eggs, 64
Parmesan aïoli, 28–9
Parmesan and bacon pancakes, 32
Parmesan and rosemary wafers, 22
pasta with broccoli, ricotta and walnuts, 51
polenta baked with Italian sausage and, 43
potato and Parmesan tart, 59
pumpkin and Gorgonzola risotto, 83
salad of winter fruit with blue cheese, 119
smoked trout rarebit, 34
Swiss chard, feta cheese and egg pie, 54
Taleggio and potato tortilla, 64
tomato and aubergine gratin, 63
trio of honey-baked Camembert, 25
warm cheese scones, 27
see also goats' cheese
cherries: sticky marzipan and cherry loaf, 131
chestnuts: chestnut and Puy lentil soup, 10–11
coffee and chestnut roulade, 153
lamb tagine with, 77
parsnip, chorizo and chestnut soup, 18
slow-cooked Brussels sprouts with, 108
chicken: chicken jalfrezi, 45
chicken, leek and tarragon pot pie, 56–7
chicken, raisin and chilli salad, 117
coq au vin, 82
country chicken, 85
poulet sauté au vinaigre, 39
quick Thai chicken curry, 45
roast chicken with bay leaves, 97
chickpeas: chickpea salad, 120
classic lamb, chickpea and lentil soup, 16
harissa-spiced chickpeas, 61
roasted early autumn vegetables with, 115
spicy carrot and chickpea tagine, 78
chillies: candied bird's eye chillies, 154
chili with all the trimmings, 75
chocolate: chocolate and Cabernet pots, 154
chocolate brandy cake, 132
chocolate chilli truffles, 154
coffee, macadamia and white chocolate chunk cookies, 127
cranberry and cherry Florentines, 127
Mexican chocolate, 167
spiced white chocolate, 162
triple chocolate brownies, 129
chorizo, parsnip and chestnut soup, 18
Christmas milk, 166
Christmas mini-muffins, 131
cider: hot rum and cider punch, 165
mulled cider, 158
slow-cooked onion and cider soup, 13
clafoutis, rhubarb, 153
cocktails, 168–9
cod: chunky fish stew, 49
coffee: coffee and chestnut roulade, 153
coffee and walnut cake, 133
coffee, macadamia and white chocolate chunk cookies, 127
egg-nog latte, 162
mocha maple coffee, 161
pumpkin latte, 162
really good coffee, 161
vodka espresso, 171
colcannon, kale, 42
coq au vin, 82
country chicken, 85
couscous, 71, 77
cranberries: Christmas mini-muffins, 131
cranberry and cherry Florentines, 127
individual caramelized pear and cranberry tarts, 139
vodka cranberry floaters, 172
croissant pudding, fig and honey, 149
croque-monsieurs, mini, 33
croquettes, potato and parsnip, 28
crumbles, 144–6
crumpets, 129
curries, 45, 60
custard, caramel, 154

D
dates: baked apples with, 151
sticky date flaky tarts, 136
dips, trio of vegetable, 26–7
drinks, 157–73
duck: a big pot of cassoulet, 80
smoked duck, mandarin and pecan salad, 117
dukkah, 23

E
eggs: egg, bacon and spinach pie, 55
egg nog, 158
egg-nog latte, 162
mountain eggs, 64
Taleggio and potato tortilla, 64
see also omelettes

F
fennel: apple and fennel puddings, 90
monkfish, fennel and saffron bourride, 19
fig and honey croissant pudding, 149
fish stew with cheese toasts, 49
French fries, 105
fruit crumble, mulled winter, 145

G
garlic sautéed green beans, 115
ginger: ginger and cinnamon biscuits, 124
gingerbread mini-muffins, 130
gooseberry and ginger wine crumble, 144
pear and ginger crumble cake, 134
stem ginger biscuits, 125
glögg, 160
goats' cheese: beetroot, goats' cheese and pine nut salad, 116
leek and walnut tart, 58
gooseberry and ginger wine crumble, 144
gratins, 63, 104, 111
gravy, 40, 95
green beans, garlic sautéed, 115
greens, wilted, 112
Guinness: black velvet, 170

H I
ham: baked and glazed ham, 97
mini croque-monsieurs, 33
mountain eggs, 64
harissa potatoes, 105
harissa-spiced chickpeas, 61
hazelnuts: dukkah, 23
honey baba, 165
hot toddy, 173
iced star biscuits, 126
Italian-style roast pork, 88

K L
kale colcannon, 42
Kalúa: brown cow, 172
lamb: classic lamb, chickpea and lentil soup, 16
lamb tagines, 76, 77
Portuguese lamb stew, 68
pot roast leg of lamb, 95

roasted rack of lamb, 96
Languedoc beef stew, 69
latte, 162
leeks: chicken, leek and tarragon pot pie, 56–7
goats' cheese, leek and walnut tart, 58
leek and potato soup, 21
lemony apple crumble tart, 139
lentils: carrot and lentil soup, 15
chestnut and Puy lentil soup, 10–11
classic lamb, chickpea and lentil soup, 16
pan-fried tuna steaks, 47
spiced tomato and lentil salad, 120
lettuce: petit pois à la Française, 106

M

malted milk, 165
marzipan and cherry loaf, 131
meatballs in red pepper sauce, 44
Mexican chocolate, 167
Mexican pork and beans, 74
milk drinks, 162–7, 172
mimosa, 168
mocha maple coffee, 161
monkfish: monkfish, fennel and saffron bourride, 19
roast monkfish with pancetta, 99
mountain eggs, 64
muffins, 130–1
mulled bloody Mary, 163
mulled cider, 158
mulled winter fruit crumble, 145
mushrooms: baked mushrooms with Manchego béchamel, 30
mushroom and thyme ragù, 52
mushroom, Cognac and cream risotto, 85
mushroom soup with Madeira, 21
mushrooms marinated with raisins, 107
steak and wild mushroom pies, 57

N O

New Orleans sazarac, 173
nuts, oven-roasted spiced, 22
omelettes: smoked salmon and chive soufflé omelette, 35
spicy potato omelette, 65
onions: crispy onion rings, 28–9
roast onion and celeriac ravioli, 50
slow-cooked onion and cider soup, 13
oranges: caramel oranges, 136
orange-mulled wine, 158
smoked duck, mandarin and pecan salad, 117

P

pancakes: fluffy potato pancakes, 34
Parmesan and bacon pancakes, 32
pancetta: roasted butternut squash and pancetta salad, 121
Savoy cabbage with bacon and cream, 109
slow-cooked Brussels sprouts with, 108
Parmesan and bacon pancakes, 32
Parmesan and rosemary wafers, 22
parsnips: parsnip, chorizo and chestnut soup, 18
potato and parsnip croquettes, 28
roasted parsnip and garlic dip, 27
pasta: mushroom and thyme ragù, 52
roast onion and celeriac ravioli, 50
spaghetti with butternut squash, 53
with broccoli, ricotta and walnuts, 51
pâté, beef and ale, 24
peaches: Bellini, 168
pears: individual caramelized pear and cranberry tarts, 139
pear and almond tart, 135
pear and ginger crumble cake, 134
pickled pears, 27
poached pear tiramisù, 150
roast pears with sweet wine, 152
winter-spiced salad, 118
peas: petit pois à la Française, 106
pecan nuts: roast pumpkin and pecan pie, 142
peppers: chili with all the trimmings, 75
meatballs in red pepper sauce, 44
pesto, 31, 50, 63
petit pois à la Française, 106
pheasant breasts, roasted, 98
pies: chicken, leek and tarragon pot pie, 56–7
dusky apple pie, 143
egg, bacon and spinach pie, 55
steak and wild mushroom pies, 57
Swiss chard, feta cheese and egg pie, 54
pine nut biscuits, snowy, 125
pistou, butternut squash with, 113
plums: baked plums in puff pastry, 141
plum and hazelnut pandowdy, 146
polenta: baked with Italian sausage and cheese, 43
herby sausages on polenta, 40
pomme purée, 104
pork: Italian-style roast pork, 88
Mexican pork and beans, 74
pork in cider, 72
pork loin roasted with rosemary and garlic, 89
roasted pork with apple and fennel puddings, 90
sage pork chops, 42
sticky pork fillet, 38
Portuguese lamb stew, 68
potatoes: buttermilk mash, 103
celeriac rösti, 41
creamy potato gratin, 104
crispy oven wedges, 31
crunchy roast potatoes, 102
fluffy potato pancakes, 34
French fries, 105
harissa potatoes, 105
kale colcannon, 42
leek and potato soup, 21
mountain eggs, 64
mustard mash, 38
perfect mashed potatoes, 103
pomme purée, 104
pork in cider with apples and, 72
potato and Parmesan tart, 59
potato and parsnip croquettes, 28
potato, bacon and Savoy cabbage soup, 17
shoestring potatoes, 105
smashed roast new potatoes, 102
spicy potato omelette, 65
Taleggio and potato tortilla, 64
poulet sauté au vinaigre, 39
prosciutto, roasted salmon wrapped in, 99
prunes: apple, prune and Armagnac filo crumble, 144
pumpkin: pumpkin and Gorgonzola risotto, 83
pumpkin latte, 162
pumpkin soup with honey and sage, 11
red curry of roasted autumn vegetables, 60
roast pumpkin and pecan pie, 142
punch, hot rum and cider, 165

R

ravioli, roast onion and celeriac, 50
rhubarb clafoutis, 153
risotto, 83–85
rösti, celeriac, 41
roulade, coffee and chestnut, 153
rum: hot buttered rum, 165
hot rum and cider punch, 165

S

saffron: saffron milk, 167
Swedish saffron cake, 133
sage pork chops, 42
salads, 116–21
salmon: herb and nut crusted fillets, 49
roasted salmon wrapped in prosciutto, 99
sandwiches: mini croque-monsieurs, 33
sausages: a big pot of cassoulet, 80
herby sausages on polenta, 40
polenta baked with Italian sausage, 43
sausages with celeriac rösti, 41
smoky sausage and bean casserole, 81
Savoy cabbage with bacon, 109
scones, warm cheese, 27
sesame seeds: dukkah, 23
shoestring potatoes, 105
smoked duck, mandarin and pecan salad, 117
smoked haddock and bean soup, 20
smoked salmon: fluffy potato pancakes with, 34
smoked salmon and chive soufflé omelette, 35
smoked trout rarebit, 34
smoky hotpot of great northern beans, 70
snowy pine nut biscuits, 125
soups, 10–21
spaghetti with butternut squash, 53
spelt toasts, 26
spinach: baked spinach mornay, 115
egg, bacon and spinach pie, 55
harissa-spiced chickpeas with, 61
salad of winter fruit with, 119
squash *see* butternut squash
steak and wild mushroom pies, 57
stews, 68–82
Swedish saffron cake, 133
sweet potatoes with thyme and chilli, 111
Swiss chard: cauliflower and Swiss chard salad, 119
Swiss chard, feta cheese and egg pie, 54

T

tagines, 76–9
Taleggio and potato tortilla, 64
tarts: apple and blueberry, 140
caramelized pear and cranberry, 139
goats' cheese, leek and walnut, 58
lemony apple crumble, 139
pear and almond, 135
potato and Parmesan, 59
real treacle tart, 137
roast pumpkin and pecan pie, 142
sticky date flaky tarts, 136
tea, spiced, 161
teacakes, toasted, 128
tiramisù, poached pear, 150
toasts, spelt, 26
tomatoes: mulled bloody Mary, 163
poulet sauté au vinaigre, 39
roasted tomato soup, 12
spiced tomato and lentil salad, 120
tomato and aubergine gratin, 63
tortilla, Taleggio and potato, 64
treacle tart, 137
trio of honey-baked Camembert, 25
truffles, chocolate chilli, 154
tuna steaks, pan-fried, 47
turkey with lemon and herb stuffing, 91
Turkish chocolate, 169

V

vegetables: roast beef with winter vegetables, 93
roasted early autumn vegetables, 115
spicy red vegetable soup, 14
trio of vegetable dips, 26–7
vegetable ragù, 71
winter vegetable gratin, 63
winter vegetable tagine, 79
Vichy carrots, 106
vodka: cocktails, 171–2
mulled bloody Mary, 163

W Y

walnuts: coffee and walnut cake, 133
goats' cheese, leek and walnut tart, 58
pasta with broccoli, ricotta and, 51
whisky: hot toddy, 173
white Russian, 171
wine: glögg, 160
orange-mulled wine, 158
winter-spiced salad, 118
winter vegetable gratin, 63
winter vegetable tagine, 79
Yorkshire puddings, herbed, 94

recipe credits

GHILLIE BASAN

chickpea salad with onions and paprika
classic lamb tagine with almonds, prunes and apricots
classic lamb, chickpea and lentil soup with cumin
lamb tagine with chestnuts, saffron and pomegranate seeds
plain, buttery couscous
spicy carrot and chickpea tagine with turmeric and coriander
spicy potato omelette

FIONA BECKETT

boeuf bourguignon
chestnut and puy lentil soup with celeriac cream
chocolate and cabernet pots
coq au vin
cranberry and cherry Florentines
crunchy roast potatoes
egg nog
ginger and cinnamon biscuits
Italian-style roast pork with white wine, garlic and fennel
Languedoc beef stew with red wine, herbs and olives
mulled cider
orange-mulled wine
pomme purée
pot roast brisket with red wine
pumpkin soup with honey and sage
roast fillet of beef with soy and butter sauce
roast monkfish with pancetta, rosemary and red wine gravy
roast pears with sweet wine, honey and pine nuts
roast pumpkin and pecan pie
smoked duck, mandarin and pecan salad with pinot noir dressing

SUSANNAH BLAKE

coffee and chestnut roulade
coffee and walnut cake
coffee, macadamia and white choc chunk cookies
mini croque-monsieurs
Parmesan and bacon pancakes with chive butter
smoked trout rarebit
stem ginger biscuits
sticky marzipan and cherry loaf
toasted teacakes

MAXINE CLARK

a big pot of cassoulet
apple, prune and Armagnac filo crumble
chocolate chilli truffles
classic blackberry and apple crumble
dukkah
fluffy potato pancakes with smoked salmon
glögg
goats' cheese, leek and walnut tart
gooseberry and ginger wine crumble
herb- and nut-crusted salmon fillets
lemony apple crumble tart
Mexican pork and beans in red chilli sauce
mulled winter fruit crumble
mushroom, cognac and cream risotto
oven-roasted spiced nuts
perfect mashed potatoes
perfect roast fillet of beef with herbed Yorkshire puddings
petits pois à la Francaise
plum and hazelnut pandowdy
polenta baked with Italian sausage and cheese
pork loin roasted with rosemary and garlic
pot roast leg of lamb with rosemary and onion gravy
potato and parmesan tart
real treacle tart with caramelized bananas
really good coffee
smoked salmon and chive soufflé omelette
spiced tea
steak and wild mushroom pies
sticky date flaky tarts with caramel oranges
tomato and aubergine gratin with tomato and chilli pesto
vichy carrots with fresh ginger

LINDA COLLISTER

chocolate brandy cake
Christmas mini-muffins
gingerbread mini-muffins
iced star biscuits
Swedish saffron cake
triple chocolate brownies

ROSS DOBSON

apple and blueberry tarts
baked brioche pudding with blackberries
baked Granny Smith and blueberry pudding
baked mushrooms with Manchego béchamel
baked spinach mornay
buttermilk mash
carrot and lentil soup
cauliflower and Swiss chard salad
chicken, leek and tarragon pot pie
creamy cauliflower and Gruyere soup
crispy onion rings with Parmesan aïoli
crispy oven wedges with home-made pesto sauce
dusky apple pie
egg, bacon and spinach pie
fig and honey croissant pudding
mushroom and thyme ragù with hand-torn pasta
pasta with broccoli, walnuts and ricotta
pear and ginger crumble cake
poached pear tiramisù
potato and parsnip croquettes
pumpkin and Gorgonzola risotto
red curry of roasted autumn vegetables
roast beef with winter vegetables and garlic crème
roasted early autumn vegetables with chickpeas
roasted pork with apple and fennel puddings
roasted tomato soup with rarebit toasts
sage pork chops with kale colcannon
salad of winter fruit with blue cheese and spinach
sausages with celeriac rösti
slow-cooked Brussels sprouts with pancetta and chestnuts
slow-cooked onion and cider soup with Gruyere toasts
smashed roast new potatoes
smoky hotpot of great northern beans
smoky sausage and bean casserole
spaghetti with butternut squash, sage and pecorino
spiced cauliflower with red peppers and peas
spicy red vegetable soup
Swiss chard, feta cheese and egg pie
taleggio and potato tortilla with red pepper tapenade
trio of vegetable dips with spelt toasts
vegetable ragù with spiced couscous
winter vegetable gratin
winter vegetable tagine with apple and mint

LYDIA FRANCE

snowy pine nut biscuits
trio of honey-baked camembert with calvados and herbs
warm cheese scones with Cheddar and pickled pears

LIZ FRANKLIN

chicken, raisin and chilli salad with hazelnut dressing
mushrooms marinated with raisins and apple cider vinegar
pan-fried tuna steaks with warm vincotto-dressed lentils
poulet sauté au vinaigre
roast onion and celeriac ravioli with warm walnut pesto
roasted butternut squash and pancetta salad with pumpkin oil and mixed spice dressing
sticky pork fillet with pecorino crust, mustard mash and balsamic onion

MANISHA GAMBHIR HARKINS

Mexican chocolate with vanilla cream
spiced tomato and lentil salad

TONIA GEORGE

herby sausages on polenta with red onion and redcurrant gravy
leek and potato soup
monkfish, fennel and saffron bourride
mushroom soup with Madeira and hazelnuts
parsnip, chorizo and chestnut soup
potato, bacon and Savoy cabbage soup
smoked haddock and bean soup
winter-spiced salad with pears, honeyed pecans and ricotta

KATE HABERSHON

crumpets

CAROLINE MARSON

baked apples with dates and sticky toffee sauce
chunky fish stew with cheese toasts
harissa-spiced chickpeas with halloumi and spinach
individual caramelized pear and cranberry tarts
quick Thai chicken curry
roasted butternut squash risotto

LOUISE PICKFORD

Campari fizz
Christmas milk
egg-nog latte
French fries
honey baba
hot buttered rum
hot rum and cider punch
malted milk
mimosa
mocha maple coffee
mulled bloody mary
pumpkin latte
saffron milk
spiced white chocolate

BEN REED

bellini
black Russian
black velvet
brandy alexander
Champagne cocktail
hot toddy
New Orleans sazarac
Turkish chocolate
vodka espresso
white Russian

FIONA SMITH

beef and ale pâté

SONIA STEVENSON

roast turkey with lemon and herb stuffing

FRAN WARDE

baked and glazed ham
beef en croûte with mustard sauce
beetroot, goats' cheese and pine nut salad with melba toasts
chicken jalfrezi
country chicken
garlic sautéed green beans
mountain eggs
Parmesan and rosemary wafers
roasted pheasant breasts with bacon, shallots and mushrooms
roasted rack of lamb with a spicy crust
roasted salmon wrapped in prosciutto
vodka cranberry floaters

LAURA WASHBURN

baked plums in puff pastry with crème fraîche
butternut squash with pistou
caramel custard
carrots with cream and herbs
cauliflower gratin
cauliflower with garlic and anchovies
chili with all the trimmings
creamy potato gratin
harissa potatoes
meatballs in red pepper sauce
pear and almond tart
pork in cider with potatoes and apples
Portuguese lamb stew with piri piri
rhubarb clafoutis
roast beetroot
roast chicken with bay leaves, thyme and lemon
savoy cabbage with bacon and cream
sweet potatoes with thyme and chilli
wilted greens

photography credits

KEY: a=above, b=below, r=right, l=left, c=centre.

MARTIN BRIGDALE

pages 1, 32, 33r, 34, 58l, 59, 73, 77, 78l, 91, 97b, 104b, 105b, 122, 125, 128 both, 131l, 132r, 135a, 136a, 137l, 137br, 139, 153, 154l

DAVID BRITTAIN

pages 70a, 130

PETER CASSIDY

pages 2, 4l, 8, 10, 11, 16l, 24, 36, 43r, 48, 50a, 61r, 65, 66, 67ac, 76r, 84, 86, 87ac, 89al, 92, 94, 119r, 120 both, 124r, 127, 138, 141bl, 142, 143l, 144, 145b, 146, 147, 150b, 151a, 152, 157al, 157ar, 158 both, 159, 167r

JEAN CAZALS

page 25r

CHRISTOPHER DRAKE

pages 85b (interior designer Carole Oulhen/+ 33 6 80 99 66 16), 109r

RICHARD JUNG

pages 9ar, 9b, 12, 13r, 14, 15, 26, 29, 30, 31a, 38, 39r, 41, 42, 47, 50b, 51, 52, 53 both, 54ar, 54b, 55, 56l, 58ar, 60l, 62, 64r, 70b, 71, 78r, 79, 81r, 83 both, 90, 93, 100, 101ac, 102, 107 main, 108b, 110, 114, 117, 119l, 121, 123a all, 134, 140, 143r, 148, 149, 150a

SANDRA LANE

pages 25al, 43l, 67ar, 95b, 96al, 97l, 98ar, 107 inset, 112al, 124l, 135b, 166al, 166ac, 169b both

TOM LEIGHTON

page 13l

WILLIAM LINGWOOD

pages 23r, 25bl, 35, 40r, 46, 58br, 69, 80, 82, 88b, 99, 101al, 104a, 154r, 155l, 156, 161r, 162 both, 163r, 164, 165 both, 166ar, 167l, 168 both, 169a, 170, 171 both, 173 both

JASON LOWE

page 85a

JAMES MERRELL

endpapers, 16r, 18l, 61l, 88a, 103a, 145a, 151b

DAVID MONTGOMERY

pages 141al

DAVID MUNNS

pages 44, 68a, 75, 105a, 111a, 112ar, 112b, 113, 141r

NOEL MURPHY

pages 9al, 22r, 23l, 57, 74, 81l, 95a, 103b, 106, 155r, 160l, 161l

WILLIAM REAVELL

pages 40l, 118, 126, 129, 131r, 132l, 133

YUKI SUGIURA

pages 17, 18r, 19, 20, 21

DEBI TRELOAR

pages 3, 5, 6, 9ac, 22l, 28, 31b, 33l, 37al, 37ac, 37b, 39l, 45, 60r, 64l, 67al, 67b, 68b, 76bl, 87al, 87ar, 87b, 89bl, 89r, 96bl, 96r, 98al, 98b, 101ar, 101b, 111b, 115, 116 both, 157b, 172

CHRIS TUBBS

pages 4r (Emily Todhunter/www.todhunterearle.com), 37ar, 49, 160r, 163l

JO TYLER

pages 76al, 123b, 136b, 166b

ALAN WILLIAMS

pages 109l, 157ac

ANDREW WOOD

page 108a (Mark Pynn/www.sunvalleyarchitect.com)

POLLY WREFORD

pages 54al, 137ar

SEASON 3

TEAMMATE

TEAMMATE

TEAMMATE

TEAMMATE

TEAMMATES FIRST DRAFT

TEAMMATES FIRST DRAFT

TEAMMATES FIRST DRAFT

TEAMMATES FIRST DRAFT

DATE

CAPTAIN

SEASON 4

TEAMMATE

TEAMMATE

TEAMMATE

TEAMMATE

TEAMMATES FIRST DRAFT

TEAMMATES FIRST DRAFT

TEAMMATES FIRST DRAFT

TEAMMATES FIRST DRAFT

What makes this Bible study so different?

- Bridges the gap between hearing and applying God's Word
- Demonstrative approach to discipleship
- Streamlines foundational Biblical teachings into one course using masculine context
- Uncompromising Biblical teaching that challenges men to face truth head on
- Models the process of the struggle with sin and the pursuit of holiness
- Identifies Pain Points that lead to habitual sin patterns and addresses them in safe environment
- Externalizes the internal through personal exploration using God's Word as the "filter"
- Creates individual intrinsic motivation via personal application
- Makes Biblical principles visual – visible faith
- Addresses obedience barriers and solves them using Biblical principles
- Skill-based application for Biblical decisions in real-life situations
- Performance-based learning to assure mastery of Biblical application with confidence and courage
- Team-based to prevent isolation
- Interactive to captivate attention – active learning
- Direct experience for maximum processing of applying Biblical principles to assure retention
- Designed to become a foundational discipleship tool/staple for local churches and men
- Uses website for connectivity, support and training — overcoming geographical challenges
- Strategically designed for cyclical discipleship to fulfill The Great Commission
- Can be used as a man's ministry discipleship tool without the red tape of going through committees

BattleZONE Training Course

Requests for information should be addressed to: **BattleZONE Ministries**
2857 Beverly
Clovis CA. 93611
info@battlezoneministries.org

There are hundreds of Scripture verses throughout this course from various translations of the Holy Bible. Please note MSG, NLT and TLB ("The Message", "The New Living Translation" and "The Living Bible") are paraphrases, not actual interpretations. Each Scripture used will be identified as follows

Acknowledgements

This training course has been a work that revealed my weaknesses and demonstrated God's grace through me and those He sent to make this program glorifying to Jesus. This has been a 4-½ year journey and many people have sacrificed to make this work a reality. I would like to thank everyone who have given input, listened to my ideas and prayed for this ministry. I owe special gratitude to:

Jesus Christ for His love and patience with me as I wrestled with Him throughout this entire process. You are my strength in my weakness. May your name be glorified and receive all the praise for changing men's lives.

My Devoted Bride, Anastasia for willingly sacrificing with me and never ceasing to give encouragement, love and support; for your continued unselfish attitude to listen, read and add to this entire course; for your perseverance to give up the "knowing" of how we were going to feed Bethany and Caleb or pay the bills. God never let us down because of your faith. I love you Favorite.

Linda Regensburger for your selfless effort and willingness to dot every 'I' and cross every 't' in the final editing process. Thanks for accepting God's assignment. You made this course better in more ways than I can ever say.

David Gagné for your amazing gift of creativity. The graphic layout is amazing. I know that you would be the first to give the Creator the glory. Thanks for using your gifts for God's glory.

Mike Strmiska for your mentorship, encouragement, confidence and love. You are truly a Godsend.

Ed Dunn for your editing efforts and your continued enthusiasm for God's work in this course.

Linda Horton for using your gifts to edit the grammar and the structure of the course in the early stages. I love your book Time & Again. Keep on believing!

Paul Martin for your willingness to step up and review the course for Biblical accuracy when Randy Alcorn asked you. You are a man of God and I love you.

Michael Alfheim for your devotion to see God work in the lives of men and your commitment to step up as the first Certified BattleZONE Coach. You are a true friend, accountability partner and disciple-maker.

Greg Bradford for your belief in this ministry and making the first printing happen. You are a man of God. Thanks for blessing me as you have.

The Meyers family for stepping up in the beginning to encourage me and this faith venture and for your help in graphic revisions. You are true stewards.

Rod Handley for your willingness to help make this program consistent and pleasing to the Lord. Thanks, brother.

Dad for your love and devotion to me as your son. You were always there for me and you still continue to hug me and tell me that you love me. You are a great Dad and amazing grandfather. Thanks for helping me make this course better. I love you Dad!

BattleZONE
Ten Week Training Course

TABLE OF CONTENTS

		PAGE
Bible Translations		1
Acknowledgements		2
Intro		3-12
Pre-Season		13-20
eXecution Threshold (XT)	Week 1	21-42
Old vs. New Nature	Week 2	43-68
Oppositional Forces	Week 3	69-94
Jesus Christ...Lord and Savior	Week 4	95-118
God the Holy Spirit	Week 5	119-142
The "Holy Playbook"—The Bible	Week 6	143-168
Faithful Obedience, Love, The Whole Armor of God and Prayer	Week 7	169-192
God's Loving Grace and Mercy	Week 8	193-220
Godly Teammates	Week 9	221-242
Spiritual Fitness Training	Week 10	243-268
BattleZONE Glossary		268-274

STRAP IT ON & GET IN THE GAME!

Dear BattleZONE Participant:
God commands all Christians to pursue a holy life:

"You shall be holy as I am holy."
I Peter 1:15-16 - NASB

Holiness means to separate oneself from sin while pursuing conformity to Jesus Christ. BattleZONE is a ten-week hands-on course intended to engage you – as a man – to pursue conformity to Christ. By using sports, coupled with the Word of God, you will learn how to live a victorious life by abiding in Jesus Christ.

BattleZONE is designed to teach men how to apply God's Word in their daily lives. This is accomplished by using a format of one leader (Captain) to up to four men (Teammates). The interactive activities make this course both fun and practical and will help you apply the Scriptures directly to your personal area(s) of daily temptation. You will learn how to lead a Spirit-filled life, and by the grace of God, overcome your personal areas of temptation, making right decisions while in your respective BattleZONEs.

The goal of BattleZONE is to train, equip and multiply male disciples for Christ or as Jesus said,

"Go out and train everyone you meet, far and near, in this way of life, marking them by baptism in the threefold name: Father, Son, and Holy Spirit. Then instruct them in the practice of all I have commanded you. I'll be with you as you do this, day after day after day, right up to the end of the age."
Matthew 28:19-20 - MSG

"Christianity is an intimate growing relationship with the person of Jesus Christ. It is not a set of doctrines to believe, habits to practice or sins to avoid. Every activity God commands is intended to enhance His love relationship with His people. God instituted His commandments as a protection for those He loves, but the commandments can become a pathway to legalism rather than an avenue for a relationship with our Father in which He protects us from harm."
Henry T. Blackaby
& Richard T. Blackaby
"Experiencing God Day by Day"
©1997 Broadman & Holman Publishers

The BattleZONE training course has a track record of building an understanding of and ability to overcome temptations with practical tools and skills that will be demonstrated and practiced during the ten weeks as follows:

10 CAPACITIES YOU WILL ACHIEVE THROUGH THIS COURSE	TOOLS USED
1. Live an obedient life in Christ	God's Game Plan for Holiness/Victory
2. Identify patterns that lead to sin	Formation Recognition Form
3. Yield to the Holy Spirit when tempted	C3-Technique
4. Develop a game plan for temptation situations	Game Plan Execution System
5. Protect yourself from spiritual attacks	Pray on the Whole Armor of God
6. Apply what the Bible teaches immediately	R.I.P.L. Effect
7. Re-establish harmony with God after sinning	Pocket GRACE-Keeper
8. Ability to select Godly Teammates	Teammate Draft/Cut Form
9. Create a spiritual training program for holiness	Daily Practice Schedule
10. Confidence to become an active disciple-maker	Post-Season Captain Commitment

Men will understand how God intended men to use the Bible as His "Playbook" to overcome the challenges of this age, with the end result of focusing on Christ—not the sin that weighs us down.

By the blood of Jesus and power and presence of the Holy Spirit, I am confident that you will enjoy this unconventional men's Bible study and obtain the spiritual skills imperative to living a holy life for God.

In Christ,

Michael C. Pouliot

Michael C. Pouliot

INTRODUCTION to the BattleZONE

Get Real!
God set the standard for truth and He expects us to follow His lead. Yet many men find themselves in church, at work and even at home being someone they are not. If men in the church continue to put up a false front, how can truth prevail? This culture of false fronts and hiding creates a hardship for Christian men and discourages them from openly discussing their temptations and receiving encouragement and coaching from their brothers in Christ. The result is isolation, which leads to character deterioration, sin, and more isolation.

Today's performance-driven culture stresses image over authenticity. Most men find it hard to expose an external weakness, but that exposure pales in comparison to being transparent with their internal struggles. These internal flaws are compounded when it comes to our spiritual issues as Christians. How can a coach help an athlete if the athlete is hiding an internal condition that affects his performance?

So what should a man do when he is tempted to sin? Is he adequately coached in fundamental Biblical knowledge and skills to be able to overcome temptation, or does he rely on his own strength? Should he be given a booklet of advice and be sent back into the game, or be trained in how to apply God's Word?

Here's a radical statement: **God wants you to leverage your God-given masculinity and need for adventure to live with reckless abandon for Jesus Christ.** BattleZONE will help you understand what it will take in order for you to become an all-out Christ-follower – an all-star player on Christ's field of honor.

Christ-Followers?
The word Christian (literally, "Little Christ") has lost its impact because of misunderstanding, overuse, cults and religious zealots. The truth is that we are not called to be Christians or become super-religious; we are called to be **Christ-Followers.** We are called to **wholeheartedly follow Jesus Christ with a warrior–like vigor.**

A football team's conditioning will always be reflected in the fourth quarter. This is a great illustration of the Biblical truth that "we reap what we sow." Minimal anything produces minimal results. True believers are called to pursue holiness with reckless abandon and live all-out for Christ.

Football, Jesus and You
During any given weekend, more than 100 million Americans watch NFL games. More than 16 million attend at least one game a year. From January 1961 through August 31, 2002, 22 of the all-time, top-50 rated television programs were Super Bowls and one was an NFC Championship game, each drawing millions of viewers. During the 2001 season alone, 16,244,538 fans came to 248 NFL games at an average ticket cost of $50, resulting in well over $8 billion in ticket sales! More amazing is that college football draws even more fans than the NFL and has larger stadiums. The top-25 largest I-A stadiums hold over 2.2 million fans. Michigan Stadium holds the most with an incredible 107,501 seats! The popularity of football reaches far beyond the United States to the entire world. The fascination with American football is amazing, but even more phenomenal is that the NFL has only been around for just over 80 years.

No big surprise – men often use football as a catalyst for discussion because it creates a common bond anchored in masculinity. Millions of Americans fixate on football to get them through the week. Instant friendships happen because of common loyalties to college and NFL teams. So much hype, emotion and energy go into this great game, breeding generations of diehard fans. College and high school football, youth Pop Warner or Pee-Wee, fantasy football leagues, team paraphernalia, gambling, sports bars and tailgate parties provide an incredible backdrop to turn the focus from great football coaches and teams to the Greatest Coach that ever walked this earth – Jesus of Nazareth.

A Standard for Training
BattleZONE is a different kind of Bible study and discipleship program – it teaches men through real situational training activities. Many men are kinesthetic (physical) learners, and learn best by doing hands-on activities, as opposed to traditional isolated visual or auditory teaching methods.

Each day, Christian men have many opportunities to execute God's will, but very often, due to lack of effective training and understanding of God's "Game Plan", experience defeat, time and again. The game of football offers a tremendous context for Christ-Followers who want to follow their Coach. Just like real players on the field, we can train hard, study our playbook, assess our opponents, learn to rely on teamwork, hold game situation simulations, and execute all of the above activities when it really counts – on game day.

BattleZONE Training Program
BattleZONE prepares men by God's loving grace to execute His will through faith, and by the power of the Holy Spirit, experience holiness.

So What Exactly Is the BattleZONE?
The BattleZONE is that moment in time when temptation is staring you right in the face. In a split second, you must choose to either execute God's will through faith and avoid sin, or give in to temptation. Every Christian man is faced with hundreds of decision points each day and must train himself to continually choose obedience (which leads to life) and avoid disobedience (which leads to death). BattleZONE uses the gridiron analogy to create a competitive, hands-on approach to maximize your Christian walk by learning how to apply Biblical principles.

Jesus, the Head Coach
The human side of Jesus demonstrated the intense BattleZONE between His external temptation to disobey God the Father or execute His will through perfect obedience:

> *"My Father, if it is possible, take this cup of suffering away from me. But let what you want be done, not what I want."*
> Matthew 26:39b - NIRV

By using football as a metaphor for the Christian life, men will better understand this intense battle internally (mind, will and emotions) and externally (physical environment, Satan and people) during their decision points.

Called To Be Holy
BattleZONE trains Christian men to approach their quest for holiness like a football team prepares for the season. A football player must be physically fit to perform well on the gridiron; a Christian man must be spiritually fit to execute God's will in his personal BattleZONEs.

The goal is for you to experience holiness by abiding in Christ. BattleZONE has three major training themes that must be seen through the lens of God's loving grace in order for you to reach maximum spiritual fitness and ultimately experience holiness: faith, spiritual training and preparation, and the continual filling and guidance of the Holy Spirit.

- **Faith** is essential to our ability to trust God's loving grace and be obedient when facing our BattleZONEs. This willing obedience should come from love, not duty or guilt.

- **Spiritual Training** and preparation using the Bible as our Holy "Playbook" will establish the foundational knowledge, skills and practical applications for holiness, allowing us to know Jesus Christ's character, which renews our minds and actions.

- The continued **filling of and leading by the Holy Spirit** empowers, guides, warns and corrects us as we strive for holiness, while deepening our relationship with Jesus Christ.

Even though the primary concern is holiness through faithful obedience, you will learn it is imperative that you don't get caught up in the training, but in Jesus Christ Himself. BattleZONE does not encourage legalism through religious do's and don'ts, but strives to transform you into a compassionate warrior for Jesus by teaching you the doctrine of grace. You will learn that a correct view of sin coupled with God's loving grace is crucial to personal holiness. Focus on pleasing God, not achieving personal victory.

For the purposes of this course you will need to be familiar with the following terms:

BattleZONE = Decision point during temptation | Victory = Holiness | Execution = Faithful obedience
Spirit-Filled = In the zone | Execution is key to victory | Obedience is key to holiness
To reach the goal line is to experience holiness

The reason for engaging in a spiritual fitness program is to become spiritually fit, which ultimately allows you to abide in Christ and experience holiness. You will know you are spiritually fit by the evidence in your life. This is accomplished by using God's game plan for holiness.

10 KEY ELEMENTS TO GOD'S GAME PLAN FOR HOLINESS

1. Jesus Christ... Lord and Savior
2. The Holy Spirit
3. The Bible – God's "Holy Playbook"
4. Faithful obedience
5. Love
6. The whole armor of God
7. Prayer
8. God's loving grace and mercy
9. Godly teammates
10. Spiritual fitness training

EVIDENCE OF SPIRITUAL FITNESS

- **Deeper Love for God's Word** *Psalm 119:97*
- **Higher Obedience** *1 John 2:3-5*
- **Strong Biblical Maturity** *1 John 2:12-14*
- **Deeper Faith** *2 Thessalonians 1:2-3*
- **Greater Love for Others** *Philippians 1:9*

Course Highlights and Goals:

- As you tackle this course and understand Christ's loving grace, you will be encouraged to develop an individual game plan that assesses your strengths and weaknesses, and a detailed scouting report on your opponents.
- You will engage in Temptation-Specific Training in preparation for overcoming your personal BattleZONEs using God's "Game Plan".
- You will learn God's ten keys for victory/holiness by applying God's "Holy Playbook" and understand how to become a 3C-Christian.
- You will also learn how to study the "Holy Playbook" using the R.I.P.L. Effect and become a student of the "game."
- You will engage in a seven game season and learn how God's loving grace and mercy can be applied moment by moment.
- You will be asked to draft new "teammates" and to prayerfully cut those who hold you back in your quest for holiness.
- You will develop your own daily practice schedule to increase your spiritual fitness level week by week, strengthening your relationship with the Lord.
- Finally, you will draft your own team and set a kick-off date for post-season play.

Become a 3C-Christian

Experiencing holiness requires you become a 3C-Christian:

Conformed to the **C**haracter of **C**hrist.

Are You Willing to Pay the Price?
This is a battle and battles are bloody. BattleZONE is not for the half-hearted, but for those who want to "sell out" to truly train themselves unto holiness and become champions of Christ.

Are you ready to become the man God called you to be? It's hard work because you will be required to "lie out for the ball" and step out of your comfort zone, exposing your greatest temptations and innermost sin.

Many Christian men are "sucking wind" because of poor conditioning – living with Christ, not in Christ. It's time for men to understand God's "Game Plan" for victory and experience holiness as God intended for all of His children. Get ready for training camp and to be blessed as God's Word penetrates your heart like a blitzing linebacker. **Let the season begin!**

BattleZONE Poem

Two natures war inside my chest
This struggle within is my greatest test;
The fight rages — old vs. new
Forcing me to choose between the two.

Tempting my fleshly desires above all,
Satan will not rest until he sees me fall.
He laughs with delight with an evil grin,
He wants nothing more than for me to sin.

Too often the old nature comes out on top.
This must cease — Lord, please let it stop.
Christ's blood covers my sins forever
Does this mean I should go on sinning?
No, not ever.

Enough excuses —
I must not give in to temptation
But execute God's will without hesitation.
God's will alone brings true satisfaction
The nature I train will determine my reaction.

Praise God in heaven for His divine plan
Accomplishing so much by sending one Man.
Through discipline, obedience and God's loving grace
I must train unto holiness to win this race.

This intense struggle will never go away
But Jesus sent the Holy Spirit to help me obey.
Yes, the Spirit 's indwelling holds the key
By yielding to Him I am guaranteed victory.

By His Grace — For His Glory
by Michael Pouliot

About BattleZONE Ministries, Inc. & the BattleZONE Training Course

To find out more and take an experiential journey through BattleZONE, log on to **www.battlezoneministries.org**. There you'll find great assessment tools like the BattleZONE Challenge, video testimonials, Show Me How To videos, webinar teachings and much more.

While online be sure to fill out the "contact us" form – it only takes a minute. We want to know you!

Currently...
BattleZONE combines basic Christian spiritual training with a cyclical discipleship strategy designed to build and reproduce strong, effective disciples of Jesus Christ. BattleZONE Ministries helps churches develop male leadership by:

- Teaching men real-life application of the Bible ("Teach Me")
- Showing men what hands-on application looks like ("Show Me")
- Coaching men through practice in a safe environment ("Coach Me")
- Releasing men to apply Biblical principles under pressure ("Release Me")
- Reproducing men through cyclical discipleship ("Reproduce Me")

A Vision for the Future
The vision of BattleZONE Ministries is to coach every willing man to live victorious in Christ. The goal of BattleZONE is to train, equip and multiply effective disciples for Christ.

The BZ Performance-Based Training Model

TEACH ME – life application of God's Word

- Build a foundation of Biblical knowledge about how to live a Christ-like life and victoriously overcome temptations. (Matthew 7:24, 2 Timothy 4:2)
- Use God's Word through the power of the Holy Spirit to transform each man's heart so he sincerely desires to pursue personal holiness. (Romans 6:17)

SHOW ME – what the application looks like

- Provide each man with a visual reference of what Biblical essentials look like in action. (Exodus 18:20, Matthew 4:19)
- Build Christ-centered masculinity in each man using visual examples of Christian essentials. (2 Timothy 3:17)

COACH ME – practice new skills in a safe environment

- Offer each man a safe environment where he can practice these new skills. (Deuteronomy 8:5, 1 Timothy 4:7)
- Provide accountability to ensure that each man's new skills are demonstrated accurately. (Luke 6:40)

RELEASE ME – applying Biblical principles under real-life pressure

- Allow each man to apply Biblical principles in real-life pressure situations (family, work, church and friends). (Proverbs 23:12, 1 John 3:24)
- Develop Christlike character by growing transparent relationships with other brothers in Christ. (Proverbs 27:17, James 5:16)

REPRODUCE ME – make disciples

- Prayerfully select men who desire to pursue holiness and reproduce disciples of Jesus. (2 Timothy 2:2)
- Carry out a cyclical discipleship strategy to fulfill the Great Commission. (Matthew 28:19)

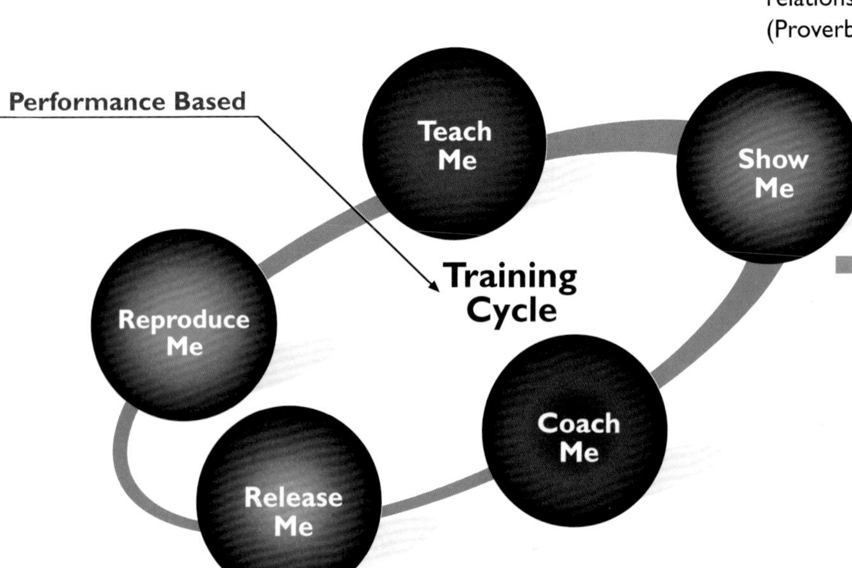

Why Do Men Like "Show Me How To's"?

Jesus Coached His Disciples

Jesus called out to them, "Come, be my disciples, and I will show you how to fish for people!"
Matthew 4:19 - NLT

Jesus showed his disciples how to do the things He did, including "fishing" for people to disciple.

Men Learn Best by Doing

Many men share a kinesthetic, or hands-on, learning style. Everything we are able to do today is because we have been taught, shown and coached.

BattleZONE Ministries is committed to showing men how to live victorious in Christ using video presentations that demonstrate the application of Biblical principles that most men only hear about—but never have scene demonstrated.

BattleZONE founder, Michael Pouliot, considered the various learning methods that use the kinesthetic training model and found that sports culture and apprenticeship training to become an electrician practice a similar model to the one Jesus used. Each uses variations of the BattleZONE Model for Discipleship; **teach me, show me, coach me, release me** and r**eproduce me.** Jesus' goal as he coached His disciples was for them to demonstrate – by their lifestyle – the teachings of the Word. They were to "DO THE WORD" under pressure, in everyday life situations.

Imagine a coach showing a quarterback how to throw a pass. The coach's goal is not to teach the player how to throw, but for the QB to be able to execute his teaching on the playing field under pressure. Jesus does not want us to simply know ***how*** to obey, but to study His teachings so we can ***do as He did*** to execute His will in real-life situations.

Throughout the BattleZONE Training Course you will see one of the many Show Me How To's that you can access on the BattleZONE website. These are free, so you can use them as personal growth tools, leadership resources or to view as a team during your BattleZONE Team Meetings.

Go to www.battlezoneministries.org > Training > Show Me How To

SHOW ME HOW TO PRAY WITH MEN

Go to www.battlezoneministries.org > Training > Show Me How To > Pray With Men

HOW TO VIDEO
How To
Pray With Men
David Murrow
"Why Men Hate Going To Church"

Prayer is a powerful way for men to connect with God. The Bible says that when two or more gather in God's name, He is there. Most men do not pray because they are uncomfortable trying to speak "Christainese" or "prayer-speak". Men also find it hard to ask for prayer in a group because it either takes too long or they feel uncomfortable and smothered. David Morrow, author of *Why Men Hate Going to Church*, shows us an alternative approach to the "prayer mushroom" called Prayer Force.

At BattleZONE Ministries...
We Show You How!

Prepare for a Battle!

When a football team is threatening to score, do their opponents ignore it? No! They dig in and fight tooth and nail to stop the other team from getting across the goal line.

Satan hates holiness. As a matter of fact, if you are a Christ-Follower he hates you. He especially hates your interest in spiritual fitness training. Satan wants to prevent you from experiencing holiness and will oppose you, your family and use people and circumstances in your life to discourage and defeat you. He will stop at nothing. He will send his evil teammates to make sure you never become Christlike. Satan roams around like a roaring lion seeking to devour men who will impact the Kingdom of God.

"Where have you come from?" the LORD asked Satan. And Satan answered the LORD, "I have been going back and forth across the earth, watching everything that's going on."
Job 1:7 - NLT

Count the Cost—Pay the Price

"And you cannot be my disciple if you do not carry your own cross and follow me. But don't begin until you count the cost."
Luke 14:27-28 - NLT

Athletes pay a price as they pursue greatness. Players make their mark on the gridiron not because they showed up on game day, but because they counted the cost and willingly chose – through blood, sweat and tears – to endure. NFL athletes who play on Sundays pay a price, just as it will cost you to become a true disciple of Jesus Christ.

When you determine to follow Christ in a wholehearted way, scripture promises that you will be persecuted. Not "may", but "will". However, we have another promise: God will give victory in the end.

You know how much persecution and suffering I have endured. You know all about how I was persecuted in Antioch, Iconium, and Lystra -- but the Lord delivered me from all of it.
2 Timothy 3:11 - NLT

The Perfect Plan—The Power of Prayer

Since Jesus paid the price in full, you must be prepared to endure the trials and temptations that will oppose you during the next 10 weeks. Be prepared for battle -- at home, at work, and in your ministry. When you chose to pursue Christlike character, you will meet serious resistance from the prince of this World (Satan), not to mention your sin nature and the World. This is a crucial battle, a battle for your soul, so you must have a team helping you cross the goal line.

There is one urgent requirement you must do prior to beginning the BattleZONE Training Course:

Recruit a team of people to faithfully pray and intercede for you daily

He will rescue us because you are helping by praying for us. As a result, many will give thanks to God because so many people's prayers for our safety have been answered.
2 Corinthians 1:11 - NLT

List at least three people below and/or a prayer team at your local church you will contact asking them to pray for you throughout the BattleZONE Training Course. Ask your wife, mom, or pastor to find your prayer team if you know you won't do it yourself. For a Microsoft Word Template, please email info@battlezoneministries.org and put "Prayer Team Recruitment Letter" in the "Re:" line of the email. See letter on the back of this page.

THIS IS A MUST! DO NOT TAKE THIS STEP LIGHTLY! JUST DO IT!

NAME:	EMAIL:	TEL:	ADDRESS:
1.			
2.			
3.			

BATTLE ZONE
MINISTRIES, INC.
We Show You How

Dear ________________________________

I have been invited to go through a men's spiritual training course called BattleZONE. This training will be challenging me to pursue a life of holiness. My first requirement for this course is to assemble a prayer team to commit to pray for me in this process as I allow God to mold me into a 3C-Christian (Conformed to the Character of Christ).

About BattleZONE
BattleZONE is designed to teach men how to apply God's Word in their daily lives. This is accomplished by using a format of one leader (captain) to up to four men (teammates). The interactive activities make this course both fun and practical and will help men apply the Scriptures directly to their personal area(s) of daily temptation. Men will learn how to lead a Spirit-filled life, and by the Grace of God, overcome their personal areas of temptation, making right decisions while in his respective BattleZONES.

The goal of BattleZONE is to train, equip and multiply male disciples for Christ or as Jesus said in *Matthew 28:19-20*:

"Go out and train everyone you meet, far and near, in this way of life,
marking them by baptism in the threefold name: Father, Son, and Holy Spirit.
Then instruct them in the practice of all I have commanded you.
I'll be with you as you do this, day after day after day, right up to the end of the age."

To find out more about BattleZONE Ministries go to **www.battlezoneministries.org**.

The Power of Prayer
Pray at all times and on every occasion in the power of the Holy Spirit. Stay alert and be persistent in your prayers for all Christians everywhere. (Ephesians 6:18 - NLT)

The author of the course is adamant about the necessity of each participant assembling a prayer team, so I am asking you to be part of my BattleZONE Prayer Team. Will you agree to pray on my behalf over the next 12 weeks? Please let me know if you could do this for me by phone or by email.

The best number to reach me is: ________________________________

My email is: ________________________________

If you agree to be on my prayer team, please pray for the following:

- God's protection over me, my family and my other relationships.
- God's guidance as I tackle my personal BattleZONEs.
- The captain/coach's faithfulness to remain diligent in his walk and preparation.
- God's clear guidance for who I am to disciple following the course.

Thank you for your consideration and your faithfulness to pray on my behalf.

In Pursuit of Holiness,

BattleZONE Pre-Season

- Pre-Season Captain's Guide
- Pre-Season Team Meeting #1 Overview
- Expectations/Confidentiality Agreement
- Captain Walk-Through
- Independent Practice

PRE-SEASON OBJECTIVES

Each man will:

1. Receive the BattleZONE training course materials.
2. Enjoy meeting each other, learning about one another, and sharing Jesus together.
3. Sign the Expectations/Confidentiality Form.
4. Establish a BattleZONE Prayer Team prior to beginning the training course.
5. Receive an overview of the BattleZONE spiritual training program.
6. Be able to demonstrate an understanding of the required independent practice materials (Plays).
7. Be able to demonstrate where the weekly Strength Training Cards are located.
8. Exchange contact information between teammates.

CAPTAIN'S TIP SHEET

This section is to assist the BattleZONE Captains as they lead their teammates through the BattleZONE Training Course.

OVERVIEW

Captains: Be sure to use the BattleZONE website (**www.battlezoneministries.org**) for resources to help equip you to be the best captain possible. We are here to serve you and help maximize your teaching skills. Also, you will find interactive tools, such as "Show Me How To" streaming video teachings, which will enrich the course, as well as downloadable forms and other course materials.

As a BattleZONE Captain, you should have already completed the BattleZONE Training Course, taken the online e-learning course or attended a weekend coaches' training camp. This strategy is crucial for you to be able to teach, and more importantly, demonstrate application skills through simulation training. The key to ongoing success is your ability to select men who will train and equip other men using BattleZONE to put the cyclical discipleship process in motion. You will learn the most by taking the role of a teacher or coach, so please encourage your men to start praying for those they will take through the course in the future. They will need to have their team drafted by Week 9.

Remember to register at **www.battlezoneministries.org** under **Coaches**.

The BattleZONE Training Course has both a "players" section and the "captain's" section each week. This is done purposefully to familiarize the "players" with the role of a "captain." The captain's section will always be bordered in gold to help you navigate each week. Remember as you train your men – they will be taking others through and any additional comments from your experiences will help equip them. Your "lens" should be one of training to release the men to train other men, not to just teach them the material.

The "players" section will be at the beginning of each week and bordered in burgundy to help them differentiate the sections. The players section will include the strength training cards, Plays, and worksheets. The strength training cards and worksheets can be downloaded at **www.battlezoneministries.org > Resources > BZ Course**.

Setting:
Where to hold BattleZONE sessions are important. Consider:

- Location: Choose a central location in someone's home, church or office boardroom.
- Confidentiality: Choose a place that is safe, secure and free from distraction. Men must feel safe.
- Time of day: If you choose to toss the football, make sure there is plenty of light and space.
- Duration: A typical session is normally one and a half to two hours long. We recommend two hours.

More Tips:

- The first meeting (Pre-Season) should be upbeat and friendly, setting the stage for men to have fun.
- Snacks are always a winner!
- Begin and close each session with prayer.
- Don't get caught up in philosophical debates... stick to what the Bible says.
- Stay focused and move the men through the materials. The "real" learning begins when the men lead.
- Pray for the meeting prior to each session.
- Pray for each man by name throughout the week.
- On occasion, one of the men may break down. When this occurs, stop, pray and encourage him, allowing the Holy Spirit to guide your decisions and prayers.
-  If a man misses a session, have him set up a make-up time with his Teammate/Captain. The Teammate/Captain is responsible to take him through the session before the next meeting.

REQUIRED:

BattleZONE PRAYER TEAM

Each man is REQUIRED to assemble a prayer team using the "Prepare for a Battle" directions on page 11 and the sample letter on page 12 in the Introduction section.

PRE-SEASON

1. Primary Purpose

The primary purpose for the Pre-Season meeting is to distribute the BattleZONE training course materials, do a walk-through and give men their Week 1 assignments.

2. Question Period

If you are able to toss footballs around, have the men partner up and play catch while you have them answer the following questions:

a. What is your favorite football team and personal football history?

b. What is your Christian history?

Captains, most training sessions will have a Warm-Up section. This will provide opportunities to prepare the men for the training session ahead.

3. Experiential Learning / Simulation Training

Tell the men that all sports teams do activities to develop specific skills such as tackling, throwing or catching. We will also do activities to help them grasp essential elements involved in a Christian's quest for holiness and purity. This is called "Experiential Learning" or Simulation-Training. You will engage the men through different exercises such as *Formation Recognition, Game Plan Execution System and Teammate Draft/Cut Forms.*

Simulations enable learning-by-doing, an approach that learning experts consider the fastest and most effective way for people to learn. People learn faster when trained using simulations because they are completely immersed in the skills, tasks or processes that they are trying to master.

4. Plays

Each Play is a method of instruction and learning that helps teammates read, prepare and present a one-page teaching on a biblical topic having to do with God's "game plan" for holiness. Four to five plays will be located at the beginning of every week. The men will be expected to read, take notes and answer the questions prior to each new training session.

The men are to take "ownership" to teach a "play" but since they never know which one you will assign them, they must be prepared to teach them all.

NOTE: As a captain, you will teach Play 1 in Week 1, so it is imperative that you model how to teach an effective play call with your men. To do so:

- Read the scripture verse out loud.
- Show the men where you highlighted, underlined or circled parts of the text that spoke to you and you wanted to share – don't assume that the men will mark up the text on their own – encourage them to do so. Let them know they will need to have reminders for when they "coach" a play or teaching.
- Read the "Highlights" out loud.
- Answer each question and facilitate brief discussion on each point.

5. Player Signing

Have the men sign the Expectations/Confidentiality Agreement Form on page 19, make a photo copy or carefully tear it out and turn into the Captain/Coach.

6. STRENGTH TRAINING CARDS

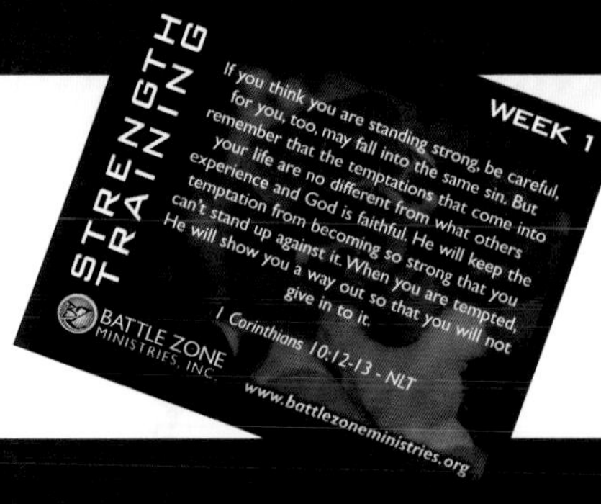

Show the men where the Strength Training Cards are located after the title page for each week. Have the men tear out , photocopy or print a full color version by going to **www.battlezoneministries.org > Resources > BZ Course > Strength Training**. Encourage the men to put the cards in a place where they will look at them regularly to read, think about and meditate on the scriptures. Start with Week 1 after the Pre-Season meeting. Don't pressure your men to memorize verses at this point – just to read and think about them.

7. BATTLEZONE SYMBOL KEY

These symbols will help you manage the course and keep your men engaged. However use your discretion – these are only suggestions.

Captain's Preparation

The Captain's Helmet symbol will prompt you to read a section. Rotation Reading will prompt you to have another teammate read a section, the Stop Watch will tell you the suggested time for a section, and the R.I.P.L. Effect will prompt you to use this Bible study skill. Please pay attention to the flow of the course. Work through the entire week's study prior to meeting with your men. How tragic would it be if a coach came to a football game completely unprepared? Likewise, preparation is essential to successfully coach men to be disciples of Christ. This preparation includes prayer, reviewing the material and taking notes. *We recommend that you start a new course each time you teach to keep you fresh.* The outline in the front of each week's materials corresponds with the "Captain's Guide" in the back. **However, it is more important to be sensitive to God's agenda. Prayerfully prepare your heart to know where God is leading each man during each session.**

8. COUNTER VERSES

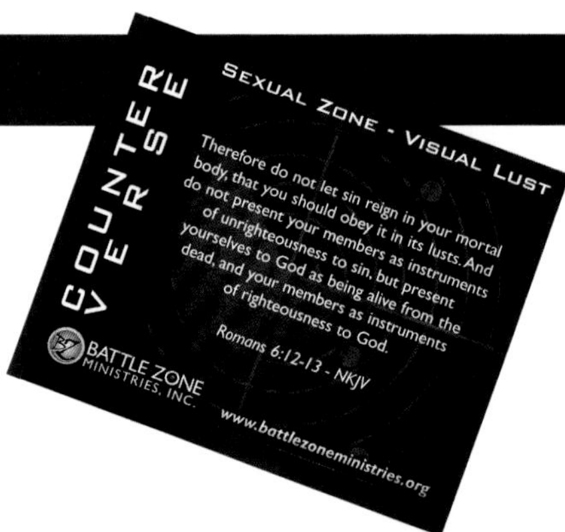

Beginning in Week 4, each player will be asked to progressively read and think about four or five scriptures or "counter verses" related with his personal BattleZONE. At the beginning of Weeks 5 through 10, he will engage in the "Two-Minute Drill" with his Teammate/Captain and recite the selected scriptures verbatim. He will then be given a score as a percentage based on his execution. He can create his own counter verses by going to **www.battlezoneministries.org** and from the Resources dropdown, open the Word document template. Then, use the link to Bible Gateway to find counter verses related to his BattleZONE and copy them into the counter verse template. This can be saved and changed or updated as often as needed.

9. CRUNCH TIME

Each week you will ask the men to describe one thing that really "hit" him during the practice session or the prior week.

10. INDEPENDENT PRACTICE

This section gives the players their weekly homework. Be purposeful about showing the men where the Independent Practice section is located, so if they forget their assignments, they will know where to look. This is the team's first assignment and it is vital that they complete them prior to Week 1.

11. Iron Sharpens Iron & BattleZONE Prayer Team

Captain for Week 1, demonstrate to the men what confessional prayer looks like. This is a time for prayer and confession. Each week we will end with a sacred time for confession either with your Teammate/Captain (TC) or as a team. This is a time to come clean of any sin you have in your life. Allow the Holy Spirit to search you and Christ's blood to cleanse you.

This section will slowly give the men an opportunity to confess their sins. It is vital that the Captain/Coach sets the pace each meeting. Next, ask for prayer requests and ask one person to pray for each situation and/or write them on the prayer request page on the Prayer Requests and Praises page located in the back of each week. If you choose to pray, for each prayer request, ask someone to pray out loud for the request so that every request is prayed for. You can also use the prayer request chart at the end of each week so you can come back to see how God answers prayer.

BattleZONE Prayer Team
Go over the BattleZONE Prayer Team **REQUIREMENT** pages located in the Introduction on pages 11 & 12. Make certain each man has a team praying for him separate from the men in the group.

Walk-Through

Captain, now is the time to do a hands-on walk-through to familiarize the men with the structure of the BattleZONE training course. Have the men turn to this page and then walk the men through the following in Week 1:

1. Week 1 Objectives
2. Strength Training Cards
3. Plays (explain their responsibility and encourage them to underline, highlight and/or circle important truths).
4. Pain Point page (encourage them to go to the BattleZONE website and take the BZ Challenge)
5. Personal Assessment Form for personal BattleZONEs
6. Captain's Guide (walk them through each component, including the prayer requests and praises)
7. Independent Practice
8. If you have access to a computer, take the men to the BattleZONE website and show them the following:
   a. BattleZONE Challenge b. Resources c. Show Me How To's d. Contact Us (encourage them to register)

Briefly review the Independent Practice section and then show the men Week 1 Plays. They will be responsible to read each Play and take notes using the Captain's Corner Personal Application page. Emphasize that they will not know which Play they will be responsible for until the training session, so each must be prepared to teach/discuss all of the Plays.

Explain what the process is if one of the men misses a training session.

Independent Practice: Ask your men to do the following before your next meeting:

1. **Read the Course Introduction** at the front of the BattleZONE Training Course manual.
2. **Visit the BattleZONE website** and **take the Bible Application Quotient (BAQ) Quiz** located under **Resources** at **www.battlezoneministries.org**.
3. **Read all five Plays** and be prepared to talk to the team, focusing on how God spoke to you as you read and meditated on His truths.
4. **Take the BattleZONE Challenge** on the website **www.battlezoneministries.org**. and either print out or e-mail the results to your Captain/Coach, and copy yourself. This will assist in the process of finding your Pain Points and BattleZONE(s).
5. **Read and think about** Week 1's Strength Training Cards as often as possible. They are located after the title page each week. Pg 23
6. **Call your Teammate/Captain (TC) at least once this week** and pray for him by name daily. Write down his name, phone number and email below:

#7. See page 11 — get prayer partners.

Teammate/Captain (T/C) NAME: ______________________

Phone:

Home: ______________ Office: ______________ Mobile: ______________

Email: ______________________________

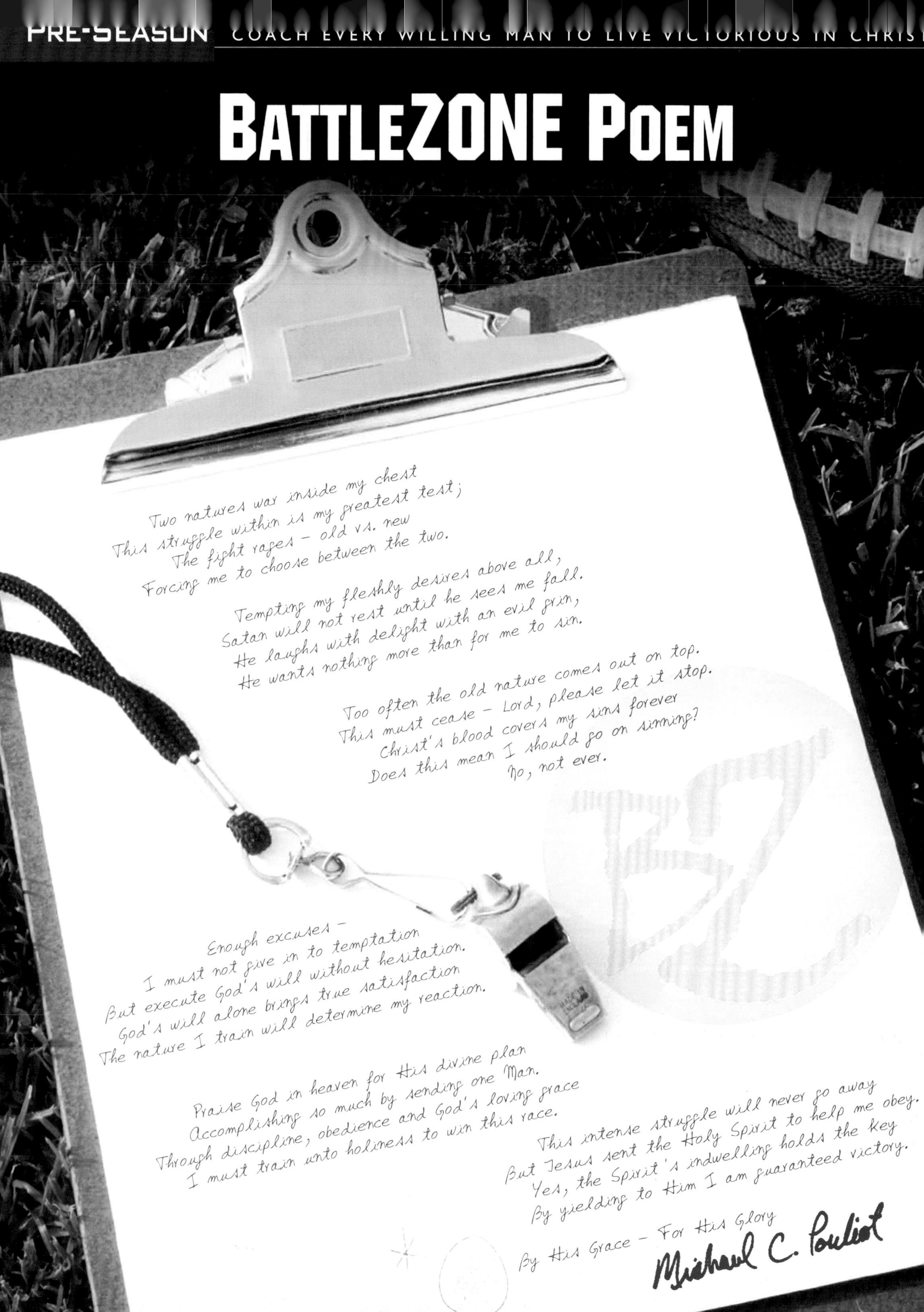
PRE-SEASON COACH EVERY WILLING MAN TO LIVE VICTORIOUS IN CHRIST
BATTLEZONE POEM
Two natures war inside my chest
This struggle within is my greatest test;
The fight rages – old vs. new
Forcing me to choose between the two.
Tempting my fleshly desires above all,
Satan will not rest until he sees me fall.
He laughs with delight with an evil grin,
He wants nothing more than for me to sin.
Too often the old nature comes out on top.
This must cease – Lord, please let it stop.
Christ's blood covers my sins forever
Does this mean I should go on sinning?
No, not ever.
Enough excuses –
I must not give in to temptation
But execute God's will without hesitation.
God's will alone brings true satisfaction
The nature I train will determine my reaction.
Praise God in heaven for His divine plan
Accomplishing so much by sending one Man.
Through discipline, obedience and God's loving grace
I must train unto holiness to win this race.
This intense struggle will never go away
But Jesus sent the Holy Spirit to help me obey.
Yes, the Spirit's indwelling holds the key
By yielding to Him I am guaranteed victory.
By His Grace – For His Glory
Michael C. Pouliot

eXecution Threshold (XT)

- BattleZONE Terms
- Holiness
- Temptation
- BattleZONE Diagram — Decision Point
- eXecution Percentage (X%) and, eXecution Threshold (XT)
- Pain Points

WEEK 1 OBJECTIVES

Each man will understand:

1. BattleZONE terminology and be able to apply the terms to Biblical principles.
2. The Biblical definition of holiness and what it means to him personally.
3. The Biblical definition of temptation and how it relates to sin and holiness in his life.
4. The BattleZONE concept as it relates to temptation and the decision point.
5. The concepts of eXecution Threshold/Percentage as they relate to obedience and sin.
6. The process of determining pain points, BattleZONEs and goals for this 10-week training course.

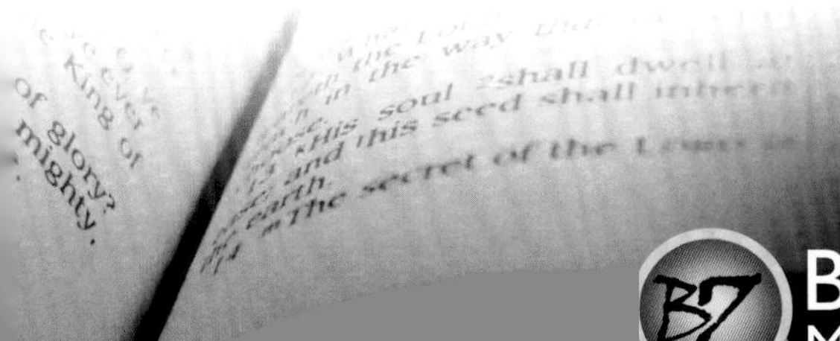

...Spend your time and energy in training yourself for spiritual fitness. Physical exercise has some value, but spiritual exercise is much more important, for it promises a reward in both this life and the next.

1 Timothy 4:7b-8 - NLT

If you think you are standing strong, be careful, for you, too, may fall into the same sin. But remember that the temptations that come into your life are no different from what others experience. And God is faithful. He will keep the temptation from becoming so strong that you can't stand up against it. When you are tempted, He will show you a way out so that you will not give in to it.

1 Corinthians 10:12-13 - NLT

But like the Holy One who called you, be holy yourselves also in all your behavior; because it is written, "You shall be holy for I am holy."

1 Peter 1:15-16 - NASB

When tempted, no one should say, "God is tempting me." For God cannot be tempted by evil, nor does he tempt anyone; but each one is tempted when, by his own evil desire, he is dragged away and enticed. Then, after desire has conceived, it gives birth to sin; and sin, when it is full grown, gives birth to death.

James 1:13-15 - NIV

"Therefore, come out from their midst and be separate," says the Lord. "and do not touch what is unclean; and I will welcome you."

2 Corinthians 6:17 - NASB

The old sinful nature loves to do evil, which is just opposite from what the Holy Spirit wants. And the Spirit gives us desires that are opposite from what the sinful nature desires. These two forces are constantly fighting each other, and your choices are never free from this conflict.

Galatians 5:17 - NLT

WEEK 1

STRENGTH TRAINING

....Spend your time and energy in training yourself for spiritual fitness. Physical exercise has some value, but spiritual exercise is much more important, for it promises a reward in both this life and the next.

I Timothy 4:7b-8 - NLT

BATTLE ZONE MINISTRIES, INC. www.battlezoneministries.org

WEEK 1

STRENGTH TRAINING

If you think you are standing strong, be careful, for you, too, may fall into the same sin. But remember that the temptations that come into your life are no different from what others experience. And God is faithful. He will keep the temptation from becoming so strong that you can't stand up against it. When you are tempted, He will show you a way out so that you will not give in to it.

I Corinthians 10:12-13 - NLT

BATTLE ZONE MINISTRIES, INC. www.battlezoneministries.org

WEEK 1

STRENGTH TRAINING

But like the Holy One who called you, be holy yourselves also in all your behavior; because it is written, "You shall be holy for I am holy."

I Peter 1:15-16 - NASB

BATTLE ZONE MINISTRIES, INC. www.battlezoneministries.org

WEEK 1

STRENGTH TRAINING

When tempted, no one should say, "God is tempting me." For God cannot be tempted by evil, nor does he tempt anyone; but each one is tempted when, by his own evil desire, he is dragged away and enticed. Then, after desire has conceived, it gives birth to sin; and sin, when it is full grown, gives birth to death.

James 1:13-15 - NIV

BATTLE ZONE MINISTRIES, INC. www.battlezoneministries.org

WEEK 1

STRENGTH TRAINING

"Therefore, come out from their midst and be separate," says the Lord. "and do not touch what is unclean; and I will welcome you."

2 Corinthians 6:17 - NASB

BATTLE ZONE MINISTRIES, INC. www.battlezoneministries.org

WEEK 1

STRENGTH TRAINING

The old sinful nature loves to do evil, which is just opposite from what the Holy Spirit wants. And the Spirit gives us desires that are opposite from what the sinful nature desires. These two forces are constantly fighting each other, and your choices are never free from this conflict.

Galatians 5:17 - NLT

BATTLE ZONE MINISTRIES, INC. www.battlezoneministries.org

NOTES

STRENGTH TRAINING

BATTLE ZONE MINISTRIES, INC. www.battlezoneministries.org

NOTES

STRENGTH TRAINING

BATTLE ZONE MINISTRIES, INC. www.battlezoneministries.org

NOTES

STRENGTH TRAINING

BATTLE ZONE MINISTRIES, INC. www.battlezoneministries.org

NOTES

STRENGTH TRAINING

BATTLE ZONE MINISTRIES, INC. www.battlezoneministries.org

NOTES

STRENGTH TRAINING

BATTLE ZONE MINISTRIES, INC. www.battlezoneministries.org

NOTES

STRENGTH TRAINING

BATTLE ZONE MINISTRIES, INC. www.battlezoneministries.org

BattleZONE Victories

Joe Fawcett
Plano, TX

I accepted Jesus Christ as my Savior on an October night in 1971, at the Billy Graham Crusade in Texas Stadium. It has taken me three decades and several years to finally realize that I truly must give God jurisdiction over every aspect of my life.

During those many tedious years of "playing church", I had never been through a discipleship program in a way that was either relevant to me or practical in its approach to and for men... until Michael took me through the "BattleZONE".

As the old cliché goes, "It's better late than never"; but it sure would've kept me out of a lot of messy defeats if I had known and used the BattleZONE's applications way back then! But thank God I am now applying them everyday and winning!

Upon completion of the ten-week course, I began to take two highly motivated men through the BattleZONE Training Course as a Certified BattleZONE Coach. I look forward to coaching many more men who are tired of the "same 'ol same 'ol" and who are now seriously ready to get into the game. Men who want to win at every aspect of the life God has so richly intended for them, and who want to disciple men with relevance and practicality.

PLAY 1 : Holiness

But like the Holy One who called you, be holy yourselves also in all your behavior; because it is written, "YOU SHALL BE HOLY, FOR I AM HOLY."

I Peter 1:15-16 - NASB

Holiness means to separate, or to be set apart. A linebacker is taught to create separation from a blocker so he can be in position to execute and make the tackle. God commands Christians to be separated from ungodliness so we can execute His perfect will.

Holiness is being fully devoted to God, set aside for God's special purpose and separated from the evils of this world. How do we do this? When we act according to God's moral commands and execute His will, we separate ourselves from the world. When we separate ourselves from the world, God can use us in a mighty way, but if we hold on to an unholy way of life, we will never experience holiness.

"Holiness…consists of that internal change of renovation of our souls whereby our minds, affections and wills are brought into harmony with God."

A.W. Pink — The Doctrine of Sanctification

(Swengel, Pennsylvania, Bible Truth Depot, 1955, pg. 25)

The word "holy" is found in the Bible more than 600 times; an entire book of the Bible (Leviticus) is devoted to the subject: "For I am the LORD your God. **You shall therefore consecrate yourselves, and you shall be holy; for I am holy.** Neither shall you defile yourselves with any creeping thing that creeps on the earth. For I am the LORD who brings you up out of the land of Egypt, to be your God. **You shall therefore be holy, for I am holy"** Leviticus 11:44-45 - NKJV.

We Must Abide or Remain in Christ

In football, a team's ability to remain ahead of their opponent results in victory. A Christian's ability to remain in Christ or be Spirit-filled, results in holiness, "If you keep My commandments, you will abide in My love, just as I have kept My Father's commandments and abide in His love." (John 15:10 NKJV). The word "abide" means to remain, and as God's men, we must train ourselves to abide in Christ. In order to abide in Him we must keep His commandments and be obedient (1 John 2:2-6). Jerry Bridges says, "Holiness is conformity to the character of God." We are to become what I call a "3C-Christian": Conformed to the Character of Christ.

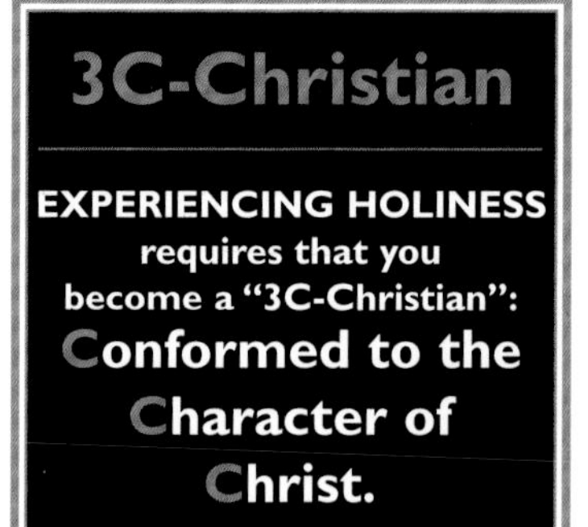

3C-Christian
EXPERIENCING HOLINESS
requires that you
become a "3C-Christian":
Conformed to the
Character of
Christ.

Pursuing Holiness

The book of Hebrews stresses the pursuit of holiness: "Pursue peace with all people, and holiness, without which no one will see the Lord" (Hebrews 12:14 NKJV). Pursuing something is an attitude combined with desire and constant action until one has reached the goal. The word pursue is a key word for reaching holiness, and this pursuit comes in the form of training. Spiritual training produces the ability to know and execute God's will. To pursue holiness, one must turn his back on sin and live by faith in the promises of Christ.

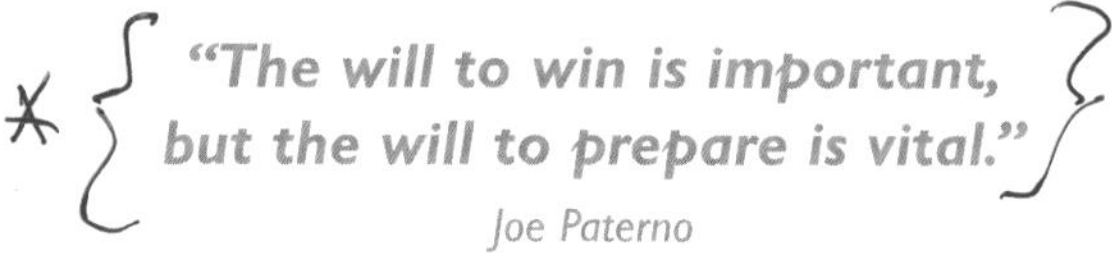

"The will to win is important, but the will to prepare is vital."

Joe Paterno

God Equips Us for Holiness

Just like football players are issued equipment to be effective on the gridiron, God gives each Christian the spiritual resources to be holy in the person of the Holy Spirit, God's loving grace, and the Holy Scriptures. We must train ourselves to use this "equipment" properly through prayer, worship, thoughts, actions, obedience and study.

We will only realize the Holy Spirit's power in our lives through our pursuit of and commitment to holiness. Remember: We are called to be holy in all of our conduct. Since we now have the Holy Spirit dwelling inside of us, we are no longer ignorant of the things of God and must begin to act accordingly.

Christ's obedience to the Father and His righteousness (not our own effort) is why we can be holy (Romans 5:19). It would be fair to say that you cannot pursue holiness while you are living in sin. So if you are living in sin, confess your sins to the Lord and to a brother in Christ today!

CAPTAIN'S CORNER
PERSONAL APPLICATION

PLAY 1: Holiness HIGHLIGHTS

- You are commanded to be holy as God is holy. This is not a suggestion.
- To pursue holiness you must abide in Christ by keeping His Commandments.
- Your desires will reveal if you are pursuing holiness.
- God equips us for holiness by giving us His Holy Spirit.

1. What does it mean to you to be holy?

fully consecrated to God - "not my will..."

2. What are your desires, goals, and ambitions that are conflicting with your pursuit of holiness?

none → laziness and procrastination
lack of discipline

CRUNCH TIME:

What did God want you to learn and do from this Play?

~~Th~~ Be Holy is more than just abstaining from sexual sin.

take my calling more seriously.

PLAY 2 : Temptation

If you think you are standing strong, be careful, for you, too, may fall into the same sin. But remember that the temptations that come into your life are no different from what others experience. And God is faithful. He will keep the temptation from becoming so strong that you can't stand up against it. When you are tempted, he will show you a way out so that you will not give in to it.

I Corinthians 10:12-13 - NLT

Stay Onsides
A defensive lineman might flinch on the snap count but stays on his side of the neutral zone, drawing no penalty. We too may flinch when we are tempted to sin, but if we catch ourselves and ask for God's help, then He promises to show us the way out so we will not sin against Him. Paul makes this clear in the passage above.

Temptation Lies Between You and Holiness
According to Dr. Bruce Wilkinson, author of Personal Holiness in Times of Temptation, *"Temptation lies between you and holiness."* Think of temptation being the opposition between you and reaching the goal line.

You Cannot Score a Touchdown (or Experience Holiness) Without Defeating Temptation. Remember: The key to winning and scoring is execution. In order to score you must defeat temptation, which stands between you and the goal line (holiness). Dr. Wilkinson also says that, "Temptations are strategic in your quest for personal holiness. **Temptations are the entry door to every sin.** At that moment during temptation you can either experience defeat or victory. Defeat in the face of temptation leads always to sin, and victory leads to life."

God Never Tempts Us to Sin.

When tempted, no one should say, "God is tempting me." For God cannot be tempted by evil, nor does he tempt anyone; but each one is tempted when, by his own evil desire, he is dragged away and enticed. Then, after desire has conceived, it gives birth to sin; and sin, when it is full-grown, gives birth to death.

James 1:13-15 - NIV

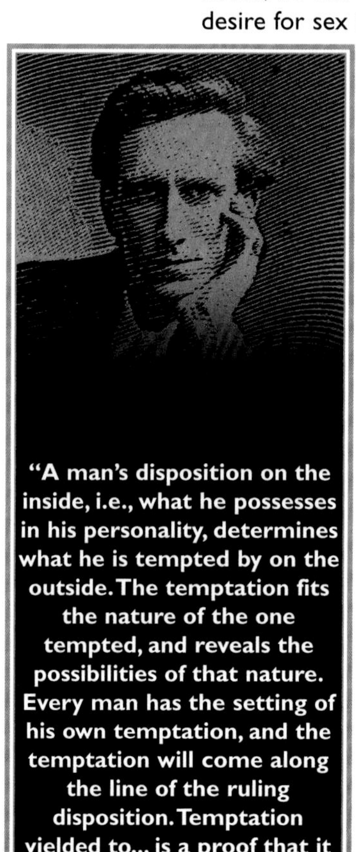

"A man's disposition on the inside, i.e., what he possesses in his personality, determines what he is tempted by on the outside. The temptation fits the nature of the one tempted, and reveals the possibilities of that nature. Every man has the setting of his own temptation, and the temptation will come along the line of the ruling disposition. Temptation yielded to... is a proof that it was timidity that prevented the sin before."

Oswald Chambers

Stay in Bounds
Sin means, "to miss the mark" or to fall short of God's standards. You sin when you give in to temptation by disobeying God's Word. These desires stem from real needs and when they are combined with unbelief, they yield inappropriate urges to step out-of-bounds. When we doubt that God can't meet all of our needs, we will try to meet them ourselves. For instance, your desire for sex is a God-given desire within the boundaries of the "Holy Playbook," the Bible. But sex outside of the marriage covenant is sin, even if the sex only happens in our mind. Likewise, the need to eat is from God, but gluttony is sin. We need food to survive, but we may want to overeat.

Temptation is not sin!
God allows temptation to strengthen and develop our spiritual fitness. When our God-given desires are brought outside of God's boundary lines or we jump off sides, we sin. When we become a child of God, He gives us a second nature of righteousness, a new heart. The problem is that our first nature, (our sin nature) draws us toward responding to life situations inappropriately. The good news is that when we recognize our new nature in Christ, understand what the Spirit of God who dwells within wants us to do, and begin to practice responding in obedience to those situations that tempt us, God's will can become our master coach.

Don't miss this point. God never tempts us to sin, but He does allow temptation so we can demonstrate our love for Him through our faithful obedience.

CAPTAIN'S CORNER
PERSONAL APPLICATION

PLAY 2: Temptation
HIGHLIGHTS

- Temptation is not sin.
- Temptation is the doorway to every sin.
- Our lustful desires tempt us to sin; God never tempts us to sin.
- Sin means to "miss the mark" or to fall short of God's standards.
- God's standards are found in the "Holy Playbook" - the Bible.
- Our sin nature must be trained to yield to our new nature via the Holy Spirit.

1. God can tempt *(Circle One)*
everyone ***no one*** ***some*** **to sin.**

2. You are tempted by your own

lustful desires

3. What are you most tempted by in your life?

Self worth (?)

4. What area in your life is compromising your walk with God? What is your repetitive sin?

lack of discipline → * I believe it is deeper and am trusting the HS to reveal it to me and help me remove it.

CRUNCH TIME:

What did God want you to learn and do from this Play?

Time will tell. – I still have to locate my areas of temptation.

PLAY 3 : BattleZONE Diagram

The old sinful nature loves to do evil, which is just opposite from what the Holy Spirit wants. And the Spirit gives us desires that are opposite from what the sinful nature desires. These two forces are constantly fighting each other, and your choices are never free from this conflict.

Galatians 5:17 - NLT

Study the diagram below and try to come up with as many key points as you can. For example, when Christians accept Jesus as their Lord and Savior, they enter a new life path and the temptation to sin increases.

"… not what I want ***BUT*** *what you want."*
Matthew 26:39b NET

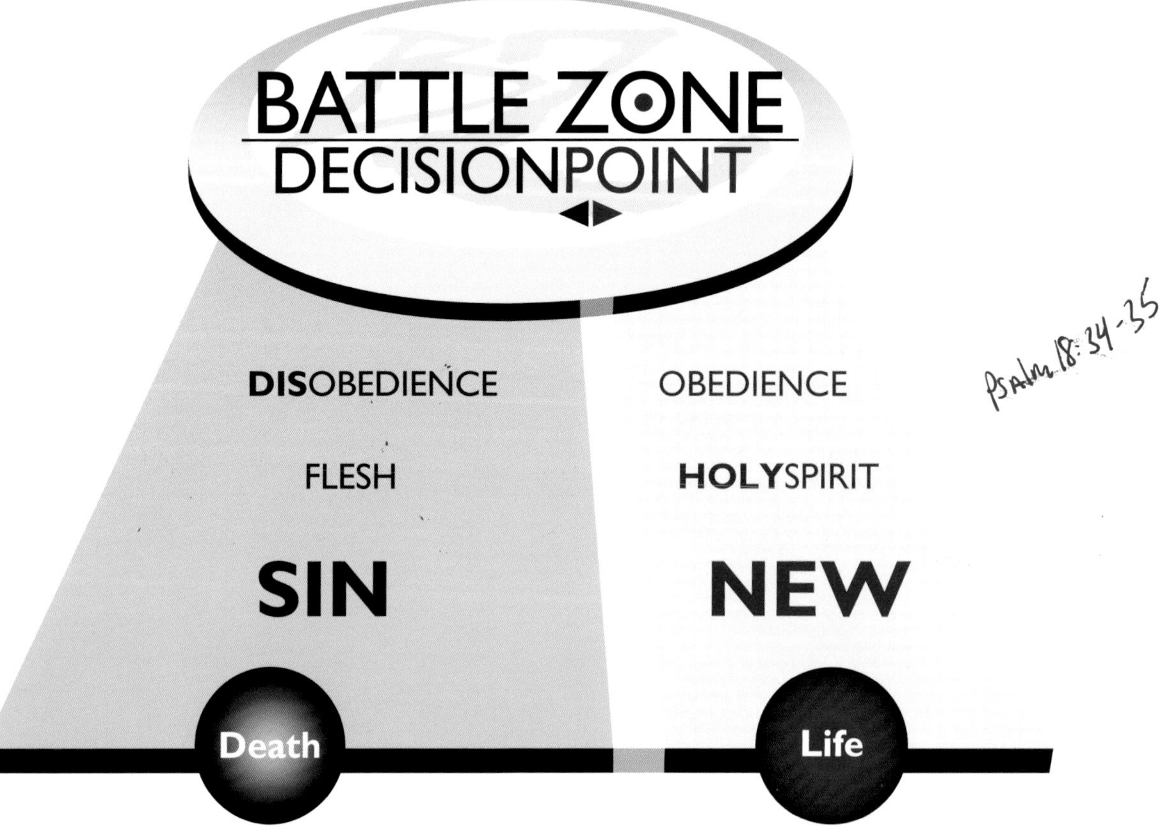

CAPTAIN'S CORNER
PERSONAL APPLICATION

PLAY 3: BattleZONE Diagram HIGHLIGHTS

- There is a constant struggle between the flesh and the Spirit at the decision point.
- Jesus struggled in His humanness to obey His Father in Heaven, yet was without sin.
- The choice of obedience is always the correct choice…always.
- Obedience compelled by love is God's desire for His children.
- You can only obey God by yielding to the Holy Spirit.

1. What did this diagram mean to you personally?

NOTHING! → It's

2. Explain a situation where you were in the BattleZONE and were struggling with your decision. What was going on internally – emotionally, spiritually, physically and psychologically?

Holy Crap! what are u asking?
Boy/Girl – should I go all the way?
"small sins up to Bit Sins"

3. Why does the path of temptation widen when you become a Christ-Follower?

your spirit is made new but
your soul + body are the same –
now there is an internal war.

4. Have you ever experienced the inner struggle when you were in your BattleZONE?

yes.

CRUNCH TIME:

What did God want you to learn and do from this Play?

learn early! → sin is sin – "a little leaven
spoils the whole loaf"
* "Do not harden your heart / sear
your conscience" – you could
be sinning and not even know it.

PLAY 4 : eXecution Threshold (XT)

"But I lavish My love on those who love Me and obey My commands, even for a thousand generations."
Exodus 20:6 - NLT

Coaching proper technique is a process and requires foundational steps in order to maintain a high execution percentage (X%) during a real-life situation. Poor X% occurs when oppositional forces exceed the skill level of your players. When this occurs, it is vital to pinpoint where the breakdown took place, the sequence of events and/or poor technique. The inability to execute a certain task under demanding circumstances or against oppositional forces is due to a breakdown in one or more areas of the system and/or a lack of proper technique. *The exact moment where one can no longer execute a skill, task or technique is the eXecution Threshold (XT).*

In order to maintain a high **eXecution Percentage (X%)** the skill level must be greater than that of the oppositional forces. When the oppositional forces are greater than the player's skill level, the result is a suboptimal X% or an inability to execute at all.

In the game of football, a QB must address factors that affect his X%. Likewise, by God's grace, Christians must develop their spiritual fitness so they can live up to God's requirements – to "be holy as He is holy" (1 Peter 1:15-16). If a Christian's **spiritual skill factors** (i.e., constant pain points, application of the Bible, yielding to the Holy Spirit, confession) are sub-optimal, they will most likely have a low X% in their most challenging BattleZONEs. But when a Christian engages in a lifelong spiritual training program that rehabs the pain point, he will, by God's grace, increase his X% in his BattleZONEs and possibly overcome them entirely.

Spiritual eXecution Threshold... is when you can no longer execute God's will consistently in your BattleZONEs.

Spiritual eXecution Percentage (SX%)

To find out your X% for your personal BattleZONEs, take the number of times you successfully executed God's will and divide it by the number of times you were tempted in that specific area. Using lust as an example, if you were successful 10 out of 20 times at turning your eyes, thoughts and attention away from the temptation to stare inappropriately at a woman, you would calculate your lust X% as 10/20 = 50% obedient. In other words, 50% of the time you were **responsibly dependent** – relying on God while taking responsible action to execute God's will obediently.

eXecution Percentage (X%) = $\frac{\text{number of successes}}{\text{total attempts}}$

X%=10/20
X%=50% for lust

Spiritual Training Program

- Study/meditate on the "Holy Playbook", the Bible
- Pray and visualize God's will
- Memorize Scripture ("Strength Train")
- Humbly submit to the Holy Spirit
- Put on the Armor of God
- Be accountable
- Pursue simplicity
- Worship
  - Privately
  - Corporately

Definitions

- **Opposition:**
  - hostile or contrary action
- **Oppositional Forces**
  - Sin nature
  - Satan
  - World
- **Skill**
  - the ability to use one's knowledge effectively and readily in execution or performance
  - a learned power of doing something competently
  - a developed aptitude or ability
- **Execution**
  - the act or mode or result of performance
- **Threshold**
  - a level, point, or value above which something is true or will take place and below which it will not occur

CAPTAIN'S CORNER
PERSONAL APPLICATION

PLAY 4: eXecution Threshold (XT) HIGHLIGHTS

- Knowing the correct technique will improve your eXecution percentage (X%).
- God expects and demands a perfect X%, so He sent the perfect sacrifice, Jesus.
- There are three oppositional forces that battle for our obedience.
- To defeat the opposition, your skill level must be higher then theirs.

1. Every time you are in your BattleZONE you have a chance to eXecute God's will. What keeps you from eXecuting God's will when you are tempted?

lack of preperation! Flesh + Soul over power spirit.

2. Why is it important to know your eXecution Threshold (XT) in your BattleZONEs?

give no place to devil!

3. If you were to be given a score right now for your obedience vs. your disobedience, what would the score be?

Poor (Average)

4. What would happen to your SX% (Spiritual Execution Percentage) if you made a decision in advance not to do a certain action? For example, you made a decision not to get a divorce, steal, cheat on taxes, or lie to make a sale at work.

it would increase – exponentialy if you took captive every thought that relates specifically to the BZ

CRUNCH TIME:

What did God want you to learn and do from this Play?

Prepare early! (Joe Paterno)

PLAY 5 : Pain Points

Above all else, guard your heart, for it affects everything you do.
Proverbs 4:23 - NLT

Where Does It Hurt?

When an athlete goes down on the field, the trainer runs out to help. The first question he asks the athlete is: **"Where does it hurt?"** The trainer's goal is to get the player back in the game as soon as possible. But the player cannot go back in if he is seriously injured. He may be able to fight through the pain but he won't be able perform to his optimal capacity. For example, if he has a sprained ankle, he won't cut well, so he may only be able to run dive plays instead of toss sweeps. **His pain hurts not only himself, but also the entire team.**

The same thing goes for Christian men: Your pain hurts God's team. When a Christian is stuck in pain, he has a hard time resisting temptation. Sin becomes a routine. That sin impacts the entire Body of Christ. This is why it's imperative for you to find your pain point. What hurts? What is your deepest felt need? For example, many men become disillusioned because their identity is based on what they do, how they perform and what others think of them. This creates a vacuum that leads to loneliness, fear, insecurity, shame, and ultimately sin. We get "hurt" when we lose sight of our identity in Christ and allow our sin nature to be the head coach in our lives. Unfortunately, far too many Christians struggle with the sin cycle of temptation-sin-confession-temptation-sin-confession, harboring pain and sin that keeps Jesus from reigning in their hearts.

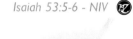

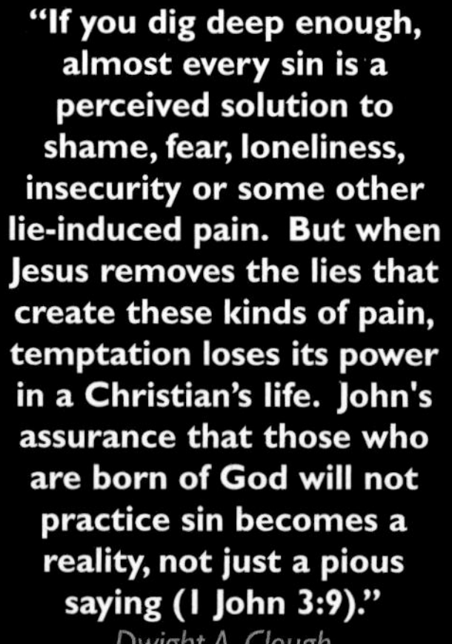
"If you dig deep enough, almost every sin is a perceived solution to shame, fear, loneliness, insecurity or some other lie-induced pain. But when Jesus removes the lies that create these kinds of pain, temptation loses its power in a Christian's life. John's assurance that those who are born of God will not practice sin becomes a reality, not just a pious saying (I John 3:9)."
Dwight A. Clough
http://www.dwightclough.com/discoveries/sin_solution.html

There is No Substitute for Christ's Reign

When a man is feeling lonely, isolated, scared, or insecure, he will be tempted to respond to these feelings with some type of sinful behavior. Sinful behavior is often the pain reliever for a pain-filled heart. In reality, **sin is a counterfeit solution to pain**. Sin is a symptom of a deeper issue – a heart lacking Christ's reign. We cannot habitually live in sin and serve the Lord simultaneously. Many Christians know in their head that what they're doing is wrong, but because their heart is filled with pain, they don't obey God's truth. Proverbs 4:23 says that above all else we should protect our heart because it affects everything we do. In other words what we do and don't do, think, say, desire all comes from the heart. A Christ-centered heart will create a Christ-centered life, but a pain-filled heart will continue to produce more and more pain and sin.

C. S. Lewis wrote that our sinful lusts are really misplaced attempts to answer deeper needs. The Scriptures do not speak to superficial needs—they speak to the deep-seated ones. The need for Christ—then for Him to rein our lives.

Sin is more than an action; it can also be inaction, beginning with unbelief. Do you know and trust God enough to believe that He alone can meet all of your needs? When you stop believing God can meet your needs, you turn **from** Christ **to** other idols (Jeremiah 2:13) to numb your pain or meet your felt needs. The beginning of the rehab process is enough faith in Christ to allow Him to reign in your heart so He can heal your pain. Jesus says,

"Come to me, all you who are weary and burdened, and I will give you rest. Take my yoke upon you and learn from me for I am gentle and humble in heart, and you will find rest for your souls. For my yoke is easy and my burden is light."
Matthew 11:28-20 - NIV

When we recognize the unconditional love of God and allow Him to heal our pain, sin loses its appeal. Sin is no longer our master because we have recognized that God is the only Master. This, in turn, causes us to get rid of the idols we turned to and turn back to God.

God is the only one who can permanently repair a damaged heart, resulting in desires that no longer turn to sin for fulfillment.

But he was pierced for our transgressions, he was crushed for our iniquities; the punishment that brought us peace was upon him, and by his wounds we are healed. We all like sheep, have gone astray, each of us has turned to his own way; and the Lord has laid on him the iniquity of us all.
Isaiah 53:5-6 - NIV 

PAIN POINTS

Pain points affect your decision points, reducing your ability to succeed in your BattleZONEs. Below is a four-step process to help you discover the main pain point in your life. While this is difficult, it is critical to this study. Ask God for His guidance. The goal is to train the pain back to health by using this course as a vehicle for God's Word. Complete as much of this as possible prior to Week 2.

1. DRIVING FORCE: What drives you as a man? **Number/rank the top five.**

- [ ] Happiness
- [ ] Image/Identity
- [ ] Money
- [ ] Performance
- [ ] Pleasure
- [ ] Power/Control
- [x] Prove someone wrong
- [x] Success
- [ ] Status
- [ ] Other good enjoyable life for my family

2. When you were a boy, who or what did you aspire to be? In other words, **what or who captured your heart?**
I don't remember any. **Was it Jesus?** ☐ Yes ☒ No
Most boys or young men do not aspire to be like Jesus because they do not know Him and His incredible masculine-super-hero attributes. What are Jesus' attributes and how do they compete with the worldly attributes you have identified above?

many times – polar opposites

When these driving forces replace your desire to be Christlike or to pursue Christlikeness, there is pain. (Jeremiah 2:13) Conflicting desires, goals and ambitions will always result in pain—which leads to or result in sin. When you pursue things that leave God on the "sidelines"—there is pain.

3. PAIN POINTS: This pain causes you to pursue things that cover the pain. These godless pursuits cause or are driven by PAIN POINTS. **Number/rank your top five PAIN POINTS** listed below:

- [ ] Addictions
- [ ] Broken Relationships
- [ ] Coping with Stress and Worry
- [ ] Depression
- [ ] Emotional Stress
- [x] Family Life and Parenting
- [ ] False Front
- [x] Guilt and Shame
- [x] Handling Money or Financial Trouble
- [ ] Illness
- [ ] Loneliness
- [ ] Managing Relationships (i.e. marriage)
- [ ] Low Self Worth
- [ ] Overweight
- [ ] Painful Past
- [ ] Sexual Dysfunction
- [ ] Workplace Problems
- [ ] Pressure to Impress Others
- [ ] Father Wounds

4. These Pain Points cause men to isolate and numb the pain with sin setting up personal BattleZONEs. These BattleZONEs fall into four distinct ZONES. Look at the Player Assessment for Personal Temptations on the next page. **If you have Internet access take the BattleZONE Challenge to help you through this process. Go to www.battlezoneministries.org and click on the BattleZONE Challenge Button on the right side bar. After you determine your top two BattleZONEs write them here:**

1) Attitude 2) ____________

BATTLEZONE CHALLENGE
Identify your personal BattleZONES, find help

5. Print BattleZONE Report and/or email to BattleZONE Ministries. Be prepared to finalize your PAIN POINT, BattleZONE and write a goal for this 10-week course.

MY GOAL FOR THIS BZ TRAINING COURSE RELATED TO MY PAIN POINT AND BATTLEZONE IS:

PLAYER ASSESSMENT FOR PERSONAL TEMPTATIONS

Circle the BattleZONEs you struggle with the most.

ATTITUDE ZONES

Anger Rage Judging
Critical Greed Envy
Jealousy Hate Murder
Impatience Laziness
Irresponsible Pride
Racism Selfishness
Unforgiveness Worry
Fear

ADDICTIVE ZONES

Alcohol Drugs Gaming
Entertainment Gambling
Overeating Overspending
Sexual Addiction Stealing
Cheating Workaholism

SEXUAL ZONES

Adultery Visual Lust
Homosexuality Porn
Cyber-sex Massage Parlors
Masterbation Webcam Sex
Premarital Sex

VERBAL ZONES

Coarse Jokes Gossip
Emotional Abuse Lying
Profanity Swearing
Verbal Abuse

PTAIN'S GUIDE

cution
hreshold (XT)

BATTLE ZONE
MINISTRIES INC

CAPTAIN'S GUIDE

BattleZONE Symbol Key

Warm-Up: Execution Threshold (XT)

This section is to assist the BattleZONE Captains as they lead their teammates through the BattleZONE Training Course

A. Assign teammates/captains (TC). You will assist one another throughout this training course.

B. Practice Field Discussion Questions (outside or inside)

1. Pretend you have a 24-inch hoop set up seven yards in front of you. What would happen to your X% if you threw a football close to the hoop?
2. What would happen to your X% when you moved away from the hoop?
3. What factors would influence your XT?
4. What factors would influence a QB's X% in the NFL? Have men brainstorm together as a group, then have them refer to **Factors Affecting X%** on the next page.
5. What factors affect a Christian's ability to obey God (X%)? Have men brainstorm together as a group, then have them refer to **Factors Affecting X%** on next page.
6. How would your proximity, or distance from the goal, affect your X% for passing the football?
7. How would your heart's proximity to Jesus affect your X% for your BattleZONES?
8. Would your X% be affected if your throwing arm was hurt?
9. How would your ability to obey Christ fully if your heart was injured or full of pain?
10. Is everyone's XT the same? Is everyone's skill level the same?

When these factors outweigh your Christian "skills" or go beyond your spiritual fitness level, or your ability/understanding, or your understanding of the Holy Spirit's role and God's grace, or your desire to willingly obey God, you sin. This point in time when you are executing or making a decision is called your BattleZONE.

Definition of the BattleZONE

The actual moment in time when you are tempted is called your BattleZONE. It's that moment when you are looking temptation in the face and have to choose between executing God's will or missing God's mark – sin.

BattleZONEs Are Different for Everyone

Obedience is your ability to execute God's will during temptation in your BattleZONE. Everyone's BattleZONES are unique and each man's XT is different for his area of temptation. This is why you each will prayerfully select your BattleZONE to tackle during this training course.

C. Go to the BattleZONE Chalk Talk and lead your Team through week 1.

Factors Affecting X%

Below are some factors comparing a quarterback's ability to complete a pass and the Christian's ability to remain obedient to God or execute God's will (X%). One or more of these factors can influence the X% to a greater or lesser degree. The key is to understand each factor and address them as needed. While addressing a specific breakdown factor, it is imperative that none of the other factors are neglected. All factors have an influence on your X%. As the quarterback of your life, victory will come only by the grace of God through hard work and spiritual discipline.

QB Passing Ability		Christian Obedience
Knowledge of technique involved in throwing a football and different elements of the game, including playbook and game plan.	 KNOWLEDGE	Understanding of the Bible in its entirety including the doctrines of the Holy Spirit, Jesus Christ and God's loving grace.
Quality coaching to teach footwork, passing technique and effective offensive strategies.	 COACHING	Truth from the Holy Spirit, Who uses Jesus as the role model to instruct and correct daily activities.
Natural ability or talent.	 ABILITY	Ability from the Holy Spirit to empower us despite our natural weaknesses.
Training program, including strength training, conditioning, flexibility, scout team, playbook study, diet and visualization.	 TRAINING	Spiritual training program, including Scripture memorization/study, worship, fellowship, accountability, prayer and yielding to the Holy Spirit's authority.
Ability to make the right adjustments before, during and after a game.	 ADJUSTMENT	Immediate confession and repentance upon disobedience, or sinning (missing God's mark) against God the Father.
Self-confidence in ability to execute and lead the team to victory.	 CONFIDENCE	Faith in God's grace allowing obedience through the power of the Holy Spirit.
Trust and belief in the owners and coaching staff's philosophies and their commitment to their QB's success.	 TRUST	Faith in God's loving grace and trust that He is always looking out for our best interests. God's love is unwavering, pure and efficient.
Supportive and highly effective teammates who execute their assignments during a play.	 TEAMMATES	The "who/what" you spend your time with including people, movies, TV, books, radio, magazines and regular and honest accountability.
Conditions in which the game is played, ranging from the weather, to crowd noise and to the field itself.	 SITUATION	The environment you allow yourself to be in, including external and internal factors. i.e. parties & HALTS, (hungry, angry, lonely, tired and stressed)
The opponent's counter-measures against the QB to prevent him from executing.	 OPPOSITION	Opposition trying to get you to sin, including your sin-nature, Satan and the World.

CHALK TALK

eXecution Threshold (XT)

1. Prayer

Have one of the men open in prayer and ask the Holy Spirit to guide and direct the session towards God's agenda.

2. Sign Confidentiality Agreement

This is located in the Pre-Season section on page 19. Have men carefully tear it out and give it to you or make a photocopy.

3. Quick Review of BattleZONE Terms

Have the men turn to this page and follow along.

Quick Review of BattleZONE Terms:

X% is the amount of times you execute or complete a task divided by the total attempts. {# executed / # attempts}

XT is the exact moment where one can no longer execute a skill, task or technique.

BZ is the moment during temptation where you must choose God's will or self-fulfillment. This is also referred to as one's personal area of temptation.

God demands a perfect eXecution percentage (X%) for each of His "players" regardless of the temptation. Jesus set the example. He also paid the price for our inability to perfectly execute. In this course, the BattleZONE is that moment in time when you are tempted to sin. "Victory" means holiness, "execution" means faithful obedience, and "being Spirit-filled" is the same as being "in the ZONE."

The key to victory is execution. Faithful obedience is the key to holiness. To reach the goal line is to experience holiness. In order to experience holiness you must be spiritually fit.

Throughout this course you will be preparing yourself through spiritual training to become spiritually fit and experience holiness. Just like the quarterback trains to increase his eXecution percentage (X%) by addressing all the factors involved in his ability to execute, you will be training to overcome your personal BattleZONEs by yielding to God's will.

4. Week 1 Plays

For Week 1 you were assigned to read and be ready to comment on five Plays. You will have TWO MINUTES to present your topic; then discuss each as a group. Please try to stay focused on what God taught you through this Play. What did God want you to learn and do?
CAPTAIN, ASSIGN EACH TEAMMATE A PLAY – THEN LET THEM TAKE THE LEAD.

PLAY 1: Holiness
As a captain, it is imperative that you model how to teach a play call with your men. To do so:

1) Read the scripture verse out loud;
2) Show the men where you highlighted, underlined or circled parts of the text that spoke to you and you wanted to share -- don't assume that these men will mark up the text on their own – encourage them to do so. Let them know that they will need to have reminders for when they "coach" a play or teaching;
3) Read the "Highlights" out loud;
4) Answer each question and facilitate brief discussion on each point.

Next, assign Plays 2 through 5 to other men. Remember to coach them as they "teach" the "plays" to their teammates. They have 2 minutes.

- **Play 2: Temptation**
- **Play 3: BattleZONE Diagram**
- **Play 4: eXecution Threshold**
- **Play 5: Pain Points**

5. Pain Points

Do as a group. Captain, please bring the team through the Pain Point Flow Chart and refer to the Player Assessment Form for Personal Temptations. **Remember to tie in the BattleZONE Challenge Results from the website.**

6. Crunch Time

Describe one thing that really "hit" each one of you during this practice session or the week readings/assignments. How did God speak to you?

7. Independent Practice

1. Wrestle with your **pain point** and ask the Lord to show you what He wants you to work on using the BattleZONE Challenge and/or the **Player Assessment Form for Personal Temptation**. Then set a goal for this course based on your pain point and personal BattleZONE. You will have to have these in writing by Week Four.
2. Read all five Plays and be prepared to teach a lesson to the team next week. Remember to circle, underline or highlight key truths as you read. Answer the questions on the page opposite to the Play. This will help you present what you learned and share how God spoke to you. Try to do one each day at a set time to establish a consistent devotional time with God.
3. Read and meditate on the **Strength Training Cards** as often as you can.
4. Call your Teammate/Captain at least once this week and pray for him daily.
5. Tear out the BattleZONE Diagram on pages 273 & 274 and display the large graphic as a reminder. Also, cut out the two small diagrams to place in your car and wallet.

Write down your Captain's phone number here: ______________________________

8. Iron Sharpens Iron (James 5:16)

Captain: For Week 1, you will demonstrate to the men what confessional prayer looks like. Each week we will end with a sacred time for confession either with your Teammate/Captain or as a team. This is a time to come clean of any sin you have in your life. Allow the Holy Spirit to search you and Christ's blood to cleanse you. Ask for prayer requests from each man and have each man record requests to use during their personal prayer time.

PRAYER REQUESTS AND PRAISES

NAME	REQUEST
	RESULT
NAME	REQUEST
	RESULT
NAME	REQUEST
	RESULT
NAME	REQUEST
	RESULT
NAME	REQUEST
	RESULT
NAME	REQUEST
	RESULT
NAME	REQUEST
	RESULT
NAME	REQUEST
	RESULT

Old vs. New

- Old Nature vs. New Nature
- Sinner or Saint?
- We Get Good at What We Practice
- Coachable vs. Prideful Spirit
- Get Real
- Dominant Reaction

Week 2 Objectives

Each man will understand:

1. The battle between the old sin nature and our new nature in the Spirit.
2. The difference between having his identity as a sinner versus a Saint.
3. That spiritual fitness training is needed to untrain the sin nature by the power of the Holy Spirit.
4. The importance of having a coachable spirit.
5. The importance of knowing his desires and how they conflict or agree with God's Word.
6. The importance of transparency as it relates to confession and holiness.
7. The importance of knowing his immediate reaction responses to temptation situations.

I will give you a new heart and put a new spirit in you; I will remove from you your heart of stone and give you a heart of flesh. And I will put my Spirit in you and move you to follow my decrees and be careful to keep my laws.
Ezekiel 36:26-27 - NIV

Spend your time and energy in training yourself for spiritual fitness. Physical exercise has some value, but spiritual exercise is much more important, for it promises a reward in both this life and the next.
I Timothy 4:7b-8 - NLT

Be humble in the presence of God's mighty power, and he will honor you when the time comes.
I Peter 5:6 - CEV

We know that the persons we used to be were nailed to the cross with Jesus. This was done so that our sinful bodies would no longer be the slaves of sin . . . Now you are set free from sin and are slaves who please God.
Romans 6:6, 18 - CEV

If you have sinned, you should tell each other what you have done. Then you can pray for one another and be healed.
James 5:16 - CEV

Since Christ suffered and underwent pain, you must have the same attitude he did; you must be ready to suffer, too. For remember, when your body suffers, sin loses its power.
I Peter 4:1 - TLB

WEEK 2

STRENGTH TRAINING

I will give you a new heart and put a new spirit in you; I will remove from you your heart of stone and give you a heart of flesh. And I will put my Spirit in you and move you to follow my decrees and be careful to keep my laws.

Ezekiel 36:26-27 - NIV

BATTLE ZONE MINISTRIES, INC. **www.battlezoneministries.org**

WEEK 2

STRENGTH TRAINING

Spend your time and energy in training yourself for spiritual fitness. Physical exercise has some value, but spiritual exercise is much more important, for it promises a reward in both this life and the next.

I Timothy 4:7b-8 - NLT

BATTLE ZONE MINISTRIES, INC. **www.battlezoneministries.org**

WEEK 2

STRENGTH TRAINING

Be humble in the presence of God's mighty power, and he will honor you when the time comes.

I Peter 5:6 - CEV

BATTLE ZONE MINISTRIES, INC. **www.battlezoneministries.org**

WEEK 2

STRENGTH TRAINING

We know that the persons we used to be were nailed to the cross with Jesus. This was done so that our sinful bodies would no longer be the slaves of sin . . . Now you are set free from sin and are slaves who please God.

Romans 6:6, 18 - CEV

BATTLE ZONE MINISTRIES, INC. **www.battlezoneministries.org**

WEEK 2

STRENGTH TRAINING

If you have sinned, you should tell each other what you have done. Then you can pray for one another and be healed.

James 5:16 - CEV

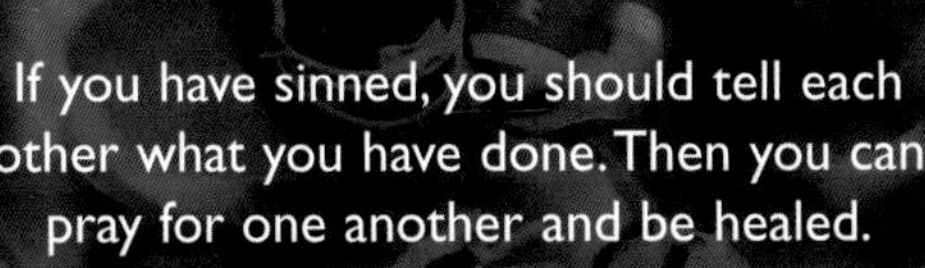

BATTLE ZONE MINISTRIES, INC. **www.battlezoneministries.org**

WEEK 2

STRENGTH TRAINING

Since Christ suffered and underwent pain, you must have the same attitude he did; you must be ready to suffer, too. For remember, when your body suffers, sin loses its power.

I Peter 4:1 - TLB

BATTLE ZONE MINISTRIES, INC. **www.battlezoneministries.org**

STRENGTH TRAINING

NOTES

BATTLE ZONE MINISTRIES, INC. www.battlezoneministries.org

STRENGTH TRAINING

NOTES

BATTLE ZONE MINISTRIES, INC. www.battlezoneministries.org

STRENGTH TRAINING

NOTES

BATTLE ZONE MINISTRIES, INC. www.battlezoneministries.org

STRENGTH TRAINING

NOTES

BATTLE ZONE MINISTRIES, INC. www.battlezoneministries.org

STRENGTH TRAINING

NOTES

BATTLE ZONE MINISTRIES, INC. www.battlezoneministries.org

STRENGTH TRAINING

NOTES

BATTLE ZONE MINISTRIES, INC. www.battlezoneministries.org

BattleZONE Victories

Michael Alfheim
Clovis, CA

I enjoy all sports and most enthusiastically soccer. There are great life truths you can learn through playing sports that carry into business, family, and day to day living. Knowing that BattleZONE Training Course uses the game of football, I really identified with the concept of training in order to perform well in the game.

After going through the course the first time, I decided to become a Certified BattleZONE Coach as an intentional element of my own spiritual training program. In addition to daily devotion, study, and prayer, BattleZONE is a critical component to my own daily spiritual fitness. The men that I lead through BattleZONE actually teach me as much as I teach them - their experiences are no different than my own in many ways; so I can encourage them as they encourage me.

As a coach I have committed use a new BattleZONE Training Course and fill it out as if I have never seen the course materials before. This approach helps me stay real with the men, not relying on "old revelation" but allowing the Spirit to teach me truth based upon my current walk and season of life. There is great joy and satisfaction as I observe men come to grips with patterns of sin that in some cases previously they didn't even know existed—then rely on God's Playbook to help them fully understand God's abundant grace and never ending mercy's.

The tools men take away from BattleZONE help them become more effective in their daily lives. The men become a captain in training as a BattleZONE graduate if they agree to carry the course forward....committing to disciple men in the Word and the teachings of Christ. The course is all about being holy, making more choices every day in line with Gods will, away from our own will. BattleZONE is helping me and other men do that more consistently every day. The men go away understanding how to apply God's Word, instead of it being an intellectual exercise.

Choosing to be a coach is a great privilege that carries responsibility, blessings, and the satisfaction of doing something really significant for the Kingdom of God. Because of my commitment to pursue holiness and live like Christ, I am prayerfully selecting men who will be disciples and GO and make more. Will you be that man?

PLAY 1 : Conflicting Desires

The old sinful nature loves to do evil, which is just opposite from what the Holy Spirit wants. And the Spirit gives us desires that are opposite from what the sinful nature desires. These two forces are constantly fighting each other, and your choices are never free from this conflict.

Galatians 5:17 - NLT

The Red Zone

The red zone is the last 20 yards on each end of the football field that the defense must protect. The intensity on the field increases as both teams battle for the goal line. When we become Christians, we immediately enter into the spiritual red zone, a battle in the heavenly realms where our opponents fight to keep us from crossing the goal by destroying our witness for Christ.

The Trench

When the defense keeps the offense from scoring on the goal line, it is known as a "goal line stand". If the spiritual battle in the heavenly realms represents the red zone, then the inner battle within every believer parallels the goal line stand in the trench. When the ball is snapped, the battle for the goal line begins; likewise when our sin nature is aroused by temptation, the battle in the spiritual trench starts. It's in the trenches where the offensive and defensive linemen fight tooth and nail for that little white line. Every time you are in your personal BattleZONE, you are to overcome your opponent's goal line stand by choosing obedience instead of self-gratification.

Take a minute to think about a time when you experienced this war between your flesh and the Spirit. What was going on inside? How did you fight? How long did you fight? Maybe it was in your motel room and you were fighting against watching pornography on cable. Whatever it was, reflect back now and try to recapture the internal war inside you.

The last few inches, or in our case, seconds, is where the battle for holiness, to obey God or not, is won or lost. The greater the temptation, the more intense the battle between the two forces becomes. In football, the entire game comes down to whether the defense kept the other team from scoring. For Christ-Followers, it all comes down to the moment when you are looking temptation in the face. How you respond in that split second will determine victory or defeat. What you desire most at that time often predicts the outcome. Christ's love should motivate us.

"No man knows how bad he is 'till he has tried very hard to be good. A silly idea is current that good people do not know what temptation means. This is an obvious lie. Only those who try to resist temptation know how strong it is. After all, you find out the strength of the German army by fighting against it, not by giving in. You find out the strength of a wind by trying to walk against it, not by lying down. A man who gives in to temptation after five minutes simply does not know what it would have been like an hour later. That is why bad people, in one sense, know very little about badness. They have lived a sheltered life by always giving in. We never find out the strength of the evil impulse inside us until we try to fight it: and Christ, because he was the only man who never yielded to temptation, is also the only man who knows to the full what temptation means--the only complete realist."

C.S. Lewis

Desire

Many football coaches say that desire is a key element for great achievement. The more you desire something, the more inner drive you have to obtain it. Paul talks about the inner desires between our sin nature and the Spirit, "...the Spirit gives us desires that are opposite from what the sinful nature desires" (Galatians 5:17). Paul assures us that although our sin nature craves evil, God gives us His Spirit that craves just the opposite. These desires are in constant conflict in Christ-Followers, and are at the core of our personal BattleZONEs. Satan and the "traitor within" (our flesh) capitalize on these conflicting desires. For example, if you desire to get drunk on weekends, that desire is in direct conflict with the Spirit (Ephesians 5:18). A great exercise to determine what your conflicting desires are is to write down the things you desire most in life, from a new plasma TV to a loved one's salvation. After you have made an extensive list of all your desires, ask God to help you see which ones are in direct conflict with His will. This is where the work begins. You must pray that God will remove those sinful, selfish desires and replace them with His desires.

Sinful Desires Sell Products

Marketing and advertising professionals know more about the power of sinful desires than Christians seem to. Just look at the way they use our sin nature to sell their products. Research shows that placing a beautiful woman in a car ad will increase sales. Why? The woman makes the car more desirable to the male target market. The less clothing the woman wears, the higher the target market's perception of the car's desirability. This is because at an emotional level, the sin nature rages with lust for the beautiful woman, subconsciously increasing the desire for the car. Instead of saying that sex sells, advertisers should just say that sin sell! From shampoo ads to yogurt, marketing and advertising entices our sin nature and uses it against us for profit.

Advertisers know this and now, so do you. 

CAPTAIN'S CORNER
PERSONAL APPLICATION

PLAY 1: Conflicting Desires HIGHLIGHTS

There is a battle for your decision every time you are tempted. Your desires will help mold your decision patterns. Every Christ-Follower has two natures that war against one another: the new nature and the old sin nature. Our choices are never free from this conflict.
Seeking and yielding to God's will for your life will help shape your desires.

1. Describe the conflict that Paul is talking about in Galatians 5:17. Do you feel equipped to overcome your sin nature's evil cravings?

2. Do you recognize the decision point where you are required to make a choice either to execute God's will or your own? How do you normally respond?

3. What are some of the personal desires you have that conflict with God's will for you?

CRUNCH TIME:

What did God want you to learn and do from this Play?

PLAY 2 : Sinner or Saint?

But I can't help myself because I'm no longer doing it. It is sin inside me that is stronger than I am that makes me do these evil things.
Romans 7:17 - TLB

Sin, Our Own Worst Enemy
Have you ever heard an announcer or coach describe a tremendously talented quarterback but who fails to perform on game-day as "his own worst enemy"? This expression refers to our self-destructive tendencies that sabotage every single attempt to win. Even when the QB has great environmental conditions, a brilliant game plan, superior teammate performance and the home field advantage, he still cannot pull off the victory. If we don't understand our new nature, we are like that quarterback – our own worst enemy. Actually, we're not the enemy – it's the sin within us that is. The most dominating "player" on your opponent's team is your sin nature.

I'm No Saint... Am I?
As we follow Paul's struggle in the above verse, we come to the conclusion that when we sin, we are not the ones doing it because we are one with Christ. However, we are always responsible for our sin. Christ cannot sin, so logically our new nature in Christ can't sin either. The power of sin in us is causing us to give in to temptation. Don't miss the importance of this. You and I are one with Christ and you are no longer the one who desires to sin – but those desires come from the power of sin that lives in you. God has promised:

"I'll give you a new heart, put a new spirit in you.
I'll remove the stone heart from your body and replace
it with a heart that's God-willed, not self-willed.
I'll put my My Spirit in you and make it possible for you
to do what I tell you and live by My commands."
Ezekiel 36:26-27 - MSG

Not only do we have a new heart, God also gives us the Holy Spirit to live inside our hearts and minds so we can know His law. What an awesome thought and privilege to know that God has such an incredible game plan that helps us defeat sin. Paul also mentions that we are a new creation when we accept Christ as our Lord and Savior (2 Corinthians 5:17, Titus 3:5). This means we now have a "coachable" heart. Our role is to yield to our Coach's authority moment by moment.

Paul teaches us in Romans 7:17 that he has separated himself from being labeled a sinner and makes it clear that sin is a power in him, not how he identified himself. The sin in him is the thing causing problems, not Paul, who is one with Christ. As Christ-Followers, we are to see ourselves as saints who, at times, allow sin's power to take over our desires, thoughts and actions. Most Christians identify themselves as sinners, instead of saints. It's time for a paradigm shift! Scripture says clearly that we are saints -- saints who allow sin to dominate our decision points when we are tempted in our BattleZONEs. The solution to overcome the power of sin has already been paid for by Jesus Christ. Jesus sent the Holy Spirit to help us execute God's will. We must train ourselves to yield to the Spirit's authority every moment of every day.

The more Christ-like you become, the clearer you will see how much of a sinner you were as well as how much sin you now allow. This spiritual sensitivity recognizes how much you need the Holy Spirit to overcome the oppositional forces that team up against you. Again, you must recognize that because of what Christ has done on the cross and your acceptance of Jesus Christ, you are no longer a sinner but a saint who gives in to sin when you allow your sin nature to dominate your choices. The word "saint" means holy one or those "set apart" because they belong to God. You are a new creation in Christ, not a creature stuck in sin! Sin is no longer your master; Christ's very nature of righteousness is! However, you must train yourself to yield to your new nature and the Holy Spirit. Our behavior doesn't make us holy – Christ does. Our job is to love Him enough to obey.

Suffering Puts Our Sin Nature to Death
Your old sin nature has been the leader for long enough. Now is the time for your old lifestyle patterns, desires and behaviors to start taking orders from your new Coach, the Holy Spirit. Your old habits are strong and will never give up without a fight, but Christ is stronger than any temptation. He proved this on the Mount of Olives and then ultimately on the cross. This will not be an easy ride, nor will you come out injury-free. Suffering is the tool that puts your flesh to death.

Since Christ suffered and underwent pain, you must have the same attitude he did; you must be ready to suffer, too. Remember, when your body suffers, sin loses its power.
1 Peter 4:1 - TLB

You are a new creation in Christ. You are not the one wanting to give in to temptation. The sin within is the culprit. Choose to allow God's Word to renew your mind about your identity. Study the Scriptures that teach about your oneness with Christ and your new identity as a saint in Jesus.

CAPTAIN'S CORNER
PERSONAL APPLICATION

PLAY 2: Sinner or Saint? HIGHLIGHTS

- Every Christ-Follower is a saint, because they have been "set apart" for God's glory.
- We are always responsible before God for our decisions, even though the sin within entices us to sin.
- Christ-Followers are one with Christ and Christ cannot sin, so when we are yielded to the Holy Spirit, we cannot sin either.
- We have been given a new heart and a new spirit called the Holy Spirit, Who is God. We are a new creation in Christ.

1. What does Paul mean when he says, *"It is sin inside me that is stronger than I am that makes me do these evil things"* (TLB, Romans 7:17)? Does this mean we are no longer responsible for the sins we commit?

2. What identity do you have of yourself, a sinner or a saint? Why?

CRUNCH TIME:

What did God want you to learn and do from this Play?

PLAY 3 : Retraining Program

...spend your time and energy in training yourself for spiritual fitness. Physical exercise has some value, but spiritual exercise is much more important, for it promises a reward in both this life and the next.

I Timothy 4:7b-8 - NLT

You Get Good at What You Practice

We were all once sinners saved by grace through faith, but now we are saints battling the sin that remains in us. We also battle old habits, whether they are thoughts, desires or behaviors, because we get good at what we practice -- even sinning. We get good at telling dirty jokes. We get good at "checking out" a woman's body without her noticing. We get good at cheating on taxes. We get good at telling lies. We get good at what we practice. If this is true, we can also get good at obedience. We can get good at yielding to the Spirit of God when we are tempted. The more you practice, the better you will get. Like tackling or blocking, the more you practice with the right coaching, the more you will improve. With the Holy Spirit as your Coach you can overcome temptation.

"Training Up" the New Nature

When you are born again and become a Christian, the Holy Spirit instantly enters your being, your eternal destiny changes – but your old sin nature remains. When you are not filled (controlled) by the Holy Spirit moment by moment but choose to reject or quench Him, the old sin nature will dominate, resulting in sin. This is why we continue to sin. In that moment of decision, God becomes abstract and less real to us and we force Him to take a backseat to our selfish desires. The temptation to sin engulfs our thoughts and our mind becomes focused on self-gratification. It's in this moment that we make the decision not to trust God to meet our needs. The power of the Holy Spirit is disarmed because our free will overrides His. When we sin, it demonstrates our sin nature is the dominating force at that moment. It is in these BattleZONEs that we must recognize and proclaim God's Word as truth: our sin nature is now dead and has no reign over our body. We are slaves to our new master, righteousness. The natural pattern to sin must be overthrown by the Word of God and retrained from our instinctive reactive patterns by the Holy Spirit. This can only be accomplished through God's loving grace and our desire to train ourselves up in God's "Holy Playbook", thus renewing our minds.

We must execute the will of God to override our old sin nature. Your spiritual training program should be designed to help you respond as Christ did, in obedience to the Father. Don't miss this crucial point. Training your new nature will simultaneously untrain your old sin nature by God's grace.

The Natural Override Principle

An example of the Natural Override Principle is the ability for a wide receiver to hang himself out by going up for the ball, knowing he is going to get drilled in the ribs by an inside linebacker. A receiver is able to retrain his brain's natural instinct to cower and protect his body from a vicious hit through repetitive training and sheer determination.

This same type of training must be practiced to disable our sin-nature. The only way we can do this is through repetitive spiritual training that starts with renewing our mind by the Word of God and ends with the action of yielding to the Holy Spirit. This is accomplished by allowing the Holy Spirit to control you as Paul states in Romans 8:9,12-14. You can override the old-nature by believing that the power of the Holy Spirit can, in fact, keep your sin nature shut down. With this conviction as the foundation, you can then practice by allowing the Holy Spirit to help you override your natural instinct to sin when you are in your personal BattleZONEs.

We can train ourselves not to look at the female jogger as we drive by in our car. We can train ourselves to hold our tongue when we want so badly to say something critical of our in-laws. We can train ourselves to not over-eat at the dinner table. The key to having a new response in these situations is allowing the Holy Spirit to override our natural habits that often lead to ungodly decisions. It is possible and yes, we are equipped to do it. Each time you are in your BattleZONE, you will have an opportunity to override your old instinct and act according to your new nature in Christ. Are you willing to train yourself for spiritual fitness?

CAPTAIN'S CORNER
PERSONAL APPLICATION

PLAY 3: Retraining Program HIGHLIGHTS

- Practicing something over and over, whether good or bad, can create a habit.
- Training yourself for spiritual fitness will reap a reward in this life and the next.
- The first step in retraining your habits is to change the way you think by developing a Biblical worldview.
- Training your new nature in Christ will simultaneously untrain your old sin nature.

1. Name one ungodly habit you have become "good" at. What can you do to untrain that habit?

2. Can you think of a time when you had to override a natural instinct? (For example, keeping quiet when you wanted to speak up, or look when you shouldn't.)

CRUNCH TIME:

What did God want you to learn and do from this Play?

PLAY 4 : Coachable Spirit

You younger men, accept the authority of the elders. And all of you, serve each other in humility, for "God sets himself against the proud, but he shows favor to the humble."
I Peter 5:5 - NLT

Low Man Always Wins
Ask any coach and they will tell you that the key to blocking or tackling is to stay low. That's because the low man always wins. Even if the other player is bigger and stronger, if you keep your hips down, head up and drive your feet, you will have the advantage. Jesus takes this same physical principle and applies it to our faith:

"To those who are open to My teaching, more understanding will be given, and they will have an abundance of knowledge. But to those who are not listening, even what they have will be taken away from them."
Matthew 13:12 - NLT

Are You Coachable?
How willing are you to be instructed, directed or prompted? The coach is responsible to call the plays; the players are responsible to execute them, no questions asked. Players are to submit to the coach even if they are afraid the play won't work. Like a football player, we too are to submit ourselves to God's play calls. The Bible says,

The wise are glad to be instructed, but babbling fools fall flat on their faces.
Proverbs 10:8 - NLT

Foolish people do not accept coaching and can actually lead others astray who follow their foolish lead:

People who accept correction are on the pathway to life, but those who ignore it will lead others astray.
Proverbs 10:17 - NLT

Pride
One thing that keeps great athletes from becoming even better is their pride. Pride can actually lead to a player's demise:

Pride goes before destruction, and haughtiness before a fall.
Proverbs 16:18 - NLT

God despises pride and we should too. When we think about the heroes of the past, the word "pride" comes up over and over. Phrases like, "he was a proud man," or "take pride in your work," or "if you want to win, you must take pride in yourself" are all too common. The word "pride" can be very confusing when it comes to the Word of God, because pride is seen as a horrendous sin against God, yet in this world, we are told it is an desirable attribute.

What if someone complements you? A simple way to prevent pride from creeping in to our hearts is to accept a complement silently with joy and then send the complement to Jesus in the form of praise and thanksgiving. Kind of like a trampoline – when the complement comes accept it and let it bounce off you to give glory to God. This way you will not take the credit for what God is allowing you to accomplish.

Failure and Becoming Coachable
So many men fail in their BattleZONEs because they have not been coached in the proper technique for overcoming temptation. Or they refuse to execute God's play calls, preferring to do it their own way, because they have not reached a point where they have a coachable spirit. This type of ignorance or attitude will lead to failure. The good news for men who are in Christ, is that God will use our multiple failures in our BattleZONEs to bring us to a point of brokenness, ultimately bringing us closer to Christ.

When we fail to be holy because we are dealing with temptation inadequately, God is patient with us, and in our despair He will teach us His ways. God demands humility and He knows it will take multiple failures in order to manifest His will in our brokenness, resulting in a coachable spirit. Only in total brokenness will you have a coachable spirit, and at your low point God will start to coach you through His Holy "Playbook". It is hard, but you will be thankful.

Be humble in the presence of God's mighty power, and he will honor you when the time comes.
I Peter 5:6 - CEV

Surrendered Obedience
As Christians, each day we must practice humility through our obedience. The ability to be humble comes from a heart that is surrendered to the fact that God knows best for you. It's through this trust in the Lord, demonstrated in our obedience, that we can continue to experience holiness. This is known as surrendered obedience – the habit of wanting God's will more than your own.

CAPTAIN'S CORNER
PERSONAL APPLICATION

PLAY 4: Coachable Spirit HIGHLIGHTS

- Jesus said if you are open to His teachings, He will give you more understanding.
- Willingness to be instructed requires humility. Your willingness to submit yourself to authority will determine your progress.
- God will break us in order to get us to depend on Him.
- Brokenness is always painful, but God always restores us if we cling to Him through surrendered obedience.

1. What does it mean to be humble in God's mighty power?

2. What is your view of the word "pride"? Is it a positive or a negative for a man to be proud?

3. Why does it seem to be so hard for men to be coached by suggestion and correction?

CRUNCH TIME:

What did God want you to learn and do from this Play?

PLAY 5 : Get Real

If you have sinned, you should tell each other what you have done.
Then you can pray for one another and be healed.
James 5:16 - CEV

Vulnerability
A man's greatest weakness is not allowing himself to be vulnerable and get real with his trusted friends. This is especially true for Christian men because God holds us to high standards. This expectation sets the scene for added pressures to "perform" as an authentic Christian. American men have been placed in a position where they are expected to operate beyond their natural abilities. They are expected to fit a mold that the world has determined instead of God's mold—the image of Christ.

Our culture stresses image over authenticity. Most men find it hard to expose an external weakness, but that exposure pales in comparison to being transparent with their internal struggles. This matter is compounded when it comes to our spiritual issues as Christians. How can a coach help an athlete if the athlete is hiding a problem? He can't! During this training course, you will have the opportunity to practice being vulnerable not only with your physical flaws, but more importantly, your emotional, psychological and spiritual ones. Remove your mask and practice being vulnerable in a masculine way.

Real Men Live Real Before God
Isolation leads to personal and relational defeat. Men need genuine friends to whom they can open up and get real. Most men are afraid of being transparent, so they create a false front and engage in image control to try and impress their "friends" and family. This is **identity isolation**. Identity isolation is a character killer and develops under the premise of performance versus character. For some men, admitting hidden faults is worse than being burned with a branding iron! It is possible to break through this wall of insecurity and pride by taking risks within a safe environment. When men embrace their God-given identities and get real, they will begin to be set free from the bondage of living a lie. Loneliness will start to lift and temptations and sin that once dominated their lives will become a distant memory – by God's grace.

Isolation... leads to secrecy

Secrecy... leads to a sick character

Sick character... leads to sick conduct and SIN

Sick conduct and SIN... leads to broken relationships with God and people.

Kenny Luck,
Every Man's Ministries

Confess Your Sins to Teammates
Another truth about being in genuine brotherhood is spiritual growth. Men who isolate experience "spiritual constipation" and don't grow into full Christ-likeness. We are told to walk in the light, and the only way to walk in the light is to come out from isolation. When we confess our sins to a trusted brother we prevent isolation.

The Bible says,

Confess to one another therefore your faults (your slips, your false steps, your offenses, your sins) and pray [also] for one another, that you may be healed and restored [to a spiritual tone of mind and heart]. The earnest (heartfelt, continued) prayer of a righteous man makes tremendous power available [dynamic in its working].
James 5:16 - AMP

We will discuss teammates in more depth in Week 9.

Dietrich Bonhoeffer, a German pastor who was imprisoned and later executed by the Nazis when he was 35, wrote "*Why is that it is often easier for us to confess our sins to God than to a brother? God is holy and sinless; He is a just judge of evil and the enemy of all disobedience. But a brother is sinful as we are. He knows from his own experience the dark night of secret sin. WHY should we not find it easier to go to a brother than to a Holy God? But if we do find it easier, we must ask ourselves whether we have not often been deceiving ourselves with our confession of sin to God, whether we have not rather been confessing our sins to ourselves and also granting ourselves absolution (forgiveness) and is not the reason perhaps for our countless relapses and the feebleness of our Christian obedience to be found precisely in the fact that we are living on self-forgiveness and not a real forgiveness? Self forgiveness can never lead to a breach with sin...*" *Life Together, pp. 115-116.*

What a powerful description of our need to confess our sins to a brother in Christ -- it keeps us from self-confession! The more you practice being vulnerable with other men, the easier it will get for you to confess your sins to them as well. This is a vital part of BattleZONE: recruiting teammates to whom you can honestly confess your sins. Do you have someone in your life like that? If you don't, begin praying for God to bring him into your life. Check out BattleZONE Life Teams at **www.battlezoneministries.org.** Just click on Life Teams.

LIFE TEAMS

CAPTAIN'S CORNER
PERSONAL APPLICATION

PLAY 5: Get Real
HIGHLIGHTS

- When men isolate, they develop sin patterns that eventually lead to sin habits that control their lives.
- Men often protect their image when they are hiding something.
- Men must develop a habit of exposing their secrets to another brother in Christ. True Transparency = True Accountability.
- Confession of sins to another Christ-Follower is a command, not a suggestion.
- Only one out of 20 Christian men say they have a best friend they can confide in. *(Source: Promise Keepers)*

1. Why do you resist exposing your flaws? Captain, go first and set the tone.

2. When do you isolate yourself? What are your choices like when you are in isolation? Are they pleasing to God?

3. Do you think men who isolate are more prone to develop patterns of sin? Describe one in your life.

CRUNCH TIME:

What did God want you to learn and do from this Play?

Reaction Training

Use these Reaction Trainer Cards to help you recognize your natural reaction when you are in your BattleZONE. Where the card says "Formation," write in where you were at physically, who you were around, your internal state (H.A.L.T.S.: Hungry, Angry, Lonely, Tired, Stressed). Jot down your reaction to the temptation. Which was/is the dominant nature? Then ask the Holy Spirit to show you a counter-reaction verse that will help you train up your new nature in Christ.

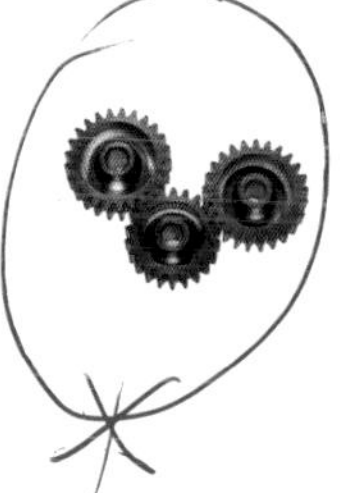

Read Matthew 4:1-11

Jesus is a great model for us when we face temptations. If we have a willing and obedient heart (as He did) and have committed the Word of God to memory (as He did), God can show us the path to follow. The Word of God is always the "counter" action for all oppositional forces. This is why memorizing Scripture is vital. Scripture stored in our heart helps us identify particular temptations for what they really are and gives us the strength to overcome them as the Spirit marries the memorized Word to our consciences and delivers us from evil. (Galatians 1:4).

WEEK 2

REACTION TRAINING

FORMATION:
At the office I am angry at a co-worker.

REACTION:
Talking behind his back, calling him names and holding a grudge.

SCRIPTURE "COUNTER" VERSE:
In your anger do not sin. Do not let the sun go down while you are still angry.
Ephesians 4:26

BATTLE ZONE MINISTRIES, INC.

www.battlezoneministries.org

WEEK 2

REACTION TRAINING

FORMATION:
In front of computer at home while alone

REACTION:
Clicked on porn pop-up

SCRIPTURE "COUNTER" VERSE:
...flee from youthful lusts...
2 Timothy 2:22

BATTLE ZONE MINISTRIES, INC. www.battlezoneministries.org

WEEK 2

REACTION TRAINING

FORMATION:
At the bar with some friends

REACTION:
Got drunk and flirted with women.

SCRIPTURE "COUNTER" VERSE:
Wine is a mocker and beer a brawler; whoever is led astray by them is not wise.
Proverbs 20:1

BATTLE ZONE MINISTRIES, INC. www.battlezoneministries.org

WEEK 2

REACTION TRAINING

FORMATION:
Wife leaves something behind at the house when I was late for engagement.

REACTION:
Angry yelling, condemnation, cursing and disrespect towards my wife.

SCRIPTURE "COUNTER" VERSE:
Love is patient, love is kind.
It is not easily angered.
1 Corinthians 13:4-5

BATTLE ZONE MINISTRIES, INC. www.battlezoneministries.org

WEEK 2

REACTION TRAINING

FORMATION:
Watching an infomercial late at night to get rich quick

REACTION:
Picked up the phone and ordered with money I do not have to spend.

SCRIPTURE "COUNTER" VERSE:
All hard work brings a profit, but mere talk leads only to poverty.
Proverbs 14:32

BATTLE ZONE MINISTRIES, INC. www.battlezoneministries.org

WEEK 2

REACTION TRAINING

FORMATION:
At the kitchen counter I open an unexpected bill that came in the mail.

REACTION:
Fear and worry.

SCRIPTURE "COUNTER" VERSE:
For you did not receive a spirit that makes you a slave again to fear, but you received the Spirit of sonship. And by him we cry, "Abba, Father."
Romans 8:15

BATTLE ZONE MINISTRIES, INC. www.battlezoneministries.org

WEEK 2

REACTION TRAINING

FORMATION:
Eating dinner at home after a tough day at work.

REACTION:
Overate until I was stuffed.

SCRIPTURE "COUNTER" VERSE:
Be careful, or your hearts will be weighed down with dissipation, drunkenness and the anxieties of life, and that day will close on you unexpectedly like a trap.
Luke 21:34

BATTLE ZONE MINISTRIES, INC. www.battlezoneministries.org

REACTION TRAINING

WEEK 2

FORMATION: At Work - accused of not doing my Job Correctly

REACTION: Try to prove accusers wrong

SCRIPTURE "COUNTER" VERSE:
- Let your yes be yes + no be no.
- Integrity of upright will guide me.

BATTLE ZONE MINISTRIES, INC. www.battlezoneministries.org

REACTION TRAINING

WEEK 2

FORMATION: Thinking of my parenting skills towards my son

REACTION: dissappointed in myself - I don't do enough.

SCRIPTURE "COUNTER" VERSE: lack wisdom? - Ask God

BATTLE ZONE MINISTRIES, INC. www.battlezoneministries.org

REACTION TRAINING

WEEK 2

FORMATION: Looking over the bills

REACTION: fear - concern - worry

SCRIPTURE "COUNTER" VERSE: Trust the Lord in all your ways lean not on your own understanding

BATTLE ZONE MINISTRIES, INC. www.battlezoneministries.org

REACTION TRAINING

WEEK 2

FORMATION:

REACTION:

SCRIPTURE "COUNTER" VERSE:

BATTLE ZONE MINISTRIES, INC. www.battlezoneministries.org

REACTION TRAINING

WEEK 2

FORMATION:

REACTION:

SCRIPTURE "COUNTER" VERSE:

BATTLE ZONE MINISTRIES, INC. www.battlezoneministries.org

REACTION TRAINING

WEEK 2

FORMATION:

REACTION:

SCRIPTURE "COUNTER" VERSE:

BATTLE ZONE MINISTRIES, INC. www.battlezoneministries.org

CAPTAIN'S GUIDE

Old vs. New

CAPTAIN'S GUIDE

BATTLEZONE SYMBOL KEY

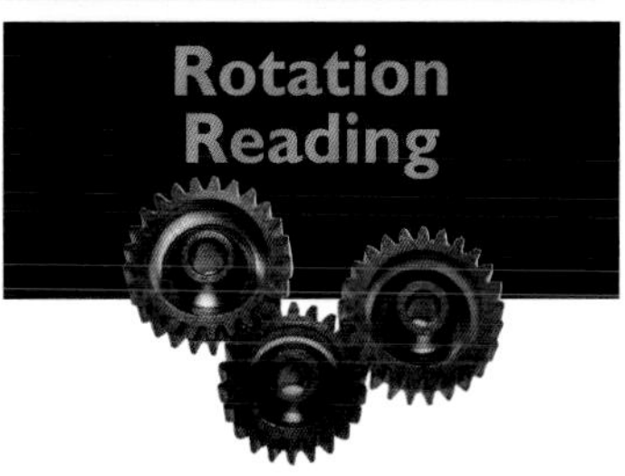

WARM-UP: OLD VS. NEW

You Get Good at What You Practice
Practice makes perfect! When you practice your sin nature, you will get good at hearing its voice and giving in to its suggestions. For instance, if you typically respond to a situation one way, it's hard to respond differently. For example, if a beautiful woman walks by and your typical response is to look her up and down as she passes, this indicates that your sin nature is dominating your response.

Warm-up Option 1:
Ask your men to toss a football back and forth to each other using their non-dominant hand. Do this for two or three minutes.
OR
Utilize the SUPER technique (page 64) to teach your men how to throw a football in a new way. Do this for two or three minutes.

When you do anything with your dominant hand, you develop a unique set of responses that your brain and body get used to. Using your dominant hand becomes a familiar pattern that develops the path of least resistance.

So how do you change? By practice and by the power of the Holy Spirit. Using your non-dominant hand in a familiar activity is similar to the transition of walking under the control of your sin nature to the control of the Holy Spirit.. For instance, to get good at throwing a football in a new way, you have to practice. Same with walking in the Spirit – it's a process of practicing new skills and responses by the power of Jesus Christ.

Warm-up Option 2:
If you don't have room to throw a football, ask your men to write their name three times using their non-dominant hand. Take two or three minutes for this activity.

Writing with your non-dominant hand is hard, isn't it? But each time you do it, it becomes a little bit easier. When you write with your dominant hand, you develop a unique set of responses that your brain and body can get used to. Writing with your dominant hand becomes a familiar pattern that develops the path of least resistance.

So how do you change? By practice and by the power of the Holy Spirit. To get good at writing in a new way, you have to practice. Writing with your non-dominant hand is similar to the transition of walking under the control of your sin nature to your new nature in Christ. Same with walking in the Spirit – it's a process of practicing new skills and new responses by the power of Jesus Christ.

This exercise illustrates why it's so difficult to "change hands" from your old natural responses to your new Christ-centered responses.

Warm Up: Old vs. New

1. Which nature is similar to throwing the football or writing your name with your dominant hand? **Old or New?** ____________

2. Can anyone think of one difficult transition you faced when you first became a Christian as you tried to respond to a situation by obeying your new nature instead of your dominant sin nature?

3. When you are in your BattleZONE which nature dominates you? **Old sin nature or new nature in Christ?**

Old- vs. New Technique

1. Which nature do you feed when practicing a new technique for throwing a football? How about when you lie, cheat or steal?

2. What are some key things you'll need to do in order to be successful at improving your new technique? (Brainstorm with your teammates.) Examples may include practicing, focus, determination, discipline, and coachability.

3. How many of you think you would want to switch back to your old way of throwing the football or writing? Why?

4. Compare this battle with the one you have between your old sin nature and your new nature in Christ when you are in your BattleZONE.

A. Go to the BattleZONE Chalk Talk and proceed to lead your team through Week 2.

New Passing Technique: S.U.P.E.R.

Coaching Clinic

This physical challenge requires a "coaching clinic" to teach you in a new passing technique.

- Each "player" must have a Teammate/captain (TC) to instruct and make adjustments while performing the QB physical execution challenge.
    - As a captain, you will improve your leadership training skills. The job of any captain is to turn potential into performance.
    - As a teammate, you will learn how to develop a coachable spirit and allow your captain to maximize your passing ability.

Shoulder is cocked and ready to throw.

Up field hip and shoulder are pointed at your target.

Palm faces away from ear with a small gap between football and palm (as you grip the ball).

Exaggerate back hip snapping forward to start the throwing motion.

Rotate hand so pinky finger is pointing up after you follow through as shoulder goes down and away. Shift weight to front foot pointing at your target.

To watch a video of S.U.P.E.R. demonstrated, go to
www.battlezoneministries.org > Resources > BZ Course > SUPER

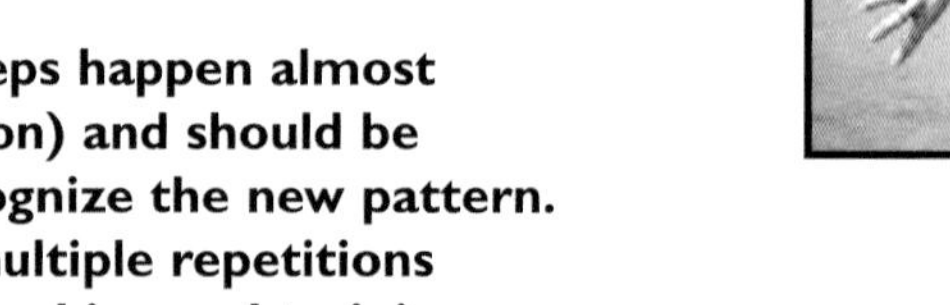

This is one fluid motion (meaning that all of the SUPER steps happen almost simultaneously as soon as the hip starts the throwing motion) and should be practiced without the ball until your brain can start to recognize the new pattern. Once your pattern is developed, start practicing through multiple repetitions throwing the football to your partner. With time, proper coaching and training, you will develop a new dominant way of throwing the football. Good luck and have fun!

CHALK TALK

Old vs. New

ast week we covered the definitions of temptation and holiness. We looked at the decision point and why it is imperative to recognize vhen you are in yours. We also looked at the link between executing and training, especially as it relates to your spiritual eXecution ercentage/threshold (X%/XT). Last, we tackled the difficult tasks of finding your pain point and your BattleZONE.

1. Prayer

Have one of the men open in prayer and ask the Holy Spirit to guide and direct the session towards God's agenda.

2. Quick Review of BattleZONE Terms

Oppositional Forces

There are three oppositional forces Christians face: Satan, the sin nature (the flesh) and the World. Their coordinated efforts are onstantly scheming to get you to fail in your BattleZONEs. This week, we will study the sin nature.

3. Week 2 Plays

For Week 2 you were assigned to read and be ready to comment on five Plays. You will have **TWO MINUTES** to present your topic; hen discuss each as a group. Please try to stay focused on what God taught you through this Play. **What did God want you to learn and do? Make sure you are underlining or highlighting key points as you read each play as well as answer questions and ake notes on the opposite page.**

CAPTAIN, ASSIGN EACH TEAMMATE A PLAY – THEN LET THEM TAKE THE LEAD.

As a captain, it is imperative that you model how to teach a play call with your men.
Take Play 1: Conflicting Desires and model by doing the following:

1) Read the scripture verse out loud;
2) Show the men where you highlighted, underlined or circled parts of the text that spoke to you and you wanted to share – don't assume that these men will mark up the text on their own – encourage them to do so. Let them know that they will need to have reminders for when they "coach" a play or teaching;
3) Read the "Highlights" from the Captain's Corner out loud;
4) Answer each question and facilitate brief discussion on each point.

Next, assign Plays 2 through 5 to the men. Remember to coach them as they "teach" the "plays" to their teammates. They have 2 minutes.

- **Play 2: Sinner or Saint?**
- **Play 3: Retraining Program**
- **Play 4: Coachable Spirit**
- **Play 5: Get Real**

4. Pain Point: BattleZONE Related to Pain Point/Course Goal

This past week, most of you wrestled with your pain point. Do you have any questions? Who had trouble nailing down his pain point? Who took the BattleZONE Challenge? Did you print your report?

Refer back to the Pain Points on page 35 in Week 1.

Let's talk about the personal BattleZONE that you prayerfully allowed God to select for you. You can still change your BattleZONE if the Holy Spirit is prompting you to get real.

5. Dominant Reactio

Get with your teammate/captain for this activity. Your captain will read some random situations. React naturally as you normally would, not how you think you should respond. Just blurt out your response at the same time to each other. For example, how would you respond to this temptation: A bank teller gives you an extra $100 bill…

Now respond to the following temptation situations as quickly as you can out loud to your TC:

a. A beer commercial flaunting women's breasts comes on TV...
b. A porn pop-up comes onto your computer screen...
c. A friend tells you a racist joke...
d. Your neighbor drives up in a car you can only dream about...
e. The guys from work invite you to the bar after a bad day...
f. You just heard your pastor is having an affair...
g. You get an unexpected bill you don't have the money to pay...
h. A beautiful woman jogs by while you're at a stoplight...
i. Your wife catches you in a lie...

6. Reaction Trainer Cards

During this practice session you have learned that throwing a football or writing your name with your non-dominant hand is difficult. You also noticed that there is a strong desire to change back to the old way because you are not as skilled. This reaction is parallel to your old nature, which wants to dominate your reactions in every situation. The old sin nature is like your old way of doing things: you are used to it and are comfortable operating with it. So in order to develop a new reaction to temptation, you must train your new nature in Christ so it becomes the dominant "hand" when you are tempted. When you give in to your old ways and sin, you must make an immediate adjustment by confessing your slip to God and turning from your sinful ways.

Captain, have the men turn to the page 58 and see read the Reaction Trainer Example. Then turn to page 59 for the Reaction Training Card Examples. Walk through a couple of examples and have the men carefully tear out the blank Reaction Trainer Card template on page 60, or download at **www.battlezoneministries.org > Resources > BZ Course > Reaction Trainer Cards**. These are to be used throughout the week to better understand your automatic reactions to certain temptation situations. You may need to show them how to find a "counter verse" for his BattleZONE by using the Bible index or **Biblegateway.com > Topical Index**.

7. Crunch Time

Have each teammate describe one thing that really "hit" him during this practice session.

8. Independent Practice

1. Finish selecting your pain point, BattleZONE and goal.
2. Read and internalize the objectives on next week's cover page.
3. Read and meditate on the set of Strength Training Cards for the next week as often as you can. You can print a full color version by going to **www.battlezoneministries.org > Resources > BZ Course > Strength Training**.
4. Use Reaction Trainer Cards to determine your immediate responses in your BattleZONE. Be sure to look up the "counter verses" based on the temptation situation.
5. Read all five of the Plays and be prepared to teach a lesson to the team next week. Share with your team how God spoke to you.
6. Call your Teammate/Captain at least once this week and pray for him daily.

9. Iron Sharpens Iron (1 John 1:9)

Captain: For Week 2, you will demonstrate to the men what confessional prayer looks like.
Each week we will end with a sacred time for confession either with your Teammate/Captain or as a team. This is a time to come clean of any sin you have in your life. Allow the Holy Spirit to search you and Christ's blood to cleanse you. Ask for prayer requests from each man and have each man record requests to use during their personal prayer time. This week, ask if anyone has done anything that compromised his walk with God? If yes, name it in general terms (i.e., lust, greed, lying). Confessional prayer can be done as a team or in private with TC.

PRAYER REQUESTS AND PRAISES

NAME Patrick
REQUEST money Camelh
RESULT

NAME Jose
REQUEST strength + encouragement – more grace
RESULT

NAME Ariel
REQUEST foster care Process – Right baby
RESULT

NAME Reve Harry
REQUEST – God's wisdom while ministering to people
RESULT Patience – w

NAME
REQUEST
RESULT

NAME
REQUEST
RESULT

NAME
REQUEST
RESULT

NAME
REQUEST
RESULT

BattleZONE Victories

Damon Schlenske
Helena, MT

"You have been called, the trumpet has sounded, and now probably for t first time in your entire life you can have total control of the "whistle."

In all of my years of seeking material to help me in my own daily spiritua walk I have finally found what I believe is a course that is "top of the educational courses" on the pyramid of spiritual learning. I compare this course to the story of Gideon, and how he (like myself and many others look for excuse after excuse not to follow the direction of God, but whe God said, "I will be with thee", fear not," Gideon began his journey to tea down all of the alters of idolatry, the walls of transgression, obstacles anc challenges that also befall all of us.

My spiritual freedom was granted me on April 18th 1979, although I was "new born" rookie I was not intimidated by what I didn't know, because realized I knew the God that would help me learn what I needed to lear I plan on using the BattleZONE Training Course to introduce a meaningf and realistic tool to those men who need to become "veterans" of their spiritual life. Having the BZ Course will enable me not only educate, but pinpoint a man's areas of pain and suffering. My excitement lies within the composition of the BZ Course, and that is it has been birthed out of the Word of God. I believe men who graduate the BZ Course will use it ove and over again through out their life. I see the BZ Course as being a generational gift from Michael Pouliot to those men who use this Biblical training tool and experience the benefits almost immediately, so they can eventually "pass" the truth onto their sons.

Without a doubt I believe that this course will give men "bonuses" never ever realized or negotiated in any other form of personal and spiritual areas of significance. Course graduates will be able to recognize, plan, attack, accept, be aware off, defend areas of pain and compromise never before possible. The BZ Course enables every single graduate to become a "Hall of Fame" coach. You will learn to activate your spiritual authority go and make disciples of all nations in the name of the Father and of the Son and of the Holy Spirit, and teaching your students them to obey everything God has commanded and to realize, possibly for the first time in your life that God is truly with you always, to the very end of the age.

Nothing has given me more gratitude then having my wife and children recognize the changes that have occurred in me since my commitment to facing my biggest challenges and temptations. One of mans greatest rewards in life is to have a wife who recognizes your efforts to change, and try to become more Christlike. The BattleZONE Training Course wil add so much to a man's personal and spiritual resume that it will affect hi entire life, what is that worth? It's priceless!

If a man is seeking to fill what ever void he has in his life then the BZ Course will ultimately be a great adjunct to the Word of God in directing his path.

My prayer is for those men that are seeking a true meaning of leadership and discipleship--that you will take the "BattleZONE Challenge" and see how incredible this course is in terms of attainable answers and positive long-term spiritual results. Like Gideon blowing his trumpet to battle, you can blow your whistle, and lead a small army of BattleZONE Alumni unto the battle field of life, and expect to be victorious. I urge men who want to see how to follow a spiritual game plan like no other--to take the BattleZONE Challenge.

Oppositional Forces

- Scouting Report
- Formation Recognition
- Ready List
- Oppositional Force #1 (Sin Nature)
- Oppositional Force #2 (Satan)
- Oppositional Force #3 (The World)
- Hate Sin and Fear the Lord

Week 3 Objectives

Each man will understand:

1. The difference between a Scouting Report and Formation Recognition as they relate to his BattleZONEs.
2. The three oppositional forces and how each works against holiness.
3. Satan's evil nature and his detailed Scouting Report.
4. Internal and External "Formations" as they relate to his BattleZONE.
5. The World's influence on the pursuit of holiness.
6. Besetting sins he doesn't hate and why.
7. How to complete a Formation Recognition Form based on a temptation situation.

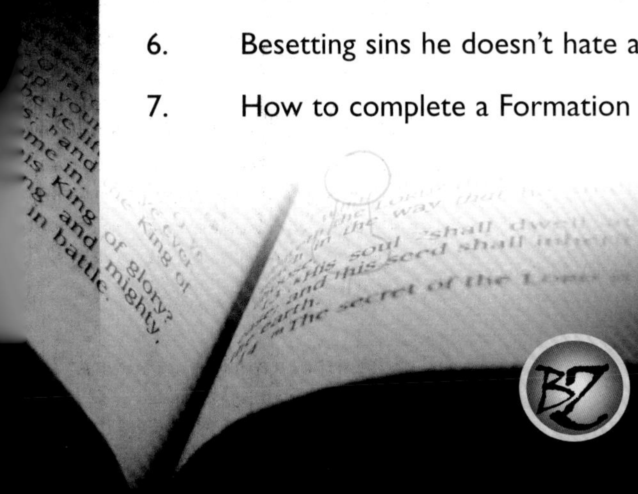

Love must be sincere. Hate what is evil; cling to what is good.
Romans 12:9 - NIV

Be of sober spirit, be on the alert. Your adversary, the devil, prowls around like a roaring lion, seeking someone to devour.
I Peter 5:8 - NASB

Therefore submit to God. Resist the devil and he will flee from you.
James 4:7 - NKJV

For the love of money is a root of all kinds of evil. Some people, eager for money, have wandered from the faith and pierced themselves with many griefs. But you, man of God, flee from all this, and pursue righteousness, godliness, faith, love, endurance and gentleness. Fight the good fight of the faith.
I Timothy 6:10-12a - NIV

Do not love the world or anything in the world. If anyone loves the world, the love of the Father is not in him. For everything in the world -- the cravings of sinful man, the lust of his eyes and the boasting of what he has and does -- comes not from the Father but from the world. The world and its desires pass away, but the man who does the will of God lives forever.
I John 2:15-17 - NIV

Search me, O God, and know my heart; test me and know my anxious thoughts. See if there is any offensive way in me, and lead me in the way everlasting.
Psalm 139:23-24 - NIV

WEEK 3

STRENGTH TRAINING

Love must be sincere. Hate what is evil; cling to what is good.

Romans 12:9 - NIV

BATTLE ZONE MINISTRIES, INC. **www.battlezoneministries.org**

WEEK 3

STRENGTH TRAINING

Be of sober spirit, be on the alert. Your adversary, the devil, prowls around like a roaring lion, seeking someone to devour.

1 Peter 5:8 - NASB

BATTLE ZONE MINISTRIES, INC. **www.battlezoneministries.org**

WEEK 3

STRENGTH TRAINING

Therefore submit to God. Resist the devil and he will flee from you.

James 4:7 - NKJV

BATTLE ZONE MINISTRIES, INC. **www.battlezoneministries.org**

WEEK 3

STRENGTH TRAINING

For the love of money is a root of all kinds of evil. Some people, eager for money, have wandered from the faith and pierced themselves with many griefs. But you, man of God, flee from all this, and pursue righteousness, godliness, faith, love, endurance and gentleness. Fight the good fight of the faith.

1 Timothy 6:10-12a - NIV

BATTLE ZONE MINISTRIES, INC. **www.battlezoneministries.org**

WEEK 3

STRENGTH TRAINING

Do not love the world or anything in the world. If anyone loves the world, the love of the Father is not in him. For everything in the world -- the cravings of sinful man, the lust of his eyes and the boasting of what he has and does -- comes not from the Father but from the world. The world and its desires pass away, but the man who does the will of God lives forever.

1 John 2:15-17 - NIV

www.battlezoneministries.org

WEEK 3

STRENGTH TRAINING

Search me, O God, and know my heart; test me and know my anxious thoughts. See if there is any offensive way in me, and lead me in the way everlasting.

Psalm 139:23-24 - NIV

www.battlezoneministries.org

NOTES
STRENGTH
TRAINING
BATTLE ZONE
MINISTRIES, INC.
www.battlezoneministries.org
NOTES
STRENGTH
TRAINING
BATTLE ZONE
MINISTRIES, INC.
www.battlezoneministries.org
NOTES
STRENGTH
TRAINING
BATTLE ZONE
MINISTRIES, INC.
www.battlezoneministries.org
NOTES
STRENGTH
TRAINING
BATTLE ZONE
MINISTRIES, INC.
www.battlezoneministries.org
NOTES
STRENGTH
TRAINING
BATTLE ZONE
MINISTRIES, INC.
www.battlezoneministries.org
NOTES
STRENGTH
TRAINING
BATTLE ZONE
MINISTRIES, INC.
www.battlezoneministries.org

SHOW ME HOW TO RECEIVE A FATHER'S BLESSING

Go to www.battlezoneministries.org > Training > Show Me How To > Fathers Blessing

HOW TO **VIDEO**

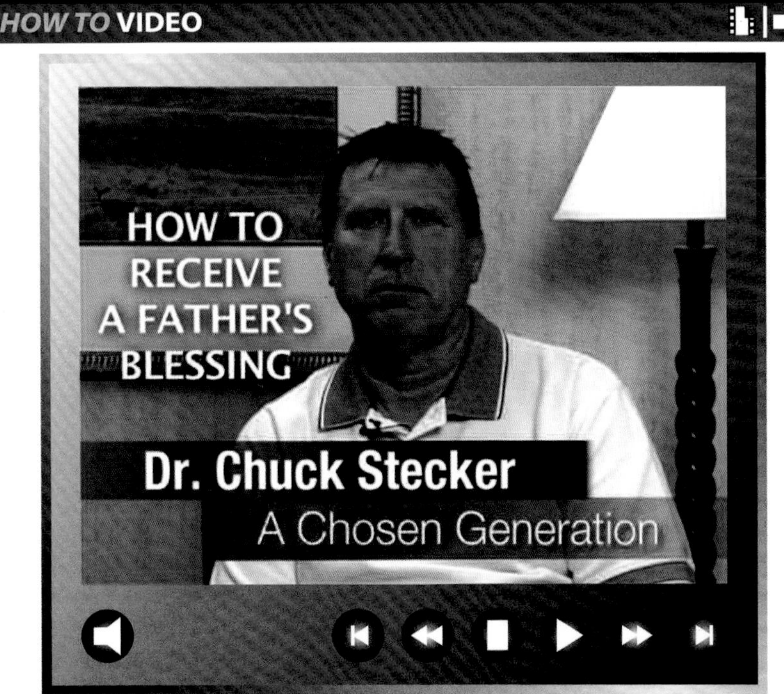

Some men have never known a father's blessing. Your identity as a son can be secured when you receive a father's blessing. Men cannot give what they do not posses. Men need to receive a father's blessing so they can be whole and pass this blessing on to their own children.

Dr. Chuck Stecker of *A Chosen Generation*, shows us how to give and receive a father's blessing. If you have never received this blessing, Dr. Stecker challenges you to find an older man of God to fill that "father" hole in your heart.

At BattleZONE Ministries...
We Show You How!

PLAY 1 : Oppositional Forces

The great dragon was hurled down–that ancient serpent called the devil, or Satan, who leads the whole world astray. He was hurled to the earth, and his angels with him.
Revelation 12:9 - NIV

Know the Competition

In order to develop an effective game plan, you must first know your competition. A coach must study his opponent's strengths, weaknesses and habits. Christians must also study the forces and strategies that interfere with our ability to execute God's will. There are three elements to this opposition – the world, the flesh (sin nature) and the Devil – just as there are three critical components to the game of football: offense, defense and special teams. The **World** is like the offense, because it is constantly trying to jam itself down your throat with materialism, consumerism, egoism and relativism, all of which attack the Biblical foundation of Jesus, the Messiah. The defense is represented by the **flesh** (or **sin nature**), which tries to keep your new nature from crossing the goal line and living holy for God. Finally, **Satan** and his demons are the "special teams" because they carry out multiple strategies to defeat you in numerous settings. As you study your opponent, and begin to understand the subtle work of the world, the flesh and the Devil, realize that your daily victory over your opponent is only possible because of God's sovereign authority.

The World

Stop loving this evil world and all that it offers you, for when you love the world, you show that you do not have the love of the Father in you. For the world offers only the lust for physical pleasure, the lust for everything we see, and pride in our possessions. These are not from the Father. They are from this evil world. And this world is fading away, along with everything it craves. But if you do the will of God, you will live forever.
I John 2:15-17 - NLT

We can't control much of what goes on in the world, but we can reduce its influence on our minds and hearts by establishing a sound defensive strategy that minimizes how deep the world penetrates into our "backfield." We can also minimize the impact the world has on us by staying clear of certain "formations" and by fleeing from things that stimulate us to sin. We can also lessen the world's impact by limiting our exposure to worldly things that stimulate our sin nature, such as advertising and TV.

The Flesh

As Christians, we can't control the world and we can't control the schemes of Satan, but we can learn to control our sin nature through spiritual fitness training and by yielding to God's Spirit. The Bible tells us that our sin nature is no longer our coach – we have a new coach called Righteousness. Henry Blackaby says,

"We must face the battle, but God promises us the victory if we remain in His will. As with the Israelites, our decision will be evident by the outcome. If you are continually being defeated by everything you face, your heart has departed from God. If you have experienced defeat in the challenges you face, examine your heart. Choose to listen to God. Then obey what He tells you, no matter what you face, and you will experience victory."
Experiencing God Day by Day, p. 288

Satan

Satan is referred to as "the anointed cherub" (Ezekiel 28:14), "the ruler of the demons" (Luke 11:15), "the god of this world" (2 Corinthians 4:4), and the "prince of the power of the air" (Ephesians 2:2). Satan has a Scouting Report **on every one of God's children** and he waits patiently to pounce on us when we are vulnerable so he can entice our sin nature to join his efforts. While we can't control the Devil, we do have a defense to ward off his vicious attacks. Satan has been given dominion over the world, but we can be protected if we understand God's game plan and stick to it. The Bible tells us to humble ourselves and resist Satan's attacks, but before we are ready for his attacks, we must first put on our spiritual equipment, the Whole Armor of God. God's "Playbook" teaches us that when we draw close to God through our spiritual training program, He will draw closer to us. God also promises that the Holy Spirit (who is in us) is more powerful than the Prince of this World, Satan.

Stop Fighting – Start Resisting

Therefore submit to God. Resist the devil and he will flee from you.
James 4:7 - NKJV

Part of Satan's deception is that he wants us to believe that we are still fighting him, and that God has not yet defeated him through Jesus' blood. This false belief alone can keep us from experiencing God's true peace. Our responsibility as believers is not to *fight* Satan, but to *resist* him. This is a subtle difference. By resisting Satan, we demonstrate that Jesus has already won the war over the ultimate adversary, but we must continually submit ourselves to Christ in order to resist Satan's attacks.

CAPTAIN'S CORNER
PERSONAL APPLICATION

PLAY 1: Oppositional Forces HIGHLIGHTS

- There are three oppositional forces that unite with the goal of getting you to sin against God.
- Satan knows your weaknesses and exploits them every chance he gets.
- Don't fight against Satan and his demons, just humble yourself to God and resist his attacks.
- The World fights against God's will for your life. We cannot love both God and the World.

1. Do you know how each one of the oppositional forces (Satan, sin nature and the World) attack you in your BattleZONE? Give one example.

CRUNCH TIME:

What did God want you to learn and do from this Play?

* Remember, we don't fight Satan we resist him as we rest in God's finished work + grace

PLAY 2 : Scouting Report

So then the dragon was furious (enraged) at the woman, and he went away to wage war on the remainder of her descendants -- [on those] who obey God's commandments and who have the testimony of Jesus Christ [and adhere to it and bear witness to Him].

Revelation 12:17 - AMP

Scouting Report

Tremendous preparation and skill go into preparing a team for game day. All football coaches prepare a "Scouting Report" for their games by studying their opponent's strengths, weaknesses and tendencies. Scouting Reports also entail an honest look at their own team's respective strengths and weaknesses compared to their opponents. Coaches who can honestly assess their personnel can create sound game plans to compensate for potential problem areas or player mismatches. In addition to formation and tendency information, scouting reports help coaches create "call sheets" or "ready lists" to help them counteract their opponent's tactics.

Scouting Report

A detailed report of the opposing team's strategies, threats, formations and tendencies used to develop a game plan and prepare players for an upcoming game.

The first step for football coaches is to create situations where their players can study and counter their opponent's offensive and defensive strategies and tendencies. Do they run a 4-4 or 5-2 defense? What are their "bread and butter" plays? Who are their greatest threats? What about their special-teams package? Hundreds of hours are spent watching game film dissecting the opponent's schemes and play tendencies. Each play is charted to give a statistical percentage of an opponent's play-calls. Coaches watch multiple game films of the opponent and chart which plays are typically called during certain downs, distances, and field positions. This results in a tendency report, which helps coaches not only understand the opponent, but also in adjusting their game plan to counteract weaknesses in personnel or in their offensive and defensive play packages. For example, if an opponent always lines up five wide receivers and throws the ball 75% of the time, it would be wise for the reviewing team to create a "nickel package" defense. A "nickel package" is five defensive backs instead of four.

Ready List

A list of several plays ready to be used in an upcoming game, tailored to an opposing team's strengths and weaknesses. Also known as an "automatic".

The Christian's Scouting Report

Just as a football team develops Scouting Reports for their opponents, Christians must also understand their opponents' strategies as well as their own vulnerabilities,

...that no advantage may be gained over us by Satan: for we are not ignorant of his devices.

2 Corinthians 2:11 - ASV

In the scripture above, Paul tells us that Satan wants to produce sin in our lives, so we should not be unaware of his devices, schemes or wiles that plot against our minds, wills and emotions. God has provided us the necessary protection through the "Holy Playbook". But, to succeed, we must study the "Playbook" in order to unmask the threats and plans of the Devil.

Satan's Ready List

Rest assured that Satan approaches his game plan in a more comprehensive, sophisticated fashion than the greatest coaching staff ever assembled. He knows your strengths, weaknesses and tendencies – not to mention his acute accuracy in play-calling to crush you during temptation. He creates his very own "ready list" for each and every one of God's children. He knows what makes you weak and how to take advantage of your tendencies. He lies, cheats and steals with the single purpose of making you fail in your BattleZONEs. The Devil has every "game film" on you and knows your tendencies and he uses them in the most deceiving ways to get you to give in to temptation and sin. (Note: The Devil also has another advantage. He can not only deceive you, but all the other parties involved – and he knows all of their weaknesses, too.)

Your BattleZONEs are where all of these opposing forces unite. This united front has one goal in mind: To make you sin and keep you from experiencing holiness.

CAPTAIN'S CORNER
PERSONAL APPLICATION

PLAY 2: Scouting Report HIGHLIGHTS

- A scouting report helps you understand your opponent and honestly examine your strengths and weaknesses.
- You must understand your personal tendencies that keep leading to sin.
- Satan has a detailed scouting report on you and he stops at nothing to entice you to sin.

1. Satan entices our sin nature by encouraging us to lie, cheat and steal. –

☐ True ☑ False

2. How does it make you feel to know that Satan has every "game film" on you and how you personally "play" the life game?

no feelings – it's part of the game.

3. Do you think your obedience to God angers Satan? Why?

yes – He hates God and everyone who is obediently serving Him.

CRUNCH TIME:

What did God want you to learn and do from this Play?

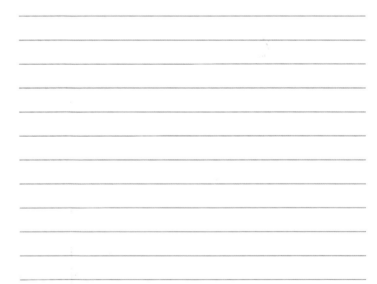

Know your enemy

Study to show yourself approved!

(• What about writing a program that isn't sport specific –)

PLAY 3 : Formation Recognition

Be well balanced (temperate, sober of mind), be vigilant and cautious at all times; for that enemy of yours, the devil, roams around like a lion roaring [in fierce hunger], seeking someone to seize upon and devour.

I Peter 5:8 - AMP

Be Alert

Peter warns us to be alert and cautious at all times, because Satan, our opponent, prowls around like a hungry lion seeking for his prey – you! He does all he can to put you in a situation that he believes is ideal for the kill. That moment has to do with the perfect situation where the Devil knows he can pounce on you and devour your witness for Christ. These situations can be your internal state of mind or emotions, and/or your physical location, the person or people you're with, and the time of day. For instance, the Devil may pounce on you when you get home from work and you're standing in your kitchen ready to overeat to soothe yourself from a stressful day.

H.A.L.T.S.

H ungry
A ngry
L onely
T ired
S tressed

The Two Areas of Formation Recognition

We sharpen our minds by understanding and studying the strategies and game plans of the Evil One and how he uses these schemes on each of us. First, let's examine external situations in your personal life that may heighten your temptation, thus leading to a low X% in your BattleZONE. The BattleZONE Scouting Report Formation Recognition Form is a tool to help you develop an alert mind so you can recognize the strategies of your opponent's attacks based on your formation, or 1) external and 2) internal situations.

External Formations

External formations involve where, when and who:

- **Where are you?**
  In a bar? At home? At a friend's house? In your car?
- **When are you there?**
  Late at night? After work? At lunch?
- **Who are you with?**
  By yourself? With a particular person? In a group?

Internal Formations

Internal Formations involve your mind and emotions, as well as internal body chemistry (for instance, blood sugar level or blood alcohol content). You may be in the H.A.L.T.S. ZONE: Hungry, Angry, Lonely, Tired or Stressed.

Have you ever seen a football game where the referee called a penalty on the defense for shouting out a false snap count that caused an offensive player to be fooled and start the play prematurely? Jesus said that His sheep recognize His voice (John 10:4-5), but there is another voice that will try to trick you into believing it came from the authentic holy source. This voice of deception is from the liar himself, Satan. Satan is the liar who shoots fiery arrows of lies and deception to try to get us to sin against God.

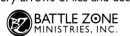

One of the biggest mistakes Christians make is believing the lies Satan plants in our minds. We mistakenly think that "flash thoughts" are our own. Since we believe these thoughts are coming from us, we automatically agree with them and accept them, without questioning the source. When you agree with the lie and accept it as your own thought, this gives the Devil the signal to send an all-out blitz of more lies that may cause you to go even further down the path of sin. Satan's lies can deceive you into sin (even though ultimately it is your choice to sin or not) and condemn you for sinning even after you have confessed your sins to God.

You will have multiple opportunities to decide whose voice you are hearing. Is it the other team trying to get you to make a mistake? Or is it the voice of truth? Each thought becomes a **decision point** in and of itself, which you can either accept or reject. When you train yourself to reject Satan's lies and correct the thought, you will allow your new nature to become dominant. Learn the R4-Technique and use it when Satan shoots his fiery arrows into your mind:

- **R**ecognize the thought (you may need to write it down) and hold it captive *(2 Corinthians 10:5)*.
- **R**emember you have the mind of Christ *(1 Corinthians 2:13b)* and a new righteous heart *(Ezekiel 36:26-27; Corinthians 5:17; Titus 3:5)*.
- **R**eject/**R**esist the lie and its source (Satan) *(James 4:7)*.
- **R**ecall God's truth *(John 8:32; 2 Timothy 3:16)*.

Remember the prevalent spiritual, environmental, psychological and emotional circumstances or "formations" that lead up to your defeat in your BattleZONEs. Do you know yours?

CAPTAIN'S CORNER
PERSONAL APPLICATION

PLAY 3: Formation Recognition HIGHLIGHTS

- Satan prowls around like a roaring lion waiting to pounce on you – be alert for his attacks.
- Certain external environments can entice us to sin.
- Certain internal conditions can entice you to sin. (H.A.L.T.S.)
- Satan can plant lies in our minds; we must hold each thought captive and ask if the thought is true, or if it is a random attack from the Devil. Reject and correct the lies.

1. Name an external formation Satan likes to see you in. Why?

?

2. Name an internal formation Satan likes to see you in. Why?

Tired = Angry

3. Do you regularly agree with the lies Satan plants in your thoughts? Give one example.

One area –
I'm not doing enough to provide for my family

CRUNCH TIME:

What did God want you to learn and do from this Play?

PLAY 4 : The World

For the love of money is a root of all kinds of evil. Some people, eager for money, have wandered from the faith and pierced themselves with many griefs. But you, man of God, flee from all this, and pursue righteousness, godliness, faith, love, endurance and gentleness. Fight the good fight of the faith. Take hold of the eternal life to which you were called when you made your good confession in the presence of many witnesses.

I Timothy 6:10-12 - NIV

Fantasy Land

Imagine being an NFL athlete making millions of dollars each year. What an incredible thought! But have you ever considered what else comes with the status of being an NFL superstar? Think of the incredible pull from the influences of the world: A twenty-something athlete with the ability to buy anything he wants, with multiple opportunities to commit adultery and be praised by men, women and children no matter what he does. Throw in the fact that some of these athletes are professing Christians. Former NFL lineman Ken Hutcherson calls Christians' moral failings in sports an all-encompassing problem. Hutcherson goes on to say in an online article on *ChristianityToday.com*, "Coddled by parents, coaches, schools, and professional teams, many spend years in 'Fantasy Land' where they will never face accountability." Last, he says, "If that maturity isn't there, that guy is going to come and speak [to Christians] when he was out the night before drinking, or sleeping with his girlfriend. Now what is that doing to an [immature Christian] who is already not making good decisions?"

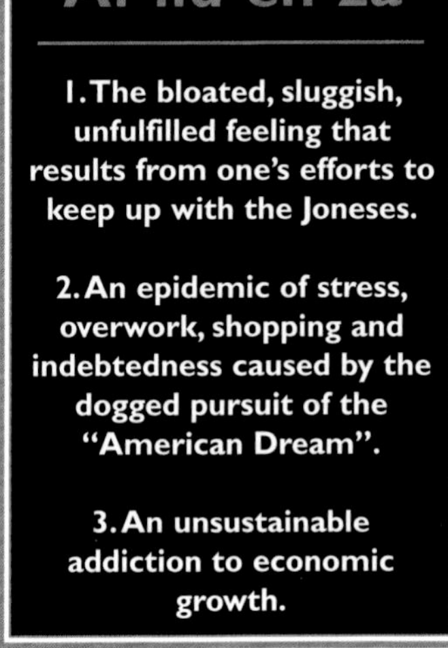

Af-flu-en-za

1. The bloated, sluggish, unfulfilled feeling that results from one's efforts to keep up with the Joneses.

2. An epidemic of stress, overwork, shopping and indebtedness caused by the dogged pursuit of the "American Dream".

3. An unsustainable addiction to economic growth.

The Bible is filled with verses that warn against the love of money, not against money itself. It's our attitude that needs watching, not our material possessions. Scripture is clear that we're to store up our treasures in heaven rather than on earth (Matthew 6:19-20). Even though money and material possessions are not evil in and of themselves, it's easy for them to become central to our everyday lives.

The World is the third oppositional force that ruthlessly tries to get our focus off of Jesus and onto worldly things. In 1997, a PBS special called "Affluenza" described the grip the world has on so many Americans. (For more on "affluenza" visit **www.pbs.org/kcts/affluenza**.) Many Christians are also caught in this "dis-ease". We discipline ourselves to pursue "stuff" rather than holiness. What about you? How does your spiritual discipline compare?

Unbelief

What causes us to be so vulnerable to worldly temptations? It can be summed up in one word: unbelief. Author and speaker Beth Moore writes in her book, *When Godly People Do Ungodly Things, Arming Yourself in the Age of Seduction* (Broadman & Holman, 2002, p. 25),

"If we searched for the root of our seasons of sin, we would find that a disastrous harvest almost always has its beginning in a deeply imbedded seed of distrust. Some level of unbelief is involved in every sin."

Moore goes on to say that unbelief gives Satan an open doorway to seduce us into a pit of sin. Often, doubt is the fuel for temptation and sin when we don't believe God will meet all our needs.

Who/what are you pursuing; The World or the Word? When we doubt God's ability to meet all of our needs, we put ourselves in a weak formation for Satan to exploit. Satan will crush us if our hearts are divided with unbelief between God's Word and the world. Don't be double-minded: When we are pursuing things of the world we cannot pursue holiness. If God's truth conflicts with a goal of yours, you must change your goal. We must stand for truth even when it conflicts with a goal, want or desire – no exceptions! God's way is always the right choice. Do you believe that?

The world is full of "eye candy" that stimulates our sin nature. That's why it's so important to be able to recognize your internal desires and pray Psalm 139:23-24. This prayer can be very painful as God reveals your selfish ambition

But if you are bitterly jealous and there is selfish ambition in your hearts, don't brag about being wise. That is the worst kind of lie. For jealousy and selfishness are not God's kind of wisdom. Such things are earthly, unspiritual, and motivated by the Devil. For wherever there is jealousy and selfish ambition, there you will find disorder and every kind of evil.

James 3:14-16 - NLT

CAPTAIN'S CORNER
PERSONAL APPLICATION

PLAY 4: The World
HIGHLIGHTS

- The love of money is the root of all kinds of evil. Money itself is not evil.
- Unbelief in God's sovereignty weakens our ability to resist temptation.
- We become dissatisfied when we are focused on worldly things.
- When we pursue things of the World we cannot pursue holiness.

1. What worldly things do you pursue more than holiness?

?

2. What lie do you believe that causes your worldly pursuit? (i.e., if I had ____________, then I would be happy).

?

3. Can you think of an area of unbelief that has you doubting God's will for your life?

CRUNCH TIME:

What did God want you to learn and do from this Play?

PLAY 5 : Should We Hate Sin?

We must desire to love God more than any evil desires. [Let your] love be sincere (a real thing); hate what is evil [loathe all ungodliness, turn in horror from wickedness], but hold fast to that which is good.

Romans 12:9 - AMP

What is Your Reaction Response to Sin?

The Bible commands us to hate what is evil. All sin is evil, so we are to hate sin. Not only are you to hate sin, you must also train yourself to despise the desires that cause you to sin. You must train yourself to hate sin as much as God does. This takes an effort of will to change your perspective.

For instance, there is an ongoing debate about alcohol consumption among Christians. The Bible does not say that alcohol is forbidden, although the Bible is clear that drunkenness is sinful (Ephesians 6:18) as is causing a weaker Christian to stumble. Some Christians stumble with drunkenness because other Christians openly drink alcohol around them, and even worse, at church functions.

Romans 8:9 tells us plainly that God commands us to love Him more than anything the world has to offer. For instance, most men love beer – everything about it: its taste, its smell, and, of course, the buzz. Again, beer is not forbidden, but drunkenness is. So how do we train ourselves to hate sin, if we love it? Through focused and disciplined training of your mind. If you struggle with drunkenness you can train your mind to hate everything about alcohol every time you think about it. Instead of dwelling on how great it would be to down a tall cool one, train yourself to think about how awful it is, if it causes you to sin against God. By God's grace, you can train yourself to hate it. The training of the mind is an act of your will, but it's by God's loving grace that you can be delivered from the BattleZONE of drunkenness.

We are promised in Galatians 5:17 that the Spirit gives us the desires that are opposite from what our sinful nature desires. However, you must take responsible steps to avoid sin physically, relationally, emotionally and mentally. The discipline of spiritual training will help you desire God more than your lusts or idols. When we pursue Christ, we will not have the desire to pursue sin.

The key to victory in any BattleZONE is the desire to execute God's will more than anything else. You can only accomplish this by training yourself to hate what is wrong and love God more than the willful acts of disobedience.

The Fear of the Lord

But to man He said, "Behold, the reverential and worshipful fear of the Lord – that is Wisdom; and to depart from evil is understanding."

Job 28:28 - AMP

Just as a coach gets angry when a player makes a mental mistake on the field, God is angered by sin. He is angered by sin because He is just and holy. The good news is that He poured out His just wrath on Jesus at Calvary.

In the first part of Job 28:28 we are told that we will gain wisdom if we fear the Lord. But what does it mean to "fear" the Lord? If God is love why should we fear Him?

To fear the Lord means that you respect Him so much and have such reverence for His authority and power that you do not want to disappoint Him by your actions. This would be like athletes not wanting to disappoint a well-respected coach, like John Wooden – his players respected him so much that they feared disappointing him out of a submissive fear, not out of terror. Remember that as Christ-Followers, when we stand before God on Judgment Day, we will be held accountable for our works. The good news for believers is that we have already been judged for our sins and forgiven because of Christ's blood that was shed on the cross. Likewise, those who are without Christ will be held accountable for all of their sins – every one of them – whether thought, deed or action.

In the second part of this verse, it is very clear that when we depart from evil deeds, we gain understanding. In other words, we understand sin and we hate it. Are you fearful of getting caught when you sin or afraid of letting the Father down? Remember when we sin, we are to confess our sins to God; He is faithful and just to cleanse and forgive us (1 John 1:9). Do you hate sin? If not this is evidence that you will never have godly wisdom. Think about that.

CAPTAIN'S CORNER
PERSONAL APPLICATION

PLAY 5: Should We Hate Sin? HIGHLIGHTS

- There is a battle for your decision every time you are tempted. Your desires will help mold your decision patterns.
- God readily gives us desires that are opposite from our sin nature desires through the Holy Spirit.
- Every Christ-Follower has two natures that war against one another; the new nature and the old sin nature. Our choices are never free from this conflict.
- Seeking and yielding to God's will for your life will help shape your desires.
- The fear of the Lord is the desire to obey God out of reverence and respect, knowing that if you sin, it does disappoint and grieves God the Holy Spirit.

1. What is one sin that you honestly do not hate?

Bad eating habits

2. What is a sin that you "snicker" at? When someone says they did something that you know offends God, whether in real life or on TV, do you "snicker"? Are you entertained by sin? Explain.

3. What does the Bible say about drunkenness? How does that compare to your personal beliefs and actions regarding alcohol?

Sin – over use of alcohol can lead to sin.

CRUNCH TIME:

What did God want you to learn and do from this Play?

BattleZONE Victories

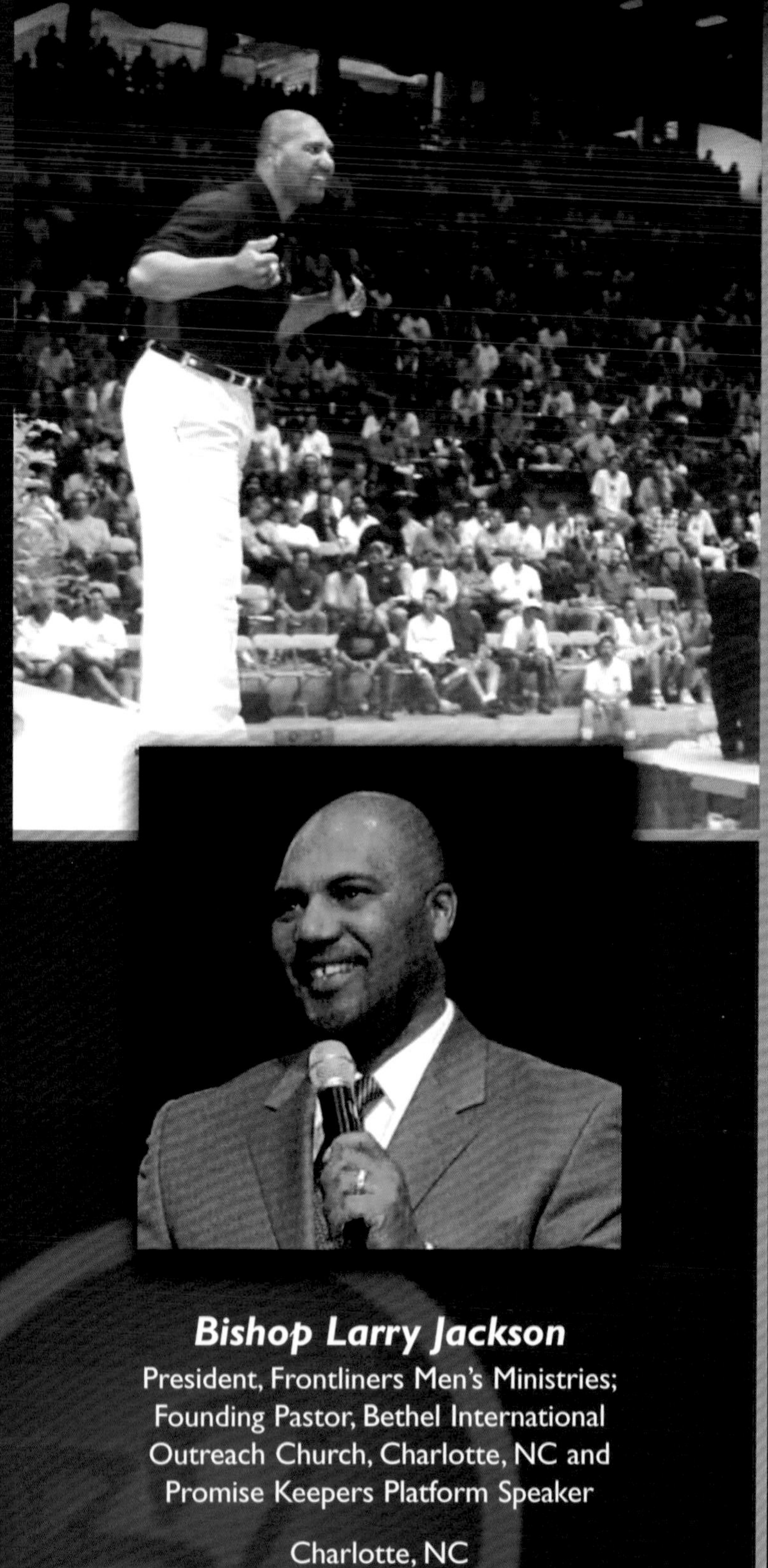

Bishop Larry Jackson
President, Frontliners Men's Ministries;
Founding Pastor, Bethel International Outreach Church, Charlotte, NC and Promise Keepers Platform Speaker

Charlotte, NC

I am convinced that God has birthed BattleZONE for this last day move of men who will come forth to lead His church. I have worked in men's ministry for over 10 years and I stay on the look out for materials that will help make my assignment easier. BattleZONE has become a tool that we use in our ministry, Frontliners to reach and increase the men we serve.

Please, do not make the mistake of thinking BattleZONE is like all of the other training programs. Michael Pouliot has tapped into the heart of God to produce a resource for the Kingdom that is second to none. For men who want to understand how to protect their families and churches as they continue to advance personally, all they need to do is get into the BattleZONE! Pastors will love the fact that this material is very balanced. It focuses on increasing men and lifting up our Savior Jesus. Pastors can release their men into the BattleZONE without them becoming weird.

I will see you in the BattleZONE!

SCOUTING REPORT
FORMATION RECOGNITION

What formation/situation are you in when you are most tempted to sin? Where are you most vulnerable to your personal BattleZONEs? Determine your internal, external and relational situations leading up to your BattleZONEs.

Formation: What is the overall situation that you are in leading up to your BattleZONE?

Internal: What are your internal thoughts, emotions and attitudes leading up to your BattleZONE?

H.A.L.T.S. Hungry Angry Lonely Tired Stressed

External: What is your surrounding environment leading up to your BattleZONE?

Relational: Who are the people you're thinking of or who you're with leading up to your BattleZONE?

OVERALL FORMATION (situation snapshot, i.e., after work when I walk in the door to my wife)

INTERNAL CONDITIONS

Hungry

Angry

Lonely

Tired

Stressed

EXTERNAL CONDITIONS

BattleZONE

RELATIONAL

BattleZONE

You can download this blank worksheet at www.battlezoneministries.org >Resources>BZ Course.

SCOUTING REPORT
FORMATION RECOGNITION

What formation/situation are you in when you are most tempted to sin? Where are you most vulnerable to your personal BattleZONEs? Determine your internal, external and relational situations leading up to your BattleZONEs.

Formation: What is the overall situation that you are in leading up to your BattleZONE?

Internal: What are your internal thoughts, emotions and attitudes leading up to your BattleZONE?

H.A.L.T.S. Hungry Angry Lonely Tired Stressed

External: What is your surrounding environment leading up to your BattleZONE?

Relational: Who are the people you're thinking of or who you're with leading up to your BattleZONE?

OVERALL FORMATION (situation snapshot, i.e., after work when I walk in the door to my wife)

INTERNAL CONDITIONS

Hungry

Angry

Lonely

Tired

Stressed

EXTERNAL CONDITIONS

BattleZONE

RELATIONAL

BattleZONE

You can download this blank worksheet at www.battlezoneministries.org >Resources>BZ Course.

CAPTAIN'S GUIDE

Oppositional Forces

CAPTAIN'S GUIDE

BattleZONE Symbol Key

Captain	Rotation Reading	Time	R.I.P.L. Effect

Warm-Up: Formation Recognition

A. Formation Recognition: If you feel you have time, take the team through the Formation Recognition Exercise below.

B. Go to the BattleZONE Chalk Talk and proceed to lead your team through Week 3.

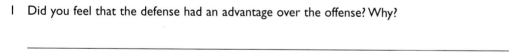

Formation Recognition

Each team has a set of offensive and defensive formations from which they attempt to execute their play calls. A well-prepared Scouting Report for the defense can have automatic blitzes or a ready list based on the weaknesses of the offensive formations. On the right are four offensive formations and a ready list of defensive blitzes based on the offenses formation.
Note: the football is the center on the offensive line.

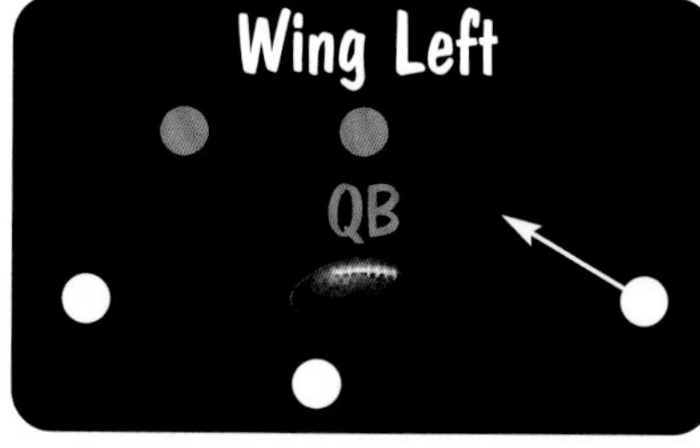

Wing Right
QB

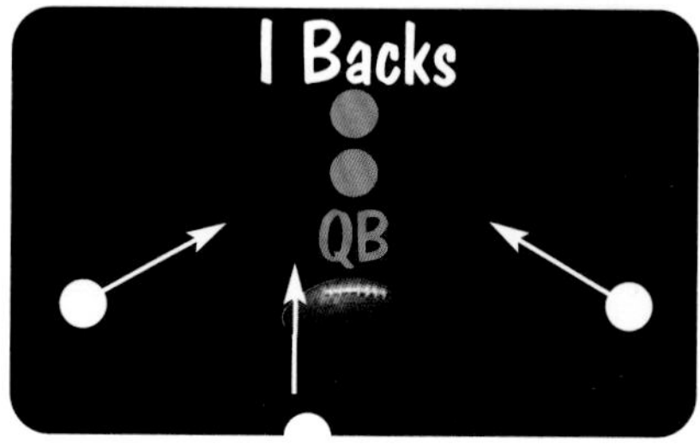

Formation	Offensive Formation	Defensive Ready List
#1	**Wing Left**	**Right outside linebacker blitz**
#2	**Wing Right**	**Left outside linebacker blitz**
#3	**Split Backs**	**Inside linebacker blitz**
#4	**I Backs**	**All linebackers blitz**

1 Did you feel that the defense had an advantage over the offense? Why?

____

____

____

Satan has a detailed "Scouting Report" on each one of us and has a "ready list" of play calls designed specifically to cater to your temptation situations. He will exploit your weak points in certain formations in order to lure your sin nature into sin, disrupting your ability to execute God's will. This, of course, will decrease your XT and X%.

2. Based on your personal BattleZONE, in what "formations" does Satan love to see you lined up? Why?

____

____

CHALK TALK

Oppositional Forces

Last week we looked at the old sin nature and the constant battle with your new nature in Christ. We also looked at your new identity in Christ as a saint and the importance of confession and vulnerability to another teammate. Last, we looked at your conditioned responses to situations or your dominant reactions to circumstances and situations.

1. PRAYER

Have one of the men open in prayer and ask the Holy Spirit to guide and direct the session towards God's agenda.

2. OPPOSITIONAL FORCES

There are three oppositional forces Christians face, whose coordinated efforts are constantly scheming to try and get you to fail in your BattleZONEs. Last week we studied the sin nature or as the Bible also calls it, the flesh. This week we will study Satan and the World in more detail.

3. WEEK 3 PLAYS

For Week 3, you were assigned to read and be ready to comment on five Plays. You will have **TWO MINUTES** to present your topic; then discuss each as a group. Please try to stay focused on what God taught you through this Play. **What did God want you to learn and do?**

CAPTAIN, ASSIGN EACH TEAMMATE A PLAY – THEN LET THEM TAKE THE LEAD.

Remember to coach them as they "teach" the "plays" to their teammates.

- **Play 1: Oppositional Forces**
- **Play 2: Scouting Report**
- **Play 3: Formation Recognition**
- **Play 4: The World**
- **Play 5: Should We Hate Sin?**

4. REACTION TRAINER CARDS

Review last week's Reaction Trainer Cards. Last week, your independent practice was to fill out the reaction training cards when you were in your BattleZONEs. This exercise was designed to help you focus in on your reaction responses to certain situations when you are tempted. Who would like to share one? (Continue to go around the room until everyone has shared their reaction responses based on their temptation situation or "formation.") Encourage them to find "counter verses" using their Bible or the link under Resources at **www.battlezoneministries.org** directly under the Counter Verse Template.

5. SCOUTING REPORT / FORMATION RECOGNITION

Answer the following questions:

1. Do you have a clear understanding of your sin tendencies, and what formations make you vulnerable to a "blitz" from the enemy? Get honest with yourself and take a close look at the areas or patterns where you are most tempted to sin.

____

____

2. What "formation" are you in when you find yourself sinning most? Is it after a bad day at work and you stop and buy a six-pack of beer? Is it when you are around a certain "friend" and you talk excessively about women other than your wife? Is it when you are hungry and you yell at your child?

____

____

The Formation Recognition Form helps you understand your patterns so you can then develop an effective game plan (in Week 5) to counteract your opponent's strategies and schemes. The Formation Recognition Forms are the first step and are designed to help you to be honest with yourself and to take a close look at the areas or patterns where you are most tempted to sin. Remember: Your opponent knows your tendencies and uses them to defeat you.

Formation Recognition Simulation

Men are more vulnerable than women in certain temptation situations. Select one temptation situation related to your individual BattleZONE. Use the Formation Recognition Form to walk you through the process. This simulation activity will be extremely helpful in uncovering the internal and external characteristics that create an environment where sin can prevail.

Get with your Teammate/Captain and select a vulnerable "formation" or temptation situation and use the Formation Recognition Form to work through one situation each. **This is leading up to the temptation situation. Do not use this form to solve it....yet!**

Captain: Briefly go over the example on the next page and explain how to fill out the Formation Recognition Form using the six steps below.

Take a few minutes to walk yourself through that situation in your mind's eye. Remember to assess external and internal oppositional factors represented by the photo (your mood, anxieties, emotional state, people you are or were with, physical location).

Formation Recognition Steps

- Step 1 Recognize your BattleZONE "formation." Where are you when you are tempted to sin?
- Step 2 Describe it in detail, including all oppositional factors that lead up to the temptation situation, (external factors, internal factors and relational factors).
- Step 3 Describe your sin nature's immediate reaction to the temptation.
- Step 4 Try to determine how Satan exploited you in this situation.
- Step 5 List what oppositional factors the World contributed to the temptation situation.
- Step 6 Determine if your relationships are stressed in any way.

Relational factors:

Refer to the state of your relationships. Relationship tension, no matter how small, can create an internal environment that can easily entice you to turn to sin. We are more vulnerable to make bad decisions when our relationships are out of whack. Maybe you had a conflict at work today or you and your wife are having a disagreement. There is a reason why we are to forgive one another and seek reconciliation when you know someone has something against you (or you have something against them). Relationships are a key trigger point for setting the stage for temptation.

Have the men turn to the blank Scouting Report Formation Recognition Form on pages 85 & 86 and proceed to complete the training exercise.

SCOUTING REPORT
FORMATION RECOGNITION

What formation/situation are you in when you are most tempted to sin? Where are you most vulnerable to your personal BattleZONE/S? Determine your internal, external and relational situations leading up to your BattleZONE/S.

Formation: What is the overall situation that you are in leading up to your BattleZONE?

Internal: What are your internal thoughts, emotions and attitudes leading up to your BattleZONE?

H.A.L.T.S. Hungry Angry Lonely Tired Stressed

External: What is your surrounding environment leading up to your BattleZONE?

Relational: Who are the people you're thinking of or who you're with leading up to your BattleZONE?

OVERALL FORMATION (situation snapshot, i.e., after work when I walk in the door to my wife)

At night after I put the kids to bed when I'm working in the home office.

INTERNAL CONDITIONS

I am struggling with feelings of anger but I don't know why.
I am feeling empty, lonely and disconnected from my wife both emotionally and sexually.
I am tired because I stay up late and get up early each day.
I am stressed because of my home life, pressures at work, my spouse's disrespect towards me.

Hungry	No
Angry	Yes
Lonely	Yes
Tired	Yes
Stressed	Yes

EXTERNAL CONDITIONS

My wife is busy doing other things and I am sitting in front of the computer in our home office alone. There is no accountability for my internet use.

BattleZONE

RELATIONAL I am having issues at work with my boss and feel unappreciated and undervalued. I feel disconnected from my spouse and this puts tremendous strain on our marriage. My wife seems to put our kids first and she demands that I act a certain way—so I can never be my true self around her. She would not understand my struggles and would look down on me even more than she does now. My mother is very ill, my sister is causing dissension in the family. My father left when I was 10 years old and I have not seen him since.

BattleZONE

You can download this blank worksheet at www.battlezoneministries.org >Resources>BZ Course.

6. Crunch Time

Have each teammate describe one thing that really "hit" him during this practice session.

7. Independent Practice

1. Read and meditate on the next week's set of Strength Training Cards as often as you can.
2. Use the Formation Recognition Form to help you understand your temptation situations as they relate to your internal and external patterns in your BattleZONES.
3. Read all four of the Plays and be prepared to teach a lesson to the team next week. Share with the men how God spoke to you.
4. Call your TC at least one time this week and pray for him daily.
5. By next week you must have in writing your:
    a. **PAIN POINT** (Refer back to the Pain Points on page 35 in Week 1)
    b. **BattleZONE** as it relates to your pain point.
    c. **Goal** for this course as it relates to your pain point.

This form can be located in Week 1 on page 35.

8. Iron Sharpens Iron (James 5:16)

Captain: Ask if anyone has done anything that compromised his walk with God this past week? If yes, name it generally (i.e., lust, greed, lying).

Also, ask for prayer requests and have one person pray for each situation until every prayer request is prayed over. Make sure to tell the men to keep them short and to the point. Use the next page to write down prayer requests and praises.

PRAYER REQUESTS AND PRAISES

AME	REQUEST
	RESULT
NAME	REQUEST
	RESULT
NAME	REQUEST
	RESULT
NAME	REQUEST
	RESULT
NAME	REQUEST
	RESULT
NAME	REQUEST
	RESULT
NAME	REQUEST
	RESULT
NAME	REQUEST
	RESULT

SHOW ME HOW TO MEMORIZE SCRIPTURE

Go to www.battlezoneministries.org > Training > Show Me How To > Memorize Scripture

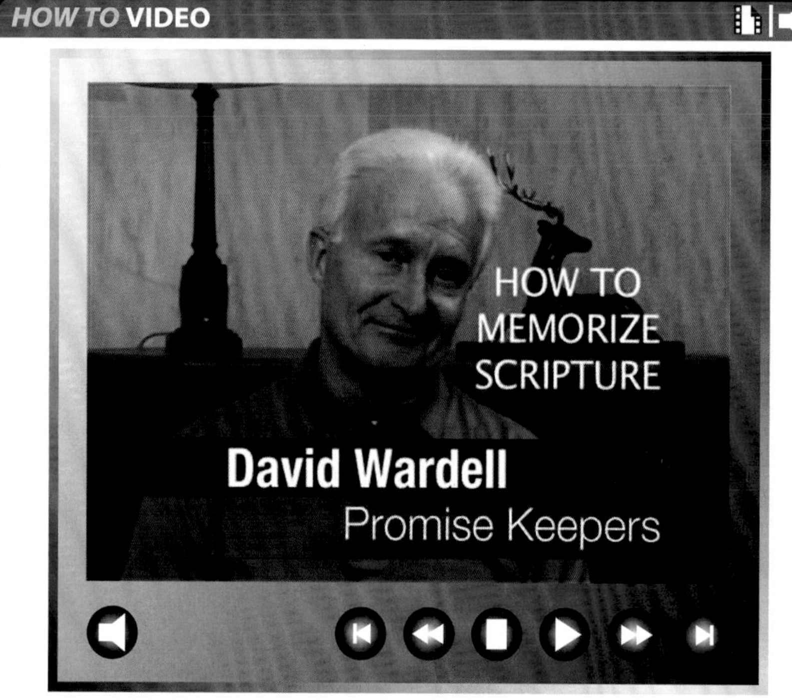

HOW TO VIDEO
HOW TO
MEMORIZE
SCRIPTURE
David Wardell
Promise Keepers

Memorizing Scripture helps us get the Word of God deep down inside of us so that we do not "depart from the Law of the Lord". How can we memorize God's Word so that we can become strong in faith and obedience? Dr. David Wardell co-founder of Promise Keepers, shows us how to "Read–Repeat–Review" in order to hide the Word of God in our hearts so we will not sin against the Lord.

**At BattleZONE Ministries...
We Show You How!**

God's "Game Plan"

Jesus Christ: Lord & Savior

- Jesus Christ: Lord & Savior – The Lead Blocker
- God's Rulebook
- Salvation = Obedience = Holiness

Week 4 Objectives

Each man will understand:

1. That Jesus Christ's atonement/sacrifice is the first component in God's "Game Plan" for holiness/victory.
2. That Jesus Christ is the only way to heaven – salvation cannot be earned.
3. That both repentance from sin and faith in Jesus Christ as Lord and Savior are required for true salvation.
4. The importance of God's Law as it applies to God's saving grace.
5. That it is impossible to execute God's will without true saving faith.
6. The Ten Commandments' role in everyday life.
7. The need for evidence of habitual obedience in his quest for holiness/victory.
8. The eternal importance of making certain his salvation.

Thou shalt have no other gods before Me.
Thou shalt not make unto thee any graven image.
Thou shalt not bow down thyself to them, nor serve them.
Thou shalt not take the name of the Lord thy God in vain.
Remember the Sabbath day to keep it holy.
Six days shalt thou labor and do all thy work.
Exodus 20: 3-9 - KJV

Honor thy father and thy mother. Thou shalt not kill.
Thou shalt not commit adultery. Thou shalt not steal.
Thou shalt not bear false witness against thy neighbor.
Thou shalt not covet they neighbor's house.
Thou shalt not covet thy neighbor's wife.
Exodus 20: 12-17 - KJV

Anyone who runs ahead and does not continue in the teaching of Christ does not have God; whoever continues in the teaching has both the Father and the Son.
2 John 1:9 - NIV

Your word I have hidden in my heart, that I might not sin against You.
Psalm 119:11 - NKJV

No one who lives in Him keeps on sinning.
No one who continues to sin has either seen Him or known Him.
1 John 3:6 - NIV

Not everyone who says to me, 'Lord, Lord,' will enter the kingdom of heaven, but only he who does the will of my Father who is in heaven.
Matthew 7:21 - NIV

WEEK 4

STRENGTH TRAINING

Thou shalt have no other gods before Me.
Thou shalt not make unto thee any graven image. Thou shalt not bow down thyself to them, nor serve them. Thou shalt not take the name of the Lord thy God in vain. Remember the Sabbath day to keep it holy.
Six days shalt thou labor and do all thy work.

Exodus 20: 3-9 - KJV

www.battlezoneministries.org

WEEK 4

STRENGTH TRAINING

Honor thy father and thy mother.
Thou shalt not kill.
Thou shalt not commit adultery.
Thou shalt not steal.
Thou shalt not bear false witness against thy neighbor.
Thou shalt not covet they neighbor's house.
Thou shalt not covet thy neighbor's wife.

Exodus 20: 12-17 - KJV

www.battlezoneministries.org

WEEK 4

STRENGTH TRAINING

Anyone who runs ahead and does not continue in the teaching of Christ does not have God; whoever continues in the teaching has both the Father and the Son.

2 John 1:9 - NIV

www.battlezoneministries.org

WEEK 4

STRENGTH TRAINING

Your word I have hidden in my heart, that I might not sin against You.

Psalm 119:11 - NKJV

www.battlezoneministries.org

WEEK 4

STRENGTH TRAINING

No one who lives in Him keeps on sinning. No one who continues to sin has either seen Him or known Him.

1 John 3:6 - NIV

www.battlezoneministries.org

WEEK 4

STRENGTH TRAINING

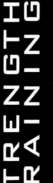

Not everyone who says to me, 'Lord, Lord,' will enter the kingdom of heaven, but only he who does the will of my Father who is in heaven.

Matthew 7:21 - NIV

www.battlezoneministries.org

NOTES

STRENGTH TRAINING

BATTLE ZONE MINISTRIES, INC. www.battlezoneministries.org

NOTES

STRENGTH TRAINING

BATTLE ZONE MINISTRIES, INC. www.battlezoneministries.org

NOTES

STRENGTH TRAINING

BATTLE ZONE MINISTRIES, INC. www.battlezoneministries.org

NOTES

STRENGTH TRAINING

BATTLE ZONE MINISTRIES, INC. www.battlezoneministries.org

NOTES

STRENGTH TRAINING

BATTLE ZONE MINISTRIES, INC. www.battlezoneministries.org

NOTES

STRENGTH TRAINING

BATTLE ZONE MINISTRIES, INC. www.battlezoneministries.org

SHOW ME HOW TO SHARE THE G.O.S.P.E.L.

Go to www.battlezoneministries.org > Training > Show Me How To > Share The Gospel

Jesus commanded us to GO and make disciples of all nations. The very first step in making disciples is to share the Gospel message. Fear of judgment and lack of training keeps most men from sharing the good news of salvation. Greg Stier, founder of *Dare2Share Ministries*, shows us how to share the Good News using an easy to remember acrostic called the G.O.S.P.E.L.

At BattleZONE Ministries...
We Show You How!

PLAY 1 : Jesus Took the Hits

But the fact is, it was our pains he carried – our disfigurements, all the things wrong with us. We thought he brought it on himself, that God was punishing him for his own failures. But it was our sins that did that to him, that ripped and tore and crushed him – our sins! He took the punishment, and that made us whole. Through his bruises we get healed. We're all like sheep who've wandered off and gotten lost. We've all done our own thing, gone our own way. And God has piled all our sins, everything we've done wrong, on him, on him. He was beaten, he was tortured, but he didn't say a word. Like a lamb taken to be slaughtered and like a sheep being sheared, he took it all in silence. Justice miscarried, and he was led off – and did anyone really know what was happening? He died without a thought for his own welfare, beaten bloody for the sins of my people.

Isaiah 53:4-8 - MSG

Jesus, the Lead Blocker

Remember the Chicago Bears of the 1980s – Jim McMahon and William "The Refrigerator" Perry? Remember when the Bears were on the goal line and 350-pound running back "The Refrigerator" lined up in the backfield? The ball was snapped and Perry opened up a hole so big you could drive a truck through it, allowing the tail back to score. What a crowd pleaser! What an all-time great football moment! "The Refrigerator's" objective was to block the opposing team's defenders so the tail back could cross the goal line and score a touchdown. Perry willingly and purposely took the hits from the defenders so his teammate could score.

In a similar fashion, Jesus took the hits you deserved so you can cross the goal line into the eternal end zone, simultaneously wiping away all penalty flags against you. Christ cleared the path by taking the punishment for all who truly believe in Him and repent of their sins. We must literally take the handoff – accepting Jesus by faith and turning from our sinful habits – allowing us to go untouched across the goal line by virtue of His effort, so we can never boast. Your performance to be saved is worthless before God. You can never earn God's loving grace. Your efforts have been nullified by Christ's blood (Isaiah 64:6 NKJV).

Can a running back take credit for crossing the goal line untouched? Of course not. His blockers literally pave the way. The only thing the running back must do is accept the ball, just as we must accept God's gracious gift of eternal salvation and forgiveness. Christ blocked God's wrath for our sins and continues to protect us from our evil opponent. The dominion of Satan and sin has been defeated.

Remember that the Gospel's message of salvation through Christ alone seals our eternal destiny and continues to free us from sin's grip,

…the blood of Jesus, his Son, purifies us from all sin.

I John 1:7b - NIV

"The law is our damnation, not our salvation. It reveals our guilt and our transgressions and it drives us to the Cross so that we may place our faith not in our efforts to keep the law, but in the efforts of Christ who perfectly kept it and died for our transgression of it; so that salvation is by faith in Jesus Christ alone… plus nothing. As our Savior said: 'It is finished!' It is enough! It is sufficient! It is done!"

D. James Kennedy

It is vital that the Gospel be foremost in our minds to remind us daily that all of our sins, past, present, and future, are forgiven by God's loving grace – the God who sent Jesus to take the hits for us.

Because of Christ's sacrificial act of obedience, we are perfect in God's sight. His wrath cannot punish us. We are clean before God, without spot or blemish, because of Jesus. We are now justified in the eyes of the Lord, "just as if" we never sinned. Jesus loved us so much that He paid the price and blocked God's wrath so we could have victory over sin and death. He cleared the path for us by making atonement (full payment) for our sins. This is a team effort of God's love, Christ's blood, our acceptance by faith and the Holy Spirit's indwelling (living in the hearts of believers the moment they accept Jesus as Lord and Savior). We can never brag about scoring the eternal touchdown.

We can now enter into God's presence, thanks to our Savior.

And so, dear brothers, now we may walk right into the very Holy of Holies, where God dwells, because of Jesus' blood.

Hebrews 10:20 - TLB

Jesus took the hits so we wouldn't have to. Thank you Jesus!

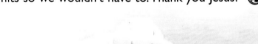

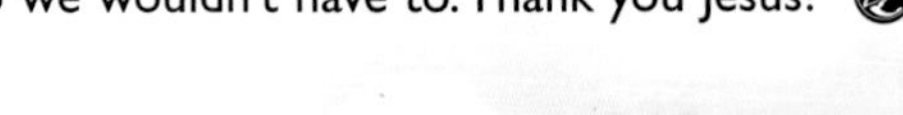

CAPTAIN'S CORNER
PERSONAL APPLICATION

PLAY 1: Jesus Took the Hits HIGHLIGHTS

- Walking an aisle, praying a prayer, or filling out a card is not what saves people. Faith in Jesus Christ, coupled with a desire to turn from a life of sin, does.
- The Gospel's message of salvation through Christ alone seals our eternal destiny and continues to free us from sin's grip.
- God's loving grace is available to us because Jesus paid for our sins on the cross so we would never have to experience God's wrath – which we so greatly deserve.

1. Who is Isaiah 53:4-8 talking about?

Jesus + us

2. Can you take credit for your salvation? If not, who can?

no - J C alone!

3. Can God's wrath be poured out on our sin, even though we are forgiven?

no. - Christ Blocked it

CRUNCH TIME:

What did God want you to learn and do from this Play?

PLAY 2 : The Rule Book Still Applies

The people trembled with fear when they heard the thunder and the trumpet and saw the lightning and the smoke coming from the mountain. They stood a long way off and said to Moses, "If you speak to us, we will listen. But don't let God speak to us, or we will die!" "Don't be afraid!" Moses replied. "God has come only to test you, so that by obeying Him you won't sin."

Exodus 20:18-20 - CEV

The Law for Our Protection

The Ten Commandments were part of the old covenant designed to help God's people live moral lives. God gave us His law to protect us from injury and harm. Football also has its own set of laws – the rulebook – that defines players' conduct and sets specific consequences for each action. For example, if the left offensive tackle moves prior to the snap, the rulebook defines it as a false start, with consequences of a five-yard penalty. It's not relative how much he moved or whether he meant to or not – the fact is, he did, and his mistake results in a penalty, because the rulebook determined in advance that when this particular action occurs, there is a consequence.

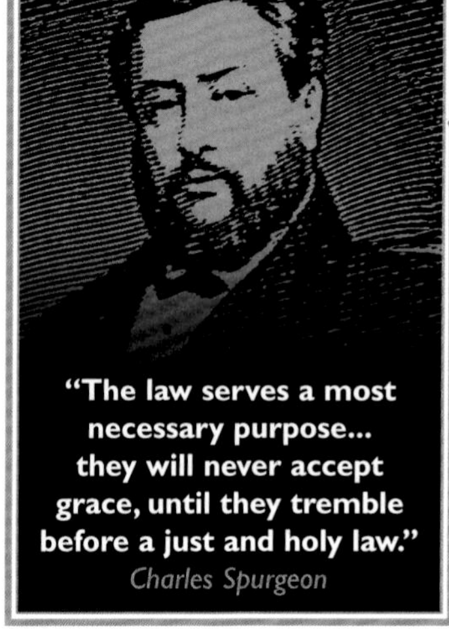

"The law serves a most necessary purpose... they will never accept grace, until they tremble before a just and holy law."
Charles Spurgeon

The player has two choices at the time of the infraction – to remain prideful and reject the penalty, or to admit his mistake and feel bad about breaking the "false-start" rule. Let's increase the stakes a little. It's the Super Bowl and the penalty was charged to the offensive lineman on fourth down and goal on the one-inch line. One second is left in the game. Instead of accepting the charge, the player throws a fit. The referee shows the last play on the Jumbotron, pulls out the rulebook and asks the lineman, "Based on what you just saw, that you clearly moved prior to the snap, and what the rulebook states, are you guilty or innocent?" With the regulation clearly stated and irrefutable evidence, the lineman hangs his head in shame.

Let's take it one step further. Suddenly, the head ref clicks on the microphone and says, "After further review, and because the player admitted his guilt and committed to not jump again, there is no penalty on the play." He goes on. "Not only will the penalty be charged to my #1 Son, but every penalty ever committed in the past and those you will commit in the future will also be charged to my #1 Son. Therefore, you have another chance to cross the goal line."

Why We Need a Sub

The reason we need a substitute (a savior) to pay our moral "fine," is because we have broken God's Law. To see how much we have transgressed the Law (the Ten Commandments), let's go over some of them. Have you ever told a lie? Have you ever stolen something? Have you ever lusted after someone? If you answered "yes" to these questions, then you're admitting that you're a lying, thieving, adulterer at heart – and you have to face God on Judgment Day! If you have used His name in vain, then you are guilty of blasphemy – you've substituted God's holy name for a curse word. Perhaps you've hated someone. Then the Bible says you are a murderer. You have violated God's holy law, and you're in big trouble. On Judgment Day, you will be found guilty and end up in hell. That's why you need the Savior. Merely being sorry for your sins, or confessing them to God won't help you. You must turn from sin (repent), and your faith must be in Jesus Christ alone. He is the only grounds for God to grant mercy towards you. If you're not sure of your salvation, make Psalm 51 your prayer (from **www.wayofthemaster.com**).

> **"The law of God expresses the mind of the Creator and is binding upon all rational creatures. It is God's unchanging moral standard for regulating the conduct of all men. Obedience to the law of God is man's first duty."**
> *Arthur Pink*

Do you have "assurance" of your salvation? The Bible says to "make your calling and election sure" (2 Peter 1:10). Here's a short checklist to make sure you are truly saved:

1. Do you know God became flesh in the person of Jesus Christ (1 Timothy 3:16) and died for the sins of the world?
2. Did you come to the Savior because you are a sinner?
3. Did you repent and put your faith in Jesus?
4. Are you convinced that He suffered and died on the Cross and that He rose again on the third day?

When a Christian sees what he has been saved from, he will realize what he has been saved for. He will have a love for God, for the unspeakable gift of the cross. It will be a continual source of joy. Gratitude will motivate him to reach out and do the will of God, to seek and save that which is lost *(Ray Comfort, Last Days Ministries).*

CAPTAIN'S CORNER
PERSONAL APPLICATION

PLAY 2: The Rule Book Still Applies HIGHLIGHTS

- God gave us His Law to protect us from injury and harm.
- The reason we need a substitute (a savior) to pay our moral "fine," is because we have broken God's Law.
- Merely being sorry for your sins, or confessing them to God won't help you on Judgment Day. You must turn from sin (repent), and your faith must be in Jesus Christ alone.

1. What is your view of God's Law (i.e., rules, legalism, protection, love)?

I am thankful for the age of Grace

2. Do you think that the Ten Commandments are still relevant today? Why or why not?

yes - it is still an excellent moral code.

3. On Judgment Day what sins would you be guilty of? Lust, blasphemy, lying, stealing?

None

CRUNCH TIME:

What did God want you to learn and do from this Play?

PLAY 3 :
Salvation = Obedience = Holiness

This Play is different because it requires you to look up multiple scriptures and interpret what God is saying to you through His Word. Can we be assured we are saved from an eternity in hell by saying a prayer, filling out a card, or walking down an aisle? These do play a part, but only if there is evidence of a changed heart. The Bible says there is evidence of being a true believer and evidence of being a nominal Christian (a Christian in name only).

Read 1 John 2:3-6

- **Verse 3** — What is the evidence that you have a true saving faith?
  Keep God's word (Commands)
- **Verse 4** — What if you claim to be a Christian but keep living in habitual sin?
  liar – deceived! – "truth not in you"
- **Verse 5** — Again, how do you know for sure that you are truly saved?
  Keep God's word
- **Verse 6** — What evidence have you to base your salvation? How do you conduct your moral life?
  the Bible! walk as Jesus walked

Read 1 John 3:3-10

- **Verse 3** — What hope is John talking about? Can you substitute the word "pure" for "holy"?
  "We shall be like Him" yes
- **Verse 4** — What action needs to be taken to break the law?
  Sin
- **Verse 5** — Who came to take away sin?
  Jesus
- **Verse 6** — What evidence do those who abide or remain or stay in Christ demonstrate? What evidence do those who do not belong to Christ demonstrate? Can a true Christian keep on sinning (habitually living in sin)?
  stop sinning – keep sinning – not happily
- **Verse 7** — Anyone who practices righteousness is said to be what?
  Righteous
- **Verse 8** — If someone continues to practice habitual, purposeful sin he belongs to whom? Who came to destroy the work of the devil?
  devil – Jesus
- **Verse 9** — Is it possible for someone to be a true Christ-Follower and continue to live in sin?
  not Happily!
- **Verse 10** — What are the two families people can belong to? Who heads these households? Whose family do you belong to if you practice righteousness? What is the evidence that you belong to God's family?
  God + Devil –

Read 2 John 9

What does this verse mean to you?
→ simple instruction – don't hate your brother.

What does it mean to abide in the doctrine or the teachings of Christ?
live your life according to them

What evidence must there be to know a person is saved?
"they'll know we are Christians by our love for each other"

John was always making sure that his brethren could tell truth from lies, true followers from false, genuine from counterfeit. John gave us several litmus tests to determine true faith from a false one. We cannot execute God's will without a true saving faith. At that time, we are assured forgiveness of our sins and simultaneously receive the indwelling of the Holy Spirit as proof of our eternal salvation. All who demonstrate genuine saving faith are adopted into God's family (John 1:12; Romans 8:16; 2 Peter 1:4). Obedience then, is the external, visible evidence of salvation. Those who are truly saved are obedient to God's Word, which requires knowledge of the Scriptures and a correct view of sin.

CAPTAIN'S CORNER
PERSONAL APPLICATION

PLAY 3: Salvation = = Obedience = Holiness HIGHLIGHTS

- A habitually sinful lifestyle that is willfully engaging in sin is evidence of the unsaved.
- We either belong to God or Satan.
- God's children cannot continue to practice willful sin.
- The genuine born-again believer demonstrates a habit of obedience.
- We can still sin as a Christ-Follower and we must pursue confession and practice obedience.

1. Have you ever questioned your salvation? When and why?

No – Not seriously

2. What evidence is there in your thoughts, attitude and behavior that you are saved?

I hate sin
* I do always those things that please the Father!

CRUNCH TIME:

What did God want you to learn and do from this Play?

PLAY 4 : Twelve Tests on Assurance

Therefore, my brothers, be all the more eager to make your calling and election sure. For if you do these things, you will never fall.
II Peter 1:10 - NIV

Blessed Assurance?
Ever heard that old hymn, "Blessed Assurance"? The first verse goes: **Blessed assurance, Jesus is mine!**
O what a foretaste of glory divine!
Heir of salvation, purchase of God,
Born of His Spirit, washed in His blood.

Do you have the blessed assurance of your salvation? Do you "know that you know that you know" you are saved? If you examine your life and see nothing but compromise and corruption, don't be surprised if you don't have any sense of spiritual security.

- Some people think they are saved because they experienced emotion and came forward during an altar call.
- Some people think they are saved because during a time of crisis they turned to God – but when the crisis passes, it's business as usual – no changed life.
- Some people think they are saved because they believe intellectually in God and His son, Jesus. Remember, Satan, too, believes (James 2:9).

True salvation requires not only belief, but also repentance, which results in transformation and evidence. God is the ultimate judge – He and only He knows who is and isn't saved. We should always continue to share Christ's love with those who say they are saved but show no evidence in their lives.

The following 12 questions will help you determine your eternal destiny.

If, after studying these scriptures and answering these questions, you still have questions about your salvation, then first read Romans 3:10. The Bible makes it clear that all have sinned and are in need of a savior. Next, you must not only give intellectual assent to the fact that Jesus Christ is Lord and Savior, but also submit your life and your will to Him and believe in His atoning work on the cross. If you are ready to make Christ your Lord and Savior, pray something like this:

Father God, I know I am a sinner. I have lied, put other things before you (idolatry) and looked with lust at others (adultery). I know that I deserve death and eternal damnation for my sin. I know I have broken your commandments and deserve your just punishment. God, right now I am trusting in Jesus Christ as my Savior. I know that Jesus is the only one who can take the punishment I deserve. I acknowledge His sacrifice for my sins and am eternally grateful. I believe that His death and resurrection provides for my forgiveness. I trust in Jesus as my personal Lord and Savior. Thank you Lord, for saving me and forgiving me! Amen!

If you made a decision for Christ today, share this with your teammates and your Teammate/Captain.

Twelve Questions to Help You Determine Your Eternal Destiny

1) Do you enjoy fellowship with Christ and His redeemed people? *(Hebrews 10:24-26; I John 1:3)*

2) Are you sensitive to your sin? *(I John 1:8, 10)*

3) Do you tend to hate the world and its evil? *(I John 2:15)*

4) Are you obedient to God's Word? *(I John 2:3-5)*

5) Do you await the coming of Jesus Christ? *(I John 3:2-3)*

6) Do you see a decreasing pattern of sin in your life? *(I John 3:5-6)*

7) Do you make sacrifices for other Christians? *(I John 3:14)*

8) Do you experience answered prayer? *(I John 3:22)*

9) Do you experience the internal work of the Holy Spirit? *(I John 3:24; I John 4:13; Rom. 8:15; Gal. 4:6)*

10) Are you able to discern between spiritual truth and spiritual error? *(I John 4:1-6)*

11) Do you believe what the Bible teaches? *(I John 5:1)*

12) Have you ever suffered for your faith? *(Matthew 13:24-30, 36-43; Philippians 1:28)*

CAPTAIN'S CORNER
PERSONAL APPLICATION

PLAY 4: Twelve Tests On Assurance HIGHLIGHTS

- If your life is only about compromise and corruption, don't be surprised if you don't feel spiritually secure.
- Walking an aisle, praying a prayer, or filling out a card is not what saves people.
- There is no such thing as a "Cultural Christian."
- There is a difference between true salvation and emotional or temporal salvation.
- The "sinner's prayer" isn't magical, but when prayed sincerely, does communicate to God that you are turning your life and will over to Him and trusting Christ alone for your salvation

1. What evidence in your life demonstrates your salvation?

Endeavoring to keep God's word.

2. Is belief in God enough to save you? Why or why not?

- Even the Devil Believes

CRUNCH TIME:

What did God want you to learn and do from this Play?

I was reminded recently that I need to open my mouth more → Ask God for things and confess what He has already done for me!

BattleZONE Victories

Robert Pouliot
San Diego, CA

My walk with God, as an adult, or should I say as a man, began with a BattleZONE course done weekly over the phone with Michael. My son had just been born and it was time for me to be born again as well. For many years prior to this point, I had been walking down the path of temptation, worldly pleasures, and sin. I would attend church almost weekly, but I felt lost, lonely, and disgusted with myself. I would sit in church and the tears would just flow down my face. My soul was crying out for help, but my flesh was still using drugs, lusting after women, and partying for days on end.

What BattleZONE has done for me, first and foremost, is to teach me that I am not alone in my struggles with temptation. All men are tempted by worldly desires. It is only through recognizing these temptations before acting upon them that we can stop the sinning. BattleZONE gave me the tools to do this. All sin begins as a thought, which then turns into a desire, that when acted upon becomes sin. It is in the moments between the temptation and the act of sinning that we must win the battle, and that is what BattleZONE is about – winning that battle. When the temptation is too strong for me to overcome alone, I now know to ask for help from the Holy Spirit; to give my temptations to God. I now have a way out. (1 Corinthians 10:12-13)

BattleZONE has also taught me that I need to make better choices about the company I keep. The people I thought were my friends were no friends at all. They were just people I partied with, people that tempted me with worldly desires.

BattleZONE has brought me into a personal relationship with God, through His Word. I wake up early each day, I put on the armor of God, and I read His Word. I feel His love and grace and it empowers me to be a better man, a better husband, and a better father. I am still tempted and I am far from perfect, but I also know that I am forgiven and that I am loved. Now I am able to share that forgiveness and love with others, and live victorious in Christ.

SEXUAL ZONE - VISUAL LUST

COUNTER VERSE

It is God's will that you should be sanctified: that you should avoid sexual immorality; that each of you should learn to control his own body in a way that is holy and honorable, not in passionate lust like the heathen, who do not know God.

I Thessalonians 4:3-5 - NIV

www.battlezoneministries.org

SEXUAL ZONE - VISUAL LUST

COUNTER VERSE

But among you there must not be even a hint of sexual immorality, or of any kind of impurity, or of greed, because these are improper for God's holy people. For of this you can be sure: No immoral, impure or greedy person—such a man is an idolater—has any inheritance in the kingdom of Christ and of God.

Ephesians 5:3, 5 - NIV

www.battlezoneministries.org

SEXUAL ZONE - VISUAL LUST

COUNTER VERSE

I made a covenant with my eyes not to look lustfully at a girl.

Job 31:1 - NIV

www.battlezoneministries.org

SEXUAL ZONE - VISUAL LUST

COUNTER VERSE

Flee from sexual immorality. All other sins a man commits are outside his body, but he who sins sexually sins against his own body.

I Corinthians 6:18 - NIV

www.battlezoneministries.org

SEXUAL ZONE - VISUAL LUST

COUNTER VERSE

Therefore do not let sin reign in your mortal body, that you should obey it in its lusts. And do not present your members as instruments of unrighteousness to sin, but present yourselves to God as being alive from the dead, and your members as instruments of righteousness to God.

Romans 6:12-13 - NKJV

www.battlezoneministries.org

SEXUAL ZONE - VISUAL LUST

COUNTER VERSE

But put on the Lord Jesus Christ, and make no provision for the flesh, to fulfill its lusts.

Romans 13:14 - NKJV

www.battlezoneministries.org

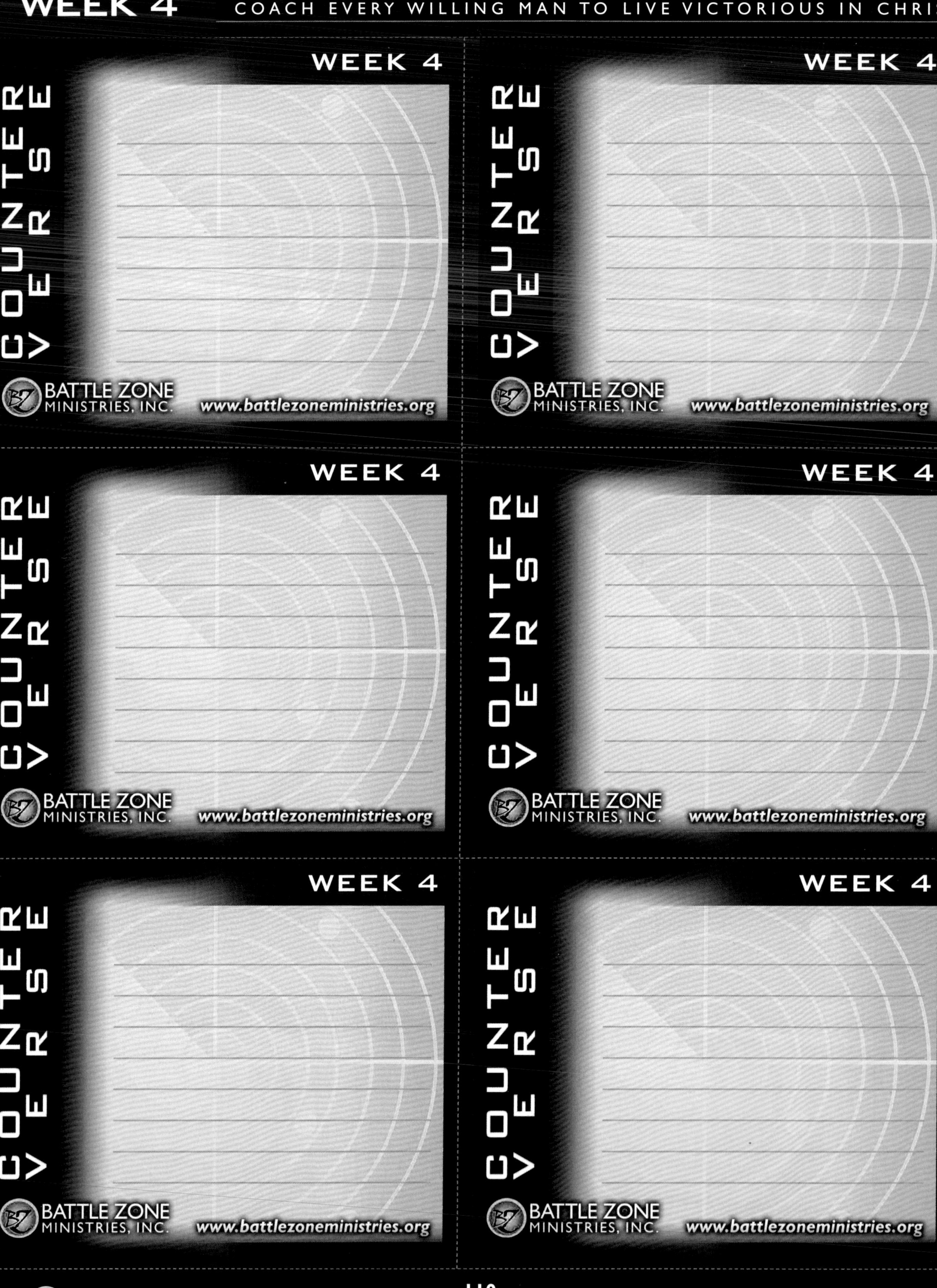
WEEK 4
COUNTER VERSE
BATTLE ZONE MINISTRIES, INC.
www.battlezoneministries.org
WEEK 4
COUNTER VERSE
BATTLE ZONE MINISTRIES, INC.
www.battlezoneministries.org
WEEK 4
COUNTER VERSE
BATTLE ZONE MINISTRIES, INC.
www.battlezoneministries.org
WEEK 4
COUNTER VERSE
BATTLE ZONE MINISTRIES, INC.
www.battlezoneministries.org
WEEK 4
COUNTER VERSE
BATTLE ZONE MINISTRIES, INC.
www.battlezoneministries.org
WEEK 4
COUNTER VERSE
BATTLE ZONE MINISTRIES, INC.
www.battlezoneministries.org

SCOUTING REPORT

FORMATION RECOGNITION

What formation/situation are you in when you are most tempted to sin? Where are you most vulnerable to your personal BattleZONEs? Determine your internal, external and relational situations leading up to your BattleZONEs.

Formation: What is the overall situation that you are in leading up to your BattleZONE?

Internal: What are your internal thoughts, emotions and attitudes leading up to your BattleZONE?

H.A.L.T.S. **Hungry** **Angry** **Lonely** **Tired** **Stressed**

External: What is your surrounding environment leading up to your BattleZONE?

Relational: Who are the people you're thinking of or who you're with leading up to your BattleZONE?

OVERALL FORMATION (situation snapshot, i.e., after work when I walk in the door to my wife)

INTERNAL CONDITIONS

Hungry

Angry

Lonely

Tired

Stressed

EXTERNAL CONDITIONS

BattleZONE

RELATIONAL

BattleZONE

SCOUTING REPORT

FORMATION RECOGNITION

What formation/situation are you in when you are most tempted to sin? Where are you most vulnerable to your personal BattleZONEs? Determine your internal, external and relational situations leading up to your BattleZONEs.

Formation: What is the overall situation that you are in leading up to your BattleZONE?

Internal: What are your internal thoughts, emotions and attitudes leading up to your BattleZONE?

H.A.L.T.S. Hungry Angry Lonely Tired Stressed

External: What is your surrounding environment leading up to your BattleZONE?

Relational: Who are the people you're thinking of or who you're with leading up to your BattleZONE?

OVERALL FORMATION (situation snapshot, i.e., after work when I walk in the door to my wife)

INTERNAL CONDITIONS

Hungry

Angry

Lonely

Tired

Stressed

EXTERNAL CONDITIONS

BattleZONE

RELATIONAL

BattleZONE

You can download this blank worksheet at www.battlezoneministries.org >Resources>BZ Course.

CAPTAIN'S GUIDE

God's "Game Plan"

Jesus Christ: Lord & Savior

CHALK TALK

BATTLEZONE SYMBOL KEY

Captain

Rotation Reading

Time

R.I.P.L. Effect

WARM-UP: JESUS CHRIST: LORD & SAVIOR

1. PRAYER

Have one of the men open in prayer and ask the Holy Spirit to guide and direct the session towards God's agenda.

2. GOD'S "GAME PLAN" - JESUS CHRIST: LORD & SAVIOR

God's "Game Plan" for Victory/Holiness – Jesus Christ: Lord & Savior
Last week, we studied Satan, the world and the importance of personally evaluating temptation situations to stay aware of Satan's cunning schemes (scouting report). This week is the first that will detail God's "Game Plan".

God assures Christians that He will give us all we need for victory over any temptation we face. We must use God's "Game Plan", not human plans (2 Corinthians 10:3-5). God's Game Plan has many components. We will cover them over the next six weeks.

True salvation through Jesus Christ: Lord & Savior, is the first component in God's "Game Plan" for holiness. The Holy Playbook is clear that no one can be holy without first accepting Jesus as Lord and Savior. This includes repenting or turning your back on a life of habitual sin. Search the Bible yourself.

What an eternal tragedy it would be if someone thought they were saved, but in fact there was never any evidence of obedience in their life. Close does not count in football or a person's eternal salvation.

God's "Game Plan" for Victory/Holiness

1. Jesus Christ: Lord and Savior	Week 4
2. God, the Holy Spirit	Week 5
3. The Holy "Playbook"—The Bible	Week 6
4. Faithful Obedience	Week 7
5. Love	Week 7
6. The Whole Armor of God	Week 7
7. Prayer	Week 7
8. God's Loving Grace and Mercy	Week 8
9. Godly Teammates	Week 9
10. Spiritual Fitness Training	Week 10

3. Week 4 Plays

For Week 4, you were assigned to read and be ready to comment on this week's Plays. You will have two minutes to present your topic; then discuss each as a group. Please try to stay focused on what God taught you through this Play. What did God want you to learn and do?

CAPTAIN, ASSIGN EACH TEAMMATE A PLAY – THEN LET THEM TAKE THE LEAD.

Remember to coach them as they "teach" the "plays" to their teammates.

- **Play 1: Jesus Took the Hits**
- **Play 2: The Rule Book Still Applies**
- **Play 3: Salvation = Obedience = Holiness**
- **Play 4: Twelve Tests on Assurance**

4. True Salvation

How do we know if we have true assurance of salvation? Scripture makes it abundantly clear that true salvation is eternally secure. However, if you look at your life and see nothing but compromise and corruption, don't be surprised if you don't have any sense of security.

Look up the following Scriptures when you can:

- John 5:24; John 3:16, 18; John 6:37-40; John 17:11, 15; John 10:27-29; I Peter 1:3-5; I John 2:1-2.

5. Pain Point

Have each teammate share their pain point, the BattleZONE linked to that point and the transformational goal they have set. Have the men turn back to pages 34 – 35 in Week 1. Here are some examples. After looking at the examples, write them all down.

Pain Point	BattleZONE	Tranformational Goal
Image/self-esteem	Critical spirit	See hisself through Jesus' eyes ~~Less focus on faults of others~~ Eph 1:18
Fear of not being enough	Image control	Free of pressure to control image
Painful past - divorce	Anger/Verbal Abuse	Live with kindness and gentleness
Broken relationships father wound	Pornography	Healing from father wound
	~~— Attitude —~~	
fear of doing more than all other family members	Anger / ~~Isolation~~	Quick to Serve His family with Joy.

6. Counter Verse – The Sword of the Spirit

True Strength

Like a football playbook holds the strategy to defeat the opponent, the sword of the Spirit (God's Word) is the perfect play call to fight off the enemy's attacks and assure God's team victory over the opposition. Much like offensive and defensive coordinators use the playbook, the Holy Spirit directs and counters in the same fashion during spiritual warfare, *"and the sword of the Spirit, which is the word of God," (Ephesians 6:17 NLT).* The exact scripture for a specific situation is like the exact play call on the gridiron – it out-maneuvers the opponent every time. Jesus is our role model for how to disarm Satan's schemes. Look at Matthew 4:1-11 – for every attack Satan used on Jesus when He came out of the wilderness after 40 days and nights of fasting, Jesus countered with a specific Scripture.

The Sword Always Defeats Satan

The result was that Satan couldn't stand up to the truth of the sword and retreated: *"Then the devil went away and angels came and cared for Jesus" (Matthew 4:12 NLT).* We have been given the two most powerful weapons in the universe – the "Holy Playbook" and the Spirit of God to prompt us when we need to pull out our sword (the perfect Scripture) to counter the opponent's attacks. Unfortunately, Christians often get defeated because they are unable to pull out their sword. Why? Because we have never picked up the Bible and put it in our hands, minds and hearts. This is why it is crucial to hide God's Word in your heart by reading and thinking about specific passages that can counteract your opponent's schemes during temptation. Have you picked up your Bible lately? Better yet, have you looked over the specific play calls that can assist you in a certain temptation situation? The Spirit of God becomes hindered by our ignorance of the Holy "Playbook." As the psalmist said, "Thy word have I hid in mine heart, that I might not sin against thee" (Psalm 119:11 KJV). Specific BattleZONEs require specific scriptures. Practice hiding God's Play Calls in your heart so the Holy Spirit can bring them to mind when you are tempted to sin.

Next, use the BattleZONE "Counter Verse" Form on page 110 and prayerfully choose three to four scriptures to hide in your heart based on your BattleZONE. See example with the BattleZONE: Visual Lust on page 109.

Counter Verse Overview

- Each teammate will be asked to recite each "counter verse" from his heart to his TC for the next six weeks at the beginning of each training session.
- Encourage men with the same BattleZONEs to share their counter verses with each other.
- Encourage the men not to focus on memorizing the verses in their heads, but read the verse out loud and think about it. This takes the pressure off men who are not "academic" by nature.
- Have the men say the "address" first (the Scripture reference), then the verse and finish with the "address." This is called the "counter verse sandwich."
- Have your teammates visit **www.battlezoneministries.org** and watch the "Show Me How To Find a Counter Verse" streaming video.
- Take this training exercise very seriously and do not allow the men to compromise the importance of reciting God's Word verbatim.

Counter Verse Options

- Have your teammates visit **www.battlezoneministries.org** and go to "Resources." Use the Counter Verse Template and the link to Bible Gateway to find verses for their specific BattleZONE(s).
- Use the Topical Index or Concordance/Dictionary in the back of your Bible or log onto BibleGateway.com and type in the keyword, i.e., lust. Then read and meditate on the scriptures after you have the Holy Spirit to help you select the one(s) He wants you to hide in your heart.
- You can use 3x5 index cards and write out the verses.
- You can also use the blank Counter Verse Template on page 110. There is a sample set of counter verses for the BattleZONE of Visual Lust on page 109.

Two-Minute Drill

- During the Two-Minute Drill, give your written verses to a teammate so he can grade you on your reciting skills. Again, these should be word for word from the Bible translation you choose.
- Upon completion of reciting your "counter verses," your TC will calculate your X% based on how many scriptures you were able to recite from memory. Then switch and let him recite his verses to you. For example if your teammate/coach recited two out of four, he will receive a 50% X%.
- Captain, will go around the room and ask each TC the X% of his teammate each week.

7. Scouting Report / Formation Recognition

Scouting Report/Formation Recognition Forms
Last week, we discussed the Formation Recognition Form to help you understand temptation situations as they relate to your internal and external patterns. What did you learn from applying this Formation Recognition concept to your personal BattleZONES this past week?

With Your TC
Get with your TC and discuss certain temptation situation or "formations" you were in recently as they relate to your personal BattleZONE. Take a few minutes to walk yourself through that situation in your mind's eye. Remember to assess your internal and external oppositional factors, such as your mood, anxieties, emotional state, people you were with, and physical location. Use the blank Formation Recognition Form on pages 111 & 112.

Formation Recognition Steps

- Step 1 Recognize your BattleZONE "formation." Where are you when you are tempted to sin?
- Step 2 Describe it in detail, including all oppositional factors that lead up to the temptation situation, (external factors, internal factors and relational factors).
- Step 3 Describe your sin nature's immediate reaction to the temptation.
- Step 4 Try to determine how Satan exploited you in this situation.
- Step 5 List what oppositional factors the World contributed to the temptation situation.
- Step 6 Determine if your relationships are stressed in any way.

After everyone completes their Formation Recognition Forms for their BattleZONE, answer the following questions:

1. What did you learn about the multiple dynamics affecting your ability to execute God's will in your BattleZONE? How would this affect your spiritual XT (eXecution threshold) and X% (eXecution percentage)?

____

2. Do you have a better understanding of your opponent's scouting report on you? Explain.

____

8. Crunch Time

Have each teammate describe one thing that really "hit" him during this practice session.

9. Independent Practice

1. Work on the process recognizing your BattleZONEs using the Formation Recognition Form on pages 111 & 112.
2. Read and meditate on the next set of Strength Training Cards for the next week as often as you can.
3. Prayerfully search God's Word for three to four counter verses to hide in your heart for use in your BattleZONEs.
4. Read all of the Plays and be prepared to teach any lesson to the team next week. Share with the men how God spoke to you.
5. Call your TC at least once this week and pray for him daily.

10. Iron Sharpens Iron (James 5:16)

Captain: Ask if anyone has done anything that compromised his walk with God during the past week. If yes, name it generally (i.e., lust, greed, lying). They may want to pray with their TC. Use the next page to write down prayer requests and praises.
NOTE: There is a great "Show Me How To" video by David Murrow, author of Why Men Hate Going to Church called, "How To Pray With Men." Watch it at **www.battlezoneministries.org > Training > Show Me How To > Pray With Men**

PRAYER REQUESTS AND PRAISES

Name	Request
	Result
Name	Request
	Result
Name	Request
	Result
Name	Request
	Result
Name	Request
	Result
Name	Request
	Result
Name	Request
	Result
Name	Request
	Result

God's "Game Plan" God, the Holy Spirit

- Grieving and Quenching the Holy Spirit
- Holy Spirit – "In the ZONE"
- Yielding to the Holy Spirit's Play Calls
- C3-Technique
- Simulation Training – Scout Team

Week 5 Objectives

Each man will understand:

1. Who the Holy Spirit is, who He is not, and His purpose in each believer's life.
2. What is means to grieve and quench the Holy Spirit.
3. That yielding to the Holy Spirit is essential for obedience or obeying God's law.
4. The importance of the Holy Spirit as He applies to salvation.
5. What results are present as a man walks by the power of the Spirit.
6. How to be filled and controlled by the Holy Spirit in his BattleZONE.
7. How to use the 3C-Technique while in his BattleZONEs.
8. How to fill out a Formation Recognition Form based on his BattleZONE.

Do not get drunk on wine, which leads to debauchery. Instead, be filled with the Spirit.
Ephesians 5:18 - NIV

But the fruit of the Spirit is love, joy, peace, patience, kindness, goodness, faithfulness, gentleness, self-control; against such things there is no law. Now those who belong to Christ Jesus have crucified the flesh with its passions and desires. If we live by the Spirit, let us also walk by the Spirit.
Galatians 5:22-25 - NASB

Do not quench the Spirit.
I Thessalonians 5:19 - NASB

Do not grieve the Holy Spirit of God by whom you were sealed for the day of redemption.
Ephesians 4:30 - NASB

Keep awake and watch and pray constantly that you may not enter into temptation; the spirit indeed is willing, but the flesh is weak.
Mark 14:38 - AMP

So I say, live by the Spirit, and you will not gratify the desires of the sinful nature. For the sinful nature desires what is contrary to the Spirit, and the Spirit what is contrary to the sinful nature. They are in conflict with each other, so that you do not do what you want. But if you are led by the Spirit, you are not under law.
Galatians 5:16-18 - NIV

WEEK 5

STRENGTH TRAINING

Do not get drunk on wine, which leads to debauchery. Instead, be filled with the Spirit.

Ephesians 5:18 - NIV

BATTLE ZONE MINISTRIES, INC. www.battlezoneministries.org

WEEK 5

STRENGTH TRAINING

But the fruit of the Spirit is love, joy, peace, patience, kindness, goodness, faithfulness, gentleness, self-control; against such things there is no law. Now those who belong to Christ Jesus have crucified the flesh with its passions and desires. If we live by the Spirit, let us also walk by the Spirit.

Galatians 5:22-25 - NASB

BATTLE ZONE MINISTRIES, INC. www.battlezoneministries.org

WEEK 5

STRENGTH TRAINING

Do not quench the Spirit.

I Thessalonians 5:19 - NASB

BATTLE ZONE MINISTRIES, INC. www.battlezoneministries.org

WEEK 5

STRENGTH TRAINING

Do not grieve the Holy Spirit of God by whom you were sealed for the day of redemption.

Ephesians 4:30 - NASB

BATTLE ZONE MINISTRIES, INC. www.battlezoneministries.org

WEEK 5

STRENGTH TRAINING

Keep awake and watch and pray constantly that you may not enter into temptation; the spirit indeed is willing, but the flesh is weak.

Mark 14:38 - AMP

BATTLE ZONE MINISTRIES, INC. www.battlezoneministries.org

WEEK 5

STRENGTH TRAINING

So I say, live by the Spirit, and you will not gratify the desires of the sinful nature. For the sinful nature desires what is contrary to the Spirit, and the Spirit what is contrary to the sinful nature. They are in conflict with each other, so that you do not do what you want. But if you are led by the Spirit, you are not under law.

Galatians 5:16-18 - NIV

BATTLE ZONE MINISTRIES, INC. www.battlezoneministries.org

STRENGTH TRAINING

NOTES

BATTLE ZONE MINISTRIES, INC. www.battlezoneministries.org

STRENGTH TRAINING

NOTES

BATTLE ZONE MINISTRIES, INC. www.battlezoneministries.org

STRENGTH TRAINING

NOTES

BATTLE ZONE MINISTRIES, INC. www.battlezoneministries.org

STRENGTH TRAINING

NOTES

BATTLE ZONE MINISTRIES, INC. www.battlezoneministries.org

STRENGTH TRAINING

NOTES

BATTLE ZONE MINISTRIES, INC. www.battlezoneministries.org

STRENGTH TRAINING

NOTES

BATTLE ZONE MINISTRIES, INC. www.battlezoneministries.org

ATHLETEZONE

Go to www.battlezoneministries.org > Training > Athlete ZONE

This unique section of the BattleZONE website features an athlete's description of his sport and then use the explanation to explain a Biblical principle helpful for pursuing holiness.

Miles McPherson, former pro football player for the San Diego Chargers and now pastor of Rock Church, introduces the purpose of the AthleteZONE. Being Spirit-filled as a Christian is like being in the ZONE as an athlete—you cannot make a mistake, or sin against God.

At BattleZONE Ministries...
We Show You How!

PLAY 1 : Don't Fumble the Ball

Do not get drunk on wine, which leads to debauchery. Instead, be filled with the Spirit.

Ephesians 5:18 - NIV

The Holy Team

Think of God as a Holy Team: **God the Father, Jesus Christ and the Holy Spirit.** Each is fully God and yet there is one God. Each is divine, but each has a distinct role in the Godhead:

God the Father, the owner of our team, Whose holiness demands we pay for sin and Whose love provided His only Son as full payment.

Jesus Christ, our Head Coach, Who willingly sacrificed His sinless life and fully satisfied God's wrath. He intercedes from heaven for Christians.

The Holy Spirit, the offensive/defensive coordinator, Who lives within all believers, leads us into all truth, convicts us of sin and is our helper. He helps us understand and recall the Playbook and gives all the glory to Jesus.

Who is the Holy Spirit?

"For there are three that bear witness in heaven: the Father, the Word, and the Holy Spirit; and these three are one. And there are three that bear witness on earth: the Spirit, the water, and the blood; and these three agree as one."

I John 5:7-8 - NKJV

Most Christians find it hard to wrap our minds around what the Bible teaches about the Holy Spirit. Several years ago, pollster George Barna surveyed a number of people who identified themselves as Christians and found that more than 80% of them believe the Holy Spirit is a symbol of God's power and presence, but not an actual person. In his book, "The Counselor: Straight Talk About the Holy Spirit by a 20th Century Prophet", A.W. Tozer said,

"Spell this out in capital letters:
THE HOLY SPIRIT IS A PERSON. He is not enthusiasm. He is not courage. He is not energy. He is not the personification of all good qualities, like Jack Frost is the personification of cold weather. Actually, the Holy Spirit is not the personification of anything – He has individuality.
He is one being and not another. He has will and intelligence. He has hearing. He has knowledge and sympathy and ability to love and see and think. He can hear, speak, desire, grieve and rejoice. He is a Person."

(Christian Publications, 1993)

Most evangelical Christians agree that the Bible is very clear in its teachings that the Holy Spirit is God and He is yet a person; and God the Father, Jesus and the Holy Spirit are each fully God, yet they are one, and each has distinct roles. This doctrine is referred to as the Trinity.

Some denominations have a different view of the Holy Spirit. This is a genuine difference of opinion, the majority of the evangelical church has held the doctrine of the Trinity since New Testament times. Without the Holy Spirit, it is impossible to be saved, execute God's will and experience holiness.

Holy Holy Holy – Don't Fumble

The Holy Spirit is the only means we have to execute God's will and be holy, because He is holy. Think of the Holy Spirit's power like a football being carried by a running back. Without the ball, a running back has no power to score. Likewise, without the power of the Holy Spirit, Christians are unable to execute God's play call and "be holy as Christ is holy" (I Peter 1:6). Take the analogy further – without the ball there is no score and without the Spirit there is no holiness/execution. A running back can burst though the line of scrimmage, break tackles, juke defenders and sprint into the endzone, but if he doesn't have the ball, it's worthless. We can serve at church, avoid sin and even exercise our spiritual gifts, but without yielding to the Spirit of God, it is all in vain. This is why we must learn to surrender to the Coach's authority by continually asking Him what play He wants us to run moment by moment, always yielding to His authority.

Surrendered to the Coach's Authority

Ephesians 5:18 tells us to be filled continually by the Holy Spirit. What does this mean? It means yielding your entire self – body, mind and will – to the Spirit of God. You are to give up everything to follow Christ, just like the disciples did in the Gospels. You may have trusted Jesus as your Savior for the promise of eternal life, but do you trust Him to rule over your life as your leader, guide, master and friend? This commitment to live with faithful attachment to Christ can only be realized through the working of the Holy Spirit. If we don't continually yield to the Spirit's authority, we end up "turning over" or fumbling His power that helps us execute God's will.

Fumble Drill

When we accept Christ as our Lord and Savior, God hands us the "Ball" or the Holy Spirit. We must continue being filled by the Spirit to avoid sinning. Train yourselves to hold onto the "Holy Ball" by continuing to be filled and controlled by the Spirit of God. When we decide to live our lives according to our own play calls, we fumble the Spirit's power. Other terms for fumbling are to grieve or quench the Spirit, severing our fellowship with Christ. Each time you sin, you grieve the Spirit (Ephesians 4:30). Every time you ignore God's "play calls," you quench the Spirit (I Thessalonians 5:19). Each time you fumble by grieving or quenching the Spirit, you allow the opponent to dominate your decisions instead of submitting to God. We fumble when we allow our selfishness to lead instead of yielding to the Holy Spirit. We fumble when we fill ourselves with anything other than the Spirit (including wine as mentioned in Ephesians 5:18.) You cannot continue to run your life, fumbling the power to faithfully obey God. How well does a team do when the running back keeps fumbling the ball? Turnovers kill a team's chance of victory. Likewise, we kill our chance of victory/holiness when we ignore the Spirit and disobey God's "Holy Playbook" by not yielding to the Holy Spirit's Power.

CAPTAIN'S CORNER
PERSONAL APPLICATION

PLAY 1: Don't Fumble the Ball HIGHLIGHTS

- The Holy Spirit is the only means we have to execute God's will and be holy, because He is holy.
- It is impossible to understand the Bible without the Holy Spirit's indwelling.
- Every time you sin, you grieve the Holy Spirit.
- Every time you ignore God's prompting, you quench the Holy Spirit.

1. Who is the Holy Spirit?

2. What does it mean to you to walk by the power of the Holy Spirit?

CRUNCH TIME:

What did God want you to learn and do from this Play?

PLAY 2 : The Holy Spirit and Salvation

Read Romans 8:1-14

Total Control

Imagine if you were an NFL quarterback and had a run where you were constantly blowing your assignments. Nothing you did turned out right. You were at an all-time low and increasingly desperate. Then you heard about a person who could guarantee an incredibly high execution percentage. The only catch was this person would have to live inside of you and have total control of your life. For this person to live in you, you must first believe in a God you can't see and believe that He allowed his only Son to die for your sins and then rise from the dead three days later. You must also believe that you have wronged Him terribly and be sorry for what you have done. You then must commit to turn from that life and live committed to Him above all other self-ambition. Would you do it? Could you allow Him to guide and direct you on life's game field, or would you struggle giving Him total control? After we are saved by God's grace, through faith in Christ, we face a similar situation. We still have the choice (free will) to either stay in control of our lives or to give full control to the third person of the Trinity, (God, the Holy Spirit).

Victory?

How can Christ Followers have victory over their most challenging BattleZONES? Only through Jesus Christ Who sent the Holy Spirit He promised (Romans 8:1-3). The Holy Spirit aids our efforts to become more spiritually fit so we are able to execute God's will in our BattleZONEs. As John MacArthur says,

"The Holy Spirit does several things to confirm that believers are not condemned: He frees us from sin and death, He enables us to fulfill the law, He changes our nature, He empowers us for victory, He confirms our adoption, and He guarantees our glory."

A New Heart and a New Spirit

Jesus sent the Holy Spirit to regenerate our hearts by fulfilling all the requirements of the Old Testament Law, and writing God's Laws on our hearts. We are reborn of the life-giving Spirit. The law of the gospel of life in Christ came to us through the Spirit and made us free from the law of sin and death. We will never be condemned because we have been set free from the law and its just punishment – death (Romans 6:23). Because of our faith in Christ, the regenerating work of the Spirit has set us free from sin's power and penalty.

Sin the Traitor Within

Sin still lives within us (Romans 7:17-18), but no longer dominates. When someone comes to a saving faith in Christ, he is set free from sin's dominion but not its presence. He will still battle with sin, but sin will not be his "master" because God is renewing his heart and giving him the ability to deny his sin nature. When God renews or regenerates the soul through the Holy Spirit, He gives the internal ability to execute His holy law. Ezekiel prophesied of the gift of the Holy Spirit, which empowers believers to obey God's Word (Ezekiel 11:19-20) and that God would give true believers a new heart (Ezekiel 36:26-27). In short, we now have the means to obey God because we have a new heart and the power of the Holy Spirit who now lives inside of every Christ-Follower. We literally have God living on the inside of us! Think about that for a minute. What an incredible truth. God is in you!

Romans 8:9 warns that anyone who doesn't have the Holy Spirit residing within him does not belong to Christ. If your life isn't showing evidence of the power and presence of God's Spirit, then you don't belong to Christ. If you aren't fulfilling God's righteous law, desiring to walk in the way of the Spirit, and seeking with your heart the things of the Spirit, then He is not in you.

God's Spirit brings us from sin to righteousness by setting us free from sin and death, enabling us to fulfill God's law, and changes our old sin nature by giving us a new heart and the Spirit of God Who lives inside of us. We become new creations inside and out.

CAPTAIN'S CORNER
PERSONAL APPLICATION

PLAY 2: The Holy Spirit and Salvation HIGHLIGHTS

- The moment you are saved, the Holy Spirit comes to dwell inside of you.
- When God renews or regenerates the soul through the Holy Spirit, He gives an internal ability to execute God's holy law.
- A person who does not have the Holy Spirit residing within does not belong to Christ.
- We become new creations inside and out because of the Holy Spirit.

1. What does the Holy Spirit's indwelling have to do with your salvation?

2. What does the Holy Spirit's indwelling have to do with your ability to avoid sin?

CRUNCH TIME:

What did God want you to learn and do from this Play?

PLAY 3 : In the ZONE with the Holy Spirit

So I advise you to live according to your new life in the Holy Spirit. Then you won't be doing what your sinful nature craves. The old sinful nature loves to do evil, which is just opposite from what the Holy Spirit wants. And the Spirit gives us desires that are opposite from what the sinful nature desires. These two forces are constantly fighting each other, and your choices are never free from this conflict. But when you are directed by the Holy Spirit, you are no longer subject to the law.

Galatians 5:16-18 - NLT

The ZONE

Elite athletes strive for a perfect performance where they perform "out of their heads", breaking personal records throughout the game. At such a time, every fine-tuned physical skill and mental discipline come together, yielding an incredible performance. Athletes call this being in the ZONE, in the flow, in a groove, on a roll, etc. When an athlete is in the ZONE, it seems he can do no wrong. He is so involved in his performance that nothing else matters because he is so focused on executing the play. Athletes recognize the ZONE as a special place where their performance is exceptional and consistent, automatic and flowing. Competition is carefree, fun and exhilarating. "Flow state is an optimal psychological experience. It's when you're functioning on auto-pilot, when everything clicks into place and goes right," says Dr. Costas Karageorghis, lecturer in sports psychology at Brunel University, Great Britain.

Christians can only execute God's will in their BattleZONEs if they are Spirit-filled or in the ZONE. When we are directed and controlled by the Holy Spirit, we are no longer enticed to sin, because the Spirit gives us desires that are opposite to what our sin nature desires. When we are in the ZONE, the Law no longer binds us because the desire to disobey God's Laws has no appeal. Now that you understand the second component of God's "Game Plan" – to be "in the ZONE" – let's see what performance benchmarks or statistics are present as a result.

"We are at this moment as close to God as we really choose to be. True, there are times when we would like to know a deeper intimacy, but when it comes to the point, we are not prepared to pay the price involved."
J. Oswald Sanders, Enjoying Intimacy with God

But the fruit of the Spirit is love, joy, peace, patience, kindness, goodness, faithfulness, gentleness, self-control; against such things there is no law. Now those who belong to Christ Jesus have crucified the flesh with its passions and desires. If we live by the Spirit, let us also walk by the Spirit.

Galatians 5:22-25 - NASB

The Fruit of the Spirit: God's Statistic

Proof is always in the performance. Every football player is judged by his performance on the gridiron. Both the coach and the player know how well they did or didn't do by looking at their individual statistics. A linebacker gets graded on multiple areas, including tackles, interceptions, forced fumbles, fumble recoveries, blocked passes and overall execution of his assignments according to the play call. God has set up a similar system to grade Christians, called the Fruit of the Spirit. When we are following God's "Game Plan" based on His "Holy Playbook," we will have the Fruit of the Spirit in our lives. When we play yielded to the Spirit of God, we cannot sin and we will reap in-the-ZONE statistics such as love, joy, peace, patience, kindness, goodness, faithfulness, gentleness, and self-control. On the contrary, when we live a life dominated by our sin nature, we reap poor statistics, (Galatians 5:19-21).

Here is the objective data you need so you can know whether you are playing well on the field according to God's "Game Plan." Do you feel joy? Are you gentle? Do you have self-control in all areas of your life? Remember: You cannot compartmentalize God into work and home, or church friends and non-church friends. Men, the goal of training for holiness is to get to the ZONE and to ultimately experience holiness. May God in His mercy allow you to become a 3C-Christian (Conformed to the Character of Christ) so you can be a living testimony, telling all who believe that total obedience to God is the greatest experience a Christian can ever have.

CAPTAIN'S CORNER
PERSONAL APPLICATION

PLAY 3: In the ZONE with the Holy Spirit HIGHLIGHTS

- Two natures are constantly fighting each other---one wants you to sin (sin nature) and the other (the new nature empowered by the Holy Spirit) wants you to obey God.
- You can only be truly obedient to God by yielding to the Holy Spirit.
- When you try to avoid sin in your own strength it may work for a while, but you will fail.
- You must practice yielding to the Holy Spirit when you are tempted to sin. This is a conscious surrendering of your desires.
- You know when you are in the Spirit by the fruit you produce.

1. What do you truly desire? Make a list (i.e., success, a new car, a friend's salvation, etc.).

2. Do these desires come from the Holy Spirit or your sin nature?

3. Describe one time when you felt the Holy Spirit's presence keeping you from sin.

CRUNCH TIME:

What did God want you to learn and do from this Play?

PLAY 4 : The Holy Spirit Defeats Sin

But I can't help myself because I'm no longer doing it. It is sin inside me that is stronger than I am that makes me do these evil things.
Romans 7:17 - TLB

What We Can't Have, We Want
Sin makes us desire what is forbidden. Think about it – if we had no way of knowing something was forbidden, it wouldn't have as much appeal. For instance, if you're on a diet and you see a Snickers bar, your desire for the Snickers increases because the diet forbids you to eat any type of candy.

Sin will use every advantage to keep us from following the Holy Spirit by using the good of the Law against us. It's like when a player gives another player a cheap shot in a pile, out of sight from referees, attempting to get the other player to retaliate. In this case, the instigator uses the rules (laws) against his opponent, just like our sin nature tries to do. He purposely arouses the other player's instinct to retaliate, trapping him by the rules of the game and receiving a 15-yard personal foul penalty.

The very nature of sin taunts us to give in to our desires in our personal BattleZONEs. We must learn God's strategy to defeat sin's power. Make no mistake -- sin's power to react against the Law is real. In football, with proper training, preparation and execution, we can defeat our natural instinct to retaliate. In our BattleZONEs, we can do the same by the power of the Spirit. We must yield to Him every moment of every day. How do you yield to the Holy Spirit? Only by training for spiritual fitness. The love of God will compel you to train and prepare yourself to hear the Spirit's voice as He calls you to execute God's will and stay in the zone.

For if you live according to [the dictates of] the flesh, you will surely die. But if through the power of the [Holy] Spirit you are [habitually] putting to death (making extinct, deadening) the [evil] deeds prompted by the body, you shall [really and genuinely] live forever.
Romans 8:13 - AMP.

Self-Effort – Sin's Power Boost
If you try to avoid sin in your own strength, you literally give your sin nature a power boost. Every time you try to avoid temptation or giving into temptation on your own, you feed your sin nature. Each and every time you try to execute God's will in your own strength, you grieve the Holy Spirit, for we can do nothing apart from Christ. In doing so, you hand the momentum over to our opponent. All you have to do is ask God for help and surrender all your feeble efforts to Him.

This may be easier said than done. Faith in action is trusting God to meet your needs instead of working in your flesh to try to fulfill them yourself. You cannot do it without total surrender. Sure, you may succeed a few times in your flesh, but success will be short-lived because the Spirit is willing, but the flesh is weak. When we don't yield to the Spirit of God, we demonstrate our pride.

Each time I sin against a Holy God, I am arrogantly telling Him, through my actions, that my ways are better than His. When we try to avoid sin in our own strength, we are telling God that we think He really can't save us from our BattleZONE and we can do it without Him. Think about how foolish this is. We can never out-do God. We can't save ourselves from God's wrath and we sure can't save ourselves from ourselves...only God can.

It is only by the power of the Holy Spirit that we can beat sin's grip and the Law, which oddly enough, strengthens the sin within us. Don't miss this point. You can never execute God's will unless you are filled, controlled and yielded to the Holy Spirit. If you try to execute God's will in your own strength, you give sin a turbo-boost and sin will always dominate in your BattleZONEs. To execute God's will, and be holy, you must be controlled by the Holy Spirit and live in the zone.

CAPTAIN'S CORNER
PERSONAL APPLICATION

PLAY 4: The Holy Spirit Defeats Sin HIGHLIGHTS

- Sin means to "miss the mark" or God's standards (Law).
- Sin uses the Law itself to makes us want what we can't or shouldn't have.
- Each and every time you try to execute God's will in your own strength, you grieve the Holy Spirit.
- We can do nothing apart from Christ.
- The only solution to overcome sin's power is Jesus Christ, Who sent us the Holy Spirit.
- Every time you sin against a Holy God, you are arrogantly telling God, through your actions, that you know better than He does.

1. How do you approach sinful desires? Do you think they come from you or your sin nature? Why?

2. Do you find yourself resisting sin or giving in because you have failed so many times before?

CRUNCH TIME:

What did God want you to learn and do from this Play?

PLAY 5 : C3-Technique

...your choices are never free from this conflict.
Galatians 5:17 - NLT

Use the C3-Technique when you are in your personal BattleZONEs.

Call a timeout and resist the tempter/temptation. *(James 4:7, 2 Timothy 2:22, Psalm 119:37)*

Confess the temptation to God in prayer and ask the Holy Spirit to show you the way of escape. *(Mark 14:38, Corinthians 10:12-13)*

Choose by faithful obedience to consciously yield to the Holy Spirit's Play Call, resulting in perfect execution of God's will. *(Romans 6:16, 8:12-14, Titus 2:11-12)*

C1

Therefore submit to God. Resist the devil and he will flee from you. — James 4:7 - NKJV

Run from anything that stimulates youthful lusts. — 2 Timothy 2:22 - NLT

Turn my eyes away from worthless things; preserve my life according to your Word. — Psalm 119:37 - NIV

C2

Keep awake and watch and pray [constantly], that you may not enter into temptation; the spirit indeed is willing, but the flesh is weak. — Mark 14:38 - AMP

If you think you are standing strong, be careful, for you, too, may fall into the same sin. But remember that the temptations that come into your life are no different from what others experience. And God is faithful. He will keep the temptation from becoming so strong that you can't stand up against it. When you are tempted, he will show you a way out so that you will not give in to it. —1 Corinthians 10:12-13 - NLT

C3

Don't you realize that whatever you choose to obey becomes your master? You can choose sin, which leads to death, or you can choose to obey God and receive his approval. — Romans 6:16 - NLT

For the grace of God has appeared, bringing salvation to all men, instructing us to deny ungodliness and worldly desires and to live sensibly, righteously and godly in the present age. — Titus 2:11-12 - NASB

So then, brethren, we are debtors, but not to the flesh [we are not obligated to our carnal nature], to live [a life ruled by the standards set up by the dictates] of the flesh. For if you live according to [the dictates of] the flesh, you will surely die. But if through the power of the [Holy] Spirit you are [habitually] putting to death (making extinct, deadening) the [evil] deeds prompted by the body, you shall [really and genuinely] live forever. For all who are led by the Spirit of God are sons of God.
— Romans 8:12-14 - AMP

In Galatians 5, Paul emphasizes the ministry of the Holy Spirit, because it is the Spirit who makes the life of faith work. A life of faith wouldn't work any better than a life of legalism if it weren't for the indwelling Holy Spirit who empowers us. Consequently, Paul calls us to yield to the spirit's control through such statements as: "We through the Spirit wait for the hope of righteousness by faith" (v. 5); "Walk in the Spirit" (v 16); "If ye be led by the Spirit, ye are not under the law" (v 18); and "If we live by the Spirit, let us also walk in the Spirit" (v 25). It is necessary for those who have been justified by faith to implement a life of faith in the energy of the Holy Spirit.

John MacArthur (from his message "Fallen from Grace" Part 1)

CAPTAIN'S CORNER
PERSONAL APPLICATION

PLAY 5: C3-Technique HIGHLIGHTS

- You must recognize when you are in a moment of decision -- whether to choose God's will or your own.
- It is vital to ask God for help in your moment of temptation, so He can show you the way of escape.
- God will always show you the way of escape when you are tempted.
- God never tempts us to sin against Him.

1. Do you recognize the moment you are about to sin? What is going on inside of you?

2. Do you actively and immediately confess to God the temptation before you and ask the Holy Spirit to help you escape?

3. Why do you think it is so important to consciously yield to the Holy Spirit when you are tempted?

CRUNCH TIME:

What did God want you to learn and do from this Play?

GAME PLAN
EXECUTION SYSTEM

NAME: Bubba Buck

YOUR BATTLEZONE: Visual Lust

FORMATION: Base this on the Scouting Report Form in Week 4.
Everywhere I go, but mostly at church and church functions.

NUTRITION HISTORY: What have you been "feeding" yourself to entice temptation?
I watch 3-4 hours of TV each night. The shows have sexy female characters. I have not had my regular devotional time in months.

OPPONENT'S STRATEGY: Exactly how does your opponent attack you to create this BattleZONE?
Stimulates my sexual desires with TV characters, which leads to an increased desire to stare at women lustfully. My ability to NOT look decreases in the direct proportion to the amount of TV. For example, when I am working in the garage at night instead of watching TV, I find it easier to turn my eyes away from women.

COUNTER-ATTACK/GAME PLAN:

C3-Technique

Call a timeout and resist the tempter/temptation.

Confess the temptation to God in prayer and ask the Holy Spirit to show you the way of escape.

Choose by faithful obedience to consciously yield to the Holy Spirit's Play Call, resulting in perfect execution of God's will.

1) Fast from TV for one week
2) Regular devotional time M, W, Su
3) Meditate on Job 31:1 daily, put in my car
4) Have my TC (teammate/captain) ask me how I am doing throughout the week.
5) Use the C3-Technique when I am in my BattleZONE.
6) Prepare my heart and mind on Sundays to desire to worship God more than I desire to look at women.
7) Have my wife pray for me daily about this sin habit.

GAME PLAN

EXECUTION SYSTEM

NAME:

YOUR BATTLEZONE:

FORMATION: Base this on the Scouting Report Form in Week 4.

NUTRITION HISTORY: What have you been "feeding" yourself to entice temptation?

OPPONENT'S STRATEGY: Exactly how does your opponent attack you to create this BattleZONE?

COUNTER-ATTACK/GAME PLAN:

C3-Technique

Call a timeout and resist the tempter/temptation.

Confess the temptation to God in prayer and ask the Holy Spirit to show you the way of escape.

Choose by faithful obedience to consciously yield to the Holy Spirit's Play Call, resulting in perfect execution of God's will.

GAME PLAN
EXECUTION SYSTEM

NAME:

YOUR BATTLEZONE:

FORMATION: Base this on the Scouting Report Form in Week 4.

NUTRITION HISTORY: What have you been "feeding" yourself to entice temptation?

OPPONENT'S STRATEGY: Exactly how does your opponent attack you to create this BattleZONE?

COUNTER-ATTACK/GAME PLAN:

C3-Technique

Call a timeout and resist the tempter/temptation.

Confess the temptation to God in prayer and ask the Holy Spirit to show you the way of escape.

Choose by faithful obedience to consciously yield to the Holy Spirit's Play Call, resulting in perfect execution of God's will.

COACH EVERY WILLING MAN TO LIVE VICTORIOUS IN CHRIST

WEEK 5

CAPTAIN'S GUIDE

God's "Game Plan"

God, the Holy Spirit

WARM-UP

BATTLEZONE SYMBOL KEY

Captain	Rotation Reading	Time	R.I.P.L. Effect

WARM-UP: GOD'S "GAME PLAN" - GOD, THE HOLY SPIRIT

A. Two-Minute Drill.

First thing, have men get together with their (TC) Teammate/Captain and go over counter verses for two minutes.

1. Captain – See the Captain's Guide in Week 4, page 116 for more direction on how to complete the counter verse exercise.
2. Some men may not have yet begun to memorize their verses. In that case, have each read out loud his counter verses for the two-minute drill. Remember to encourage men to state the verse's "address," recite the Scripture and then state the verse's "address" again.
3. Some men may not have looked up any verses. Encourage these men to find one verse with his teammate/Captain and write it on a blank counter verse form. Make sure the other teammate has an opportunity to recite his (give one minute) and then switch.

B. Go to the BattleZONE Chalk Talk and proceed to lead your Team through Week 5.

CHALK TALK

God's "Game Plan"

1. PRAYER

Have one of the men open in prayer and ask the Holy Spirit to guide and direct the session towards God's agenda.

2. GOD'S "GAME PLAN" - GOD, THE HOLY SPIRIT

Last week, we studied the first component to God's "Game Plan", which is Jesus Christ, Lord, and Savior. You can't be holy without true salvation, which is demonstrated by a life of obedience. Jesus Christ paid the price for our sins, so we can be seen as holy and blameless to God the Father.

We also practiced understanding Temptation Situations or Formations that put you in vulnerable situations where you are more likely to fail in your BattleZONEs. This week, we will cover the next component of God's "Game Plan" – God, the Holy Spirit.

The second component of God's "Game Plan" for holiness/victory is the power of the Holy Spirit.

In the ZONE (Spirit-filled)
We can never attain holiness without the indwelling of the Holy Spirit. The ultimate goal of this training course is to teach you to experience holiness – or be Spirit-filled and in the ZONE.

When the Holy Spirit controls us, we allow ourselves to yield to His authority, which develops our faithful obedience out of a sincere love for Jesus. God's Game Plan is perfect; all we have to do is yield.

Check the play call with the Playbook.
You can always tell if the play you hear is from the Holy Spirit. If it's consistent with the "Holy Playbook", it's from the Coach.

For example, if someone says "It must be God's will that I move in with my girlfriend because it worked out so perfectly," they are clearly tuned in to I-ME FM and not God's truth channel. We will study the "Holy Playbook" in Week 6.

1. What are some things in your life that get you out of tune with God's voice?

____

____

3. WEEK 5 PLAYS

For Week 5 you were assigned to read and be ready to comment on five Plays. You will have **TWO MINUTES** to present your topic; then discuss each as a group. Please try to stay focused on what God taught you through this Play. **What did God want you to learn and do?**

CAPTAIN, ASSIGN EACH TEAMMATE A PLAY – THEN LET THEM TAKE THE LEAD.
Remember to coach them as they "teach" the "plays" to their teammates.

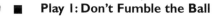

- **Play 1: Don't Fumble the Ball**
- **Play 2: The Holy Spirit and Salvation**
- **Play 3: In the ZONE with the Holy Spirit**
- **Play 4: The Holy Spirit Defeats Sin**
- **Play 5: C3-Technique**

4. Simulation Training

In his book *Crunch Time*, Jim Grassi says "... most NFL teams spend a lot of time in classroom situations, reviewing all the possibilities that exist. In addition to chalk talks, diagrams, films, videos and Polaroids, today's classrooms have sophisticated computers that allow the players to see field situations in several different dimensions." This classroom activity is called Situation-Specific Training (SST) and is carried out onto a live demonstration on the field called "scout team," giving players an experiential look at what they may encounter and how to respond.

Likewise, the specific technique characterizing your formations in your BattleZONEs is called Temptation-Specific Training (TST). This may feel awkward, but stretch yourself and give TST your very best effort.

5. Game Plan Execution System

Turn to your BattleZONE Game Plan Execution System on pages 135 & 136. This is a tool to help you put into practice God's "Game Plan" for executing His will in your BattleZONEs. Page 134 gives you an example form to reference.

Based on last week's Scouting Report Formation Recognition Forms, we will develop a game plan to defeat your opponents in your personal BattleZONEs.

One skill we will be using is called the C3-Technique.

Captain, go over C3-Technique Form on Play 5, and briefly match it to the Scriptures indicated there. Next, turn to the Game Plan Execution System example on page 134 and walk the men through it. Review the Game Plan Execution System form with the team. Create a "snap shot" of each teammate's temptation situation and his respective BattleZONE.

Next, have teammates prepare themselves to use the C3-Technique in a Temptation Specific Training exercise with their blank Game Plan Execution System Form on pages 135 & 136. Give them 5 minutes to complete the form with their TC. Give them another 5 minutes to practice. Have everyone stand up with their TC as they practice their temptation situation while using the C3-Technique. **Make sure each man uses the same language for the technique (C1 = Call a time out; C2 = Confess; and C3 = Choose).**

Captain, as a team, have the men give some highlights and use their comments as coaching opportunities. Help walk the entire group through their temptation situations/BattleZONE using the C3-Technique.

To see the C3-Technique in action go to

www.battlezoneministries.org > Training > Show Me How To > Yield to the Spirit

6. Crunch Time

Have each teammate describe one thing that really "hit" him during this practice session.

7. Independent Practice

Captain: Tell your teammates that the training is getting more strenuous – from here on out, they should plan on adding between half an hour to an hour to their independent practice.

1. Continue to refine your new "Game Plan Execution System" in your BattleZONE using pages135 & 136. Implement the C3-Technique discussed on page 132.

2. Read and meditate on the next set of Strength Training Cards for the next week as often as you can.

3. Prayerfully search God's Word for three to four counter verses that you can memorize when you are in your BattleZONEs. Remember to use the BZ website as a tool to find the most appropriate counter verses. You should have two or three by now.

4. Read all five of the Plays and be prepared to teach a lesson to the team next week. Share with the men how God spoke to you.

5. In Week 6, you will be practicing a new skill called the R. I. P. L. Effect where you will learn how to study God's play calls and become a student of the Word. Be prepared to spend 30 minutes longer doing your assignments, so plan ahead and do one Play per day instead of at the last minute.

6. Call your Teammate/Captain at least once this week and pray for him daily.

8. Iron Sharpens Iron (James 5:16)

Captain: Ask if anyone has done anything that compromised his walk with God during the past week. If yes, name it generally (i.e., lust, greed, lying). They may want to partner with teammate/captain.

Use the next page to write down the prayer requests and praises.

PRAYER REQUESTS AND PRAISES

Name	Request
	Result
Name	Request
	Result
Name	Request
	Result
Name	Request
	Result
Name	Request
	Result
Name	Request
	Result
Name	Request
	Result
Name	Request
	Result

God's "Game Plan" The "Holy Playbook"

- Know the Bible – Know Jesus
- Student of the Game
- Milk is for Babies
- R. I. P. L. Effect
- Execution Breakdowns
- C3-Technique using the Game Plan Execution System

Week 6 Objectives

Each man will understand:

1. That Jesus Christ came to live out the Word of God in the flesh and left a living example to follow.
2. That He commanded us to become students of the Word.
3. That we will grow into spiritually fit warriors for Christ as we grow in understanding and begin living out the Word.
4. How to use inductive study using the R. I. P. L. Effect.
5. How to use the C3-Technique in his respective BattleZONE(s).

And the Word became flesh and dwelt among us, and we beheld His glory, the glory as of the only begotten of the Father, full of grace and truth.
John 1:1 - NKJV

This Book of the Law shall not depart from your mouth, but you shall meditate in it day and night, that you may observe to do according to all that is written in it. For then you will make your way prosperous, and then you will have good success.
Joshua 1:8 - NKJV

But solid food is for the mature, who by constant use have trained themselves to distinguish good from evil.
Hebrews 5:14 - NIV

But obey God's word. Do not just listen to it. If you just listen to it, you fool yourselves.
James 1:22 - WE

Be diligent to present yourself approved to God as a workman who does not need to be ashamed, handling accurately the word of truth.
2 Timothy 2:15 - NASB

All Scripture is God-breathed and is useful for teaching, rebuking, correcting and training in righteousness.
2 Timothy 3:16 - NLT

WEEK 6

STRENGTH TRAINING

And the Word became flesh and dwelt among us, and we beheld His glory, the glory as of the only begotten of the Father, full of grace and truth.

John 1:1 - NKJV

BATTLE ZONE MINISTRIES, INC. www.battlezoneministries.org

WEEK 6

STRENGTH TRAINING

This Book of the Law shall not depart from your mouth, but you shall meditate in it day and night, that you may observe to do according to all that is written in it. For then you will make your way prosperous, and then you will have good success.

Joshua 1:8 - NKJV

BATTLE ZONE MINISTRIES, INC. www.battlezoneministries.org

WEEK 6

STRENGTH TRAINING

But solid food is for the mature, who by constant use have trained themselves to distinguish good from evil.

Hebrews 5:14 - NIV

BATTLE ZONE MINISTRIES, INC. www.battlezoneministries.org

WEEK 6

STRENGTH TRAINING

But obey God's word. Do not just listen to it. If you just listen to it, you fool yourselves.

James 1:22 - WE

BATTLE ZONE MINISTRIES, INC. www.battlezoneministries.org

WEEK 6

STRENGTH TRAINING

Be diligent to present yourself approved to God as a workman who does not need to be ashamed, handling accurately the word of truth.

2 Timothy 2:15 - NASB

BATTLE ZONE MINISTRIES, INC. www.battlezoneministries.org

WEEK 6

STRENGTH TRAINING

All Scripture is God-breathed and is useful for teaching, rebuking, correcting and training in righteousness.

2 Timothy 3:16 - NLT

BATTLE ZONE MINISTRIES, INC. www.battlezoneministries.org

NOTES
STRENGTH TRAINING
BATTLE ZONE MINISTRIES, INC.
www.battlezoneministries.org
NOTES
STRENGTH TRAINING
BATTLE ZONE MINISTRIES, INC.
www.battlezoneministries.org
NOTES
STRENGTH TRAINING
BATTLE ZONE MINISTRIES, INC.
www.battlezoneministries.org
NOTES
STRENGTH TRAINING
BATTLE ZONE MINISTRIES, INC.
www.battlezoneministries.org
NOTES
STRENGTH TRAINING
BATTLE ZONE MINISTRIES, INC.
www.battlezoneministries.org
NOTES
STRENGTH TRAINING
BATTLE ZONE MINISTRIES, INC.
www.battlezoneministries.org

SHOW ME HOW TO MEDITATE

Go to www.battlezoneministries.org > Training > Show Me How To > Meditate On Scripture

Meditating on Scripture is an important means of ensuring that God's Word gets deep down inside of us so we won't "depart from the Law of the Lord". How can we meditate on God's Word day and night to become strong in faith and obedience? Brian Doyle, of *Vision New England Men's Ministries*, takes us through foundational teaching and illustrates one way to meditate on Scripture.

At BattleZONE Ministries...
We Show You How!

PLAY 1 : Applying the "Holy Playbook"

And the Word became flesh and dwelt among us, and we beheld His glory, the glory as of the only begotten of the Father, full of grace and truth.
John 1:14 - NKJV

Jesus is the "Holy Playbook"
Every game plan and every playbook are merely extensions of the coach. If you want to know the coach, just look at the playbook. A player who accepts the playbook accepts the coach. Christians are called to do the same -- without compromise. We must accept the Word of God and the God of the Word, not man-made versions of either. When you know the Bible, you know God, but you cannot intimately know God without knowing the Bible. When Jesus was born to the Virgin Mary, He was the Word Who became flesh. Do you want to know Jesus?

Then you need to know the Bible. In order to know Him, you must first accept Him – all of Him and what the Bible says about Him: that He is fully human and fully God.

All Scripture is God-breathed and is useful for teaching, rebuking, correcting and training in righteousness.
2 Timothy 3:16 - NLT

"Read whatever chapter of Scripture you will, and be ever so delighted with it – yet it will leave you as poor, as empty and unchanged as it found you unless it has turned you wholly and solely to the Spirit of God, and brought you into full union with and dependence upon Him."
William Law, *The Power of the Spirit* (Fort Washington, PA: Christian Literature Crusade, 1971), p.19

The foundation for every game plan is the playbook. A player cannot execute the game plan without knowing the playbook. To fully understand the playbook, a football player must apply it, not just read it. To be effective, he must execute the play calls on the field. If an athlete approached his playbook casually, instead of studying it under the assumption he will have to put it into use on the field, the playbook would not likely spur the optimum desired performance.

God's "Playbook" outlines the game plan for all Christians. God coached Joshua on how he should read the Scriptures,

"This Book of the Law shall not depart from your mouth, but you shall meditate on it day and night, that you may observe to do according to all that is written in it. For then you will make your way prosperous, and then you will have good success."
Joshua 1:8 - NKJV

Application Expectation
In this passage, God commands Joshua to observe and to do, to read God's Word and do what it says. In other words, he is reading it — to do it. A football player knows his chance of starting depends on his knowledge of the playbook. When there is a known **application expectation,** the player's learning intensity increases, and maximizes his understanding. If you approach any type of material and see it as information only, you will not absorb it or process it to the fullest. God has made it clear that our approach to the Bible must be to do all that is written in it, not just to read it as informative, or pick and choose what we will do. The Bible is not a multiple-choice quiz nor does it offer a "have it your way" Burger King kind of doctrine; we are to do all of what it says and obediently follow God's Game Plan.

Self-Deception
Throughout the Bible – just like today – people sat and listened to God's Word without any intention of being obedient.

And they come to you as people come, and they sit before you as my people, and they hear what you say but they will not do it; for with lustful talk in their mouths they act; their heart is set on their gain. And behold, you are to them like one who sings lustful songs with a beautiful voice and plays well on an instrument, for they hear what you say, but they will not do it.
Ezekiel 33:31-32 - ESV

But obey God's word. Do not just listen to it. If you just listen to it, you fool yourselves.
James 1:22 - WE

Approach God's Word with the intention of **doing** it. If you don't, the only person you're fooling is yourself. Reading the Word or hearing the Word doesn't create obedience. We must intentionally obey.

CAPTAIN'S CORNER
PERSONAL APPLICATION

PLAY 1: Applying the "Holy Playbook" HIGHLIGHTS

- Jesus is the Living Word Who became flesh and lived with us.
- Jesus is the Word of God -- when we know the Bible we know Jesus.
- God has made it clear that our approach to the Bible must be to do all that is written in it, not just to read it as informative, or pick and choose what we will do.
- "But obey God's word. Do not just listen to it. If you just listen to it, you fool yourselves." James 1:22 - WE

1. How well would your favorite team do if the players had no clue about the coaches' game plan or if they never even looked at the playbook?

2. What is your approach to reading the Bible? Is it as an FYI (for your information) or to live it out?

3. When you read the Bible, how do you know when God is speaking to you personally?

CRUNCH TIME:

What did God want you to learn and do from this Play?

PLAY 2 : Becoming a Student of the Game

We have much to say about this, but it is hard to explain because you are slow to learn. In fact, though by this time you ought to be teachers, you need someone to teach you the elementary truths of God's word all over again. You need milk, not solid food! Anyone who lives on milk, being still an infant, is not acquainted with the teaching about righteousness. But solid food is for the mature, who by constant use have trained themselves to distinguish good from evil.

Hebrews 5:11-14 - NIV

Attack Your Faith

In the game of football, the aggressor usually wins. Linemen must attack their opponents during a drive block and defenders must aggressively attack the ball carrier. A player cannot rely on his teammates to do his assignment for him on the gridiron, nor can he depend on his coach to make a tackle. Likewise, Christians must be responsible for their own study of the Word – not solely depend on others to teach them. To become a spiritually fit or mature Christian you must own it and live it. Walk the talk!

Milk is for Babies

Babies need to be bottle-fed milk.

A sign of growth is when they learn to feed themselves.

A sign of growing maturity is when they move from milk to solid food.

Student of the Game

Players who become students of the game often become coaches later in their careers. However, just because someone plays football doesn't automatically make him a student of the game. There is also a major difference between performing a play and understanding the facets of the play, just as there is a gap between knowing basic scriptural doctrines and becoming a student of the Word. In football, this gap exists because many players rely on their coaches to be the teacher, never assuming personal responsibility to study for themselves. A similar gap occurs among Christians who never mature spiritually. To become a spiritually fit warrior for Christ, you must not merely read the "Holy Playbook" or study what someone else has written about it – you must study it for yourself and be a student of the Word. Unlike a bird, you can't digest someone else's food for them. You have to eat your own food – chew on it – and then digest it yourself.

Your words were found, and I ate them, and your words became to me a joy and the delight of my heart, for I am called by your name, O Lord, God of hosts.

Jeremiah 15:16 - ESV

Pastors Only?

Some Christians excuse themselves from their lack of study by claiming they are not "called" to be students of the Word. This is a lie from Satan himself. In Joshua 1:8, it is very clear that we are to study God's Word day and night. The difference between a mature Christian and an immature one is whether they have taken the personal responsibility to become a student of the Word, or remain on the "bottle", always expecting to be fed. Can you to think of one mature Christian who is not a student of the Word. Compare this person with someone you know who has been a Christian for years, yet has failed to advance from milk to solid food. This type of Christian is easily led astray by false teachers:

"For false christs and false prophets will rise and show signs and wonders to deceive, if possible, even the elect."

Mark 13:22 - NKJV.

We can't discern the truth from the counterfeit unless we study God's Word ourselves. A milk-fed believer is also more likely to buy in to worldly thinking, beliefs and behaviors. Unfortunately, this type of Christian infects the body of Christ because he does not train himself to recognize the difference between right and wrong, "But solid food is for the mature, who by constant use have trained themselves to distinguish good from evil" Hebrews 5:14 NIV. This type of believer has to go over the basics of Christianity over and over again,

So come on, let's leave the preschool fingerpainting exercises on Christ and get on with the grand work of art. Grow up in Christ. The basic foundational truths are in place: turning your back on 'salvation by self-help' and turning in trust toward God.

Hebrews 6:1 MSG.

Passive Spectator or Active Participant

The gap between the mature and immature Christian is the same as the difference between a player and a coach. The mature Christian and the coach have become students themselves. Spiritual maturity is a process (Mark 4:26-29). Those who become spiritually mature have one thing in common: they are active students of the Word. They refuse to be passive learners who sit back and "receive" the Word with a bottle. It's a team effort to mature in Christ (1 Corinthians 3:6-8).

Do you have diaper rash? 

CAPTAIN'S CORNER
PERSONAL APPLICATION

PLAY 2: Becoming a Student of the Game HIGHLIGHTS

- Christians must be responsible for their own study of the Word—not be solely dependent on Bible teachers or pastors.
- Spiritual maturity is a process and requires study and meditation on God's Word.
- A mature Christ-Follower takes responsibility for "feeding" himself.
- Immature Christians tend to be easily led astray by false teaching and/or are easily drawn to worldly attitudes, beliefs and behaviors.

1. Who is responsible for your understanding of the Bible? Why?

2. Do you think there is a direct correlation between your knowledge of the Bible and your spiritual maturity? Explain your answer.

CRUNCH TIME:

What did God want you to learn and do from this Play?

PLAY 3 :
R.I.P.L. Effect – Introduction

Do not merely listen to the word, and so deceive yourselves. Do what it says.
James 1:22 - NIV

The Miraculous Bible
The Bible is made up of 66 books written by dozens of different people, all of whom were inspired by the Holy Spirit to write each word and each line. Think of it as the Holy Spirit giving dictation to each of the writers. God intentionally worked through the ages to create the Bible as a complete message to His children. Each word has a role, but there are certain words, phrases or themes that define the true meaning of the passage. If you were to remove a significant word or phrase from a passage, the entire meaning of the passage would be changed or misinterpreted. Each passage in the "Holy Playbook" has a significant purpose in the context of God's "Game Plan". The passage is there to give specific instruction in a specific situation for a specific set of "players."

When studying the Bible, interpret each verse in context, as well as in relation to thousands of other verses. We should never take a part of a verse out of context to make a personal point. Scripture determines doctrine, not the other way around. We must apply *scriptura scripturam interpretar*, a Latin phrase meaning "scripture interprets scripture". If we claim the Bible is God's Word, then we should follow what it says, not try to make it say what we want to follow. A failure to recognize this "unity-of-doctrine" principle can lead to incorrect interpretation. The revealed Word does not hang by itself, but fits within a given structure, tied by historical events of God's intervention with the world (the Kingdom of God). Revelation comes within this given structure to give it continuity and clarity.

Pray Before Study
We should always pray prior to studying God's "Playbook" to make sure we bring Him into our study and humble ourselves to the Holy Spirit's illumination of the Word. Many Christians read the Bible devotionally. While this isn't bad in itself, if we are serious about becoming students of the Word, we must first read Scriptures academically and then apply it to our lives.

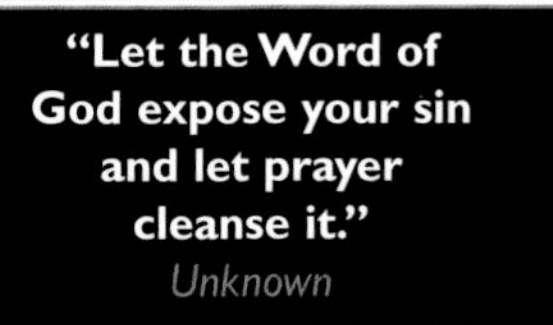
"Let the Word of God expose your sin and let prayer cleanse it."
Unknown

R. I. P. L. Effect
This symbol will prompt you to use the BattleZONE Bible Study Technique in your quest to become a student of the Word. R. I. P. L. stands for:

Read it: Read the passage carefully. What does the passage say literally? Don't try to put the passage in your own words – don't paraphrase and don't interpret it. Look at it full in the face and see exactly what it says word for word. Resist the temptation during this step to apply the text to you, which comes later.

Interpret it: Interpret the passage in its context. What does the passage mean? What are the repeating words, phrases or themes? As you read, it's a good idea to highlight or underline repeating phrases, words, ideas or themes.

- Read the Bible like an announcer doing a play-by-play on ESPN – ask who, what, when, where, why and how. (For instance, most Bibles have an overview about the author, background, setting and historical relevance of the book before the actual Scripture. This will answer some of the questions. Sometimes, as in the case of Hebrews, the author of the book isn't known for sure.
  - Who is talking? Who is God or the person talking to?
  - Who are the people involved?
  - What is being said?
  - When is this being said (time and the place)? Again, this can often be found in the overview at the beginning of the book.
  - Where is the setting? Again, this most often can be found in the overview.
  - Why was this written? This may take some work. For example, the book of Romans was written by the Apostle Paul to teach the great truths of the gospel of grace to believers.
  - Cross-reference the passage. Try to determine what God was saying in that moment in time – not what He's saying to you right now. Resist the temptation to read it as a devotional.

Personalize it: Now is the time to personalize the passage to your current life. How is the Holy Spirit prompting you to respond to the passage? This is when you ask what God is saying to you and what He wants you to get out of the passage.

Live it: Live out the passage obediently. What must you do to live the passage in your daily life? What act of faithful obedience must you do right now to live the passage in your life? Do you need to make an adjustment in your thinking and/or living? Write out what you must do; then ask someone to hold you accountable.

CAPTAIN'S CORNER
PERSONAL APPLICATION

PLAY 3: R.I.P.L. Introduction HIGHLIGHTS

- The Bible comprises 66 books; we are to interpret all verses in relation to the others, not take a part of a verse out of context to make a personal point.
- Most people read the Bible as a devotional only, which may create a superficial understanding of God's "Playbook".
- Scripture determines doctrine, not the other way around.
- Failing to recognize this "unity-of-doctrine" principle can lead to incorrect interpretation.

1. When you read the Bible, do you read it as a devotional (thinking how it applies to you)? Explain.

2. Have you ever taken a passage of the Bible out of context or twisted Scripture to meet your point of view? Explain.

3. Can you think of a time when you didn't want to know whether something you were doing was sin (i.e., many men avoid the topics of masturbation, drunkenness and Biblical forgiveness)?

Give an example of something you do not want to know more about.

CRUNCH TIME:

What did God want you to learn and do from this Play?

PLAY 4 : R.I.P.L. – Example

Be diligent to present yourself approved to God as a workman who does not need to be ashamed, handling accurately the word of truth.
2 Timothy 2:15 - NASB

We are to present ourselves to God as workmen who can hold our heads high because we train ourselves to read the Bible. "Handling accurately" implies there is to be proper interpretation; "be diligent" implies there are obstacles and difficulties involved; "need not be ashamed" suggests that good interpretation is achievable.

R. I. P. L. Effect
This symbol will prompt you to use the BattleZONE Bible Study Technique in your quest to become a student of the Word. R.I.P.L. stands for:

Read it: Read the passage carefully. What does the passage say literally? List the literal facts in the column on the right. Don't try to put the passage in your own words – don't paraphrase and don't interpret it. Look at it full in the face and see exactly what it says.

Interpret it: Interpret the passage in its context. What does the passage mean? What are the repeating words, phrases or themes? As you read, it's a good idea to highlight or underline repeating phrases, words, ideas or themes.

- Read the Bible like an announcer doing a play-by-play on ESPN – ask who, what, when, where, why and how.
- Cross-reference the passage. Try to determine what God was saying in that moment in time – NOT what He's saying to you right now.

Personalize it: Now is the time to personalize the passage to your current life. How is the Holy Spirit prompting you to respond to the passage? This is when you ask what God is saying to you and what He wants you to get out of the passage.

Live it: Live out the passage obediently. What must you do to live the passage in your daily life? What act of faithful obedience must you do right now to live the passage in your life?

Practice applying the R.I.P.L. Effect using Joshua 1:8

"This Book of the Law shall not depart from your mouth, but you shall meditate in it day and night, that you may observe to do according to all that is written in it. For then you will make your way prosperous, and then you will have good success."
Joshua 1:8 - NKJV

Read it: What does the passage say literally? List the facts in the column on the right.

____

Interpret it: What did God intend the passage to mean for the time and place?

____

- **Who:** Who is talking? To whom is God talking/writing?

  ____

- **What:** What is the subject matter? What are His main points?

  ____

- **When:** When did the book take place in the course of the Bible and in Joshua's life? This information is usually found at the beginning of the book, depending on the type of Bible you're using.

  ____

- **Where:** Where did this take place? Where specifically is God talking to Joshua?

  ____

- **Why:** Why did God say this to Joshua?

  ____

- **How:** How was Joshua supposed to accomplish what God commanded?

  ____

Personalize it: What does this passage say to you personally as if God were talking to you?

____

Live it: What must you do today to live this passage in your life?

____

List the literal facts:

The book of the law shall not depart from your mouth.

You shall meditate on it day and night.

Observe to do according to ALL that is written in it.

____

____

____

____

____

References:

____

____

CAPTAIN'S CORNER
PERSONAL APPLICATION

PLAY 4: R.I.P.L. Effect
Joshua 1:8
HIGHLIGHTS

- It is important to read the Bible in the time, setting and context of the author's writings. What is God saying in that moment?
- After you understand the literal context of the passage you can personalize the passage to your life.
- Always end your study with practical application – ask what you must do to live out the passage(s) and what God is saying to you personally.

1. What does it mean to meditate on God's Word day and night?

2. Do you read the Bible as if you are going to "do it"? Why or why not?

CRUNCH TIME:

What did God want you to learn and do from this Play?

PLAY 5 : Execution Breakdown

Search me, O God, and know my heart; test me and know my anxious thoughts. See if there is any offensive way in me, and lead me in the way everlasting.
Psalm 139: 23-24 - NIV

Execution Breakdowns
Execution is the key to winning. When a team fails to execute, the coaches try to find where the breakdown took place. For example, if the QB is sacked, the coaches will analyze the play that was called, the players' individual assignments and the opponent's defensive rushing scheme. If no breakdowns were apparent, they will look into the secondary where the receivers are running their routes. From this second-tier analysis, they conclude that the breakdown occurred when the receiver ran the wrong route, causing the timing to be thrown off for the secondary receivers, which ultimately caused the sack. This could be classified as a coverage sack.

When we fail to execute God's will in our BattleZONEs, we too must analyze the sequence of events to determine where the breakdowns took place. We must continually ask ourselves, "Where did the breakdown occur?" Say my BattleZONE is lust and I fail to execute during a trip to the grocery store where I see an attractive woman. I purposefully make my way near her to get a better look at her body. I have sinned against God in this moment and I failed to execute God's will, because I lusted after this woman. I chose to fulfill my lust-rush instead of God's will. Where did the breakdown occur? Let's take a look at the checklist below to analyze the sequence of events that led up to my sin.

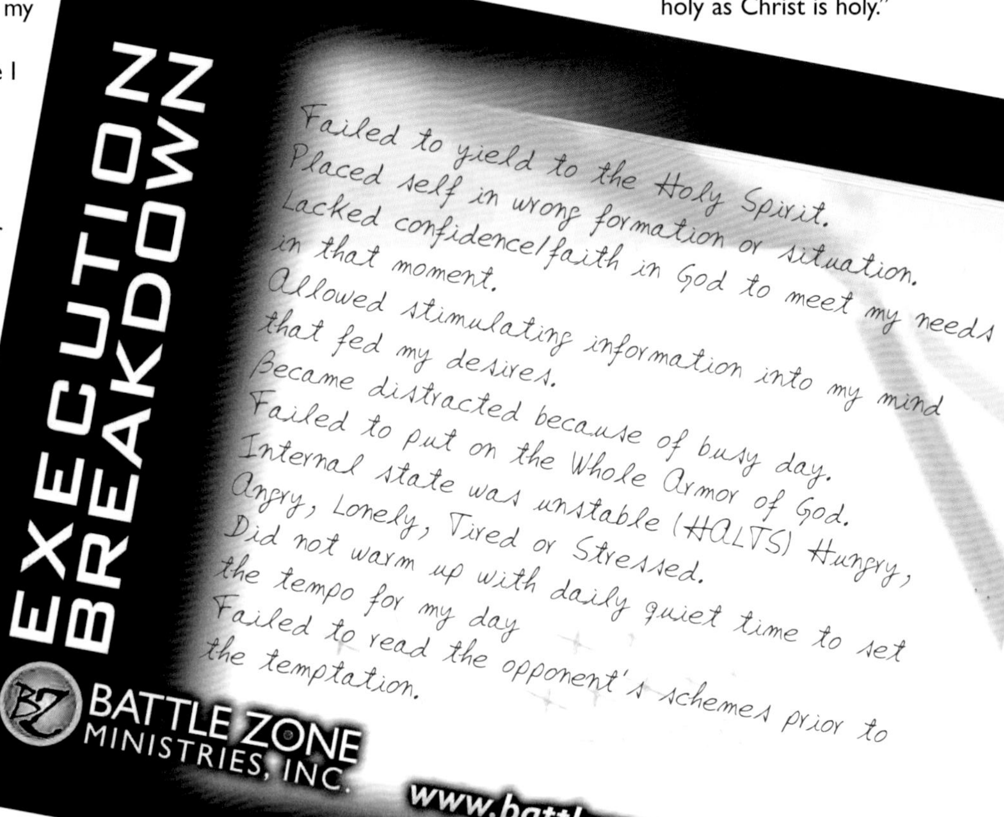

EXECUTION BREAKDOWN
Failed to yield to the Holy Spirit.
Placed self in wrong formation or situation.
Lacked confidence/faith in God to meet my needs in that moment.
Allowed stimulating information into my mind that fed my desires.
Became distracted because of busy day.
Failed to put on the Whole Armor of God.
Internal state was unstable (HALTS) Hungry, Angry, Lonely, Tired or Stressed.
Did not warm up with daily quiet time to set the tempo for my day
Failed to read the opponent's schemes prior to the temptation.
BATTLE ZONE MINISTRIES, INC.
www.battlezoneministries.org

I checked the first box because every time I sin, I fail to yield to the Holy Spirit. We cannot sin if the Holy Spirit controls us, because He is Holy, and when He is in charge, His holiness cannot be tainted by sin. I also checked the third box because I was more interested in self-gratification than yielding to God. In other words, I did not believe He could fulfill my immediate need so I lusted for that particular woman. I checked the fourth box because

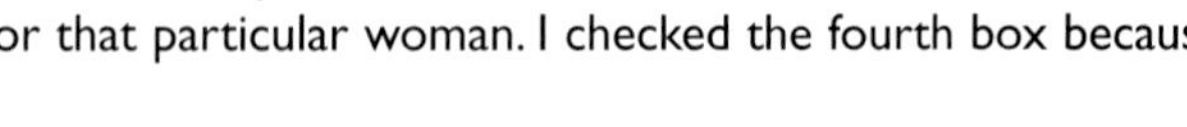

I had watched a TV show with provocatively dressed women. This fed my sin nature and I knew it was my main breakdown. I checked boxes 7 and 8, because I slept in and skipped my quiet time with the Lord, and then I went to the grocery store hungry and stressed.

Hopefully, this example provides an idea of the process needed to identify the types of breakdowns that interfere with your ability to execute God's will. Develop your own "BattleZONE breakdown checklist" so you can constantly assess your key reasons for breakdowns. Try downloading the BZ Breakdown Checklist at **www.battlezoneministries.org > Resources > BZ Course > BZ Checklist** or use 3 x 5 note cards. During this process, you will be able to determine what specific training you should focus on to increase your spiritual fitness. This, in turn, will eventually lead to a higher X% (eXecution percentage) in your BattleZONE(s). By God's loving grace, you can "be holy as Christ is holy."

CAPTAIN'S CORNER
PERSONAL APPLICATION

PLAY 5: Execution Breakdowns HIGHLIGHTS

- When there is a failure to execute, the causes of the breakdown should be analyzed.
- Use the BattleZONE Breakdown Checklist to help analyze when we fail to execute God's will in our BattleZONE(s).
- Success execution comes through reflective thinking and problem solving.

1. List five or more reasons why it is important to develop your own BattleZONE Breakdown Checklist.

1.

2.

3.

4.

5.

6.

7.

CRUNCH TIME:

What did God want you to learn and do from this Play?

GAME PLAN
EXECUTION SYSTEM

C3-Technique

Call a timeout and resist the tempter/temptation.

Confess the temptation to God in prayer and ask the Holy Spirit to show you the way of escape.

Choose by faithful obedience to consciously yield to the Holy Spirit's Play Call, resulting in perfect execution of God's will.

NAME: Mark Mister

YOUR BATTLEZONE: Anger

FORMATION RECOGNITION: Base this on the Scouting Report Form in Week 4.
External: At home, driving my car, and at work. Internal: Hunger–I skip breakfast and get really cranky before lunch. I may miss lunch all together. / Angry–while driving. I understand road rage and it scares me. Lonely–I feel like I am alone trying to live. How can that be, I am around people all day. Tired–I stay up late watching the evening news
Stressed–I feel stressed all day and feel like I am trapped in the rat race.

NUTRITION HISTORY: What have you been "feeding" yourself to entice temptation?
My thoughts are constantly filled with worry and fear. I watch the news every morning before work, after work and right before I go to bed.

OPPONENT'S STRATEGY: Exactly how does your opponent's attack you to create this BattleZONE?
Satan wants to get me thinking about all the things I can't control. If I let negative thoughts enter my mind I allow them to affect my mood, attitude and decisions.

COUNTER-ATTACK/GAME PLAN: 1. Start reading Christian books and/or the Bible in the evening. 2. Meet with my accountability partner and talk about my anger. 3. Use the C-3 Technique when I am in my BattleZONE of anger. 4. Deal with some of my fears and worries about life. 5. Listen to Christian Christian music in the car so I am not yelling and cursing all the time at other ~~idiots~~ drivers

READY LIST: Pre-planned decisions of how you will respond "automatically" to a certain situation

SITUATION	PRE-PLANNED RESPONSE/"AUTOMATIC"	READY LIST
In the car when a driver does something stupid	Listen to Christian music... Do morning devotionals prior to leaving each day	A list of several plays ready to be used in an upcoming game, tailored to an opposing team's strengths and weaknesses. Also known as an "automatic."
At home when something goes wrong	Use the C-3 Technique and walk away before my anger causes me to say and throw things. Get more sleep and eat breakfast.	
At work when I am pressured to get a job done	Get more organized so I am not spending so much time trying to find things. C-3 Technique. Trust God that he will help me get it done.	

BATTLE ZONE MINISTRIES, INC.

GAME PLAN

EXECUTION SYSTEM

C3-Technique

Call a timeout and resist the tempter/temptation.

Confess the temptation to God in prayer and ask the Holy Spirit to show you the way of escape.

Choose by faithful obedience to consciously yield to the Holy Spirit's Play Call, resulting in perfect execution of God's will.

NAME:

YOUR BATTLEZONE:

FORMATION RECOGNITION: Base this on the Scouting Report Form in Week 4.

NUTRITION HISTORY: What have you been "feeding" yourself to entice temptation?

OPPONENT'S STRATEGY: Exactly how does your opponent's attack you to create this BattleZONE?

COUNTER-ATTACK/GAME PLAN:

READY LIST: Pre-planned decisions of how you will respond "automatically" to a certain situation

SITUATION	PRE-PLANNED RESPONSE/"AUTOMATIC"

READY LIST

A list of several plays ready to be used in an upcoming game, tailored to an opposing team's strengths and weaknesses. Also known as an "automatic."

GAME PLAN
EXECUTION SYSTEM

C3-Technique

Call a timeout and resist the tempter/temptation.

Confess the temptation to God in prayer and ask the Holy Spirit to show you the way of escape.

Choose by faithful obedience to consciously yield to the Holy Spirit's Play Call, resulting in perfect execution of God's will.

NAME:

YOUR BATTLEZONE:

FORMATION RECOGNITION: Base this on the Scouting Report Form in Week 4.

NUTRITION HISTORY: What have you been "feeding" yourself to entice temptation?

OPPONENT'S STRATEGY: Exactly how does your opponent's attack you to create this BattleZONE?

COUNTER-ATTACK/GAME PLAN:

READY LIST: Pre-planned decisions of how you will respond "automatically" to a certain situation

SITUATION	PRE-PLANNED RESPONSE/"AUTOMATIC"

READY LIST

A list of several plays ready to be used in an upcoming game, tailored to an opposing team's strengths and weaknesses. Also known as an "automatic."

WEEK 6
EXECUTION BREAKDOWN
BATTLE ZONE MINISTRIES, INC.
www.battlezoneministries.org
WEEK 6
EXECUTION BREAKDOWN
BATTLE ZONE MINISTRIES, INC.
www.battlezoneministries.org
WEEK 6
EXECUTION BREAKDOWN
BATTLE ZONE MINISTRIES, INC.
www.battlezoneministries.org
WEEK 6
EXECUTION BREAKDOWN
BATTLE ZONE MINISTRIES, INC.
www.battlezoneministries.org
WEEK 6
EXECUTION BREAKDOWN
BATTLE ZONE MINISTRIES, INC.
www.battlezoneministries.org
WEEK 6
EXECUTION BREAKDOWN
BATTLE ZONE MINISTRIES, INC.
www.battlezoneministries.org

WEEK 6

EXECUTION BREAKDOWN

BATTLE ZONE MINISTRIES, INC. www.battlezoneministries.org

WEEK 6

EXECUTION BREAKDOWN

BATTLE ZONE MINISTRIES, INC. www.battlezoneministries.org

WEEK 6

EXECUTION BREAKDOWN

BATTLE ZONE MINISTRIES, INC. www.battlezoneministries.org

WEEK 6

EXECUTION BREAKDOWN

BATTLE ZONE MINISTRIES, INC. www.battlezoneministries.org

WEEK 6

EXECUTION BREAKDOWN

BATTLE ZONE MINISTRIES, INC. www.battlezoneministries.org

WEEK 6

EXECUTION BREAKDOWN

BATTLE ZONE MINISTRIES, INC. www.battlezoneministries.org

CAPTAIN'S GUIDE

God's "Game Plan" The "Holy Playbook" – The Bible

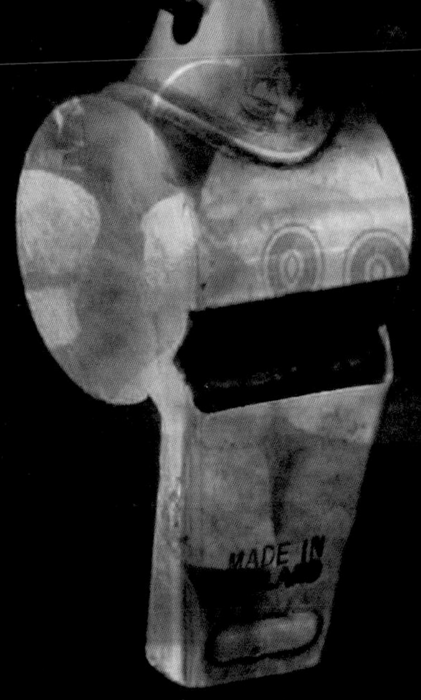

WARM-UP

BATTLEZONE SYMBOL KEY

WARM-UP: GOD'S "GAME PLAN" - THE "HOLY PLAYBOOK"

A. Two-Minute Drill: First thing, have the men get together with their Teammate/Captain and go over counter verses for about 2 minutes total.

- Captain: see the Captain's Guide page 116 in Week 4 for more direction on how to complete the counter verse exercise.
- Some men may not have begun to memorize their verses. In that case, have him read his counter verse(s) out loud for 2 minutes straight. Encourage them to use the "counter verse sandwich" – (verse "address", scripture and verse "address").
- Some men may not have looked up any verses. Simply encourage each of these men and his teammate to find one together and write it on a 3x5 note card. Make sure the other teammate has an opportunity to recite his (give 2 minutes each and then switch).

B. Next, complete the Play Call example activity below.

In football, every offensive play call has a specific purpose and is interpreted exactly the same by the offensive players. The play call tells each player where to line up, what his assignment is and what happens prior to the play (like a motion back or a shift). God's play calls also have specific purpose and it is our job to be able to understand exactly what God wants His children to do during each play.

Below is an offensive passing play call. Each aspect of the play call tells a specific player what his task is for that play. When a player does not understand his assignment, the entire play can be a disaster, creating a poor X% (eXecution percentage).

- Trips Right -- dictates that three receivers line up on the right side of the ball.
- R Zoom -- dictates that the "R" or running back goes in motion.
- The "219" is part of the passing tree number system used for passing routs. All routs are the same for the "X", "Y", & "Z" receivers. All even numbers go towards the center of the field and all odd numbered routs are towards the sidelines.
- "219"- dictates that the "X" receiver or the inside trips receiver runs a "2" or slant rout. The "Y" receiver or middle receiver runs a "1" or a quick 5 yard out rout. The "Z" or the far outside receiver runs "9" or a streak.
- The "R Bench" tells the "R" or running back to run towards the bench on the sidelines.
- There are 10 different routs from "0" to "9."

1. How do you think play calls in football compare to God's "play calls" in the "Holy Playbook"?

2. Do you think there is a purpose for each word God writes?

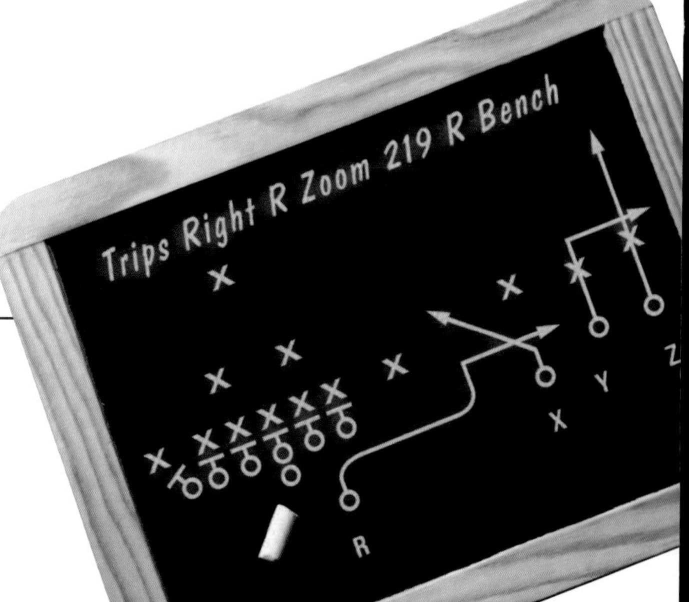

C. Go to the BattleZONE Chalk Talk and proceed to lead your team through Week 6.

CHALK TALK
The "Holy Playbook" – the Bible

1. PRAYER

Have one of the men open in prayer and ask the Holy Spirit to guide and direct the session towards God's agenda.

2. GOD'S "GAME PLAN" - GOD'S "PLAYBOOK" – THE BIBLE

Last week, we studied God's second component in His "Game Plan" for victory/holiness, God the Holy Spirit. Jesus sent the Comforter that leads us into all truth and He gives us the Power to execute God's will in our most challenging BattleZONEs. This week we will cover the third component in God's Game Plan for holiness/victory, The "Holy Playbook"—The Bible.

3. THE BIBLE

The third component of God's "Game Plan" to holiness/victory is The "Holy Playbook"—The Bible.

The Bible
No one knows exactly how many Bibles are sold annually because many publishers guard their sales figures – but the total is in the tens of millions, making the Bible the world's best-selling book *(Chicago Free Press, November 12, 2000).* Paradoxically, at the same time, many people say they don't understand the Bible; others criticize it and don't believe its truth.

Miles Coverdale taught the following rules of interpretation. "It shall greatly help ye to understand scripture, if thou mark not only what is spoken or wrytten, but of whom, and to whom, with what words, at what time, where, to what intent, with what circumstances, considering what goeth before and what followeth."

4. WEEK 6 PLAYS

For Week 6 you were assigned to read and be ready to comment on five Plays. You will have TWO MINUTES to present your topic; then discuss each as a group. Please try to stay focused on what God taught you through this Play. **What did God want you to learn and do?**

Captain make sure to take the lead on Play 4—R.I.P.L. Effect.

CAPTAIN, ASSIGN EACH TEAMMATE A PLAY – THEN LET THEM TAKE THE LEAD.

- **Play 1: Applying the "Holy Playbook"**
- **Play 2: The "Holy Playbook" – Becoming a Student of the Game**
- **Play 3: R.I.P.L. Effect – Introduction**
- **Play 4: R.I.P.L. Effect – Joshua 1:8 (Captain, lead this one)**
- **Play 5: Execution Breakdowns**

5. GAME PLAN EXECUTION

Give one example of how you used the C3-Technique last week. Use the C3-Technique language. **Notice that there is a new section called the Ready List on the bottom of the form on pages 159 & 160. Turn there now.**

Do the Ready List in class together. See sample on page 158.
Continue to work on your BattleZONE Game Plan Execution System this week.
We will do another Simulation Training next week, so please be prepared to demonstrate one example from a real life temptation situation.

6. Crunch Time

Have each teammate describe one thing that really "hit" him during this practice session.

7. Independent Practice

1. Continue and refine your new Game Plan Execution System in your BattleZONE and continue to practice the C3-Technique during the week.

2. Read and meditate on the next set of Strength Training Cards for the next week as often as possible.

3. Prayerfully search God's Word for three to four counter verses that you can hide them in your heart for use in your BattleZONE(s).

4. Read all five Plays and be prepared to teach the team next week. Be prepared to share with your teammates how God spoke to you. Remember to underline, highlight and take notes as you go.

5. You will be required to do the R.I.P.L. Effect for one play call in Week 7. Add 30 minutes to you time.

6. Pray who God wants you to "draft" so you can lead them through BattleZONE. Write their name(s) down for next week. You will be asked to have the name(s) and a start date finalized by Week 9. My First BattleZONE Draft on page 199 will walk you through the process to ensure that you draft the team God wants.

7. Call your TC at least once this week and pray for him daily.

8. Iron Sharpens Iron (James 5:16)

Captain: Ask if anyone has done anything that compromised his walk with God during the past week. If yes, name it generally (i.e., lust, greed, lying). The men can get with their TC or do as a team. Ask for prayer requests and ask one person to pray for each situation until every request is prayed over and/or write the prayer requests on the next page.

PRAYER REQUESTS AND PRAISES

NAME	
	REQUEST
	RESULT
NAME	REQUEST
	RESULT
NAME	REQUEST
	RESULT
NAME	REQUEST
	RESULT
NAME	REQUEST
	RESULT
NAME	REQUEST
	RESULT
NAME	REQUEST
	RESULT
NAME	REQUEST
	RESULT

BATTLEZONE VICTORIES

Chad Jorgenson
Antioch, CA

I have been a Christian for nearly 15 years and I like to believe that I was doing a pretty good job living the Christian life. I was striving to emulate the godly attributes outlined in Timothy & Titus, as well as the lives of those men I consider mentors.

If you're like me you may have encountered a handful of godly men over the course of your life that discipled you in one way or another. PRAISE GOD for them! They have given you an invaluable gift. But, when asked directly who showed you how to live out your faith daily, you may be surprised by your answer. I was!

I was recently asked that question, point blank, during a conference in March 2006. That was my first exposure to BattleZONE Ministries. Out of a list of 20 actions essential to living my life in a way pleasing to God, that is Holy - set apart for Christ, I honestly had to say no one had ever shown me how. I was astonished.

It was then that God made it clear to me that pretty good wasn't good enough. I was not effectively impacting the world around me for Christ. I needed to act! I needed to train myself, and I needed to train other men. So, when asked they could answer that question with an emphatic YES, and say Chad showed me how! That, in a nutshell, is what BattleZONE Ministries is all about to me.

God is using BattleZONE in my life to open my eyes. He is radically changing my view of not only my personal walk with Christ, but also of the men around me both Christian and unbeliever alike. I, like many men, was a passive participant in my Christian walk. Now, it is crystal clear to me that men need to be actively pursuing righteousness! That is precisely why I'm becoming a Certified BattleZONE Coach.

As I've thought about this over the course of the past three months I truly believe there are two primary reasons for this passive mentality. First, the vast majority of men are isolated and do not have a model to follow or vital relationships with other men. This is essential. I believe you cannot live a holy, victorious life that pleases God without other men meaningfully involved in your life.

And second, most men do not have the tools required to actively train themselves. Michael's passion is to transform men into reproducing disciples of Jesus Christ. To accomplish that, he has created a set of training techniques to practice living holy lives. I have never come across such a powerful set of tools designed specifically to help men train themselves on a daily basis in the pursuit of righteousness! This is what sets BattleZONE apart from most other studies – its more than just knowledge – it trains your heart and mind through daily practice!

What God is doing through BattleZONE Ministries is truly amazing. I strongly encourage you to tackle your BattleZONE today. It is my prayer that you will yield your heart to God completely and begin your pursuit. Then just watch in wonder and amazement at what He will do through you!

Start today by taking the BattleZONE Challenge at **www.battlezoneministries.org.**

God's "Game Plan" Faithful Obedience, Love, The Armor of God & Prayer

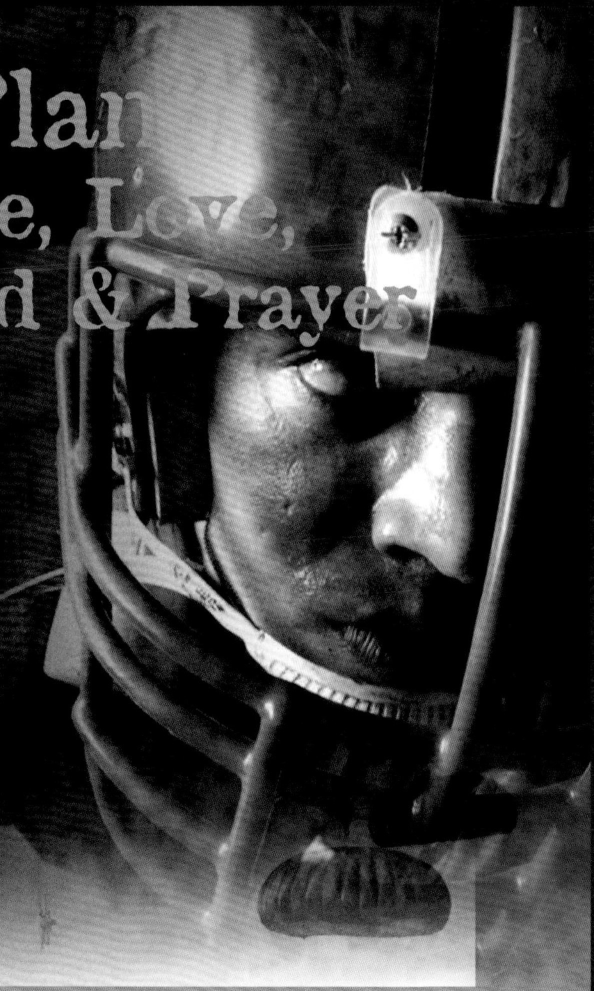

- The "Pocket"
- Faithful Obedience
- Faith Training
- Love
- The Armor of God
- Prayer

Week 7 Objectives

Each man will understand:

1. The importance of faith as it relates to obedience and executing God's will.
2. That God gives us faith but we must trust Him to build our "faith muscles".
3. The importance of Godly love and how it relates to the pursuit of holiness/victory.
4. How to arm himself with the Armor of God.
5. How to use the R. I. P. L. Effect on a passage of scripture.
6. How to use the Game Plan Execution System in real-life temptation situations.

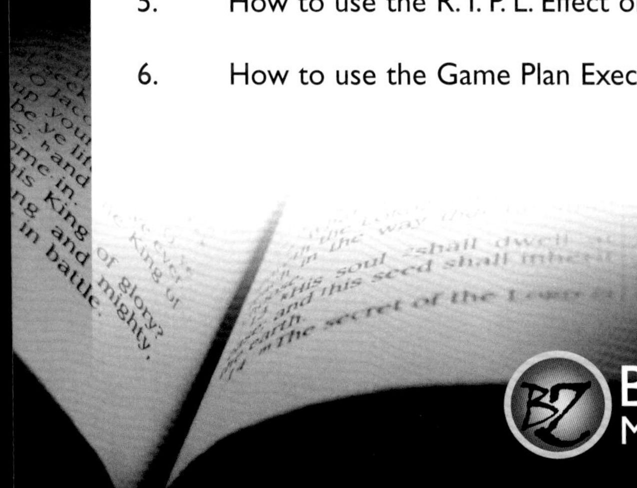

Let love be your highest goal.
I Corinthians 14:1 - NLT

The love of Christ compels us.
2 Corinthians 5:14 - NKJV

Pray without ceasing.
I Thessalonians 5:17 - KJV

What is faith? It is the confident assurance that something we want is going to happen. It is the certainty that what we hope for is waiting for us, even though we cannot see it up ahead.
Hebrews 11:1 - TLB

A final word: Be strong with the Lord's mighty power. Put on all of God's armor so that you will be able to stand firm against all strategies and tricks of the Devil. For we are not fighting against people made of flesh and blood, but against the evil rulers and authorities of the unseen world, against those mighty powers of darkness who rule this world, and against wicked spirits in the heavenly realms.
Ephesians 6:10-12 - NLT

Use every piece of God's armor to resist the enemy in the time of evil, so that after the battle you will still be standing firm. Stand your ground, putting on the sturdy belt of truth and the body armor of God's righteousness. For shoes, put on the peace that comes from the Good News, so that you will be fully prepared.
Ephesians 6:13-15 - NLT

In every battle you will need faith as your shield to stop the fiery arrows aimed at you by Satan. Put on salvation as your helmet, and take the sword of the Spirit, which is the word of God. Pray at all times and on every occasion in the power of the Holy Spirit. Stay alert and be persistent in your prayers for all Christians everywhere.
Ephesians 6: 16-18 - NLT

You can never please God without faith, without depending on him. Anyone who wants to come to God must believe that there is a God and that He rewards those who sincerely look for Him.
Hebrews 11:6 - TLB

WEEK 7

STRENGTH TRAINING

Let love be your highest goal.

1 Corinthians 14:1 - NLT

The love of Christ compels us.

2 Corinthians 5:14 - NKJV

BATTLE ZONE MINISTRIES, INC. **www.battlezoneministries.org**

WEEK 7

STRENGTH TRAINING

Pray without ceasing.

1 Thessalonians 5:17 - KJV

What is faith? It is the confident assurance that something we want is going to happen. It is the certainty that what we hope for is waiting for us, even though we cannot see it up ahead.

Hebrews 11:1 - TLB

BATTLE ZONE MINISTRIES, INC. **www.battlezoneministries.org**

WEEK 7

STRENGTH TRAINING

A final word: Be strong with the Lord's mighty power. Put on all of God's armor so that you will be able to stand firm against all strategies and tricks of the Devil. For we are not fighting against people made of flesh and blood, but against the evil rulers and authorities of the unseen world, against those mighty powers of darkness who rule this world, and against wicked spirits in the heavenly realms.

Ephesians 6:10-12 - NLT

BATTLE ZONE MINISTRIES, INC. **www.battlezoneministries.org**

WEEK 7

STRENGTH TRAINING

Use every piece of God's armor to resist the enemy in the time of evil, so that after the battle you will still be standing firm. Stand your ground, putting on the sturdy belt of truth and the body armor of God's righteousness. For shoes, put on the peace that comes from the Good News, so that you will be fully prepared.

Ephesians 6:13-15 - NLT

BATTLE ZONE MINISTRIES, INC. **www.battlezoneministries.org**

WEEK 7

STRENGTH TRAINING

In every battle you will need faith as your shield to stop the fiery arrows aimed at you by Satan. Put on salvation as your helmet, and take the sword of the Spirit, which is the word of God. Pray at all times and on every occasion in the power of the Holy Spirit. Stay alert and be persistent in your prayers for all Christians everywhere.

Ephesians 6: 16-18 - NLT

BATTLE ZONE MINISTRIES, INC. **www.battlezoneministries.org**

WEEK 7

STRENGTH TRAINING

You can never please God without faith, without depending on him. Anyone who wants to come to God must believe that there is a God and that He rewards those who sincerely look for Him.

Hebrews 11:6 - TLB

BATTLE ZONE MINISTRIES, INC. **www.battlezoneministries.org**

NOTES

STRENGTH TRAINING

BATTLE ZONE MINISTRIES, INC. www.battlezoneministries.org

NOTES

STRENGTH TRAINING

BATTLE ZONE MINISTRIES, INC. www.battlezoneministries.org

NOTES

STRENGTH TRAINING

BATTLE ZONE MINISTRIES, INC. www.battlezoneministries.org

NOTES

STRENGTH TRAINING

BATTLE ZONE MINISTRIES, INC. www.battlezoneministries.org

NOTES

STRENGTH TRAINING

BATTLE ZONE MINISTRIES, INC. www.battlezoneministries.org

NOTES

STRENGTH TRAINING

BATTLE ZONE MINISTRIES, INC. www.battlezoneministries.org

PRACTICE: R.I.P.L. Effect

Practice the R. I. P. L. Effect using Hebrews 12:1-2 — Faithful Obedience

First, look up Hebrews 12:1-2 in your Bible. Next, use the R. I. P. L. Effect chart below:

R. I. P. L. Effect
This symbol will prompt you to use the BattleZONE Bible Study Technique in your quest to become a student of the Word. R.I.P.L. stands for:

Read it: Read the passage carefully. What does the passage say literally? List the literal facts on the column on the right. Don't try to put the passage in your own words – don't paraphrase and don't interpret it. Look at it full in the face and see exactly what it says.

Interpret it: Interpret the passage in its context. What does the passage mean? What are the repeating words, phrases or themes? As you read, it's a good idea to highlight or underline repeating phrases, words, ideas or themes.

- Read the Bible like an announcer doing a play-by-play on ESPN – ask who, what, when, where, why and how.
- Cross-reference the passage. Try to determine what God was saying in that moment in time – NOT what He's saying to you right now.

Personalize it: Now is the time to personalize the passage to your current life. How is the Holy Spirit prompting you to respond to the passage? This is when you ask what God is saying to you and what He wants you to get out of the passage.

Live it: Live out the passage obediently. What must you do to live the passage in your daily life? What act of faithful obedience must you do right now to live the passage in your life?

Read it: What does the passage say literally? List the facts in the column on the right.

____

Interpret it: What did God intend the passage to mean for the time and place?

____

- **Who:** Who is talking? To whom is God/the author talking/writing?

____

- **What:** What is the subject matter? What are His main points?

____

- **When:** When did the book take place historically? This information is usually found at the beginning of the book, depending on the type of Bible you're using.

____

- **Where:** Where did this take place?

____

- **Why:** Why did God/the author say this to the writer or the people?

____

- **How:** How were the readers supposed to accomplish what God wanted?

____

Personalize it: What does this passage say to you personally as if God were talking to you?

____

Live it: What must you do today to live this passage in your life?

____

List the literal facts:

____

References:

____

PLAY 1 : Faithful Obedience

What is faith? It is the confident assurance that something we want is going to happen. It is the certainty that what we hope for is waiting for us, even though we cannot see it up ahead.

Hebrews 11:1 - TLB

Staying in the Pocket

A quarterback must have faith in his team to stand tall in the pocket and execute the pass play call. He must trust that his team will protect him from harm and give him a safe zone where he can increase his execution percentage. In the midst of the pocket, even with a tremendous battle going on around him, he must have faith and carry out the coach's play call with precision and confidence.

The QB gets into trouble when he takes his eyes off the receivers and starts to look at his opponents. At this moment, he mustn't try to make things happen on his own. He has been taught to complete the pass regardless of the physical consequences. Even if he gets pummeled, he gets up, brushes himself off and is encouraged because the receiver completed the pass downfield. If he steps outside the pocket, his protection is minimized.

Likewise, when we step outside of God's pocket of protection and disobey His commandments, or live inauthentic Christian lives, we will not be blessed. When we stay in His pocket of protection by executing His will by the power of the Holy Spirit, He will bless us. The QB is trained to follow the coach's play call because with obedience comes execution. God works the same way, always blessing obedience.

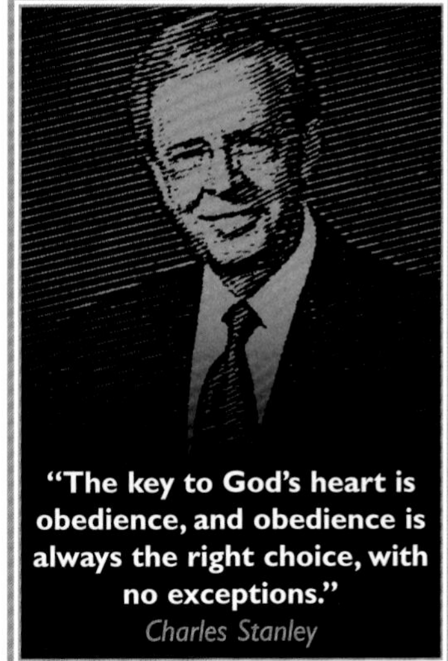

"The key to God's heart is obedience, and obedience is always the right choice, with no exceptions."

Charles Stanley

The Big Lie Called Satisfy

In the moment of temptation, we are faced with the big lie that the sin before us will satisfy. Consider the lie that looking at pornography will satisfy your need for sexual fulfillment. The truth is that it does just the opposite. Porn entices your sin nature's desire for more lustful images, which may lead you to masturbate (while thinking of a woman other than your wife), or even sex outside of marriage. Both of these actions are the sin of adultery.

The real truth is that God is the only one who can satisfy every one of your needs. You may not think so at the time, but you must believe that nothing and no one can satisfy your needs other than Jesus Christ. This is where faith comes in. You must have a solid core belief that God is bigger than the sin before you. Believe He can satisfy your exact need at the exact time; even though you may suffer in your decision to obey, God will always give you the strength and the means to obey Him over your temptation.

According to Jerry Bridges,

"...if you do not believe you are dead to sin's guilt, you cannot trust Christ for the strength to subdue its power in your life."

Jerry Bridges

(Growing Your Faith: How to Mature in Christ, NavPress, 2004, p. 113).

Faithful Obedience

Faithful obedience is the ability to make decisions because you are in the will of God, knowing that He will bless you even if it means giving up something you desire more than being obedient to God (like a pornographic picture). **Faithful obedience is doing the hard thing and experiencing discomfort knowing God's way is better than the temptation set before you.** Faith is the ability to make a decision not to sin and then walk away from the temptation knowing God's way is best. God will meet all of your needs – no exceptions!

"...obedience is the pathway to holiness—a holy life being essentially an obedient life—we may say that no one will become holy apart from a life of faith. Faith is not only necessary to salvation; but it is also necessary to live a life pleasing to God. Faith enables us to claim the promises of God—but is also enables us to obey the commands of God. Faith enables us to obey when obedience is costly or seems unreasonable to the natural mind"

Jerry Bridges

(The Pursuit of Holiness, NavPress, 2003, p. 170)

CAPTAIN'S CORNER
PERSONAL APPLICATION

PLAY 1: Faithful Obedience HIGHLIGHTS

- God will bless obedience. It may not come in the form of material blessing, but He is faithful to an obedient Christ-Follower.
- God is always bigger than the sin before you.
- Faithful obedience is doing the hard thing and experiencing discomfort knowing God's way is best.

1. Would it help you to avoid sin if you knew God's will for the situation? Why or why not?

2. What is the desire you have that you are not willing to believe God can meet – and that leads to a particular temptation?

3. Do you believe faith and obedience are linked? Why or why not?

CRUNCH TIME:

What did God want you to learn and do from this Play?

PLAY 2 : Faith Training

You can never please God without faith, without depending on him. Anyone who wants to come to God must believe that there is a God and that he rewards those who sincerely look for him.
Hebrews 11:6 - TLB

Flex Your Faith

We go to the gym and do squats, curls, pull-downs and chest presses in order to strengthen and give definition to our muscles. We ride bikes or run or box to strengthen our cardiovascular system. This in itself isn't bad, but there is a kind of workout that is even more valuable than physical exercise.

Physical exercise has some value, but spiritual exercise is much more important, for it promises a reward in both this life and the next.
I Timothy 1:8 - NLT

Exercising our faith is vital to becoming a strong man of God. Temptation-Specific Training (TST) allows Christians an opportunity to exercise faith. Everyone has multiple opportunities during the day to trust God to meet our needs when we are tempted instead of failing to execute God's will in our personal BattleZONEs. The late Bill Bright said,

"Faith must have an object, and the object of my faith is God and His inspired Word. The right view of God generates faith. Faith is like a muscle: it grows with exercise. The more we see God accomplish in and through our lives, the more we can be assured that He will accomplish as we trust and obey Him more. There is nothing mysterious about faith. It is simply a matter of getting to know God whom we worship, His holy inspired Word, claiming His promises, expecting the results of those promises, claimed by a life that lives in faith and obedience"
Bill Bright
(The Holy Spirit, The Key to Supernatural Living, New Life Publications, 2003, p 149)

"Reason is the greatest enemy that faith has..."
Table Talk, 1569

"God our Father has made all things depend on faith so that whoever has faith will have everything, and whoever does not have faith will have nothing."
(On Christian Liberty)
Marin Luther

Faith is paramount for experiencing holiness. Faith is belief in action or, as one English teacher once said, "I want to be a Christian verb."

Basic Training

A muscular faith is one that truly believes God will meet all of your needs – believing this deeply, down to your very core. The Holy Spirit ministers to us, giving us a blessed assurance even when we doubt God's faithfulness. We must also remember that all faith is a gift from God and it's only in His timing that He gives us a deeper faith. Faith trained by God's loving grace manifests itself in obedience, which demonstrates love for God. In the midst of a BattleZONE, we are given an opportunity to exercise our faith by God's loving grace. When we choose to execute God's will over our own selfish desires, we build our faith in the Faithful One. On the other hand, when we lack the faith or Temptation-Specific Training that helps build faith, we can experience sin.

Wimpy Faith

Unbelief is the single most damaging factor in poor execution and is the opposite of faith. Satan lies and says Jesus can't possibly meet our needs – even the immediate ones in our BattleZONEs – to get Christians out of God's will. God tells us that everything we do should be done in faith or it is sin. So what exactly does that mean? Simply put, if we do not have the will of God at the forefront of our decision-making process, we will sin. This includes our compulsive desires to overeat, drink, or purchase something. Jesus said, "Your will, not mine be done."

For instance, what if the Raiders had doubts about the coaches' game plan? Wouldn't this effect their performance? If you are wavering in your belief and have limited knowledge of the Bible, you will be crushed in your BattleZONEs. Think about it. If you believe that looking at a few pictures of naked women does not compromise your marriage, you are dead wrong.

But when you follow your own wrong inclinations, your lives will produce these evil results: impure thoughts, eagerness for lustful pleasure.
Galatians 5:19 - TLB

If you believe that getting drunk is no big deal because Jesus drank wine, you are deceived and you will fail to execute God's will in the BattleZONE of drunkenness.

And do not be drunk with wine, in which is dissipation; but be filled with the Spirit.
Ephesians 5:18 - NKJV

What great opportunities for your opponent to use wimpy faith against you.

Never settle for wimpy faith, because God has given you the desire to train for spiritual fitness.

Let's work out! 

CAPTAIN'S CORNER
PERSONAL APPLICATION

PLAY 2: Faith Training HIGHLIGHTS

- The Holy Spirit ministers to you, giving a blessed assurance, even when you doubt God's faithfulness.
- All faith is a gift from God; it's only in His timing that He gives us a deeper faith.
- When you lack faith that God can meet all your needs, you can experience sin.
- Unbelief is the single most damaging factor in poor execution and leads to a lack of faith.

1. Do you trust God to meet all your needs? Why or why not? Explain.

2. Search your heart... do you disbelieve any of God's promises? Which one in particular?

3. Would you consider yourself a Christian noun or verb? In other words, do you do God's Word?

CRUNCH TIME:

What did God want you to learn and do from this Play?

PLAY 3 : Love

Let love be your highest goal.
I Corinthians 14:1 - NLT

The love of Christ compels us.
2 Corinthians 5:14 - NKJV

What Motivates You?
All coaches look for ways to ignite the inner fire that motivates players to train in a way that allows them to perform better on the gridiron. Jon Gruden, Head Coach of the 2003 Super Bowl champions Tampa Bay Buccaneers, "...can flat out motivate you," according to Trent Dilfer, who spoke at a men's Christian retreat in California. Motivation is an essential element in any venture. Finding out what motivates someone is the key to a sales manager's team's effectiveness, as it is to the Christian walk. In a murder trial, the prosecution always tries to explore and expose the motive. Once a motive is found, they have a better chance of winning the case.

Let the Love of Christ Compel You
Christ's love should be our single motive for spiritual training and holiness. In 2 Corinthians 5:14 ("the love of Christ compels us"), the word "compels" is similar to "motivates" or "urges". The love of Christ should motivate us to execute God's will, living obedient lives. The correct view of Christ's love should motivate us to want to train for spiritual fitness. The correct view of the pursuit of Christ should motivate us to pursue Christ in the correct way. An incorrect attitude towards the pursuit of Christ can lead to legalism and even heresy.

"Love, to be real, must cost. It must hurt. It must empty us of self."
Mother Theresa
USA Today, Nov. 17, 1986

Our old nature's motives are always (even at our best) tainted with wickedness, because our old hearts are deceitful and wicked. But God has given us a new heart:

I'll give you a new heart, put a new spirit in you. I'll remove the stone heart from your body and replace it with a heart that's God-willed, not self-willed.
Ezekiel 36:26 - MSG

Christ's motives are always pure. In order to execute God's "Game Plan" with pure motives, we must be in Christ, because Christ is pure truth. We must be controlled by the power of the Holy Spirit.

The Apostle Paul was motivated by Christ's love, not the drive to be more holy. When we are motivated by a place or destination, e.g. "getting" to holiness, we miss out on the person, Jesus Christ. Jerry Bridges says,

"We believers do need to be challenged to a life of committed discipleship, but that challenge needs to be based on the Gospel, not on duty or guilt. Duty or guilt may motivate us for a while, but only a sense of Christ's love for us will motivate us for a lifetime. As we continually reflect upon that Gospel, the Holy Spirit floods our hearts with a sense of God's love to us in Christ. And that sense of His love motivates us in a compelling way to live for Him."
Jerry Bridges
(The Discipline of Grace, God's Role and Our Role in the Pursuit of Holiness, NavPress, 1994, p. 24)

We are to boast not of our performance but of Christ. When the Motivator isn't our motivation, we begin to boast of our performance, dismiss God's loving grace and become spiritually proud.

God is Unconditional Love
You cannot truly love without knowing the loving Father. The more you strive to give your life over to Him, the more you will desire to love others and by faith, execute God's will. The greatest commandment is to love God and your neighbor as yourself (Matthew 22:36-40). When you see Christ's unconditional love, how even in your darkest sins, He loves you unconditionally, this love will compel you to move from training for spiritual fitness out of duty to training for love's sake. Christ's love compels us to obedience. If you love Him, you will want to obey His commandments. When you desire to obey His commandments, you will be able to execute His will in your BattleZONEs. Make love your highest goal.

Faith expresses itself through love (Galatians 5:6), resulting in obedience, which leads to holiness. You will know that you are making progress because you will begin to love God and others more, demonstrated through self-sacrifice and reflecting the fruit of the Spirit.

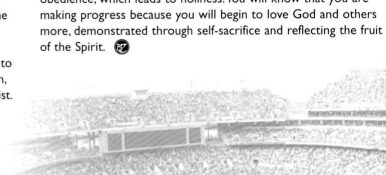

CAPTAIN'S CORNER
PERSONAL APPLICATION

PLAY 3: Love
HIGHLIGHTS

- The correct view of Christ's love will motivate you to train for spiritual fitness.
- The correct view of the pursuit of Christ will motivate you to pursue Christ in the correct way.
- The greatest commandments are to love God totally and your neighbor as yourself.
- Faith expresses itself through love, resulting in obedience, which leads to holiness.

1. What compels you towards an obedient life of faith?

2. Do the goals you have for your family, career, health, finances and spiritual growth demonstrate that they are compelled by Christ's love? If not write a new goal for each of the areas to reflect Christlike motivation.

CRUNCH TIME:

What did God want you to learn and do from this Play?

PLAY 4 : The Armor of God

Read Ephesians 6:10-18

Gear Up (Put on the Armor)
Football is a contact sport with tremendous high-speed collisions. Players use their bodies as weapons of mass destruction (WMDs) to demoralize, pound, and ultimately defeat their opponents. Christians are in a battle much like the physical one that takes place on the gridiron, but the one we face is far more dangerous and can be much more damaging if a single piece of "equipment" is left in the locker room. This battle is not physical in nature, but is an invisible war in the spiritual realm.

Protection from Spiritual Injuries
This powerful war going on in the spiritual realm is real whether you believe it or not. God commands us to put on the whole Armor of God to protect us against spiritual injury. Paul exhorts us

Finally, my brethren, be strong in the Lord and in the power of His might. Put on the whole armor of God, that you may be able to stand against the wiles of the devil.
Ephesians 6:10-11

We are instructed to put on the whole Armor of God (not just pieces of it) so we can stand against the Devil's strategies and tricks. Each piece of the Armor is necessary to fight the Devil, just like each piece of equipment has a specific and critical function for a football player.

An Invisible Battle
Paul goes on to say we are not in a physical battle, but an invisible one against the powers of darkness in the unseen world

For we do not wrestle against flesh and blood, but against principalities, against powers, against the rulers of the darkness of this age, against spiritual hosts of wickedness in the heavenly places.
Ephesians 6:12 - NIV

The weapons from Satan's arsenal are spiritual, not physical. They are evil and cunning in their very nature. These spiritual weapons attack our thoughts, tempting us to cheat, act proud, lie and scheme. Because we belong to Christ, God's angels physically protect us. They fight in the perimeter surrounding us, in the heavenly places talked about in verse 12. Unlike the Holy Spirit, Who protects our conscience, these angels fight the powers of darkness 24/7/365 literally holding back the powers of hell. They are sent by God to protect His children.

Each of the six pieces of God's Armor points back to Jesus, leaving us to conclude that not only is Jesus the ultimate victor over Satan, but that Christ continues to protect us from the enemy's evil schemes here on earth in our day-to-day BattleZONEs. Let's take a look at the six pieces of God's Armor and how they link to Jesus.

ONLINE VIDEO

Watch streaming video teaching of how to put on the whole Armor of God at **www.battlezoneministries.org > Training > ShowMeHow > PutOnTheArmor > default.aspx**

PUT ON JESUS CHRIST AS THE WHOLE ARMOR OF GOD

WHOLE ARMOR OF GOD	LINK TO JESUS	SCRIPTURE
Belt of Truth	Jesus is Truth	John 14:6
Breastplate of Righteousness	Jesus is Righteousness	Jeremiah 23:6
Shoes of the Gospel of Peace	Jesus is the Prince of Peace	Isaiah 9:6
Shield of Faith	Jesus is Who we put our faith in	Acts 3:16
Helmet of Salvation	Jesus is our Salvation/Savior	Psalms 27:1/Isaiah 60:16
Sword of the Spirit/Word of God	Jesus is the Living Word	John 1:14

Jesus said to him, "I am the way, the truth, and the life. No one comes to the Father except through Me." — John 14:6 NKJV

In His days, Judah will be saved, and Israel will dwell safely; now this is His name by which He will be called: THE LORD OUR RIGHTEOUSNESS. — Jeremiah 23:6 NKJV

For unto us a Child is born, unto us a Son is given; and the government will be upon His shoulder. And His name will be called Wonderful, Counselor, Mighty God, Everlasting Father, Prince of Peace. — Isaiah 9:6 NKJV

Jesus' name has healed this man -- and you know how lame he was before. Faith in Jesus' name – faith given us from God –a has caused this perfect healing. — Acts 3:16 TLB

The Lord is my light and my salvation; he protects me from danger -- whom shall I fear? — Psalm 27:1 TLB

"I, the Lord, am your Savior..." — Isaiah 60:16 TLB

And the Word became flesh and dwelt among us, and we beheld His glory, the glory as of the only begotten of the Father, full of grace and truth. — John 1:14 NKJV

CAPTAIN'S CORNER
PERSONAL APPLICATION

PLAY 4: The Armor of God HIGHLIGHTS

- There is a powerful war going on in the spiritual realm between Satan and his demons and God's angels.
- Spiritual weapons attack your thoughts, tempting you to cheat, act proud, lie, and scheme.
- There are six pieces of God's Armor; every piece points back to Jesus.
- Praying on the Whole Armor of God is vital to defeating Satan's schemes.

1. What is your honest belief about spiritual warfare? How did you reach this conclusion?

2. What does Paul mean by the spiritual realm where principalities, powers, rulers of the darkness of this age and spiritual hosts of wickedness live in the heavenly places live?

CRUNCH TIME:

What did God want you to learn and do from this Play?

PLAY 5 : Prayer

And He came to the disciples and found them sleeping. And He said to Peter, "So, could you not watch with Me one hour? Watch and pray that you may not enter into temptation. The spirit indeed is willing, but the flesh is weak." Again, for the second time, He went away and prayed, "My Father, if this cannot pass unless I drink it, Your will be done."

Matthew 26:40-42 – ESV (emphasis the author's)

Focus, Prayer and the Holy Spirit

Prayer is also key to overcoming our personal BattleZONEs. When we ask God for help, we admit that we are weak and He alone can rescue us from the sin set before us. While Jesus was agonizing in the garden on the Mount of Olives, He asked the disciples to stay alert and pray,

"Keep alert and pray. Otherwise temptation will overpower you. For though the spirit is willing enough, the body is weak!"

Matthew 26:41

Jesus coached His team by teaching that the key to avoiding temptation is keeping alert and praying. By keeping alert, Jesus meant for us to stay focused, always assessing the surrounding oppositional circumstances. In other words, be aware of the formations you are in. We are to know our weaknesses and take precautions and sometimes we are to literally run away:

Run from anything that stimulates youthful lusts.

2 Timothy 2:22 - NLT

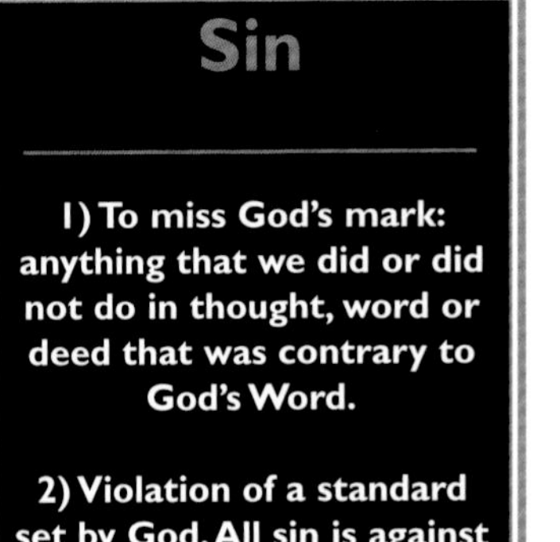

Sin

1) To miss God's mark: anything that we did or did not do in thought, word or deed that was contrary to God's Word.

2) Violation of a standard set by God. All sin is against the law-giver and grieves the Holy Spirit.

Jesus knows temptation can strike at any moment, especially in our areas of weakness. Therefore, we can take Matthew 26:41 and apply it to all of our personal BattleZONEs as well. We must stay alert not only in our own areas of weakness, but also be aggressively scanning the field for the opponent's attack strategies.

Be careful! Watch out for the attacks from the Devil, your great enemy. He prowls around like a roaring lion looking for some victim to devour.

I Peter 5:8 - NLT

Prayer is no substitute for hard work, prayer is the work. God does things in and through our lives by prayer that He does in no other way. As we pray and as our attention is turned toward God, we become more receptive to aligning our lives with His will.

Oswald Chambers — My Utmost for His Highest

Prayer is the Christian's secret weapon over temptation. We must strive to maintain regular, adequate time in prayer. Minimal, harried prayer time will cause our spiritual lives to unwind and cause us to take the shape of this world, instead of God's Word. Prayer is an intimate conversation with God, a one-on-one session with the loving Owner of the team. We must discipline ourselves to get past the distractions that keep us from connecting intimately with God during prayer. As you train yourself to connect with God, your prayer life and your relationship with God will flourish. This intimate time will also build your trust in Him because you will see that He truly does answer your prayers when you walk by faith in obedience to His Word. When we have nothing to hide from God, we want to talk to Him all day long. We are told in I Thessalonians 5:17 to "pray without ceasing," which literally means to talk to God all day long and invite Him into every decision.

Leather Knees?

What is your prayer time like? Do you spend unhurried, adequate time in prayer so you can hear your Father's voice? Develop a disciplined prayer schedule so God can transform you. Prayer is for the past, present and future. We pray for the past to ask God to forgive our sins; we pray in the present so God can help us not fall into temptation; we pray for the future for others and ourselves to become **3C-Christians – C**onformed to the **C**haracter of **C**hrist. A fruitful prayer life takes work and effort. Train yourself to be a prayer warrior. A coach looks for evidence that his athletes are spending enough time in the weight room by looking at the calluses on his hands; God does not look for leather knees; He looks at our hearts, which are transformed by spending time in prayer with Him.

Jesus taught His disciples a format for prayer.

P.R.A.Y.E.R.S. — Matthew 6:5-15

v9:	**P**raise God
v10:	**R**ealign your will with God's
v11:	**A**sk for 1) others 2) self
v12:	**Y**esterday's sin confession
v13:	**E**xamine relationships for unforgiveness
v14a:	**R**epress temptations
v14b:	**S**afety from Satan

'APTAIN'S CORNER
PERSONAL APPLICATION

'LAY 5: Prayer HIGHLIGHTS

When you are tempted, **run!**
When you are tempted **pray!**
When you are tempted **yield** to the Holy Spirit.
Prayer is an intimate conversation with God, a one-on-one session with the loving Owner of the team.
Unhurried, adequate time in prayer will help you set your moral compass each day and give you strength when you are tempted.

. What relationship is there between prayer and temptation?

. How often do you try to avoid sinning in your own strength? Give one example.

. What are the obstacles in your prayer life? How will you overcome them?

CRUNCH TIME:

What did God want you to learn and do from this Play?

BattleZONE Victories

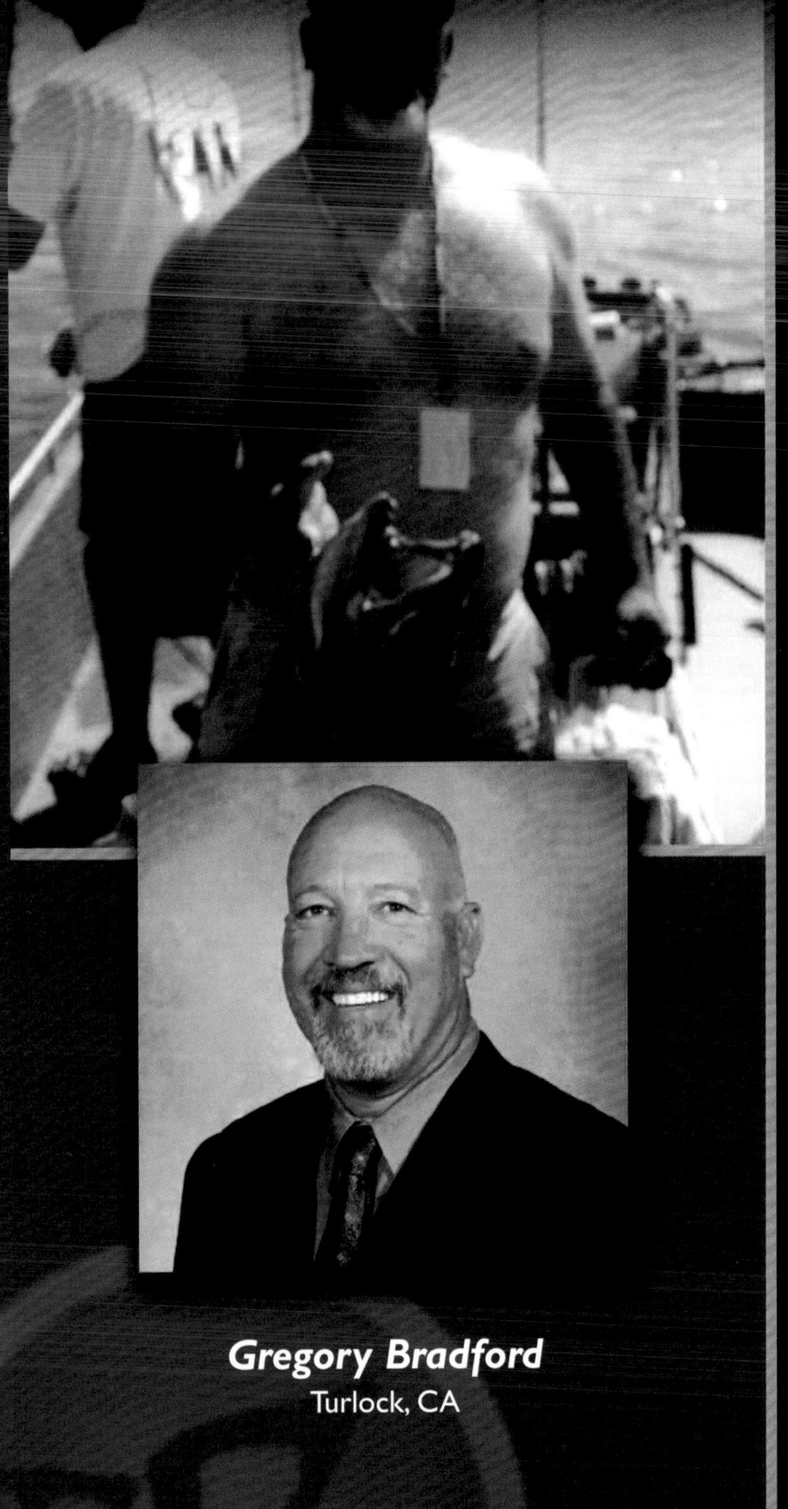

Gregory Bradford
Turlock, CA

I have been in the church since I was 13 years old. By the time I had turned 16, I had given my life to Christ. Over the last 32 years, I have served as a teacher, leader, deacon, assistant pastor (and a pew sitter!) During these years, like all men, there have been times of victory and defeat when faced with the temptation. How can a Christian man live a consistent victorious life over sin?

Thankfully, I was introduced to BattleZONE Ministries while attending a men's ministry conference. After going through BattleZONE and using the tools it provides, I am convinced that a man can live that consistent victorious life. The Battlezone strategy creates training ground to build up Christian men that who will one day go out and disciple other men.

It is impossible to sit on the fence after experiencing the BattleZONE Training Course. Have you given your life to Jesus Christ? Are you living a the holy life which God expects? I urge you to enter the BattleZONE – you will never be the same.

Thank you BattleZONE.

NAME:

YOUR BATTLEZONE:

C3-Technique

Call a timeout and resist the tempter/temptation.

Confess the temptation to God in prayer and ask the Holy Spirit to show you the way of escape.

Choose by faithful obedience to consciously yield to the Holy Spirit's Play Call, resulting in perfect execution of God's will.

FORMATION RECOGNITION: Base this on the Scouting Report Form in Week 4.

NUTRITION HISTORY: What have you been "feeding" yourself to entice temptation?

OPPONENT'S STRATEGY: Exactly how does your opponent attack you to create this BattleZONE?

CONSEQUENCES: Visualize and ponder the consequences of your disobedience/sin.

COUNTER-ATTACK/GAME PLAN:

READY LIST: Pre-planned decisions of how you will respond "automatically" to a certain situation

SITUATION	PRE-PLANNED RESPONSE/"AUTOMATIC"	READY LIST
		A list of several plays ready to be used in an upcoming game, tailored to an opposing team's strengths and weaknesses. Also known as an "automatic."

C3-Technique

Call a timeout and resist the tempter/temptation.

Confess the temptation to God in prayer and ask the Holy Spirit to show you the way of escape.

Choose by faithful obedience to consciously yield to the Holy Spirit's Play Call, resulting in perfect execution of God's will.

NAME:

YOUR BATTLEZONE:

FORMATION RECOGNITION: Base this on the Scouting Report Form in Week 4.

NUTRITION HISTORY: What have you been "feeding" yourself to entice temptation?

OPPONENT'S STRATEGY: Exactly how does your opponent attack you to create this BattleZONE?

CONSEQUENCES: Visualize and ponder the consequences of your disobedience/sin.

COUNTER-ATTACK/GAME PLAN:

READY LIST: Pre-planned decisions of how you will respond "automatically" to a certain situation

SITUATION	PRE-PLANNED RESPONSE/"AUTOMATIC"

READY LIST

A list of several plays ready to be used in an upcoming game, tailored to an opposing team's strengths and weaknesses. Also known as an "automatic."

CAPTAIN'S GUIDE

God's "Game Plan"

Faithful Obedience, Love, The Armor of God & Prayer

WARM-UP

BattleZONE Symbol Key

Captain

Rotation Reading

Time

R.I.P.L. Effect

Warm-Up: God's "Game Plan": Faithful Obedience, Love, the Armor of God & Prayer

A. Two-Minute Drill: First thing, have men get together with their TC and go over "counter verses" for 2 minutes total.

B. The Pocket of Protection on this page can be used as another tool to teach God's will. Use at your discretion.

C. After the Pocket Warm-Up, go to the BattleZONE Chalk Talk and proceed to lead your team through Week 7.

Warm-Up Activity — The Pocket Pass Protection

In order for the QB to have a high X% for pass completions he must have great pass protection. Pass protection allows the QB to scan the field for his most advantageous receiver, as well as set his feet and accurately deliver the football. An offensive strategy that helps protect the QB is called a "pocket." A pocket is an area on the offensive side of the ball where the quarterback can safely set up for the pass. The offensive team forms a pocket to protect the QB from the opposition's attacks. When the pocket collapses, the QB is either sacked, forced to throw the football prematurely, or scrambles to avoid a sack. Part of God's "Game Plan" is to create a "pocket" of protection for his Team even during our most intense battles with temptation (I Corinthians 10:13). Our role is to yield to the Holy Spirit's play call and have faith in our loving Father to stand in the pocket and follow through on execution, regardless of the cost. (If you choose, have players do a similar walk-through to demonstrate this blocking philosophy. Everyone blocks to his outside and creates a safe pocket for the QB to throw in.)

- Do you trust God enough to stay in the "pocket" and execute His plays by being obedient, regardless of the hit you'll take?

The Pocket

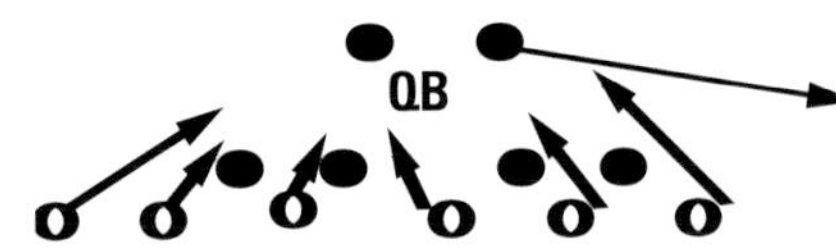

Doubt

The smallest bit of doubt or double-mindedness can cause a QB to perform poorly. Likewise, doubt or distrust in God's loving sovereignty can lead to disobedience during temptation.

- Do you doubt that God will fulfill your desire during your BattleZONE? Explain.
- Do you look for the "pocket" of protection or the way of escape during your BattleZONEs?
- Can the QB execute a pass play as well if he steps out of the "pocket" of protection?
- Can you execute God's will if you step outside of His "pocket" of protection?

CHALK TALK
Faithful Obedience, Love, the Armor of God & Prayer

1. PRAYER

Have one of the men open in prayer and ask the Holy Spirit to guide and direct the session towards God's agenda.

2. GOD'S "GAME PLAN" - FAITHFUL OBEDIENCE, LOVE, THE ARMOR OF GOD & PRAYER

Last week, we studied the third component in God's "Game Plan" for victory/holiness – The "Holy Playbook" (The Bible). God has provided us with His "Playbook" to execute His will in our most challenging BattleZONEs. However, in order to accurately execute His plays, we must know His play calls and apply them to our daily lives.

This week, we will cover the next components in God's "Game Plan" for holiness/victory: Faithful Obedience, Love, the Armor of God and Prayer. Faith is a gift from God and its theme runs deep through all of these components. Faith helps us to be obedient; faith expresses itself in love; faith shields us from Satan's attacks; and faith is demonstrated through prayer.

The Pocket of Faith
God creates a "pocket" of protection around Christians, so when we are tempted, we will not give in to it. We are to stand firm and resist the attacks from our opponent by relying on God's "Game Plan" for victory. God assures Christians that He will give us all we need for victory over any temptation we face. We must use God's "Game Plan", not human plans (2 Corinthians 10:3-5).

3. R.I.P.L. EFFECT

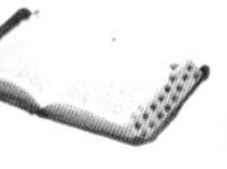

For Week 7 you were assigned to complete one R. I. P. L. Effect on faith.

- First, we will read the R. I. P. L. Effect verse, Hebrews 12:1-2. Who would like to start going through God's meaning in the verse, starting with **R**ead?

Captain, continue to move the group through the rest of the R. I. P. L. Effect.

4. WEEK 7 PLAYS

For Week 7 you were assigned to read and be ready to comment on five Plays. You will have two minutes to present your topic. Comment on two things that hit you in the five Plays. What did God want you to learn and live out? We have shortened the time for this to have more time to cover other material.

CAPTAIN, ASSIGN EACH TEAMMATE A PLAY – THEN LET THEM TAKE THE LEAD.

- **PLAY 1: Faithful Obedience**
- **PLAY 2: Faith Training**
- **PLAY 3: Love**
- **PLAY 4: The Armor of God**
- **PLAY 5: Prayer**

Show Me How To: Pray on the Whole Armor of God
Captain, demonstrate to the men how to pray on the Whole Armor of God. Then have the men get with their teammate/captain and demonstrate how to put on the Whole Armor of God. (Captain, if you have access to the Internet you can show the men the streaming video teaching about putting on the armor at **www.battlezoneministries.org > Training > Show Me How To > Put on the Armor.**

5. Game Plan Execution System

Turn to your BattleZONE Game Plan Execution System on pages 185 & 186. Get with your TC and walk through this system using a temptation situation from the past week. Talk through it first and then each of you should demonstrate to one another using the C3-Technique. This should take 10 minutes total.

6. BattleZONE Draft

Captain: have the men turn to the My First BattleZONE Draft Form on page 199 in Week 8. Then walk the men through the page explaining their first "draft" expectations and the Season Flow Chart on the inside back cover. This will help the men track their generational discipleship.

7. Crunch Time

Have each teammate describe one thing that really "hit" him during this practice session.

8. Independent Practice

1. Continue and refine your new Game Plan Execution System in your BattleZONE and practice the C3-Technique on pages 185 & 186.

2. Read and meditate on the next set of Strength Training Cards for the next week as often as you can.

3. Prayerfully search God's Word for three to four counter verses that you can hide in your heart when you are in your BattleZONEs. You should have two or three memorized by now.

4. Read all five Plays and be prepared to teach the team next week. Share with your teammates how God spoke to your heart. .

5. Read the two "overtime" Plays in Week 8.

6. Complete your study of the scripture passage using the R. I. P. L. Effect and be prepared to discuss it with the team.

7. Call your TC at least once this week and pray for him daily.

8. **Prayerfully fill out the My First BattleZONE Draft Form on page 199 in Week 8.**

9. Iron Sharpens Iron (James 5:16)

Captain: Ask if anyone has done anything that compromised his walk with God this past week. If yes, this week encourage each man to name it specifically and to step out and confess his sins. The men can get with their Teammate/Captain or do as a team. Ask for prayer requests and ask one person to pray for each situation until every request is prayed over and/or write the prayer requests on the next page.

PRAYER REQUESTS AND PRAISES

NAME REQUEST

RESULT

NAME REQUEST

RESULT

NAME REQUEST

RESULT

NAME REQUEST

RESULT

NAME REQUEST

RESULT

NAME REQUEST

RESULT

NAME REQUEST

RESULT

NAME REQUEST

RESULT

BattleZONE Victories

Peter Reta
Las Vegas, NV

I was doing the Christian thing, going to church, weekly men's group and I was involved in teaching summer Sunday school. However, to be honest I was still struggling with the same sin. I desperately needed something more. I needed someone to show me how to stop this habitual sin and start living for Christ. I prayed and asked God to help me.

Then, I got a call from a friend. He told me that he just went through a class called BattleZONE. He thought this class would help me to get to the next level in my Christian walk. To be honest, the first thought that came to my mind was, "I am way to busy." At the same time, pride came to me, why is my friend asking me to take this class? Does he see something in me that tipped him off that I need this class or is he just being a friend? Come to find out, he was just being a friend. So I reluctantly told him that I would try it out.

I remember the first day I went to the class. I told the "captain" that I hoped that I would be focused and committed enough to finish the entire course. BattleZONE Training Course, not only changed my life, it changed my heart and motivated me to pursue God like never before. BattleZONE showed me how to use all kinds of tools based on Biblical principles and certain Scriptures to fight the battle that I was struggling with. It also taught me that I am not alone and that other men are also battling the same wars. I think what every man faces the question of significance, Who am I and do I really matter? Well the answer is ____________________. I will let God tell you in His timing. I encourage you to go through the BattleZONE Training Course and God will show you the answer—like He showed me.

I am now committed to become a Certified BattleZONE Coach and take other men through this Bible-based curriculum. I have found a passion for men's ministry and God is using BattleZONE as a vehicle to disciple men to become more like Jesus. I have found significance to the glory of God.

God's "Game Plan" God's Loving Grace & Mercy

- God's Powerful Grace
- God's Forgiving Mercy
- Confession – God's Adjustment for Sin
- BattleZONE Grace Board
- BattleZONE Seven-Game Season

WEEK 8 OBJECTIVES

Each man will understand:

1. God's loving grace as it relates to salvation, obedience and holiness.
2. The Holy Spirit's role in God's day-to-day grace.
3. God's loving mercy as it relates to confession and holiness.
4. How to verbalize the difference between God's loving grace and mercy.
5. The difference between God's powerful grace and forgiving mercy.
6. That God's loving grace and mercy always out-perform any individual's own performance.
7. How to use the Pocket GRACE Keeper and his BattleZONE Grace Board.

For the grace of God that brings salvation has appeared to all men. It teaches us to say "No" to ungodliness and worldly passions, and to live self-controlled, upright and godly lives in this present age.

Titus 2:11-12 - NIV

But by the grace (the unmerited favor and blessing) of God I am what I am, and His grace toward me was not [found to be] for nothing (fruitless and without effect). In fact, I worked harder than all of them [the apostles], though it was not really I, but the grace (the unmerited favor and blessing) of God which was with me.

1 Corinthians 15:10 - AMP

But if we confess our sins to him, he is faithful and just to forgive us and cleanse us from every wrong.

1 John 1:9 - NLT

Being confident of this very thing, that He who has begun a good work in you will complete it until the day of Jesus Christ.

Philippians 1:6 - NKJV

He who conceals his sins does not prosper, but whoever confesses and renounces them finds mercy.

Proverbs 28:13 - NIV

WEEK 8

STRENGTH TRAINING

For the grace of God that brings salvation has appeared to all men. It teaches us to say "No" to ungodliness and worldly passions, and to live self-controlled, upright and godly lives in this present age.

Titus 2:11-12 - NIV

BATTLE ZONE MINISTRIES, INC. www.battlezoneministries.org

WEEK 8

STRENGTH TRAINING

But by the grace (the unmerited favor and blessing) of God I am what I am, and His grace toward me was not [found to be] for nothing (fruitless and without effect). In fact, I worked harder than all of them [the apostles], though it was not really I, but the grace (the unmerited favor and blessing) of God which was with me.

1 Corinthians 15:10 - AMP

BATTLE ZONE MINISTRIES, INC. www.battlezoneministries.org

WEEK 8

STRENGTH TRAINING

But if we confess our sins to him, he is faithful and just to forgive us and cleanse us from every wrong.

1 John 1:9 - NLT

BATTLE ZONE MINISTRIES, INC. www.battlezoneministries.org

WEEK 8

STRENGTH TRAINING

So let us come boldly to the very throne of God and stay there to receive his mercy and to find grace to help us in our times of need.

Hebrews 4:16 - TLB

BATTLE ZONE MINISTRIES, INC. www.battlezoneministries.org

WEEK 8

STRENGTH TRAINING

Being confident of this very thing, that He who has begun a good work in you will complete it until the day of Jesus Christ.

Philippians 1:6 - NKJV

BATTLE ZONE MINISTRIES, INC. www.battlezoneministries.org

WEEK 8

STRENGTH TRAINING

He who conceals his sins does not prosper, but whoever confesses and renounces them finds mercy.

Proverbs 28:13 - NIV

BATTLE ZONE MINISTRIES, INC. www.battlezoneministries.org

NOTES

STRENGTH TRAINING

BATTLE ZONE MINISTRIES, INC. www.battlezoneministries.org

NOTES

STRENGTH TRAINING

BATTLE ZONE MINISTRIES, INC. www.battlezoneministries.org

NOTES

STRENGTH TRAINING

BATTLE ZONE MINISTRIES, INC. www.battlezoneministries.org

NOTES

STRENGTH TRAINING

BATTLE ZONE MINISTRIES, INC. www.battlezoneministries.org

NOTES

STRENGTH TRAINING

BATTLE ZONE MINISTRIES, INC. www.battlezoneministries.org

NOTES

STRENGTH TRAINING

BATTLE ZONE MINISTRIES, INC. www.battlezoneministries.org

SHOW ME HOW TO PUT ON THE ARMOR OF CHRIST

Go to www.battlezoneministries.org > Training > Show Me How To > Put On The Armor

What does it mean to "put on the armor of Christ"? Surveys show that most men who seek to follow Christ are uncertain what this means or how to do it. BattleZONE Ministries founder, Michael Pouliot, provides foundational teaching and illustrates this important spiritual formation practice. After you watch this video, you will know how to put on the Whole Armor of God, as described in Ephesians 6:10-18.

At BattleZONE Ministries...
We Show You How!

PRACTICE: R.I.P.L. Effect

Practice the R. I. P. L. Effect using Titus 2:11-12 – God's Loving Grace

First, look up Titus 2:11-12 in your Bible. Next, use the R.I.P.L. Effect chart below:

R. I. P. L. Effect
This symbol will prompt you to use the BattleZONE Bible Study Technique in your quest to become a student of the Word. R.I.P.L. stands for:

Read it: Read the passage carefully. What does the passage say literally? List the literal facts in the column on the right. Don't try to put the passage in your own words – don't paraphrase and don't interpret it. Look at it full in the face and see exactly what it says.

Interpret it: Interpret the passage in its context. What does the passage mean? What are the repeating words, phrases or themes? As you read, it's a good idea to highlight or underline repeating phrases, words, ideas or themes.

- Read the Bible like an announcer doing a play-by-play on ESPN – ask who, what, when, where, why and how.
- Cross-reference the passage. Try to determine what God was saying in that moment in time – NOT what He's saying to you right now.

Personalize it: Now is the time to personalize the passage to your current life. How is the Holy Spirit prompting you to respond to the passage? This is when you ask what God is saying to you and what He wants you to get out of the passage.

Live it: Live out the passage obediently. What must you do to live the passage in your daily life? What act of faithful obedience must you do right now to live the passage in your life?

Read it: What does the passage say literally? List the facts in the column on the right.

____

Interpret it: What did God intend the passage to mean for the time and place?

____

- **Who:** Who is talking? To whom is God talking/writing?

____

- **What:** What is the subject matter? What are Paul's main points?

____

- **When:** When did the book take place historically? This information is usually found at the beginning of the book, depending on the type of Bible you're using.

____

- **Where:** Where did this take place? Where specifically is Paul writing to Titus?

____

- **Why:** Why did God say this to Paul and to Titus?

____

- **How:** How were Titus and other readers supposed to accomplish what God wanted?

____

Personalize it: What does this passage say to you personally as if God were talking to you?

____

Live it: What must you do today to live this passage in your life?

____

List the literal facts:

____

____

____

____

____

____

____

____

____

____

____

____

____

References:

____

____

MY FIRST BATTLEZONE DRAFT

CAPTAIN(S)

/

TEAMMATE	TEAMMATE	TEAMMATE	TEAMMATE
TEL:	TEL:	TEL:	TEL:
EMAIL:	EMAIL:	EMAIL:	EMAIL:

DATE: / TIME: / LOCATION:

Jesus came to them and said: "I have been given all authority in heaven and on earth! Go to the people of all nations and make them my disciples. Baptize them in the name of the Father, the Son, and the Holy Spirit, and teach them to do everything I have told you. I will be with you always, even until the end of the world."

Matthew 28:18-20 - CEV

"The job of a football coach is to make men do what they don't want to do in order to achieve what they've always wanted to be."
Tom Landry
Former Coach, Dallas Cowboys

You and many others heard what I taught. Now you must teach these things to men who can be trusted, men who will be able to teach them to other people also.

2 Timothy 2:2 - WE

We proclaim Him, admonishing every man and teaching every man with all wisdom, so that we may present every man complete in Christ. For this purpose also I labor, striving according to His power, which mightily works within me.

Colossians 1:28-29 - NASB

"Christians are called to pursue Spiritual Disciplines... something they would not naturally do... in order to become what they've always wanted to be... like Jesus Christ."
Donald Whitney

You are not done with this course until you have made disciples in post-season play. Jesus' call to His disciples, "Follow me, and I will make you fishers of men", indicates that He was moving them to the next level of spiritual growth – teaching them to be fishers of men and to live holy lives. God's team has a tremendous shortage of men who are committed to live holy lives and willing to pour themselves into other men as mentor/coaches... training them to live by the power of the Holy Spirit moment by moment and ultimately become 3C-Christians.

Use this form to prayerfully draft your first team to take through the BattleZONE Training Course. Ask God who He wants on your team. Then establish your "season opener" or date, "stadium location" or meeting place, your "kick-off time" or when you will meet and your "coaching staff" or TC – if you choose to team teach.

Some men decide to start with a "pre-season game" and take one or two men through the training. Others dive right in and take a full team of four men through. Others do a "scrimmage game", or one-on-one, either in person or over the phone with a trusted friend.

Use the inside and backside cover pages to track your teams and see how you did with your draft. Did you choose men who were committed to make disciples of Jesus who make disciples?

As iron sharpens iron, one man sharpens another.

Proverbs 27:17 - NLT

Plan to Win—Order your BattleZONE Training Course and Pocket GRACE-Keepers online. Go to **www.battlezoneministries.org > Store > BZ Direct Products**. Send the direct URL below to your Drafted Teammates via email so they can order directly.
http://battlezone.echurchnetwork.net/Store/BZDirectProducts/default.aspx

PLAY 1 : God's Powerful Grace

But by the grace (the unmerited favor and blessing) of God I am what I am, and His grace toward me was not [found to be] for nothing (fruitless and without effect). In fact, I worked harder than all of them [the apostles], though it was not really I, but the grace (the unmerited favor and blessing) of God which was with me.

I Corinthians 15:10 - AMP

Transforming Grace

The Apostle Paul's words in the passage above give testimony to God's powerful loving grace that transformed him into a spiritually fit warrior for Christ. The grace that saves (Ephesians 2:8-9) and transforms us into spiritually fit individuals is the same loving grace that changed Saul the sinner into Paul the saint. Paul acknowledges that although he worked hard, it was God's loving grace that gave him the strength and power to change. Paul clearly points out that his transformation into a spiritually fit Christian was the work of God's unmerited favor (or grace) through the power of the Holy Spirit; his job was to follow God's game plan for his life. (See also 2 Timothy 2:1; 2 Corinthians 12:1; Acts 13:43).

The Power of Freedom

For the purposes of BattleZONE, God's powerful grace is manifested when we are "In the Zone" or filled and controlled by the Holy Spirit, who helps us to execute God's will. The same powerful grace that saved us from God's wrath also saves us from our selfish disobedience in our BattleZONEs. God demonstrated the ultimate proof of His loving grace by sending His only Son to the cross to die for our sins. The power of God who raised Christ from the dead allows us to share in His glory and defeat evil. Your attitude and understanding about the doctrine of God's loving grace is paramount to understanding what true victory over your personal BattleZONE means. Christians who fail to understand and embrace this doctrine will grow proud and will fall from grace (not saving grace but powerful grace) because they are trying to obey God in their flesh (Galatians 5:4-5). It is Christ in us manifested by the power of the Holy Spirit who gives us victory over death, temptation and sin. In order for us to train for spiritual fitness without falling into legalism, pride, guilt or performance, we must accept God's powerful grace as the only catalyst for holiness. When we are tempted in our BattleZONEs, God wants us to rely on His power and grace to help us avoid grieving the Holy Spirit.

"You were saved by grace, and you are to live by grace – God's free favor on your behalf. If you try to add works to grace, you destroy grace. Everyone would be required to be a legalist to keep saved."
John MacArthur

God's Grace and Power

For the grace of God that brings salvation has appeared to all men. It teaches us to say "No" to ungodliness and worldly passions, and to live self-controlled, upright and godly lives in this present age.

Titus 2:11-12 - NIV

God's loving grace teaches us to say no to ungodliness; the Holy Spirit empowers us to say yes to God's will. This sanctification process is only accomplished when we join the Holy Spirit in His righteousness. Remember, we are no longer slaves to sin, but to the Spirit of righteousness living inside of us. We no longer must depend on external laws to make us do good, but the internal power of the Spirit of God.

God's loving grace is bigger than our worst performance. God can never be outdone by our best performance. We are to see our relationship with God as perfect through Jesus Christ, never changing and always full of abundant grace. Jerry Bridges says,

"Your worst days are never so bad that you are beyond the reach of God's grace. And your best days are never so good that you are beyond the need of God's grace."
Jerry Bridges
(The Disciplines of Grace, NavPress, 1994, pg. 21)

Bridges also says, "Because we are focusing on our performance, we forget the meaning of grace: God's unmerited favor to those who deserve only His wrath. Pharisee-type believers unconsciously think they have earned God's blessing through their behavior. Guilt-laden believers are quite sure they have forfeited God's blessing through their lack of discipline or their disobedience. Both have forgotten the meaning of grace because they have moved away from the gospel and have slipped into a performance relationship with God" *(Disciplines, ibid.)*.

Because of what Jesus did on the cross, God loves us unconditionally regardless of our performance or what our critics may say.

CAPTAIN'S CORNER
PERSONAL APPLICATION

PLAY 1: God's Powerful Grace HIGHLIGHTS

- There is a perfect tension between relying on God's powerful grace and working hard to serve Christ.
- God's powerful grace is manifested when we are "In the Zone' or filled and controlled by the Holy Spirit.
- It is Christ in us manifested by the power of the Holy Spirit Who gives us victory over death, temptation and sin.
- God's loving grace is bigger than our worst performance.
- God can never be outdone by our best performance.

1. In what area of your Christian walk are you trying to add works to gain God's favor/blessings?

2. How is sailing a ship similar to your reliance on God's powerful grace?

3. Is your tendency to be more legalistic or free-choice in your Christian walk? Do you execute God's will by the power of the Holy Spirit or in your flesh? Do you need to make an adjustment?

CRUNCH TIME:

What did God want you to learn and do from this Play?

PLAY 2 : God's Forgiving Mercy

So let us come boldly to the very throne of God and stay there to receive his mercy and to find grace to help us in our times of need.

Hebrews 4:16 - TLB

Repent!

If we confess our sins, God willingly and even enthusiastically forgives us when we sin against Him. Because of His sovereignty, He can use our unrighteous sins for His glory, despite the grief they caused the Holy Spirit. We must go boldly before His throne in prayer and willingly accept His mercy (withheld punishment) and find His grace (unmerited favor) through our transgressions.

God is never through with our spiritual fitness program:

Being confident of this very thing, that He who has begun a good work in you will complete it until the day of Jesus Christ.

Philippians 1:6 - NKJV

He has begun a good work in you, by His loving grace and mercy. He has been and always will be your spiritual growth coach who picks you back up when you fall into temptation. When we fail to execute God's will in our BattleZONES we can still embrace His forgiving mercy by remembering Christ's blood and by confessing our sins.

Mercy: Withheld Punishment

He saved us, not because of any works of righteousness that we had done, but because of His own pity and mercy, by [the] cleansing [bath] of the new birth (regeneration) and renewing of the Holy Spirit.

Titus 3:5 - AMP

Imagine that if at the end of a long football career, a long-time veteran is standing before the owner of the team awaiting judgment for all of his mistakes and penalties. To his surprise, the owner says that all of his penalties have been wiped clean and there are no statistics for any of his personal fouls, holdings, off-sides, or roughing the quarterback. He has literally forgotten them, just as if they never happened. On the gridiron, penalties are unacceptable but they still happen. Likewise, sin is unacceptable to God, but when we deal with sin as God instructs us, we can still experience holiness. God does not expect us to be perfect, but He does expect us to strive for holiness as we depend on His loving grace through the power of the Holy Spirit.

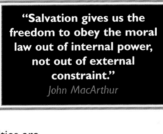

"Salvation gives us the freedom to obey the moral law out of internal power, not out of external constraint."

John MacArthur

God has demonstrated His forgiving mercy through His Son, Jesus. This is the same forgiving mercy that forgave all of our sins when we first believed, and still forgives us from our daily sins if we confess them (1 John 1:9). Each time you are in your BattleZONE and choose to sin against God, if you confess your sin you are viewed by God as forgiven because of Christ's sacrificial blood, and the regeneration or new birth of the Holy Spirit. But, when you sin, you grieve the Holy Spirit, and in order to continue to be "In the ZONE" you must confess your disobedience against God. Upon confession you are restored and able to maintain harmony with God, allowing Christ's blood to continue to cleanse you.

Stop the Momentum

When you fall into sin because you have allowed yourself to be in a certain "formation" or because of poor spiritual execution, you can immediately stop the other team's (sin nature, Satan and/or the World) momentum by immediately confessing your sins to God. If you ignore the transgression and allow the other team to keep their momentum, you will be defeated again and again. The enemy will continue to pound you into the ground because you are allowing yourself to get further away from your source of strength, the Holy Spirit. Unconfessed sin can also dull our spiritual discernment, which can ultimately lead to more sin. God's forgiving mercy renews our spiritual character, bringing us back into fellowship with God.

CAPTAIN'S CORNER
PERSONAL APPLICATION

PLAY 2: God's Forgiving Mercy HIGHLIGHTS

- When you fail to execute God's will in your BattleZONEs you can still embrace His forgiving mercy by remembering Christ's blood and by confessing your sins.
- When you sin, you grieve the Holy Spirit.
- Unconfessed sin can dull your spiritual discernment, which can ultimately lead to more sin.

1. What is your pattern of confession when you sin?

2. Think of a time when someone you loved betrayed you. Did this grieve you? Explain.

3. If repetitive sin is a pattern in your life, what must you do to regain fellowship and harmony with God?

CRUNCH TIME:

What did God want you to learn and do from this Play?

PLAY 3 :
God's Adjustment for Sin – Confession

But if we confess our sins to him, he is faithful and just to forgive us and cleanse us from every wrong.
I John 1:9 - NLT

Search Me, O God
If you quiet your mind and humbly ask God to reveal your sins, the Holy Spirit will show them to you. If the Holy Spirit doesn't bring sins to your remembrance and you are honestly asking for cleansing, then don't obsess. God is faithful; He will tell you when you sin, if you truly are allowing Him to search your heart. Godly guilt is based on the Holy Spirit's conviction. Satan's whispers cause you to constantly repeat a confession because you feel guilty over and over again.

Search me, O God, and know my heart: try me, and know my thoughts: and see if there be any wicked way in me, and lead me in the way everlasting.
Psalms 139:23-24 - KJV

Are you courageous enough to pray this prayer?

True Confessions
God sees sin as an offense against His holy nature; we must view sin through the same lens, not simply as a "mistake". Sin has consequences and disrupts our harmony with God. When we have unconfessed sin, we separate ourselves from the Lord and allow more sin to creep in, like a ball rolling down hill picks up speed and is harder to stop. Unconfessed sin quenches the Holy Spirit and gives Satan a foothold in our lives. So, what is confession and how do we do it? Confession is agreeing with God's Word about your behavior. After confession, we need to repent, or turn away from sin, making an about-face. If you've ever seen a defensive-back intercept the deep ball on the run and then transition his feet so he can turn and head the opposite direction towards his opponent's goal line, you've seen a great model of genuine repentance.

Confess sin specifically. Saying something like "God, please forgive me of all my sins today" doesn't do it. It would be like a coach sending in a player by saying "run a play." In today's NFL, such a general play call wouldn't fly. Would you send your wife to Home Depot with a note that says, "Get me some tools, wood, and fasteners"?

Confession = Ownership
Own your sin by agreeing with God, Confess to Him that you chose your selfish desire over His will – don't try to dance around it. Specific confession is painful and makes the sin less desirable the next time. It might go something like this: "Lord please forgive me for my selfishness to my wife tonight. I felt your Spirit nudging me to get up and help her, but I was only interested in my own selfish needs. I'm sorry for quenching your Holy Spirit. Have mercy on me. Help me yield next time to Your holy prompting." That's a lot different than "Lord, forgive me for all my sins today." Which confession would you accept if a friend stole money from you – "Forgive me dude, I needed money" or "I lied to you and stole from you and I was wrong, selfish and I am sincerely sorry. I broke your trust and I will never do it again"? Confess personally, not generally. "We" and "they" confessions try to spread the pain of sin around like Adam and Eve did in the Garden of Eden, putting on fig leaves to hide the obvious. You alone are responsible for your choices. **Always remember that Jesus' blood cleanses us from sin, not confession itself.** Our relationship is a one-time acceptance of Jesus, but our fellowship is continually renewed as we bring our sins to the foot of the Cross. If we confess, God's loving mercy always shines through.

LEVELS OF CONFESSION

LEVEL 0 — **Denial, Blame-Game or Comparison: It's no big deal. __________ made me do it. Compared to him, I'm doing great.**

LEVEL I — **Mistake: Maybe I made a mistake and did something wrong. I'm sorry for getting caught. Besides, I'm only human. I really don't want to change.**

LEVEL II — **No Risk, Admittance: I sinned today. General catch all – sorry for all my sins.**

LEVEL III — **Low Risk, Simple Confession: I sinned against God by (here you name surface specific sins that may be socially acceptable – lying, anger, lust). You really don't plan on changing. This takes very little courage and trust.**

LEVEL IV — **Medium Risk, Repentance: I sinned against God by (specific details), and am truly sorry for grieving the Holy Spirit. I will not do this again and will do whatever it takes to change my behavior. This takes moderate courage and trust.**

LEVEL V — **High Risk, Repentance: I sinned against God (specific details that incur deep shame and reveal darkness -- deep secret sins like pornography addiction, homosexuality, business fraud, tax evasion, adultery). I will not do this again and will do whatever it takes to change my behavior. This takes tremendous courage and may be inconceivable to tell someone else.**

CAPTAIN'S CORNER
PERSONAL APPLICATION

PLAY 3: Adjustment for Sin — Confession HIGHLIGHTS

- If you quiet your mind and humbly ask God to reveal your sins, the Holy Spirit will show them to you.
- God sees sin as an offense against His holy nature; we must view sin through the same lens, not simply as a "mistake".
- Confession is agreeing with God's Word about your behavior. Repentance is turning away from sin, making an about-face.

1. What is the difference between confession and admission?

2. What keeps you from asking God to search your heart and point out everything that offends Him?

3. Write down an example of how you confess your sins. Analyze your confession.

CRUNCH TIME:

What did God want you to learn and do from this Play?

PLAY 4 :
God's Adjustment for Sin — Punt

But if we judged ourselves, we would not come under judgment.
I Corinthians 11:31 - NIV

A Fresh Start
A punt is a built-in momentary surrender, the proof that your opponent has beaten you for the time being. When a football team's offense executes poorly, a wise team will take advantage of this temporary surrender by punting so they can regroup and get a fresh start. The offensive team has the ability to punt so they don't dig themselves into a hole with poor field position. Punting the ball never means that an offense is totally defeated. It just means that by punting, they acknowledge the other team's successful strategy. When a team is deep in its own territory and decides to "go for it" on fourth down -- but fails to convert the first down -- it gives the opponent the field position advantage. By choosing to punt, the team will be able to gain a renewed spirit by making offensive adjustments and receiving a fresh series of downs. What if Christ-Follower's had a similar built-in way to "punt" without being totally defeated? What if men were able to avoid "poor field position" and regain a fresh series of downs? We do! It's called confession.

Punt — Confession
Confession does the same thing for Christians as punting does in football. In football, a punt is part of the rules and should never be seen as defeat. Every team takes advantage of the rule and leverages punting into their strategy. Likewise, we must never see sin as total defeat because within God's rules, He has designed a way to get out of sin, just like an offense punts to get out of field trouble. God's plan is for us to confess our sins to Him so we will get out of sin trouble. Christian men must avoid "poor sin position" by confessing their sins to God, or "spiritually punting," before they get pinned against their own goal line. The "spiritual punt" is a way for men to regroup and strategize for their next series of downs. Ask questions like: What formation was I in? Where was my formation weakness? What counter play did my opponent run against me?

If a football team has three downs before they punt, does that mean we get three sins before we have to "punt? No! Unlike football, we must "punt" immediately when the Holy Spirit convicts us. One unconfessed sin can pick up momentum, as we saw with King David's sin of adultery, which led to murder and multiple other sins against God. We do not get three sins before we need to "punt" or confess to the Lord.

Remember: "punting" does not mean defeat, but instead signifies that at that time, your opponents executed better than your team did. Even though we have unlimited access to confession, it is not in the best interests of an individual (or a team) to keep putting themselves in a position where they have to punt. In other words, we should not let sin abound, so we can "punt" more. The team who punts most has to work the most on execution.

Confession Increases Time of Possession
If confession does not come out of true repentance, it is just an admission. Henry Blackaby and Claude King say that

> ***"Confession is not a sign of weakness, it is evidence of your refusal to allow sin to remain in your life."***
> *Experiencing God,*
> *(Broadman & Holman, 1998, p. 272)*

Refuse to allow anything to pollute the temple of the Holy Spirit by keeping sin from "renting a room". Frequent confession is proof that you truly understand the true meaning of sin and that sin must be acknowledged seriously. Without the ability to punt, a team would dig itself further into enemy territory. When we refuse to "spiritually punt," we separate ourselves further from the will of God and the Holy Spirit's ability to lead us toward the goal line of experiencing holiness.

Punting is a way to humble ourselves before God and admit that we have fallen into temptation and sin. If a team fails to get a first down, they must punt to have any chance of victory. Christ-Followers must punt because God has made provision for us to regroup and be empowered by the power of the Holy Spirit for the next possession. The only way to avoid punting during a possession is by simply allowing the Holy Spirit to possess all of you. This yields perfect execution (100X%). You must train to allow the Holy Spirit to possess your every thought, desire and action. If you are unwilling to allow the Holy Spirit to possess any part of you, then you will punt every single series. The key for time of possession is confession. The more you submit yourself and confess your sins before God, the more of you He will possess.

CAPTAIN'S CORNER
PERSONAL APPLICATION

PLAY 4: God's Adjustment for Sin —Punt HIGHLIGHTS

- Confession does the same thing for Christians as punting does in football – it allows a time to regroup and be empowered by the power of the Holy Spirit.
- Frequent confession is proof that you truly understand the true meaning of sin and that sin must be acknowledged seriously.
- The only way to avoid punting during a possession is by simply allowing the Holy Spirit to possess all of you, which yields perfect execution (100X%).

1. Do you take sin lightly in your life by admitting your sin to God and then falling back into the same sin over and over again? Why?

2. Think of a time you had unconfessed sin in your life and it picked up momentum. What could you have done differently?

3. Do you secretly believe that confession is a sign of weakness? Why?

CRUNCH TIME:

What did God want you to learn and do from this Play?

PLAY 5 : God's Powerful Grace (Team Grace) & Forgiving Mercy (Team Mercy)

For the grace of God that brings salvation has appeared to all men. It teaches us to say "No" to ungodliness and worldly passions, and to live self-controlled, upright and godly lives in this present age.

Titus 2:11-12 - NIV

So let us come boldly to the very throne of God and stay there to receive his mercy and to find grace to help us in our times of need.

Hebrews 4:16 - TLB

He who conceals his sins does not prosper, but whoever confesses and renounces them finds mercy.

Proverbs 28:13 - NIV

"What's the Score, God?"

It's always amazing: If there's a football game on TV or radio, the first question anybody asks when they come into the room is: "What's the score?" The score is the indicator of who's winning and who's losing. It's a measure of progress, an instant evaluator, and one that provides a snapshot of who is dominating at the time.

If men are so interested in game scores, why aren't we so concerned with our obedience to Christ? Why don't we stop and ask with the same frequency, "What's the score, God? How am I doing on the field today? Am I ahead or behind?" The Apostle Paul encourages us to examine ourselves so God will not have to,

For if we would judge ourselves,
we would not be judged.
I Corinthians 11:31 - NKJV

When you stop and ask God "What's the score?" you allow the Holy Spirit to point out your poor execution so you can confess and make adjustments. No matter how far behind you find yourself, you must examine your eXecution percentage, (X%) and ask, "What's the score, God?"

The BattleZONE Grace Board

On the BattleZONE Grace Board, there are two teams – the Burgundy Team Grace is God's powerful grace and the Gold Team Mercy is God's forgiving mercy. You will be encouraged to keep score of God's loving grace in your life by using the Grace Board. The BattleZONE Grace Board is like a journal, except you don't have to write as much. The Grace Board is a tool that helps to measure what is truly going on in the life of a Christ-Follower, but unlike a scoreboard, which keeps track of who's winning and losing, the Grace Board tracks God's loving grace and mercy in your life. This is simply an awareness tool to help you see clearly.

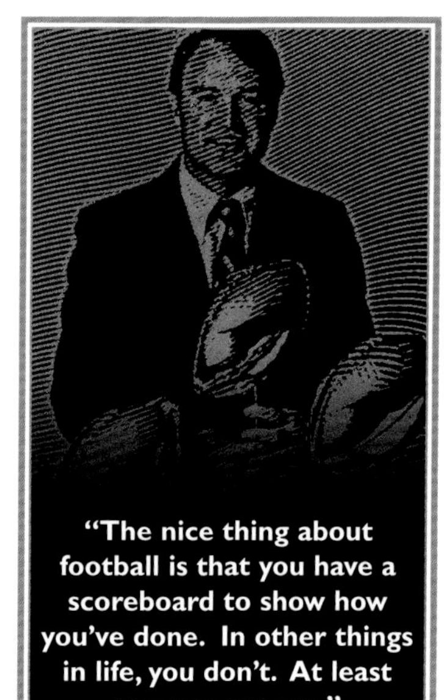

"The nice thing about football is that you have a scoreboard to show how you've done. In other things in life, you don't. At least one you can see."
Chuck Noll

TEAM GRACE	**While in Your BattleZONE / Experience God's Grace / Yield to Spirit by faith / Execute God's will**
TEAM MERCY	**While in Your BattleZONE / Sin by choosing self / Immediate confession / Accept God's Mercy**

The BattleZONE Grace Board will help you see three important principles in your quest for holiness:

- **Powerful grace**, Titus 2:11-12: In the midst of your BattleZONEs, God's powerful grace is demonstrated when you trust the Holy Spirit to show you the way of escape, surrendering your prideful attempts to execute God's will on your own. When this occurs, one point will be rewarded to the Burgundy Team Grace. Keep in mind that if you avoid sin in your own self-efforts you are strengthening your opponent's sin nature, and no point will be awarded to the Team Grace.
- **Forgiving mercy**, Hebrews 4:16; Proverbs 28:13: When you fail to execute God's will in your BattleZONE and sin, you grieve the Holy Spirit. God's forgiving mercy is demonstrated after you confess your transgressions against God. When this occurs, one point will be rewarded to the Gold Team Mercy. Remember, because of Christ's atonement on the cross, God the Father sees you as He sees Jesus, holy and blameless, regardless of your sinful actions. However, in order for you to restore the intimate harmony and fellowship with God, you must confess your sin with truthful sorrow.
- **Accountability**, I Corinthians 11:31: Last, the Grace Board is intended to be a physical tool that holds you accountable in your daily walk with God. It is designed to assist you to mindfully live according to the Holy Spirit's "play calls". Therefore, you must study your "Playbook" to know what God considers sin and regularly allow the Holy Spirit to search you for unconfessed sin. The Grace Board reminds you to live by faith and selflessly yield to the power of the Holy Spirit, trusting God for His provision when you are tempted to provide it yourself.

CAPTAIN'S CORNER
PERSONAL APPLICATION

PLAY 5: God's Powerful Grace (Team Grace) & Forgiving Mercy (Team Mercy) HIGHLIGHTS

- The Apostle Paul encourages us to examine ourselves so God will not have to.
- God's powerful grace is demonstrated when you trust the Holy Spirit to show you the way of escape, surrendering your prideful attempts to execute God's will on your own.
- When you fail to execute God's will in your BattleZONE and sin, you grieve the Holy Spirit.
- God's forgiving mercy is demonstrated after you confess your transgressions against God.

1. How often do you truly examine yourself using God's Word?

2. If you were to give yourself a score today, who would be ahead, Team Grace or Team Mercy?

3. What is your attitude towards being held accountable for your life decisions? Explain.

4. Do you feel that it is wrong to focus on sin or should we focus on Jesus alone? Explain.

CRUNCH TIME:

What did God want you to learn and do from this Play?

OVERTIME 1 :
God's Adjustments for Sin—The Big IF

But if we confess our sins to him, he is faithful and just to forgive us and cleanse us from every wrong.
I John 1:9 - NLT

Remember or Forget
Some of you might be wondering, "So what happens if we don't confess our sins to God? Doesn't He cleanse us and forgive us?"

God is omniscient (I John 3:20), or all knowing. God knows every thought before we have one, including our most sinful thoughts. God knows everything we are going to do in advance, including our sins, yet He still loves us unconditionally. There is some debate among evangelical Christians about this topic and we will try and explain the issue of sin and confession, as we understand it. For instance, there is a passage that says, God remembers our sins no more:

> ***"I, even I, am he who blots out your transgressions, for my own sake, and remembers your sins no more."***
> *Isaiah 43:25 - NIV*

There are similar Scriptures in Hebrews:

> ***"For I will forgive their wickedness and will remember their sins no more."***
> *Hebrews 8:12 - NIV*

> ***"...Their sins and lawless acts I will remember no more."***
> *Hebrews 10:17 - NIV*

The interpretation of these passages hangs on the word "remember." In Isaiah 43:25, the Hebrew word for remember is **zâkar**, which means to make mention (of), be mindful, recount, or record. Merriam-Webster Online Dictionary defines **remember** as: "To bring to mind or think of again <*remembers* the old days>, to keep in mind for attention or consideration <*remembers* friends at Christmas>, to exercise or have the power of memory."

Remembering is not only willful recall, but can be the act of "making mention of" or bringing the past up again. Whether God "remembers" our sins or not is conditionally based on I John's, "if" we confess "then" He will forgive and cleanse us. Most theologians believe this is in reference to fellowship and harmony, rather than salvation. If the Holy Spirit convicts you of sin and you choose not to confess it, then your harmony with God will be disrupted. King David is a perfect example of this disharmony after he refused to confess his sin of adultery with Bathsheba. For nearly a year, David suffered physically, emotionally and spiritually all because his fellowship with God was broken from his willful disobedience and refusal to confess his sins. God demands purity, and when we pollute ourselves with sin, the Spirit of God (who is purely holy), cannot minister and coach us to His full capability until we deal with our sins.

Perhaps the meaning of the word "remember" is being confused with the word "forget". Not remembering something and forgetting something are quite different. You cannot forget something by the act of your will but you can choose not to remember. Merriam-Webster Online Dictionary defines **forget** as: "To lose the remembrance of...be unable to think of, or recall <I forget his name>." Forgetting just happens, but remembering is an act of the will. Remembering is an active, conscious effort to recall something, like a phone number or someone's name. For instance, no matter how hard you try, you might not be able to recall your phone number in college, but you can choose to not remember or recall the score of a bad loss suffered by your high school football team – because you choose not to.

God chooses, by an act of His will, not to remember our sins. This is conditional upon our primary confession of Jesus Christ as our Lord and Savior and a continual confession process as we sin. Yes, Jesus' blood covers all our sins once and for all, but if we sin against God and the Holy Spirit convicts us of that sin, we must confess it to God so He can cleanse us, choose not to remember it again, and we can become in harmony with Him. Christ's blood is continually cleansing us from sin because we are continually sinning against God. No matter if it's a conscious or unconscious sin, Christ's blood is continually cleansing us as we bring our sins to the Cross.

OVERTIME 2 :
God's Game Ball – His Loving Grace

...yet He has now reconciled you in His fleshly body through death, in order to present you before Him holy and blameless and beyond reproach -- if indeed you continue in the faith firmly established and steadfast, and not moved away from the hope of the Gospel that you have heard, which was proclaimed in all creation under heaven, and of which I, Paul, was made a minister.

Colossians 1:22-23 - NASB

The MVP

After every NFL game, it is tradition for the winning head coach to give the game ball to the player he believes performed best on the field. The entire team stands around in the locker room waiting with anticipation to find out whom the head coach will choose as most deserving of the coveted game ball. As the tension builds, the coach says a few inspiring words of praise for the individual he is about to reward. He finally announces the most deserving player, the entire team cheers and the coach hands him the game ball. What a joy, not only for the deserving player, but also for the proud coach. Even though the coach knows the player made some mistakes, he has chosen to overlook them.

God in His loving grace is constantly awarding his "players" the game ball, not because of their performance on the field, but because every player on His team is considered an MVP (most valuable player). We have the privilege of gathering around Him after each "game" in genuine excitement knowing He has already graciously forgiven our sins.

Now imagine if the player said, "Coach, I don't deserve the game ball because I threw an interception, misread the defense twice and caused one delay-of-game penalty. I am a failure. I let you and the team down, never mind that we won and I had over 400 total yards offense. I don't deserve it because I failed to perfectly execute your play calls four times."

Some, if not most, Christians feel this way in their perception of God's loving grace – that receiving His grace is based on our performance. The truth is, we are all undeserving of God's loving grace, but now that we are one with Christ, we must learn to get excited to go before God's throne and confess our sins, not because we committed them, but because He waits anxiously to forgive us and reestablish fellowship. It is crucial to keep in mind that we will be forgiven immediately, and better yet, that we have already been forgiven because of Christ's blood.

We should celebrate our forgiveness and embrace the fact that God's "Game Plan" for poor execution is confession and repentance. How much more willing would you be to confess your sins to God if you knew in advance that He has already decided to give you the game ball after every game? Don't you see that God's loving grace forgives us even when we blow it? God has no favorites on His team. He gives every player the game ball because of His unwavering mercy and grace. This is Who God is. It's His nature. He will always respond consistently with His perfect character. Our reward is our ability to confess and repent of our mistakes and still get the game ball – not because we deserve it, but because we are one with Christ and share in His perfect glory. Sure, we are to be sincerely sorry for sinning against a Holy God and grieving the Holy Spirit, but as we bring it to God in prayer through confession, we should be excited, knowing He has already forgiven us.

Do you have the perspective that God's loving grace is always bigger than all of your sins combined? Those who hesitate to confess their sins to God have a wrong view of His loving mercy. Think about it for a minute: Every time you sin against God, and grieve the Holy Spirit, shouldn't you get excited to accept His forgiveness? This doesn't mean that we should have a cavalier attitude toward sin. We should always respond to sin appropriately when we see both our sin and God's loving grace.

It's as if there should be one word for it, like SINGRACE. This understanding can be hard for some of us because we may feel like it's a cop-out, or that we now have a license to sin. Wrong again. Sin is deadly serious because it disrupts our harmony with the Holy Spirit. The point here is to embrace the freedom to be completely honest with God in confession and not hold back anything, or procrastinate with your confession. You can have the freedom to say, "God, I lied to my wife," instead of, "I stretched the truth," or "I was looking at my co-worker lustfully," instead of saying, "I was admiring her clothes." By embracing God's loving grace, you don't have to sugarcoat your sin – you can say it like it is.

We not only can celebrate in our victories, but because of the Gospel of Jesus Christ, we are able to celebrate even when we give into temptation and sin, because the blood of Jesus allows us to celebrate our confessions to God. "So let us come boldly to the very throne of God and stay there to receive his mercy and to find grace to help us in our times of need" Hebrews 4:16 TLB. This is the Good News of the Gospel.

God sees us as holy and blameless, without a single fault as we stand before Him, because of the blood of Jesus. Like the old hymn says, "What can wash away my sin? Nothing but the blood of Jesus."

Christ's blood constantly cleanses us from our sins before God. God sees us without spot or blemish, as white as the driven snow. Imagine that even in our darkest hour, God's loving grace washes away our sins through the sacrificial blood of His Son. Praise God for His forgiving mercy.

GraceBoard Directions and Examples

Use the Pocket GRACE Keeper (see below) to keep score of God's grace and His mercy in your BattleZONEs by clicking the appropriate button. You click the Team Grace button when you are tempted to sin in your BattleZONE and choose to exercise your faith that God will meet all your needs, giving the Burgundy Team one point. By doing this, you execute God's will in the power of the Holy Spirit by resisting the temptation to sin, experiencing God's grace. Click the Team Mercy button when you are tempted to sin in your BattleZONE and you choose to meet your own needs giving in to temptation by sinning against the Holy Spirit, AND immediately humbly confess your sin to God and receive His Mercy – the Gold Team scores one point. REMEMBER CHRIST'S BLOOD HAS ALREADY COVERED YOU. At the end of your game day, calculate your eXecution percentage (X%) by taking your total TEAM Grace and dividing it by your total Team Grace and Team Mercy score, {TG ÷ (TG + TM) = X%}. Next, at the end of the day, transfer your scores from the Pocket Grace Keeper to the appropriate column on the GRACE Board for 7-14 consecutive days. Make an "x" in the shield when you put on your "equipment" – the Armor of God at the start of each game day. Put an "x" in the shield called "Spiritual Training" to chart your training and preparation efforts for each game. See examples below.

While in Your BattleZONE / Experience God's Grace / Yield to Spirit by faith / Execute God's will

TEAM MERCY While in Your BattleZONE / Sin by choosing self / Immediate confession / Accept God's Mercy

Remember, the key to victory (holiness) is execution (obedience), so record a score only when you are in your BattleZONEs and are tempted to sin. Use the C3-Technique each time you are tempted. When you do sin, be sure to make "adjustments" according to God's Word by immediately confessing your sin to God and asking Him for forgiveness. The longer you leave unconfessed sin in your heart, the greater chance your opponent has to defeat you and you may receive God's chastisement. Be honest: you are always in the game.

08/05	Game 5		05	X%=	38	☒	☒	Extra prayer time
08/06	Game 6		11	X%=	42	☒	☒	Lied at work
08/07	Game 7		03	X%=	8	☐	☐	Told dirty jokes

"It is by our actions that we know that we are living in the truth, so we will be confident when we stand before the Lord" — I John 3:19 - NLT

GraceBoard Directions and Examples

Use the Pocket GRACE Keeper (see below) to keep score of God's grace and His mercy in your BattleZONEs by clicking the appropriate button. You click the Team Grace button when you are tempted to sin in your BattleZONE and choose to exercise your faith that God will meet all your needs, giving the Burgundy Team one point. By doing this, you execute God's will in the power of the Holy Spirit by resisting the temptation to sin, experiencing God's grace. Click the Team Mercy button when you are tempted to sin in your BattleZONE and you choose to meet your own needs giving in to temptation by sinning against the Holy Spirit, **AND** immediately humbly confess your sin to God and receive His Mercy – the Gold Team scores one point. **REMEMBER CHRIST'S BLOOD HAS ALREADY COVERED YOU.** At the end of your game day, calculate your eXecution percentage (X%) by taking your total TEAM Grace and dividing it by your total Team Grace and Team Mercy score, {TG ÷ (TG + TM) = X%}. Next, at the end of the day, transfer your scores from the Pocket Grace Keeper to the appropriate column on the GRACE Board for 7-14 consecutive days. Make an "x" in the shield when you put on your "equipment" – the Armor of God at the start of each game day. Put an "x" in the shield called "Spiritual Training" to chart your training and preparation efforts for each game. See examples below.

TEAM GRACE While in Your BattleZONE / Experience God's Grace / Yield to Spirit by faith / Execute God's will

TEAM MERCY While in Your BattleZONE / Sin by choosing self / Immediate confession / Accept God's Mercy

Remember, the key to victory (holiness) is execution (obedience), so record a score only when you are in your BattleZONEs and are tempted to sin. Use the C3-Technique each time you are tempted. When you do sin, be sure to make "adjustments" according to God's Word by immediately confessing your sin to God and asking Him for forgiveness. The longer you leave unconfessed sin in your heart, the greater chance your opponent has to defeat you and you may receive God's chastisement. Be honest: you are always in the game.

Date	Game	TG	TM	X%=			
08/05	Game 5		05	X%= 38	☒	☒	Extra prayer time
08/06	Game 6		11	X%= 42	☒	☒	Lied at work
08/07	Game 7		03	X%= 8	☐	☐	Told dirty jokes

"It is by our actions that we know that we are living in the truth, so we will be confident when we stand before the Lord" — I John 3:19 - NLT

GraceBoard Directions and Examples

Use the Pocket GRACE Keeper (see below) to keep score of God's grace and His mercy in your BattleZONEs by clicking the appropriate button. You click the Team Grace button when you are tempted to sin in your BattleZONE and choose to exercise your faith that God will meet all your needs, giving the Burgundy Team one point. By doing this, you execute God's will in the power of the Holy Spirit by resisting the temptation to sin, experiencing God's grace. Click the Team Mercy button when you are tempted to sin in your BattleZONE and you choose to meet your own needs giving in to temptation by sinning against the Holy Spirit, **AND** immediately humbly confess your sin to God and receive His Mercy – the Gold Team scores one point. **REMEMBER CHRIST'S BLOOD HAS ALREADY COVERED YOU.** At the end of your game day, calculate your eXecution percentage (X%) by taking your total TEAM Grace and dividing it by your total Team Grace and Team Mercy score, {TG ÷ (TG + TM) = X%}. Next, at the end of the day, transfer your scores from the Pocket Grace Keeper to the appropriate column on the GRACE Board for 7-14 consecutive days. Make an "x" in the shield when you put on your "equipment" – the Armor of God at the start of each game day. Put an "x" in the shield called "Spiritual Training" to chart your training and preparation efforts for each game. See examples below.

TEAM GRACE While in Your BattleZONE / Experience God's Grace / Yield to Spirit by faith / Execute God's will

TEAM MERCY While in Your BattleZONE / Sin by choosing self / Immediate confession / Accept God's Mercy

Remember, the key to victory (holiness) is execution (obedience), so record a score only when you are in your BattleZONEs and are tempted to sin. Use the C3-Technique each time you are tempted. When you do sin, be sure to make "adjustments" according to God's Word by immediately confessing your sin to God and asking Him for forgiveness. The longer you leave unconfessed sin in your heart, the greater chance your opponent has to defeat you and you may receive God's chastisement. Be honest: you are always in the game.

Date	Game	TG	TM	X%=			
08/05	Game 5		05	X%= 38	☒	☒	Extra prayer time
08/06	Game 6		11	X%= 42	☒	☒	Lied at work
08/07	Game 7		03	X%= 8	☐	☐	Told dirty jokes

"It is by our actions that we know that we are living in the truth, so we will be confident when we stand before the Lord" — I John 3:19 - NLT

GraceBoard Directions and Examples

Use the Pocket GRACE Keeper (see below) to keep score of God's grace and His mercy in your BattleZONEs by clicking the appropriate button. You click the Team Grace button when you are tempted to sin in your BattleZONE and choose to exercise your faith that God will meet all your needs, giving the Burgundy Team one point. By doing this, you execute God's will in the power of the Holy Spirit by resisting the temptation to sin, experiencing God's grace. Click the Team Mercy button when you are tempted to sin in your BattleZONE and you choose to meet your own needs giving in to temptation by sinning against the Holy Spirit, **AND** immediately humbly confess your sin to God and receive His Mercy – the Gold Team scores one point. **REMEMBER CHRIST'S BLOOD HAS ALREADY COVERED YOU.** At the end of your game day, calculate your eXecution percentage (X%) by taking your total TEAM Grace and dividing it by your total Team Grace and Team Mercy score, {TG ÷ (TG + TM) = X%}. Next, at the end of the day, transfer your scores from the Pocket Grace Keeper to the appropriate column on the GRACE Board for 7-14 consecutive days. Make an "x" in the shield when you put on your "equipment" – the Armor of God at the start of each game day. Put an "x" in the shield called "Spiritual Training" to chart your training and preparation efforts for each game. See examples below.

TEAM GRACE While in Your BattleZONE / Experience God's Grace / Yield to Spirit by faith / Execute God's will

TEAM MERCY While in Your BattleZONE / Sin by choosing self / Immediate confession / Accept God's Mercy

Remember, the key to victory (holiness) is execution (obedience), so record a score only when you are in your BattleZONEs and are tempted to sin. Use the C3-Technique each time you are tempted. When you do sin, be sure to make "adjustments" according to God's Word by immediately confessing your sin to God and asking Him for forgiveness. The longer you leave unconfessed sin in your heart, the greater chance your opponent has to defeat you and you may receive God's chastisement. Be honest: you are always in the game.

Date	Game	TG	TM	X%=			
08/05	Game 5		05	X%= 38	☒	☒	Extra prayer time
08/06	Game 6		11	X%= 42	☒	☒	Lied at work
08/07	Game 7		03	X%= 8	☐	☐	Told dirty jokes

"It is by our actions that we know that we are living in the truth, so we will be confident when we stand before the Lord" — I John 3:19 - NLT

GraceBoard Directions and Examples

Use the Pocket GRACE Keeper (see below) to keep score of God's grace and His mercy in your BattleZONEs by clicking the appropriate button. You click the Team Grace button when you are tempted to sin in your BattleZONE and choose to exercise your faith that God will meet all your needs, giving the Burgundy Team one point. By doing this, you execute God's will in the power of the Holy Spirit by resisting the temptation to sin, experiencing God's grace. Click the Team Mercy button when you are tempted to sin in your BattleZONE and you choose to meet your own needs giving in to temptation by sinning against the Holy Spirit, **AND** immediately humbly confess your sin to God and receive His Mercy – the Gold Team scores one point. **REMEMBER CHRIST'S BLOOD HAS ALREADY COVERED YOU.** At the end of your game day, calculate your eXecution percentage (X%) by taking your total TEAM Grace and dividing it by your total Team Grace and Team Mercy score, {TG ÷ (TG + TM) = X%}. Next, at the end of the day, transfer your scores from the Pocket Grace Keeper to the appropriate column on the GRACE Board for 7-14 consecutive days. Make an "x" in the shield when you put on your "equipment" – the Armor of God at the start of each game day. Put an "x" in the shield called "Spiritual Training" to chart your training and preparation efforts for each game. See examples below.

TEAM GRACE While in Your BattleZONE / Experience God's Grace / Yield to Spirit by faith / Execute God's will

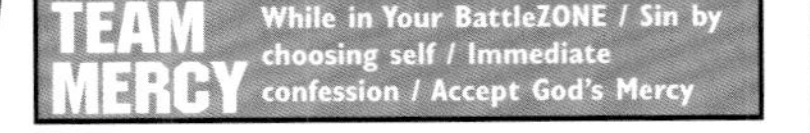

TEAM MERCY While in Your BattleZONE / Sin by choosing self / Immediate confession / Accept God's Mercy

Remember, the key to victory (holiness) is execution (obedience), so record a score only when you are in your BattleZONEs and are tempted to sin. Use the C3-Technique each time you are tempted. When you do sin, be sure to make "adjustments" according to God's Word by immediately confessing your sin to God and asking Him for forgiveness. The longer you leave unconfessed sin in your heart, the greater chance your opponent has to defeat you and you may receive God's chastisement. Be honest: you are always in the game.

Date	Game	TG	TM	X%=			
08/05	Game 5		05	X%= 38	☒	☒	Extra prayer time
08/06	Game 6		11	X%= 42	☒	☒	Lied at work
08/07	Game 7		03	X%= 8	☐	☐	Told dirty jokes

"It is by our actions that we know that we are living in the truth, so we will be confident when we stand before the Lord" — I John 3:19 - NLT

GraceBoard Directions and Examples

Use the Pocket GRACE Keeper (see below) to keep score of God's grace and His mercy in your BattleZONEs by clicking the appropriate button. You click the Team Grace button when you are tempted to sin in your BattleZONE and choose to exercise your faith that God will meet all your needs, giving the Burgundy Team one point. By doing this, you execute God's will in the power of the Holy Spirit by resisting the temptation to sin, experiencing God's grace. Click the Team Mercy button when you are tempted to sin in your BattleZONE and you choose to meet your own needs giving in to temptation by sinning against the Holy Spirit, **AND** immediately humbly confess your sin to God and receive His Mercy – the Gold Team scores one point. **REMEMBER CHRIST'S BLOOD HAS ALREADY COVERED YOU.** At the end of your game day, calculate your eXecution percentage (X%) by taking your total TEAM Grace and dividing it by your total Team Grace and Team Mercy score, {TG ÷ (TG + TM) = X%}. Next, at the end of the day, transfer your scores from the Pocket Grace Keeper to the appropriate column on the GRACE Board for 7-14 consecutive days. Make an "x" in the shield when you put on your "equipment" – the Armor of God at the start of each game day. Put an "x" in the shield called "Spiritual Training" to chart your training and preparation efforts for each game. See examples below.

TEAM GRACE While in Your BattleZONE / Experience God's Grace / Yield to Spirit by faith / Execute God's will

TEAM MERCY While in Your BattleZONE / Sin by choosing self / Immediate confession / Accept God's Mercy

Remember, the key to victory (holiness) is execution (obedience), so record a score only when you are in your BattleZONEs and are tempted to sin. Use the C3-Technique each time you are tempted. When you do sin, be sure to make "adjustments" according to God's Word by immediately confessing your sin to God and asking Him for forgiveness. The longer you leave unconfessed sin in your heart, the greater chance your opponent has to defeat you and you may receive God's chastisement. Be honest: you are always in the game.

Date	Game	TG	TM	X%=			
08/05	Game 5		05	X%= 38	☒	☒	Extra prayer time
08/06	Game 6		11	X%= 42	☒	☒	Lied at work
08/07	Game 7		03	X%= 8	☐	☐	Told dirty jokes

"It is by our actions that we know that we are living in the truth, so we will be confident when we stand before the Lord" — I John 3:19 - NLT

GraceBoard Directions and Examples

Use the Pocket GRACE Keeper (see below) to keep score of God's grace and His mercy in your BattleZONEs by clicking the appropriate button. You click the Team Grace button when you are tempted to sin in your BattleZONE and choose to exercise your faith that God will meet all your needs, giving the Burgundy Team one point. By doing this, you execute God's will in the power of the Holy Spirit by resisting the temptation to sin, experiencing God's grace. Click the Team Mercy button when you are tempted to sin in your BattleZONE and you choose to meet your own needs giving in to temptation by sinning against the Holy Spirit, **AND** immediately humbly confess your sin to God and receive His Mercy – the Gold Team scores one point. **REMEMBER CHRIST'S BLOOD HAS ALREADY COVERED YOU.** At the end of your game day, calculate your eXecution percentage (X%) by taking your total TEAM Grace and dividing it by your total Team Grace and Team Mercy score, {TG ÷ (TG + TM) = X%}. Next, at the end of the day, transfer your scores from the Pocket Grace Keeper to the appropriate column on the GRACE Board for 7-14 consecutive days. Make an "x" in the shield when you put on your "equipment" – the Armor of God at the start of each game day. Put an "x" in the shield called "Spiritual Training" to chart your training and preparation efforts for each game. See examples below.

TEAM GRACE While in Your BattleZONE / Experience God's Grace / Yield to Spirit by faith / Execute God's will

TEAM MERCY While in Your BattleZONE / Sin by choosing self / Immediate confession / Accept God's Mercy

Remember, the key to victory (holiness) is execution (obedience), so record a score only when you are in your BattleZONEs and are tempted to sin. Use the C3-Technique each time you are tempted. When you do sin, be sure to make "adjustments" according to God's Word by immediately confessing your sin to God and asking Him for forgiveness. The longer you leave unconfessed sin in your heart, the greater chance your opponent has to defeat you and you may receive God's chastisement. Be honest: you are always in the game.

Date	Game	TG	TM	X%=			
08/05	Game 5		05	X%= 38	☒	☒	Extra prayer time
08/06	Game 6		11	X%= 42	☒	☒	Lied at work
08/07	Game 7		03	X%= 8	☐	☐	Told dirty jokes

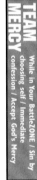

"It is by our actions that we know that we are living in the truth, so we will be confident when we stand before the Lord" — I John 3:19 - NLT

DATE	GAME	TEAM GRACE	TEAM MERCY	TG / TG + TM = X%	Armor Ephesians 6	Spiritual Training	NOTES
	Game 1			X%=	☐	☐	
	Game 2			X%=	☐	☐	
	Game 3			X%=	☐	☐	
	Game 4			X%=	☐	☐	
	Game 5			X%=	☐	☐	
	Game 6			X%=	☐	☐	
	Game 7			X%=	☐	☐	
	Game 8			X%=	☐	☐	
	Game 9			X%=	☐	☐	
	Game 10			X%=	☐	☐	
	Game 11			X%=	☐	☐	
	Game 12			X%=	☐	☐	
	Game 13			X%=	☐	☐	
	Game 14			X%=	☐	☐	
	Game 15			X%=	☐	☐	
	Game 16			X%=	☐	☐	
	Game 17			X%=	☐	☐	
	Game 18			X%=	☐	☐	
	Game 19			X%=	☐	☐	
	Game 20			X%=	☐	☐	
	Game 21			X%=	☐	☐	
	Game 22			X%=	☐	☐	
	Game 23			X%=	☐	☐	
	Game 24			X%=	☐	☐	
	Game 25			X%=	☐	☐	
	Game 26			X%=	☐	☐	
	Game 27			X%=	☐	☐	
	Game 28			X%=	☐	☐	
Season Record		TG	TM	Grand Total X% =			

DATE	GAME	TEAM GRACE	TEAM MERCY	TG / TG + TM = X%	Armor Ephesians 6	Spiritual Training	NOTES
	Game 1			X%=	☐	☐	
	Game 2			X%=	☐	☐	
	Game 3			X%=	☐	☐	
	Game 4			X%=	☐	☐	
	Game 5			X%=	☐	☐	
	Game 6			X%=	☐	☐	
	Game 7			X%=	☐	☐	
	Game 8			X%=	☐	☐	
	Game 9			X%=	☐	☐	
	Game 10			X%=	☐	☐	
	Game 11			X%=	☐	☐	
	Game 12			X%=	☐	☐	
	Game 13			X%=	☐	☐	
	Game 14			X%=	☐	☐	
	Game 15			X%=	☐	☐	
	Game 16			X%=	☐	☐	
	Game 17			X%=	☐	☐	
	Game 18			X%=	☐	☐	
	Game 19			X%=	☐	☐	
	Game 20			X%=	☐	☐	
	Game 21			X%=	☐	☐	
	Game 22			X%=	☐	☐	
	Game 23			X%=	☐	☐	
	Game 24			X%=	☐	☐	
	Game 25			X%=	☐	☐	
	Game 26			X%=	☐	☐	
	Game 27			X%=	☐	☐	
	Game 28			X%=	☐	☐	
Season Record		TG	TM	Grand Total X% =			

DATE	GAME	TEAM GRACE	TEAM MERCY	TG / TG + TM = X%	Armor Ephesians 6	Spiritual Training	NOTES
	Game 1			X%=	☐	☐	
	Game 2			X%=	☐	☐	
	Game 3			X%=	☐	☐	
	Game 4			X%=	☐	☐	
	Game 5			X%=	☐	☐	
	Game 6			X%=	☐	☐	
	Game 7			X%=	☐	☐	
	Game 8			X%=	☐	☐	
	Game 9			X%=	☐	☐	
	Game 10			X%=	☐	☐	
	Game 11			X%=	☐	☐	
	Game 12			X%=	☐	☐	
	Game 13			X%=	☐	☐	
	Game 14			X%=	☐	☐	
	Game 15			X%=	☐	☐	
	Game 16			X%=	☐	☐	
	Game 17			X%=	☐	☐	
	Game 18			X%=	☐	☐	
	Game 19			X%=	☐	☐	
	Game 20			X%=	☐	☐	
	Game 21			X%=	☐	☐	
	Game 22			X%=	☐	☐	
	Game 23			X%=	☐	☐	
	Game 24			X%=	☐	☐	
	Game 25			X%=	☐	☐	
	Game 26			X%=	☐	☐	
	Game 27			X%=	☐	☐	
	Game 28			X%=	☐	☐	
Season Record		TG	TM	Grand Total X% =			

DATE	GAME	TEAM GRACE	TEAM MERCY	TG / TG + TM = X%	Armor Ephesians 6	Spiritual Training	NOTES
	Game 1			X%=	☐	☐	
	Game 2			X%=	☐	☐	
	Game 3			X%=	☐	☐	
	Game 4			X%=	☐	☐	
	Game 5			X%=	☐	☐	
	Game 6			X%=	☐	☐	
	Game 7			X%=	☐	☐	
	Game 8			X%=	☐	☐	
	Game 9			X%=	☐	☐	
	Game 10			X%=	☐	☐	
	Game 11			X%=	☐	☐	
	Game 12			X%=	☐	☐	
	Game 13			X%=	☐	☐	
	Game 14			X%=	☐	☐	
	Game 15			X%=	☐	☐	
	Game 16			X%=	☐	☐	
	Game 17			X%=	☐	☐	
	Game 18			X%=	☐	☐	
	Game 19			X%=	☐	☐	
	Game 20			X%=	☐	☐	
	Game 21			X%=	☐	☐	
	Game 22			X%=	☐	☐	
	Game 23			X%=	☐	☐	
	Game 24			X%=	☐	☐	
	Game 25			X%=	☐	☐	
	Game 26			X%=	☐	☐	
	Game 27			X%=	☐	☐	
	Game 28			X%=	☐	☐	
Season Record		TG	TM	Grand Total X% =			

DATE	GAME	TEAM GRACE	TEAM MERCY	TG / TG + TM = X%	Armor Ephesians 6	Spiritual Training	NOTES
	Game 1			X%=	☐	☐	
	Game 2			X%=	☐	☐	
	Game 3			X%=	☐	☐	
	Game 4			X%=	☐	☐	
	Game 5			X%=	☐	☐	
	Game 6			X%=	☐	☐	
	Game 7			X%=	☐	☐	
	Game 8			X%=	☐	☐	
	Game 9			X%=	☐	☐	
	Game 10			X%=	☐	☐	
	Game 11			X%=	☐	☐	
	Game 12			X%=	☐	☐	
	Game 13			X%=	☐	☐	
	Game 14			X%=	☐	☐	
	Game 15			X%=	☐	☐	
	Game 16			X%=	☐	☐	
	Game 17			X%=	☐	☐	
	Game 18			X%=	☐	☐	
	Game 19			X%=	☐	☐	
	Game 20			X%=	☐	☐	
	Game 21			X%=	☐	☐	
	Game 22			X%=	☐	☐	
	Game 23			X%=	☐	☐	
	Game 24			X%=	☐	☐	
	Game 25			X%=	☐	☐	
	Game 26			X%=	☐	☐	
	Game 27			X%=	☐	☐	
	Game 28			X%=	☐	☐	
Season Record		TG	TM	Grand Total X% =			

DATE	GAME	TEAM GRACE	TEAM MERCY	TG / TG + TM = X%	Armor Ephesians 6	Spiritual Training	NOTES
	Game 1			X%=	☐	☐	
	Game 2			X%=	☐	☐	
	Game 3			X%=	☐	☐	
	Game 4			X%=	☐	☐	
	Game 5			X%=	☐	☐	
	Game 6			X%=	☐	☐	
	Game 7			X%=	☐	☐	
	Game 8			X%=	☐	☐	
	Game 9			X%=	☐	☐	
	Game 10			X%=	☐	☐	
	Game 11			X%=	☐	☐	
	Game 12			X%=	☐	☐	
	Game 13			X%=	☐	☐	
	Game 14			X%=	☐	☐	
	Game 15			X%=	☐	☐	
	Game 16			X%=	☐	☐	
	Game 17			X%=	☐	☐	
	Game 18			X%=	☐	☐	
	Game 19			X%=	☐	☐	
	Game 20			X%=	☐	☐	
	Game 21			X%=	☐	☐	
	Game 22			X%=	☐	☐	
	Game 23			X%=	☐	☐	
	Game 24			X%=	☐	☐	
	Game 25			X%=	☐	☐	
	Game 26			X%=	☐	☐	
	Game 27			X%=	☐	☐	
	Game 28			X%=	☐	☐	
Season Record		TG	TM	Grand Total X% =			

God's "Game Plan"

God's Loving Grace & Mercy

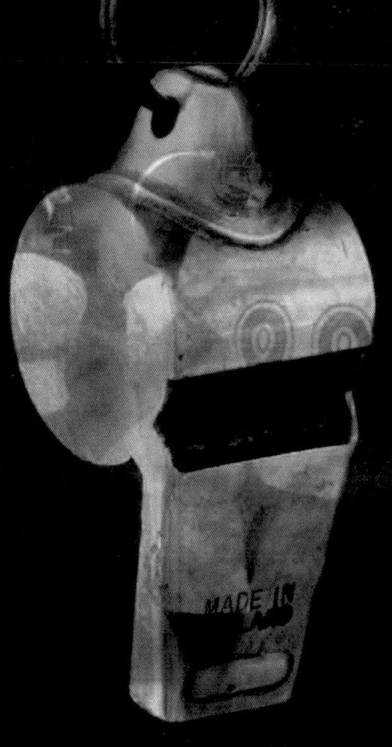

WARM-UP

BattleZONE Symbol Key

Captain	Rotation Reading	Time	R.I.P.L. Effect

Warm-Up: God's "Game Plan": God's Loving Grace & Mercy

A. Two-Minute Drill: First thing, have each man get together with his TC and go over "counter verses" for about 2 minutes total.

B. Go to the BattleZONE Chalk Talk and proceed to lead your team through Week 8.

CHALK TALK

God's "Game Plan": God's Loving Grace & Mercy

1. Prayer

Have one of the men open in prayer and ask the Holy Spirit to guide and direct the session towards God's agenda.

2. God's "Game Plan"

Last week, we studied the fourth through seventh components in God's "Game Plan" for victory/holiness: Faithful Obedience, Love, The Whole Armor of God and Prayer. We need to trust God in our BattleZONEs, be compelled by our love for Jesus, arm ourselves for spiritual battle and pray without stopping.

This week we will cover the next component in God's "Game Plan" for holiness/victory: God's loving grace and mercy.

3. R.I.P.L. Effect

For Week 8, you were assigned to complete one R. I. P. L. Effect on how God's loving grace teaches us to say no to ungodliness and yes to Godly living faith.

First, we will go over your R. I. P. L. Effect verse Titus 2:11-12. Who would like to start going through God's meaning in the verse, starting with Read? Captain, continue to move the group through the rest of the R. I. P. L. Effect.

4. Week 8 Plays

For Week 8 you were assigned to read and be ready to comment on five Plays. You will have two minutes to present your topic; then discuss each as a group. Please try to stay focused on what God taught you through this Play. What did God want you to learn and do?

CAPTAIN, ASSIGN EACH TEAMMATE A PLAY – THEN LET THEM TAKE THE LEAD.

- **PLAY 1: God's Powerful Grace**
- **PLAY 2: God's Forgiving Mercy**
- **PLAY 3: God's Adjustment for Sin**
- **PLAY 4: God's Adjustment for Sin – Punt**
- **PLAY 5: God's Powerful Grace (Team Grace) & Forgiving Mercy (Team Mercy)**

5. BattleZONE Grace Board

The BattleZONE Grace Board

The Grace Board helps you track God's loving grace and mercy in your BattleZONEs while simultaneously holding you accountable for disobedience. God's loving grace and mercy always prevail and always win. We are to trust Him daily by our faithful obedience in all of our BattleZONEs so we can continue to experience and enjoy His fellowship and blessings. (*Since he did not spare even his own Son for us but gave him up for us all, won't he also surely give us everything else? Romans 8:32 - TLB*).

Over the next seven days, you will "play" seven "games". Each day is a "game" and you will record your scores accordingly. Remember that God's grace and mercy covers us because of what Jesus did on the cross.

This is not a legalistic instrument, but rather a tool to help us better grasp God's loving grace and mercy in our everyday temptations. Some of you may have had a skewed view of sin. This tool is to be seen as a positive way to watch God work in your life, even after you sin and ask for forgiveness.

TG
03
BATTLE ZONE
MINISTRIES, INC.
05
TM

Captain, have the men look at the BattleZONE Grace Board on pages 212 – 214. Review the directions located on page 212 along with the 3 example "games." Explain the importance of the Grace Board and how to keep score using the Pocket GRACE Keeper. They can tear out, photocopy or download more Grace Boards and also order additional Pocket GRACE Keepers at **www.battlezoneministries.org > Store > BZ Products Direct**

Have the men get out their Pocket GRACE Keepers at this time. Demonstrate how to keep score and walk through some specific examples using their personal BattleZONEs. Encourage the men to go beyond their selected BattleZONE and use the Grace Board for all their areas of temptation. This will help the men grasp the depth of God's loving grace and mercy.

As a Christian, you are constantly scoring "points" because God's loving grace and mercy give you the power to obey and cover all of your sins. The truth is that because you are in Christ, God's loving grace and mercy always wins. No matter if the Burgundy Team scores or the Gold Team scores, God's loving grace and mercy prevail.

When you execute God's will in your BattleZONE, God's grace scores. When you sin and confess it, God's mercy scores, because of what Jesus did on the cross at Calvary. In Christ, grace and mercy always prevail.

Top 10 Reasons Why You Should Keep a Grace Board

1. God commands you to confess your sins to Him.
2. It forces you to face the truth daily and not slip into denial.
3. You can make adjustments when you know the score.
4. Competition creates focus and increased effort.
5. Satan does not want you to keep score.
6. You begin to depend on your teammates more, recognizing you can't do it alone.
7. You maximize your walk with God because of your desire to obey His commands.
8. It increases your understanding of God's "Playbook" and desire to read it obediently.
9. You begin to see your incredible need for Christ and His atonement for your many sins.
10. You begin to love God more because you see the abundance of His grace and mercy for your multitude of sins.

6. BattleZONE Draft

If the men have not started their First Team Draft on page 199 in Week 8, spend some time now helping with their draft pick(s). Remember, a great BattleZONE captain, soon to be a coach, is someone who will coach men do what they don't want to do so he can be all that God has made him for – to be a disciple maker.

Plan to Win—Order your BattleZONE Training Course and Pocket GRACE-Keepers online.

Go to **www.battlezoneministries.org > Store > BZ Direct Products**. Send the direct URL below to your Drafted Teammates via email so they can order directly.

http://battlezone.echurchnetwork.net/Store/BZDirectProducts/default.aspx

7. Crunch Time

Have each teammate describe one thing that really "hit" him during this practice session.

8. Independent Practice

1. Continue to practice the C3-Technique in your BattleZONEs and use the Grace Board and Pocket GRACE Keeper to track God's loving grace and mercy for seven full days.

2. Read and meditate on the next set of Strength Training Cards for Week 9 as often as you can.

3. Prayerfully search God's Word for three to four "counter verses" you can memorize when you are in your BattleZONEs. You should have three to four hidden in your heart by now.

4. Read all five Plays and be prepared to teach them to the team next week. Share with the men how God spoke to your heart.

5. Complete your study of the scripture passage using the R. I. P. L. Effect and be prepared to discuss it with the team.

6. Call your TC at least once this week and pray for him daily.

9. Iron Sharpens Iron (James 5:16)

Captain: Ask if anyone has done anything that compromised his walk with God this past week. If yes, this week encourage each man to name it specifically and to step out and confess his sins. The men can get with their Teammate/Captains or do as a team. Ask for prayer requests and ask one person to pray for each situation until every request is prayed over and/or write the prayer requests on the next page.

PRAYER REQUESTS AND PRAISES

AME REQUEST

RESULT

AME REQUEST

RESULT

NAME REQUEST

RESULT

NAME REQUEST

RESULT

NAME REQUEST

RESULT

NAME REQUEST

RESULT

NAME REQUEST

RESULT

NAME REQUEST

RESULT

BATTLEZONE VICTORIES

Rod Handley
Founder and President
of Character That Counts
Lee's Summit, MO

The Need for Teamwork
(excerpt from Character Counts: Who's Counting Yours?)
www.characterthatcounts.org

As a former athlete, I participated on a number of both excellent and terrible teams. It was very easy to distinguish the difference. The poor teams were filled with individuals seeking personal gain, a lack of concern for others on the team, virtually no discipline, rampant hypocrisy and lots of backbiting and unrest. On the other hand, the good teams exhibited humility, confidence in the other members, an attitude of togetherness, a commitment to a greater cause and a belief in one another.

Teamwork is a concept which God has stressed since the beginning of time. In the Garden of Eden God saw that man needed a "suitable helper." Moses had his brother Aaron help him lead people out of Egypt toward the Promised Land. David and Jonathan had a special friendship which encouraged and challenged one another; later Nathan played an important part in David's life, as he was willing to confront him openly regarding David's sin with Bathsheba. Daniel had three close friends, Shadrach, Meschach and Abednego, to stand beside him. Paul had his special missionary companions of Barnabus, Silas and Timothy. Jesus not only had His 12 disciples but an even closer intimate friendship with Peter, James and John. In fact, examine the Bible, and look for people who lived out their faith in God alone. You will not find anyone who successfully navigated their life without a support system.

Sometimes the "supporting" person was visible and at other times they were out of the limelight. Being sent out "two by two" has always been a Biblical pattern. No person can, or is meant to, live the Christian life alone. Eventually, our heart will turn towards evil. Jeremiah 17:9 says, "The heart is deceitful above all things and beyond cure. Who can understand it?"

A Biblical view of teamwork is best understood through the word "interdependence." The Body of Christ is not characterized by dependence. Dependence keeps people from wholeness. Dependence means you are unable to function as an autonomous free agent. Dependence is crippling, not freeing. In contract, independence is not characteristic of a believer either. We are not loners living out a private, eccentric, aloof Christian life. It is not just "God and me." Rather it is meant to be a life of interrelatedness and affirmation. We are neither dependent or independent but interdependent. Dependence produces weak, incomplete people. Independence produces proud, pretentious people. Interdependence produces whole, loving, serving people. Interdependence is the Body using the individual's gifts for the sake of the whole. It is the Body cooperating together in love, to see people coming to Christian maturity in accountable, interdependent relationships.

God never intended for us to live our Christianity out as a Lone Ranger. Even the modern day Lone Ranger had his sidekick Tonto and his beloved horse Silver. "A cord of three strands is not quickly broken," says the author of Ecclesiastes. In other words, we can't walk through life solo. Today, God intends for us to not live an independent lifestyle but one of complete dependence upon Him and interdependence on others around us.

God's "Game Plan" Godly Teammates

- Drafting Godly Teammates
- Cutting Ungodly Teammates
- Renewing Your Mind
- Thought Replacement
- Grace Board Review/TST
- Next Season's Draft Picks

WEEK 9 OBJECTIVES

Each man will understand:

1. The importance of Godly teammates in his journey towards Christ-likeness.
2. The importance of his role to his teammates.
3. How God says to handle ungodly teammates, which include certain people, some types of media and thoughts.
4. God's command to confess sins to a Godly teammate.
5. How a man's thought life relates to holiness.
6. The skill of thought replacement.
7. The Holy Spirit's role in his thought life.
8. How to cut and draft teammates in pursuing holiness.
9. Who his teammates will be so he can lead them through the BZ Training Course.

Under His direction, the whole body is fitted together perfectly. As each part does its own special work, it helps the other parts grow, so that the whole body is healthy and growing and full of love.
Ephesians 4:16 - NLT

Friends love through all kinds of weather, and families stick together in all kinds of trouble.
Proverbs 17:17 - MSG

Become wise by walking with the wise; hang out with fools and watch your life fall to pieces.
Proverbs 13:20 - MSG

My child, if sinners entice you,turn your back on them.
Proverbs 1:10 - NLT

For the weapons of our warfare are not merely human, but they have divine power to destroy strongholds. We destroy arguments and every proud obstacle raised up against the knowledge of God, and we take every thought captive to obey Christ.
2 Corinthians 10:4-5 - NRSV

Here, my brothers, are some things I want you to think about. Think about things that are true, honest, right, clean and pure, things that are lovely, and things that are good to talk about. If they are good, and if they bring praise to God, think about these things.
Philippians 4:8 - WE

As iron sharpens iron, one man sharpens another.
Proverbs 27:17 - NLT

A person standing alone can be attacked and defeated, but two can stand back-to-back and conquer. Three are even better, for a triple-braided cord is not easily broken.
Ecclesiastes 4:12 - NLT

Do not be conformed to this world, but be transformed by the renewing of your minds, so that you may discern what is the will of God -- what is good and acceptable and perfect.
Romans 12:2 - NRSV

WEEK 9

STRENGTH TRAINING

Under His direction, the whole body is fitted together perfectly. As each part does its own special work, it helps the other parts grow, so that the whole body is healthy and growing and full of love.

Ephesians 4:16 - NLT

www.battlezoneministries.org

WEEK 9

STRENGTH TRAINING

Friends love through all kinds of weather, and families stick together in all kinds of trouble.
Proverbs 17:17 - MSG

Become wise by walking with the wise; hang out with fools and watch your life fall to pieces.
Proverbs 13:20 - MSG

My child, if sinners entice you, turn your back on them.
Proverbs 1:10 - NLT

www.battlezoneministries.org

WEEK 9

STRENGTH TRAINING

For the weapons of our warfare are not merely human, but they have divine power to destroy strongholds. We destroy arguments and every proud obstacle raised up against the knowledge of God, and we take every thought captive to obey Christ.

2 Corinthians 10:4-5 - NRSV

www.battlezoneministries.org

WEEK 9

STRENGTH TRAINING

Here, my brothers, are some things I want you to think about. Think about things that are true, honest, right, clean and pure, things that are lovely, and things that are good to talk about. If they are good, and if they bring praise to God, think about these things.

Philippians 4:8 - WE

www.battlezoneministries.org

WEEK 9

STRENGTH TRAINING

As iron sharpens iron,
one man sharpens another.
Proverbs 27:17 - NLT

A person standing alone can be attacked and defeated, but two can stand back-to-back and conquer. Three are even better, for a triple-braided cord is not easily broken.
Ecclesiastes 4:12 - NLT

www.battlezoneministries.org

WEEK 9

STRENGTH TRAINING

Do not be conformed to this world, but be transformed by the renewing of your minds, so that you may discern what is the will of God – what is good and acceptable and perfect.

Romans 12:2 - NRSV

www.battlezoneministries.org

NOTES
STRENGTH TRAINING
BATTLE ZONE MINISTRIES, INC.
www.battlezoneministries.org
NOTES
STRENGTH TRAINING
BATTLE ZONE MINISTRIES, INC.
www.battlezoneministries.org
NOTES
STRENGTH TRAINING
BATTLE ZONE MINISTRIES, INC.
www.battlezoneministries.org
NOTES
STRENGTH TRAINING
BATTLE ZONE MINISTRIES, INC.
www.battlezoneministries.org
NOTES
STRENGTH TRAINING
BATTLE ZONE MINISTRIES, INC.
www.battlezoneministries.org
NOTES
STRENGTH TRAINING
BATTLE ZONE MINISTRIES, INC.
www.battlezoneministries.org

PRACTICE: R.I.P.L. Effect

Practice the R. I. P. L. Effect using Galatians 6:1-2 – Godly Teammates

First, look up Galatians 6:1-2 in your Bible. Next, use the R. I. P. L. Effect chart below:

R. I. P. L. Effect
This symbol will prompt you to use the BattleZONE Bible Study Technique in your quest to become a student of the Word. R.I.P.L. stands for:

Read it: Read the passage carefully. What does the passage say literally? List the literal facts in the column on the right. Don't try to put the passage in your own words – don't paraphrase and don't interpret it. Look at it full in the face and see exactly what it says.

Interpret it: Interpret the passage in its context. What does the passage mean? What are the repeating words, phrases or themes? As you read, it's a good idea to highlight or underline repeating phrases, words, ideas or themes.

- Read the Bible like an announcer doing a play-by-play on ESPN – ask who, what, when, where, why and how.
- Cross-reference the passage. Try to determine what God was saying in that moment in time – NOT what He's saying to you right now.

Personalize it: Now is the time to personalize the passage to your current life. How is the Holy Spirit prompting you to respond to the passage? This is when you ask what God is saying to you and what He wants you to get out of the passage.

Live it: Live out the passage obediently. What must you do to live the passage in your daily life? What act of faithful obedience must you do right now to live the passage in your life?

Read it: What does the passage say literally? List the facts in the column on the right.

____

Interpret it: What did God intend the passage to mean for the time and place?

____

- **Who:** Who is talking? To whom is God/the author talking/writing?

____

- **What:** What is the subject matter? What are Paul's main points?

____

- **When:** When did the book take place historically? This information is usually found at the beginning of the book, depending on the type of Bible you're using.

____

- **Where:** Where did this take place? What's the location?

____

- **Why:** Why did God say this to Paul? Why did Paul write this to the Galatians?

____

- **How:** How were the readers supposed to accomplish what God wanted?

____

Personalize it: What does this passage say to you personally as if God were talking to you?

____

Live it: What must you do today to live this passage in your life?

____

List the literal facts:

____

References:

____

PLAY 1 : Practice Becoming a Sacrificial Teammate

Don't think only of your own good. Think of other Christians and what is best for them.

I Corinthians 10:24 - NLT

True Teammates

A true teammate is one who is more concerned for the welfare and success of the guy next to him than he is for himself. Perhaps the most unselfish position in football is the offensive lineman. You can probably count the number of offensive linemen who have held out for more money on one hand. They are the epitome of selflessness in the NFL. They hardly ever score a touchdown, get picked for MVP or complain that they are not "getting the play call to their side" like most of the ball-handlers. How often does the press interview an offensive lineman after a 500-yard total offensive performance? When is the last time you saw an offensive lineman with a lucrative product endorsement contract? Rarely, if ever, do they get the recognition they deserve. They simply do their best to make others successful. If God were to select a position He would most like us to emulate with our attitude, it would probably be the offensive lineman.

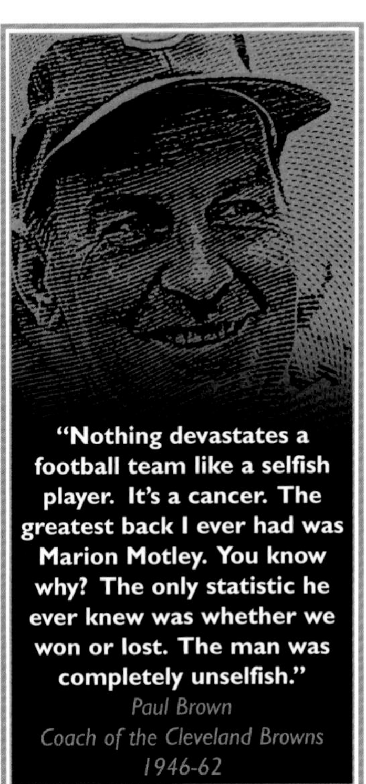

"Nothing devastates a football team like a selfish player. It's a cancer. The greatest back I ever had was Marion Motley. You know why? The only statistic he ever knew was whether we won or lost. The man was completely unselfish."
Paul Brown
Coach of the Cleveland Browns
1946-62

Iron Sharpens Iron

As iron sharpens iron,
one man sharpens another.

Proverbs 27:17 - NLT

For iron to sharpen iron, there must be friction. Unfortunately, too many men are looking for teammates who will tell them what they want to hear and end up avoiding the needed friction to sharpen them. True teammates provide accountability. In order to be held accountable, you must be willing to ask someone who loves and cares for you to help you in your personal BattleZONEs.

Brothers, if someone is caught in a sin, you who are spiritual should restore him gently. But watch yourself, or you also may be tempted. Carry each other's burdens, and in this way you will fulfill the law of Christ.

Galatians 6:1-2 - NIV

A true teammate will "call you" on your excuses and make you stronger.

"My best friend is the one who will bring out the best in me."
Henry Ford

Instead, we will speak the truth in love, becoming more and more in every way like Christ, who is the head of his body the church. Under His directions the whole body is fitted together perfectly. As each part does its own special work, it helps the other parts grow, so that the whole body is healthy and growing and full of love.

Ephesians 4:15-16 - NLT

They will stand with you as you allow the Holy Spirit to deliver you from your BattleZONEs and hold you up when you are defeated.

A person standing alone can be attacked and defeated, but two can stand back-to-back and conquer. Three are even better, for a triple-braided cord is not easily broken.

Ecclesiastes 4:12 - NLT

Sacrificial Teammates

We see in Romans the incredible attitude of the Apostle Paul towards weaker Christians. In Romans 15:2-3 he says, "We should please others. If we do what helps them, we will build them up in the Lord." For even Christ didn't please himself. As the Scriptures say, "Those who insult you are also insulting me." By following Jesus' example, you, too, are called to serve others and to spend your life and energy bringing them closer to the Lord. If a teammate struggles with alcohol and you don't, you shouldn't drink or even mention that you drink alcohol around him. If a brother struggles with gluttony and you don't, don't take him to an all-you-can-eat buffet. Do these things out of love, not pity:

Perhaps you feel it is all right for you to do it. But be careful! It might make the weak Christian do wrong.

I Corinthians 8:9 - WE

Opportunity for Sacrificial Love

True Christian love is sacrificial, and if there is no sacrifice on your part, you cannot say you love as the Bible defines it. Your actions, not words, demonstrate love. Your level of love can be measured by your level of self-sacrifice. Even when it makes your skin crawl and everything in you is fighting to do your own thing, you must break your "me" nature and start building your "them" nature. It is a sacrifice to help your neighbor move furniture when you could be golfing. But, by helping your neighbor and sacrificing your own agenda, you have an opportunity to die to yourself and demonstrate sacrificial love. This is a process. Start practicing overriding your selfish desires by helping someone else, looking at it as an opportunity to demonstrate Christlike, selfless love.

CAPTAIN'S CORNER
PERSONAL APPLICATION

PLAY 1: Practice Becoming a Sacrificial Teammate HIGHLIGHTS

- True teammates provide accountability.
- A true teammate will "call you" on your excuses and make you stronger.
- By following Jesus' example, you are called to serve others and to spend your life and energy bringing them closer to the Lord.
- Your actions, not words, demonstrate love.

1. Is it easy or difficult for you to think of others before yourself? Explain.

2. What would prevent you from allowing another Christ-Follower to "sharpen" you?

CRUNCH TIME:

What did God want you to learn and do from this Play?

PLAY 2 : Drafting the Right Teammates

In these days he went out to the mountain to pray, and all night he continued in prayer to God. And when day came, he called his disciples and chose from them twelve, whom he named apostles.

Luke 6:12-13 - ESV

Your Teammates Influence You

You become like the five people you hang around most. Stop and think about this – these "people" can be actual persons (friends and/or co-workers) or radio personalities, writers, television characters/personalities and/or sports figures – even a "voice in your head." Whomever you spend your time with will determine who you become, and whomever you have spent your time with in the past is a part of who you are today.

> **"The only difference between who you are today and who you'll become in five years will come from the books you read and the people you spend your time with."**
>
> *Charles "Tremendous" Jones*

This is also true with an 11-man football team. A true football saying is "you are only as strong as your weakest position." A free safety that gets beat all the time will bring the whole team down. This is also true in real life. When you choose to live a life dominated by sin, the consequences impact more than just yourself. They affect your family, your friendships, and the other people with whom you spend time. Just ask the 2005-06 Philadelphia Eagles what T.O. (Terrell Owens - one of their teammates) did to their team.

Jesus knew the importance of having the right people on His team (Luke 6:12-13). The importance of surrounding yourself with teammates who help you reach the goal line is crucial, so you must be very selective. One bad teammate can bring the entire team down. Remember a teammate can be a friend, a co-worker, and certain family members. Teammates can also be television programs, radio talk shows, magazines, music, the Internet, cultural image of success, and your thought-life. Who or what in your life is holding you back from becoming a 3C-Christian? Who or what is hindering you from moving forward in your spiritual training program towards holiness? What must you do to free yourself from this negative influence? If you are serious about personal holiness, then you will recognize that some of these influences will have to be cut from your team. However, regarding personal relationships, be sure to seek wise council before making a rash decision – don't take this lesson as license to file for divorce or do anything contradictory to God's Word.

Confessing Sin to Your Teammates

Confess to one another therefore your faults (your slips, your false steps, your offenses, your sins) and pray [also] for one another, that you may be healed and restored [to a spiritual tone of mind and heart]. The earnest (heartfelt, continued) prayer of a righteous man makes tremendous power available [dynamic in its working].

James 5:16 - AMP

How can you tell if you are creating a strong Christian team around you? By making sure that you are confessing your sins to at least one of your teammates. The Bible says we are to confess our sins to one another and pray for each other. The more you practice being vulnerable with other men, the easier it gets to confess your sins to them, as well. This is a vital part of BattleZONE – recruiting teammates to whom you can confess your sins honestly and allow them to hold you accountable. Do you have a relationship like that? If you don't, begin praying for God to bring him into your life.

David's Warriors – 1 Chronicles 12

King David surrounded himself with great warriors who ultimately made up his team. He drafted these men based on the following qualities:

- They were fearless veterans, "brave and experienced warriors" (12:8).
- They were the best at what they did because they spent years perfecting their fighting skills, "expert with both shield and spear" (12:8).
- They were tough competitors, "fierce as lions" (12:8).
- They were well conditioned, "as swift as a deer" (12:8).
- They were such great leaders that even "the weakest among them could take on a hundred, and the strongest could take on a thousand" (12:14).
- They had undivided loyalty to David (12:33). 

CAPTAIN'S CORNER
PERSONAL APPLICATION

PLAY 2: Drafting the Right Teammates HIGHLIGHTS

- One bad teammate can bring an entire team down.
- You must cut certain bad influences from your team in order to have any chance of personal holiness.
- The Bible says you are to confess your sins to one another and to pray for each other.
- The more you practice being vulnerable with other men, the easier it gets to confess your sins.
- Surround yourself with men who are committed to holiness.

1. What or who has influenced your life? Has this been a positive or negative influence? How?

2. Is it difficult for you to confess your sins to another man? Why?

CRUNCH TIME:

What did God want you to learn and do from this Play?

PLAY 3 : Choosing the Right Mental Teammates

Do not be conformed to this world, but be transformed by the renewing of your minds, so that you may discern what is the will of God what is good and acceptable and perfect.
Romans 12:2 - NSRV.

Stinkin' Thinkin'
Your most important teammate could be your own thoughts. The mind is the breeding ground for all human action. Before you can take action, an idea must first enter your mind. The eye is one "spoon" that feeds the mind. Every image that your eye sees is stored in your super-computer-like brain and can be recalled under the right conditions. Jesus knew the power of the mind and warned that if left unchecked, it will lead to full-fledged sin. For instance, if you look at a woman (including pictures or movies) in an unholy way, it feeds your mind lustful trash, enticing your sin nature to desire more lustful images. This may then lead to more disobedience as you fulfill those lusts.

Controlling the Line of Scrimmage (Renewing Your Mind)
We are commanded to be transformed (reshaped) into our new nature in Christ by renewing our minds. A football team can score a touchdown only by crossing the goal line. Likewise, Christians can only be transformed by renewing their minds with the truth. So how do you renew your mind? Follow God's "Game Plan" for spiritual fitness outlined in the Holy "Playbook" and prayerfully draft new teammates while cutting those persons/things that infect you. You cannot renew your mind with Godly wisdom by listening to worldly music, watching secular TV, reading secular magazines and/or hanging around "cultural-Christians". ***Jesus hung out with sinners because He was spiritually mature enough to do so. Some Christians are not able to be around the ungodly because they are not spiritually mature and may easily fall under the influences of the World (for example, rationalizing their behavior by saying they are witnessing while getting drunk).***

Each year, sports psychologists make millions of dollars helping athletes train their minds to improve performance. This type of "mind training" isn't new:

For as he thinketh in his heart, so [is] he.
Proverbs 23:7a - KJV

We become what we focus on.
The line of scrimmage in a football game is where the battle is won or lost. A team that controls the line of scrimmage controls the game. This also holds true in our BattleZONEs. The one who has control over your thoughts will win. Your line of scrimmage is your mind. The best performing receivers in the NFL are constantly thinking about catching a pass, running a rout, blocking techniques and scoring. The battle for our mind must be dominated by actively, not passively, checking every thought and comparing it with the Word of God.

For the weapons of our warfare are not merely human, but they have divine power to destroy strongholds. We destroy arguments and every proud obstacle raised up against the knowledge of God, and we take every thought captive to obey Christ.
2 Corinthians 10:4-5 - NRSV

For example, you are to take every argument for why you might think it's OK to watch television shows that stimulate your lustful sin nature and sift those arguments through the "sieve" of God's Word.

The battle for your thoughts is the main game plan Satan has for destroying our Christian witness. Satan cannot control us physically, but he does influence our minds which influences our actions. If our minds want to lie because Satan has inserted a corrupt thought, we must surrender to the Holy Spirit at that moment, or we will lose control of our mental "line-of-scrimmage." The Devil wants us to have teammates who sabotage our ability to execute the Holy Spirit's play calls. **Satan knows that if he can get into your mind for a minute, he can infect your heart for days.** Think of it like a tiny virus that enters your body and destroys your heart with the deadly wages of sin. Jesus knew that in order to protect your heart, you must first protect your mind:

"It is the thought-life that defiles you."
Mark 7:20 - NLT

Don't take this half-heartedly. Your mind is the first line in spiritual warfare. This is why we must put on the whole armor of God each day when we wake, to protect us from the enemy's attacks.

For more on starting an accountability group, visit **www.battlezoneministries.org** and click on **"Release Me"** or **"Life Teams"**. There you'll find an array of downloadable resources to help you begin.

CAPTAIN'S CORNER
PERSONAL APPLICATION

PLAY 3: Drafting the Right Mental Teammates HIGHLIGHTS

- Jesus knew the power of the mind and warned that if left unchecked, it will lead to full-fledged sin.
- You are commanded to be transformed into your new nature in Christ by the renewing of your mind.
- The battle for your mind must be actively dominated by Godly thoughts, checking every thought and comparing it with the Word of God.
- Satan cannot control us physically, but he influences our mind, which influences our actions.

1. Do you find yourself entertaining evil or ungodly thoughts that contradict God's Word? Explain.

2. Is your thinking more like the World or the Word? Please ask someone who knows you to answer this question, as well.

3. When an ungodly thought pops into your head, where do you think it comes from?

CRUNCH TIME:

What did God want you to learn and do from this Play?

PLAY 4 : Thought Replacement Skill

Here, my brothers, are some things I want you to think about. Think about things that are true, honest, right, clean and pure, things that are lovely, and things that are good to talk about. If they are good, and if they bring praise to God, think about these things.

Philippians 4:8 - WE

Use this simple tool to help you "be transformed by the renewing of your mind." Each time you have a thought that the Holy Spirit prompts you to understand is ungodly, replace it with a Godly thought. Take a blank sheet of paper and make a "T" using the entire page, labeling the left hand side "Unholy Thought of Lie" and the right hand side "Godly Thought or Truths". See examples below:

UNHOLY THOUGHT OR LIE	GODLY THOUGHT OR TRUTHS
It's OK to get drunk...no one would know.	*The Bible says not to get drunk... but instead to be filled with the Holy Spirit.* Ephesians 5:18
It's no big deal that I am late again to my meeting; they are late a lot too."	*God wants me to be godly and honest in all of my actions. I am to honor Him in everything I do.* I Samuel 2:30
We're going to get married in a few months anyway; it doesn't matter if we wait to have sex or not.	*God says that sex outside of marriage is wrong. He commands me to stay pure.* I Corinthians 6:18
The government has enough tax money – it doesn't matter if I cut corners on my tax return this year.	*Cheating is really stealing. God says stealing is wrong.* Romans 2:21
I'm not lusting – I'm just looking. After all, I'm not blind.	*Jesus said that looking at a woman lustfully is the same as having sex with her – just in my heart.* Matthew 5:28
It's not a lie – I'm just leaving out the details so they don't get upset.	*The Bible says I should speak clearly and truthfully.* James 5:12
I'm not being proud – I'm just good at what I do and I have good self-esteem.	*God wants me to be humble.* Philippians 2:3
I have every right to be angry.	*God says I shouldn't sin when I'm angry and that I shouldn't let the sun go down on my anger.* Ephesians 4:26
It's just another piece of cake – so what?	*God has created my body to be the temple of the Holy Spirit. I should take care of it and submit myself to Him.* I Corinthians 6:19
It's not gossip – I'm just sharing a prayer request.	*If the person wants prayer from the Body, they'll ask themselves. Meanwhile, I can keep their confidence and pray for them myself.* Proverbs 11:13

CAPTAIN'S CORNER
PERSONAL APPLICATION

PLAY 4: Thought Replacement Skill HIGHLIGHTS

- Every time an ungodly thought enters your mind, process it through the filter of God's Word.
- If you are willing, the Holy Spirit will prompt you about when a thought is ungodly.
- By comparing your ungodly thoughts to God's Word, your thinking will be reshaped and your mind renewed.

1. Why is it important for your mind to be renewed if you are to experience holiness?

2. What is the one lie in your thought life that you struggle with most? Why?

CRUNCH TIME:

What did God want you to learn and do from this Play?

PLAY 5 : BattleZONE Life Team's Prevent Isolation

Two are better than one, Because they have a good reward for their labor. For if they fall, one will lift up his companion. But woe to him who is alone when he falls, For he has no one to help him up. Though one may be overpowered by another, two can withstand him. And a threefold cord is not quickly broken.
Ecclesiastes 4:9-10,12 - NKJV

Teamwork
A quarterback can never win a game on his own. It takes the entire team working together as one unit using one playbook. The quarterback is also accountable to the coach, teammates and the owner for his performance. Popular media has emphasized that real men need no one and that "need" is a four-letter word. This *Lone Ranger lie* is causing men to stumble into sin and despair.

Brotherhood = Life Team's
Men view distance as safe. Men feel safe in isolation because their natural tendency is to deal with their problems alone. However, God designed men to do life together, and since all men stumble, we need another brother there to pick us back up. This kind of brotherhood takes time and commitment. Wise men have recognized the importance of getting together with other men in a safe environment, where they can encourage and challenge each other (Hebrews 10:23-25). We need a place where we can be ourselves and sharpen each other in the process. The truth is, we need accountability to pursue holiness. Most men can encourage and challenge one another to joyfully obey God's Word, not just stop their outward acts of sin. All counsel given in your team must be filtered through Scripture. Another truth about being in real brotherhood is spiritual growth. Men who isolate experience spiritual constipation and they don't grow into full Christ-likeness—because they get "stuck." We are told to walk in the light, and the only way to walk in the light is to come out from isolation by getting into a life team with other men who desire holiness as much as you.

T.E.A.M.

Together
Everyone
Accomplishes
More

What is Masculine Accountability?
The perception of the word "accountability" has turned many men away from experiencing true Christian brotherhood and spiritual maturity. Jim Clayton, in an article entitled: Accountability: *Pursuing Vital Relationships* said; "**Accountability is not:** Guys getting together and talking about how often they have sex with their wives. It is not guys getting in touch with their 'inner child.' It is not simply another support group or Bible study. It is not wimps getting together and whining about how unfair life is. It is not men sitting around bashing women. **Accountability is:** A few men getting together to share their lives. Guys getting to know each other beyond the casual and superficial; beyond 'sports and the weather.' Brothers allowing themselves to be challenged, and held to a higher standard than the world would dictate. Men being honest with each other about their struggles and shortfalls. Guys praying together, and for each other. Brothers growing together toward Christ-likeness, reaching their full potential as men of God. And all of this takes place in an atmosphere of love and acceptance, without judgment."

The Importance of a BattleZONE LifeTeam
The best time for accountability is when we least need it. The BattleZONE Life Team strategy is designed to get men connected in groups of three to four (one Team Captain and two to three other men). Christian accountability involves processing God's Word and Biblical principles in community through real-life ups-and-downs. This process tackles a variety of life events like a new job promotion or a family crisis, to dealing with sin habits like drunkenness, pornography and lying. The benefit is not only the change in behavior, but also the deep root-work of changing a man's soul, a spiritual transformation that desires God's will over his own.

BattleZONE Life Teams are created to help men avoid isolation and develop their character in community. There is no other way to fight the good fight and remain standing. Be strong and courageous! Take the steps necessary to select, establish, sustain and grow your BattleZONE Life Team.

If you are not on a team, please get on one. To learn more about starting a BZ Life Team go to **www.battlezoneministries.org > Life Teams.** There you will find useful tools to help men start, maintain and grow their own accountability group. There are downloads and other tools, like the BZ Accountability Calculator to help you and your Life Team win the battle faced by every man.

Also, go to **www.battlezoneministries.org > Training > Show Me How To > Accountability Group** to view Rod Handley of Character that Counts demonstration on how to ask to join your accountability group.

And let us consider how we may spur one another on toward love and good deeds. Let us not give up meeting together, as some are in the habit of doing, but let us encourage one another...
Hebrews 10:24-25a - NIV

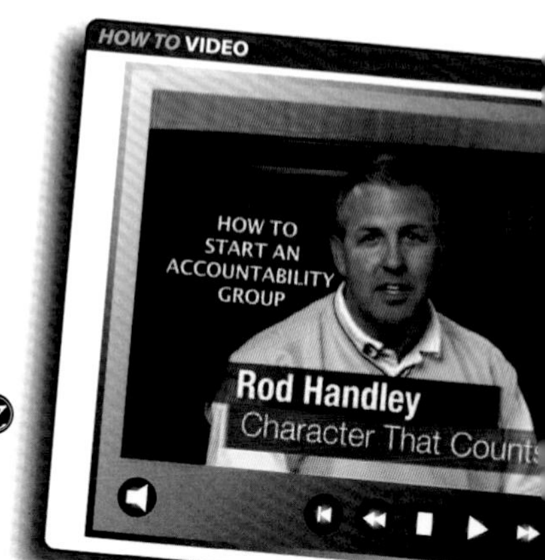

CAPTAIN'S CORNER
PERSONAL APPLICATION

PLAY 5: BattleZONE Life Teams Prevent Isolation HIGHLIGHTS

- God created men to be on a team to sharpen each other and lend a hand when a brother falls.
- Accountability is a good thing – not a sissy thing.
- Life Teams should consist of three to four men. Two is not enough and five is too many.
- The best time to form a BZ Life Team is when life is going well vs. when you are in a crisis.

1. What good is isolation?

2. How does isolation harm men?

3. What is your experience of desire for masculine accountability?

WHAT'S THE BIG DEAL WITH ISOLATION?

Isolation **leads to the wrong desires**
Wrong desires **lead to deception.**
Satan pounces on you when you're deceived.
Deception **leads to sin.**
Sin **leads to departure from God's ways (disobedience).**
Departure from God's ways **leads to temporary disobedient delight (false joy).**
Disobedient delight **leads to depression.**
Depression **leads to despair and disappointment**
Despair and disappointment **lead to disaster and death.**

(adopted from Charles Stanley message entitled, The Pathway to Spiritual Independence)

CRUNCH TIME:

What did God want you to learn and do from this Play?

TEAMMATE DRAFT
CUT FORM

It is said that you become like the five people you hang around most. Use this form to expand your list beyond personal relationships to include television, books, magazines, movies, music, radio programs and/or mental goals/fantasies you spend the most time with throughout the day. As Captain, the goal for the player(s) who cannot be "cut" from your team is to help them to reach their goals by encouraging them and sacrificially serving them in love. In other words, you can develop them into godly teammates.

T.E.A.M.M.A.T.E.S.

T	rustworthy:	Confidential in all discussions
E	ncouraging:	Lifts you up and believes in you
A	ccountable:	Holds you to God's ways lovingly
M	otivating:	Their words make you want to be holy
M	ale:	Must be male; exclude your wife/girlfriend
A	dvice giver:	Not afraid to tell you what they think
T	ruthful:	Speak the truth in love
E	xcuse blocker:	Won't tolerate rationalizations or excuses
S	pirit-filled:	Must be a Christian walking with Jesus

HOLDING Keeping another player from advancing by literally holding him back with one's hand(s).

Fill in your new recruits using the huddle below. Be sure to use T.E.A.M.M.A.T.E.S. as a guide for the draft.

FRIENDS

TV & MOVIES

AUTHORS / BOOKS

FAMILY

RADIO

CAPTAIN YOU

MENTAL THOUGHTS

CO-WORKERS

MENTOR / COACH

HOBBIES

OTHER

WHO OR WHAT SHOULD GET CUT FROM YOUR TEAM?

1. __________
2. __________
3. __________
4. __________
5. __________
6. __________
7. __________
8. __________
9. __________
10. __________

CAPTAIN'S GUIDE

God's "Game Plan"
Godly Teammates

WARM-UP

BattleZONE Symbol Key

Captain	Rotation Reading	Time	R.I.P.L. Effect

Warm-Up: God's "Game Plan": Godly Teammates

A. **Two-minute Drill: First thing, have each man get together with his TC and review this week's counter verses for two minutes.**

B. **Go to the BattleZONE Chalk Talk and proceed to lead your team through Week 9.**

CHALK TALK

God's "Game Plan": Godly Teammates

1. Prayer

Have one of the men open in prayer and ask the Holy Spirit to guide and direct the session towards God's agenda.

2. God's "Game Plan": Godly Teammates

Last week, we studied the eighth component in God's "Game Plan" for victory/holiness; **God's loving grace and mercy**. We must understand the power of God's loving grace in our BattleZONEs and His loving mercy when we fail to execute His will.

This week we will cover the next component in God's "Game Plan" for holiness/victory, **Godly teammates.**

Part of God's "Game Plan" is for his "players" to work together as a team, united with one mind and one purpose…to glorify His Son, Jesus. The Bible refers to God's team as the Body of Christ, each with a special purpose.

Just like each player on the football field has a purpose in the overall game plan, God's "Game Plan" gives each of us our "positions" to carry out His plan on earth. God also commands us to work together in love, peace and unity. As the Body of Christ, we are interdependent and must not act alone. A player on the field must not act alone by doing his own thing; a team is only effective when it works together. Likewise, we must rely on other Christian teammates in our quest for holiness, or we will be crushed! Not only does God want us to work together as a team, but He also wants us to build each other up, hold one another accountable, pray for one another and live at peace with each other.

T.E.A.M.M.A.T.E.S.

T rustworthy
E ncouraging
A ccountable
M otivating
M ale
A dvice giver
T ruthful
E xcuse-blocker
S pirit-filled

Teammates

Under his direction, the whole body is fitted together perfectly. As each part does its own special work, it helps the other parts grow, so that the whole body is healthy and growing and full of love. — Ephesians 4:16 - NLT

This week, we will study the importance of who and what you surround yourself, and who/what you allow to influence your thinking and daily decisions. Selecting the right players can make all the difference in a football team's overall success, and likewise, your success as a Christian. Make no mistake: the right teammates will help you succeed with God's "Game Plan".

Here are five verses that give clear insight into what God thinks about selecting Godly teammates:

- *Blessed (happy fortunate, prosperous, and enviable) is the man who walks and lives not in the counsel of the ungodly [following their advice, their plans and purposes], nor stands [submissive and inactive] in the path where sinners walk, nor sits down [to relax and rest] where the scornful [and the mockers] gather.* — Psalms 1:1 - AMP
- *Become wise by walking with the wise; hang out with fools and watch your life fall to pieces.* — Proverbs 13:20 - MSG
- *My child, if sinners entice you, turn your back on them.* — Proverbs 1:10 - NLT
- *They will act as if they are religious, but they will reject the power that could make them godly. You must stay away from people like that.* — 2 Timothy 3:5 - NLT
- *Do not let anyone fool you. Bad people can make those who want to live good become bad.* — 1 Corinthians 15:33 - NLV

3. R.I.P.L. Effect

This week, we will skip discussing the R. I. P. L. Effect on Galatians 6:1-2 because of limited time.

4. Week 9 Plays

For Week 9 you were assigned to read and be ready to comment on five Plays. You will have two minutes to present your topic; then discuss each as a group. Please try to stay focused on what God taught you through this Play. **What did God want you to learn and do?**

CAPTAIN, ASSIGN EACH TEAMMATE A PLAY – THEN LET THEM TAKE THE LEAD.

- **Play 1: Practice Becoming a Sacrificial Teammate**
- **Play 2: Drafting the Right Teammates**
- **Play 3: Choosing the Right Mental Teammates**
- **Play 4: Thought Replacement Skill**
- **Play 5: BattleZONE Life Team's Prevent Isolation**

5. Team Draft / Cut

To determine your eleven-person team, fill out the "Teammate Assessment Form" on page 236 (see example on the next page). This will allow you to examine who and what is affecting your quest for holiness in positive and negative ways and is a crucial step in the process of victory over temptation. You may find that some of the people, TV shows, music and media with which you spend your time are keeping you from being successful in your daily battles with temptation. In this case, it is imperative to do the following:

1. DRAFT new players onto your team who are committed to helping you be holy. To get you started, consider having lunch with another wise Christian man every week; start listening to Christian radio; listen to Christian music that glorifies God and edifies your spirit; read Christian personal growth books; join a men's Bible study; start a BZ Life Team.

2. CUT the teammates from your life who you know are hindering your ability to avoid temptation – or at least limit your time around them. This is not advice to get a divorce or cut off relationships with family, friends and co-workers. The "cutting" process should be done only after prayerful consideration and seeking wise counsel from other Christians. Your goal is to assemble a team that makes you a better "player" and in turn contributes to your holiness.

TEAMMATE DRAFT

CUT FORM

It is said that you become like the five people you hang around most. Use this form to expand your list beyond personal relationships to include television, books, magazines, movies, music, radio programs and/or mental goals/fantasies you spend the most time with throughout the day. As Captain, the goal for the player(s) who cannot be "cut" from your team is to help them to reach their goals by encouraging them and sacrificially serving them in love. In other words, you can develop them into godly teammates.

T.E.A.M.M.A.T.E.S.

T rustworthy:	Confidential in all discussions
E ncouraging:	Lifts you up and believes in you
A ccountable:	Holds you to God's ways lovingly
M otivating:	Their words make you want to be holy
M ale:	Must be male; exclude your wife/girlfriend
A dvice giver:	Not afraid to tell you what they think
T ruthful:	Speak the truth in love
E xcuse blocker:	Won't tolerate rationalizations or excuses
S pirit-filled:	Must be a Christian walking with Jesus

HOLDING Keeping another player from advancing by literally holding him back with one's hand(s).

Fill in your new recruits using the huddle below. Be sure to use T.E.A.M.M.A.T.E.S. as a guide for the draft.

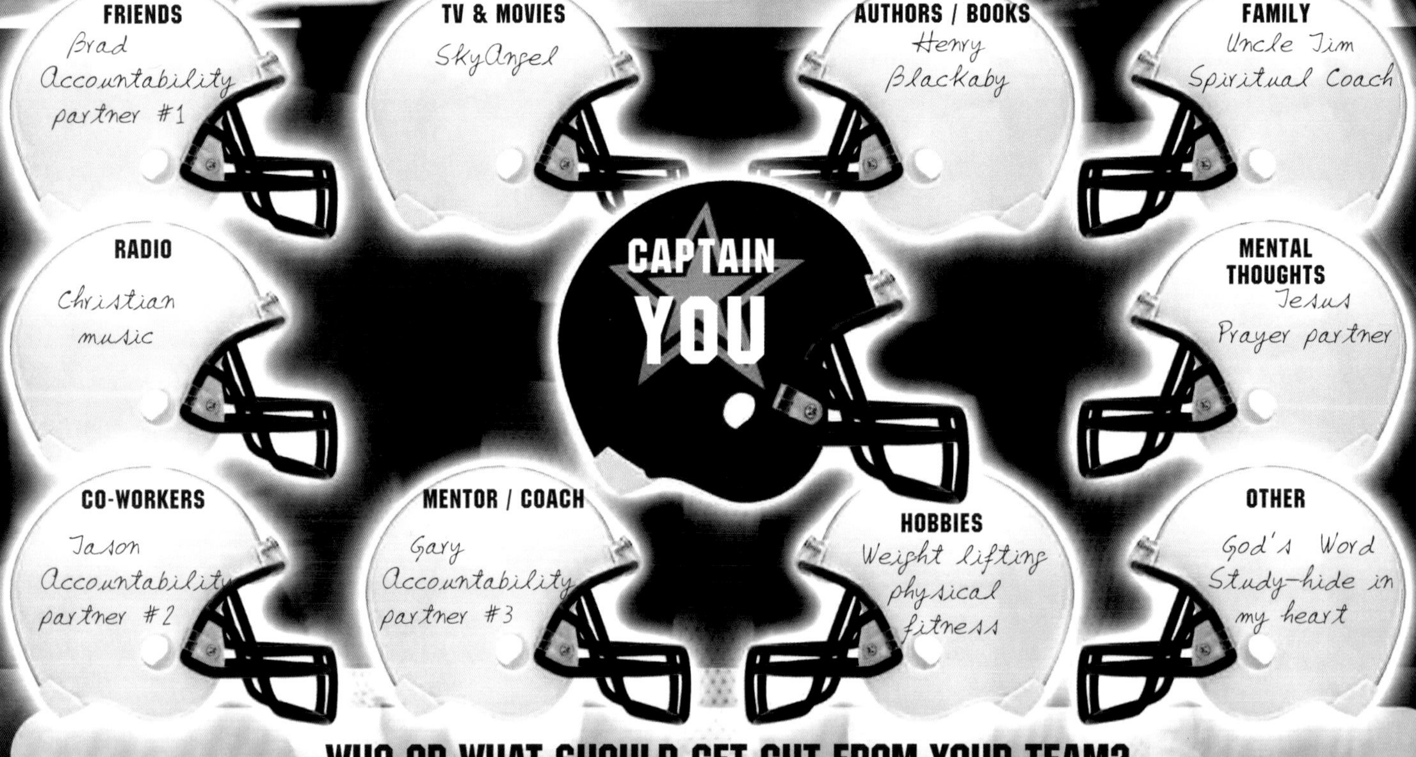

WHO OR WHAT SHOULD GET CUT FROM YOUR TEAM?

1. SmutTV
2. Magazines
3. Porn
4. Chat Rooms
5. Worry
6. Anger
7. Kyle J.
8. Hangouts A & B
9. www.???
10. Books with sex scenes

6. BattleZONE Grace Board

Grace Board 7 Game Discussion

Now it's time to recap your last seven "Games." Take out your Grace Board and Pocket GRACE Keeper.

Captain, proceed to have an open discussion about experiences the men had using the Grace-Board, including challenges and victories.

One at a time, tell us about your "games" this past week. Share one temptation situation when you were in your BattleZONE and Team Grace scored... then give one example when Team Mercy scored. Be sure to verbally demonstrate how you used the C3-Technique when Team—Grace Scored.

7. Crunch Time

Have each teammate describe one thing that really "hit" him during this practice session.

8. Independent Practice

1. Continue to practice the C3-Technique in your BattleZONEs and use the Grace Board and Pocket GRACE Keeper to track God's loving grace and mercy for the remaining seven days if your choose.
2. Read and internalize the objectives on next week's cover page.
3. Read and meditate on next week's set of Strength Training Cards as often as you can.
4. You should have three to four "counter verses" hidden in your heart by now. If not, continue to read and think about them at least 5 times each, everyday this next week.
5. Read all four Plays and be prepared to teach them to the team next week. Share with the men how God spoke to you.
6. Write down the pros and cons of the BattleZONE Training Course and complete the evaluation form found on page 257 and tear out or make a photo copy to hand in next week.
7. Go to **www.battlezoneministries.org** and take the electronic post-test – it will take five minutes.
8. Write down the final names of the team you've drafted to lead through BattleZONE Training Course on page 199 in Week 8. Include the start date and location. Have the Captain/Coach sign his name in your book, your commitment to follow through. Remember you can team-teach, take someone through over the phone or start a team of four. Prayerfully ask God what you should do.
9. Call your TC at least once this week and pray for him daily.

MY FIRST BATTLEZONE DRAFT

TEAMMATE
TEL.
EMAIL.
DATE. / TIME.

CAPTAIN(S)

TEAMMATE
TEL.
EMAIL.
/ LOCATION.

TEAMMATE
TEL.
EMAIL.

TEAMMATE
TEL.
EMAIL.

Jesus came to them and said: "I have been given all authority in heaven and on earth! Go to the people of all nations and make them my disciples. Baptize them in the name of the Father, the Son, and the Holy Spirit, and teach them to do everything I have told you. I will be with you always, even until the end of the world."
Matthew 28:18-20 - CEV

You and many others heard what I taught. Now you must teach these things to men who can be trusted, men who will be able to teach them to other people also.
2 Timothy 2:2 - WE

We proclaim Him, admonishing every man and teaching every man with all wisdom, so that we may present every man complete in Christ. For this purpose also I labor, striving according to His power, which mightily works within me.
Colossians 1:28-29 - NASB

"The job of a football coach is to make men do what they don't want to do in order to achieve what they've always wanted to be."
Tom Landry
Former Coach, Dallas Cowboys

"Christians are called to pursue Spiritual Disciplines... something they would not naturally do... in order to become what they've always wanted to be... like Jesus Christ."
Donald Whitney

You are not done with this course until you have made disciples in post-season play. Jesus' call to His disciples, "Follow me, and I will make you fishers of men", indicates that He was moving them to the next level of spiritual growth – teaching them to be fishers of men and to live holy lives. God's team has a tremendous shortage of men who are committed to live holy lives and willing to pour themselves into other men as mentor/coaches... training them to live by the power of the Holy Spirit moment by moment and ultimately become 3C-Christians.

Use this form to prayerfully draft your first team to take through the BattleZONE Training Course. Ask God who He wants on your team. Then establish your "season opener" or date, "stadium location" or meeting place, your "kick-off time" or when you will meet and your "coaching staff" or TC – if you choose to team teach.

Some men decide to start with a "pre-season game" and take one or two men through the training. Others dive right in and take a full team of four men through. Others do a "scrimmage game", or one-on-one, either in person or over the phone with a trusted friend.

Use the inside and backside cover pages to track your teams and see how you did with your draft. Did you choose men who were committed to make disciples of Jesus who make disciples?

As iron sharpens iron, one man sharpens another.
Proverbs 27:17 - NLT

Plan to Win—Order your BattleZONE Training Course and Pocket GRACE-Keepers online. Go to **www.battlezoneministries.org > Store > BZ Direct Products**. Send the direct URL below to your Drafted Teammates via email so they can order directly.
http://battlezone.echurchnetwork.net/Store/BZDirectProducts/default.aspx

BATTLE ZONE MINISTRIES, INC.

9. Iron Sharpens Iron (James 5:16)

Captain: Ask if anyone has done anything that compromised his walk with God this past week. If yes, this week encourage each man to name it specifically and to step out and confess his sins. The men can get with their Teammate/Captain or do as a team. Ask for prayer requests and ask one person to pray for each situation until every request is prayed over and/or write the prayer requests on the next page.

PRAYER REQUESTS AND PRAISES

Name	Request
	Result
Name	Request
	Result
Name	Request
	Result
Name	Request
	Result
Name	Request
	Result
Name	Request
	Result
Name	Request
	Result
Name	Request
	Result

God's "Game Plan"
Spiritual Fitness Training

- Training for Spiritual Fitness
- Maturity: Moving from a Recruit to a Seasoned Veteran
- Preventing Spiritual Atrophy
- Multiplying 3C-Christians into 3C-Disciples
- BattleZONE Hand-off

Week 10 Objectives

Each man will understand:

1. That he must train himself to become a spiritually fit warrior for Jesus.
2. The three levels of Christian maturity and how to determine at which level he is.
3. That he is commanded to make disciples by teaching them to obey God's Word.
4. How to complete a spiritual training practice schedule.
5. That he has not completed this course until he has taken his own team through it.

...Spend your time and energy training yourself for spiritual fitness.

I Timothy 4:7 - NLT

You and many others heard what I taught. Now you must teach these things to men who can be trusted, men who will be able to teach them to other people also.

2 Timothy 2:2 - WE

Do you not know that in a race all the runners run, but only one gets the prize? Run in such a way as to get the prize. Everyone who competes in the games goes into strict training. They do it to get a crown that will not last; but we do it to get a crown that will last forever.

I Corinthians 9:24-25 - NIV

Jesus came to them and said: "I have been given all authority in heaven and on earth! Go to the people of all nations and make them my disciples. Baptize them in the name of the Father, the Son, and the Holy Spirit, and teach them to do everything I have told you. I will be with you always, even until the end of the world."

Matthew 28:18-20 - CEV

Therefore I do not run like a man running aimlessly; I do not fight like a man beating the air. No, I beat my body and make it my slave so that after I have preached to others, I myself will not be disqualified for the prize.

I Corinthians 9:26-27 - NIV

. . . set your sights on the realities of heaven, where Christ sits at God's right hand in the place of honor and power. Let heaven fill your thoughts. Do not think only about things down here on earth.

Colossians 3:1(b)-2 - NLT

WEEK 10

STRENGTH TRAINING

...Spend your time and energy training yourself for spiritual fitness.

I Timothy 4:7 - NLT

BATTLE ZONE MINISTRIES, INC. www.battlezoneministries.org

WEEK 10

STRENGTH TRAINING

You and many others heard what I taught. Now you must teach these things to men who can be trusted, men who will be able to teach them to other people also.

2 Timothy 2:2 - WE

BATTLE ZONE MINISTRIES, INC. www.battlezoneministries.org

WEEK 10

STRENGTH TRAINING

Do you not know that in a race all the runners run, but only one gets the prize? Run in such a way as to get the prize. Everyone who competes in the games goes into strict training. They do it to get a crown that will not last; but we do it to get a crown that will last forever.

I Corinthians 9:24-25 - NIV

BATTLE ZONE MINISTRIES, INC. www.battlezoneministries.org

WEEK 10

STRENGTH TRAINING

Jesus came to them and said: "I have been given all authority in heaven and on earth! Go to the people of all nations and make them my disciples. Baptize them in the name of the Father, the Son, and the Holy Spirit, and teach them to do everything I have told you. I will be with you always, even until the end of the world."

Matthew 28:18-20 - CEV

BATTLE ZONE MINISTRIES, INC. www.battlezoneministries.org

WEEK 10

STRENGTH TRAINING

Therefore I do not run like a man running aimlessly; I do not fight like a man beating the air. No, I beat my body and make it my slave so that after I have preached to others, I myself will not be disqualified for the prize.

I Corinthians 9:26-27 - NIV

BATTLE ZONE MINISTRIES, INC. www.battlezoneministries.org

WEEK 10

STRENGTH TRAINING

...set your sights on the realities of heaven, where Christ sits at God's right hand in the place of honor and power. Let heaven fill your thoughts. Do not think only about things down here on earth..

Colossians 3:1(b)-2 - NLT

BATTLE ZONE MINISTRIES, INC. www.battlezoneministries.org

NOTES

STRENGTH TRAINING

BATTLE ZONE MINISTRIES, INC. www.battlezoneministries.org

NOTES

STRENGTH TRAINING

BATTLE ZONE MINISTRIES, INC. www.battlezoneministries.org

NOTES

STRENGTH TRAINING

BATTLE ZONE MINISTRIES, INC. www.battlezoneministries.org

NOTES

STRENGTH TRAINING

BATTLE ZONE MINISTRIES, INC. www.battlezoneministries.org

NOTES

STRENGTH TRAINING

BATTLE ZONE MINISTRIES, INC. www.battlezoneministries.org

NOTES

STRENGTH TRAINING

BATTLE ZONE MINISTRIES, INC. www.battlezoneministries.org

SHOW ME HOW TO CARE FOR MEN

Go to www.battlezoneministries.org > Training > Show Me How To > Care For Men

HOW TO **VIDEO**

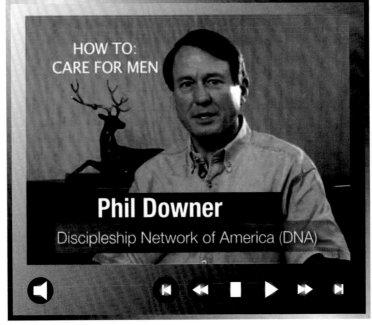

HOW TO:
CARE FOR MEN

Phil Downer
Discipleship Network of America (DNA)

It's not easy to get beyond the "mask" most men wear. We are quick to say, "Hi, how are you doing?" but do we really mean it? In this *Show Me How To*, Phil Downer of *Discipleship Network of America (DNA)*, gives men practical guidance on how to move beyond the mask and begin to really care for one another.

At BattleZONE Ministries...
We Show You How!

PLAY 1 : We Must Train to Become Spiritually Fit

...Spend your time and energy training yourself for spiritual fitness.
I Timothy 4:7 - NLT

High Expectations
Much like an NFL coach has for his players, God has high expectations for His children. Christians are called to be spiritually fit warriors for Christ – 3C-Christians. We must train ourselves for spiritual fitness just as a football player trains himself for physical fitness. A spiritual training program should be designed to help you respond to life as Christ did, obediently to His Father.

"We are at this moment as close to God as we really choose to be. True, there are times when we would like to know a deeper intimacy, but when it comes to the point, we are not prepared to pay the price involved."
J. Oswald Sanders
"Enjoying Intimacy with God"

Training Your New Nature Will Simultaneously Weaken Your Old Sin Nature
Spiritual fruit comes from intentional training for Godly living. Just like a coach knows if a player worked out in the off-season by his strength, cardiovascular fitness and quickness, God knows who is "disciplining his body, training it to do what it should," (1 Corinthians 9:27) to be His hands and feet.

Choose to be Spiritually Fit
Jerry Bridges in his book, *Growing Your Faith, How to Mature in Christ*, says,

"Life is a constant series of choices from the time we arise in the morning until we go to bed at night. Many of these choices have moral consequences."

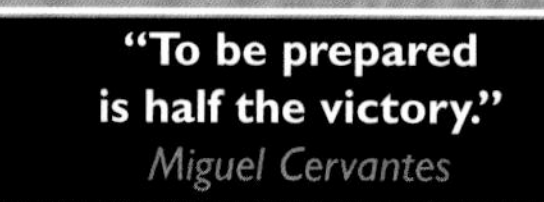
"To be prepared is half the victory."
Miguel Cervantes

"The pursuit of holiness involves a constant series of such choices. We choose in every situation which direction we will go, towards sin or towards holiness. It is through these choices we develop Christlike habits of living. Habits are developed by repetition, and it is the area of moral choices that we develop spiritual habit patterns."

In other words, the more you choose to execute God's will, the stronger your spiritual habits will become. The more you choose to sin, the deeper and more ingrained your likelihood to sin is, simply because unchecked sin always leads to more sin. Spiritual training is the key to experiencing holiness. Bridges continues:

"Sin tends to cloud our reason, dull our consciences, stimulate our sinful desires, and weaken our wills. Because of this, each sin we commit reinforces the habit of sinning and makes it easier to give in to that temptation the next time we encounter it. On the other hand, making right choices tends to strengthen our resolve against sin."

In other words, you get good at what you practice. Practice sinning and you will get better at it; practice holiness through the power of the Holy Spirit and you will get good at executing God's will. The way you train your reactions to a situation will determine which nature is spiritually dominant.

What Does This Spiritual Training Program Look Like?
Renowned Christian author Hank Hanegraaff says

"...those who wish to emulate Jesus Christ do not become Christlike by simply taking on the appearance of Christianity, nor do they win the good fight by merely mouthing Christian slogans. Instead they become Christlike by offering themselves to God 'as living sacrifices' (Romans 12:1). Prayer, fasting and sacrifice characterized the life of Christ. In like fashion, such spiritual disciplines must characterize the lives of those who sincerely desire to become Christlike. Spiritual disciplines are, in effect, spiritual exercises. As the physical disciplines of weightlifting and running promote strength and stamina, so the spiritual disciplines of abstinence (solitude, sacrifice, simplicity, etc.) and engagement (study, service, submission, etc.) promote righteousness. Tom Landry, former coach of the Dallas Cowboys, is often quoted saying, 'The job of a football coach is to make men do what they don't want to do in order to achieve what they've always wanted to be.' In much the same way, says Donald Whitney, 'Christians are called to make themselves do something they would not naturally do—pursue the Spiritual Disciplines—in order to become what they've always wanted to be, that is like Jesus Christ'."

Hank Hanegraff continues by saying, "The problem with contemporary Christianity is that a vast majority of Christians have never made the transition from declaration to discipleship. Thus, they have never become slaves of righteousness." (*The Covering, W Publishing Group, August 2002, pp. 51–52*)

CAPTAIN'S CORNER
PERSONAL APPLICATION

PLAY 1: We Must Train to Become Spiritually Fit HIGHLIGHTS

- Training your new nature will simultaneously weaken your old sin nature.
- In every situation you make a choice – either holiness or sin.
- The more you train yourself by making Godly choices, the stronger will be your desire to obey God.

1. Would you agree that it takes training to become fit... and better yet, skill-specific training to increase your spiritual XT and X%? Why?

2. Make a list of reasons why spiritual fitness training is necessary for holiness.

3. What are you doing today to strengthen your spiritual muscle?

CRUNCH TIME:

What did God want you to learn and do from this Play?

PLAY 2 : Maturing in Your Faith

I write to you, little children, because your sins are forgiven you for His name's sake. I write to you, fathers, because you have known Him who is from the beginning. I write to you, young men, because you have overcome the wicked one. I write to you, little children, because you have known the Father. I have written to you, fathers, because you have known Him who is from the beginning. I have written to you, young men, because you are strong, and the word of God abides in you, and you have overcome the wicked one.

I John 2:12-14 - NKJV

A Specific Progression

In the verses above, John writes about three stages in the Christian life: little children, young men and fathers. This is the specific progression of growth in every Christian who is maturing spiritually. Jesus also addressed these three distinct stages as the seed, the corn and the full ear of corn (Mark 4:38). Jesus uses the analogy of agriculture; John uses the analogy of human growth. In BattleZONE, we use the analogy of football, where recruits are the newly saved, rookies are little children, players are the young men and the seasoned veteran is like the father.

The Recruit (verse 12) is someone who has been recently *"recruited"* onto God's team (saved). This has nothing to do with age, but simply that we are all God's children at every point in our faith.

The Rookie (verse 13) is a *"milk bottle"* believer. The word John uses in the Greek for *"little children"* is completely different than the word he uses in verse 12. The little child does not have the Word of God abiding in him strongly – he only understands the basics. Therefore, he is "*tossed to and fro, and carried about with every wind of doctrine*" (Ephesians 4:14). He knows about God and Jesus, but unfortunately does not yet know God's "Playbook" very well. This is the key to Christian growth – getting new converts in the Word right away so they are not confused by false teachings.

The Player (verse 14) is someone who has overcome the wicked one (Satan), *"because you are strong, and the word of God abides in you"*. This is key to understanding how to get to the next level in your spiritual fitness. You are strong and obey God's Word because you know what it says and you do what God expects. You must also understand Satan's strategies. The Player has struggled with Satan's temptations and won. A Rookie gets tossed around by the opposing team because he's new to the game – he doesn't know the "Playbook" so he doesn't have a strong knowledge of the Coach's game plan. The Player has a solid foundation in the Holy "Playbook" and does not get tossed aside by the Evil One's wicked lies and schemes. The Player has trained himself to recognize certain "formations" and adjust his play accordingly. As Rookies learn about Jesus, they grow in their ability to win battles with temptation.

The Seasoned Veteran (verse 14) is mature in his faith, *"because you have known Him who is from the beginning."* This means more than just knowing Who God is, but knowing Him intimately because you spend time talking with Him in prayer and learning about Him through Bible study and meditation. You worship Him (service) and faithfully obey Him by Spirit-filled living.

"Spiritual growth progresses from knowing that you are a Christian, to knowing the Word of God, to knowing God Himself. As you focus on the glory of God and begin to give Him the honor He is due, you will find that you are being changed into His very image from one level of glory to the next. That is spiritual growth."

John MacArthur 

Place an "X" on the line below where you feel you are in your spiritual fitness level.

How can you get to the next level?

Can a coach give what he does not possess himself?

Can you disciple/coach others to move from rookie to player to veteran?

RECRUITED SAVED — ROOKIE (LEVEL 1) — PLAYER (LEVEL 2) — SEASONED VETERAN (LEVEL 3)

CAPTAIN'S CORNER
PERSONAL APPLICATION

PLAY 2: Maturing in Your Faith HIGHLIGHTS

- According to John there are three stages of a Christian maturity: little children, young men and fathers.
- The little child does not have the Word of God abiding in him strongly – he only understands the basics.
- The young man is someone who has overcome Satan, "because he is strong, and the word of God abides in him."
- The father is mature in faith, and knows God intimately.

1. If you were a coach of a children's football team, how would you train them to understand the basics of the game?

2. Why did you put an "X" in the location you did on the opposite page?

3. Does the Word of God abide in you strongly and have you overcome Satan's evil temptations?

4. Can you think of someone you know who is a "seasoned veteran" as I John 2:14 describes.

CRUNCH TIME:

What did God want you to learn and do from this Play?

PLAY 3 : Discipline Yourself to Win the Race

You've all been to the stadium and seen the athletes race. Everyone runs; one wins. Run to win. All good athletes train hard. They do it for a gold medal that tarnishes and fades. You're after one that's gold eternally. I don't know about you, but I'm running hard for the finish line. I'm giving it everything I've got. No sloppy living for me! I'm staying alert and in top condition. I'm not going to get caught napping, telling everyone else all about it and then missing out myself.

I Corinthians 9:24-27 - MSG

Strength Training – No Pain, No Gain

No one can get strong by reading about weightlifting. You must engage yourself in the discipline of lifting weights, experiencing the pain necessary for your muscles to grow. In order to get consistently stronger, one cannot go through the same routine, but must add weight and reps, pushing to failure for muscle growth to occur. The Bible says Jesus learned obedience through His suffering; we, too, must be willing to suffer in our obedience. God teaches us through real-life situations, primarily the difficult and challenging ones.

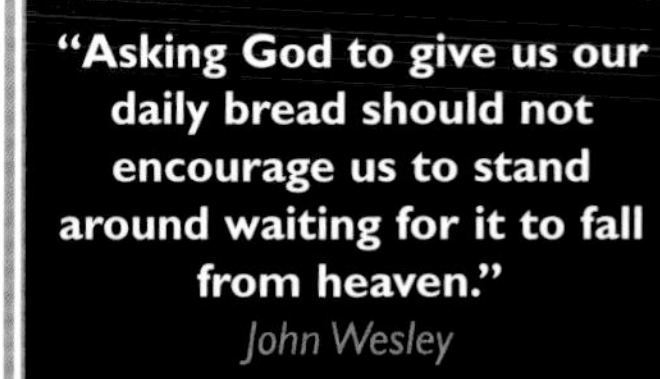

"Asking God to give us our daily bread should not encourage us to stand around waiting for it to fall from heaven."
John Wesley

Desire is Demonstrated by Discipline: Responsibly Dependent

It all comes down to preparation, and to prepare for victory you must be disciplined. It's not an easy stroll in the park... it can flat-out hurt! It is our responsibility to execute the play call, but it is the Holy Spirit who calls the right play at the right time and gives us the power to execute it... even when it hurts. It hurts to say "no" to a big promotion at work, because you know God wants you around your family more. When you first start tithing, it hurts to allow God to determine how you should spend His money. However, we can do all things through Christ, who gives us the strength to execute His will.

"Discipline is that act of inducing pain and stress in one's life in order to grow into greater toughness, capacity, endurance, or strength. So spiritual discipline is that effort pressing the soul into greater effort so that it will enlarge its capacity to hear God speak and, as a result, to generate inner force (spiritual energy) that will guide and empower one's mind and outer life."

Gordon MacDonald
"The Life God Blesses"
Thomas Nelson Publishers, Nashville, TN, 1994, p. 41

"The harder we work, the luckier we get."
Vince Lombardi

Spiritual Atrophy – Use It or Lose It

In the field of kinesiology, there is a theory called the "Principle of Adaptation," which states that human muscles adapt to the forces or pressures put on them. That is why football players lift weights – to strengthen their muscles, ligaments and bones. If you don't challenge the muscle with heavy loads or worse yet, don't use them at all, they will atrophy or literally deteriorate. Unless you train regularly to be spiritually fit, you will begin to suffer from spiritual atrophy. Dozens of football players are cut every year during training camp because they failed to train in the off-season. They got lazy and lost their edge.

There is no off-season for Christians. We must keep training to stay spiritually fit year-round.

Unlike salvation, which is a one-time act of faith and repentance, spiritual fitness isn't something you get once and keep forever – you must continue to train yourself for holiness. Yet, we must never set aside God's amazing grace in our pursuit of holiness.

A pure desire to engage in spiritual training exemplifies your love for God, which compels us to want to spend time with Christ getting to know Him at a deeper level. We are to enjoy our relationship with Christ, not dread it. By training for spiritual fitness, we get to know the Man who gave His life for us and can begin to taste His divine love, which will always compel us to train. Allow Jesus Christ to become your "Personal Spiritual Fitness Trainer" so you will never experience spiritual atrophy, enjoy spiritual rewards and ultimately experience holiness as a 3C-Christian.

CAPTAIN'S CORNER
PERSONAL APPLICATION

PLAY 3: Discipline Yourself to Win the Race HIGHLIGHTS

- The Bible says Jesus learned obedience through His suffering.
- God teaches you through real-life situations, especially the difficult and challenging ones.
- A pure desire to engage in spiritual training exemplifies your love for God, which compels you to want to spend time with Christ, getting to know Him at a deeper level.

1. How would your favorite team perform if they didn't engage in a strength training program?

2. What is your understanding of the doctrine of suffering as it relates to spiritual growth? Explain.

3. What is getting in your way from a disciplined spiritual strength training program?

4. Where does God's grace factor in to your spiritual training program?

CRUNCH TIME:

What did God want you to learn and do from this Play?

PLAY 4 : Multiplying 3C-Christian Disciples

We proclaim Him, admonishing every man and teaching every man with all wisdom, so that we may present every man complete in Christ. For this purpose also I labor, striving according to His power, which mightily works within me.
Colossians 1:28-29 - NASB

Disciple Making
We are to proclaim Jesus as the only way to heaven, warn everyone that an eternity in hell awaits those who do not become Christ-Followers, instruct everyone in the ways of God, so those who choose Jesus can be presented to God as mature 3C-Christians. We are to work hard so the Holy Spirit's power can be even more effective at creating mature Christians. This is how we make disciples.

Commissioned to Lead by Teaching
You and many others heard what I taught. Now you must teach these things to men who can be trusted, men who will be able to teach them to other people also.
2 Timothy 2:2 - WE

Jesus came to them and said: I have been given all authority in heaven and on earth! Go to the people of all nations and make them my disciples. Baptize them in the name of the Father, the Son, and the Holy Spirit, and teach them to do everything I have told you. I will be with you always, even until the end of the world.
Matthew 28:18-20 CEV

Below is a section of a teaching from John MacArthur that so perfectly describes what it means to "teach" or make disciples of all nations.

The command to *"teach [make disciples of] all nations"* (Matthew 28:19) requires obedience. Mark 16:15 commands us to *"go... into all the world, and preach the gospel to every creature."* In the words of Luke, *"Repentance and remission of sins should be preached in his name among all nations."* (Luke 24:47).

"Teaching them to observe all things whatsoever I have commanded you." (Matthew 28:19-20) Since the new convert desires to learn so he can obey, he needs to be taught "all the counsel of God" (Acts 20:27). One cannot be a disciple apart from a life of obedience and a desire to follow Him as Lord. Jesus said to the people gathered on the mountain that they were to teach everything He had commanded them. He previously said, *"The Holy Spirit... shall teach you all things, and bring all things to your remembrance, whatever I have said unto you"* (John 14:26), and the Bible writers wrote it all down. The Spirit has made that teaching available to every believer in the Word of God. Each believer is to submit himself to it in obedience. Hebrews 5:9 says, *"Being made perfect, he became the author of eternal salvation unto all them that obey him."* True converts are those who obey Christ. Romans 6:13 says, *"Yield yourselves unto God, as those that are alive from the dead, and your members as instruments of righteousness unto God."* That speaks of an obedient faith. Many people claim to follow Jesus. But our Lord often spoke of the marks of a genuine disciple to expose those whose discipleship was only a facade. That distinction has often been overlooked in contemporary Christianity.

Are you ready to lead by example and commit to make disciples? Don't let fear, worry or busyness get in your way of becoming a BattleZONE Captain. Remember, you are a captain in training until you lead one group or one individual through the BZ Training Course. The process to becoming a Certified BattleZONE Coach is on the opposite page. Our nation is starving for men who are sold out for Jesus. Will you step up and fill the gap by becoming a man who lives by faithful obedience – and trains other men to become 3C-Christians by reproducing reproducers?

3C-Christian
Conformed to the Character of Christ.

For more on how to become a Certified BattleZONE Coach, go to **www.battlezoneministries.org**. Under the "Coaches" drop-down menu, click on "Be a Coach" and then "Coach Sign-up".

CAPTAIN'S CORNER
PERSONAL APPLICATION

PLAY 4: Multiplying 3C-Christian Disciples HIGHLIGHTS

- You are commanded to go and make disciples.
- We are to teach God's truth to other men who can turn around and teach those truths to others.
- A disciple is someone who teaches, shows and coaches someone how to follow Christ.
- Teaching someone else is the highest form of learning.
- **There are four steps to becoming a Certified BattleZONE Coach:**

STEP 1:
FIRST complete the BattleZONE Training Course. This can be accomplished in several ways:

a. Complete a Coach-specific BattleZONE Training Camp.
b. Go through the course lead by a BattleZONE Captain or Coach. Do this:
  i. In a team
  ii. One-on-one
  iii. Over the phone
  iv. E-learning on the web
  v. Webinar format

STEP 2:
You must teach a BattleZONE Training Course either by yourself or by partnering with another man who has gone through the course. You may take someone through the course three ways:

a. Live with a team
b. Live one-on-one
c. Over the phone

STEP 3:
You must complete the BattleZONE Online Forms

a. Register as a BattleZONE participant
b. Register the Coach who took you through the BZ Training Course
c. Register the team/individual you took through the Course
d. Have your pastor complete the BattleZONE letter of recommendation.

STEP 4:
Sign the BattleZONE Ministries Coach's Covenant and fax it to the corporate office (559-297-8710).

1. How would you define the word "disciple"?

2. The Bible commands us to go and make disciples. How does this command apply to you?

3. Do you have someone in your life who you would like to disciple you? If so, who is he? If not, what do you need to do today to find a spiritual mentor?

4. What is getting in the way for you to embrace the role of becoming a disciple maker? List the reasons below:

CRUNCH TIME:

What did God want you to learn and do from this Play?

SHOW ME HOW TO FIND YOUR GREATER "YES"

Go to www.battlezoneministries.org > Training > Show Me How To > Find Greater Yes

HOW TO **VIDEO**
HOW TO FIND YOUR GREATER "YES"!
Dan Erickson
People Matter - Ministries

Men often find their identity in what they do. This is superficial and temporary. The average man makes a living–but not a life, which leads to frustration and discontentment. God has created each of us with a destiny and a purpose. Dan Erickson of *People Matter Ministries*, shows us how to find our "Greater Yes" by using Ephesians 2:10 to address four essential questions a man must ask himself to find his purpose that will echo in eternity.

At BattleZONE Ministries...
We Show You How!

BattleZONE Questionnaire

Name: ____________

Date: ____________

Directions: Circle "0" if you Strongly Disagree; 1-2 if you Disagree Somewhat; 3 if you are Neutral; 4 if you agree; and 5 if you Strongly Agree.

1. I felt this study was an effective way to teach me about temptation and holiness.

0 1 2 3 4 5

2. I understand the direct link between my Pain Point(s) and my BattleZONEs, and found the online BattleZONE Challenge helpful.

0 1 2 3 4 5

3. I am more confident in my understanding and ability to be Spirit-filled or to walk by the power of the Holy Spirit.

0 1 2 3 4 5

4. I found it helpful to role-play through my personal BattleZONEs or engage in Temptation-Specific Training.

0 1 2 3 4 5

5. I have a better understanding of the oppositional forces (sin nature, Satan, the World) with which I battle competing for my choices.

0 1 2 3 4 5

6. I have a better understanding of how to apply (application expectation) God's Word to my daily life.

0 1 2 3 4 5

7. I have a better understanding about the Holy Spirit's role in my ability to "be holy as Christ is holy."

0 1 2 3 4 5

8. I recognize even more, the importance of putting on the whole Armor of God daily... as God's protection against Satan's attacks.

0 1 2 3 4 5

9. I have a better understanding of faith as it relates to obedience.

0 1 2 3 4 5

10. I have a better understanding of God's grace and mercy as they relate to executing God's will and forgiveness of my sins.

0 1 2 3 4 5

11. I feel more confident in my ability to obey God.

0 1 2 3 4 5

12. I understand the importance of surrounding myself with Godly influences more than I did before.

0 1 2 3 4 5

13. I felt that the BattleZONE Grace-Board was helpful in practicing yielding to God's will by the power of the Holy Spirit.

0 1 2 3 4 5

14. I would recommend this Bible study to other men I know.

0 1 2 3 4 5

15. How would you rank this Bible study compared to other studies you've done?

LAST **TOP**

0 1 2 3 4 5

Please explain your ranking:

____

____

What is one thing that you learned from BattleZONE that has changed your ability to "be holy as Christ is holy?"

____

____

How can this study improve? Please be specific. Use extra pages if necessary to share all your thoughts.

____

____

Thank you for taking the time to provide this valuable feedback to help improve this course.

Your BattleZONE Teammate in Christ
By His Grace — For His Glory,
Michael C. Pouliot

Notes:

DAILY PRACTICE SCHEDULE

EDD'S (EVERYDAY DRILLS)

TIME	**STUDY PLAYBOOK** (Bible)
TIME	**CONDITIONING** (Prayer/Meditation)
TIME	**DAILY DIET/NUTRITION** (What are you "feeding" yourself?)
TIME	**CHALK-TALKS** (Church & Bible Studies)
TIME	**STRENGTH TRAINING** (Memory verses)
TIME	**TEMPTATION SPECIFIC TRAINING/TST** (Practice situational temptations)
TIME	**TEAM UP** (Meet weekly with other men for accountability)

DAILY PRACTICE SCHEDULE

EDD'S (EVERYDAY DRILLS)

TIME	
TIME	**STUDY PLAYBOOK** (Bible)
TIME	**CONDITIONING** (Prayer/Meditation)
TIME	**DAILY DIET/NUTRITION** (What are you "feeding" yourself?)
TIME	**CHALK-TALKS** (Church & Bible Studies)
TIME	**STRENGTH TRAINING** (Memory verses)
TIME	**TEMPTATION SPECIFIC TRAINING/TST** (Practice situational temptations)
TIME	**TEAM UP** (Meet weekly with other men for accountability)

COACH EVERY WILLING MAN TO LIVE VICTORIOUS IN CHRIST **WEEK 10**

God's "Game Plan"

Spiritual Fitness Training

WARM-UP

BATTLEZONE SYMBOL KEY

Captain	Rotation Reading	Time	R.I.P.L. Effect

WARM-UP: GOD'S "GAME PLAN": SPIRITUAL FITNESS TRAINING

A. Two-minute Drill: First thing, have each man get together with his TC and go over counter verses
1. Captain — make sure each teammate has an opportunity to recite his verses.
2. Make sure each teammate has an opportunity to recite his verses.

B. Have the men tear out or make a photo copy of their evaluations on page 257 to hand in to you. Make sure they took the Post-Test on the BattleZONE website under Resources > Post-Test.

C. Go to the BattleZONE Chalk Talk and proceed to lead your team through Week 10.

CHALK TALK

God's "Game Plan": Spiritual Fitness Training

1. PRAYER

Have one of the men open in prayer and ask the Holy Spirit to guide and direct the session towards God's agenda.

2. GOD'S "GAME PLAN": SPIRITUAL FITNESS TRAINING

Remember last week, we studied then ninth component in His "Game Plan" for victory/holiness: Godly Teammates. We must surround ourselves with other Christ-Followers, confess our sins, renew our minds with God's Word and allow the Holy Spirit to call the plays.

This week, we will cover the next component in God's "Game Plan" for victory/holiness: Spiritual Fitness Training.

Wrap-up Summary

Throughout this spiritual training course, we have learned that God commands us to "be holy as Christ is holy" (1 Peter 1:16). Our choices are never free from the oppositional forces enticing us to sin, (Galatians 5:17), which unite as one team: our own sin nature, the World and Satan.

We also learned that God has graciously drafted us onto His team and we signed His eternal contract using faith as our pen and Christ's blood as the ink. By doing so, God has given us His infallible Scriptures as our "Holy Playbook" which is also our "Rulebook"– that keeps us from stepping out of bounds and/or off-sides. This "Playbook" gives us a flawless "Game Plan" to defeat our opponent and stay penalty-free.

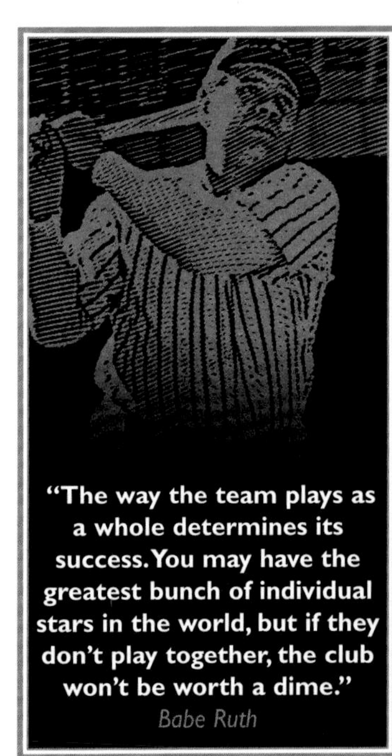

"The way the team plays as a whole determines its success. You may have the greatest bunch of individual stars in the world, but if they don't play together, the club won't be worth a dime."
Babe Ruth

3. Week 10 Plays

For Week 10 you were assigned to read and be ready to comment on four Plays. You will have two minutes to present your topic; then discuss each as a group. Please try to stay focused on what God taught you through this Play. **What did God want you to learn and do?**

CAPTAIN, ASSIGN EACH TEAMMATE A PLAY – THEN LET THEM TAKE THE LEAD.

- **Play 1: We Must Train to Become Spiritually Fit**
- **Play 2: Maturing in Your Faith**
- **Play 3: Discipline Yourself to Win the Race**
- **Play 4: Multiplying 3C-Christian Disciples**

4. BattleZONE Grace-Board

Final Grace-Board Discussion and Recap
Take out your Grace-Board and Pocket GRACE Keeper. One at a time, please share how this experiential tool made an impact on your spiritual life. How has it helped you understand God's grace and God's mercy?

Have one team/partner role-play quickly through a scenario using the C3-Technique.

Undefeated

So, what do you think? With God on our side like this, how can we lose?
Romans 8:31 MSG

Jesus had one focus: to do His Father's will. The crowds, the Pharisees, or the size of His task did not distract Jesus; He concentrated on the will of God. Jesus was undefeated because He trained daily to prepare for His daily battles and temptations. He remained undefeated because He relied on the Holy Spirit's power.

Jesus was born a winner, never lost a battle, died a winner, rose from the dead a winner and He sits at the right hand of His Father, victorious. Jesus Christ is undefeated, and since we are one with Christ... we too share in His glory! Praise be to God in the highest!

Focus

...set your sights on the realities of heaven, where Christ sits at God's right hand in the place of honor and power. Let heaven fill your thoughts. Do not think only about things down here on earth.
Colossians 3:1b-2 - NLT

Even though we spent a lot of time learning about temptations, the true key to living a holy life is to keep focused on Christ who always obeys God's will. Now that you have a solid understanding of the incredible oppositional forces we are up against as Christ-Followers, try to avoid focusing only on your personal areas of temptation or your sins – focus on Christ and get to know Him more and more each day.

The BattleZONE Training Course is a tool to help apply God's "Game Plan" to all areas of your life by focusing on Jesus, so you will be compelled by His unconditional love to continually strive to pursue and ultimately experience holiness. This can only be obtained by God's loving grace through the power of the Holy Spirit.

5. BattleZONE Daily Practice Schedule

A schedule is crucial to spiritual fitness and football. Have each teammate fill out their Daily Practice Schedule on pages 259 & 260. See example on the following page.

Do this with your TC and be prepared to discuss your schedule with the entire team. You will have about 10 minutes to complete your Daily Practice Schedule.

DAILY PRACTICE SCHEDULE

EDD'S (EVERYDAY DRILLS)

TIME 5:00am

STUDY PLAYBOOK (Bible) Read one chapter of Proverbs for the corresponding day of the month--on March 22, I will read Proverbs 22. Then read and meditate on one paragraph of Scripture. Then read a meaningful section of the Bible based on a life circumstance I am in. OR do Bible study homework.

TIME 5:30am

CONDITIONING (Prayer/Meditation) Pray using the format Jesus taught His disciples in Matthew 6 (see Week 7, Play #5). Then read and meditate on one paragraph of Scripture based on a life circumstance or leading from the Holy Spirit.

(To see how to meditate on Scripture go to www.battlezoneministries.org > Show Me How To > Meditate on Scripture)

TIME Daily

DAILY DIET/NUTRITION (What are you "feeding" yourself?) Use the 80/20 Rule when listening to radio in my car. 80% Christ focused (Christian music and Bible teaching) and 20% World (sports, news, weather and clean music). TV-Ask myself would I let my 5-year-old daughter watch this show? If the answer is no, then I probably should not watch it. Also, stimulating TV, with beautiful women, will rev up my lust engine.

TIME Varies

CHALK-TALKS (Church & Bible Studies) Sunday fellowship and Worship. Strategically select one to two church-studies per year-depending on season of life and time availability.

TIME Daily

STRENGTH TRAINING (Memory verses) Read specific meaningful Scripture and hide God's Word in my heart. Use cards to carry around with me and place where I will be reminded to read them over and over again.

Go to www.battlezoneministries.org

Click on RESOURCES to create my own Counter Verse memory cards

TIME Daily

TEMPTATION SPECIFIC TRAINING/TST (Practice situational temptations) Depending on my walk with God, in times of continuing struggle with a specific temptation, I will complete another BattleZONE Game Plan Execution System Form. I will share it with my wife and my BZ Life Team.

To download a blank form go to www.battlezoneministries.org > resources > BZ Course > Forms > BZ Ex System

TIME 6 to 7:30 AM Every Thursday

TEAM UP (Meet weekly with other men for accountability) Meet weekly with my BZ Life Teammates in a location where we feel safe to pray and get real about life issues.

Go to www.battlezoneministries.org

Click on Life Teams to learn how to put together an accountability group.

6. Final Crunch Time

Captain, have the men turn back to page 35 in Week 1 and see how they did at reaching their Goal based on their Pain Point and BattleZONE. Then ask each man what most impacted them during the course and write it on page 266.

Submit your own BattleZONE Victory Testimonial. See page 267 for details.

7. BattleZone Final Commissioning

Final Commission: Go and Make Disciples

Men, you have endured through a tremendous amount of information learning about God's "Game Plan" for personal holiness – just like an NFL team going through an entire 16 regular season games, only to get to where it really counts—post-season play. Sure, they are tired and beat-up, but they must press on to get the reward they have worked so hard for—the Vince Lombardi Super Bowl Trophy. You, too, must press on into the BattleZONE Post-Season where it really counts. Now that you have completed this training program, take what you have learned, practiced and applied and teach others to do the same.

You are not done with this course until you have made disciples in post-season play. Jesus' call to His disciples – "Follow me, and I will make you fishers of men" – indicates that He was moving them to the next level of spiritual growth, teaching them to be fishers of men and to live holy lives. God's team has a tremendous shortage of Godly men (Levels II and III) who are committed to live holy lives and willing to pour themselves into other men as mentor/coaches...training them to live by the power of the Holy Spirit moment by moment and ultimately become 3C-Christians.

Decide today that you will leave here a "captain" on God's team who will lead others to become spiritually fit warriors for Jesus, getting to the next level as maturing, holy Christian men. You are a "captain" when you are actively discipling men through the BattleZONE Training Course in post-season play.

Captains have the men show you their final team and start date from Week 8, page 199. Also, have the men turn in their BattleZONE Evaluation Questionnaire.

BattleZONE Dinner:

It makes it very special for you to host a BattleZONE potluck dinner with the wives to complete the "hand-off" with the certificates.

A final dinner of fellowship can be a blessed way of sending your team out.

BattleZONE "Hand-Off"

Now it's time to gather as a group and hand out the BattleZONE completion certificates. As men are called to the front, it's tradition to give their certificate like a football hand-off. **(CAPTAIN: Download certificate forms from the BattleZONE website under the COACH's tab).** The hand-off symbolizes the team captain handing-off the "ball" making each teammate a captain in training until they take another group or another man through the BattleZONE Training Course.

Men will only be officially commissioned as a BattleZONE team captain when they are actively taking another man or group of men through this spiritual training course.

Captain: First, read the quote from President Roosevelt.
Next, say something specific about each one of the men before you call them up for their hand-off.

After you have successfully taken a group or individuals through the BattleZONE Training Course, you will then receive an Official Certified BattleZONE Coaching Certificate. See Play 4 on page 255 to review the requirements of becoming a Certified BattleZONE Coach.

As a Certified BattleZONE Coach, you will have demonstrated you have become a true student of the Word of God and you are applying God's teachings to your everyday life. Because you have been chosen by God to be a disciple maker, you can strategically select men throughout the world to train to become Certified BattleZONE Coaches.

"Theodore Roosevelt reportedly observed that there has never yet been a man who led a life of ease whose name is worth remembering. He said, "I wish to preach, not the doctrine of ignoble ease, but the doctrine of the strenuous life."

From President Roosevelt's address to the Hamilton Club Chicago, April 10, 1899

We can do it because of Jesus – we can do it in team – we can do it because we are commanded to do so—we can do it by God's grace.

GO—make disciples!

BattleZONE Final Praise Reports

Name	Praises

BATTLEZONE VICTORIES

Your Name
City, State

What's Your Story?

Submit your BattleZONE victory testimony in 200 to 400 words. By sending us your testimony, you are agreeing that we can post it on the BattleZONE website as an inspiration to other men. (You can even print this full color page and frame God's work in your life as a landmark of His grace.) See other BattleZONE Victories for examples.

Email the following to **info@battlezoneministries.org**

1) 200 to 400 word testimonial saved as a Word file, stating how the BattleZONE Training Course impacted your life.

2) Head shot in high resolution (3 Mega Pixel camera or better) saved as a JPG file.

3) Action photo in high resolution (3 Mega Pixel camera or better) saved as a JPG file.

BattleZONE Victories

Michael Cancio
Tacoma, WA

I came to Christ initially when I was 21, at a church revival with the wife of my youth, serving our country as a soldier in the United States Army. Through many mountain and valley experiences, I was challenged to a deeper relationship with Christ and a committed responsibility to my wife of 24 years and my family.

As I strive to have a closer walk with Christ, my Christian experience has been one of gradual maturity. For many years my life has been lived in selfishness and deceit. In recent years I have started a process of recognizing and changing my unhealthy and unrighteous behavior. Like BattleZONE teaches, I am in pursuit of the holiness God wants to see in me.

Learning and using the tools presented in BattleZONE has helped me walk in the daily battles of this life. Accountability and truth have helped me fight the good fight every day. Trust and obedience to Christ will produce the fruit necessary to build His kingdom. I am encouraged and ready to teach men to walk in this life daily as committed soldiers in

God's army, Yahweh of Armies, is mustering the army for the battle.

Isaiah 13:4 WEB

GLOSSARY

GLOSSARY OF BATTLEZONE TERMS

3C-Christian:
Conformed to the Character of Christ. A 3C-Christian is what being a disciple is all about. Becoming a 3C-Christian is the ultimate goal in our pursuit of holiness.

Two-Minute Drill:
At the beginning of Weeks 5 through 10, each man will get with his TC and recite his "counter verses" based on their individual BattleZONE. This will help men hide God's Word in their hearts so that they will not sin against Him.

BattleZONE:
The actual moment in time when you are tempted. It's that moment when you are looking temptation in the face and must choose between executing God's will or sin. It is the moment during temptation where you must choose God's will or self-fulfillment. This is also referred to as one's personal area of temptation. BattleZONEs are different for everyone. BattleZONEs (or Decision Points) are made at different points during the time leading up to sin. The decision not to cheat on your taxes could have been made years earlier, yet when you are doing your taxes and money is tight, you may enter a final BattleZONE or Decision Point when you are tempted to cheat.

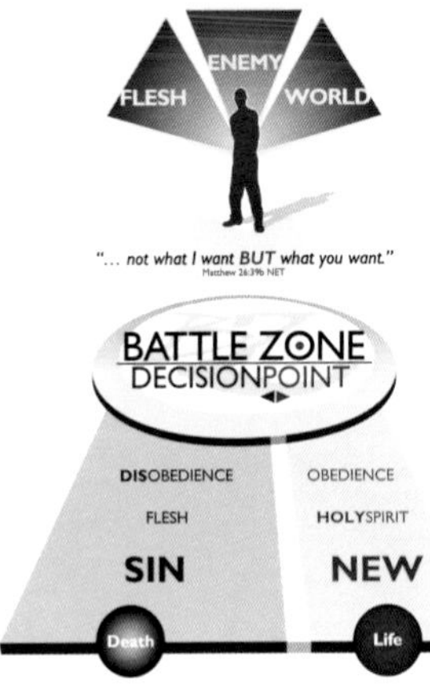

BattleZONE Draft Form:
This form, located in Week 8, will help you determine your first BattleZONE team that you will take through the training course.

C3-Technique:
A tool to help you yield to the Holy Spirit when you are tempted to sin in your BattleZONE. **C1 = Call** a time out and recognize you are being prompted by God to pray. **C2 = Confess** to God that you are being tempted to sin and what you are feeling in that moment. **C3 = Choose** to Consciously yield to the Holy Spirit and choose God's will over your desire to sin against Him.

Captain:
The man who facilitates and takes a leadership role to encourage, equip and train the other men taking the BattleZONE Training Course. You must go through the course first as a participant before you can be a captain.

Captain's Corner:
Page adjacent to the Plays where important Biblical principles (Highlights) are located, as well as questions and an area for notes.

Captain's Guide:
This section is for the captain (the facilitator of the BattleZONE Training Course). This section will have a burgundy outline to help the captain/coach differentiate the two sections.

Chalk Talk:
The area in the BattleZONE Training Course that helps the captain/coach walk the men through each week's training sessions. This is located directly after the Warm-up in the Captain's Guide.

Coach:
A BattleZONE Coach has first, gone through the training course as a participant. Next, he has successfully taken men through as a captain/facilitator. He then has applied to become a Certified BattleZONE Coach and received an endorsement from his pastor. To become a BattleZONE Coach, you must be certified by BattleZONE Ministries.

Counter Verses:
Starting in Week 4, each player will be asked to progressively memorize (hide in his heart) three to five Scriptures or "counter verses" related to his BattleZONE. At the beginning of Weeks 5 through 10, he will engage in the "Two-Minute Drill" with his Teammate/Captain and recite the selected Scriptures verbatim. He will then be given a score as a percentage.

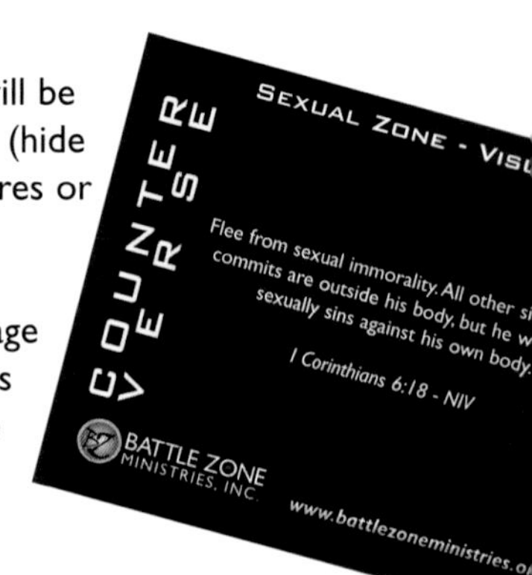

Crunch Time:
The time each week when you ask your men to describe one teaching and or Scripture that really hit them during the practice session.

Daily Practice Schedule Form:
This form is located in Week 10 and will help each man develop a Spiritual Training Program for holiness. It is vital that the form be filled out specifically with times and locations. This will ensure a greater chance of applying the spiritual disciplines. Set realistic goals based on personal circumstances.

Decision Point:
The point where we are forced to make a decision to obey God or not. This is otherwise known as the BattleZONE. This decision point can come days before an actual temptation, as well as in the heat of the moment. This is where the C3-Technique is to be applied.

Execution:
To successfully complete a desired task, goal or outcome as an action.

eXecution percentage (X%):
{#executed / #attempts} The number of times a task is executed (completed) divided by the total attempts.

$$\text{eXecution Percentage (X\%)} = \frac{\text{number of successes}}{\text{total attempts}}$$

X%=10/20 — X%=50% completed passes

Execution Breakdown:
A method to look back and evaluate a situation where you sinned against God, with the sole purpose of learning from the error and developing a "ready list" to be better prepared next time the situation occurs.

eXecution Threshold:
The exact moment where one can no longer execute a skill, task or technique.

Experiential:
Simulations enable learning-by-doing, an approach that experts consider the fastest **Learning/Simulation** and most effective way for people – **especially men** – to learn.

External Conditions:
The environment and circumstances you find yourself in when you are tempted to sin against God. This includes where you are, who you are with, the time of day and why you are there.

Faithful Obedience:
Trusting God enough to do His will and obey Him in all aspects of life, knowing that His way is better than yours.

Formation Recognition:
The overall situation you are in when you are in your BattleZONE. This is a high-level analysis of where you are, who you are with and the time of day.

Game Plan Execution System Form:
This form combines the Scouting Report Formation Recognition Form and assists you in developing a game plan to overcome the oppositional forces in your BattleZONEs. This form helps you determine your overall formation (internal, external and relational factors), your nutrition history (what you have been "feeding" your mind and heart), your opponent's strategy (how Satan, your sin nature and the World try to entice you to sin), your counter-attack (a game plan to overcome putting yourself in the situation where you are tempted) and your "ready list" (a pre-plan to determine how you will respond to the situation and or how you will avoid the situation all together).

Get Real:
The expectation and culture of BattleZONE participants to develop a safe environment so men can share struggles, sins, and life events in an authentic way. In other words, getting real is removing the mask that comes with identity control in order to be like Christ.

GRACE Board:
This is a tracking device to be used in tandem with the Pocket GRACE Keeper. This will assist the men in tracking how they experienced God's grace and mercies throughout a seven-day stretch. This will also allow them to take an objective look at how they are doing at yielding to the Holy Spirit when tempted, praying on God's Armor and spending daily time with God in His Word.

God's Will:
The perfect and loving ways of God. As Christ-Followers, we are to seek and align our wills with God's. This is true for major life decisions and moments when we are tempted to sin.

Holiness:
To separate or to be set apart.

Independent Practice:
Assignment given to individual teammates that they must complete prior to the next team meeting.

Internal Conditions:
During temptation there are several internal (head, heart, and attitude) that may be contributing to the decision. Internal conditions can be categorized in an acrostic called H.A.L.T.S. (Hungry, Angry, Lonely, Tired, Stressed). A man who is aware of internal conditions during his BattleZONEs can develop a plan to minimize their impact on his decisions when he is tempted.

Obedience:
The act of executing God's will by yielding to the Holy Spirit.

Oppositional Forces:
The forces which encourage us not to follow God's will: Sin nature, Satan and the World.

Opposition:
Hostile or contrary action or forces.

Pain Points:
Your pain point is the part of your life that hurts, present or past. It could also be defined as a "felt need". If it touched or talked about, it causes stress, shame or guilt. Most often, your pain point(s) will be covered by distractions, rationalizations, anger or sin. Pain Point(s) affect(s) decision points -- reducing your X% and XT (eXecution percentage and eXecution threshold). Pain points trigger the flesh into sinning to "feel" better. For example, a difficult marriage can trigger the desire to turn to porn, drugs or excessive entertainment.

Plays:
A method of instruction and learning that aids each teammate to read, prepare and present a one-page teaching on a Biblical topic having to do with God's "Game Plan" for Holiness/Victory.

Pocket GRACE Keeper:
This is a tool to help men recognize that God's powerful grace and His loving mercy are ongoing and necessary for a proper view of sin. This tool is to be used in a positive light, not as a legalistic "sin counter". Some men have an unhealthy view of God's grace and mercy and this tool will help then experience God's plan for sin and temptation.

Reaction Trainer Cards:
These cards are located in Week 2 and will help you to become aware of your automatic reactions to temptation situations. They are also used to start the process of selecting "counter verses" based on individual BattleZONEs.

Relational Factors:
The personal effects from past, present and future relationship tension. Is there any relationship "out-of-whack"? These could include a father wound, a co-worker, your children, a friend, your spouse or even a relationship with someone who is now deceased.

R.I.P.L. Effect:
This is a practical tool to help study the Bible in its context and help the reader apply it to real life. R.I.P.L. means: **Read** the passage in context first; **Interpret** the passage in context; **Personalize** the verse as if it was being said to you; and **Live** the passage through faithful obedience.

Rotation Reading:
A method that ensures each BattleZONE participant is actively engaged in the readings. This symbol helps the captain remember to ask men to participate in the training sessions each week.

Spiritual eXecution Threshold (XT):
The point where you can no longer execute God's will consistently in your BattleZONEs.
See eXecution Percentage (X%)

Saint:
A holy one or one "set apart" for God.

Scouting Report Formation Recognition Form:
A form used to identify patterns that lead up to temptation situations. This form will help men process their overall situation, external circumstances, internal conditions and relational factors. The purpose of this form is to help men become aware of his patterns that lead to sin. This form is the first step in developing a game plan to help gain victory over his BattleZONEs.

Skill:
The ability to use one's knowledge effectively and readily in execution or performance; a learned power of doing something competently; a developed aptitude or ability.

Simulation Training:
The active experiential engagement in a real situation for the purpose of developing knowledge and skills to respond appropriately. Football teams use a method called scout team to give the players a real look at how their opponents will respond to a certain play call.

Sin:
To miss the mark that God has set; to go against God's will in thought, word or deed.

Spiritual Execution Percentage (SX%):
A term to identify the total number of times you were tempted divided by the number of times you yielded to God's will and obeyed. For example, you were tempted to lie 10 times in one day. You yielded to the Holy Spirit five times and lied five times, resulting in a 50% SX%. This is an awareness tool to be used in a short time period, not a legalistic method for self-defeat.

Strength Training Cards:
Scripture memory verses located after the title page of each week's lesson. Each teammate should tear them out and carry the cards with him to read, memorize and meditate on one verse each week.

Symbol Key:
These symbols are to help the captain/coach manage the course as he takes his players through the Captain's Guide.

Team Grace:
This term refers to the times when you are tempted to sin and ask the Holy Spirit to show you a way out and He does. You yield to Him and gain victory. This helps men understand that God's grace does not stop with salvation but must be relied on moment by moment to obey Him.

Team Mercy:
This term refers to the times when you are tempted and choose to sin against God, but then in sorrow ask God to forgive you and restore harmony in your relationship with Christ. God's mercy yearns for us to come before Him and restore our fellowship with Him.

Teammate Draft Cut Form:
This form is located in Week 9 and is used to help you select people, books, and resources that will help you in your pursuit of holiness, as well as cut those that hold you back.

Temptation Specific Training (TST):
An experiential exercise to determine a Bible-based game plan based on a specific situation where you are tempted to sin. This is most effective when role-played, but can also be effective if visualized successfully doing God's will in a BattleZONE.

Threshold:
A level, point or value above which something is true or will take place and below which it is not or will not be true.

Warm-Up:
A term used in this course to help the captain/coach get the men prepared for the training session. This is located at the beginning of the Captain's Guide each week. This section can include activities, counter verse two-minute drills and/or a short lesson.

The old sinful nature loves to do evil, which is just opposite from what the Holy Spirit wants. And the Spirit gives us desires that are opposite from what the sinful nature desires. These two forces are constantly fighting each other, and your choices are never free from this conflict.

Galatians 5:17 - NLT

"... not what I want ***BUT*** *what you want."*
Matthew 26:39b NET

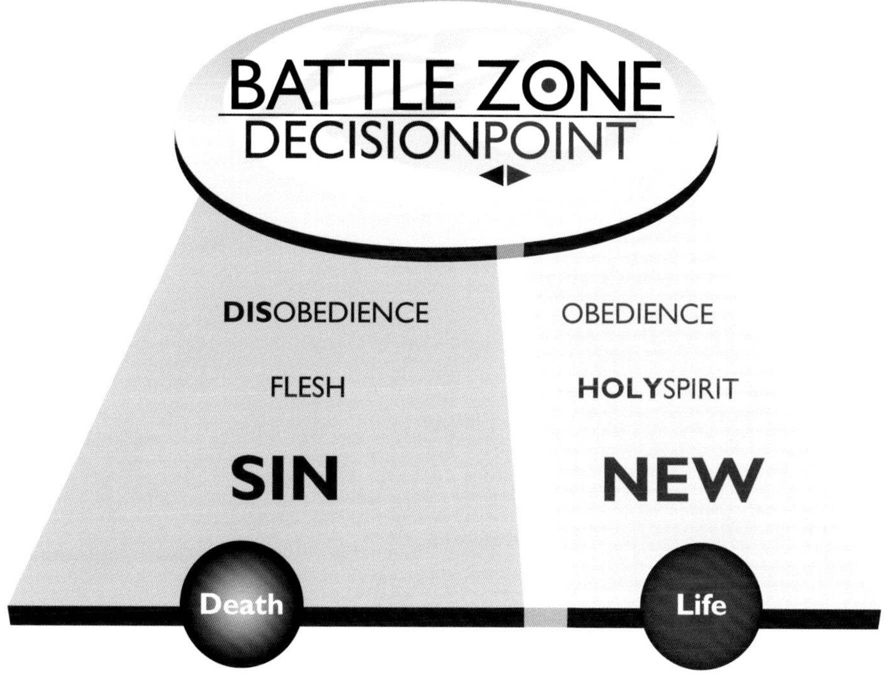

www.battlezoneministries.org

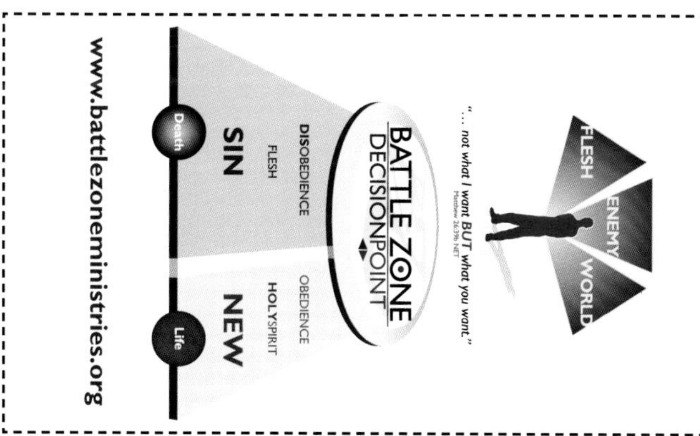

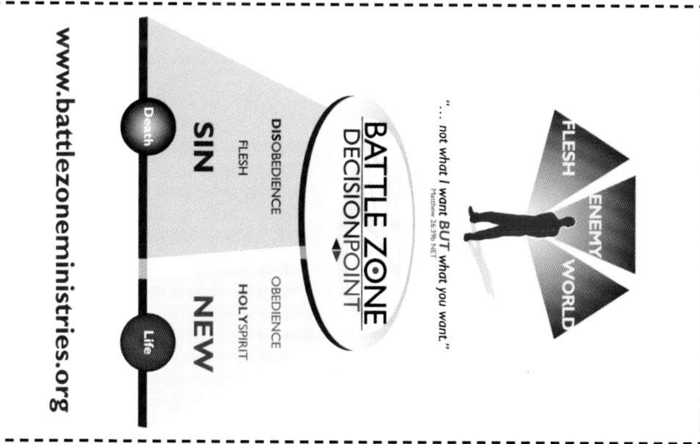

The old sinful nature loves to do evil, which is just opposite from what the Holy Spirit wants. And the Spirit gives us desires that are opposite from what the sinful nature desires. These two forces are constantly fighting each other, and your choices are never free from this conflict.
Galatians 5:17 - NLT

"... not what I want ***BUT*** *what you want."*
Matthew 26:39b NET

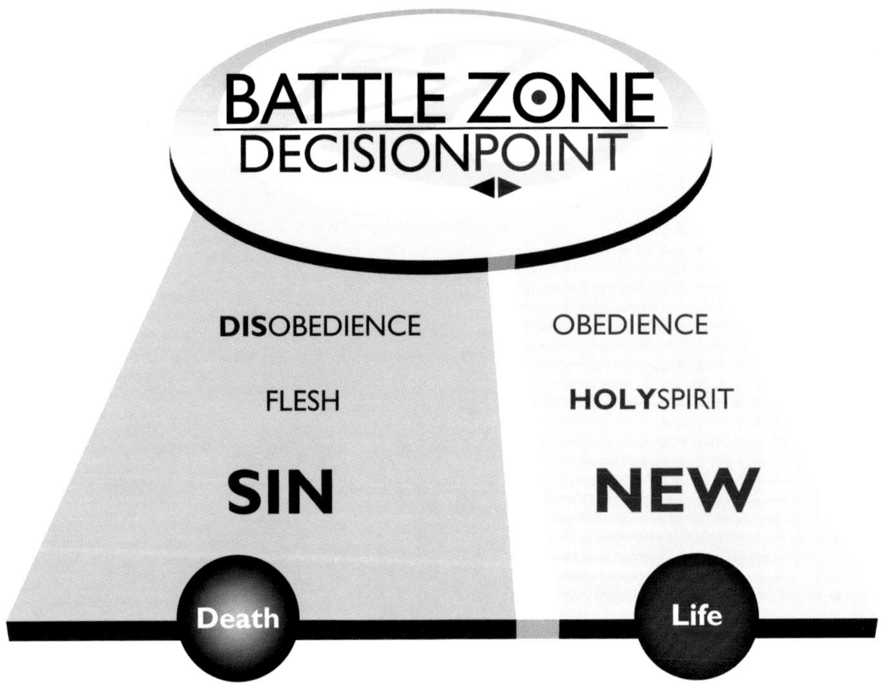

www.battlezoneministries.org

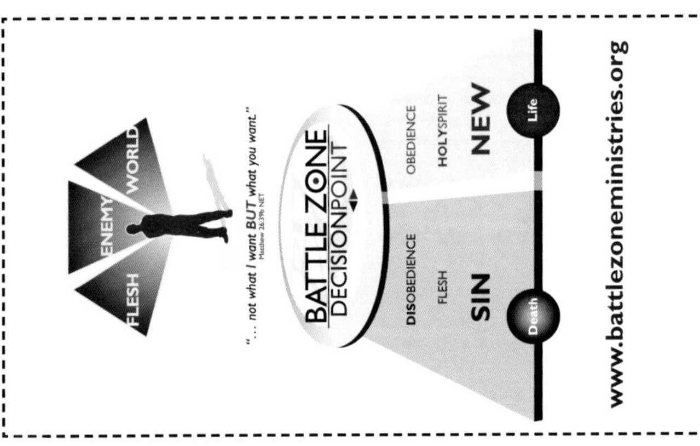

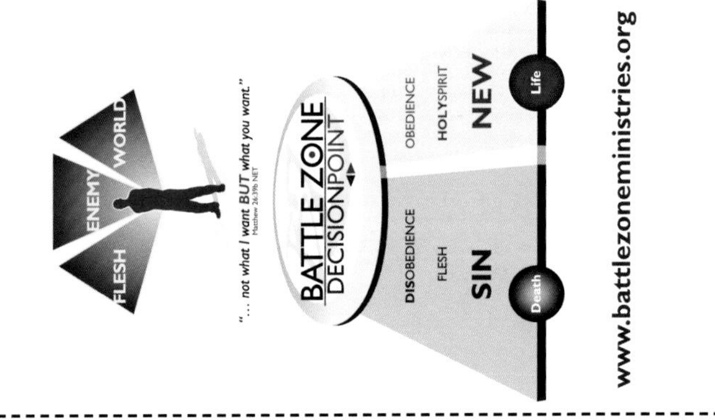

BATTLEZONE PRESIDENT BIO

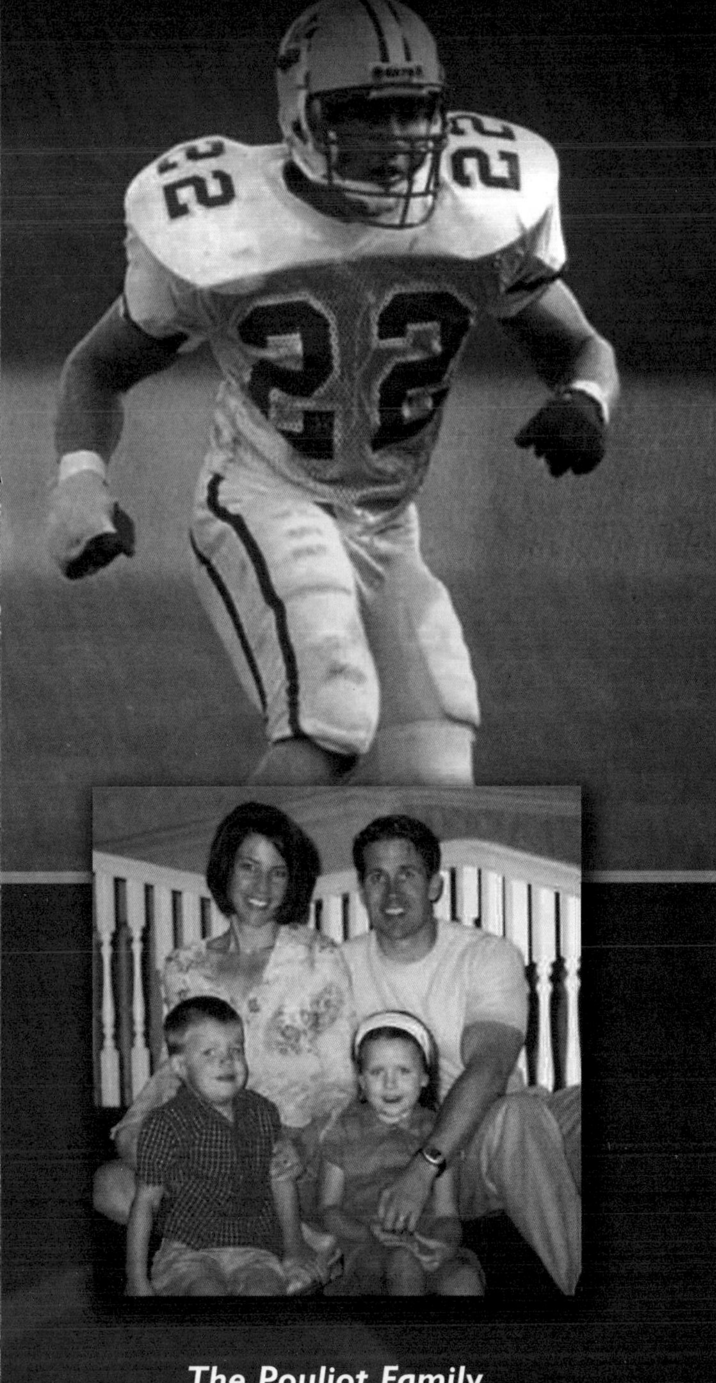

The Pouliot Family
Clovis, CA
Top L-R: Anastasia, Michael
Bottom L-R: Caleb, Bethany

Michael was born and raised in Helena, Montana and is the youngest of three siblings. He has been married for over a decade to his best friend, Anastasia. He and his wife are the proud parents of four children, Bethany (6) and Caleb (4) who bless them daily and Baby Joe and his sibling who reside in heaven. The Pouliot's live in Clovis, California.

Michael's personal mission statement is; *"To know God's will and to do it, as I lead my family and others to live a life of holiness submitted to Christ."*

He is committed to lead his family using the Bible as his Playbook, the Holy Spirit as his coach, and Jesus as his role model.

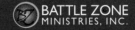

Michael has been involved in ministry for 10 years and is deeply concerned with the majority of men who lack the commitment to live a life that glorifies God. He is an Elder-Shepherd in training at his local church, New Harvest, and serves as the men's ministry "point-man" under the leadership of his friend and pastor, Mitch Ribera. Michael has been accepted by the National Coalition of Men's Ministry (NCMM) as a Certified Men's Ministry Coach. Michael is also the President of BattleZONE Ministries Inc., a nonprofit Christian ministry to men.

Michael is a graduate of Montana State University where he earned his bachelor's degree in dietetics while playing football as an inside linebacker. He has his Master's in Business Administration from the Craig School of Business at California State University, Fresno and is a registered dietitian, speaker, trainer and writer. Michael is a student of the Scripture and frequently attends conferences to learn better how to help others apply God's Word. Both Michael and Anastasia plan on pursuing their doctorates in ministry when the Lord releases them in His perfect timing.

SEASON 5

CAPTAIN

DATE

TEAMMATE

TEAMMATE

TEAMMATE

TEAMMATE

TEAMMATES FIRST DRAFT

TEAMMATES FIRST DRAFT

TEAMMATES FIRST DRAFT

TEAMMATES FIRST DRAFT

SEASON 6

CAPTAIN

DATE

TEAMMATE

TEAMMATE

TEAMMATE

TEAMMATE

TEAMMATES FIRST DRAFT

TEAMMATES FIRST DRAFT

TEAMMATES FIRST DRAFT

TEAMMATES FIRST DRAFT